ACCA

PAPER F9

FINANCIAL MANAGEMENT

BPP Learning Media is an **ACCA Approved Content Provider**. This means we work closely with ACCA to ensure this Study Text contains the information you need to pass your exam.

In this Study Text, which has been reviewed by the **ACCA examination team**, we:

- **Highlight** the **most important elements** in the syllabus and the **key skills** you need
- **Signpost** how each chapter links to the syllabus and the study guide
- **Provide** lots of **exam focus points** demonstrating what is expected of you in the exam
- **Emphasise key points** in regular **fast forward summaries**
- **Test your knowledge** in **quick quizzes**
- **Examine your understanding** in our **practice question bank**
- **Reference** all the **important topics** in our **full index**

BPP's **Practice & Revision Kit** also supports this paper.

FOR EXAMS FROM IN SEPTEMBER 2016, DECEMBER 2016, MARCH 2017 AND JUNE 2017

BPP LEARNING MEDIA

First edition 2007
Ninth edition February 2016

ISBN 9781 4727 4426 5
(Previous ISBN 9781 4727 2678 0)

e-ISBN 9781 4727 4668 9

British Library Cataloguing-in-Publication Data

A catalogue record for this book
is available from the British Library

Published by

BPP Learning Media Ltd
BPP House, Aldine Place
London W12 8AA

www.bpp.com/learningmedia

Printed in the United Kingdom by

RICOH UK Limited
Unit 2
Wells Place
Merstham
RH1 3LG

Your learning materials, published by BPP Learning
Media Ltd, are printed on paper obtained from traceable
sustainable Media Ltd, are printed on paper obtained
from traceable sustainable sources.

We are grateful to the Association of Chartered Certified
Accountants for permission to reproduce past
examination questions. The suggested solutions in the
practice answer bank have been prepared by BPP
Learning Media Ltd, unless otherwise stated.

BPP
LEARNING MEDIA

Contents

Helping you to pass

BPP Learning Media – ACCA Approved Content Provider

As ACCA's **Approved Content Provider**, BPP Learning Media gives you the **opportunity** to use study materials reviewed by the ACCA examination team. By incorporating the examination team's comments and suggestions regarding the depth and breadth of syllabus coverage, the BPP Learning Media Study Text provides excellent, **ACCA-approved** support for your studies.

The PER alert

Before you can qualify as an ACCA member, you not only have to pass all your exams but also fulfil a three year **practical experience requirement** (PER). To help you to recognise areas of the syllabus that you might be able to apply in the workplace to achieve different performance objectives, we have introduced the 'PER alert' feature. You will find this feature throughout the Study Text to remind you that what you are **learning to pass** your ACCA exams is **equally useful to the fulfilment of the PER requirement**.

Your achievement of the PER should now be recorded in your online *My Experience* record.

Tackling studying

Studying can be a daunting prospect, particularly when you have lots of other commitments. The **different features** of the Study Text, the **purposes** of which are explained fully on the **Chapter features** page, will help you whilst studying and improve your chances of **exam success**.

Developing exam awareness

Our Study Texts are completely **focused** on helping you pass your exam.

Our advice on **Studying F9** outlines the **content** of the paper, the **necessary skills** you are expected to be able to demonstrate and any **brought forward knowledge** you are expected to have.

Exam focus points are included within the chapters to highlight when and how specific topics were examined, or how they might be examined in the future.

Using the syllabus and study guide

You can find the syllabus and study guide on pages xi–xxi of this Study Text.

Testing what you can do

Testing yourself helps you develop the skills you need to pass the exam and also confirms that you can recall what you have learnt.

We include **Questions** – lots of them – both within chapters and in the **Practice Question Bank**, as well as **Quick Quizzes** at the end of each chapter to test your knowledge of the chapter content.

Chapter features

Each chapter contains a number of helpful features to guide you through each topic.

Topic list

Topic list	Syllabus reference

What you will be studying in this chapter and the relevant section numbers, together with ACCA syllabus references.

Introduction

Puts the chapter content in the context of the syllabus as a whole.

Study Guide

Links the chapter content with ACCA guidance.

Exam Guide

Highlights how examinable the chapter content is likely to be and the ways in which it could be examined.

Knowledge brought forward from earlier studies

What you are assumed to know from previous studies/exams.

FAST FORWARD

Summarises the content of main chapter headings, allowing you to preview and review each section easily.

Examples

Demonstrate how to apply key knowledge and techniques.

Key terms

Definitions of important concepts that can often earn you easy marks in exams.

Exam focus points

When and how specific topics were examined, or how they may be examined in the future.

Formula to learn

Formulae that are not given in the exam but which have to be learnt.

PER alert

Gives you a useful indication of syllabus areas that closely relate to performance objectives in your Practical Experience Requirement (PER).

Question

Gives you essential practice of techniques covered in the chapter.

Case Study

Real world examples of theories and techniques.

Chapter Roundup

A full list of the Fast Forwards included in the chapter, providing an easy source of review.

Quick Quiz

A quick test of your knowledge of the main topics in the chapter.

Practice Question Bank

Found at the back of the Study Text with more comprehensive chapter questions. Cross referenced for easy navigation.

Studying F9

This paper examines a wide range of financial management topics, many of which will be completely new to you. You will need to be competent at a range of quite tricky calculations as well as being able to explain and discuss financial management techniques and issues.

The F9 examination team

The ACCA examination team expects you to be able to perform and comment on calculations, exercise critical abilities, clearly demonstrate understanding of the syllabus and use question information.

Syllabus update

The F9 syllabus has been updated for the September 2016 sitting onwards. The syllabus changes are summarised below.

Summary of changes to F9

There have been no amendments to the F9 syllabus since the last 2015-2016 syllabus. However, the format of the exam has changed. See page ix.

BPP
LEARNING MEDIA

1 What F9 is about

The aim of this syllabus is to develop the knowledge and skills expected of a finance manager in relation to investment, financing and dividend policy decisions.

F9 is a middle level paper in the ACCA qualification structure. There are some links to material you have covered in F2, particularly short-term decision-making techniques. The paper with a direct link following F9 is P4 which thinks strategically and considers wider environmental factors. F9 requires you to be able to apply techniques and think about their impact on the organisation.

2 What skills are required?

- You are expected to have a core of management accounting knowledge from Paper F2.
- You will be required to carry out calculations, with **clear workings** and a logical structure.
- You will be required to **interpret** data.
- You will be required to **explain** management accounting techniques and **discuss** whether they are appropriate for a particular organisation.
- You must be able to **apply** your skills in a practical context.

3 How to improve your chances of passing

- There is no choice in this paper; all questions have to be answered. You must therefore study the **entire syllabus**; there are no shortcuts.
- The first section of the paper consists of 15 multiple choice questions, worth two marks each. These will inevitably cover a wide range of the syllabus.
- Practising questions under timed conditions is essential. BPP's **Practice & Revision Kit** contains 2 mark, 10 mark and 20 mark questions to help you practise this.
- Questions in Sections B and C will be based on simple scenarios and answers to Section C questions must be **focused** and **specific** to the organisation.
- **Answer plans** in Section C will help you to focus on the requirements of the question and enable you to manage your time effectively.
- **Answer all parts** of the questions in Section C. Even if you cannot do all of the calculation elements, you will still be able to gain marks in the discussion parts.
- Make sure your answers focus on **practical applications of management accounting**, common sense is essential!
- Keep an eye out for **articles**, as the **examination team** will use the articles to communicate with students.
- Read journals etc to pick up on ways in which real organisations apply management accounting and think about your own organisation if that is relevant.

4 Brought forward knowledge

You will need to have a good working knowledge of certain management accounting techniques from F2. In particular, you will need to be familiar with the capital budgeting process, and be able to apply the concepts of interest and discounting. This includes being able to calculate annuities and perpetuities, and to use the discount and annuity tables to calculate net present values.

This Study Text revises these topics and brought forward knowledge is identified. If you struggle with the examples and questions used, you must go back and revisit your previous work. The ACCA examination team will assume you know this material and it may form part of an exam question.

The exam paper and exam formulae

Format of the paper

From September 2016, the exam will be 3 hours and 15 minutes in duration. The exam paper is divided into three sections.

Section A consists of 15 multiple choice questions of two marks each. These questions can be on any part of the syllabus.

Section B consists of 15 mini scenario based multiple choice questions of two marks each. These questions can be on any part of the syllabus.

Section C consists of 2 constructive response questions of 20 marks, and answers to the questions will require a mixture of calculations and discussion. The 20 mark questions will cover Parts C, D and E of the syllabus.

All questions are compulsory.

The exam will cover as much of the syllabus as possible.

Computer Based Examination

ACCA have announced that they intend to commence the launch of computer-based exams (CBEs) for F5–F9 towards the end of 2016. At the time of going to print the exact details had not been confirmed. Paper-based examinations will be run in parallel while the CBEs are phased in and BPP materials have been designed to support you, whichever exam option you choose.

Exam formulae

Set out below are the **formulae you will be given in the exam**. If you are not sure what the symbols mean, or how the formulae are used, you should refer to the appropriate chapter in this Study Text.

	Chapter in Study Text
Economic order quantity	**5**

$$= \sqrt{\frac{2C_0D}{Ch}}$$

Miller-Orr Model	**6**

$$\text{Return point} = \text{Lower limit} + \left(\frac{1}{3} \times \text{spread}\right)$$

$$\text{Spread} = 3\left[\frac{\frac{3}{4} \times \text{transaction cost} \times \text{variance of cash flows}}{\text{interest rate}}\right]^{\frac{1}{3}}$$

The Capital Asset Pricing Model	**15**

$$E(r_i) = R_f + \beta_i(E(r_m) - R_f)$$

The asset beta formula	**16**

$$\beta_a = \left[\frac{V_e}{(V_e + V_d(1-T))}\beta_e\right] + \left[\frac{V_d(1-T)}{(V_e + V_d(1-T))}\beta_d\right]$$

The Growth Model

$$P_0 = \frac{D_0(1+g)}{(r_e - g)}$$

Gordon's growth approximation

$$g = br_e$$

The weighted average cost of capital

$$WACC = \left[\frac{V_e}{V_e + V_d}\right] k_e + \left[\frac{V_d}{V_e + V_d}\right] k_d (1-T)$$

The Fisher formula

$$(1 + i) = (1 + r)(1 + h)$$

Purchasing power parity and interest rate parity

$$S_1 = S_0 \times \frac{(1+h_c)}{(1+h_b)} \qquad F_0 = S_0 \times \frac{(1+i_c)}{(1+i_b)}$$

Syllabus and Study Guide

The F9 syllabus and Study Guide can be found below.

Syllabus

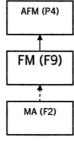

AIM

To develop the knowledge and skills expected of a finance manager, in relation to investment, financing, and dividend policy decisions.

MAIN CAPABILITIES

On successful completion of this paper candidates should be able to:

A Discuss the role and purpose of the financial management function
B Assess and discuss the impact of the economic environment on financial management
C Discuss and apply working capital management techniques
D Carry out effective investment appraisal
E Identify and evaluate alternative sources of business finance
F Discuss and apply principles of business and asset valuations
G Explain and apply risk management techniques in business.

RELATIONAL DIAGRAM OF MAIN CAPABILITIES

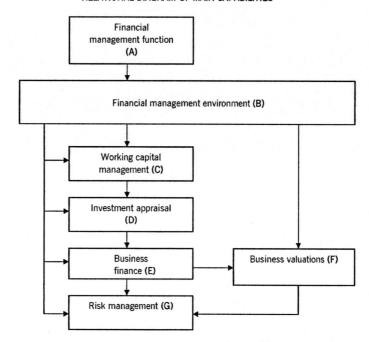

RATIONALE

The syllabus for Paper F9, *Financial Management*, is designed to equip candidates with the skills that would be expected from a finance manager responsible for the finance function of a business. It prepares candidates for more advanced and specialist study in Paper P4, *Advanced Financial Management*

The paper, therefore, starts by introducing the role and purpose of the financial management function within a business. Before looking at the three key financial management decisions of investing, financing, and dividend policy, the syllabus explores the economic environment in which such decisions are made.

The next section of the syllabus is the introduction of investing decisions. This is done in two stages - investment in (and the management of) working capital and the appraisal of long-term investments.

The next area introduced is financing decisions. This section of the syllabus starts by examining the various sources of business finance, including dividend policy and how much finance can be raised from within the business. It also looks at the cost of capital and other factors that influence the choice of the type of capital a business will raise. The principles underlying the valuation of business and financial assets, including the impact of cost of capital on the value of business, is covered next.

The syllabus finishes with an introduction to, and examination of, risk and the main techniques employed in the management of such risk.

DETAILED SYLLABUS

A   Financial management function

1.   The nature and purpose of financial management

2.   Financial objectives and relationship with corporate strategy

3.   Stakeholders and impact on corporate objectives

4.   Financial and other objectives in not-for-profit organisations

B   Financial management environment

1.   The economic environment for business

2.   The nature and role of financial markets and institutions

3.   The nature and role of money market

C   Working capital management

1.   The nature, elements and importance of working capital

2.   Management of inventories, accounts receivable, accounts payable and cash

3.   Determining working capital needs and funding strategies

D   Investment appraisal

1.   Investment appraisal techniques

2.   Allowing for inflation and taxation in investment appraisal

3.   Adjusting for risk and uncertainty in investment appraisal

4.   Specific investment decisions (lease or buy; asset replacement, capital rationing)

E   Business finance

1.   Sources of, and raising business finance

2.   Estimating the cost of capital

3.   Sources of finance and their relative costs

4.   Capital structure theories and practical considerations

5.   Finance for small- and medium-sized entities

F   Business valuations

1.   Nature and purpose of the valuation of business and financial assets

2.   Models for the valuation of shares

3.   The valuation of debt and other financial assets

4.   Efficient market hypothesis (EMH) and practical considerations in the valuation of shares

G   Risk management

1.   The nature and types of risk and approaches to risk management

2.   Causes of exchange rate differences and interest rate fluctuations

3.   Hedging techniques for foreign currency risk

4.   Hedging techniques for interest rate risk

APPROACH TO EXAMINING THE SYLLABUS

The syllabus is assessed by a three-hour 15 minutes paper-based examination, All questions are compulsory.

All questions are compulsory. It will contain both computational and discursive elements.
Some questions will adopt a scenario/case study approach.

Section A of the exam comprises 15 multiple choice questions of 2 marks each.

Section B of the exam comprises three scenarios consisting of 15 multiple choice questions of 2 marks each

Section C contains two 20 mark questions.

The two 20 mark questions will mainly come from working capital management, investment appraisal and business finance areas of the syllabus. The section A and section B questions can cover any areas of the syllabus.

Candidates are provided with a formulae sheet and tables of discount and annuity factors

Study Guide

A FINANCIAL MANAGEMENT FUNCTION

1. The nature and purpose of financial management

a) Explain the nature and purpose of financial management.[1]

b) Explain the relationship between financial management and financial and management accounting.[1]

2. Financial objectives and the relationship with corporate strategy

a) Discuss the relationship between financial objectives, corporate objectives and corporate strategy.[2]

b) Identify and describe a variety of financial objectives, including: [2]
   i) shareholder wealth maximisation
   ii) profit maximisation
   iii) earnings per share growth

3. Stakeholders and impact on corporate objectives

a) Identify the range of stakeholders and their objectives [2]

b) Discuss the possible conflict between stakeholder objectives [2]

c) Discuss the role of management in meeting stakeholder objectives, including the application of agency theory.[2]

d) Describe and apply ways of measuring achievement of corporate objectives including: [2]
   i) ratio analysis, using appropriate ratios such as return on capital employed, return on equity, earnings per share and dividend per share
   ii) changes in dividends and share prices as part of total shareholder return

e) Explain ways to encourage the achievement of stakeholder objectives, including: [2]
   i) managerial reward schemes such as share options and performance-related pay
   ii) regulatory requirements such as corporate governance codes of best practice and stock exchange listing regulations

4. Financial and other objectives in not-for-profit organisations

a) Discuss the impact of not-for-profit status on financial and other objectives.[2]

b) Discuss the nature and importance of Value for Money as an objective in not-for-profit organisations.[2]

c) Discuss ways of measuring the achievement of objectives in not-for-profit organisations.[2]

B FINANCIAL MANAGEMENT ENVIRONMENT

1. The economic environment for business

a) Identify and explain the main macroeconomic policy targets.[1]

b) Define and discuss the role of fiscal, monetary, interest rate and exchange rate policies in achieving macroeconomic policy targets.[1]

c) Explain how government economic policy interacts with planning and decision-making in business.[2]

d) Explain the need for, and the interaction with, planning and decision-making in business of: [1]
   i) competition policy
   ii) government assistance for business
   iii) green policies
   iv) corporate governance regulation.[2]

2. The nature and role of financial markets and institutions

a) Identify the nature and role of money and capital markets, both nationally and internationally.[2]

b) Explain the role of financial intermediaries.[1]

c) Explain the functions of a stock market and a corporate bond market.[2]

d) Explain the nature and features of different securities in relation to the risk/return trade-off. [2]

3. The nature and role of money market

a) Describe the role of the money markets in: [1]
   i) Providing short-term liquidity to the private sector
      and the public sector
   ii) Providing short-term trade finance
   iii) Allowing an organisation to manage its exposure to foreign currency risk and interest rate risk.

b) Explain the role of banks and other financial institutions in the operation of the money markets. [2]

c) Explain the characteristics and role of the principal money market instruments: [2]
   i) Interest-bearing instruments
   ii) Discount instruments
   iii) Derivative products.

C   WORKING CAPITAL MANAGEMENT

1. The nature, elements and importance of working capital

a) Describe the nature of working capital and identify its elements. [1]

b) Identify the objectives of working capital management in terms of liquidity and profitability, and discuss the conflict between them. [2]

c) Discuss the central role of working capital management in financial management. [2]

2. Management of inventories, accounts receivable, accounts payable and cash

a) Explain the cash operating cycle and the role of accounts payable and accounts receivable. [2]

b) Explain and apply relevant accounting ratios, including: [2]
   i)   current ratio and quick ratio
   ii) inventory turnover ratio, average collection period and average payable period
   iii) sales revenue/net working capital ratio

c) Discuss, apply and evaluate the use of relevant techniques in managing inventory, including the Economic Order Quantity model and Just-in-Time techniques. [2]

d) Discuss, apply and evaluate the use of relevant techniques in managing accounts receivable, including:
   i) assessing creditworthiness [1]
   ii) managing accounts receivable [1]
   iii) collecting amounts owing [1]
   iv) offering early settlement discounts [2]
   v) using factoring and invoice discounting [2]
   vi) managing foreign accounts receivable [2]

e) Discuss and apply the use of relevant techniques in managing accounts payable, including:
   i)   using trade credit effectively [1]
   ii) evaluating the benefits of discounts for early settlement and bulk purchase [2]
   iii) managing foreign accounts payable [1]

f) Explain the various reasons for holding cash, and discuss and apply the use of relevant techniques in managing cash, including: [2]
   i)   preparing cash flow forecasts to determine future cash flows and cash balances
   ii) assessing the benefits of centralised treasury management and cash control
   iii) cash management models, such as the Baumol model and the Miller-Orr model
   iv) investing short-term

3. Determining working capital needs and funding strategies

a) Calculate the level of working capital investment in current assets and discuss the key factors determining this level, including: [2]
   i)   the length of the working capital cycle and terms of trade
   ii) an organisation's policy on the level of investment in current assets
   iii) the industry in which the organisation operates

b) Describe and discuss the key factors in determining working capital funding strategies, including: [2]
   i)   the distinction between permanent and fluctuating current assets

ii) the relative cost and risk of short-term and long-term finance

iii) the matching principle

iv) the relative costs and benefits of aggressive, conservative and matching funding policies

v) management attitudes to risk, previous funding decisions and organisation size [1]

D INVESTMENT APPRAISAL

1. Investment appraisal techniques

a) Identify and calculate relevant cash flows for investment projects.[2]

b) Calculate payback period and discuss the usefulness of payback as an investment appraisal method.[2]

c) Calculate discounted payback and discuss its usefulness as an investment appraisal method.[2]

d) Calculate return on capital employed (accounting rate of return) and discuss its usefulness as an investment appraisal method.[2]

e) Calculate net present value and discuss its usefulness as an investment appraisal method.[2]

f) Calculate internal rate of return and discuss its usefulness as an investment appraisal method.[2]

g) Discuss the superiority of discounted cash flow (DCF) methods over non-DCF methods.[2]

h) Discuss the relative merits of NPV and IRR.[2]

2. Allowing for inflation and taxation in DCF

a) Apply and discuss the real-terms and nominal-terms approaches to investment appraisal.[2]

b) Calculate the taxation effects of relevant cash flows, including the tax benefits of tax allowable depreciation and the tax liabilities of taxable profit.[2]

c) Calculate and apply before- and after-tax discount rates.[2]

3. Adjusting for risk and uncertainty in investment appraisal

a) Describe and discuss the difference between risk and uncertainty in relation to probabilities and increasing project life.[2]

b) Apply sensitivity analysis to investment projects and discuss the usefulness of sensitivity analysis in assisting investment decisions.[2]

c) Apply probability analysis to investment projects and discuss the usefulness of probability analysis in assisting investment decisions.[2]

d) Apply and discuss other techniques of adjusting for risk and uncertainty in investment appraisal, including:
i) simulation [1]
ii) adjusted payback [1]
iii) risk-adjusted discount rates [2]

4. Specific investment decisions (Lease or buy; asset replacement; capital rationing)

a) Evaluate leasing and borrowing to buy using the before-and after-tax costs of debt.[2]

b) Evaluate asset replacement decisions using equivalent annual cost and equivalent annual benefit.[2]

c) Evaluate investment decisions under single-period capital rationing, including:[2]
i) the calculation of profitability indexes for divisible investment projects
ii) the calculation of the NPV of combinations of non-divisible investment projects
iii) a discussion of the reasons for capital rationing

E BUSINESS FINANCE

1. Sources of and raising business finance

a) Identify and discuss the range of short-term sources of finance available to businesses, including: [2]
i) overdraft

ii) short-term loan
iii) trade credit
iv) lease finance

b) Identify and discuss the range of long-term sources of finance available to businesses, including: [2]
   i) equity finance
   ii) debt finance
   iii) lease finance
   iv) venture capital

c) Identify and discuss methods of raising equity finance, including: [2]
   i) rights issue
   ii) placing
   iii) public offer
   iv) stock exchange listing

d) Identify and discuss methods of raising short and long term Islamic finance including[1]
   i) major difference between Islamic finance and the other forms of business finance.
   ii) The concept of riba (interest) and how returns are made by Islamic financial securities.
   iii) Islamic financial instruments available to businesses including
      i) murabaha (trade credit)
      ii) ijara (lease finance)
      iii) mudaraba (equity finance)
      iv) sukuk (debt finance)
      v) musharaka (venture capital)

(note: calculations are not required)

e) Identify and discuss internal sources of finance, including:[2]
   i) retained earnings
   ii) increasing working capital management efficiency
   iii) the relationship between dividend policy and the financing decision
   iv) the theoretical approaches to, and the practical influences on, the dividend decision, including legal constraints, liquidity, shareholding expectations and alternatives to cash dividends

2. Estimating the cost of capital

a) Estimate the cost of equity including.[2]

i) Application of the dividend growth model and discussion of its weaknesses.
ii) Explanation and discussion of systematic and unsystematic risk.
iii) Relationship between portfolio theory and the capital asset pricing model (CAPM)
iv) Application of the CAPM, its assumptions, advantages and disadvantages

b) Estimating the cost of debt
   i) irredeemable debt
   ii) redeemable debt
   iii) convertible debt
   iv) preference shares
   v) bank debt

c) Estimating the overall cost of capital including.[2]:
   i) Distinguishing between average and marginal cost of capital
   ii) Calculating the weighted average cost of capital (WACC) using book value and market value weightings

3. Sources of finance and their relative costs

a) Describe the relative risk-return relationship and the relative costs of equity and debt.[2]

b) Describe the creditor hierarchy and its connection with the relative costs of sources of finance.[2]

c) Identify and discuss the problem of high levels of gearing [2]

d) Assess the impact of sources of finance on financial position, financial risk and shareholder wealth using appropriate measures, including[2]:
   i) ratio analysis using statement of financial position gearing, operational and financial gearing, interest coverage ratio and other relevant ratios
   ii) cash flow forecasting
   iii) leasing or borrowing to buy

e) Impact of cost of capital on investments including.[2]
   i) the relationship between company value and cost of capital.
   ii) the circumstances under which WACC can be used in investment appraisal

iii) the advantages of the CAPM over WACC in determining a project-specific cost of capital

iv) the application of CAPM in calculating a project-specific discount rate.

4. **Capital structure theories and practical considerations**

a) Describe the traditional view of capital structure and its assumptions.[2]

b) Describe the views of Miller and Modigliani on capital structure, both without and with corporate taxation, and their assumptions.[2]

c) Identify a range of capital market imperfections and describe their impact on the views of Miller and Modigliani on capital structure.[2]

d) Explain the relevance of pecking order theory to the selection of sources of finance.[1]

5. **Finance for small and medium sized entities (SMEs)**

a) Describe the financing needs of small businesses.[2]

b) Describe the nature of the financing problem for small businesses in terms of the funding gap, the maturity gap and inadequate security.[2]

c) Explain measures that may be taken to ease the financing problems of SMEs, including the responses of government departments and financial institutions.[1]

d) Identify and evaluate the financial impact of sources of finance for SMEs, including sources already referred to in syllabus section E1 and also [2]
    i) Business angel financing
    ii) Government assistance
    iii) Supply chain financing
    iv) Crowdfunding / peer-to-peer funding

F **BUSINESS VALUATIONS**

1. **Nature and purpose of the valuation of business and financial assets**

a) Identify and discuss reasons for valuing businesses and financial assets.[2]

b) Identify information requirements for valuation and discuss the limitations of different types of information.[2]

2. **Models for the valuation of shares**

a) Asset-based valuation models, including:[2]
    i) net book value (statement of financial position) basis.
    ii) net realisable value basis.
    iii) net replacement cost basis.

b) Income-based valuation models, including:[2]
    i) price/earnings ratio method.
    ii) earnings yield method.

c) Cash flow-based valuation models, including:[2]
    i) dividend valuation model and the dividend growth model.
    ii) discounted cash flow basis.

3. **The valuation of debt and other financial assets**

a) Apply appropriate valuation methods to:[2]
    i) irredeemable debt
    ii) redeemable debt
    iii) convertible debt
    iv) preference shares

4. **Efficient Market Hypothesis (EMH) and practical considerations in the valuation of shares**

a) Distinguish between and discuss weak form efficiency, semi-strong form efficiency and strong form efficiency [2]

b) Discuss practical considerations in the valuation of shares and businesses, including:[2]
    i) marketability and liquidity of shares
    ii) availability and sources of information
    iii) market imperfections and pricing anomalies
    iv) market capitalisation

c) Describe the significance of investor speculation and the explanations of investor decisions offered by behavioural finance [1]

G RISK MANAGEMENT

1. The nature and types of risk and approaches to risk management

a) Describe and discuss different types of foreign currency risk:[2]
   i) translation risk
   ii) transaction risk
   iii) economic risk

b) Describe and discuss different types of interest rate risk:[1]
   i) gap exposure
   ii) basis risk

2. Causes of exchange rate differences and interest rate fluctuations

a) Describe the causes of exchange rate fluctuations, including:
   i) balance of payments [1]
   ii) purchasing power parity theory [2]
   iii) interest rate parity theory [2]
   iv) four-way equivalence [2]

b) Forecast exchange rates using:[2]
   i) purchasing power parity
   ii) interest rate parity

c) Describe the causes of interest rate fluctuations, including: [2]
   i) structure of interest rates and yield curves
   ii) expectations theory
   iii) liquidity preference theory
   iv) market segmentation

3. Hedging techniques for foreign currency risk

a) Discuss and apply traditional and basic methods of foreign currency risk management, including:
   i) currency of invoice [1]
   ii) netting and matching [2]
   iii) leading and lagging [2]
   iv) forward exchange contracts [2]
   v) money market hedging [2]
   vi) asset and liability management [1]

b) Compare and evaluate traditional methods of foreign currency risk management.[2]

c) Identify the main types of foreign currency derivatives used to hedge foreign currency risk and explain how they are used in hedging.[1] (No numerical questions will be set on this topic)

4. Hedging techniques for interest rate risk

a) Discuss and apply traditional and basic methods of interest rate risk management, including:
   i) matching and smoothing [1]
   ii) asset and liability management [1]
   ii) forward rate agreements [2]

b) Identify the main types of interest rate derivatives used to hedge interest rate risk and explain how they are used in hedging.[1] (No numerical questions will be set on this topic)

SUMMARY OF CHANGES TO F9

There are changes to the syllabus to reflect the latest business and educational developments affecting this paper. These are summarised in the table below.
ACCA periodically reviews its qualification syllabuses so that they fully meet the needs of stakeholders such as employers, students, regulatory and advisory bodies and learning providers

Amendments /additions

There have been no amendments to the F9 study guide from the 2015 – 2016 study guide.

P
A
R
T

A

Financial management function

Financial management and financial objectives

Topic list	Syllabus reference
1 The nature and purpose of financial management	A1(a), (b)
2 Financial objectives and the relationship with corporate strategy	A2 (a), (b)
3 Stakeholders	A3 (a), (b), (c)
4 Measuring the achievement of corporate objectives	A3 (d)
5 Encouraging the achievement of stakeholder objectives	A3 (e)
6 Not for profit organisations	A4 (a), (b), (c)

Introduction

In Parts A and B of this Study Text we examine the work of the financial management function and the framework within which it operates.

In this chapter, after introducing the **nature and purpose of financial management**, we consider the **objectives** of organisations. We go on to examine the influence of **stakeholders** on stakeholder objectives.

The final part of this chapter examines objectives in **not for profit** organisations.

Study guide

		Intellectual level
A	**Financial management function**	
1	**The nature and purpose of financial management**	
(a)	Explain the nature and purpose of financial management.	1
(b)	Explain the relationship between financial management and financial and management accounting.	1
2	**Financial objectives and the relationship with corporate strategy**	
(a)	Discuss the relationship between financial objectives, corporate objectives and corporate strategy.	2
(b)	Identify and describe a variety of financial objectives, including:	2
(i)	Shareholder wealth maximisation	
(ii)	Profit maximisation	
(iii)	Earnings per share growth	
3	**Stakeholders and impact on corporate objectives**	
(a)	Identify the range of stakeholders and their objectives.	2
(b)	Discuss the possible conflict between stakeholder objectives.	2
(c)	Discuss the role of management in meeting stakeholder objectives, including the application of agency theory.	2
(d)	Describe and apply ways of measuring achievement of corporate objectives including:	2
(i)	Ratio analysis, using appropriate ratios such as return on capital employed, return on equity, earnings per share and dividend per share	
(ii)	Changes in dividends and share prices as part of total shareholder return	
(e)	Explain ways to encourage the achievement of stakeholder objectives, including:	2
(i)	Managerial reward schemes such as share options and performance-related pay	
(ii)	Regulatory requirements such as corporate governance codes of best practice and stock exchange listing regulations	
4	**Financial and other objectives in not for profit organisations**	
(a)	Discuss the impact of not for profit status on financial and other objectives.	2
(b)	Discuss the nature and importance of value for money as an objective in not for profit organisations.	2
(c)	Discuss ways of measuring the achievement of objectives in not for profit organisations.	2

Exam guide

The material in this chapter is examinable as an entire discussion question or as a question involving calculations such as ratios and discussion. When doing a ratio analysis question, you must make sure you **apply** your answer to the organisation in the question. The organisation will not necessarily be a publicly quoted company with shareholders.

1 The nature and purpose of financial management

Financial management decisions cover **investment** decisions, **financing** decisions, **dividend** decisions and **risk management**.

1.1 What is financial management?

Financial management can be defined as the management of the finances of an organisation in order to achieve the financial objectives of the organisation. The usual assumption in financial management for the private sector is that the objective of the company is to **maximise shareholders' wealth**.

1.2 Financial planning

The financial manager will need to **plan** to ensure that enough funding is available at the right time to meet the needs of the organisation for short-, medium- and long-term capital.

(a)   In the short term, funds may be needed to pay for purchases of inventory, or to smooth out changes in receivables, payables and cash: the financial manager must ensure that **working capital requirements** (ie requirements for day to day operations) are met.

(b)   In the medium or long term, the organisation may have planned purchases of **non-current assets**, such as plant and equipment, for which the financial manager must ensure that **funding** is available.

The financial manager contributes to decisions on the uses of funds raised by **analysing financial data** to **determine uses** which meet the **organisation's financial objectives**. Is project A to be preferred over project B? Should a new asset be bought or leased?

1.3 Financial control

The **control** function of the financial manager becomes relevant for funding which has been raised. Are the various activities of the organisation meeting its objectives? Are assets being used efficiently? To answer these questions, the financial manager may **compare data** on **actual performance** with **forecast performance**. Forecast data will have been prepared in the light of past performance (historical data) modified to reflect expected future changes. Future changes may include the effects of economic development, for example an economic recovery leading to a forecast upturn in revenues.

1.4 Financial management decisions

The financial manager makes decisions relating to **investment**, **financing** and **dividends**. The **management of risk** must also be considered.

Investments in assets must be **financed** somehow. Financial management is also concerned with the **management of short-term funds** and with how funds can be raised over the long term.

The retention of profits is a financing decision. The other side of this decision is that if profits are retained, there is less to pay out to shareholders as dividends, which might deter investors. An appropriate balance needs to be struck in addressing the **dividend decision**: how much of its profits should the company pay out as dividends and how much should it retain for investment to provide for future growth and new investment opportunities?

We shall be looking at various aspects of the investment, financing and dividend decisions of financial management throughout this Study Text.

Examples of different types of investment decision	
Decisions **internal** to the business enterprise	• Whether to undertake new projects • Whether to invest in new plant and machinery • Research and development decisions • Investment in a marketing or advertising campaign
Decisions involving **external parties**	• Whether to carry out a takeover or a merger involving another business • Whether to engage in a joint venture with another enterprise
Disinvestment decisions	• Whether to sell off unprofitable segments of the business • Whether to sell old or surplus plant and machinery • The sale of subsidiary companies

Question

Disposal of surplus assets

'The financial manager should identify surplus assets and dispose of them'. Why?

Answer

A surplus asset earns no return for the business. The business is likely to be paying the 'cost of capital' in respect of the money tied up in the asset, ie the money which it can realise by selling it.

If surplus assets are sold, the business may be able to invest the cash released in more productive ways, or alternatively it may use the cash to cut its liabilities. Either way, it will enhance the return on capital employed for the business as a whole.

Although selling surplus assets yields short-term benefits, the business should not jeopardise its activities in the medium or long term by disposing of productive capacity until the likelihood of it being required in the future has been fully assessed.

1.5 Management accounting, financial accounting and financial management

Of course, it is not just people **within** an organisation who require information. Those **external** to the organisation, such as banks, shareholders, tax authorities, trade payables and government agencies, all desire information too.

Management accountants provide **internally used** information. The **financial accounting function** provides **externally used** information. The management accountant is not concerned with the calculation of earnings per share for the statement of profit or loss and the financial accountant is not concerned with the variances between budgeted and actual labour expenditure.

Management information provides a **common source** from which financial accounts and management accounts are prepared. The **differences** between the two types of accounts arise in the manner in which the common source of data is **analysed**.

Financial accounts	Management accounts
Financial accounts **detail the performance of an organisation over a defined period and the state of affairs at the end of that period.**	Management accounts are **used to aid management to record, plan** and **control activities** and **to help the decision-making process.**
Limited companies must, **by law**, prepare financial accounts.	There is **no legal requirement** to prepare management accounts.

Financial accounts	Management accounts
The **format** of published financial accounts is determined by **law** and by **accounting standards**. In principle the accounts of different organisations can therefore be easily compared.	The **format** of management accounts is entirely at management discretion: **no strict rules** govern the way they are prepared or presented.
Financial accounts **concentrate on the business as a whole**, aggregating revenues and costs from different operations, and are an end in themselves.	Management accounts can **focus on specific areas** of an organisation's activities. Information may aid a decision rather than be an end product of a decision.
Most financial accounting information is of a **monetary** nature.	Management accounts incorporate **non-monetary** measures.
Financial accounts present an essentially **historic** picture of **past** operations.	Management accounts are both a **historical** record and a **future** planning tool.

As we have seen, financial management is **the management of finance**. Finance is used by an organisation just as, for example, labour is used by an organisation. Finance therefore needs management in a similar way to labour. The management accounting function provides information to ensure the effective management of labour and, in the same way, the financial management function provides information on, for example, projected cash flows to aid the **effective** management of finance.

2 Financial objectives and the relationship with corporate strategy

6/09

FAST FORWARD

Strategy is a course of action to achieve an objective. There are three main levels of strategy in an organisation.

- Corporate: the general direction of the whole organisation
- Business: how the organisation or its business units tackle particular markets
- Operational/functional: specific strategies for different departments of the business

2.1 Strategy

Strategy may be defined as a course of action, including the specification of resources required, to achieve a specific objective.

Strategy can be **short term** or **long term**, depending on the time horizon of the objective it is intended to achieve.

This definition also indicates that since strategy depends on objectives or targets, the obvious starting point for a study of strategy is the **identification and formulation of objectives**.

Key term

Corporate strategy is concerned with the overall purpose and scope of the organisation and how value will be added to the different parts (business units) of the organisation.   *(Johnson, Scholes and Whittington)*

2.2 Corporate objectives

FAST FORWARD

Corporate objectives are relevant for the organisation as a whole, relating to key factors for business success.

Corporate objectives are those which are concerned with the firm as a whole. Objectives should be **explicit, quantifiable** and **capable of being achieved**. The corporate objectives outline the expectations of the firm and the strategic planning process is concerned with the means of achieving the objectives.

Objectives should relate to the **key factors for business success**, which are typically as follows.

- Profitability (return on investment)
- Market share
- Growth
- Cash flow
- Customer satisfaction
- The quality of the firm's products
- Industrial relations
- Added value

2.3 Financial objectives   6/13

Financial targets may include targets for: **earnings; earnings per share; dividend per share; gearing level; profit retention; operating profitability.**

The usual assumption in financial management for the private sector is that the primary financial objective of the company is to **maximise shareholders' wealth.**

2.3.1 Shareholder wealth maximisation   12/08, 6/10, 12/11, 12/13

Exam focus point

The December 2011 exam required candidates to compare and contrast the financial objectives of a company and a not for profit organisation. Make sure that you can explain the benefits of financial objectives, and are able to apply your knowledge to different situations. The December 2013 exam approached the subject from a different angle. The question asked for ways in which directors of a company could be encouraged to achieve maximisation of shareholder wealth. This required a bit of common sense. The two main ways are via managerial reward schemes such as share option schemes, and through regulatory requirements such as corporate governance codes.

If the financial objective of a company is to maximise the value of the company, and in particular the value of its ordinary shares, we need to be able to put values on a company and its shares. How do we do it?

Three possible methods for the valuation of a company might occur to us.

(a)   **Statement of financial position (balance sheet) valuation**

Here assets will be valued on a **going concern basis**. Certainly, investors will look at a company's statement of financial position. If retained profits rise every year, the company will be a profitable one. Statement of financial position values are not a measure of 'market value', although retained profits might give some indication of what the company could pay as dividends to shareholders.

(b)   **Break-up basis**

This method of valuing a business is only of interest when the business is threatened with **liquidation**, or when its management is thinking about selling off individual assets to raise cash.

(c)   **Market values**

The market value is the price at which buyers and sellers will trade stocks and shares in a company. This is the method of valuation which is most relevant to the financial objectives of a company.

(i)   When shares are traded on a recognised stock market, such as the stock exchange, the market value of a company can be measured by the **price** at which shares are currently being traded.

(ii)   When shares are in a private company, and are not traded on any stock market, there is no easy way to measure their market value. Even so, the financial objective of these companies should be to **maximise** the **wealth** of their **ordinary shareholders**.

The wealth of the shareholders in a company comes from:

- **Dividends** received
- **Market value** of the shares

A shareholder's **return** on investment is obtained in the form of:

- **Dividends** received
- **Capital gains** from increases in the market value of their shares

If a company's shares are traded on a stock market, the wealth of shareholders is increased when the share price goes up. The price of a company's shares will go up when the company makes attractive profits, which it pays out as **dividends** or **reinvests** in the business to achieve future profit growth and dividend growth. However, to increase the share price the company should achieve its attractive profits without taking **business risks** and **financial risks** which worry shareholders.

If there is an increase in earnings and dividends, management can hope for an increase in the share price too, so that shareholders benefit from both **higher revenue** (dividends) and also **capital gains** (higher share prices). **Total shareholder return** is a measure which combines the increase in share price and dividends paid and can be calculated as:

$$(P_1 - P_0 + D_1) / P_0$$

Where P_0 is the share price at the beginning of the period

P_1 is the share price at the end of period

D_1 is the dividend paid

Question · Total shareholder return

A shareholder purchased 1,000 shares in SJG Co on 1 January at a market price of $2.50 per share. On 31 December the shares had an ex-div market value of $2.82 per share. The dividend paid during the period was $0.27 per share. What is the total shareholder return and what are the elements of total shareholder return?

Answer

The total shareholder return is:

($2.82 – $2.50 + $0.27) / $2.50 = 0.24 or 24%

This is made up of the capital gain $(P_1 - P_0) / P_0 = (\$2.82 - \$2.50) / \$2.50 = 0.13$ or 13%
and the dividend yield $D_1 / P_0 = \$0.27 / \$2.50 = 0.11$ or 11%

Exam focus point

Students often forget to use P_0 as the denominator when calculating the total shareholder return. The start of the period share price needs to be used, as the return being calculated is the return on the share price paid at the start of the period.

Management should set **targets** for factors which they can influence directly, such as **profits** and **dividend growth**. A financial objective might be expressed as the aim of increasing profits, earnings per share and dividend per share by, say, 10% a year for each of the next five years.

2.3.2 Profit maximisation

In much economic theory, it is assumed that the firm behaves in such a way as to **maximise profits**, where profit is viewed in an economist's sense. Unlike the accountant's concept of cost, total costs by this economist's definition include an element of reward for the risk-taking of the entrepreneur, called 'normal profit'.

Where the entrepreneur is in **full managerial control** of the firm, as in the case of a small owner-managed company or partnership, the economist's assumption of profit maximisation would seem to be very reasonable. Remember though that the economist's concept of profits is broadly in terms of **cash**, whereas accounting profits may not equate to cash flows.

Even in companies owned by shareholders but run by non-shareholding managers, if the manager is serving the company's (ie the shareholders') interests, we might expect that the profit maximisation assumption should be close to the truth.

Although profits do matter, they are not the best measure of a company's achievements.

(a) Accounting profits are not the same as 'economic' profits. Accounting profits can be **manipulated** to some extent by choices of accounting policies.

| Question | Manipulation of profits |

Can you give three examples of how accounting profits might be manipulated?

| Answer |

Here are some examples you might have chosen.

(a) Provisions, such as provisions for depreciation or anticipated losses
(b) The capitalisation of various expenses, such as development costs
(c) Adding overhead costs to inventory valuations

(b) Profit does not take account of **risk**. Shareholders will be very interested in the level of risk, and maximising profits may be achieved by increasing risk to unacceptable levels.

(c) Profits on their own take no account of the **volume of investment** that it has taken to earn the profit. Profits must be related to the volume of investment to have any real meaning. Hence measures of financial achievement include:

    (i) Accounting return on capital employed
    (ii) Earnings per share
    (iii) Yields on investment, eg dividend yield as a percentage of stock market value

(d) Profits are reported every year (with half-year interim results for quoted companies). They are measures of **short-term** performance, whereas a company's performance should ideally be judged over the longer term.

2.3.3 Earnings per share growth   12/08, 6/09, 6/13, 6/14

Key term

> **Earnings per share** is calculated by dividing the net profit or loss attributable to ordinary shareholders by the weighted average number of ordinary shares.

Earnings per share (EPS) is widely used as a measure of a company's performance and is of particular importance in comparing results over a period of several years. A company must be able to sustain its earnings in order to pay dividends and reinvest in the business so as to achieve future growth. Investors also look for **growth** in the EPS from one year to the next.

Question

Walter Wall Carpets made profits before tax in 20X8 of $9,320,000. Tax amounted to $2,800,000.

The company's share capital is as follows.

	$
Ordinary shares (10,000,000 shares of $1)	10,000,000
8% preference shares	2,000,000
	12,000,000

Calculate the EPS for 20X8.

Answer

	$
Profit before tax	9,320,000
Less tax	2,800,000
Profits after tax	6,520,000
Less preference dividend (8% of $2,000,000)	160,000
Earnings attributable to ordinary shareholders	6,360,000
Number of ordinary shares	10,000,000
EPS	63.6c

Question

Grasshopper made earnings attributable to shareholders of $8,250,000 in 20X8 and $8,880,000 in 20X9. The company's share capital was 12 million ordinary shares of $1 each in both years.

Calculate the EPS for 20X8 and 20X9 and EPS growth in relative and absolute terms.

Answer

	$
Earnings attributable to ordinary shareholders (20X8)	8,250,000
Number of ordinary shares	12,000,000
EPS (20X8)	68.8c
Earnings attributable to ordinary shareholders (20X9)	8,880,000
Number of ordinary shares	12,000,000
EPS (20X9)	74.0c
EPS growth (absolute) (74.0 – 68.8)	5.2c
EPS growth (relative) (5.2/68.8)	7.6%

Note that:

(a)   EPS is a figure based on **past data**, and

(b)   It is **easily manipulated** by changes in accounting policies and by mergers or acquisitions.

The use of the measure in calculating management bonuses makes it particularly liable to manipulation. For example, EPS can be increased via a share consolidation (exchanging a number of existing shares for one new share without altering the total value of the shareholding). The attention given to EPS as a performance measure by City analysts is arguably disproportionate to its true worth. Investors should be more concerned with future earnings, but of course estimates of these are more difficult to reach than the readily available figure.

2.3.4 Other financial targets

In addition to targets for earnings, EPS and dividend per share, a company might set **other financial targets**, such as:

(a) A restriction on the company's level of **gearing**, or debt. For example, a company's management might decide:

    (i) The ratio of long-term debt capital to equity capital should never exceed, say, 1:1.

    (ii) The cost of interest payments should never be higher than, say, 25% of total profits before interest and tax.

(b) A target for **profit retentions**. For example, management might set a target that dividend cover (the ratio of distributable profits to dividends actually distributed) should not be less than, say, 2.5 times.

(c) A target for **operating profitability**. For example, management might set a target for the profit/sales ratio (say, a minimum of 10%) or for a return on capital employed (say, a minimum ROCE of 20%).

These financial targets are not primary financial objectives, but they can act as subsidiary targets or constraints which should help a company to achieve its main financial objective without incurring excessive risks. They are usually measured over a year rather than over the long term.

Remember, however, that short-term measures of return can encourage a company to pursue **short-term** objectives at the expense of **long-term** ones, for example by deferring new capital investments, or spending only small amounts on research and development and on training.

A major problem with setting a number of different financial targets, either primary targets or supporting secondary targets, is that they might not all be consistent with each other. When this happens, some compromises will have to be accepted.

2.3.5 Example: Financial targets

Lion Grange Co has recently introduced a formal scheme of long-range planning. Sales in the current year reached $10,000,000, and forecasts for the next five years are $10,600,000, $11,400,000, $12,400,000, $13,600,000 and $15,000,000. The ratio of net profit after tax to sales is 10%, and this is expected to continue throughout the planning period. Total assets less current liabilities will remain at around 125% of sales. Equity in the current year is $8.75m.

It was suggested at a recent board meeting that:

(a) If profits rise, dividends should rise by at least the same percentage.

(b) An earnings retention rate of 50% should be maintained ie a payment ratio of 50%.

(c) The ratio of long-term borrowing to long-term funds (debt plus equity) is limited (by the market) to 30%, which happens also to be the current gearing level of the company.

You are required to prepare a financial analysis of the draft long-range plan.

Solution

The draft financial plan for profits, dividends, assets required and funding can be drawn up in a table, as follows.

	Current year $m	Year 1 $m	Year 2 $m	Year 3 $m	Year 4 $m	Year 5 $m
Sales	10.00	10.60	11.40	12.40	13.60	15.00
Net profit after tax	1.00	1.06	1.14	1.24	1.36	1.50
Dividends (50% of profit after tax)	0.50	0.53	0.57	0.62	0.68	0.75
Total assets less current liabilities	12.50	13.25	14.25	15.50	17.00	18.75
Equity (increased by retained earnings)	8.75	9.28	9.85	10.47	11.15	11.90
Maximum debt (30% of long-term funds, or 3/7 × equity)	3.75	3.98	4.22	4.49	4.78	5.10
Funds available	12.50	13.26	14.07	14.96	15.93	17.00
(Shortfalls) in funds *	0.00	0.00	(0.18)	(0.54)	(1.07)	(1.75)

* Given maximum gearing of 30% and no new issue of shares = funds available minus net assets required.

Question — Dividends and gearing

Suggest policies on dividends, retained earnings and gearing for Lion Grange, using the data above.

Answer

The financial objectives of the company are not compatible with each other. Adjustments will have to be made.

(a) Given the assumptions about sales, profits, dividends and net assets required, there will be an **increasing shortfall of funds** from year 2 onwards, unless new shares are issued or the gearing level rises above 30%.

(b) In years 2 and 3, the shortfall can be eliminated by **retaining a greater percentage** of profits, but this may have a serious **adverse effect** on the share price. In years 4 and 5, the shortfall in funds cannot be removed even if dividend payments are reduced to nothing.

(c) The **net asset turnover** (sales/capital employed) appears to be **low**. The situation would be eased if investments were able to generate a higher volume of sales, so that fewer non-current assets and less working capital would be required to support the projected level of sales.

(d) If asset turnover cannot be improved, it may be possible to **increase the profit to sales ratio** by reducing costs or increasing selling prices.

(e) If a new issue of shares is proposed to make up the shortfall in funds, the amount of funds required must be considered very carefully. Total **dividends** would have to be **increased** in order to pay dividends on the new shares. The company seems unable to offer prospects of suitable dividend payments, and so raising new equity might be difficult.

(f) It is conceivable that extra funds could be raised by issuing new debt capital, so that the level of gearing would be over 30%. It is uncertain whether investors would be prepared to lend money so as to increase gearing. If more funds were borrowed, profits after interest and tax would fall so that the share price might also be reduced.

Tate & Lyle is 'a leading global provider of ingredients and solutions to the food, beverage and other industries'. Their corporate strategy is as follows.

'Our vision is to become the leading global provider of speciality food ingredients and solutions. Over the last three years we have been taking a number of steps to realise this vision through our business transformation programme. The first part of the transformation, which is now complete, was about realigning and focusing our resources on growing our Speciality Food Ingredients business unit.

The second part is about getting the right enabling platform in place. We have made good progress including the move to a new operating model comprising two global business units, implementing a global Shared Service Centre and the initial roll-out of our global IS/IT system.'

http://annualreport2013.tateandlyle.com <accessed 21/01/14>

2.4 Non-financial objectives

A company may have important **non-financial objectives** which must be satisfied in order to ensure the continuing participation of all stakeholders. Without their participation, financial objectives such as maximising shareholder wealth may be compromised in the future. Examples of non-financial objectives are as follows.

(a) **The welfare of employees**

A company might try to provide good wages and salaries, comfortable and safe working conditions, good training and career development, and good pensions. If redundancies are necessary, many companies will provide generous redundancy payments, or spend money trying to find alternative employment for redundant staff.

(b) **The welfare of management**

Managers will often take decisions to improve their own circumstances, even though their decisions will incur expenditure and so reduce profits. High salaries, company cars and other perks are all examples of managers promoting their own interests.

(c) **The provision of a service**

The major objectives of some companies will include fulfilment of a responsibility to provide a service to the public. Examples are the privatised British Telecom and British Gas. Providing a service is of course a key responsibility of government departments and local authorities.

(d) **The fulfilment of responsibilities towards customers**

Responsibilities towards customers include providing in good time a product or service of a quality that customers expect, and dealing honestly and fairly with customers. Reliable supply arrangements and after-sales service arrangements are important.

(e) **The fulfilment of responsibilities towards suppliers**

Responsibilities towards suppliers are expressed mainly in terms of trading relationships. A company's size could give it considerable power as a buyer. The company should not use its power unscrupulously. Suppliers might rely on receiving prompt payment, in accordance with the agreed terms of trade.

(f) **The welfare of society as a whole**

The management of some companies are aware of the role that their company has to play in exercising corporate social responsibility. This includes compliance with applicable laws and regulations but is wider than that. Companies may be aware of their responsibility to minimise pollution and other harmful 'externalities' (such as excessive traffic) which their activities generate. In delivering 'green' environmental policies, a company may improve its corporate image as well as reducing harmful externality effects. Companies also may consider their 'positive' responsibilities, for example to make a contribution to the community by local sponsorship.

Other non-financial objectives are **growth**, **diversification** and **leadership in research and development**.

Non-financial objectives do not negate financial objectives, but they do suggest that the simple theory of company finance, that the objective of a firm is to maximise the wealth of ordinary shareholders, is too narrow. Financial objectives may have to be **compromised** in order to satisfy non-financial objectives.

3 Stakeholders

Stakeholders are individuals or groups who are affected by the activities of the firm. They can be classified as **internal** (employees and managers), **connected** (shareholders, customers and suppliers) and **external** (local communities, pressure groups, government).

Key term

There is a variety of different groups or individuals whose interests are directly affected by the activities of a firm. These groups or individuals are referred to as **stakeholders** in the firms.

The various stakeholder groups in a firm can be classified as follows.

Stakeholder groups	
Internal	Employees and pensioners Managers Directors
Connected	Shareholders Debt holders (bondholders) Customers Bankers Suppliers Competitors
External	Government Pressure groups Local and national communities Professional and regulatory bodies

3.1 Objectives of stakeholder groups

The various groups of stakeholders in a firm will have different goals which will depend in part on the particular situation of the enterprise. Some of the more important aspects of these different goals are as follows.

(a) **Ordinary (equity) shareholders**

Ordinary (equity) shareholders are the providers of the risk capital of a company. Usually their goal will be to maximise the wealth which they have as a result of the ownership of the shares in the company.

(b) **Trade payables (creditors)**

Trade payables have supplied goods or services to the firm. Trade payables will generally be profit-maximising firms themselves and have the objective of being paid the full amount due by the date agreed. On the other hand, they usually wish to ensure that they continue their trading relationship with the firm and may sometimes be prepared to accept later payment to avoid jeopardising that relationship.

(c) **Long-term payables (creditors)**

Long-term payables, which will often be banks, have the objective of receiving payments of interest and capital on the loan by the due date for the repayments. Where the loan is secured on assets of the company, the lender will be able to appoint a receiver to dispose of the company's assets if the company defaults on the repayments. To avoid the possibility that this may result in a loss to the

lender if the assets are not sufficient to cover the loan, the lender will wish to minimise the risk of default and will not wish to lend more than is prudent.

(d) **Employees**

Employees will usually want to maximise their rewards paid to them in salaries and benefits, according to the particular skills and the rewards available in alternative employment. Most employees will also want continuity of employment.

(e) **Government**

Government has objectives which can be formulated in political terms. Government agencies impinge on the firm's activities in different ways including through taxation of the firm's profits, the provision of grants, health and safety legislation, training initiatives, and so on. Government policies will often be related to macroeconomic objectives, such as sustained economic growth and high levels of employment.

(f) **Management**

Management has, like other employees (and managers who are not directors will normally be employees), the objective of maximising its own rewards. Directors, and the managers to whom they delegate responsibilities, must manage the company for the benefit of shareholders. The objective of reward maximisation might conflict with the exercise of this duty.

3.2 Stakeholder groups, strategy and objectives

The actions of stakeholder groups in pursuit of their various goals can exert influence on strategy and objectives. The greater the power of the stakeholder, the greater their influence will be. Each stakeholder group will have different expectations about what it wants, and the **expectations of the various groups may conflict**. Each group, however, will influence strategic decision making.

3.3 Shareholders and management

Although ordinary shareholders (equity shareholders) are the owners of the company to whom the board of directors are accountable, the actual powers of shareholders tend to be restricted, except in companies where the shareholders are also the directors. The **day to day** running of a company is the responsibility of **management**. Although the company's results are submitted for shareholders' approval at the annual general meeting (AGM), there is often apathy and acquiescence in directors' recommendations.

Shareholders are often ignorant about their company's current situation and future prospects. They have no right to inspect the books of account, and their forecasts of future prospects are gleaned from the annual report and accounts, stockbrokers, investment journals and daily newspapers. The relationship between management and shareholders is sometimes referred to as an **agency relationship**, in which managers act as agents for the shareholders.

Key term

> **Agency relationship**: a description of the relationship between management and shareholders expressing the idea that managers act as agents for the shareholder, using delegated powers to run the company in the shareholders' best interests.

However, if managers hold none or very few of the equity shares of the company they work for, what is to stop them from working inefficiently?

One power that shareholders possess is the right to **remove** the **directors** from office. But shareholders have to take the initiative to do this and, in many companies, the shareholders lack the energy and organisation to take such a step. Even so, directors will want the company's report and accounts, and the proposed final dividend, to meet with shareholders' approval at the AGM.

Another reason why managers might do their best to improve the financial performance of their company is that managers' pay is often related to the **size** or profitability of the company. Managers in very big companies, or in very profitable companies, will normally expect to earn higher salaries than managers in smaller or less successful companies. There is also an argument for giving managers some **profit-related**

pay, or providing incentives which are related to profits or share price. We will come back to this in Section 5 of this chapter.

3.4 Shareholders, managers and the company's long-term creditors

The relationship between long-term creditors (payables) of a company, the management and the shareholders of a company encompasses the following factors.

(a) Management may decide to raise finance for a company by taking out long-term or medium-term loans or issuing bonds in the case of larger companies. They might well be taking **risky investment decisions** using outsiders' money to finance them.

(b) Investors who provide debt finance will rely on the company's management to generate enough net cash inflows to make **interest payments on time**, and eventually to repay loans.

However, long-term creditors will often take **security** for their loan, perhaps in the form of a fixed charge over an asset (such as a mortgage on a building). Bonds are also often subject to certain restrictive covenants, which restrict the company's rights to borrow more money until the loan notes have been repaid.

If a company is unable to pay what it owes its creditors, the creditors may decide to **exercise their security** or perhaps eventually apply for the company to be **wound up**.

(c) The money that is provided by long-term creditors will be invested to earn profits, and the profits (in excess of what is needed to pay interest on the borrowing) will provide **extra dividends** or retained profits for the shareholders of the company. In other words, shareholders will expect to increase their wealth using creditors' money.

3.5 Shareholders, managers and government

The Government does not have a direct interest in companies (except for those in which it actually holds shares). However, the Government does often have a strong indirect interest in companies' affairs.

(a) **Taxation**

The Government raises taxes on sales and profits and on shareholders' dividends. It also expects companies to act as tax collectors for income tax and sales tax (VAT). The **tax structure** might influence investors' preferences for either dividends or capital growth.

(b) **Encouraging new investments**

The Government might provide **funds** towards the cost of some investment projects. It might also encourage private investment by offering **tax incentives**.

(c) **Encouraging a wider spread of share ownership**

In the UK, the Government has made some attempts to encourage more private individuals to become company shareholders by means of **attractive privatisation issues** (such as in the electricity, gas and telecommunications industries) and tax incentives, such as tax-free savings accounts (Individual Savings Accounts or ISAs) to encourage individuals to invest in shares.

(d) **Legislation**

The Government also influences **companies**, and the **relationships** between shareholders, creditors, management, employees and the general public through legislation, including the Companies Acts, legislation on employment, health and safety regulations, legislation on consumer protection and consumer rights and environmental legislation.

(e) **Economic policy**

A government's economic policy will affect business activity. For example, **exchange rate policy** will have implications for the revenues of exporting firms and for the purchase costs of importing firms. Policies on **economic growth, inflation, employment, interest rates**, and so on are all relevant to business activities.

4 Measuring the achievement of corporate objectives

Performance measurement is a part of the system of financial control of an enterprise as well as being important to investors.

4.1 Measuring financial performance   6/11

As part of the system of financial control in an organisation, it will be necessary to have ways of measuring the progress of the enterprise, so that managers know how well the company is doing. A common means of doing this is through **ratio analysis**, which is concerned with comparing and quantifying relationships between financial variables, such as those variables found in the statement of financial position and statement of profit or loss of the enterprise.

Exam focus point

The ACCA examination team has said, more than once, that knowledge of how to calculate and interpret key ratios is a weak point for many candidates. Make sure that it is one of your strong points. In reviewing ratio analysis below, we are in part revising material included in previous papers including F5.

4.2 The broad categories of ratios

Ratios can be grouped into the following four categories.

- **Profitability and return**
- **Debt and gearing**
- **Liquidity**
- **Shareholders' investment** ratios ('stock market ratios')

The key to obtaining meaningful information from ratio analysis is **comparison**: comparing ratios **over a number of periods** within the same business to establish whether the business is improving or declining, and **comparing ratios between similar businesses** to see whether the company you are analysing is better or worse than average within its own business sector.

4.3 Ratio pyramids

The Du Pont system of ratio analysis involves constructing a pyramid of interrelated ratios as shown below.

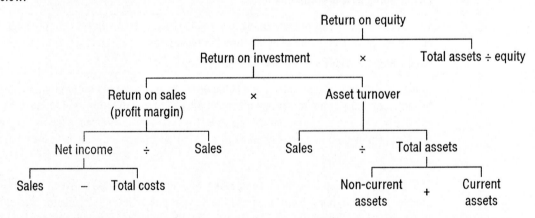

Such ratio pyramids help in providing for an overall management plan to achieve profitability, and allow the interrelationships between ratios to be checked.

4.4 Profitability

A company ought of course to be profitable if it is to maximise shareholder wealth, and obvious checks on profitability are:

(a) Whether the company has made a profit or a loss on its ordinary activities

(b) By how much this year's profit or loss is bigger or smaller than last year's profit or loss

Profit before taxation is generally thought to be a better figure to use than profit after taxation, because there might be unusual variations in the tax charge from year to year which would not affect the underlying profitability of the company's operations.

Another profit figure that should be considered is **profit before interest and tax (PBIT)**. This is the amount of profit which the company earned before having to pay interest to the providers of loan capital. This is also a good measure of operating profit, the profit that the company is making from its business operations. By providers of loan capital, we usually mean **longer-term** loan capital, such as loan notes and medium-term bank loans.

4.4.1 Profitability and return: the return on capital employed

You cannot assess profits or profit growth properly without relating them to the amount of funds (the capital) employed in making the profits. The most important profitability ratio is therefore **return on capital employed (ROCE)**, also called **return on investment (ROI)**.

Key terms

> Return on capital employed = $\dfrac{\text{PBIT}}{\text{Capital employed}}$
>
> Capital employed = Shareholders' funds **plus** long-term liabilities
>
> = Total assets less current liabilities

4.4.2 Evaluating the ROCE

What does a company's ROCE tell us? What should we be looking for? There are three comparisons that can be made.

(a) The **change** in ROCE from one year to the next

(b) The ROCE being **earned** by **other companies**, if this information is available

(c) A comparison of the ROCE with **current market borrowing rates** (warning: this needs to be interpreted with care, as ROCE will often reflect higher risk than borrowing rates)

    (i) What would be the **cost of extra borrowing** to the company if it needed more loans, and is it earning a ROCE that suggests it could make high enough profits to make such borrowing worthwhile?

    (ii) Is the company making a ROCE which suggests that it is making **profitable use** of its **current borrowing**?

4.4.3 Secondary ratios

We may analyse the ROCE by looking at the kinds of interrelationships between ratios used in ratio pyramids, which we mentioned earlier. We can thus find out why the ROCE is high or low, or better or worse than last year. **Profit margin** and **asset turnover** together explain the ROCE, and if the ROCE is the primary profitability ratio, these other two are the secondary ratios. The relationship between the three ratios is as follows.

Profit margin × asset turnover = ROCE

$$\frac{\text{PBIT}}{\text{Sales revenue}} \times \frac{\text{Sales revenue}}{\text{Capital employed}} = \frac{\text{PBIT}}{\text{Capital employed}}$$

It is also worth commenting on the **change in revenue (turnover)** from one year to the next. Strong sales growth will usually indicate volume growth as well as revenue increases due to price rises, and volume growth is one sign of a prosperous company.

4.4.4 Return on equity

Another measure of the firm's overall performance is **return on equity**. This compares net profit after tax with the equity that shareholders have invested in the firm.

This ratio shows the earning power of the shareholders' book investment and can be used to compare two firms in the same industry. A high return on equity could reflect the firm's good management of expenses and ability to invest in profitable projects. However, it could also reflect a higher level of debt finance (gearing) with associated higher risk (see Section 4.5).

Note that shareholders' equity includes reserves and is not limited to the ordinary share account.

4.4.5 Gross profit margin, the net profit margin and profit analysis

Depending on the format of the statement of profit or loss, you may be able to calculate the **gross profit margin** and also the **net profit margin**. Looking at the two together can be quite informative.

4.4.6 Example: Profit margins

A company has the following summarised statements of profit or loss for two consecutive years.

	Year 1	Year 2
	$	$
Sales revenue	70,000	100,000
Less cost of sales	42,000	55,000
Gross profit	28,000	45,000
Less expenses	21,000	35,000
Net profit	7,000	10,000

Although the net profit margin is the same for both years at 10%, the gross profit margin is not.

In year 1 it is: $\dfrac{28,000}{70,000} = 40\%$ and in year 2 it is: $\dfrac{45,000}{100,000} = 45\%$

Is this good or bad for the business? An increased profit margin must be good because this indicates a wider gap between selling price and cost of sales. However, given that the net profit ratio has stayed the same in the second year, expenses must be rising. In year 1 expenses were 30% of revenue, whereas in year 2 they were 35% of revenue. This indicates that administration or selling and distribution expenses may require tighter control.

A percentage analysis of profit between year 1 and year 2 is as follows.

	Year 1	Year 2
	%	%
Cost of sales as a % of sales	60	55
Gross profit as a % of sales	40	45
	100	100
Expenses as a % of sales	30	35
Net profit as a % of sales	10	10
Gross profit as a % of sales	40	45

4.5 Debt and gearing ratios

Debt ratios are concerned with how much the company owes in relation to its size and whether it is getting into heavier debt or improving its situation. **Financial gearing** (often simply referred to as 'gearing') is the amount of debt finance a company uses relative to its equity finance.

(a) When a company is heavily in debt, and seems to be getting even more heavily into debt, banks and other would-be lenders are very soon likely to **refuse further borrowing**.

(b) When a company is earning only a modest profit before interest and tax, and has a heavy debt burden, there will be **very little profit** left over for shareholders after the interest charges have been paid.

The main debt and gearing ratios are covered in Chapter 14.

4.6 Liquidity ratios: cash and working capital

Profitability is of course an important aspect of a company's performance, and debt or gearing is another. Neither, however, directly addresses the key issue of **liquidity**. A company needs liquid assets so that it can meet its debts when they fall due. The main liquidity ratios will be described in Chapter 4.

4.7 Shareholders' investment ratios   6/08

FAST FORWARD

Indicators such as **dividend yield, EPS, P/E ratio** and **dividend cover** can be used to assess investor returns.

Returns to shareholders are obtained in the form of **dividends** received and/or **capital gains** from increases in market value.

A company will only be able to raise finance if investors think that the returns they can expect are satisfactory in view of the risks they are taking. We must therefore consider how investors appraise companies. We will concentrate on quoted companies.

Information that is relevant to market prices and returns is available from published stock market information, and in particular from certain **stock market ratios**.

Key terms

> Cum dividend or **cum div** means the purchaser of shares is entitled to receive the next dividend payment.
>
> Ex dividend or **ex div** means that the purchaser of shares is not entitled to receive the next dividend payment.

The relationship between the cum-div price and the ex-div price is:

Market price per share (ex div) = Market price per share (cum div) – forthcoming dividend per share.

When stock market share prices are quoted, shares go from being cum div to ex div on a given day, and shareholders buying the shares from the time they go ex div are not entitled to the next dividend pay-out, which will happen soon.

4.7.1 The dividend yield

Key term

> $$\text{Dividend yield} = \frac{\text{Dividend per share}}{\text{Ex-div market price per share}}$$

The dividend yield is the return a shareholder is currently expecting on the shares of a company.

(a) The dividend per share is taken as the dividend for the previous year.
(b) Ex div means that the share price does not include the right to the most recent dividend.

Shareholders look for **both dividend yield and capital growth**. Obviously, dividend yield is therefore an important aspect of a share's performance.

In the year to 30 September 20X8, an advertising agency declares an interim ordinary dividend of 7.4c per share and a final ordinary dividend of 8.6c per share. Assuming an ex-div share price of 315 cents, what is the dividend yield?

Answer

The total dividend per share is (7.4 + 8.6) = 16 cents

$$\frac{16}{315} \times 100 = 5.1\%$$

4.7.2 Earnings per share (EPS)

Key term

$$\text{Earnings per share} = \frac{\text{Profit distributable to ordinary shareholders}}{\text{Weighted average number of ordinary shares}}$$

The use of earnings per share was discussed in Section 2.3.3 of this chapter.

4.7.3 The price earnings ratio

Key term

$$\text{Price earnings ratio} = \frac{\text{Market price of share}}{\text{EPS}}$$

The **price earnings (P/E) ratio** is a useful yardstick for assessing the relative worth of a share.

This is the same as:

$$\frac{\text{Total market value of equity}}{\text{Total earnings}}$$

The **value of the P/E ratio** reflects the **market's appraisal** of the share's **future prospects**. It is an important ratio because it relates two key considerations for investors, the market price of a share and its earnings capacity.

4.7.4 Example: Price earnings ratio

A company has recently declared a dividend of 12c per share. The share price is $3.72 cum div and earnings for the most recent year were 30c per share. Calculate the P/E ratio.

Solution

$$\text{P/E ratio} = \frac{\text{MV ex div}}{\text{EPS}} = \frac{\$3.60}{30c} = 12$$

The ex-div price should be used, as this reflects the underlying value of the share.

4.7.5 Changes in EPS: the P/E ratio and the share price   12/08

An approach to assessing what share prices ought to be, which is often used in practice, is a P/E ratio approach.

(a)   The relationship between the **EPS** and the **share price** is measured by the **P/E ratio**.

(b) The **P/E ratio** tends to change gradually and is reasonably consistent between companies operating in similar businesses.

(c) So if the **EPS goes up** or **down**, the **share price** should be expected to **move up or down** too, and the new share price will be the new EPS multiplied by the constant P/E ratio.

For example, if a company had an EPS last year of 30c and a share price of $3.60, its P/E ratio would have been 12. If the current year's EPS is 33c, we might expect that the P/E ratio would remain the same, 12, and so the share price ought to go up to 12 × 33c = $3.96.

<table>
<tr><td>**Exam focus point**</td><td>The ACCA examination team has commented that students have had problems with these ratios and emphasised how important it is to be familiar with them.</td></tr>
</table>

Question
Shareholder ratios

The directors of X are comparing some of the company's year-end statistics with those of Y, the company's main competitor. X has had a fairly normal year in terms of profit but Y's latest profits have been severely reduced by an exceptional loss arising from the closure of an unsuccessful division. Y has a considerably higher level of financial gearing than X.

The board is focusing on the figures given below.

	X	Y
Share price	450c	525c
Nominal value of shares	50c	100c
Dividend yield	5%	4%
Price/earnings ratio	15	25
Proportion of profits earned overseas	60%	0%

In the course of the discussion a number of comments are made, including those given below.

Required

Discuss comments (a) to (d), making use of the above data where appropriate.

(a) 'There is something odd about the P/E ratios. Y has had a particularly bad year. Its P/E should surely be lower than ours.'

(b) 'One of the factors which may explain Y's high P/E is the high financial gearing.'

(c) 'The comparison of our own P/E ratio and dividend yield with those of Y is not really valid. The shares of the two companies have different nominal values.'

(d) 'These figures will not please our shareholders. The dividend yield is below the return an investor could currently obtain on risk-free government bonds.'

Answer

(a) **P/E ratio**

The **P/E ratio** measures the **relationship** between the **market price** of a share and the **earnings per share**. Its calculation involves the use of the share price, which is a reflection of the market's expectations of the future earnings performance, and the historic level of earnings.

If Y has just suffered an abnormally bad year's profit performance which is not expected to be repeated, the market will price the share on the basis of its expected future earnings. The earnings figure used to calculate the ratio will be the historical figure which is lower than that forecast for the future, and thus the ratio will appear high.

(b) **Financial gearing**

The **financial gearing** of the firm expresses the **relationship** between **debt** and **equity** in the capital structure. A high level of gearing means that there is a high ratio of debt to equity. This means that the company carries a high fixed interest charge, and thus the amount of earnings available to equity will be more variable from year to year than in a company with a lower gearing level. Thus the shareholders will carry a higher level of risk than in a company with lower gearing. All other things being equal, it is therefore likely that the share price in a highly geared company will be lower than that in a low geared firm.

The historical P/E ratio is dependent on the **current share price** and the **historical level of earnings**. A high P/E ratio is therefore more likely to be found in a company with low gearing than in one with high gearing. In the case of Y, the high P/E ratio is more probably attributable to the depressed level of earnings than to the financial structure of the company.

(c) **Comparison of ratios**

The ratios are calculated as follows.

$$\text{P/E ratio} \quad = \quad \frac{\text{Market share price}}{\text{Earnings per share}}$$

$$\text{Dividend yield} \quad = \quad \frac{\text{Dividend per share}}{\text{Market share price}}$$

Even if the shares have a **nominal value** (which isn't the case in every country) this nominal value is **irrelevant** in calculating the ratios. This can be proved by calculating the effect on the ratios of a share split – the ratios will be unchanged. Thus if all other factors (such as accounting conventions used in the two firms) are equal, a direct comparison of the ratios is valid.

(d) **Comparison with risk-free securities**

As outlined in (c) above, the **dividend yield** is the relationship between the **dividend per share** and the **current market price** of the share. The market price of the share reflects investor expectations about the future level of earnings and growth. If the share is trading with a low dividend yield, this means that investors have positive growth expectations after taking the level of risk into account. Although government bonds carry little risk, they are unlikely to offer significant growth potential either, and this means that the share will still be more attractive even after the low dividend yield has been taken into account.

5 Encouraging the achievement of stakeholder objectives
12/08, 6/12, 12/13

5.1 Managerial reward schemes

FAST FORWARD

It is argued that management will only make **optimal** decisions if they are monitored and appropriate incentives are given.

The agency relationship arising from the separation of ownership from management is sometimes characterised as the **'agency problem'**. For example, if managers hold none or very little of the equity shares of the company they work for, what is to stop them from working inefficiently, not bothering to look for profitable new investment opportunities or giving themselves high salaries and perks?

Key term

> **Goal congruence** is accordance between the objectives of agents acting within an organisation and the objectives of the organisation as a whole.

Goal congruence may be better achieved and the 'agency problem' better dealt with by offering organisational **rewards** (more pay and promotion) for the achievement of certain levels of performance. The conventional theory of reward structures is that if the organisation establishes procedures for **formal measurement** of performance, and rewards individuals for **good performance**, individuals will be more likely to direct their efforts towards achieving the organisation's goals.

Examples of such remuneration incentives are:

(a) **Performance-related pay**

Pay or bonuses are usually related to the size of profits, but other performance indicators may be used.

(b) **Rewarding managers with shares**

This might be done when a private company 'goes public' and managers are invited to subscribe for shares in the company at an attractive offer price. In a **management buy-out** or buy-in (the latter involving purchase of the business by new managers; the former by existing managers), managers become owner-managers.

Shares and share options are also often included as part of the remuneration package for employees and managers in listed businesses. Ideally these will be given in many small tranches to incentivise building value over time.

(c) **Executive share option plans (ESOPs)**

In a share option scheme, selected employees are given a number of share options, each of which gives the holder the right after a certain date to subscribe for shares in the company at a fixed price. The value of an option will increase if the company is successful and its share price goes up.

Exam focus point

The December 2013 exam contained a question asking for ways in which directors of a company could be encouraged to achieve maximisation of shareholder wealth. The two main ways are via managerial reward schemes and through regulatory requirements such as corporate governance codes. Please read the article on ACCA's website called 'Myopic management'.

5.1.1 Beneficial consequences of linking reward schemes and performance

(a) Performance-related pay may give individuals an incentive to achieve a good performance level.

(b) Effective schemes also succeed in attracting and keeping the employees that are valuable to the organisation.

(c) By tying an organisation's key performance indicators to a scheme, it is clear to all employees what level of performance is expected of them and helps communicate their role in attempting to create organisational success.

(d) By rewarding performance, an effective scheme creates an organisation focused on continuous improvement.

(e) Schemes based on shares can motivate employees/managers to act in the long-term interests of the organisation by doing things to increase the organisation's market value.

5.1.2 Problems associated with reward schemes

(a) A serious problem that can arise is that performance-related pay and performance evaluation systems can **encourage dysfunctional behaviour**. Many investigations have noted the tendency of managers to pad their budgets either in anticipation of cuts by superiors or to make subsequent variances more favourable.

(b) Perhaps of even more concern are the numerous examples of managers making **decisions that are contrary to the wider purposes of the organisation**.

(c) Schemes designed to **ensure long-term achievements** (that is, to combat short-termism or myopic management) **may not motivate** since effort and reward are too distant in time from each other (or managers may not think they will be around that long!).

(d) It is questionable whether any performance measures or set of measures can provide a **comprehensive assessment of what a single person achieves** for an organisation. There will always be a lack of goal congruence, employees being committed to what is measured, rather than the objectives of the organisation.

(e)   **Self-interested performance** may be encouraged at the **expense of teamwork**.

(f)   High levels of output (whether this is number of calls answered or production of product X) may be achieved at the expense of **quality**.

(g)   In order to make bonuses more accessible, **standards and targets may have to be lowered**, with knock-on effects on quality.

(h)   They **undervalue intrinsic rewards** (which reflect the satisfaction that an individual experiences from doing a job and the opportunity for growth that the job provides) given that they promote extrinsic rewards (bonuses and so on).

5.2 Regulatory requirements

FAST FORWARD ▶▶

The achievement of stakeholder objectives can be **enforced** using regulatory requirements such as **corporate governance** codes of best practice and stock exchange **listing regulations**.

5.2.1 Corporate governance

FAST FORWARD ▶▶

Good corporate governance involves ensuring the effectiveness of **risk management** and **internal control**, **accountability** to shareholders and other stakeholders, and conducting business in an **ethical and effective way**.

Key term

> **Corporate governance** is the system by which organisations are directed and controlled.

There are a number of key elements in corporate governance.

(a)   The **management and reduction of risk** is a fundamental issue in all definitions of good governance, whether explicitly stated or merely implied.

(b)   The notion that **overall performance is enhanced** by **good organisational structures** and **management** practice within set best practice guidelines underpins most definitions.

(c)   Good governance provides a **framework** for an organisation to pursue its strategy in an **ethical and effective** way from the perspective of all stakeholder groups affected, and offers safeguards against misuse of resources, physical or intellectual.

(d)   Good governance is not just about externally established codes but also requires a willingness to **apply the spirit** as well as the letter of the law.

(e)   **Accountability** is generally a major theme in all governance frameworks.

Corporate governance codes of good practice generally cover the following areas.

(a)   The board should be responsible for taking major **policy** and **strategic** decisions.

(b)   Directors should have a **mix of skills** and their **performance** should be assessed regularly.

(c)   Appointments should be conducted by formal procedures administered by a **nomination committee**.

(d)   **Division of responsibilities** at the head of an organisation is most simply achieved by separating the roles of chairman and chief executive.

(e)   **Independent non-executive directors** have a key role in governance. Their number and status should mean that their views carry significant weight.

(f)   Directors' remuneration should be set by a **remuneration committee** consisting of independent non-executive directors.

(g)   Remuneration should be dependent on **organisation** and **individual performance**.

(h)   Accounts should disclose **remuneration policy** and (in detail) the **packages of individual directors**.

(i)   Boards should regularly review **risk management** and **internal control**, and carry out a wider review annually, the results of which should be disclosed in the accounts.

(j)   Audit committees of independent non-executive directors should liaise with external auditors, supervise internal audit, and review the annual accounts and internal controls.

(k)   The board should maintain a regular dialogue with shareholders, particularly institutional shareholders. The annual general meeting is a significant forum for communication.

(l)   Annual reports must **convey** a **fair and balanced view** of the organisation. This might include whether the organisation has complied with governance regulations and codes, and give specific disclosures about the board, internal control reviews, going concern status and relations with stakeholders.

5.2.2 Stock exchange listing regulations

A stock exchange employs **rules and regulations** to ensure that the stock market operates **fairly** and **efficiently** for all parties involved.

A stock exchange is an organisation that provides a marketplace in which to trade shares. It also sets rules and regulations to ensure that the stock market operates both efficiently and fairly for all parties involved.

The stock exchange operates as two different markets.

*   It is a market for issuers who wish to raise equity capital by offering shares for sale to investors (a primary market). Such companies are **listed** on the stock exchange.

*   It is also a market for investors who can buy and sell shares at any time, without directly affecting the entities in which they are buying the shares (a secondary market).

To be listed on a stock exchange, a stock must meet the **listing requirements** laid down in the listing rules in its approval process.

6 Not for profit organisations

Not for profit and public sector organisations have their own objectives, generally concerned with achieving specified objectives effectively and efficiently.

6.1 Not for profit sectors

Although most people would know one if they saw it, there is a surprising problem in clearly defining what counts as a **not for profit (NFP) organisation**. Local authority services, for example, would not be setting objectives in order to arrive at a profit for shareholders, but nowadays they are being increasingly required to apply the same disciplines and processes as companies which are oriented towards straightforward profit goals.

 Case Study

Oxfam operates around 700 shops in Britain, and these operate at a profit. The Royal Society for the Protection of Birds owns and operates an internet and mail order trading company which operates profitably and effectively.

Bois proposes that a **not for profit organisation** be defined as: ' ... an organisation whose attainment of its prime goal is not assessed by economic measures. However, in pursuit of that goal it may undertake profit-making activities.'

The not for profit sector may involve a number of different kinds of organisation with, for example, differing legal status – charities, statutory bodies offering public transport or the provision of services such as leisure, health or public utilities.

The tasks of setting objectives and developing strategies and controls for their implementation can all help in improving the performance of charities and NFP organisations.

6.2 Objectives

The primary objective of many NFP organisations will be the effective provision of a service, not the creation of profit. This has implications for reporting of results. The organisation will need to be open and honest in showing how it has managed its budget and allocated funds raised. **Efficiency and effectiveness** are particularly important in the use of donated funds, but there is a danger that **resource efficiency** becomes more important than **service effectiveness**.

Here are some possible objectives for a NFP organisation.

(a) Surplus maximisation (equivalent to profit maximisation eg a charity shop)
(b) Revenue maximisation (as for a commercial business eg a charity shop)
(c) Usage maximisation (for example, leisure centre swimming pool usage)
(d) Usage targeting (matching the capacity available, for example, in a government-funded hospital)
(e) Full/partial cost recovery (minimising subsidy)
(f) Budget maximisation (maximising what is offered)
(g) Producer satisfaction maximisation (satisfying the wants of staff and volunteers)
(h) Client satisfaction maximisation (the police generating the support of the public)

6.3 Value for money

Value for money is getting the best possible combination of services from the least resources.

It is reasonable to argue that not for profit organisations **best serve society's interests** when the **gap** between the **benefits** they provide and the **cost** of providing those benefits is **greatest**. This is commonly termed **value for money** and is not dissimilar from the concept of profit maximisation, apart from the fact that society's interests are being maximised rather than profit.

Value for money can be defined as getting the best possible combination of services from the least resources, which means maximising the benefits for the lowest possible cost.

This is usually accepted as requiring the application of economy, effectiveness and efficiency (sometimes known as the 3Es).

(a) **Economy** (spending money frugally)
(b) **Efficiency** (getting out as much as possible for what goes in)
(c) **Effectiveness** (getting done, by means of (a) and (b), what was supposed to be done)

More formally, these criteria can be defined as follows.

Effectiveness is the extent to which declared objectives/goals are met.
Efficiency is the relationship between inputs and outputs.
Economy is attaining the appropriate quantity and quality of inputs at the lowest cost to achieve a certain level of outputs.

6.4 Example: Economy, efficiency, effectiveness

(a) **Economy.** This dimension relates to the cost of inputs. Economy within a school could be measured, for example, by comparing average salaries per teacher with earlier years and budgets.

(b) **Efficiency.** The efficiency with which a school's IT laboratory is used might be measured in terms of the proportion of the school week for which it is used.

(c) **Effectiveness.** The effectiveness of a school's objective to produce quality teaching could be measured by the proportion of students going on to higher or further education.

6.5 Performance measures

Value for money as a concept **assumes** that there is a **yardstick** against which to measure the overall performance of an organisation. It can be **difficult to determine** where there is value for money, however.

(a) Not for profit organisations tend to have **multiple objectives**, so that even if they can all be clearly identified it is impossible to say which is the overriding objective.

(b) **Outputs can seldom be measured** in a way that is generally agreed to be meaningful. (Are good exam results alone an adequate measure of the quality of teaching? How does one quantify the easing of pain following a successful operation?) For example, in a publicly funded healthcare system, success may be measured in terms of fewer patient deaths per hospital admission, shorter waiting lists for operations, average speed of patient recovery, and so on.

Here are a number of possible solutions to these problems.

(a) Performance can be judged in terms of **inputs**. This is very common in everyday life. If somebody tells you that their suit cost $750, for example, you would generally conclude that it was an extremely well-designed and good quality suit, even if you did not think so when you first saw it. The **drawback**, of course, is that you might also conclude that the person wearing the suit had been cheated or was a fool, or you may think that no piece of clothing is worth $750. It is similar with the inputs and outputs of a non profit seeking organisation.

(b) Accept that performance measurement must to some extent be subjective. **Judgements** can be made **by experts**.

(c) Most not for profit organisations do not face competition but this does not mean that they are all unique. Bodies like local governments, health services, and so on can **compare** their performance **against each other** and **against the historical results** of their predecessors. **Unit cost measurements** like 'cost per patient day' or 'cost of borrowing one library book' can be established to allow organisations to assess whether they are doing better or worse than their counterparts. Care must be taken not to read too much into limited information, however.

6.6 Example: Performance measures

Although output of not for profit organisations is difficult to measure in a way that is generally agreed to be meaningful, it is not impossible. Outputs of a university might be measured in terms of the following.

Broader performance measures

- Proportion of total undergraduate population attending the university (by subject)
- Proportion of students graduating and classes of degrees obtained
- Amount of private sector research funds attracted
- Number of students finding employment after graduation
- Number of publications/articles produced by teaching staff

Operational performance measures

- Unit costs for each operating 'unit'
- Staff: student ratios; staff workloads
- Class sizes
- Availability of computers; good library stock
- Courses offered

6.7 Example: Inputs and outputs

Suppose that at a cost of $40,000 and 4,000 hours (**inputs**) in an average year, two policemen travel 8,000 miles and are instrumental in 200 arrests (**outputs**). A large number of **possibly meaningful measures** can be derived from these few figures, as the table below shows.

		$40,000	4,000 hours	8,000 miles	200 arrests
Cost ($)	$40,000		$40,000/4,000 = $10 per hour	$40,000/8,000 = $5 per mile	$40,000/200 = $200 per arrest
Time (hours)	4,000	4,000/$40,000 = 6 minutes patrolling per $1 spent		4,000/8,000 = ½ hour to patrol 1 mile	4,000/200 = 20 hours per arrest
Miles	8,000	8,000/$40,000 = 0.2 of a mile per $1	8,000/4,000 = 2 miles patrolled per hour		8,000/200 = 40 miles per arrest
Arrests	200	200/$40,000 = 1 arrest per $200	200/4,000 = 1 arrest every 20 hours	200/8,000 = 1 arrest every 40 miles	

These measures do not necessarily identify cause and effect or personal responsibility and accountability. Actual performance needs to be **compared**:

- With **standards**, if there are any
- With similar **external activities**
- With similar **internal activities**
- With **targets**
- With **indices**
- Over time – **as trends**

Chapter Roundup

- Financial management decisions cover **investment** decisions, **financing** decisions, **dividend** decisions and **risk management.**

- **Strategy** is a course of action to achieve an objective. There are three main levels of strategy in an organisation.

    - Corporate: the general direction of the whole organisation
    - Business: how the organisation or its business units tackle particular markets
    - Operational/functional: specific strategies for different departments of the business

- **Corporate objectives** are relevant for the organisation as a whole, relating to key factors for business success.

- Financial targets may include targets for: **earnings; earnings per share; dividend per share; gearing level; profit retention; operating profitability.**

    The usual assumption in financial management for the private sector is that the primary financial objective of the company is to **maximise shareholders' wealth.**

- **Stakeholders** are individuals or groups who are affected by the activities of the firm. They can be classified as **internal** (employees and managers), **connected** (shareholders, customers and suppliers) and **external** (local communities, pressure groups, government).

- **Performance measurement** is a part of the system of financial control of an enterprise as well as being important to investors.

- Indicators such as **dividend yield**, **EPS**, **P/E ratio** and **dividend cover** can be used to assess investor returns.

- It is argued that management will only make **optimal** decisions if they are monitored and appropriate incentives are given.

- The achievement of stakeholder objectives can be **enforced** using regulatory requirements such as **corporate governance** codes of best practice and stock exchange **listing regulations**.

- Good corporate governance involves ensuring the effectiveness of **risk management** and **internal control,** **accountability** to shareholders and other stakeholders, and conducting business in an **ethical and effective way.**

- A stock exchange employs **rules and regulations** to ensure that the stock market operates **fairly** and **efficiently** for all parties involved.

- Not for profit and public sector organisations have their own objectives, generally concerned with achieving specified objectives effectively and efficiently.

- **Value for money** is getting the best possible combination of services from the least resources.

1   Give a definition of financial management.

2   What three broad types of decision does financial management involve?

3   What main financial objective does the theory of company finance assume that a business organisation has?

4   If earnings per share fall from one year to the next, so will the level of dividends.

☐ True

☐ False

5   Tick which are stakeholder groups for a company.

Employees ☐

Ordinary shareholders ☐

The Board of Directors ☐

Trade payables (suppliers) ☐

6   Return on capital employed = $\dfrac{?}{?}$

7   Which of the following are examples of financial objectives that a company might choose to pursue?

A   Provision of good wages and salaries
B   Restricting the level of gearing to below a specified target level
C   Dealing honestly and fairly with customers on all occasions
D   Producing environmentally friendly products

8   **Fill in the blank.**

.... is accordance between the objectives of agents acting within an organisation.

9   What are the 'Three Es' of value for money?

E ....

E ....

E ....

10   In the context of managing performance in not for profit organisations, which of the following definitions is incorrect?

A   Value for money means providing a service in a way which is economical, efficient and effective.

B   Economy means doing things cheaply: not spending $2 when the same thing can be bought for $1.

C   Efficiency means doing things quickly: minimising the amount of time that is spent on a given activity.

D   Effectiveness means doing the right things: spending funds so as to achieve the organisation's objectives.

Answers to Quick Quiz

1   The management of the finances of an organisation in order to achieve the financial objectives of the organisation

2   Investment decisions, financing decisions, dividend decisions

3   To maximise the wealth of the company's ordinary shareholders

4   False. Dividends may still be maintained from payments out of profits retained in earlier periods.

5   You should have ticked all four boxes.

6    $$\frac{\text{Profit before interest and tax}}{\text{Capital employed}}$$

7   B   This is a financial objective that relates to the level of risk that the company accepts.

8   Goal congruence

9   Efficiency. Economy. Effectiveness

10   C   Efficiency means doing things well: getting the best use out of what money is spent on.

Now try the questions below from the Practice Question Bank

Number	Level	Marks	Approximate time
Section A Q1	Examination	2	4 mins
Section A Q2	Examination	2	4 mins
Section A Q3	Examination	2	4 mins

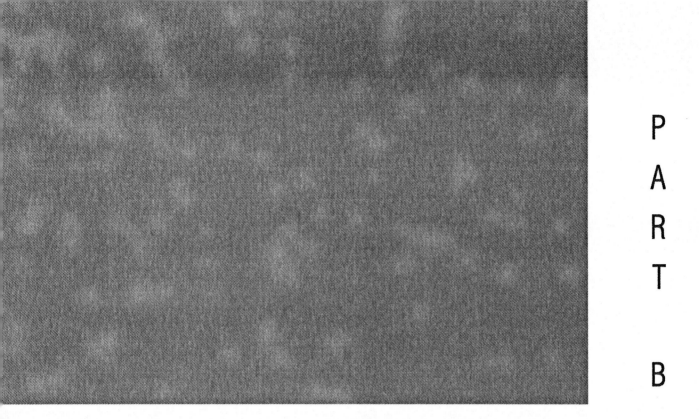

Financial management environment

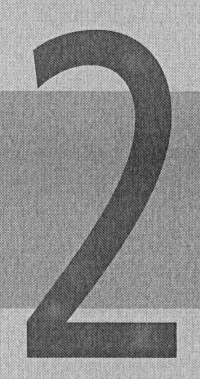

The economic environment for business

Topic list	Syllabus reference
1 Outline of macroeconomic policy	B1 (a)
2 Fiscal policy	B1 (b), (c)
3 Monetary policy	B1 (b), (c)
4 Exchange rates	B1 (b), (c)
5 Competition policy	B1 (d)
6 Government assistance for business	B1 (d)
7 Green policies	B1 (d)
8 Corporate governance regulation	B1 (d)

Introduction

A business will strive to achieve its objectives, but it has to do so in an economy which the Government will try to steer to achieve its own objectives. In this chapter we're moving away from the **microeconomics** of the individual business to the **macroeconomics** of the economy as a whole. The business (and you as an individual) will need to understand how government policies can impact on different aspects of the economy, and the implications for the business's own activities and future plans.

The main **macroeconomic policy** tools we will look at are **fiscal, monetary, interest rate**, and **exchange rate** policy. We will also look at the impact that specific government policies have on businesses.

Study guide

		Intellectual level
B1	**The economic environment for business**	
(a)	Identify and explain the main macroeconomic policy targets.	1
(b)	Define and discuss the role of fiscal, monetary, interest rate and exchange rate policies in achieving macroeconomic policy targets.	1
(c)	Explain how government economic policy interacts with planning and decision-making in business.	2
(d)	Explain the need for, and the interaction with, planning and decision-making in business of:	1
(i)	Competition policy	2
(ii)	Government assistance for business	2
(iii)	Green policies	2
(iv)	Corporate governance regulation	2

Exam guide

The emphasis in the exam will be on discussing how economic conditions or policies affect particular businesses, for example the impact of a change in interest rates.

1 Outline of macroeconomic policy

Macroeconomic policy involves:

- Policy **objectives** – the ultimate aims of economic policy
- Policy **targets** – quantified levels or ranges which policy is intended to achieve
- Policy **instruments** – the tools used to achieve objectives

Achievement of **economic growth, low inflation, full employment** and **balance of payments stability** are policy objectives.

Policy targets might be set for **economic growth** or the **rate of inflation**, for example.

1.1 Microeconomics, macroeconomics and economic policy

Key terms

Microeconomics is concerned with the economic behaviour of individual firms and consumers or households. **Macroeconomics** is concerned with the economy at large, and with the behaviour of large aggregates such as the national income, the money supply and the level of employment.

A government is concerned with how the economy is behaving as a whole, and therefore with **macroeconomic variables**.

Macroeconomic policy can affect planning and decision-making in various ways, for example via interest rate changes, which affect borrowing costs and required rates of return.

Note also that a government might adopt policies which try to exert influence at the **microeconomic** level. Examples include policies to restrict the maximum hours an individual can work or the imposition of a minimum wage.

1.2 Economic policies and objectives

The policies pursued by a government may serve various objectives.

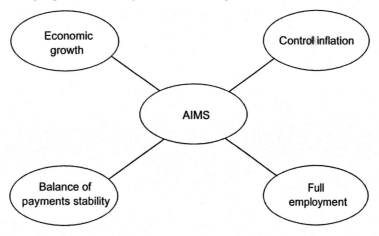

(a)   **Economic growth**
'Growth' implies an increase in national income in 'real' terms (increases caused by price inflation are not real increases at all). It is usually interpreted as a rising standard of living.

(b)   **Control price inflation**
This means managing price inflation to a low, stable level. Inflation is viewed as a problem because, if a country has a higher rate of inflation than its major trading partners, its exports will become relatively expensive. It leads to a redistribution of income and wealth in ways which may be undesirable. In times of high inflation, substantial labour time is spent on planning and implementing price changes.

(c)   **Full employment**
Full employment does not mean that everyone who wants a job has one all the time, but it does mean that unemployment levels are low, and involuntary unemployment is short term.

(d)   **Balance of payments stability**
The wealth of a country relative to others, a country's creditworthiness as a borrower, and the goodwill between countries in international relations might all depend on the achievement of an external trade balance over time. Deficits in external trade, with imports exceeding exports, might also be damaging for the prospects of economic growth.

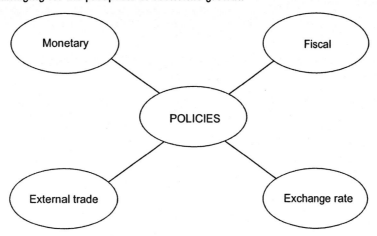

To try to achieve its objectives, a government will use a number of different policy tools or policy instruments. These include the following.

(a) **Monetary policy**

Monetary policy aims to influence monetary variables such as the rate of interest and the money supply in order to achieve targets set for employment, inflation, economic growth and the balance of payments.

(b) **Fiscal policy**

Fiscal policy involves using government spending and taxation in order to influence aggregate demand in the economy.

(c) **Exchange rate policy**

Some economists argue that economic objectives can be achieved through management of the exchange rate by the Government. The strength or weakness of sterling's value, for example, will influence the volume of UK imports and exports, the balance of payments and interest rates.

(d) **External trade policy**

A government might have a policy for promoting economic growth by stimulating exports; for example, by managing the exchange rate to make exports cheaper for foreign purchasers. Another argument is that there should be import controls to provide some form of protection for domestic manufacturing industries by making the cost of imports higher and the volume of imports lower. Protection could encourage domestic output to rise, stimulating the domestic economy.

These **policy tools** are not mutually exclusive and a government might adopt a policy mix of monetary policy, fiscal policy and exchange rate policy and external trade policy in an attempt to achieve its intermediate and ultimate economic objectives.

1.3 Conflicts in policy objectives and instruments

Macroeconomic policy aims cannot necessarily all be sustained together for a long period of time; attempts to achieve one objective will often have adverse effects on others, sooner or later.

(a) There may be a **conflict** between **steady balanced growth** in the economy and **full employment**. Although a growing economy should be able to provide more jobs, there is some concern that since an economy must be modernised to grow and modern technology is labour saving, it might be possible to achieve growth without creating many more jobs, and so keeping unemployment at a high level.

(b) In the UK, **problems** with **creating more employment** and **steady growth** in the economy have been a lack of domestic and global demand following the global financial crisis, the balance of payments, the foreign exchange value of sterling, inflation and the money supply. The objectives of lower unemployment and economic growth have been difficult to achieve because of the problems and conflicts with secondary objectives.

   (i) To create jobs and growth, there must be an **increase in aggregate demand**. When demand picks up there will be a surge in imports, with foreign goods bought by UK manufacturers (eg raw materials) and consumers.

   (ii) For example, in the UK, the high rate of imports creates a **deficit in the balance of payments**, which in turn will weaken sterling and raise the cost of imports, thus giving some impetus to price rises.

   (iii) To maintain the value of a country's currency, **interest rates** might need to be kept **high**, and high interest rates appear to **deter** companies from **investing**.

In practice, achieving the best mix of economic policies also involves a number of problems, such as the following.

- Inadequate **information**
- **Time lags** between use of policy and effects being noticeable
- **Political pressure** for short-term solutions

- Unpredictable **side effects** of policies
- The influence of **other countries**
- **Conflict** between policy instruments

2 Fiscal policy

Fiscal policy seeks to influence the economy by managing the amounts which the Government spends and the amounts it collects through taxation. Fiscal policy can be used as an instrument of **demand management**.

2.1 Fiscal policy and demand management

Key term

Fiscal policy is action by the Government to spend money, or to collect money in taxes, with the purpose of influencing the condition of the national economy.

A government might intervene in the economy by:

(a)   **Spending more money** and **financing this expenditure** by **borrowing**

(b)   **Collecting more in taxes without increasing public spending**

(c)   **Collecting more in taxes** in order to **increase public spending**, thus diverting income from one part of the economy to another

Government spending is an **'injection'** into the economy, adding to total demand for goods and services in the economy (known as aggregate demand) and therefore national income, whereas taxes are a 'withdrawal' from the economy. Fiscal policy can thus be used as an instrument of demand management ie deliberate policies to stimulate and control the level of aggregate demand in an economy. Too little demand creates unemployment, too much creates inflation.

Fiscal policy appears to offer a method of **managing aggregate demand** in the economy.

(a)   If the Government spends more – for example, on public works such as hospitals, roads and sewers – without raising more money in taxation (ie by borrowing more) it will **increase expenditure** in the economy, and so **raise demand**.

(b)   If the Government kept its own spending at the same level but **reduced** the levels of taxation, it would **also stimulate demand** in the economy because firms and households would have more of their own money after tax for consumption or saving/investing. This is an expansionary policy.

(c)   In the same way, a government can **reduce demand** in the economy by **raising taxes** or **reducing its expenditure**. This is a contractionary policy.

2.2 Fiscal policy and business

Fiscal policy affects business enterprises in both service and manufacturing industries in various ways. For example:

(a)   By influencing the level of **aggregate demand (AD)** for goods and services in the economy, macroeconomic policy **affects** the **environment** for business. Business planning should take account of the likely effect of changes in AD for sales growth. For example, a drop in AD might mean lower demand from customers for a business's products and services. Business planning will be easier if government policy is relatively stable.

(b)   Tax changes brought about by **fiscal policy** affect businesses. For example, labour costs will be affected by changes in **employment taxes**. For example, if indirect taxes such as sales tax or excise duty rise, either the additional cost will have to be absorbed or the rise will have to be passed on to consumers in the form of higher prices.

3 Monetary policy

Monetary policy aims to influence monetary variables such as the rate of interest and the money supply in order to achieve targets set, such as targets for the rate of inflation.

Money is important because:

(a) It **'oils the wheels'** of **economic activity**, providing an easy method for exchanging goods and services (ie buying and selling).

(b) The total amount of money in a national economy may have a **significant influence** on **economic activity and inflation.**

3.1 The role and aims of monetary policy

Key term

Monetary policy is the regulation of the economy through control of the monetary system by operating on such variables as the money supply, the level of interest rates and the conditions for availability of credit.

The **effectiveness** of monetary policy will depend on:

(a) Whether the **targets** of **monetary policy** are **achieved successfully**

(b) Whether the **success** of **monetary policy** leads on to the **successful achievement** of the **intermediate target** (eg lower inflation)

(c) Whether the **successful achievement** of the **intermediate target** (eg lower inflation) leads on to the **successful achievement** of the **overall objective** (eg stronger economic growth)

3.2 Targets of monetary policy

Targets of monetary policy are likely to relate to the volume of national income and expenditure.

- Growth in the size of the money supply

- The level of interest rates

- The volume of credit, or growth in the volume of credit

- The volume of expenditure in the economy (ie national income or gross national product (GNP) itself)

3.3 The money supply as a target of monetary policy

To monetarist economists, the **money supply** is a possible intermediate **target** of economic policy. This is because they claim that an increase in the money supply will raise prices and money incomes, and this in turn will raise the demand for money to spend.

3.4 Interest rates as a target for monetary policy

The authorities may decide that **interest rates** themselves should be a target of monetary policy. This would be appropriate if it is considered that there is a **direct relationship** between interest rates and the **level of expenditure** in the economy.

It certainly seems logical that interest rates should have a strong influence on economic activity.

However, although empirical evidence suggests there is some connection between interest rates and investment (by companies) and consumer expenditure, the connection is not a stable and predictable one. Some economists argue that the key element affecting investment is **business confidence** rather than the level of interest rates. Interest rate changes are only likely to affect the level of expenditure after a considerable time lag.

In 1997 the British Government gave responsibility for setting short-term interest rates to the central bank, the Bank of England. The Bank sets rates at a level which it considers appropriate, given the inflation rate target set by the Government. For example, if inflation is forecast to be excessive, increasing interest rates

should increase saving, reduce borrowing and reduce investment, thus reducing aggregate demand in the economy. With lower aggregate demand, there is less pressure for suppliers to increase prices as they struggle to hit sales targets, so inflationary pressure is reduced. The purpose of having the central bank setting interest rates is to remove the risk of **political influence** over the decisions. In the **European Monetary Union** (where the **euro** is the common currency), the interest rates that prevail are effectively set at the European level.

3.5 Interest rate policy and business   12/08

Interest rate changes brought about by government policy affect the **borrowing costs** of business. Increases in interest rates will mean that **fewer investments** show positive returns, deterring companies from borrowing to finance expansion. Increases in interest rates will also exert a **downward pressure on share prices**, making it more difficult for companies to raise monies from new share issues. Businesses will also be squeezed by **decreases in consumer demand** that result from increases in interest rates.

Question   Interest rate levels

Outline the effects on the economy of a policy of high interest rates to dampen demand and inflation.

Answer

An increase in interest rates is thought to reduce the money supply through demand for credit in the economy, thereby reducing the level of effective demand. This will, in turn, decrease inflation and improve the balance of payments (the latter by lowering the price of exports, increasing demand for them and simultaneously increasing the relative price of imports, reducing demand for them, and freeing more domestic output for sale abroad). Aggregate expenditure in the economy will decrease for various reasons.

(a)   A higher interest rate **encourages savings** at the expense of consumer expenditure.

(b)   Higher interest rates will **increase mortgage payments** and will thus reduce the amount of disposable income in the hands of home buyers for discretionary spending.

(c)   The higher cost of consumer credit will **deter borrowing** and **spending** on consumer durables.

(d)   Higher prices of goods due to higher borrowing costs for industry will also **reduce some consumer expenditure** in the economy.

Investment expenditure may also decline for two reasons.

(a)   Higher interest rates **deter some investment** due to increased borrowing costs.

(b)   Higher interest rates may make the **corporate sector pessimistic** about future business prospects and the economy. This may further reduce investment in the economy.

To the extent that higher domestic interest rates lead to an appreciation of the exchange rate, this should reduce inflation by lowering the cost of imported items. Exporters will experience pressure on their costs as a result of the more competitive price conditions they face, and may be less willing to concede high wage demands, thus wage inflation may be constrained. The desired outcomes of the authorities' interest rate policy noted above may be negated by the following effects of higher interest rates.

(a)   Higher interest results in **greater interest income** for savers, who may increase their spending due to this interest windfall.

(b)   Since **mortgage payments** are generally a significant part of domestic household expenditure, any increase in them will be reflected immediately in reported inflation. This could lead to higher wage demands in the economy, and may result in a wage-price spiral.

(c)   By encouraging capital inflows, higher interest rates will tend to lead to an **appreciation of the currency's exchange rate**. This makes exports more expensive and imports less expensive.

(d)   A reduction in investment may **decrease the pressure of demand** in the economy but at the same time will set in motion a process which in the future could reduce the economy's potential for production.

(e)   To the extent that higher interest rates squeeze demand in the economy, they will **reduce employment**, decreasing the proceeds of taxation and increasing government expenditure on the unemployed.

Case Study

US interest rates left unchanged by Federal Reserve

Analysts were divided over whether the Federal Reserve would raise interest rates or keep them as they have been since December 2008. In fact, they left them unchanged with the aim of keeping them low until employment levels increase. The inflation target is 2% but this has been kept down by cheaper oil and the strong dollar. Before interest rates are raised, the Federal Reserve wants to be 'reasonably confident' that inflation will increase.

Source: *www.bbc.co.uk* 17 September 2015

4 Exchange rates

FAST FORWARD

Exchange rates are determined by **supply and demand**, even under fixed exchange rate systems.

Governments can intervene to influence the exchange rate by, for example, **adjusting interest rates**. Government policies on exchange rates might be **fixed or floating exchange rates** as two extreme policies, but 'in-between' schemes have been more common.

Key term

An **exchange rate** is the rate at which one country's currency can be traded in exchange for another country's currency.

Dealers in foreign exchange make their profit by buying currency at one exchange rate, and selling it at a different rate. This means that there is a **selling rate** and a **buying rate** for a currency.

4.1 Factors influencing the exchange rate for a currency

The exchange rate between two currencies is determined primarily by supply and demand in the foreign exchange markets. Demand comes from individuals, firms and governments who want to buy a currency and supply comes from those who want to sell it.

Supply and demand in turn are subject to a number of influences.

- The rate of inflation, compared with the rate of inflation in other countries
- Interest rates, compared with interest rates in other countries
- The balance of payments
- Speculation
- Government policy on intervention to influence the exchange rate

Other factors influence the exchange rate through their relationship with the items identified above.

(a)   **Total income and expenditure** (demand) in the **domestic economy** determines the demand for goods. This includes imported goods and demand for goods produced in the country which would otherwise be exported if demand for them did not exist in the home markets.

(b) **Output capacity** and the **level of employment** in the domestic economy might influence the balance of payments because, if the domestic economy has full employment already, it will be unable to increase its volume of production for exports.

(c) The **growth** in the **money supply** influences interest rates and domestic inflation.

We will look at the cause of exchange rate fluctuations in more detail in Chapter 19.

4.2 Consequences of an exchange rate policy

Reasons for a policy of controlling the exchange rate are as follows.

(a) To **rectify a balance of trade deficit**, by trying to bring about a fall in the exchange rate

(b) To **prevent a balance of trade surplus** from getting too large, by trying to bring about a limited rise in the exchange rate

(c) To **stabilise the exchange rate** of the currency, as exporters and importers will then face less risk of exchange rate movements wiping out their profits; a stable currency increases confidence in the currency and promotes international trade.

4.3 Fixed exchange rates

A government may try to keep the exchange rate at a fixed level against a major currency such as the US dollar, or may try to keep it within a specified value range. However, if a government cannot control inflation, the **real value** of its currency would not remain fixed. If one country's rate of inflation is higher than others, its export prices will become uncompetitive in overseas markets and the country's trade deficit will grow (or its trade surplus will diminish). Devaluation of the currency would be necessary for a recovery. For example, a government may work to move the exchange rate from $2:£1 to $1:£1 so that exports become less expensive.

If exchange rates are fixed, any changes in **(real) interest rates** in one country will create pressure for the **movement of capital** into or out of the country. Capital movements would put pressure on the country's exchange rate to change. It follows that if exchange rates are fixed and capital is allowed to move freely between countries (ie there are no exchange controls) all countries must have consistent policies on interest rates.

4.4 Floating exchange rates

Key term

> **Floating exchange rates** are exchange rates which are allowed to fluctuate according to demand and supply conditions in the foreign exchange markets.

Floating exchange rates are at the opposite end of the spectrum to fixed rates. At this extreme, exchange rates are completely left to the free play of demand and supply market forces, and there is no official financing at all. The ruling exchange rate is, therefore, at equilibrium by definition.

In practice, many governments seek to combine the advantages of exchange rate stability with flexibility and to avoid the disadvantages of both rigidly fixed exchange rates and free floating. **Managed** (or dirty) **floating** refers to a system whereby exchange rates are allowed to float, but from time to time the authorities will intervene in the foreign exchange market:

- To use their official reserves of foreign currencies to buy their own domestic currency
- To sell their domestic currency to buy more foreign currency for the official reserves

Buying and selling in this way would be intended to influence the exchange rate of the domestic currency. Governments do not have official reserves large enough to dictate exchange rates to the market, and can only try to 'influence' market rates with intervention.

Speculation in the capital markets often has a much bigger short-term impact than changes in fundamental supply and demand.

4.5 European Economic and Monetary Union

There are three main aspects to the European Monetary Union.

(a) **A common currency** (the euro)

(b) **A European Central Bank**. The European Central Bank has several roles:

    (i) Issuing the common currency

    (ii) Conducting monetary policy on behalf of the central government authorities

    (iii) Acting as lender of last resort to all European banks

    (iv) Managing the exchange rate for the common currency

(c) A **centralised monetary policy** applies across all the countries in the union. This involves the surrender of control over aspects of economic policy and therefore surrender of some political sovereignty by the Government of each member state to the central government body of the union.

4.6 Exchange rates and business

A change in the exchange rate will affect the **relative prices** of domestic and foreign produced goods and services.

A lower exchange rate	A higher exchange rate
Domestic goods are cheaper in foreign markets so demand for exports increases.	Domestic goods are more expensive in foreign markets so demand for exports falls.
Foreign goods are more expensive so demand for imports falls.	Foreign goods are cheaper so demand for imports rises.
Imported raw materials are more expensive so costs of production rise.	Imported raw materials are cheaper so costs of production fall.

Fluctuating exchange rates create **uncertainties** for businesses involved in international trade. A service industry is less likely to be affected because it is less likely to be involved in substantial international trade.

International trading companies can do a number of things to reduce their **risk of suffering losses** on foreign exchange transactions, including the following.

(a) Many companies buy currencies **'forward'** at a fixed and known price.

(b) **Dealing in a 'hard' currency** may lessen the risks attached to volatile currencies.

(c) **Operations can be managed** so that the proportion of sales in one currency are matched by an equal proportion of purchases in that currency.

(d) **Invoicing can be in the domestic currency**. This means that the customer bears all the foreign exchange risk, however, and, in industries where customers have high bargaining power, this may be an unacceptable arrangement. Furthermore, there is the risk that sales will be adversely affected by high prices, reducing demand.

(e) **Activities can be outsourced** to the local market. Many of the Japanese car firms which have invested in the UK in recent years have made efforts to obtain many of their inputs, subject to quality limits, from local suppliers. Promotional activities can also be sourced locally.

(f) Firms can aim at **segments** in the market which are not particularly price sensitive. For example, many German car marques such as Mercedes have been marketed in the US on the basis of quality and exclusivity. This is a type of strategy based on differentiation focus.

Foreign currency risk will be covered in more detail in Chapter 19.

5 Competition policy

5.1 Regulation and market failure

The Government influences markets in various ways, one of which is through direct **regulation** (eg the **Competition and Markets Authority** in the UK).

Key term

Market failure is said to occur when the market mechanism (the interaction of supply and demand to result in a market clearing price and quantity supplied/demanded) fails to result in economic efficiency, and therefore the outcome is sub-optimal.

An important role of the Government is the **regulation of private markets** where these fail to bring about an **efficient** use of resources. In response to the existence of market failure, and as an alternative to taxation and public provision of production, the state often resorts to regulating economic activity in a variety of ways. Of the various forms of market failure, the following are the cases where regulation of markets can often be the most appropriate policy response.

(a) **Imperfect competition**
Where one company's large share or complete domination of the market is leading to **inefficiency** or **excessive profits**, the state may intervene, for example through controls on prices or profits, in order to try to reduce the effects of this power.

(b) **Social costs**
A possible means of dealing with the problem of social costs or **externalities** is via some form of regulation. Regulations might include, for example, controls on emissions of pollutants, restrictions on car use in urban areas, the banning of smoking in public buildings, or compulsory car insurance.

(c) **Imperfect information**
Regulation is often the best form of government action whenever informational inadequacies are undermining the efficient operation of private markets. This is particularly so when consumer choice is being distorted.

(d) **Equity**
The Government may also resort to regulation to **improve social justice**.

5.2 Types of regulation

Regulation can be defined as any form of state interference with the operation of the free market. This could involve regulating demand, supply, price, profit, quantity, quality, entry, exit, information, technology, or any other aspect of production and consumption in the market.

In many markets the participants (especially the firms) may decide to maintain a system of voluntary **self-regulation**, possibly in order to try to avert the imposition of government controls. Areas where self-regulation often exists include the professions (eg the Law Society, the British Medical Association and other professional bodies).

5.3 Monopolies and mergers

Key term

In a pure **monopoly**, there is only one firm in the market, the sole producer of a good, which has no closely competing substitutes.

A monopoly situation can have some advantages.

(a) In certain industries arguably only by achieving a monopoly will a company be able to benefit from the kinds of **economies of scale** (benefits of conducting operations on a large scale) that can minimise prices.

(b) Establishing a monopoly may be the best way for a business to **maximise its profits**.

However, monopolies often have several adverse consequences.

(a)   Companies can impose **higher prices** on consumers.

(b)   The lack of incentive of competition may mean companies have **no incentive** to **improve their products** or **offer a wider range of products**.

(c)   There is no pressure on the company to **improve the efficiency** of its **use of resources**.

In practice, government policy is concerned not just with situations where one firm has a 100% market share but also with other situations where an organisation has a significant market share.

The Competition and Markets Authority can also be asked to investigate what could be called **'oligopoly situations'** involving explicit or implicit collusion between firms, who together control the market.

The investigation is not automatic. Once the case has been referred, the Authority must decide whether or not the monopoly is acting **'against the public interest'**.

In its report, the Competition and Markets Authority will say if a monopoly situation has been found to exist and, if so, will make recommendations to deal with it. These may involve various measures.

- Price cuts
- Price and profit controls
- Removal of entry barriers
- The breaking up of the firm (rarely)

 Case Study

The healthcare giant Johnson & Johnson has become the latest foreign company to be accused of misconduct in China.

A ruling by a Shanghai court ordered the US company to pay $85,000 (£56,000) to a local distributor for violating anti-monopoly laws.

Two subsidiaries of the company were accused of setting a minimum price for the sale of surgical instruments.

Multinationals have faced increased scrutiny from the Chinese authorities.

Last month, two foreign milk suppliers announced price cuts after the Government launched an investigation into possible price fixing.

Source: www.bbc.co.uk 2 August 2013

A prospective **merger** between two or more companies may be referred to the Competition and Markets Authority for investigation if a larger company will gain more than 25% market share and where a merger appears likely to lead to a substantial lessening of competition in one or more markets in the UK.

Again, referral to the Competition and Markets Authority is not automatic and, since the legislation was first introduced, only a small proportion of all merger proposals have been referred.

If a potential merger is investigated, the Authority again has to determine whether or not the merger would be against the public interest. As with monopolies, it will assess the relative benefits and costs in order to arrive at a decision.

 Question

Competition

Look through newspapers or on the internet for a report on the activities of the Competition and Markets Authority. Why is the investigation being carried out and how was it initiated?

5.4 Restrictive practices

Some countries have legislation which deals with restrictive practices that distort, restrict or prevent competition. A notable example of a restrictive practice would be agreements with direct competitors resulting in them colluding to the disadvantage of the consumer (eg price-fixing agreements). The legislation may also deal with abuse of dominant position offences, such as predatory pricing (charging low prices to unfairly destroy competition) or refusing to supply so as to restrict competition.

5.5 European Union competition policy

As a member of the European Union (EU), the UK is also now subject to EU competition policy. This is enshrined in Articles 85 (dealing with restrictive practices) and 86 (concerned with monopoly) of the Treaty of Rome.

5.6 Deregulation

Deregulation or 'liberalisation' is, in general, the opposite of regulation. Deregulation can be defined as the removal or weakening of any form of statutory (or voluntary) regulation of free **market activity**. Deregulation allows **free market forces** more scope to determine the outcome.

Deregulation, whose main aim is to **introduce more competition** into an industry by removing statutory or other entry barriers, has the following potential benefits.

(a) **Improved incentives for internal/cost efficiency**
Greater competition compels managers to try harder to keep down costs.

(b) **Improved allocative efficiency**
Competition keeps down prices closer to marginal cost, and firms therefore produce closer to the socially optimal output level.

In some industries it could have certain disadvantages, including the following.

(a) **Loss of economies of scale**
If increased competition means that each firm produces less output on a smaller scale, unit costs will be higher.

(b) **Lower quality or quantity of service**
The need to reduce costs may lead firms to reduce quality or eliminate unprofitable but socially valuable services.

(c) **Need to protect competition**
It may be necessary to implement a regulatory regime to protect competition where inherent forces have a tendency to eliminate it, for example if there is a dominant firm already in the industry, as in the case of British Telecom. In this type of situation, effective 'regulation for competition' will be required, ie regulatory measures aimed at maintaining competitive pressures, whether existing or potential.

5.7 Privatisation

FAST FORWARD

Privatisation is a policy of introducing private enterprise into industries which were previously state-owned or state-operated.

Privatisation takes three broad forms.

(a) The **deregulation of industries**, to allow private firms to compete against state-owned businesses where they were not allowed to compete before (for example, deregulation of bus and coach services; deregulation of postal services)

(b) **Contracting out work** to **private firms**, where the work was previously done by government employees – for example, refuse collection or hospital laundry work

(c) **Transferring the ownership** of **assets from** the **state to private shareholders**

Privatisation can improve efficiency in one of two ways.

(a) If the effect of privatisation is to **increase competition**, the effect might be to reduce or eliminate allocative inefficiency.

(b) The effect of denationalisation might be to make the **industries more cost-conscious**, because they will be directly answerable to shareholders, and under scrutiny from stock market investors.

There are other possible advantages of privatisation.

(a) It provides an **immediate source of money** for the Government.

(b) It reduces **bureaucratic and political meddling** in the industries concerned.

(c) It encourages **wider share ownership**. Denationalisation is one method of creating wider share ownership, as the sale of BT, British Gas and some other nationalised industries have shown in the UK.

There are arguments against privatisation too.

(a) State-owned industries are more likely to respond to the **public interest**, ahead of the profit motive. For example, state-owned industries are more likely to cross-subsidise unprofitable operations from profitable ones.

(b) Encouraging private competition to state-run industries might be **inadvisable** where significant economies of scale can be achieved by monopoly operations.

(c) There is also an argument that privatised businesses act as monopolists or oligopolists.

6 Government assistance for business

6.1 Official aid schemes

The freedom of European governments to offer cash **grants and other forms of direct assistance** to business is **limited by European Union** policies designed to prevent the distortion of free market competition.

A government may provide finance to companies in cash grants and other forms of official direct assistance, as part of its policy of helping to develop the national economy, especially in high technology industries and in areas of high unemployment.

Government incentives might be offered on:

(a) A **regional basis**, giving help to firms that invest in an economically depressed area of the country

(b) A **selective national basis**, giving help to firms that invest in an industry that the Government would like to see developing more quickly, for example robotics or fibre optics

In Europe, such assistance is increasingly limited by European Union policies designed to prevent the distortion of free market competition. The UK Government's powers to grant aid for modernisation and development are now severely restricted.

7 Green policies

There are a number of policy approaches to **pollution**, such as **polluter pays policies, subsidies** and direct **legislation**.

The environment is increasingly seen as an important issue facing managers in both the public and private sectors. The problems of pollution and the environment appear to call for international co-operation between governments. Pollutants expelled into the atmosphere in the UK are said to cause acid rain to fall in Scandinavia, for example.

7.1 Pollution policy

Key term

> **Externalities** are positive or negative effects on third parties resulting from production and consumption activities.

Pollution, for example from exhaust gas emissions or the dumping of waste, is often discussed in relation to environmental policy. If polluters take little or no account of their actions on others, this generally results in the output of polluting industries being greater than is optimal.

One solution is to levy a tax on polluters equal to the cost of removing the effect of the externality they generate: the **polluter pays principle**. This will encourage firms to cut emissions and provides an incentive for them to research ways of permanently reducing pollution.

Apart from the imposition of a tax, there are a number of other measures open to the Government in attempting to reduce pollution. One of the main measures available is the application of **subsidies** which may be used either to persuade polluters to reduce output and hence pollution, or to assist with expenditure on production processes, such as new machinery and air cleaning equipment, which reduce levels of pollution.

7.2 Legislation

An alternative approach used in the UK is to impose **legislation** laying down regulations governing waste disposal and atmospheric emissions. Waste may only be disposed of with prior consent and if none is given, or it is exceeded, the polluter is fined. There may also be attempts with this type of approach to specify standards of, for example, air and water quality with appropriate penalties for not conforming to the required standards.

Case Study

The European Council's Directive (implemented in 1999 and amended in 2008) states:

'Member States must ensure that existing landfill sites may not continue to operate unless they comply with the provisions of the Directive as soon as possible. Member States must report to the Commission every three years on the implementation of the Directive. On the basis of these reports, the Commission must publish a Community report on the implementation of the Directive.'

This led to the Landfill (England & Wales) Regulations 2002 being brought into force in the UK. This, in turn, was implemented through the Government's Waste Strategy.

- Landfill Regulations require a reduction in the quantity of biodegradable and recyclable household waste being disposed of via landfill.

- Local councils are required to increase recycling and composting of household waste to meet rising targets over a number of years. How they achieve this is their responsibility.

- Recycling/composting EU target for 2020 is 50%

7.3 Advantages of 'environmentally friendly policies' for a business

There may be various reasons why a business may gain from adopting a policy of strict compliance with environmental regulations, or of going further and taking voluntary initiatives to protect aspects of the environment.

(a) If potential customers perceive the business to be environmentally friendly, some may be **more inclined** to **buy its products**.

(b) A corporate image which embraces environmentally friendly policies may **enhance relationships** with the **public in general** or with local communities.

(c)   People may prefer to work for an **environmentally friendly** business.

(d)   **'Ethical' investment funds** may be more likely to buy the firm's shares.

The case study below highlights the dangers for a company of not displaying environmentally friendly policies.

Case Study

In September 2015, the world's largest car maker, Volkswagen, made headlines when it was discovered that it had deceived US regulators in exhaust emissions tests. Devices were installed in test vehicles which gave better emissions results than would be achieved when the vehicles were actually used on the road. Volkswagen set aside €6.5bn to cover the costs of the scandal and the CEO resigned.

Source: *www.bbc.co.uk* 23 September 2015

8 Corporate governance regulation

FAST FORWARD

> Corporate governance impacts on the way companies make decisions, their financial organisation and their relations with investors and auditors.

In Chapter 1, Section 5.2.1, we looked at how corporate governance is used to enforce the achievement of stakeholder objectives. Corporate governance has emerged as a major issue in the last 20 years in the light of several high profile collapses. Guidance has been given because of the lack of confidence perceived in financial reporting and in the ability of auditors to provide the assurances required by the users of financial accounts.

8.1 Impact of corporate governance requirements on businesses

The **consequences of failure to obey** corporate governance regulations should be considered along with failure to obey any other sort of legislation.

Businesses that fail to comply with the law run the risk of **financial penalties** and the financial consequences of accompanying **bad publicity**.

In regimes where corporate governance principles are **guidelines** rather than regulations, businesses will consider what the consequences might be of non-compliance, in particular the **impact on share prices**.

Obedience to requirements or guidelines can also have consequences for businesses. Compliance may involve **extra costs**, including extra procedures and investment necessary to conform; for example, the creation of sufficiently independent board committees relating to remuneration, nomination and audit.

Chapter Roundup

- Macroeconomic policy involves:
    - Policy **objectives** – the ultimate aims of economic policy
    - Policy **targets** – quantified levels or ranges which policy is intended to achieve
    - Policy **instruments** – the tools used to achieve objectives

  Achievement of **economic growth, low inflation, full employment** and **balance of payments stability** are policy objectives.

  Policy targets might be set for **economic growth** or the **rate of inflation**, for example.

- **Fiscal policy** seeks to influence the economy by managing the amounts which the Government spends and the amounts it collects through taxation. Fiscal policy can be used as an instrument of **demand management**.

- **Monetary policy** aims to influence monetary variables such as the rate of interest and the money supply in order to achieve targets set, such as targets for the rate of inflation.

- Exchange rates are determined by **supply and demand**, even under fixed exchange rate systems.

  Governments can intervene to influence the exchange rate by, for example, **adjusting interest rates**. Government policies on exchange rates might be **fixed or floating exchange rates** as two extreme policies, but 'in-between' schemes have been more common.

- The Government influences markets in various ways, one of which is through direct **regulation** (eg the **Competition and Markets Authority** in the UK).

- **Privatisation** is a policy of introducing private enterprise into industries which were previously state-owned or state-operated.

- The freedom of European governments to offer cash **grants and other forms of direct assistance** to business is **limited by European Union** policies designed to prevent the distortion of free market competition.

- There are a number of policy approaches to **pollution**, such as **polluter pays policies, subsidies** and direct **legislation**.

- **Corporate governance** impacts on the way companies make decisions, their financial organisation and their relations with investors and auditors.

1 What are likely to be the main aims of a government's economy policy?

2 What is the difference between fiscal policy and monetary policy?

3 What effect does a high interest rate have on the exchange rate?

4 Name five factors that can influence the level of exchange rates.

5 Give four reasons for government intervention in markets.

6 What is the situation called when there is only one firm, the sole producer of a good, which has no closely competing substitutes?

    A   Duopoly
    B   Oligopoly
    C   Monopoly
    D   Totopoly

7 Fill in the blank.

   .... are positive or negative effects on third parties resulting from production and consumption activities.

8 Fill in the blank.

   Corporate governance is ....

1   Main objectives include:

    (a)   Economic growth

    (b)   Control of price inflation

    (c)   Full employment

    (d)   Balance between imports and exports

2   A government's fiscal policy is concerned with taxation, borrowing and spending and their effects on the economy. Monetary policy is concerned with money and interest rates.

3   It attracts foreign investment, thus increasing the demand for the currency. The exchange rate rises as a result.

4   (a)   Comparative inflation rates

    (b)   Comparative interest rates

    (c)   Balance of payments

    (d)   Speculation

    (e)   Government policy

5   (a)   Imperfect competition

    (b)   Social costs/externalities

    (c)   Imperfect information

    (d)   Equity

6   C   Monopoly

7   Externalities

8   The system by which companies are directed and controlled

Now try the question below from the Practice Question Bank

Number	Level	Marks	Approximate time
Section A Q4	Examination	2	4 mins
Section A Q5	Examination	2	4 mins
Section A Q6	Examination	2	4 mins

Financial markets, money markets and institutions

Topic list	Syllabus reference
1 Financial intermediaries	B2 (b)
2 Financial markets	B2 (a), B3 (a), (b)
3 International money and capital markets	B2 (a), (c)
4 Rates of interest and rates of return	B2 (d)
5 Money market instruments	B3 (c)

Introduction

Having discussed the scope of financial management and the objectives of firms and other organisations in Chapter 1, we now introduce the framework of **markets** and **institutions** through which the financing of a business takes place.

Study guide

		Intellectual level
B2	**The nature and role of financial markets and institutions**	
(a)	Identify the nature and role of money and capital markets, both nationally and internationally.	2
(b)	Explain the role of financial intermediaries.	1
(c)	Explain the functions of a stock market and a corporate bond market.	2
(d)	Explain the nature and features of different securities in relation to the risk/return tradeoff.	2
B3	**The nature and role of money markets**	
(a)	Describe the role of the money markets in:	1
(i)	Providing short-term liquidity to the private sector and the public sector	
(ii)	Providing short-term trade finance	
(b)	Explain the role of banks and other financial institutions in the operation of the money markets.	2
(c)	Explain the characteristics and role of the principal money-market instruments:	2
(i)	Interest-bearing instruments	
(ii)	Discount instruments	
(iii)	Derivative products	

Exam guide

You are unlikely to be asked a whole longer question on financial markets and institutions. You might, however, be asked a part question or Section A multiple choice question that relates to the circumstances of a particular company, for instance how they could raise funds using a stock market.

1 Financial intermediaries

1.1 The role of a financial intermediary

FAST FORWARD

A **financial intermediary** links those with surplus funds (eg **lenders**) to those with fund deficits (eg potential **borrowers**) thus providing **aggregation** and **economies of scale**, **risk pooling** and **maturity transformation**.

Key term

A **financial intermediary** is an institution bringing together providers and users of finance, either as broker or as principal.

A **financial intermediary** links lenders with borrowers, by obtaining deposits from lenders and then re-lending them to borrowers.

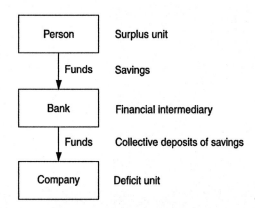

Not all intermediation takes place between savers and investors. Some institutions act mainly as **intermediaries** between **other institutions**. Financial intermediaries may also lend abroad or borrow from abroad.

1.1.1 Examples of financial intermediaries

- Commercial banks
- Finance houses
- Mutual societies
- Institutional investors eg pension funds and investment funds

1.2 The benefits of financial intermediation

Financial intermediaries perform the following functions.

(a) They provide obvious and **convenient** ways in which a lender can save money. Instead of having to find a suitable borrower for their money, the lender can deposit their money with a financial intermediary. All the lender has to do is decide for **how long** they might want to lend the money, and **what sort of return** they require, and they can then choose a financial intermediary that offers a **financial instrument** to suit their requirements.

(b) Financial intermediaries also provide a **ready source of funds** for **borrowers**. Even when money is in short supply, a borrower will usually find a financial intermediary prepared to lend some.

(c) They can **aggregate** smaller savings deposited by savers and lend on to borrowers in larger amounts.

(d) **Risk** for individual lenders is reduced by **pooling**. Since financial intermediaries lend to a large number of individuals and organisations, any losses suffered through default by borrowers or capital losses are effectively pooled and **borne** as **costs** by the intermediary. Such losses are **shared among lenders in general**.

(e) By pooling the funds of large numbers of people, some financial institutions are able to give investors access to **diversified portfolios** covering a varied range of different securities, such as unit trusts and investment trusts.

(f) Financial intermediaries, most importantly, provide **maturity transformation**, ie borrowing money on shorter timeframes than they lend out. They bridge the gap between the wish of most lenders for **liquidity** and the desire of most borrowers for **loans** over longer periods.

2 Financial markets

2.1 Financial markets

Financial markets are the markets where individuals and organisations with surplus funds lend funds to other individuals and organisations that want to borrow.

This function is shown diagrammatically below.

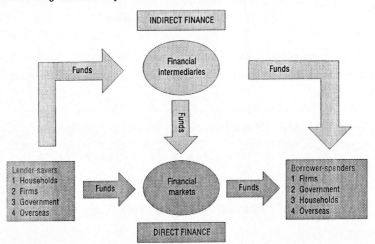

Those who have saved and are lending funds, the 'lender savers', are on the left, and those who must borrow funds to finance their spending, the 'borrower spenders', are on the right. The principal lender-savers are **households**, as well as **overseas institutions** and their **governments**, who sometimes also find themselves with excess funds and so lend them out. The most important borrower-spenders are corporations and governments, although individuals also borrow to finance the acquisition of durable goods or houses. The arrows show that funds flow from **lender-savers** to **borrower-spenders** via two routes.

The first route is the direct finance route at the bottom of the diagram, when borrowers borrow funds directly from lenders in financial markets by selling them **securities** (also called **financial instruments**), which are **claims** on the **borrowers' future income** or **assets**.

Securities are **assets** for the **buyer** but **liabilities** for the seller. For example, if British Airways needs to borrow funds to pay for a new aircraft, it might borrow the funds from a saver by **selling** the saver a **bond**, a **debt security** that promises to make payments periodically for a specified period of time.

The channelling of funds from **savers** to **spenders** is a crucial function for the economy because the people who save are frequently not the same people who have profitable investment opportunities available to them, ie the entrepreneurs. Without financial markets, it is hard to transfer funds from a person with surplus funds and no investment opportunities to one who has investment opportunities but no funds. They would be unable to transact and both would be worse off as a result. Financial markets are thus essential to promoting **economic efficiency**.

Financial markets can be classified in several ways. We will look at the main classifications below in turn.

- Capital and money markets
- Primary and secondary markets
- Exchange-traded and over the counter markets

2.2 Capital markets and money markets

Capital markets are markets for medium-term and long-term capital.

Money markets are markets for short-term capital.

Differences in maturity between short term, medium term and long term

| Year 0 | Year 1 | Year 5 | Year 10 |

```
Short term
        Medium term
                                        Long term
```

'Maturity' means the time when the financial instrument reaches its settlement date. Money market instruments and loans have a maturity of up to one year.

2.2.1 The money markets

Money markets are markets for:

- Trading short-term financial instruments
- Short-term lending and borrowing

The money markets are **operated** by the **banks** and other **financial institutions**. Although the money markets largely involve borrowing and lending by banks, some large companies, as well as the Government, are involved in money market operations.

The primary market is known as the **official market**, the other markets as the **parallel** or **wholesale markets**.

Types of market	
Primary market	Capital market where new securities are issued and sold to investors
Interbank market	Banks lend short-term funds to each other
Eurocurrency market	Banks lend and borrow in foreign currencies
Certificate of deposit market	Market for trading in Certificates of Deposit (negotiable instruments acknowledging deposits)
Local authority market	Local authorities borrow short-term funds by issuing and selling short-term debt instruments
Finance house market	Dealing in short-term loans raised from money markets by finance houses
Inter-company market	Direct short-term lending between treasury departments of large companies
	Commercial paper (short-term unsecured borrowing by businesses with high credit ratings) and bills

We will introduce the principal money market instruments in Section 5 below. The sources of short-term finance will be discussed in more detail in Chapter 12.

2.2.2 The capital markets

FAST FORWARD

A stock market (in the UK: the **main market** plus the Alternative Investment Market (**AIM**)) acts as a **primary market** for raising finance, and as a **secondary market** for the trading of existing securities.

Securities are tradable financial instruments. They can take the form of **equity** (such as shares), **debt** (such as bonds and loan notes) or **derivatives**.

Capital markets are markets for trading in **long-term finance**, in the form of long-term financial instruments such as equities and corporate bonds.

In the UK, the principal capital markets are:

(a)   The Stock Exchange **'main market'** (for companies with a full stock market listing)
(b)   The more loosely regulated 'second tier' **Alternative Investment Market (AIM)**

Firms obtain long-term or medium-term capital in one of the following ways.

(a) They may raise **share capital**. Most new issues of share capital are in the form of ordinary share capital. Firms that issue ordinary share capital are inviting investors to take an **equity stake** in the business, or to increase their existing equity stake.

(b) They may raise **debt capital**. Long-term debt capital might be raised in the form of loan notes, corporate bonds, loan notes or convertible bonds.

We will look at sources of long-term finance in more detail in Chapter 12.

2.3 Primary and secondary markets

FAST FORWARD

Primary markets enable organisations to raise new finance. **Secondary markets** enable investors to buy and sell existing investments to each other.

The financial markets serve two main purposes.

(a) As **primary markets** they enable organisations to **raise new finance**, by issuing new shares or new bonds. In the UK, a company must have public company status (be a publicly listed company, or 'plc') to be allowed to raise finance from the public on a capital market.

(b) As **secondary markets** they enable existing investors to buy and **sell existing investments**, should they wish to do so. The marketability of securities is a very important feature of the capital markets, because investors are more willing to buy stocks and shares if they know that they could sell them easily, should they wish to.

Here are two examples of how primary and secondary markets work.

Primary markets: When one company wants to **take over** another, it is common to do so by issuing shares to finance the takeover. Takeovers by means of a share exchange are only feasible if the shares that are offered can be readily traded on a stock market, and so have an identifiable market value.

Secondary markets: When a company comes to the stock market for the first time, and 'floats' its shares on the market, the owners of the company can **realise** some of the **value of their shares** in cash, because they will offer a proportion of their personally held shares for sale to new investors.

2.4 Exchange-traded instruments and over the counter markets

FAST FORWARD

Secondary markets may be organised on **exchanges** or may consist of **over the counter** (OTC) transactions.

Secondary markets for financial securities can be organised on **exchanges**, where buyers and sellers of securities buy and sell securities in one location, the exchange. Examples of exchanges include the London Stock Exchange and the New York Stock Exchange for the trading of shares, the Chicago Board of Trade for the trading of commodities and derivatives, and the London International Financial Futures and Options Exchange (LIFFE) for the trading of derivatives.

Alternatively, secondary markets can operate as **over the counter (OTC)** markets, where transactions do not involve buying and selling through an exchange, but customers **negotiate individual transactions**, usually with a financial intermediary such as a bank.

Securities that are issued in an over the counter market can be negotiable or non-negotiable.

- **Negotiable** securities can be resold.
- **Non-negotiable** securities cannot be resold.

2.5 Institutional investors

Institutional investors are institutions which have large amounts of funds which they want to invest, and they will invest in stocks and shares or any other assets which offer satisfactory returns and security or lend money to companies directly. The institutional investors are the biggest investors in the stock markets.

The major institutional investors in the UK are **pension funds, insurance companies, investment trusts, unit trusts** and **venture capital organisations**. Of these, pension funds and insurance companies have the largest amounts of funds to invest.

2.6 Capital market participants

The various participants in the capital markets are summarised in the diagram below.

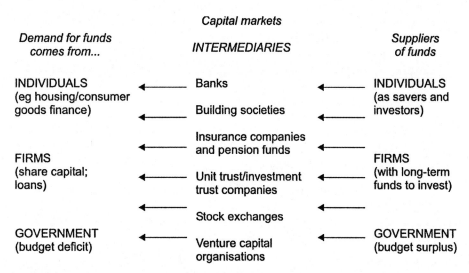

2.7 Securitisation

Securitisation is the process of converting **illiquid assets** into **marketable asset-backed securities**. The development of **securitisation** has led to **disintermediation** and a reduction in the day to day role of financial intermediaries, as borrowers can reach lenders directly after securitisation.

Securitisation is the process of converting **illiquid assets** into **marketable securities**. These securities are backed by specific assets and are normally called **asset-backed securities** (ABS).

The oldest and historically most common type of asset securitisation is the **mortgage-backed bond** or **security (MBS)**. Very simplistically, the process is as follows.

(1)   A financial entity can purchase a number of mortgage loans from banks.

(2)   The entity pools the mortgage loans together.

(3)   The entity issues bonds to institutional investors. The money raised from issuing the bonds is used to pay for the mortgage loans.

(4)   The institutional investors now have the right to receive the principal and interest payments made on the mortgage.

Today, virtually anything that has a cash flow (for example, a loan, a public works project, or a receivable balance) is a candidate for securitisation.

The development of securitisation has led to **disintermediation** and a reduction in the role of financial intermediaries, as borrowers can reach lenders directly. For example, once banks have securitised mortgages and sold them on, they have been removed from the link between lender and borrower.

Key term

Disintermediation describes a decline in the traditional deposit and lending relationship between banks and their customers and an increase in direct relationships between the ultimate suppliers and users of financing.

3 International money and capital markets

FAST FORWARD

International money and capital markets are available for larger companies wishing to raise larger amounts of finance.

Larger companies are able to borrow funds on the **eurocurrency markets** (which are international money markets) and on the markets for **eurobonds** (international capital markets).

Exam focus point

Don't suggest these international markets as possible sources of finance for a **smaller** business in an exam answer.

3.1 Eurocurrency markets

A UK company might borrow money from a bank or from the investing public, in sterling. But it might also borrow in a foreign currency, especially if it trades abroad, or if it already has assets or liabilities abroad denominated in a foreign currency.

When a company borrows in a foreign currency, the loan is known as a **eurocurrency loan**.

Key term

Eurocurrency is currency which is held by individuals and institutions outside the country of issue of that currency.

For example, if a UK company borrows US$50,000 from its bank, the loan will be a 'eurodollar' loan. London is a major centre for eurocurrency lending and companies with foreign trade interests might choose to borrow from their bank in another currency.

The **eurocurrency markets** involve the depositing of funds with a bank outside the country of the currency in which the funds are denominated and re-lending these funds for a fairly short term, typically three months. Most eurocurrency transactions in fact take place between banks of different countries and take the form of negotiable certificates of deposit.

3.2 International bond markets

Large companies may arrange borrowing facilities from their bank, in the form of bank loans or bank overdrafts. Alternatively, however, they may prefer to borrow from private investors. In other words, instead of obtaining a £10,000,000 bank loan, a company might issue bonds, in order to borrow directly from investors, with:

(a)   The bank merely **arranging the transaction**, finding investors who will take up the bonds that the borrowing company issues

(b)   **Interest** being payable to the **investors themselves**, not to a bank

A strong international market has built up which allows very large companies to borrow in this way, long term or short term. As well as eurobonds, there is also a less highly developed market in international equity share issues (**'euro-equity'**).

Key term

A **eurobond** is a bond denominated in a currency which often differs from that of the country of issue.

Eurobonds are, in effect, long-term loans raised by international companies or other institutions and sold to investors in several countries at the same time. Such bonds can be sold by one holder to another. The term of a eurobond issue is typically 10 to 15 years.

Eurobonds may be the most suitable source of finance for a large organisation with an excellent credit rating, such as a large successful multinational company, which:

(a)   Requires a **long-term loan** to **finance a big capital expansion** programme; the loan may be for at least 5 and up to 20 years

(b)   Requires **borrowing** which is **not subject to the national exchange** controls of any government

In addition, domestic capital issues may be regulated by the Government or central bank, with an orderly queue for issues. In contrast, eurobond issues can be made whenever market conditions seem favourable.

A borrower who is contemplating a eurobond issue must consider the **exchange risk** of a long-term foreign currency loan. If the money is to be used to purchase assets that will earn revenue in a currency **different to that of the bond issue**, the borrower will run the risk of losses from unfavourable exchange rate movements.

If the money is to be used to purchase assets which will earn revenue in the **same currency**, the borrower can match these revenues with payments on the bond, and so remove or reduce the exchange risk.

An **investor** subscribing to a bond issue will be concerned about the following factors.

(a)   **Security**
       The borrower must be of **high quality** (ie have a high credit rating).

(b)   **Marketability**
       Investors may wish to have a **ready market** in which bonds can be bought and sold. If the borrower is of high quality the bonds or notes will be readily negotiable.

(c)   **Anonymity**
       Investors in eurobonds tend to be attracted to the potential **anonymity** of this type of issue, as the bonds are generally issued to bearer.

(d)   **The return on the investment**
       This is often paid tax free.

4 Rates of interest and rates of return

Interest rates are effectively the 'prices' governing lending and borrowing. The borrower pays interest to the lender at a certain percentage of the capital sum, as the price for the use of the funds borrowed. As with other prices, supply and demand effects apply. For example, the higher the rates of interest that are charged, the lower the demand will be for funds from borrowers.

4.1 The pattern of interest rates

FAST FORWARD

> **Interest rates** on financial assets are influenced by the **risk** of the assets, the **duration** of the lending and their maturity.

The pattern of interest rates refers to the variety of interest rates on different financial assets, and the margin between interest rates on lending and deposits that are set by banks. Note that the **pattern of interest rates** is a different thing from the **general level of interest rates**.

Why are there such a large number of interest rates? In other words, how is the **pattern** of interest rates to be explained? The answer to this question relates to several factors.

(a)   **Risk**
       There is a trade-off between risk and return. Higher-risk borrowers must pay higher yields on their borrowing, to compensate lenders for the greater credit risk involved. Banks will assess the creditworthiness of the borrower, and set a rate of interest on its loan at a certain mark-up above its base rate.

(b)   **Need to make a profit on re-lending**
       Financial intermediaries make their profits from re-lending at a higher rate of interest than the cost of their borrowing. For example, the interest rate charged on bank loans exceeds the rate paid on deposits and the mortgage rate charged by mutual societies exceeds the interest rate paid on deposits.

(c)   **Duration of the lending**
       The term of the loan or asset will affect the rate of interest charged on it. In general, longer-dated assets will earn a higher yield than similar short-dated assets but this is not always the case. The differences in rates are therefore due to the differences in the **term structure** of interest rates.

(d) **Size of the loan or deposit**
The yield on assets might vary with the size of the loan or deposit. Administrative cost savings help to allow **lower rates of interest** to be charged by banks **on larger loans** and **higher rates of interest** to be paid on **larger time deposits**.

(e) **Different types of financial asset**
Different types of financial asset attract **different rates of interest**. This is partly because different types of asset attract different sorts of lender/investor. For example, bank deposits attract individuals and companies, whereas long-dated government securities are particularly attractive to various institutional investors.

The rates of interest paid on government borrowing provide benchmarks for other interest rates. For example:

(a) Clearing banks might set the three months interbank rate (LIBOR) at about 1% above the Treasury bill rate.

(b) Banks in turn lend (wholesale) at a rate higher than LIBOR.

LIBOR or the London Interbank Offered Rate is the rate of interest at which banks borrow from each other in the London interbank market.

We will look at interest rates in more detail in Chapter 20.

4.2 The risk-return trade-off

There is a **trade-off** between **risk and return**. Investors in riskier assets expect to be compensated for the risk. In the case of ordinary shares, investors hope to achieve their return in the form of an increase in the share price (a capital gain) as well as from dividends.

We have explained how rates of interest, and therefore rates of return to lenders, will be affected by the risk involved in lending. The idea of a risk-return trade-off can, however, be extended beyond a consideration of interest rates.

An investor has the choice between different forms of investment. The investor may earn interest by depositing funds with a financial intermediary who will lend on to, say, a company, or it may invest in corporate bonds. Alternatively, the investor may invest directly in a company by purchasing shares in it.

The current market price of a security is found by discounting the future expected earnings stream at a rate suitably adjusted for risk. This means that investments carrying a **higher degree of risk** will demand a **higher rate of return**. This rate of return or yield has two components.

- **Annual income** (dividend or interest)
- **Expected capital gain**

Some of the main forms of investment are listed below in ascending order of risk.

(a) **Government bonds**
The risk of default is negligible. Hence this tends to form the **base level** for returns in the market.

(b) **Company bonds**
Although there is some risk of default on company bonds, they are often **secured** against corporate assets.

(c) **Preference shares**
These are generally riskier than bonds since they rank behind debt in the event of a liquidation, although they rank ahead of **ordinary shares**. The return takes the form of a **fixed percentage dividend** based on the par value of the share.

(d) **Ordinary shares**
Ordinary shares carry a high level of risk. Dividends are paid out of distributable profits after all other liabilities have been paid and can be subject to **large fluctuations** from year to year. However,

there is the potential for significant **capital appreciation** in times of growth. In general, the level of risk will vary with the operational and financial **gearing** of the company and the nature of the markets in which it operates.

4.3 The reverse yield gap

Because debt involves lower risk than equity investment, we might expect yields on debt to be lower than yields on shares. More usually, however, the opposite applies and the yields on shares are lower than on low-risk debt; this situation is known as a **reverse yield gap**. A reverse yield gap can occur because shareholders may be willing to accept lower returns on their investment in the short term, in anticipation that they will make capital gains in the future.

4.4 Interest rates and shareholders' required rates of return   12/08

Given that equity shares and interest-earning investments stand as alternatives from the investor's point of view, changes in the general level of interest rates can be expected to have an effect on the rates of return which shareholders will expect.

If the return expected by an investor from an equity investment (ie an investment in shares) is 11% and the dividend paid on the shares is 15 cents every year, the market value of one share will be 15 cents/11% = $1.36.

Suppose that interest rates on debt investments then fall. The option of putting the funds on deposit has become less attractive and as a result the shareholders' required return may also fall to, say, 9%. Then the market value of one share will increase to 15 cents/9% = $1.67.

You can see from this that an **increase** in the shareholders' **required rate of return** (perhaps resulting from an increase in the general level of interest rates) will lead to a **fall** in the **market value** of the share.

5 Money market instruments

Performance objective 9 requires you to 'value projects, financial securities and instruments and advise on their costs and benefits to the organisation'. This section introduces various money market instruments and how they can be used to cover liabilities. The various features of each instrument will be useful in practice to determine the best one to use in different situations, not only to cover the risk involved but also to cover the risk for the required period.

Money market instruments are traded over the counter between institutional investors. They include **interest-bearing** instruments, **discount** instruments and **derivatives** and can be either negotiable or non-negotiable.

We looked at money markets in Section 2 above. Money markets are over the counter markets and the transactions take place between **institutions** rather than individual investors. Money market instruments can be either **negotiable** or **non-negotiable**.

The table below shows some of the money market instruments in the UK.

Interest-bearing instruments	Discount instruments	Derivatives
Money Market Deposits	Treasury Bill (T-bill)	Forwards and Futures
Certificate of Deposit (CD)	Banker's Acceptance (BA)	Swaps
Repurchase Agreement (Repo)	Commercial Paper (CP)	Options

Interest-bearing instruments pay interest. The investor receives face value plus interest at maturity.

Discount instruments do not pay interest. They are issued and traded at a **discount to the face value** and they are redeemed at their par value at maturity. The discount is equivalent to interest and is the difference

between the issue price of the instrument and the redemption price at maturity. For example, if a bill is issued at a price of 98.50, it is issued at a discount of 1.50 and redeemed at maturity at a price of 100.00. The discount of 1.50 represents interest on the investment of 98.50.

Derivatives allow the buyer and seller to agree today to buy or sell an asset at some time in the future at an agreed fixed price.

5.1 Money market deposits

Money market deposits are **very short-term loans** between banks and depositors. These deposits can either be **fixed deposits**, where the rate of interest and maturity dates are agreed at the time of the transaction, or **call deposits** where the interest is variable and the deposit can be terminated if notice is given. The table below shows examples of market rates for money market instruments.

	Overnight	7 days' notice	1 month	3 months	6 months	1 year
Interbank Sterling	$5\frac{3}{32} - 5$	$6 - 5\frac{3}{4}$	$6\frac{15}{16} - 6\frac{1}{16}$	$6\frac{3}{16} - 6\frac{1}{16}$	$6\frac{5}{16} - 6\frac{3}{16}$	$6\frac{3}{8} - 6\frac{1}{4}$

The table quotes **two rates**. The first figure in each column shows the **interest rate** at which a bank will **lend money**. This is called the **offer price**. The second number is the **rate** at which the bank will pay to **borrow money**. This is called the **bid price**. Note that while the convention in London is to quote **Offer/Bid**, in most other markets including the US what is quoted is **Bid/Offer**.

The rate at which banks borrow from each other in the London market is of particular importance for the money market. This is called LIBOR and is the most widely used reference rate for short-term interest rates globally for the settlement of money market derivatives. LIBOR rates are calculated for ten currencies including the US dollar, pound sterling and the euro. The following table shows examples of LIBOR rates for three currencies for different maturities.

	EUR	USD	GBP
Overnight	3.413	5.289	5.141
1 week	3.592	5.305	5.150
1 month	3.653	5.350	5.241
3 months	3.672	5.360	5.279
9 months	3.851	5.313	5.420
12 months	3.898	5.250	5.459

The LIBOR rates at **different maturities** define the **short-term yield curve** which is shown below.

LIBOR Yield Curve

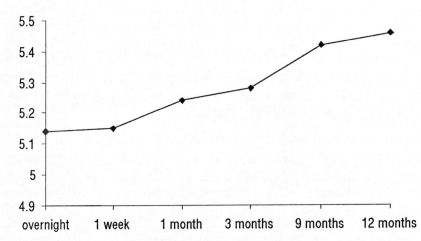

The LIBOR yield curve can also be used to estimate the **forward yield curve** which gives the interest rate between two future periods. The forward yield curve is used to price many money market derivatives.

5.2 Certificates of deposit

> A **certificate of deposit (CD)** is a certificate of receipt for funds deposited at a bank (or other financial institution) for a specified term and paying interest at a specified rate.

Certificates of deposit can be either **negotiable** or **non-negotiable**. The holder of a **negotiable CD** has two options: to hold it until maturity, receiving the interest and the principal, or to sell it before maturity at the market price. A typical range of dollar certificates of deposit in terms of coupon and maturity is shown below, together with the corresponding yield.

Term	Coupon	Annual percentage yield
3 Months	5.950	6.080
3 Months	6.150	6.290
3 Months	6.200	6.350
6 Months	6.200	6.300
6 Months	6.300	6.400
9 Months	6.400	6.450

The coupon is expressed as an annual percentage rate and needs to be adjusted to reflect the fact that its maturity is less than a year. **Sterling CDs** assume there are **365 days** in the year, while **US CDs** assume **360 days**. For example, if the coupon on three-month US dollar CDs is 5.950%, this means that the interest payment after three months will be (one quarter) 1.4875%. Converting this to an annual percentage yield:

$(1.014875)^4 - 1 = 0.0608$ or 6.08%

The value of the CD on maturity = face value $\times \left[1 + \left(\text{coupon rate} \times \text{days to maturity} \div \text{days in the year} \right) \right]$

Question

Maturity value

Consider a Sterling CD with a face value of £1,000,000 issued on 1 March 20X0 maturing on 1 September 20X0 (184 days later). The coupon is 7% pa. Calculate the maturity value of the CD.

Answer

$$\text{Value at maturity} = £1,000,000 \times \left[1 + \left(0.07 \times \left[184 \div 365 \right] \right) \right]$$
$$= £1,035,288$$

5.3 Repos

> A **repurchase agreement** is an agreement between two counterparties under which one counterparty agrees to sell a financial instrument to the other on an agreed date for an agreed price, and simultaneously agrees to buy back the instrument from the counterparty at a later date for an agreed higher price.

A repurchase agreement is in effect a loan secured by a marketable financial instrument, usually a treasury bill or a bond. The typical term is up to 180 days but is often much shorter. It is an attractive instrument because it can accommodate a wide spectrum of short-term maturities. A repo involves two sets of transactions.

- First on the start date, the dealer sells the security for cash.
- On maturity, the dealer will repay the cash with interest and take back the security.

The flows in a repo are shown in the following diagram.

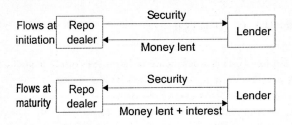

 Question — Repo cash flows

A company enters into a repo agreement with a bank and it sells $10,000,000 of government bonds with an obligation to repurchase the security in 60 days. If the repo rate is 8.2% what is the repurchase price of the bond? Assume a 365-day year.

Answer

The repurchase price of the bonds is the sale price plus the interest on the cash received.

$$\text{Interest} = \$10,000,000 \times 0.082 \times \frac{60}{365} = \$134,794.52$$

Repurchase price = $10,000,000 + $134,794.52 = $10,134,794.52

Key term

> A **reverse repurchase** agreement (reverse repo) is an agreement for the purchase of an instrument with the simultaneous agreement to resell the instrument at an agreed future date and agreed price.

In a **reverse repo**, the dealer purchases the security initially and then sells it on maturity. Because the two parties in a **repo** agreement act as a buyer and a seller of the security, a **repo** to one party is a **reverse repo** to the other.

5.4 Treasury bills

Treasury bills are debt instruments issued by the Government with maturities ranging from one month to one year. Most are issued with a maturity of 91 days.

5.5 Commercial paper

Commercial paper (CP) is **short-term unsecured corporate debt** with maturity up to 270 days. The typical term of this debt is 30 or 60 days. Commercial paper can only be issued by large organisations with good credit ratings, normally to fund short-term expenditure.

A bank organises a CP programme for a large company with a duration of several years. Within the term of the programme, the company can make issues of CP, up to the maximum limit permitted by the programme. The bank administers the programme for its corporate client, selling each issue of CP and repaying the CP investors at redemption date.

CP is issued at a discount that reflects the prevailing interest rates.

Formula to learn

> $$\text{Yield on commercial paper} = \frac{\text{Number of days in the year}}{\text{Days held}} \times \frac{\text{Selling price} - \text{Purchase price}}{\text{Purchase price}}$$

5.6 Banker's acceptance

Key term

> **Banker's acceptances** (BAs) are negotiable bills guaranteed by a bank.

Banker's acceptances are issued by firms to finance commercial transactions, such as imports or the purchase of goods.

A bill of exchange is a short-term debt instrument that is issued ('drawn') by one person on another (the 'drawee'). When issued it is in effect a 'You Owe Me' instrument. The bill is then accepted by the drawee (who notifies acceptance by signing the bill), when it becomes a promise to pay – an 'I Owe You'.

A BA is a bill of exchange accepted by a bank. By accepting the bill, the bank is making a promise to pay. If the bank is well established, a BA therefore has low credit risk.

A bank may agree to accept bills on behalf of a client in a BA acceptance facility. The client has to repay the bank for the payments made by the bank to settle its BAs, but is financed by the bank between the time of accepting the bill and the time of its settlement.

The drawer of the bill can hold the bill until maturity, when the bank will settle the bill and make the payment. Alternatively the drawer can sell the bill to another investor at a discount, to raise immediate cash. The bank then pays the bill holder at maturity.

The name 'banker's acceptance' derives from the fact that the bank has guaranteed the payment to the holder of the banker's acceptance; that is, the bank has accepted responsibility for the payment. Banks guarantee the payment by the company for a fee.

Banker's acceptances are sold on a **discounted basis**, like T-bills and commercial paper. Because banker's acceptances are negotiable instruments, they can be bought and sold until they mature. The **rates** on banker's acceptances are **low** because, as they are guaranteed by a bank, the credit risk is low.

UK Banker's Acceptance are calculated on a **Actual/365 days** basis while in the US they are calculated on an **Actual/360 days** basis.

The typical term of BAs is **30 to 180 days**.

5.7 Futures, forwards and options

Imagine a farmer growing a crop of wheat. To grow such a crop costs money: money for seed, labour, fertiliser, and so on. All this expenditure takes place with no certainty that when the crop is eventually harvested the price at which the wheat is sold will cover these costs. This is obviously a risky thing to do and many farmers will be unwilling to take on this burden. How can this uncertainty be avoided?

By using futures or options, the farmer will be able to **agree today a price** at which the crop will ultimately be sold, in perhaps four or six months' time. This enables the farmer to achieve a minimum sale price for their crop. They are no longer subject to fluctuations in wheat prices. They know what price their wheat will bring and can thus plan their business accordingly.

From their origins in the agricultural world, futures and options have become available on a wide range of other assets, from commodities, such as metals and crude oil, to financial products, such as currencies, bonds and equities. To understand futures and options properly requires some application. There is much terminology to master, and definitions to be understood, but at heart they are really quite simple. They are products which allow you to **fix today the price at which assets may be bought or sold at a future date**. Futures and options are sometimes called derivatives, as their price is derived from an underlying asset.

5.7.1 Futures

A future is an agreement to buy or sell a standard quantity of a specified asset on a fixed future date at a price agreed today. As they are standardised, they can be and are exchange traded.

There are two parties to a futures contract, namely a buyer and a seller.

- The buyer of a future enters into an **obligation** to buy on a specified future date.
- The seller of a future is under an **obligation** to sell on a specified future date.

These obligations relate to a **standard quantity** of a **specified asset** on a **fixed future date** at a **price agreed today**. These details of the future contract are contained within the **contract specification**.

5.7.2 Forwards

A **forward** is an agreement over the counter (ie off-exchange) between two parties to make or take delivery of an asset for an agreed price at a future date. In principal, then, the nature of the transaction is very similar to a futures contract. However, because this is an 'over the counter' transaction between two parties, all terms of the contract can be tailored individually to meet the buyer's and seller's needs.

The key advantage of forwards is that they allow much **greater flexibility** to suit particular circumstances. This will enable a hedger to tailor their derivative hedge to their exact requirements. (Hedging is a way of protecting against financial loss by making an investment to reduce the risk of an uncertain market.)

The main disadvantages are a lack of liquidity in comparison to exchange-traded futures, and increased credit risk for both buyer and seller, as there is no clearing house to act as a central counterparty. This is known as counterparty risk.

5.7.3 Options

An option is a contract that confers the right, but not the obligation, to buy or sell an asset at a given price (**exercise price** or **strike price**) on or before a given date. Options are entered into at a cost, called the **premium**.

The right to buy is known as a **call option**.

The right to sell is known as a **put option**.

Chapter Roundup

- A **financial intermediary** links those with surplus funds (eg **lenders**) to those with fund deficits (eg potential **borrowers**) thus providing **aggregation** and **economies of scale**, **risk pooling** and **maturity transformation**.

- **Financial markets** are the markets where individuals and organisations with surplus funds lend funds to other individuals and organisations that want to borrow.

- **Capital markets** are markets for medium-term and long-term capital.

  Money markets are markets for short-term capital.

- A stock market (in the UK: the **main market** plus the Alternative Investment Market **(AIM)**) acts as a **primary market** for raising finance, and as a **secondary market** for the trading of existing securities.

  Securities are tradable financial instruments. They can take the form of **equity** (such as shares), **debt** (such as bonds and loan notes) or **derivatives**.

- **Primary markets** enable organisations to raise new finance. **Secondary markets** enable investors to buy and sell existing investments to each other.

- Secondary markets may be organised on **exchanges** or may consist of **over the counter** (OTC) transactions.

- **Securitisation** is the process of converting **illiquid assets** into **marketable asset-backed securities**. The development of **securitisation** has led to **disintermediation** and a reduction in the day to day role of financial intermediaries, as borrowers can reach lenders directly after securitisation.

- **International money and capital markets** are available for larger companies wishing to raise larger amounts of finance.

- **Interest rates** on financial assets are influenced by the **risk** of the assets, the **duration** of the lending and their maturity.

- There is a **trade-off** between **risk and return**. Investors in riskier assets expect to be compensated for the risk. In the case of ordinary shares, investors hope to achieve their return in the form of an increase in the share price (a capital gain) as well as from dividends.

- **Money market instruments** are traded over the counter between institutional investors. They include **interest-bearing** instruments, **discount** instruments and **derivatives** and can be either negotiable or non-negotiable.

1   Identify five types of financial intermediaries.

2   For short-term borrowing, a company will go to the **money markets/capital markets**. (Which?)

3   (a)   From which does the **demand** for capital markets funds come: Individuals/Firms/Government? (Delete any that do not apply.)

     (b)   From which does the **supply** of capital market funds come: Individuals/Firms/Government? (Delete any that do not apply.)

4   Is the stock exchange a money market?

5   Fill in the blank.

     If an Indian company borrows US dollars in Australia, the loan is known as a .... loan.

6   Which of the following types of investment carries the highest level of risk?

     A   Company bonds
     B   Preference shares
     C   Government bonds
     D   Ordinary shares

Answers to Quick Quiz

1   Any five of: banks; mutual societies; insurance companies; pension funds; unit trust companies; investment trusts; stock exchanges; venture capital organisations.

2   Money markets

3   (a) and (b): You should have deleted none.

4   No. The stock exchange is a capital market, not a money market.

5   Eurocurrency

6   D   Ordinary shares

Now try the questions below from the Practice Question Bank

Number	Level	Marks	Approximate time
Section A Q7	Examination	2	4 mins
Section A Q8	Examination	2	4 mins
Section A Q9	Examination	2	4 mins

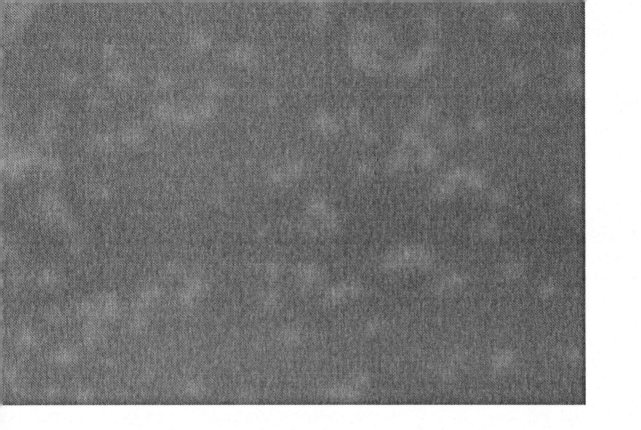

P
A
R
T

C

Working capital management

Working capital

Topic list	Syllabus reference
1 The nature of working capital	C1 (a)
2 Objectives of working capital management	C1 (b)
3 Role of working capital management	C1 (c)
4 The cash operating cycle	C2 (a)
5 Liquidity ratios	C2 (b)

Introduction

Part C of this Study Text covers the crucial topic of working capital management.

In this chapter, we consider functions of the financial manager relating to the **management of working capital** in general terms including the elements of working capital and the objectives and role of working capital management.

This chapter also explains the cash operating cycle and working capital ratios.

In later chapters, we shall be looking at specific aspects of the management of **cash, accounts receivable and payable** and **inventories**.

Study guide

		Intellectual level
C1	**The nature, elements and importance of working capital**	
(a)	Describe the nature of working capital and identify its elements.	1
(b)	Identify the objectives of working capital management in terms of liquidity and profitability, and discuss the conflict between them.	2
(c)	Discuss the central role of working capital management in financial management.	2
C2	**Management of inventories, accounts receivable, accounts payable and cash**	
(a)	Explain the cash operating cycle and the role of accounts payable and accounts receivable.	2
(b)	Explain and apply relevant accounting ratios, including:	2
(i)	Current ratio and quick ratio	
(ii)	Inventory turnover ratio, average collection period and average payable period	
(iii)	Sales revenue/net working capital ratio	

Exam guide

Working capital is highly examinable and has appeared in every exam so far. Questions are likely to be a mixture of calculations and discussion. Always make sure your discussion and explanations are applied to the specific organisation in the question.

1 The nature of working capital

FAST FORWARD

The amount tied up in **working capital** is equal to the value of raw materials, work in progress, finished goods inventories and accounts receivable less accounts payable. The size of this net figure has a direct effect on the **liquidity** of an organisation.

Key term

Net working capital of a business is its current assets less its current liabilities.

KEY CURRENT ASSETS AND LIABILITIES	
Current assets	**Current liabilities**
Cash	Trade accounts payable
Inventory of raw materials	Taxation payable
Inventory of work in progress	Dividend payments due
Inventory of finished goods	Short-term loans
Amounts receivable from customers	Long-term loans maturing within one year
Marketable securities	Lease rentals due within one year

BPP
LEARNING MEDIA

1.1 Working capital characteristics of different businesses 6/11

Different businesses will have different working capital characteristics. There are three main aspects to these differences.

(a) Holding inventory (from their purchase from external suppliers, through the production and warehousing of finished goods, up to the time of sale)

(b) Taking time to pay suppliers and other accounts payable (creditors)

(c) Allowing customers (accounts receivable) time to pay

Here are some examples.

(a) Supermarkets and other retailers receive much of their sales in cash or by credit card or debit card. However, they typically buy from suppliers on credit. They may therefore have the advantage of significant cash holdings, which they may choose to invest.

(b) A company which supplies to other companies, such as a wholesaler, is likely to be selling and buying mainly on **credit**. Co-ordinating the flow of cash may be quite a problem. Such a company may make use of short-term borrowings (such as an overdraft) to manage its cash.

(c) Smaller companies with a limited trading record may face particularly severe problems. Lacking a long track record, such companies may find it difficult to obtain credit from suppliers. At the same time, customers will expect to receive the length of credit period that is normal for the particular business concerned. The firm may find itself squeezed in its management of cash.

Exam focus point

> Some aspect of working capital management is likely to be included in every paper.

2 Objectives of working capital management

12/07, 6/08, 6/10

FAST FORWARD

> The two main objectives of working capital management are to ensure that it has **sufficient liquid resources** to continue in business and to **increase its profitability**.

Every business needs adequate **liquid resources** to maintain day to day cash flow. It needs enough to pay wages, salaries and accounts payable if it is to keep its workforce and ensure its supplies.

Maintaining adequate working capital is not just important in the short term. Adequate liquidity is needed to ensure the **survival** of the business in the long term. Even a profitable company may fail without adequate cash flow to meet its liabilities.

On the other hand, an excessively conservative approach to working capital management resulting in high levels of cash tied up in excessive inventories/receivables will harm profits, as excessive investment in these assets does not yield additional return.

These two objectives will often **conflict**, as liquid assets give the lowest returns.

Exam focus point

> In June 2008, the ACCA examination team asked for a discussion of the key factors which determine the level of investment in current assets. Answers often referred incorrectly to working capital funding strategies illustrating that it is essential to answer the specific requirements of the question.

3 Role of working capital management

FAST FORWARD

> A business needs to have **clear policies** for the management of each component of working capital.

Working capital management is a key factor in an organisation's long-term success. A business must therefore have clear policies for the management of each component of working capital. The management

BPP
LEARNING MEDIA

of cash, marketable securities, accounts receivable, accounts payable and other means of short-term financing is the **direct** responsibility of the financial manager and it requires continuous day to day supervision.

Question

What differences would there be in working capital policies for a manufacturing company and a food retailer?

Answer

The manufacturing company will need to invest heavily in spare parts and may be owed large amounts of money by its customers. The food retailer will have a large inventory of goods for resale but will have low/no accounts receivable.

The manufacturing company will therefore need a carefully considered policy on the management of accounts receivable which will need to reflect the credit policies of its close competitors.

The food retailer will be more concerned with inventory management.

4 The cash operating cycle   6/08, 6/13, 6/14

Key term

> The **cash operating cycle** is the period of time which elapses between the point at which cash begins to be expended on the production of a product and the collection of cash from a customer.

The connection between investment in working capital and cash flow may be illustrated by means of the **cash operating cycle** (also called the **working capital cycle**, **trading cycle** or **cash conversion cycle**).

The cash operating cycle in a manufacturing business equals:

	Months
The average time that raw materials remain in inventory	X
Less the time taken to pay suppliers (ie period of credit taken from suppliers)	X
Plus the time taken to produce the goods	X
Plus the time taken by customers to pay for the goods	X
Cash cycle	X

If the turnover periods for inventories and accounts receivable lengthen (ie inventories and receivables levels increase), or the payment period to accounts payable shortens (ie payables level falls), then the cash operating cycle will lengthen and the investment in working capital will increase.

The length of the cash operating cycle is often dictated by the industry. For example, a construction business may have a long cash operating cycle because of the high level of work in progress. Restaurant businesses usually have short cash operating cycles because they have short inventory periods and customers pay by cash or debit or credit card.

Note also that it is possible to have a negative cash operating cycle. The bookseller and retailer Amazon has a negative cash operating cycle because of short inventory periods and fast payments from customers. When Amazon ships a book, for example, it charges the customer's credit card and gets paid by the credit card company within a day.

4.1 Example: Cash operating cycle

Wines Co buys raw materials from suppliers that allow Wines 2.5 months' credit. The raw materials remain in inventory for one month, and it takes Wines two months to produce the goods. The goods are sold within a couple of days of production being completed and customers take on average 1.5 months to pay.

Required

Calculate Wines's cash operating cycle.

Solution

We can ignore the time that finished goods are in inventory, as it is no more than a couple of days.

	Months
The average time that raw materials remain in inventory	1.0
Less the time taken to pay suppliers	(2.5)
The time taken to produce the goods	2.0
The time taken by customers to pay for the goods	1.5
Cash cycle	2.0

The company's cash operating cycle is two months. This can be illustrated diagrammatically as follows.

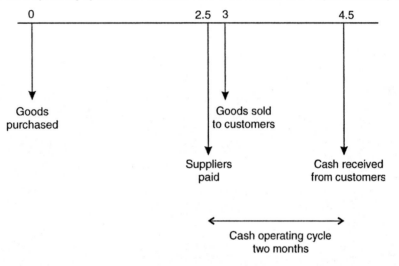

The cash operating cycle is the period between the suppliers being paid and the cash being received from the customers.

5 Liquidity ratios   6/08, 6/12, 6/13, 6/14

FAST FORWARD

Working capital ratios may help to indicate whether a company is **over-capitalised**, with excessive working capital, or if a business is likely to fail. A business which is trying to do too much too quickly with too little long-term capital is **overtrading**.

5.1 The current ratio

The **current ratio** is the standard test of liquidity.

Key term

> **Current ratio** = $\dfrac{\text{Current assets}}{\text{Current liabilities}}$

A company should have enough current assets that give a promise of 'cash to come' to meet its commitments to pay its current liabilities. Superficially, a ratio in excess of 1 implies that the organisation has enough cash and near-cash assets to satisfy its immediate liabilities. However, interpretation needs to be conducted with care. Too high a ratio implies that too much cash may be tied up in receivables and inventories. What is 'comfortable' varies between different types of business.

5.2 The quick ratio

Quick ratio or acid test ratio = $\dfrac{\text{Current assets less inventories}}{\text{Current liabilities}}$

Companies are unable to convert all their current assets into cash very quickly. In some businesses where inventory turnover is slow, most inventories are not very liquid assets, and the cash cycle is long. For these reasons, we calculate an additional liquidity ratio, known as the quick ratio or acid test ratio.

This ratio should ideally be at least 1 for companies with a slow inventory turnover. For companies with a fast inventory turnover, a quick ratio can be less than 1 without suggesting that the company is in cash flow difficulties.

5.3 The accounts receivable payment period

Accounts receivable days or accounts receivable payment period, or average collection period =

$\dfrac{\text{Trade receivables}}{\text{Credit sales revenue}} \times 365 \text{ days}$

This is a rough measure of the average length of time it takes for a company's accounts receivable to pay what they owe.

The trade accounts receivable are not the **total** figure for accounts receivable in the statement of financial position, which includes prepayments and non-trade accounts receivable. The trade accounts receivable figure will be itemised in an analysis of the total accounts receivable, in a note to the accounts.

The estimate of accounts receivable days is only approximate.

(a) The **statement of financial position value** of accounts receivable might be **abnormally high** or low compared with the 'normal' level the company usually has. This may apply especially to smaller companies, where the size of year-end accounts receivable may largely depend on whether a few or even a single large customer pay just before or just after the year end.

(b) Revenue (turnover) in the statement of profit or loss excludes sales tax, but the accounts receivable figure in the statement of financial position includes sales tax. We are not strictly comparing like with like. In addition, accounts receivable from the statement of financial position is at a point and may not be typical.

5.4 The inventory turnover period

Inventory turnover = $\dfrac{\text{Cost of sales}}{\text{Average inventory}}$

The inventory turnover period can also be calculated:

Inventory turnover period (finished goods) = $\dfrac{\text{Average inventory}}{\text{Cost of sales}} \times 365 \text{ days}$

Raw materials inventory holding period = $\dfrac{\text{Average raw materials inventory}}{\text{Annual purchases}} \times 365 \text{ days}$

Average production (work-in-progress) period = $\dfrac{\text{Average WIP}}{\text{Cost of sales}} \times 365 \text{ days}$

These indicate the average number of days that items of inventory are held for. As with the average accounts receivable collection period, these are only approximate figures, but ones which should be reliable enough for finding changes over time. Average inventory is often calculated as (opening + closing balance) / 2 although other methods of estimating a typical value may be used.

A lengthening inventory turnover period indicates:

(a) A **slowdown** in **trading**, or

(b) A **build-up** in **inventory levels**, perhaps suggesting that the investment in inventories is becoming excessive

If we add together the inventory days and the accounts receivable days, this should give us an indication of how soon inventory is convertible into cash, thereby giving a further indication of the **company's liquidity**.

5.5 The accounts payable payment period

Key term

$$\text{Accounts payable payment period} = \frac{\text{Average trade payables}}{\text{Purchases or Cost of sales}} \times 365 \text{ days}$$

The accounts payable payment period often helps to assess a company's liquidity; an increase in accounts payable days is often a sign of lack of long-term finance or poor management of current assets, resulting in the use of extended credit from suppliers, increased bank overdraft, and so on.

All the ratios calculated above will **vary by industry**; hence **comparisons** of ratios calculated with other similar companies in the same industry are important.

You may need to use the following periods to calculate the operating cycle.

	Days
Raw materials inventory holding period	X
Accounts payable payment period	(X)
Average production period	X
Inventory turnover period (Finished goods)	X
Accounts receivable payment period	X
Operating cycle	X

5.6 The sales revenue/net working capital ratio

The ratio of $\dfrac{\text{Sales revenue}}{\text{Current assets} - \text{Current liabilities}}$

shows the level of working capital supporting sales. Working capital must **increase in line with sales** to avoid liquidity problems and this ratio can be used to forecast the level of working capital needed for a projected level of sales.

5.7 The need for funds for investment in current assets

These liquidity ratios are a guide to the risk of cash flow problems and insolvency. If a company suddenly finds that it is **unable to renew** its **short-term liabilities** (for example, if the bank suspends its overdraft facilities), there will be a **danger of insolvency** unless the company is able to turn enough of its current assets into cash quickly.

Current liabilities are often a cheap method of finance (trade accounts payable do not usually carry an interest cost). Companies may therefore consider that, in the interest of higher profits, it is worth accepting some risk of insolvency by increasing current liabilities, taking the maximum credit possible from suppliers.

5.8 Working capital needs of different types of business   6/11

Different industries have different optimum working capital profiles, reflecting their methods of doing business and what they are selling.

(a) Businesses with a lot of **cash sales** and few credit sales should have **minimal accounts receivable**.

(b) Businesses that exist solely to trade will only have **finished goods in inventory**, whereas **manufacturers** will have **raw materials** and **work in progress** as well. In addition, some finished goods, notably foodstuffs, have to be sold within a few days because of their perishable nature.

(c) **Large companies** may be able to use their strength as customers to obtain **extended credit periods** from their suppliers. By contrast small companies, particularly those that have recently started trading, may be required to pay their suppliers immediately.

(d) Some businesses will be receiving **most of their monies** at **certain times** of the year, while incurring expenses throughout the year. Examples include travel agents who will have peaks reflecting demand for holidays during the summer and at Christmas.

5.9 Over-capitalisation and working capital

If there are excessive inventories, accounts receivable and cash, and very few accounts payable, there will be an overinvestment by the company in current assets. Working capital will be excessive and the company in this respect will be over-capitalised.

Indicators of over-capitalisation	
Sales/working capital	Compare with previous years or similar companies. A low or falling ratio may indicate over-capitalisation.
Liquidity ratios	Compare with previous years or similar companies.
Turnover periods	Long turnover periods for inventory and accounts receivable or short credit period from suppliers may be unnecessary. Working capital requirements can be reduced by improving these turnover times.

5.10 Example: Working capital ratios

Calculate liquidity and working capital ratios from the following accounts of a manufacturer of products for the construction industry, and comment on the ratios.

	20X3	20X2
	$m	$m
Sales revenue	2,065.0	1,788.7
Cost of sales	1,478.6	1,304.0
Gross profit	586.4	484.7
Current assets		
Inventories	119.0	109.0
Accounts receivable (note 1)	400.9	347.4
Short-term investments	4.2	18.8
Cash at bank and in hand	48.2	48.0
	572.3	523.2
Accounts payable: amounts falling due within one year		
Loans and overdrafts	49.1	35.3
Corporation taxes	62.0	46.7
Dividend	19.2	14.3
Accounts payable (note 2)	370.7	324.0
	501.0	420.3
Net current assets	71.3	102.9

Notes

		20X3	20X2
		$m	$m
1	Trade accounts receivable	329.8	285.4
2	Trade accounts payable	236.2	210.8

Solution

	20X3	20X2
Current ratio	$\dfrac{572.3}{501.0} = 1.14$	$\dfrac{523.2}{420.3} = 1.24$
Quick ratio	$\dfrac{453.3}{501.0} = 0.90$	$\dfrac{414.2}{420.3} = 0.99$
Accounts receivable payment period	$\dfrac{329.8}{2,065.0} \times 365 = 58 \text{ days}$	$\dfrac{285.4}{1,788.7} \times 365 = 58 \text{ days}$
Inventory turnover period	$\dfrac{119.0}{1,478.6} \times 365 = 29 \text{ days}$	$\dfrac{109.0}{1,304.0} \times 365 = 31 \text{ days}$
Accounts payable turnover period	$\dfrac{236.2}{1,478.6} \times 365 = 58 \text{ days}$	$\dfrac{210.8}{1,304.0} \times 365 = 59 \text{ days}$
Sales revenue/net working capital	$\dfrac{2,065.0}{572.3 - 501.0} = 28.96$	$\dfrac{1,788.7}{523.2 - 420.3} = 17.38$

(a) The company is a manufacturing group serving the construction industry, and so would be expected to have a comparatively lengthy accounts receivable turnover period, because of the relatively poor cash flow in the construction industry.

(b) The company compensates for this by ensuring that they do not pay for raw materials and other costs before they have sold their inventories of finished goods (hence the similarity of accounts receivable and accounts payable turnover periods).

(c) The company's current and quick ratios have fallen but are still reasonable, and the quick ratio is not much less than the current ratio. This suggests that inventory levels are strictly controlled, which is reinforced by the low inventory turnover period.

(d) The ratio of sales revenue/net working capital indicates that working capital has not increased in line with sales. This may forecast future liquidity problems.

It would seem that working capital is tightly managed to avoid the poor liquidity which could be caused by a high accounts receivable turnover period and comparatively high accounts payable. However, revenue has increased but net working capital has declined due in part to the fall in short-term investments and the increase in loans and overdrafts.

> **Exam focus point**
>
> The ACCA examination team may give you industry averages for ratios and expect you to compare performance against what could be expected using financial analysis, including ratio analysis.
>
> In June 2008, candidates were required to work backwards from provided ratios to calculate receivables, inventory, etc. This requires a very good familiarity with all of the ratios.

5.11 Overtrading   12/08, 6/12

In contrast with over-capitalisation, overtrading happens when a business tries to **do too much too quickly with too little long-term capital**, so that it is trying to support too large a volume of trade with the capital resources at its disposal.

Even if an overtrading business operates at a profit, it could easily run into serious trouble because it is **short of cash**. Such liquidity troubles stem from the fact that it does not have enough capital to provide the cash to pay its debts as they fall due.

Symptoms of overtrading are as follows.

(a) There is a **rapid increase** in **sales revenue**.

(b) There is a **rapid increase** in the **volume of current assets** and possibly also non-current assets. **Inventory turnover** and **accounts receivable turnover** might slow down, in which case the rate of increase in inventories and accounts receivable would be even greater than the rate of increase in sales.

(c) There is only a **small increase** in **equity capital** (perhaps through retained profits). Most of the increase in assets is financed by credit, especially:

   (i) **Trade accounts payable** – the payment period to accounts payable is likely to lengthen

   (ii) A **bank overdraft**, which often reaches or even exceeds the limit of the facilities agreed by the bank

(d) Some **debt ratios** and **liquidity ratios** alter dramatically.

   (i) The **proportion** of **total assets** financed by proprietors' capital falls, and the proportion financed by credit rises.

   (ii) The current ratio and the quick ratio fall.

   (iii) The business might have a **liquid deficit**; that is, an excess of current liabilities over current assets.

<table>
<tr><td>Exam focus point</td><td>This list of signs is important; you must be aware of why businesses run into financial difficulties. In the exam you might be expected to diagnose overtrading from information given about a company.</td></tr>
</table>

5.12 Example: Overtrading

Great Ambition Co appoints a new managing director who has great plans to expand the company. They want to increase revenue by 100% within two years, and to do this they employ extra sales staff. They recognise that customers do not want to have to wait for deliveries, and so they decide that the company must build up its inventory levels. There is a substantial increase in the company's inventories. These are held in additional warehouse space which is now rented. The company also buys new cars for its extra sales representatives.

The managing director's policies are immediately successful in boosting sales, which double in just over one year. Inventory levels are now much higher, but the company takes longer credit from its suppliers, even though some suppliers have expressed their annoyance at the length of time they must wait for payment. Credit terms for accounts receivable are unchanged, and so the volume of accounts receivable, like the volume of sales, rises by 100%.

In spite of taking longer credit, the company still needs to increase its overdraft facilities with the bank, which are raised from a limit of $40,000 to one of $80,000. The company is profitable, and retains some profits in the business, but profit margins have fallen. **Gross profit margins** are lower because some prices have been reduced to obtain extra sales. **Net profit margins** are lower because overhead costs are higher. These include sales representatives' wages, car expenses and depreciation on cars, warehouse rent and additional losses from having to write off out of date and slow-moving inventory items.

The statement of financial position of the company might change over time from (A) to (B).

	Statement of financial position (A)		Statement of financial position (B)	
	$	$	$	$
Non-current assets		160,000		210,000
Current assets				
Inventory	60,000		150,000	
Accounts receivable	64,000		135,000	
Cash	1,000		–	
Current assets		125,000		285,000
Total assets		285,000		495,000
Share capital	10,000		10,000	
Retained profits	200,000		205,000	
Total equity		210,000		215,000
Current liabilities				
Bank	25,000		80,000	
Accounts payable	50,000		200,000	

BPP LEARNING MEDIA

	Statement of financial position (A)		Statement of financial position (B)	
	$	$	$	$
Total liabilities		75,000		280,000
Total equity and liabilities		285,000		495,000

	Statement of profit or loss (A)	Statement of profit or loss (B)
	$	$
Sales	$1,000,000	$2,000,000
Gross profit	$200,000	$300,000
Net profit	$50,000	$20,000

In situation (B), the company has **reached** its **overdraft** limit and has **four times** as many **accounts payable** as in situation (A) but with only **twice the sales revenue. Inventory levels** are much **higher**, and **inventory turnover** is **lower**.

The company is overtrading. If it had to pay its next trade account, or salaries and wages, before it received any income, it could not do so without the bank allowing it to exceed its overdraft limit. The company is profitable, although profit margins have fallen, and it ought to expect a prosperous future. But if it does not sort out its cash flow and liquidity, it will not survive to enjoy future profits.

Suitable solutions to the problem would be implementing measures to reduce the degree of overtrading.

(a) **New capital** from the shareholders could be injected.

(b) **Better control** could be applied to inventories and accounts receivable. The company could **abandon ambitious plans** for increased sales and more non-current asset purchases until the business has had time to consolidate its position, and build up its capital base with retained profits.

A business seeking to increase its revenue too rapidly without an adequate capital base is not the only **cause of overtrading. Other causes** are as follows.

(a) When a business repays a loan, it often replaces the old loan with a new one (refinancing). However a business might **repay a loan without replacing it**, with the consequence that it has **less long-term capital** to finance its current level of operations.

(b) A business might be profitable, but in a period of **inflation**, its **retained profits** might be **insufficient** to pay for **replacement** non-current assets and inventories, which now cost more because of inflation.

Chapter Roundup

- The amount tied up in **working capital** is equal to the value of raw materials, work in progress, finished goods inventories and accounts receivable less accounts payable. The size of this net figure has a direct effect on the **liquidity** of an organisation.

- The two main objectives of working capital management are to ensure that it has **sufficient liquid resources** to continue in business and to **increase its profitability**.

- A business needs to have **clear policies** for the management of each component of working capital.

- **Working capital ratios** may help to indicate whether a company is **over-capitalised**, with excessive working capital, or if a business is likely to fail. A business which is trying to do too much too quickly with too little long-term capital is **overtrading**.

Quick Quiz

1   Which of the following is the most likely to be a symptom of overtrading?

    A   Static levels of inventory turnover
    B   Rapid increase in profits
    C   Increase in the level of the current ratio
    D   Rapid increase in sales

2   The cash operating cycle is:

          A The time   [   ]

   Less   B The time   [   ]

   Plus   C The time   [   ]

   Plus   D The time   [   ]

    Fill in the blanks.

3   Fill in the blanks with the following:

    Current liabilities; current assets; inventories

$$\text{Quick ratio} = \frac{\text{.........................less.........................}}{\text{...}}$$

4   Which of the following describes **over-capitalisation** and which describes **overtrading**?

    A   A company with excessive investment in working capital

    B   A company trying to support too large a volume of trade with the capital resources at its disposal

5   Which of the following statements best defines the current ratio?

    A   The ratio of current assets to current liabilities
          For the majority of businesses it should be at least 2.

    B   The ratio of current assets to current liabilities
          For the majority of businesses it should be at least 1.

    C   The ratio of current assets excluding inventory
          For the majority of businesses it should be at least 1.

    D   The ratio of current assets excluding inventory to current liabilities
          For the majority of businesses it should be at least 2.

6   The accounts receivable payment period is a calculation of the time taken to pay by all accounts receivable.

True ☐

False ☐

7   What are the two most likely reasons for a lengthening inventory turnover period?

8   What is the working capital requirement of a company with the following average figures over a year?

	$
Inventory	3,750
Trade accounts receivable	1,500
Cash and bank balances	500
Trade accounts payable	1,800

1   D   Rapid increase in sales

2   A   The time raw materials remain in inventory
    B   The time period of credit taken from suppliers
    C   The time taken to produce goods
    D   The time taken by customers to pay for goods

3   Quick ratio = $\dfrac{\text{Current assets less inventories}}{\text{Current liabilities}}$

4   A   Over-capitalisation
    B   Overtrading

5   B   Current assets to current liabilities: 1

6   False. The calculation normally only includes trade accounts receivable.

7   (a)   A slowdown in trading
    (b)   A build-up of inventory levels

8   Working capital requirement = current assets less current liabilities

    = 3,750 + 1,500 + 500 − 1,800
    = $3,950

Now try the questions below from the Practice Question Bank

Number	Level	Marks	Approximate time
Section A Q10	Examination	2	4 mins
Section A Q11	Examination	2	4 mins
Section A Q12	Examination	2	4 mins
Section C Q1	Examination	20	39 mins

Managing working capital

Topic list	Syllabus reference
1 Managing inventories	C2 (c)
2 Managing accounts receivable	C2 (d)
3 Managing accounts payable	C2 (e)

Introduction

This chapter deals with specific techniques in the management of accounts receivable, accounts payable and inventory. These include overall **credit control policies** (should the business offer credit – if so, how much and to whom), and ensuring amounts owed are not excessive.

While working through this chapter, try not to think of accounts receivable and accounts payable in isolation; they are part of working capital, each element of which will have **knock-on effects** when there is a change in another. For example, an increase in the credit period taken by accounts receivable will reduce the amount of cash available to pay accounts payable and invest in inventory.

Study guide

		Intellectual level
C2	**Management of inventories, accounts receivable, accounts payable and cash**	
(c)	Discuss, apply and evaluate the use of relevant techniques in managing inventory, including the economic order quantity model and Just-in-Time techniques.	2
(d)	Discuss, apply and evaluate the use of relevant techniques in managing accounts receivable, including:	
(i)	Assessing creditworthiness	1
(ii)	Managing accounts receivable	1
(iii)	Collecting amounts owing	1
(iv)	Offering early settlement discounts	2
(v)	Using factoring and invoice discounting	2
(vi)	Managing foreign accounts receivable	2
(e)	Discuss and apply the use of relevant techniques in managing accounts payable, including:	
(i)	Using trade credit effectively	1
(ii)	Evaluating the benefits of discounts for early settlement and bulk purchase	2
(iii)	Managing foreign accounts payable	1

Exam guide

Questions in this area are likely to be a mixture of calculations and discussion. The material in this chapter is highly examinable.

1 Managing inventories   12/07, 6/08, 12/10, 6/11, 12/13

FAST FORWARD

An **economic order quantity** can be calculated as a guide to minimising costs in managing **inventory** levels. However, **bulk discounts** can mean that a different order quantity minimises inventory costs.

Almost every company carries inventories of some sort, even if they are only inventories of consumables such as stationery. For a manufacturing business, inventories in the form of **raw materials, work in progress** and **finished goods** may amount to a substantial proportion of the total assets of the business.

Some businesses attempt to control inventories on a scientific basis by balancing the costs of inventory shortages against those of inventory holding. The 'scientific' control of inventories may be analysed into three parts.

(a)   The **economic order quantity (EOQ) model** can be used to decide the optimum order size for inventories which will minimise the costs of ordering inventories plus inventory holding costs.

(b)   If **discounts for bulk purchases** are available, it may be cheaper to buy inventories in large order sizes so as to obtain the discounts.

(c)   Uncertainty in the demand for inventories and/or the supply lead time may lead a company to decide to hold **buffer inventories** in order to reduce or eliminate the risk of 'stock-outs' (running out of inventory).

INVENTORY COSTS	
Holding costs	The cost of capital Warehousing and handling costs Deterioration Obsolescence Insurance Pilferage
Procuring costs	Ordering costs Delivery costs
Shortage costs	Contribution from lost sales Extra cost of emergency inventory Cost of lost production and sales in a stock-out
Purchase cost of inventory	Relevant particularly when calculating discounts for bulk quantity purchases

1.1 The basic EOQ formula
6/08, 12/10

Key term

> The **economic order quantity (EOQ)** is the optimal ordering quantity for an item of inventory which will minimise costs.

Let D = usage in units for one period (the demand)

C_0 = cost of placing one order
C_h = holding cost per unit of inventory for one period
Q = re-order quantity
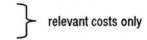 relevant costs only

Assume that demand is constant, the lead time is constant or zero and purchase costs per unit are constant (ie no bulk discounts).

The total annual cost of having inventory is:

(a) Holding costs (holding cost per unit × average inventory) + ordering costs

$$\frac{Q}{2} \times C_h + \frac{C_0 \times D}{Q}$$

The more orders are made each year the higher the ordering costs, but the lower the holding costs (as less inventory is held).

(b) The objective is to minimise $T = \frac{Q}{2} \times C_h + \frac{C_0 \times D}{Q}$

The order quantity, EOQ, which will minimise these total costs is:

Formula to learn

$$EOQ = \sqrt{\frac{2C_0 D}{C_h}}$$

At the EOQ level, total holding costs per period equal the total ordering costs in the period.
The EOQ assumes that there are no bulk purchase discounts for large quantity orders; therefore purchasing costs are the same regardless of the order quantity.

Exam focus point

> The EOQ formula will be given to you in the exam, but make sure you know what each letter represents and how to do the calculation quickly and accurately.

1.2 Example: Economic order quantity

The demand for a commodity is 40,000 units a year, at a steady rate. It costs $20 to place an order, and 40c to hold a unit for a year. Find the order size to minimise inventory costs, the number of orders placed each year, the length of the inventory cycle and the total costs of holding inventory for the year.

Solution

$$Q = \sqrt{\frac{2C_0 D}{C_h}} = \sqrt{\frac{2 \times 20 \times 40,000}{0.4}} = 2,000 \text{ units.}$$

This means that there will be:

$$\frac{40,000}{2,000} = 20 \text{ orders placed each year.}$$

The inventory cycle is therefore:

$$\frac{52 \text{ weeks}}{20 \text{ orders}} = 2.6 \text{ weeks.}$$

Total costs will be $(20 \times \$20) + \left(\frac{2,000}{2} \times 40c\right) = \$800$ a year.

1.3 Uncertainties in demand and lead times: a re-order level system

FAST FORWARD

Uncertainties in demand and lead times taken to fulfil orders mean that inventory will be ordered once it reaches a re-order level (maximum usage × maximum lead time).

Key term

Re-order level = maximum usage × maximum lead time.

The re-order level is the measure of inventory at which a replenishment order should be made.

(a) If an order is placed **too late**, the organisation may run out of inventory, **a stock-out**, resulting in a loss of sales and/or a loss of production.

(b) If an order is placed **too soon**, the organisation will hold too much inventory, and inventory holding costs will be excessive.

Use of a re-order level builds in a measure of safety inventory and minimises the risk of the organisation running out of inventory. This is particularly important when the volume of demand or the supply lead time are uncertain.

The **average annual** cost of such a safety inventory would be:

Quantity of safety inventory (in units) × Inventory holding cost per unit per annum

The diagram below shows how the inventory levels might fluctuate with this system. Points marked 'X' show the re-order level at which a new order is placed. The number of units ordered each time is the EOQ. Actual inventory levels sometimes fall below the safety inventory level, and sometimes the resupply arrives before inventories have fallen to the safety level. On average, however, extra inventory holding will approximate the safety inventory. The size of the safety inventory will depend on whether stock-outs (running out of inventory) are allowed.

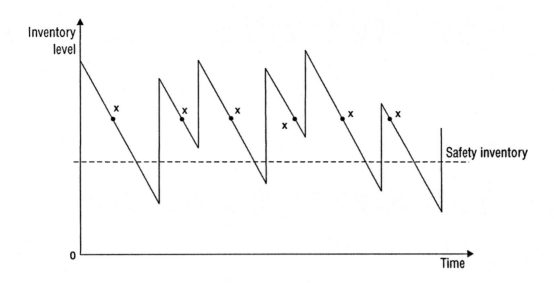

1.4 Maximum and buffer safety inventory levels

> **Maximum inventory level** = re-order level + re-order quantity − (minimum usage × minimum lead time)

The maximum level acts as a warning signal to management that inventories are reaching a potentially wasteful level.

> **Minimum inventory** or **buffer safety inventory** = re-order level − (average usage × average lead time)

The buffer safety level acts as a warning to management that inventories are approaching a dangerously low level and that stock-outs are possible.

> **Average inventory** = buffer safety inventory + $\dfrac{\text{re-order amount}}{2}$

This formula assumes that inventory levels fluctuate evenly between the buffer safety (or minimum) inventory level and the highest possible inventory level (the amount of inventory immediately after an order is received, safety inventory and re-order quantity).

1.5 Example: Maximum and buffer safety inventory

A company has an inventory management policy which involves ordering 50,000 units when the inventory level falls to 15,000 units. Forecast demand to meet production requirements during the next year is 310,000 units. You should assume a 50-week year and that demand is constant throughout the year. Orders are received two weeks after being placed with the supplier. What is the average inventory level?

Solution

Average usage per week = 310,000 units/50 weeks = 6,200 units

Average lead time = 2 weeks

Re-order level = 15,000 units

Buffer safety inventory = re-order level − (average usage × average lead time)

= 15,000 − (6,200 × 2) = 2,600 units

Average inventory = buffer safety inventory + $\dfrac{\text{re-order amount}}{2}$

= 2,600 + $\dfrac{50,000}{2}$ = 27,600 units

This approach assumes that a business wants to minimise the risk of stock-outs at all costs. In the modern manufacturing environment stock-outs can have a disastrous effect on the production process.

If, however, you are given a question where the risk of stock-outs is assumed to be worth taking, and the costs of stock-outs are quantified, the re-order level may not be calculated in the way described above. For **each possible re-order level**, and therefore each **possible level** of buffer inventory, **calculate**:

- The **costs of holding buffer inventory** per annum

- The **costs of stock-outs** (Cost of one stock-out × expected number of stock-outs per order × number of orders per year)

The expected number of stock-outs per order reflects the various levels by which demand during the lead time could exceed the re-order level.

1.6 Example: Possibility of stock-outs

If re-order level is 4 units, but there is a probability of 0.2 that demand during the lead time would be 5 units, and 0.05 that demand during the lead time would be 6 units, then expected number of stock-outs = $((5 - 4) \times 0.2) + ((6 - 4) \times 0.05) = 0.3$.

(Stock-outs are defined as the number of units not available in inventory when required.)

1.7 The effect of discounts

The solution obtained from using the simple EOQ formula may need to be modified if bulk discounts (also called quantity discounts) are available. To decide mathematically whether it would be worthwhile taking a discount and ordering larger quantities, it is necessary to minimise:

Total purchasing costs + Ordering costs + Inventory holding costs.

The total cost will be minimised:

- At the pre-discount EOQ level, so that a discount is not worthwhile; or
- At the minimum order size necessary to earn the discount.

1.8 Example: Bulk discounts

The annual demand for an item of inventory is 125 units. The item costs $200 a unit to purchase, the holding cost for one unit for one year is 15% of the unit cost and ordering costs are $300 an order. The supplier offers a 3% discount for orders of 60 units or more, and a discount of 5% for orders of 90 units or more. What is the cost-minimising order size?

Solution

(a)   The EOQ ignoring discounts is:

$$\sqrt{\frac{2 \times 300 \times 125}{15\% \text{ of } 200}} = 50 \text{ units}$$

	$
Purchases (no discount) 125 × $200	25,000
Holding costs ($^{50}/_2$) 25 units × 15% × $200	750
Ordering costs 2.5 orders × $300	750
Total annual costs	26,500

(b)   With a discount of 3% and an order quantity of 60 units costs are as follows.

	$
Purchases $25,000 × 97%	24,250
Holding costs 30 units × 15% of 97% of $200	873
Ordering costs 2.08 orders × $300	625
Total annual costs	25,748

(c) With a discount of 5% and an order quantity of 90 units costs are as follows.

	$
Purchases $25,000 × 95%	23,750.0
Holding costs 45 units × 15% of 95% of $200	1,282.5
Ordering costs 1.39 orders × $300	416.7
Total annual costs	25,449.2

The cheapest option is to order 90 units at a time.

Question
Bulk orders

Question: Bulk orders

A company uses an item of inventory as follows.

Purchase price:	$96 per unit
Annual demand:	4,000 units
Ordering cost:	$300
Annual holding cost:	10% of purchase price
Economic order quantity:	500 units

Should the company order 1,000 units at a time in order to secure an 8% discount?

Answer

The total annual cost at the economic order quantity of 500 units is as follows.

	$
Purchases 4,000 × $96	384,000
Ordering costs $300 × (4,000/500)	2,400
Holding costs $96 × 10% × (500/2)	2,400
	388,800

The total annual cost at an order quantity of 1,000 units would be as follows.

	$
Purchases $384,000 × 92%	353,280
Ordering costs $300 × (4,000/1,000)	1,200
Holding costs $96 × 92% × 10% × (1,000/2)	4,416
	358,896

The company should order the item 1,000 units at a time, saving $(388,800 - 358,896) = $29,904 a year.

1.9 Just-in-time (JIT)
12/10

Some manufacturing companies have sought to reduce their inventories of raw materials and components to as low a level as possible. **Just-in-time procurement** is a term which describes a policy of obtaining goods from suppliers at the latest possible time (ie when they are needed) and so avoiding the need to carry any materials or components inventory.

Just-in-time production describes manufacturing to order. As orders are received, manufacturing is triggered to fulfil those orders. This enables better product customisation, less/no risk of obsolescence and few holding costs. It does, however, imply a flexible manufacturing process (in terms of what and how much is made) with follow-on considerations for employment terms. In addition, idle time may need to be tolerated (although managed to a practical minimum).

Introducing JIT might bring the following potential benefits.

- Reduction in inventory holding costs
- Reduced manufacturing lead times
- Improved labour productivity
- Reduced scrap/rework/warranty costs

Reduced inventory levels mean that a lower level of investment in working capital will be required.

JIT will not be appropriate in some cases. For example, a restaurant might find it preferable to use the traditional economic order quantity approach for staple non-perishable food inventories but adopt JIT for perishable and 'exotic' items. In a hospital, a stock-out could quite literally be fatal and so JIT would be quite unsuitable.

<table>
<tr><td>Exam focus point</td><td>You may be required to evaluate the benefits of introducing a JIT arrangement, given certain assumptions about the costs and benefits.</td></tr>
</table>

 ### Case Study

Japanese car manufacturer Toyota was the first company to develop JIT (JIT was originally called the Toyota Production System). After the end of the world war in 1945, Toyota recognised that it had much to do to catch up with the US automobile manufacturing industry. The company was making losses. In Japan, however, consumer demand for cars was weak, and consumers were very resistant to price increases. Japan also had a bad record for industrial disputes. Toyota itself suffered from major strike action in 1950.

The individual credited with devising JIT in Toyota from the 1940s was Taiichi Ohno, and JIT techniques were developed gradually over time.

Ohno identified seven wastes and worked to eliminate them from operations in Toyota. Measures that were taken by the company included the following.

(a) The aim of reducing costs was of paramount importance in the late 1940s. Toyota was losing money, and market demand was weak, preventing price rises. The only way to move from losses into profits was to cut costs, and cost reduction was probably essential for the survival of the company.

(b) The company aimed to level the flow of production and eliminate unevenness in the work flow. Production levelling should help to minimise idle time while at the same time allowing the company to achieve its objective of minimum inventories.

(c) The factory layout was changed. Previously all machines, such as presses, were located in the same area of the factory. Under the new system, different types of machines were clustered together in production cells.

(d) Machine operators were retrained.

(e) Employee involvement in the changes was seen as being particularly important. Teamwork was promoted.

(f) The **kanban system** was eventually introduced, but a major problem with its introduction was the elimination of defects in production. The kanban system is a 'pull' system of production scheduling. Items are only produced when they are needed. If a part is faulty when it is produced, the production line will be held up until the fault is corrected.

2 Managing accounts receivable

2.1 Total credit

FAST FORWARD

> Giving credit has a cost: the value of the interest charged on an overdraft to fund the period of credit, or the interest lost on the cash not received and deposited in the bank. An increase in profit from extra sales resulting from offering credit could offset this cost.

Credit is offered to customers to win sales and sales mean profits. But there is a cost to giving credit. The benefits should exceed the costs.

2.2 Effect on profit of extending credit

One of the main costs of offering credit is the interest expense. How can we assess the effect on profit?

Let us assume that the Zygo Company sells widgets for $1,000, which enables it to earn a profit, after all other expenses except interest, of $100 (ie a 10% margin).

(a) Aibee buys a widget for $1,000 on 1 January 20X1, but does not pay until 31 December 20X1. Zygo relies on overdraft finance, which costs it 10% pa. The effect is:

	$
Net profit on sale of widget	100
Overdraft cost $1,000 × 10% pa	(100)
Actual profit after 12 months' credit	Nil

In other words, the entire profit margin has been wiped out in 12 months.

(b) If Aibee had paid after six months, the effect would be:

	$
Net profit	100
Overdraft cost $1,000 × 10% pa × $^6/_{12}$ months	(50)
	50

Half the profit has been wiped out. (**Tutorial note**. The interest cost might be worked out in a more complex way to give a more accurate figure.)

(c) If the cost of borrowing had been 18%, then the profit would have been absorbed before seven months had elapsed. If the net profit were 5% and borrowing costs were 15%, the interest expense would exceed the net profit after four months.

Question — Cost of receivables

Winterson Tools has an average level of accounts receivable of $2m at any time representing 60 days outstanding. (Their credit terms are 30 days.) The firm borrows money at 10% a year. The managing director is proud of the credit control: 'I only had to write off $10,000 in bad debts last year,' they said proudly. Are they right to be proud?

Answer

The managing director may be proud of the low level of bad debts but customers are taking an extra month to pay and this has a cost. At any one time, there is $1m more money outstanding than there should be ($^{30}/_{60}$ days × $2m) and this costs $100,000 in interest charges (10% × $1m).

The level of total credit can then have a significant effect on **profitability**. That said, if credit considerations are included in pricing calculations, extending credit can, in fact, increase profitability. If offering credit generates extra sales, then those extra sales will have additional repercussions on:

(a) The amount of inventory maintained in the warehouse, to ensure that the extra demand must be satisfied

(b) The amount of money the company owes to its accounts payable (as it will be increasing its supply of raw materials)

2.3 Credit control policy   12/10

Several factors should be considered by management when a policy for **credit control** is formulated. These include:

(a) The administrative costs of **debt collection**

(b) The procedures for **controlling credit** to individual customers and for debt collection

(c) The amount of **extra capital required** to finance an extension of total credit – there might be an increase in accounts receivable, inventories and accounts payable, and the net increase in working capital must be financed

(d) The cost of the **additional finance** required for any increase in the volume of accounts receivable (or the savings from a reduction in accounts receivable) – this cost might be bank overdraft interest, or the cost of long-term funds (such as loan inventory or equity)

(e) Any **savings or additional expenses** in operating the credit policy (for example the extra work involved in pursuing slow payers)

(f) The **ways** in which the credit policy could be **implemented** – for example:

   (i) Credit could be eased by giving accounts receivable a longer period in which to settle their accounts – the cost would be the resulting increase in accounts receivable.

   (ii) A discount could be offered for early payment – the cost would be the amount of the discounts taken.

(g) The **effects of easing credit**, which might be to encourage a higher proportion of bad debts, and an increase in sales volume. Provided that the extra gross contribution from the increase in sales exceeds the increase in fixed cost expenses, bad debts, discounts and the finance cost of an increase in working capital, a policy to relax credit terms would be profitable.

2.4 Assessing creditworthiness   6/15

FAST FORWARD

> In managing **accounts receivable**, the **creditworthiness** of customers needs to be assessed. The risks and costs of a customer defaulting will need to be balanced against the profitability of the business provided by that customer.

Credit control involves the initial investigation of potential credit customers and the continuing control of outstanding accounts. The main points to note are as follows.

(a) New customers should give two **good references**, including one from a bank, before being granted credit.

(b) **Credit ratings** might be **checked** through a credit rating/reference agency.

(c) A **new customer's credit limit** should be **fixed** at a **low level** and only increased if their payment record subsequently warrants it.

(d) For large value customers, a **file** should be **maintained** of any available financial information about the customer. This file should be reviewed regularly. Information is available from the company's annual report and accounts.

(e)   Government departments can sometimes advise on overseas companies.

(f)   **Press comments** may give information about what a company is currently doing (as opposed to the historical results in Extel cards or published accounts which only show what the company has done in the past).

(g)   The company could send a member of staff to **visit** the company concerned, to get a first-hand impression of the company and its prospects. This would be advisable in the case of a prospective major customer.

An organisation might devise a **credit-rating system** for new individual customers that is based on characteristics of the customer (such as whether the customer is a homeowner, and the customer's age and occupation). Points or ratings would be awarded according to the characteristics of the customer, and the amount of credit that is offered would depend on their credit score.

2.5 Managing accounts receivable

FAST FORWARD

Regular monitoring of accounts receivable is very important. Individual accounts receivable can be assessed using a **customer history analysis** and a **credit rating system**. The overall level of accounts receivable can be monitored using an **aged accounts receivable listing** and **credit utilisation report**, as well as reports on the level of bad debts.

(a)   **Accounts receivable payment records** must be **monitored** continually. This depends on successful sales ledger administration.

(b)   Credit monitoring can be simplified by a system of **in-house credit ratings**. For example, a company could have five credit-risk categories for its customers. As mentioned above, these credit categories or ratings could be used to decide either individual credit limits for customers within that category or the frequency of the credit review.

(c)   A **customer's payment record** and the **accounts receivable aged analysis** should be examined regularly, as a matter of course. Breaches of the credit limit, or attempted breaches of it, should be brought immediately to the attention of the credit controller.

2.5.1 Policing total credit

The total amount of credit offered, as well as individual accounts, should be policed to ensure that the senior management policy with regard to the total credit limits is maintained. A **credit utilisation report** can indicate the extent to which total limits are being utilised. An example is given below.

Customer	Limit	Utilisation	
	$'000	$'000	%
Alpha	100	90	90
Beta	50	35	70
Gamma	35	21	60
Delta	250	125	50
	435	271	
		62.2%	

This might contain other information, such as days sales outstanding.

Reviewed in aggregate, this can reveal the following.

(a)   The **number of customers** who might **want more credit**

(b)   The **extent** to which the **company is exposed to accounts receivable**

(c)   The **'tightness'** of the policy (It might be possible to increase profitable sales by offering credit. On the other hand, perhaps the firm offers credit too easily.)

It is possible to design credit utilisation reports to highlight other trends.

(a) The **degree of exposure** to **different countries**

(b) The **degree of exposure** to **different industries** (some countries or industries may be worthy of more credit; others may be too risky)

Credit utilisation can also be analysed by industry within country or by country within industry. It is also useful to relate credit utilisation to total sales.

2.5.2 Extension of credit

To determine whether it would be profitable to extend the level of total credit, it is necessary to assess:

- The **extra sales** that a **more generous credit policy would stimulate**
- The **profitability** of the **extra sales**
- The **extra length** of the **average debt collection period**
- The **required rate of return** on the investment in additional accounts receivable

2.5.3 Example: A change in credit policy

Russian Beard Co is considering a change of credit policy which will result in an increase in the average collection period from one to two months. The relaxation in credit is expected to produce an increase in sales in each year amounting to 25% of the current sales volume.

Selling price per unit	$10
Variable cost per unit	$8.50
Current annual sales	$2,400,000

The required rate of return on investments is 20%. Assume that the 25% increase in sales would result in additional inventories of $100,000 and additional accounts payable of $20,000.

Advise the company on whether or not to extend the credit period offered to customers, if:

(a) All customers take the longer credit of two months

(b) Existing customers do not change their payment habits, and only new customers take a full two months' credit

Solution

The change in credit policy is justifiable if the rate of return on the additional investment in working capital would exceed 20%.

Extra profit

Contribution/sales ratio	15%
Increase in sales revenue	$600,000
Increase in contribution and profit	$90,000

(a) *Extra investment, if all accounts receivable take two months' credit*

	$
Average accounts receivable after the sales increase (2/12 × $3,000,000)	500,000
Less current average accounts receivable (1/12 × $2,400,000)	200,000
Increase in accounts receivable	300,000
Increase in inventories	100,000
	400,000
Less increase in accounts payable	20,000
Net increase in working capital investment	380,000

Return on extra investment $\dfrac{\$90,000}{\$380,000} = 23.7\%$

(b) *Extra investment, if only the new accounts receivable take two months' credit*

	$
Increase in accounts receivable (2/12 of $600,000)	100,000
Increase in inventories	100,000
	200,000
Less increase in accounts payable	20,000
Net increase in working capital investment	180,000

Return on extra investment $\dfrac{\$90,000}{\$180,000} = 50\%$

In both case (a) and case (b) the new credit policy appears to be worthwhile.

Question	Extension of credit

Enticement Co currently expects sales of $50,000 a month. Variable costs of sales are $40,000 a month (all payable in the month of sale). It is estimated that if the credit period allowed to accounts receivable were to be increased from 30 days to 60 days, sales volume would increase by 20%. All customers would be expected to take advantage of the extended credit. If the cost of capital is 12½% a year, is the extension of the credit period justifiable in financial terms?

Answer	

	$
Current accounts receivable (1 month)	50,000
Accounts receivable after implementing the proposal (2 months)	120,000
Increase in accounts receivable	70,000
Financing cost (× 12½%)	8,750
Annual contribution from additional sales (12 months × 20% × $10,000)	24,000
Annual net benefit from extending credit period	15,250

2.6 Collecting amounts owing

FAST FORWARD

The **benefits** of action to collect debts must be greater than the **costs** incurred.

The overall **debt collection policy** of the firm should be such that the administrative costs and other costs incurred in debt collection do not exceed the benefits from incurring those costs. Beyond a certain level of spending, however, additional expenditure on debt collection would not have enough of an effect on bad debts or on the average collection period to justify the extra administrative costs.

Collecting debts is a two-stage process.

(a) Having agreed credit terms with a customer, a business should issue an invoice and expect to receive payment when it is due. **Issuing invoices** and **receiving payments** is the task of sales ledger staff. They should ensure that:

(i) The customer is **fully aware** of the terms.
(ii) The **invoice is correctly drawn up** and issued promptly.
(iii) They are aware of any **potential quirks** in the customer's system.
(iv) **Queries are resolved quickly.**
(v) **Monthly statements** are **issued promptly**.

(b)   If payments become overdue, priority ones should be 'chased'. Procedures for pursuing overdue debts must be established, for example:

(i)   **Instituting reminders or final demands**
These should be sent to a named individual, asking for repayment by return of post. A second or third letter may be required, followed by a final demand stating clearly the action that will be taken. The aim is to goad customers into action, perhaps by threatening not to sell any more goods on credit until the debt is cleared.

(ii)   **Chasing payment by telephone**
The telephone is of greater nuisance value than a letter, and the greater immediacy can encourage a response. It can be time consuming, however, particularly because of problems in getting through to the right person.

(iii) **Making a personal approach**
Personal visits can be very time consuming and tend only to be made to important customers who are worth the effort.

(iv)   **Notifying debt collection section**
This means not giving further credit to the customer until they have paid the due amounts.

(v)   **Handing over debt collection to specialist debt collection section**
Certain, generally larger, organisations may have a section to collect debts under the supervision of the credit manager.

(vi)   **Instituting legal action to recover the debt**
Premature legal action may unnecessarily antagonise important customers.

(vii) **Hiring external debt collection agency to recover debt**
Again this may upset customers.

2.7 Early settlement discounts   12/10, 6/11, 12/13

FAST FORWARD ▶▶

Early settlement discounts may be employed to shorten average credit periods and to reduce the investment in accounts receivable and therefore **interest costs** of the finance invested in trade receivables. The benefit in interest cost saved should exceed the cost of the discounts allowed.

To see whether the offer of a **settlement discount** (for early payment) is financially worthwhile we must compare the cost of the discount with the benefit of a reduced investment in accounts receivable.

Varying the discount allowed for early payment of debts affects the **average collection period** and affects the **volume of demand** (and possibly, therefore, indirectly affects bad debt losses). We shall begin with examples where the offer of a discount for early payment does not affect the volume of demand.

2.8 Example: Settlement discount

Lowe and Price Co has annual credit sales of $12,000,000, and 3 months are allowed for payment. The company decides to offer a 2% discount for payments made within 10 days of the invoice being sent, and to reduce the maximum time allowed for payment to 2 months. It is estimated that 50% of customers will take the discount. If the company requires a 20% return on investments, what will be the effect of the discount? Assume that the volume of sales will be unaffected by the discount.

Solution

Our approach is to calculate:

(a)   The profits forgone by offering the discount
(b)   The interest charges saved or incurred as a result of the changes in the cash flows of the company

Thus:

(a) The volume of accounts receivable, if the company policy remains unchanged, would be:

$3/12 \times \$12,000,000 = \$3,000,000$.

(b) If the policy is changed the volume of accounts receivable would be:

$(10/365 \times 50\% \times \$12,000,000) + (2/12 \times 50\% \times \$12,000,000) = \$164,384 + \$1,000,000$

$= \$1,164,384$.

(c) There will be a reduction in accounts receivable of $1,835,616.

(d) Since the company can invest at 20% a year, the value of a reduction in accounts receivable (a source of funds) is 20% of $1,835,616 each year in perpetuity, that is, $367,123 a year.

(e) *Summary*

	$
Value of reduction in accounts receivable each year	367,123
Less discounts allowed each year (2% × 50% × $12,000,000)	120,000
Net benefit of new discount policy each year	247,123

An extension of the payment period allowed to accounts receivable may be introduced in order to increase sales volume.

2.9 Percentage cost of an early settlement discount

The **percentage cost** of an early settlement discount to the company giving it can be estimated by the formula:

$$\left\{\left[\left(\frac{100}{(100-d)}\right)^{\frac{365}{t}}\right]-1\right\}\%$$

Where d = the discount offered (5% = 5, etc)

 t = the reduction in the payment period in days that is necessary to obtain the early payment discount

 Question   **Cost of discount**

A company offers its goods to customers on 30 days' credit, subject to satisfactory trade references. It also offers a 2% discount if payment is made within ten days of the date of the invoice.

Required

Calculate the cost to the company of offering the discount, assuming a 365 day year.

Answer

The percentage cost of the discount $= \left[\dfrac{100}{(100-2)}\right]^{365/20} - 1$

$= 1.02041^{18.25} - 1$

$= 1.446 - 1$

$= 44.6\%$

2.10 Bad debt risk

Different credit policies are likely to have differing levels of bad debt risk. The higher revenue resulting from easier credit terms should be sufficiently profitable to exceed the cost of:

- Additional bad debts, and
- The additional investment necessary to achieve the higher sales.

2.10.1 Example: Receivables management

Grabbit Quick Co achieves current annual sales of $1,800,000. The cost of sales is 80% of this amount, but bad debts average 1% of total sales, and the annual profit is as follows.

	$
Sales	1,800,000
Less cost of sales	1,440,000
	360,000
Less bad debts	18,000
Profit	342,000

The current debt collection period is one month, and the management consider that, if credit terms were eased (Option A), the effects would be as follows.

	Present policy	Option A
Additional sales (%)	–	25%
Average collection period	1 month	2 months
Bad debts (% of sales)	1%	3%

The company requires a 20% return on its investments. The costs of sales are 75% variable and 25% fixed. Assume there would be no increase in fixed costs from the extra revenue and that there would be no increase in average inventories or accounts payable. Which is the preferable policy, Option A or the present one?

Solution

The increase in profit before the cost of additional finance for Option A can be found as follows.

(a)

	$
Increase in contribution from additional sales	
25% × $1,800,000 × 40%*	180,000
Less increase in bad debts (3% × $2,250,000) – $18,000	49,500
Increase in annual profit	130,500

* The contribution/sales ratio is 100% – (75% × 80%) = 40%

(b)

	$
Proposed investment in accounts receivable $2,250,000 × 1/6	375,000
Less current investment in accounts receivable $1,800,000 × 1/12	150,000
Additional investment required	225,000
Cost of additional finance at 20%	$45,000

(c)   As the increase in profit exceeds the cost of additional finance, Option A should be adopted.

2.10.2 Credit insurance

Companies may be able to obtain credit insurance against certain approved debts going bad through a specialist credit insurance firm. A company cannot insure against all its bad debt losses, but may be able to insure against losses above a 'normal' level.

When a company arranges **credit insurance**, it must submit specific proposals for credit to the insurance company, stating the name of each customer to which it wants to give credit and the amount of credit it wants to give. The insurance company will accept, amend or refuse these proposals, depending on its assessment of each of these customers.

FAST FORWARD

Some companies use either **factoring** or **invoice discounting** to improve liquidity or to reduce administration costs. **Insurance**, particularly of overseas debts, can also help reduce the risk of bad debts.

A **factor** is defined as 'a doer or transactor of business for another', but a factoring organisation specialises in trade debts, and manages the debts owed to a client (a business customer) on the client's behalf.

Key term

> **Factoring** is an arrangement to have debts collected by a factor company, which advances a proportion of the money it is due to collect.

2.11.1 Aspects of factoring

The main aspects of factoring include the following.

(a) **Administration** of the client's invoicing, sales accounting and debt collection service

(b) **Credit protection** for the client's debts, whereby the factor takes over the risk of loss from bad debts and so 'insures' the client against such losses. This is known as a **non-recourse** service. However, if a **non-recourse** service is provided, the factor, not the firm, will decide what action to take against non-payers.

(c) Making **payments** to the client **in advance** of collecting the debts. This is sometimes referred to as 'factor finance' because the factor is providing cash to the client against outstanding debts.)

2.11.2 Benefits of factoring

Exam focus point

> The ACCA examination team noted in the December 2011 exam that a number of candidates found it difficult to identify the benefits of factoring. Make sure you are familiar with the benefits listed below, in order to gain maximum marks in a knowledge-based part of a question.

The **benefits of factoring** for a business customer include the following.

(a) The business receives early payment for most of its receivables in the form of finance from the factor. It can use this money to **pay** its **suppliers**.

(b) **Optimum inventory levels** can be **maintained**, because the business will have enough cash to pay for the inventories it needs.

(c) **Growth** can be **financed** through **sales** rather than by injecting fresh external capital.

(d) The business gets **finance linked** to its **volume of sales**. In contrast, overdraft limits tend to be determined by historical statements of financial position.

(e) The **managers** of the business **do not** have to **spend** their **time** on the problems of **slow-paying accounts receivable**. Factoring organisations are also likely to employ staff who are experienced and skilled at collecting payments from customers and chasing overdue payments.

(f) The business does **not incur** the **costs** of **running** its own **sales ledger department**, and can use the **expertise** of debtor management that the factor has.

An important **disadvantage** is that credit customers will be making payments direct to the factor, which is likely to present a negative picture of the firm's **attitude to customer relations**. It may also indicate that the firm is in need of rapid cash, raising questions about its **financial stability**.

2.11.3 Example: Factoring

A company makes annual credit sales of $1,500,000. Credit terms are 30 days, but its debt administration has been poor and the average collection period has been 45 days with 0.5% of sales resulting in bad debts which are written off.

A factor would take on the task of debt administration and credit checking, at an annual fee of 2.5% of credit sales. The company would save $30,000 a year in administration costs. The payment period would be 30 days.

The factor would also provide an advance of 80% of invoiced debts at an interest rate of 14% (3% over the current base rate). The company can obtain an overdraft facility to finance its accounts receivable at a rate of 2.5% over base rate.

Should the factor's services be accepted? Assume a constant monthly revenue.

Solution

It is assumed that the factor would advance an amount equal to 80% of the invoiced debts, and the balance 30 days later.

(a) The current situation is as follows, using the company's debt collection staff and a bank overdraft to finance all debts.

Credit sales	$1,500,000 pa
Average credit period	45 days

The annual cost is as follows.

	$
45/365 × $1,500,000 × 13.5% (11% + 2.5%)	24,966
Bad debts 0.5% × $1,500,000	7,500
Administration costs	30,000
Total cost	62,466

(b) *The cost of the factor.* 80% of credit sales financed by the factor would be 80% of $1,500,000 = $1,200,000. For a consistent comparison, we must assume that 20% of credit sales would be financed by a bank overdraft. The average credit period would be only 30 days. The annual cost would be as follows.

	$
Factor's finance 30/365 × $1,200,000 × 14%	13,808
Overdraft 30/365 × $300,000 × 13.5%	3,329
	17,137
Cost of factor's services: 2.5% × $1,500,000	37,500
Cost of the factor	54,637

(c) *Conclusion.* The factor is cheaper. In this case, the factor's fees exactly equal the savings in bad debts ($7,500) and administration costs ($30,000). The factor is then cheaper overall because it will be more efficient at collecting debts. The advance of 80% of debts is not needed, however, if the company has sufficient overdraft facility because the factor's finance charge of 14% is higher than the company's overdraft rate of 13.5%.

An **alternative way** of carrying out the calculation is to consider the changes in costs that using a factor will mean.

	$
Effect of reduction in collection period $\frac{45-30}{365}$ × $1,500,000 × 13.5%	8,322
Extra interest cost of factor finance 30/365 × $1,200,000 × (14 – 13.5)%	(493)
Cost of factor's services 2.5% × $1,500,000	(37,500)
Savings in bad debts 0.5% × $1,500,000	7,500
Savings in company's administration costs	30,000
Net benefit of using factor	7,829

Check: $62,466 – $54,637 = $7,829

2.12 Invoice discounting

> **Invoice discounting** is the purchase (by the provider of the discounting service) of trade debts at a discount. Invoice discounting enables the company from which the debts are purchased to raise working capital.

Invoice discounting is related to factoring and many factors will provide an invoice discounting service. It is the purchase of a selection of invoices, at a discount. The invoice discounter does not take over the administration of the client's sales ledger.

A client should only want to have some invoices discounted when he has a temporary cash shortage, and so invoice discounting tends to consist of one-off deals. **Confidential invoice discounting** is an arrangement whereby a debt is confidentially assigned to the factor, and the client's customer will only become aware of the arrangement if they do not pay their debt to the client.

If a client needs to generate cash, they can approach a factor or invoice discounter, who will offer to purchase selected invoices and advance up to 75% of their value. At the end of each month, the factor will pay over the balance of the purchase price, less charges, on the invoices that have been settled in the month.

Exam focus point

> Don't confuse invoice discounting with early settlement discounts. They are not the same thing.

2.13 Managing foreign accounts receivable

Exam focus point

> You may find it useful to read the article called Management of Foreign Accounts Receivable on the ACCA website.

FAST FORWARD

> **Exporters** have to address the problems of **larger inventories and accounts receivable**, and an **increased risk** of bad debts due to the transportation time and additional paperwork involved in sending goods abroad.

Foreign debts raise the following special problems.

(a) When goods are sold abroad, the customer might ask for credit. Exports take time to arrange, and there might be complex paperwork. Transporting the goods can be slow, if they are sent by sea. These **delays** in **foreign trade** mean that exporters often build up large investments in inventories and accounts receivable. These working capital investments have to be financed somehow.

(b) The **risk of bad debts** can be **greater** with foreign trade than with domestic trade. If a foreign debtor refuses to pay a debt, the exporter must pursue the debt in the debtor's own country, where procedures will be subject to the laws of that country.

Some businesses may decide to **trust** the foreign receivable and not take any special measures to reduce the non-payment risk. This method is known as **open account**.

However, there are several measures available to exporters to help overcome risks of non-payment.

2.13.1 Reducing the investment in foreign accounts receivable

A company can reduce its investment in foreign accounts receivable by insisting on **earlier payment** for goods. Another approach is for an exporter to arrange for a bank to give **cash for a foreign debt** sooner than the exporter would receive payment in the normal course of events. There are several ways in which this might be done.

(a) **Advances against collections**. Where the exporter asks their bank to handle the collection of payment (of a bill of exchange or a cheque) on their behalf, the bank may be prepared to make an

BPP
LEARNING MEDIA

Part C Working capital management | **5: Managing working capital**   **111** advance to the exporter against the collection. The amount of the advance might be 80% to 90% of the value of the collection.

(b) **Negotiation of bills or cheques**. This is similar to an advance against collection, but would be used where the bill or cheque is payable outside the exporter's country (for example in the foreign buyer's country).

(c) **Discounting bills of exchange**. This is where the customer agrees to accept a bill of exchange drawn on the customer by the exporter. The exporter's bank may buy the bill before it is due for payment (at a discount to face value) and credit the proceeds from this sale to the company's account.

(d) **Documentary credits**. These are described below.

(e) **Forfaiting**. This is also described below.

2.13.2 Reducing the bad debt risk

Methods of minimising bad debt risks are broadly similar to those for domestic trade. An exporting company should vet the creditworthiness of each customer, and grant credit terms accordingly.

2.13.3 Export factoring

The functions performed by an **overseas factor** or **export factor** are essentially the same as with the factoring of domestic trade debts, which was described earlier in this chapter.

Factoring can be more expensive than credit insurance (explained below) and may not be available in all countries.

2.13.4 Documentary credits

Documentary credits ('letters of credit') provide a method of payment in international trade, which gives the exporter a secure risk-free method of obtaining payment.

The process works as follows:

(a) The buyer (a foreign buyer or domestic importer) and the seller (a domestic exporter or foreign supplier) first of all agree a contract for the sale of the goods, which provides for payment through a documentary credit.

(b) The **buyer** then requests a bank in their country to issue a **letter of credit** in favour of the exporter. The bank which issues the letter of credit is known as the issuing bank.

(c) The issuing bank, by issuing its letter of credit, guarantees payment to the exporter on condition that the exporter complies with certain specified conditions in the letter of credit (relating to such matters as presenting documentation for the export shipment and shipping the goods before a latest shipment date).

(d) The goods are despatched and the shipping documentation is sent to the purchaser's bank.

(e) The bank issues a banker's acceptance.

(f) The seller either keeps the banker's acceptance until maturity or sells it at a discount on the money market.

A documentary credit arrangement must be made between the exporter, the buyer and participating banks **before the export sale takes place**. Documentary credits are slow to arrange, administratively cumbersome and inflexible. For example, the exact conditions of the letter of credit must be met. If the letter of credit states that shipping documents are required, then the seller would be unable to claim payment if the goods were sent by air. Despite these drawbacks, letters of credit might be considered essential where the risk of non-payment is high.

2.13.5 Forfaiting

Key term

> **Forfaiting** is a method of export finance whereby a bank purchases from a company a number of sales invoices, usually obtaining a guarantee of payment of the invoices.

Forfaiting is the most common method of providing **medium-term** (say, three to five years) export finance. It has normally been used for export sales involving **capital goods** (such as machinery), where payments will be made over a number of years. It is usually available for large amounts (over $250,000), but only in the major convertible currencies.

The forfaiter buys the foreign accounts receivable from a seller at a discount and takes on all of the credit risk from the transaction (without recourse). The receivables then become a form of debt instrument which can be sold on the money market.

Forfaiting can be an expensive choice, and arranging it takes time. However, it can be a useful way of enabling trade to occur in cases where other methods of ensuring payment and smooth cash flow are not certain, and in cases where trade may not be possible by other means.

2.13.6 Countertrade

Countertrade is a means of financing trade in which goods are exchanged for other goods. Three parties might be involved in a 'triangular' deal. Countertrade is thus a form of **barter** and can involve complex negotiations and logistics. One of the main problems with countertrade is that the value of the goods received in exchange may be uncertain.

2.13.7 Export credit insurance

Key term

> **Export credit insurance** is insurance against the risk of non-payment by foreign customers for export debts.

You might be wondering why export credit insurance should be necessary, when exporters can pursue **non-paying customers** through the courts in order to obtain payment. The answer is that:

(a) If a credit customer defaults on payment, the task of pursuing the case through the courts will be lengthy, and it might be a long time before payment is eventually obtained.

(b) There are various reasons why non-payment might happen. For example, the seller can be insured against slow payment, insolvency, certain political risks and changes in import or export regulations.

Not all exporters take out export credit insurance because premiums are very high and the benefits are sometimes not fully appreciated. If they do, they will obtain an insurance policy from a private insurance company that deals in export credit insurance. Note that insurance does not usually cover 100% of the value of the foreign sales.

2.13.8 General policies for overseas accounts receivable

There are also a number of general credit control policies that can be particularly important when dealing with overseas customers.

(a) Prior to the sale, the customer's **credit rating** should be **checked**, and the terms of the contract specified. One key term may be demanding the use of a **letter of credit** as a condition for the transaction. The terms of the **remittance** and the bank to be used should be specified.

(b) The **paperwork** relating to the sales should be carefully completed and checked, in particular the shipping and delivery documentation.

(c) Goods should only be released to the custody of the buyer if payment has been made, or is sufficiently certain, either because of the customer's **previous record** or because the customer has arranged for its bank to accept a bill of exchange on behalf of the buyer.

(d) Receipts should be **rapidly processed** and late **payments chased**.

3 Managing accounts payable

Performance objective 10 requires you to 'prepare and monitor an organisation's cash flow, credit facilities and advise on appropriate actions'. This section covers the management of accounts payable and credit terms.

FAST FORWARD

Effective management of **trade accounts payable** involves seeking satisfactory credit terms from supplier, getting credit extended during periods of cash shortage and maintaining good relations with suppliers.

Exam focus point

It may seem an obvious point, but take care not to confuse accounts receivable and accounts payable, as many students do under exam pressure.

3.1 Management of trade accounts payable

The management of trade accounts payable involves:

- Attempting to obtain **satisfactory credit** from suppliers

- Attempting to **extend credit** during periods of cash shortage, without damaging a good business relationship with the supplier

- Maintaining **good relations** with regular and important suppliers

If a supplier offers a discount for the early payment of debts, the evaluation of the decision whether or not to **accept the discount** is similar to the **evaluation of the decision** whether or not to **offer a discount**. One problem is the mirror image of the other. The methods of evaluating the offer of a discount to customers were described earlier.

3.1.1 Trade credit

Taking credit from suppliers is a normal feature of business. Nearly every company has some trade accounts payable waiting for payment. It is particularly important to small and fast-growing firms. Trade credit is a source of short-term finance because it helps to keep working capital down. It is usually a cheap source of finance, since suppliers rarely charge interest. The costs of making maximum use of trade credit include the loss of suppliers' goodwill, and the loss of any available cash discounts for the early payment of debts.

3.1.2 The cost of lost early payment discounts

The cost of lost cash discounts can be calculated by comparing the saving from the discount with the opportunity cost of investing the cash used.

The cost of lost cash discounts can also be estimated by the formula:

$$\left\{ \left[\left(\frac{100}{(100-d)} \right)^{\frac{365}{t}} \right] - 1 \right\}\%$$

Where d is the % discount, d = 5 for 5%

     t is the reduction in the payment period in days which would be necessary to obtain the early payment discount, final date to obtain discount – final date for payment

This is the same formula that was used for accounts receivable.

3.2 Example: Trade credit

X Co has been offered credit terms from its major supplier of 2/10, net 45. That is, a cash discount of 2% will be given if payment is made within ten days of the invoice, and payments must be made within 45 days of the invoice. The company has the choice of paying 98c per $1 on day 10 (to pay before day 10

would be unnecessary), or to invest the 98c for an additional 35 days and eventually pay the supplier $1 per $1. The decision as to whether the discount should be accepted depends on the opportunity cost of investing 98c for 35 days. What should the company do?

Solution

Suppose that X Co can invest cash to obtain an annual return of 25%, and that there is an invoice from the supplier for $1,000. The two alternatives are as follows.

	Refuse discount $	Accept discount $
Payment to supplier	1,000.0	980
Return from investing $980 between day 10 and day 45:		
$980 \times 35/365 \times 25\%$	23.5	—
Net cost	976.5	980

It is cheaper to refuse the discount because the investment rate of return on cash retained, in this example, exceeds the saving from the discount.

Although a company may delay payment beyond the final due date, thereby obtaining even longer credit from its suppliers, such a policy would generally be inadvisable. Unacceptable delays in payment will **worsen the company's credit rating**, and additional credit may become difficult to obtain.

3.3 Managing foreign accounts payable

Foreign accounts payable will be subject to **exchange rate risk**. Companies expecting to pay foreign currency in the future will be concerned about the possibility of domestic currency **depreciating** against the foreign currency, making the cost of the supplies more expensive.

Companies sometimes pay into an overseas bank account today and then let the cash earn some interest so they can pay off the invoice in the future. This method of avoiding exchange rate risk is called **leading**.

The management of exchange rate risk is covered in Chapter 19.

- An **economic order quantity** can be calculated as a guide to minimising costs in managing **inventory** levels. However, **bulk discounts** can mean that a different order quantity minimises inventory costs.

- **Uncertainties** in demand and lead times taken to fulfil orders mean that inventory will be ordered once it reaches a re-order level (maximum usage × maximum lead time).

- Giving credit has a cost: the value of the interest charged on an overdraft to fund the period of credit, or the interest lost on the cash not received and deposited in the bank. An increase in profit from extra sales resulting from offering credit could offset this cost.

- In managing **accounts receivable**, the **creditworthiness** of customers needs to be assessed. The risks and costs of a customer defaulting will need to be balanced against the profitability of the business provided by that customer.

- Regular monitoring of accounts receivable is very important. Individual accounts receivable can be assessed using a **customer history analysis** and a **credit rating system**. The overall level of accounts receivable can be monitored using an **aged accounts receivable listing** and **credit utilisation report**, as well as reports on the level of bad debts.

- The **benefits** of action to collect debts must be greater than the **costs** incurred.

- **Early settlement discounts** may be employed to shorten average credit periods and to reduce the investment in accounts receivable and therefore **interest costs** of the finance invested in trade receivables. The benefit in interest cost saved should exceed the cost of the discounts allowed.

- Some companies use either **factoring** or **invoice discounting** to improve liquidity or to reduce administration costs. **Insurance**, particularly of overseas debts, can also help reduce the risk of bad debts.

- **Exporters** have to address the problems of **larger inventories and accounts receivable**, and an **increased risk** of bad debts due to the transportation time and additional paperwork involved in sending goods abroad.

- Effective management of **trade accounts payable** involves seeking satisfactory credit terms from supplier, getting credit extended during periods of cash shortage and maintaining good relations with suppliers.

Quick Quiz

1 The basic EOQ formula for inventory indicates whether bulk discounts should be taken advantage of.

   True ☐

   False ☐

2 Identify the potential benefits of JIT manufacturing.

3 PB Co uses 2,500 units of component X per year. The company has calculated that the cost of placing and processing a purchase order for component X is $185, and the cost of holding one unit of component X for a year is $25.

   What is the economic order quantity (EOQ) for component X and, assuming a 52-week year, what is the average frequency at which purchase orders should be placed?

4 The economic order quantity model can be used to determine:

Order quantity	Buffer inventory	Re-order level
Yes/No	Yes/No	Yes/No

5 What service involves collecting debts of a business, advancing a proportion of the money it is due to collect?

6 What service involves advancing a proportion of a selection of invoices, without administration of the sales ledger of the business?

7 Which of the following is a **disadvantage** to a company of using a factor for its accounts receivable?

   A   It is easier to finance growth through sales.
   B   Managers spend less time on slow paying accounts receivable.
   C   Credit customers pay direct to the factor.
   D   It is easier to pay suppliers promptly to obtain discounts.

8 Which of the following does **not** determine the amount of credit offered by a supplier?

   A   The credit terms the supplier obtains from its own suppliers
   B   The ease with which the buyer can go elsewhere
   C   The supplier's total risk exposure
   D   The number of purchases made by the buyer each year

9 If a customer decided to pass up the chance of a cash discount of 1% in return for reducing their average payment period from 70 to 30 days, what would be the implied cost in interest per annum?

1   False. It may be necessary to modify the formula to take account of bulk discounts.

2   (a)   Reduction in inventory holding costs
    (b)   Reduced manufacturing lead times
    (c)   Improved labour productivity
    (d)   Reduced scrap/warranty/rework/costs
    (e)   Price reductions on purchased materials
    (f)   Reduction in the number of accounting transactions

3   C $EOQ = \sqrt{\dfrac{2C_0D}{C_h}}$

Economic order quantity $= \sqrt{\dfrac{2 \times 185 \times 2,500}{25}}$

    = 192 units

Frequency of ordering $= \dfrac{192}{2,500}$

    = 4 weeks

4   The EOQ model finds order quantity only, not buffer inventory and re-order level.

5   Factoring

6   Invoice discounting

7   C   This may present a negative picture of the company to customers.

8   D   The number of purchases (although the amount of annual purchases may well be a factor)

9   Cost $= \left\{ \left[\left(\dfrac{100}{(100-d)} \right)^{\frac{365}{t}} \right] - 1 \right\} \%$

    $= \left[\dfrac{100}{(99)} \right]^{\frac{365}{40}} - 1$

    $= 1.01^{9.125} - 1 = 9.5\%$

Now try the questions below from the Practice Question Bank

Number	Level	Marks	Approximate time
Section A Q13	Examination	2	4 mins
Section C Q2	Introductory	N/A	39 mins
Section C Q3	Introductory	N/A	39 mins

Working capital finance

Topic list	Syllabus reference
1 The management of cash	C2 (f)
2 Cash flow forecasts	C2 (f)
3 Treasury management	C2 (f)
4 Cash management models	C2 (f)
5 Investing surplus cash	C2 (f)
6 Working capital funding strategies	C3 (a), (b)

Introduction

This chapter concludes our study of working capital management methods by considering how cash is managed. This involves looking at the various **reasons for holding cash**, the **preparation of cash flow forecasts** and relevant techniques for **managing cash**. We revisit how working capital needs are determined and finally in this area we consider working capital **funding strategies**.

Study guide

		Intellectual level
C2	**Management of inventories, accounts receivable, accounts payable and cash**	
(f)	Explain the various reasons for holding cash, and discuss and apply the use of relevant techniques in managing cash, including:	2
(i)	Preparing cash flow forecasts to determine future cash flows and cash balances	
(ii)	Assessing the benefits of centralised treasury management and cash control	
(iii)	Cash management models, such as the Baumol model and the Miller-Orr model	
(iv)	Investing short-term	
C3	**Determining working capital needs and funding strategies**	
(a)	Calculate the level of working capital investment in current assets and discuss the key factors determining this level, including:	2
(i)	The length of the working capital cycle and terms of trade	
(ii)	An organisation's policy on the level of investment in current assets	
(iii)	The industry in which the organisation operates	
(b)	Describe and discuss the key factors in determining working capital funding strategies, including:	2
(i)	The distinction between permanent and fluctuating current assets	
(ii)	The relative cost and risk of short-term and long-term finance	
(iii)	The matching principle	
(iv)	The relative costs and benefits of aggressive, conservative and matching funding policies	
(v)	Management attitudes to risk, previous funding decisions and organisation size	1

Exam guide

The material covered in this chapter is again highly examinable. Any of the calculations could form part or all of a question and you also need to be able to explain the meaning of your answers.

Performance objective 10 requires you to 'prepare and monitor an organisation's cash flow, credit facilities and advise on appropriate actions'. This chapter covers the management of cash and cash flow forecasts.

1 The management of cash

1.1 Why organisations hold cash   12/12

The economist John Maynard Keynes identified three reasons for holding cash.

(a)   Firstly, a business needs cash to meet its **regular commitments** of paying its accounts payable, its employees' wages, its taxes, its annual dividends to shareholders, and so on. This reason for holding cash is what Keynes called the **transactions motive**.

(b)   Keynes identified the **precautionary motive** as a second motive for holding cash. This means that there is a need to maintain a 'buffer' of cash for **unforeseen contingencies**. In the context of a

business, this buffer may be provided by an **overdraft facility**, which has the advantage that it will cost nothing until it is actually used.

(c) Keynes identified a third motive for holding cash – the **speculative motive**. Some businesses hold surplus cash as a speculative asset in the hope that interest rates will rise. However, many businesses would regard large long-term holdings of cash as not prudent.

How much cash should a company keep on hand or 'on short call' at a bank? The more cash on hand, the easier it will be for the company to meet its bills as they fall due and to take advantage of discounts.

However, holding cash or near equivalents to cash has a cost – the **loss of earnings** which would otherwise have been obtained by using the funds in another way. The financial manager must try to **balance liquidity with profitability**.

1.2 Cash flow problems

Cash flow problems can arise in various ways.

(a) **Making losses**

If a business is continually making losses, it will eventually have cash flow problems. If the loss is due to a large depreciation charge, the cash flow troubles might only begin when the business needs to replace non-current assets.

(b) **Inflation**

In a period of inflation, a business needs **ever-increasing amounts** of cash just to replace used-up and worn-out assets. A business can be making a profit in historical cost accounting terms, but still not be receiving enough cash to buy the replacement assets it needs.

(c) **Growth**

When a business is growing, it needs to **acquire more non-current assets**, and to **support higher amounts of inventories and accounts receivable**. These additional assets must be paid for somehow (or financed by accounts payable).

(d) **Seasonal business**

When a business has seasonal or cyclical sales, it may have cash flow difficulties at certain times of the year, when:

(i) Cash inflows are low, but

(ii) Cash outflows are high, perhaps because the business is building up its inventories for the next period of high sales.

(e) **One-off items of expenditure**

A single non-recurring item of expenditure may create a cash flow problem. Examples include the repayment of loan capital on maturity of the debt or the purchase of an exceptionally expensive item, such as a freehold property.

2 Cash flow forecasts   12/14

Cash flow forecasts show the expected receipts and payments during a forecast period and are a vital management control tool, especially during times of recession.

Key term

A **cash flow forecast** is a detailed forecast of cash inflows and outflows incorporating both revenue and capital items.

A cash flow forecast is thus a statement in which estimated future **cash receipts** and **payments** are tabulated in such a way as to show the forecast **cash balance** of a business at defined intervals. For

example, in December 20X2 an accounts department might wish to estimate the cash position of the business during the three following months, January to March 20X3. A cash flow forecast might be drawn up in the following format.

	Jan $	Feb $	Mar $
Estimated cash receipts			
From credit customers	14,000	16,500	17,000
From cash sales	3,000	4,000	4,500
Proceeds on disposal of non-current assets		2,200	
Total cash receipts	17,000	22,700	21,500
Estimated cash payments			
To suppliers of goods	8,000	7,800	10,500
To employees (wages)	3,000	3,500	3,500
Purchase of non-current assets		16,000	
Rent and rates			1,000
Other overheads	1,200	1,200	1,200
Repayment of loan	2,500		
	14,700	28,500	16,200
Net surplus/(deficit) for month	2,300	(5,800)	5,300
Opening cash balance	1,200	3,500	(2,300)
Closing cash balance	3,500	(2,300)	3,000

In the example above (where the figures are purely for illustration) the accounts department has calculated that the cash balance at the beginning of the flow forecast period, 1 January, will be $1,200. Estimates have been made of the cash which is likely to be received by the business (from cash and credit sales, and from a planned disposal of non-current assets in February). Similar estimates have been made of cash due to be paid out by the business (payments to suppliers and employees, payments for rent, rates and other overheads, payment for a planned purchase of non-current assets in February and a loan repayment due in January).

From these estimates it is a simple step to calculate the excess of cash receipts over cash payments in each month. In some months cash payments may exceed cash receipts and there will be a **deficit** for the month; this occurs during February in the above example because of the large investment in non-current assets in that month.

The last part of the cash flow forecast above shows how the business's estimated cash balance can then be rolled along from month to month. Starting with the opening balance of $1,200 at 1 January a cash surplus of $2,300 is generated in January. This leads to a closing January balance of $3,500 which becomes the opening balance for February. The deficit of $5,800 in February throws the business's cash position into overdraft and the overdrawn balance of $2,300 becomes the opening balance for March. Finally, the healthy cash surplus of $5,300 in March leaves the business with a favourable cash position of $3,000 at the end of the flow forecast period.

<table>
<tr><td>Exam focus point</td><td>When preparing cash flow forecasts, it is vital that your work is clearly laid out, and referenced to workings where appropriate.</td></tr>
</table>

2.1 The usefulness of cash flow forecasts 12/14

The cash flow forecast is one of the most important planning tools that an organisation can use. It shows the cash effect of all plans made within the flow forecasting process and its preparation can therefore lead to a modification of flow forecasts if it shows that there are insufficient cash resources to finance the planned operations.

It can also **give management an indication of potential problems that could arise and allows them the opportunity to take action to avoid such problems**. A cash flow forecast can show four positions. Management will need to take appropriate action depending on the potential position.

Cash position	Appropriate management action
Short-term surplus	Pay accounts payable early to obtain discount Attempt to increase sales by increasing accounts receivable and inventories Make short-term investments
Short-term deficit	Increase accounts payable by delaying payments to suppliers Reduce accounts receivable by improving collection of overdue payments Arrange a bank overdraft facility, or increase the limit on an existing facility
Long-term surplus	Make long-term investments Expand Diversify Replace/update non-current assets Distribute the surplus to shareholders
Long-term deficit	Raise long-term finance (such as via issue of share capital) Consider shutdown/disinvestment opportunities

Exam focus point

A cash flow forecast question could ask you to prepare the cash flow forecast and then recommend appropriate action for management. Ensure your advice takes account both of whether there is a surplus or deficit and whether the position is long or short term.

2.2 What to include in a cash flow forecast

A cash flow forecast is prepared to show the **expected receipts of cash and payments of cash** during a budget period.

It should be obvious that the **profit or loss made by an organisation during an accounting period does not reflect its cash flow position for the following reasons.**

(a) Not all cash receipts affect statement of profit or loss income.

(b) Not all cash payments affect statement of profit or loss expenditure.

(c) Some costs in the statement of profit or loss, such as profit or loss on sale of non-current assets or depreciation, are not cash items but are costs derived from accounting conventions.

(d) The timing of cash receipts and payments may not coincide with the recording of statement of profit or loss transactions. For example, a charge for rent or electricity might be made in respect of 20X6 and shown in the statement of profit or loss for that year, but paid in 20X7.

To ensure that there is sufficient cash in hand to cope adequately with planned activities, management should therefore prepare and pay close attention to a cash flow forecast rather than a statement of profit or loss.

Exam focus point

Clear workings and assumptions are very important in a cash flow forecast.

2.3 Example: Cash flow forecast

Peter Blair has worked for some years as a sales representative, but has recently been made redundant. He intends to start up in business on his own account, using $15,000 which he currently has invested with a building society. Peter maintains a bank account showing a small credit balance, and he plans to approach his bank for the necessary additional finance. Peter provides the following additional information.

(a) Arrangements have been made to purchase non-current assets costing $8,000. These will be paid for at the end of September and are expected to have a five-year life, at the end of which they will possess a nil residual value.

(b) Inventories costing $5,000 will be acquired on 28 September and subsequent monthly purchases will be at a level sufficient to replace forecast sales for the month.

(c) Forecast monthly sales are $3,000 for October, $6,000 for November and December, and $10,500 from January 20X4 onwards.

(d) Selling price is fixed at the cost of inventory plus 50%.

(e) Two months' credit will be allowed to customers but only one month's credit will be received from suppliers of inventory.

(f) Running expenses, including rent but excluding depreciation of non-current assets, are estimated at $1,600 per month.

(g) Blair intends to make monthly cash drawings of $1,000.

Required

Prepare a cash flow forecast for the six months to 31 March 20X4.

Solution

The opening cash balance at 1 October is $7,000 which consists of Peter's initial $15,000 less the $8,000 expended on non-current assets purchased in September. Cash receipts from credit customers arise two months after the relevant sales.

Payments to suppliers are a little more tricky. We are told that cost of sales is 100/150 × sales. Thus for October cost of sales is 100/150 × $3,000 = $2,000. These goods will be purchased in October but not paid for until November. Similar calculations can be made for later months. The initial inventory of $5,000 is purchased in September and consequently paid for in October.

Depreciation is not a cash flow and so is *not* included in a cash flow forecast.

CASH FLOW FORECAST FOR THE SIX MONTHS ENDING 31 MARCH 20X4

	Oct $	Nov $	Dec $	Jan $	Feb $	Mar $
Payments						
Suppliers	5,000	2,000	4,000	4,000	7,000	7,000
Running expenses	1,600	1,600	1,600	1,600	1,600	1,600
Drawings	1,000	1,000	1,000	1,000	1,000	1,000
	7,600	4,600	6,600	6,600	9,600	9,600
Receipts						
Accounts receivable	–	–	3,000	6,000	6,000	10,500
Surplus/(shortfall)	(7,600)	(4,600)	(3,600)	(600)	(3,600)	900
Opening balance	7,000	(600)	(5,200)	(8,800)	(9,400)	(13,000)
Closing balance	(600)	(5,200)	(8,800)	(9,400)	(13,000)	(12,100)

2.4 Cash flow forecasts and an opening statement of financial position

You might be given a cash flow forecast question in which you are required to analyse an opening statement of financial position to decide how many outstanding accounts receivable will pay what they owe in the first few months of the cash flow forecast period, and how many outstanding accounts payable must be paid.

Suppose that a statement of financial position as at 31 December 20X4 shows accounts receivable of $150,000 and trade accounts payable of $60,000. The following information is also relevant.

- Accounts receivable are allowed two months to pay.
- 1½ months' credit is taken from trade accounts payable.
- Sales and materials purchases were both made at an even monthly rate.

Let's try to ascertain the months of 20X5 in which the accounts receivable will eventually pay and the accounts payable will be paid.

(a) Since accounts receivable take two months to pay, the $150,000 of accounts receivable in the statement of financial position represents credit sales in November and December 20X4, who will pay in January and February 20X5 respectively. Since sales in 20X4 were at an equal monthly rate, the cash flow forecast should plan for receipts of $75,000 each month in January and February from the accounts receivable in the opening statement of financial position.

(b) Similarly, since accounts payable are paid after $1\frac{1}{2}$ months, the statement of financial position accounts payable will be paid in January and the first half of February 20X5, which means that flow forecasted payments will be as follows.

	$
In January (purchases in second half of Nov and first half of Dec 20X4)	40,000
In February (purchases in second half of Dec 20X4)	20,000
Total accounts payable in the statement of financial position	60,000

(The accounts payable of $60,000 represent $1\frac{1}{2}$ months' purchases, so that purchases in 20X4 must be $40,000 per month, which is $20,000 per half month.)

2.5 Example: A month by month cash flow forecast

From the following information which relates to George and Zola Co you are required to prepare a month by month cash flow forecast for the second half of 20X5 and to append such brief comments as you consider might be helpful to management.

(a) The company's only product, a vest, sells at $40 and has a variable cost of $26 made up of material $20, labour $4 and overhead $2.

(b) Fixed costs of $6,000 per month are paid on the 28th of each month.

(c) Quantities sold/to be sold on credit

May	Jun	Jul	Aug	Sep	Oct	Nov	Dec
1,000	1,200	1,400	1,600	1,800	2,000	2,200	2,600

(d) Production quantities

May	Jun	Jul	Aug	Sep	Oct	Nov	Dec
1,200	1,400	1,600	2,000	2,400	2,600	2,400	2,200

(e) Cash sales at a discount of 5% are expected to average 100 units a month.

(f) Customers settle their accounts by the end of the second month following sale.

(g) Suppliers of material are paid two months after the material is used in production.

(h) Wages are paid in the same month as they are incurred.

(i) 70% of the variable overhead is paid in the month of production, the remainder in the following month.

(j) Corporation tax of $18,000 is to be paid in October.

(k) A new delivery vehicle was bought in June. It cost $8,000 and is to be paid for in August. The old vehicle was sold for $600, the buyer undertaking to pay in July.

(l) The company is expected to be $3,000 overdrawn at the bank at 30 June 20X5.

(m) No increases or decreases in raw materials, work in progress or finished goods are planned over the period.

(n) No price increases or cost increases are expected in the period.

Solution

Cash flow forecast for 1 July to 31 December 20X5

	Jul $	Aug $	Sep $	Oct $	Nov $	Dec $	Total $
Receipts							
Credit sales	40,000	48,000	56,000	64,000	72,000	80,000	360,000
Cash sales	3,800	3,800	3,800	3,800	3,800	3,800	22,800
Sale of vehicle	600	–	–	–	–	–	600
	44,400	51,800	59,800	67,800	75,800	83,800	383,400
Payments							
Materials	24,000	28,000	32,000	40,000	48,000	52,000	224,000
Labour	6,400	8,000	9,600	10,400	9,600	8,800	52,800
Variable overhead (W)	3,080	3,760	4,560	5,080	4,920	4,520	25,920
Fixed costs	6,000	6,000	6,000	6,000	6,000	6,000	36,000
Corporation tax				18,000			18,000
Purchase of vehicle		8,000					8,000
	39,480	53,760	52,160	79,480	68,520	71,320	364,720
Receipts less payments	4,920	(1,960)	7,640	(11,680)	7,280	12,480	18,680
Balance b/f	(3,000)	1,920	(40)	7,600	(4,080)	3,200	(3,000)
Balance c/f	1,920	(40)	7,600	(4,080)	3,200	15,680	15,680

Working

	Jun $	Jul $	Aug $	Sep $	Oct $	Nov $	Dec $
Variable overhead production cost	2,800	3,200	4,000	4,800	5,200	4,800	4,400
70% paid in month		2,240	2,800	3,360	3,640	3,360	3,080
30% in following month		840	960	1,200	1,440	1,560	1,440
		3,080	3,760	4,560	5,080	4,920	4,520

Comments

(a) There will be a small overdraft at the end of August but a much larger one at the end of October. It may be possible to delay payments to suppliers for longer than two months or to reduce purchases of materials or reduce the volume of production by running down existing inventory levels.

(b) If neither of these courses is possible, the company may need to negotiate overdraft facilities with its bank.

(c) The cash deficit is only temporary and by the end of December there will be a comfortable surplus. The use to which this cash will be put should ideally be planned in advance.

Exam focus point

You may be asked to prepare a cash flow forecast, and also consider the effects on the flow forecast or particular figures in it of the original assumptions changing.

Question
Cash budget

You are presented with the following forecasted cash flow data for your organisation for the period November 20X1 to June 20X2. It has been extracted from functional flow forecasts that have already been prepared.

	Nov X1 $	Dec X1 $	Jan X2 $	Feb X2 $	Mar X2 $	Apr X2 $	May X2 $	Jun X2 $
Sales	80,000	100,000	110,000	130,000	140,000	150,000	160,000	180,000
Purchases	40,000	60,000	80,000	90,000	110,000	130,000	140,000	150,000
Wages	10,000	12,000	16,000	20,000	24,000	28,000	32,000	36,000
Overheads	10,000	10,000	15,000	15,000	15,000	20,000	20,000	20,000
Dividends		20,000						40,000
Capital expenditure			30,000			40,000		

You are also told the following.

(a) Sales are 40% cash, 60% credit. Credit sales are paid two months after the month of sale.
(b) Purchases are paid the month following purchase.
(c) 75% of wages are paid in the current month and 25% the following month.
(d) Overheads are paid the month after they are incurred.
(e) Dividends are paid three months after they are declared.
(f) Capital expenditure is paid two months after it is incurred.
(g) The opening cash balance is $15,000.

The managing director is pleased with the above figures, as they show sales will have increased by more than 100% in the period under review. In order to achieve this they have arranged a bank overdraft with a ceiling of $50,000 to accommodate the increased inventory levels and wage bill for overtime worked.

Required

(a) Prepare a cash flow forecast for the six-month period January to June 20X2.
(b) Comment on your results in the light of the managing director's comments and offer advice.

Answer

(a)

	January $	February $	March $	April $	May $	June $
Cash receipts						
Cash sales	44,000	52,000	56,000	60,000	64,000	72,000
Credit sales	48,000	60,000	66,000	78,000	84,000	90,000
	92,000	112,000	122,000	138,000	148,000	162,000
Cash payments						
Purchases	60,000	80,000	90,000	110,000	130,000	140,000
Wages: 75%	12,000	15,000	18,000	21,000	24,000	27,000
Wages: 25%	3,000	4,000	5,000	6,000	7,000	8,000
Overheads	10,000	15,000	15,000	15,000	20,000	20,000
Dividends			20,000			
Capital expenditure			30,000			40,000
	85,000	114,000	178,000	152,000	181,000	235,000
b/f	15,000	22,000	20,000	(36,000)	(50,000)	(83,000)
Net cash flow	7,000	(2,000)	(56,000)	(14,000)	(33,000)	(73,000)
c/f	22,000	20,000	(36,000)	(50,000)	(83,000)	(156,000)

(b) The overdraft arrangements are quite inadequate to service the cash needs of the business over the six-month period. If the figures are realistic then action should be taken now to avoid difficulties in the near future. The following are **possible courses of action**.

(i) **Activities** could be **curtailed**.

(ii) **Other sources of cash** could be explored, for example a long-term loan to finance the capital expenditure and a factoring arrangement to provide cash due from accounts receivable more quickly.

(iii) Efforts to increase the **speed of debt collection** could be made.

(iv) **Payments to accounts payable** could be delayed.

(v) The **dividend payments** could be **postponed** (the figures indicate that this is a small company, possibly owner managed).

(vi) Staff might be persuaded to work at a **lower rate** in return for, say, an annual bonus or a profit-sharing agreement.

(vii) **Extra staff** might be taken on to reduce the amount of overtime paid.

(viii) The **inventory holding policy** should be **reviewed**; it may be possible to meet demand from current production and minimise cash tied up in inventories.

2.6 Methods of easing cash shortages

FAST FORWARD

Cash shortages can be eased by postponing capital expenditure, selling assets, taking longer to pay accounts payable and pressing accounts receivable for earlier payment.

The steps that are usually taken by a company when a need for cash arises, and when it cannot obtain resources from any other source, such as a loan or an increased overdraft, are as follows.

(a) **Postponing capital expenditure**

Some new non-current assets might be needed for the **development and growth of the business**, but some capital expenditures might be postponable without serious consequences. If a company's policy is to replace company cars every two years, but the company is facing a cash shortage, it might decide to replace cars every three years.

(b) **Accelerating cash inflows which would otherwise be expected in a later period**

One way would be to press accounts receivable for earlier payment. Often, this policy will result in a **loss of goodwill** and problems with customers. It might be possible to encourage credit customers to pay more quickly by offering discounts for earlier payment.

(c) **Reversing past investment decisions by selling assets previously acquired**

Some assets are less crucial to a business than others. If cash flow problems are severe, the option of selling investments or property might have to be considered. Sale and leaseback of property could also be considered.

(d) **Negotiating a reduction in cash outflows to postpone or reduce payments**

There are several ways in which this could be done.

(i) **Longer credit** might be taken from suppliers. Such an extension of credit would have to be negotiated carefully: there would be a risk of having further supplies refused.

(ii) **Loan repayments** could be rescheduled by agreement with a bank.

(iii) A **deferral** of the payment of **company tax** might be agreed with the taxation authorities. However, they will charge interest on the outstanding amount of tax.

(iv) **Dividend payments** could be **reduced**. Dividend payments are discretionary cash outflows, although a company's directors might be constrained by shareholders' expectations, so that they feel obliged to pay dividends even when there is a cash shortage.

2.7 Deviations from expected cash flows

Cash flow forecasts, whether prepared on an annual, monthly, weekly or even daily basis, can only be estimates of cash flows. Even the best estimates will not be exactly correct, so deviations from the cash flow forecast are inevitable.

A cash flow forecast model could be constructed, using a PC and a spreadsheet package, and the **sensitivity** of cash flow forecasts to changes in estimates of sales, costs, and so on could be analysed. By planning for different eventualities, management should be able to prepare **contingency measures** in advance and also **appreciate** the **key factors** in the cash flow forecast.

A knowledge of the **probability distribution** of possible outcomes for the cash position will allow a **more accurate estimate** to be made of the minimum cash balances, or the borrowing power necessary, to provide a satisfactory margin of safety. Unforeseen deficits can be hard to finance at short notice, and advance planning is desirable.

3 Treasury management

A large organisation will have a **treasury department** to manage liquidity, short-term investment, borrowings, foreign exchange risk and other, specialised areas such as forward contracts and futures.

Key term

Treasury management can be defined as: 'The corporate handing of all financial matters, the generation of external and internal funds for business, the management of currencies and cash flows, and the complex strategies, policies and procedures of corporate finance.' *(Association of Corporate Treasurers)*

Large companies rely heavily on the financial and currency markets. These markets are volatile, with interest rates and foreign exchange rates changing continually and by significant amounts. To manage cash (funds) and currency efficiently, many large companies have set up a separate treasury department.

A treasury department, even in a large organisation, is likely to be quite small, with a staff of perhaps three to six qualified accountants, bankers or corporate treasurers working under the treasurer.

3.1 Centralisation of the treasury department

The following are advantages of having a specialist **centralised treasury department**.

(a)   **Centralised liquidity management**

   (i)   Avoids having a mix of cash surpluses and overdrafts in different localised bank accounts
   (ii)   Facilitates bulk cash flows, so that lower bank charges can be negotiated

(b)   Larger volumes of cash are available to invest, giving better **short-term investment opportunities** (for example money markets, high-interest accounts and CDs).

(c)   Any **borrowing** can be **arranged in bulk**, at lower interest rates than for smaller borrowings, and perhaps on the eurocurrency or eurobond markets.

(d)   **Foreign exchange risk management** is likely to be improved in a group of companies. A central treasury department can **match foreign currency income** earned by one subsidiary with **expenditure** in the same currency by another subsidiary. In this way, the risk of losses on adverse exchange rate movements can be avoided without the expense of forward exchange contracts or other hedging methods.

(e)   A specialist treasury department can employ **experts** with knowledge of dealing in forward contracts, futures, options, eurocurrency markets, swaps, and so on. Localised departments could not have such expertise.

(f)   The centralised pool of **funds required for precautionary purposes** will be **smaller** than the sum of separate precautionary balances which would need to be held under decentralised treasury arrangements.

(g)   Through having a separate **profit centre**, attention will be focused on the contribution to group profit performance that can be achieved by good cash, funding, investment and foreign currency management.

Possible advantages of **decentralised** cash management are as follows.

(a)   Sources of finance can be **diversified** and can match **local assets**.

(b)   **Greater autonomy** can be given to **subsidiaries** and divisions because of the closer relationships they will have with the decentralised cash management function.

(c)   A decentralised treasury function may be **more responsive** to the needs of individual operating units.

(d)   Since cash balances will not be aggregated at group level, there will be **more limited opportunities** to invest such balances on a short-term basis.

4 Cash management models

Optimal **cash** holding levels can be calculated from formal models, such as the **Baumol model** and the **Miller-Orr** model.

A number of different cash management models indicate the **optimum amount of cash** that a company should hold.

4.1 The Baumol model

The **Baumol model** is based on the idea that deciding on optimum cash balances is like deciding on optimum inventory levels. It assumes that cash is steadily consumed over time and a business holds a stock of marketable securities that can be sold when cash is needed. The cost of holding cash is the opportunity cost, ie the interest forgone from not investing the cash. The cost of placing an order is the administration cost incurred when selling the securities.

The Baumol model uses an equation of the same form as the EOQ formula for inventory management which we looked at earlier.

Similarly to the EOQ, costs are minimised when:

$$Q = \sqrt{\frac{2CS}{i}}$$

Where S = the amount of cash to be used in each time period
C = the cost per sale of securities
i = the interest cost of holding cash or near cash equivalents
Q = the total amount to be raised to provide for S

4.1.1 Example: Baumol approach to cash management

Finder Co faces a fixed cost of $4,000 to obtain new funds. There is a requirement for $24,000 of cash over each period of one year for the foreseeable future. The interest cost of new funds is 12% per annum; the interest rate earned on short-term securities is 9% per annum. How much finance should Finder raise at a time?

Solution

The cost of holding cash is 12% − 9% = 3%

The optimum level of Q (the 'reorder quantity') is:

$$\sqrt{\frac{2 \times 4,000 \times 24,000}{0.03}} = \$80,000$$

The optimum amount of new funds to raise is $80,000. This amount is raised every 80,000 ÷ 24,000 = 3$\frac{1}{3}$ years.

4.1.2 Drawbacks of the Baumol model

The inventory approach illustrated above has the following drawbacks.

(a) In reality, it is unlikely to be **possible** to **predict amounts required** over future periods with much certainty.

(b) No **buffer inventory** of cash is allowed for. There may be costs associated with running out of cash.

(c) There may be other **normal costs** of holding cash which increase with the average amount held.

Exam focus
point

The examiner's report for the June 2015 exam noted that many students were unable to correctly apply the Baumol model to find the optimum amount of short-term investments to convert into cash. Although the Baumol formula is not on the formula sheet, the EOQ formula is. You need to treat the fixed cost of

getting cash from short-term investments as the ordering cost. You also need to treat the penalty or opportunity cost of holding cost as the inventory holding cost. If you can't remember this then you need to memorise the Baumol formula instead.

4.2 The Miller-Orr model

In an attempt to produce a more realistic approach to cash management, various models more complicated than the inventory approach have been developed. One of these, the **Miller-Orr model**, manages to achieve a reasonable degree of realism while not being too elaborate.

We can begin looking at the Miller-Orr model by asking what will happen if there is no attempt to manage cash balances. Clearly, the cash balance is likely to 'meander' upwards or downwards. The Miller-Orr model imposes limits to this meandering.

If the cash balance reaches an **upper limit** (point A) the firm **buys sufficient securities** to return the cash balance to a normal level (called the 'return point'). When the cash balance reaches a lower limit (point B), the firm sells securities to bring the balance back to the return point.

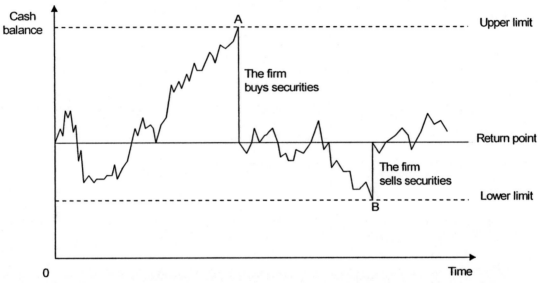

How are the upper and lower limits and the return point set? Miller and Orr showed that the answer to this question depends on the **variance of cash flows, transaction costs** and **interest rates**. If the day to day variability of cash flows is high or the transaction cost in buying or selling securities is high, then wider limits should be set. If interest rates are high, the limits should be closer together.

To keep the interest costs of holding cash down, the return point is set at one-third of the distance (or 'spread') between the lower and the upper limit.

Formula to learn

Return point = Lower limit + ($\frac{1}{3}$ × spread)

The formula for the spread is:

$$\text{Spread} = 3 \left(\frac{3}{4} \times \frac{\text{Transaction cost} \times \text{Variance of cash flows}}{\text{Interest rate}} \right)^{\frac{1}{3}}$$

To use the Miller-Orr model, it is necessary to follow the steps below.

Step 1   Set the **lower limit** for the **cash balance**. This may be zero, or it may be set at some minimum safety margin above zero.

Step 2   **Estimate** the **variance** of **cash flows**, for example from sample observations over a 100-day period.

Step 3   **Note the interest rate** and the **transaction cost** for each sale or purchase of securities (the latter is assumed to be fixed).

Step 4   **Compute the upper limit** and the **return point** from the model and implement the limits strategy.

You may be given the information to help you through the early steps, as in the question below.

Question   Miller-Orr model

The following data applies to a company.

1   The minimum cash balance is $8,000.

2   The variance of daily cash flows is 4,000,000, equivalent to a standard deviation of $2,000 per day.

3   The transaction cost for buying or selling securities is $50. The interest rate is 0.025% per day.

You are required to formulate a decision rule using the Miller-Orr model.

Answer

The spread between the upper and lower cash balance limits is calculated as follows.

$$\text{Spread} = 3\left(\frac{3}{4} \times \frac{\text{Transaction cost} \times \text{Variance of cash flows}}{\text{Interest rate}}\right)^{\frac{1}{3}}$$

$$= 3\left(\frac{3}{4} \times \frac{50 \times 4,000,000}{0.00025}\right)^{\frac{1}{3}} = 3 \times (6 \times 10^{11})^{\frac{1}{3}} = 3 \times 8,434.33$$

$$= \$25,303, \text{ say } \$25,300$$

The upper limit and return point are now calculated.

Upper limit   = lower limit + $25,300   = $8,000 + $25,300 = $33,300
Return point   = lower limit + 1/3 × spread = $8,000 + 1/3 × $25,300 = $16,433, say $16,400

The decision rule is as follows. If the cash balance reaches $33,300, buy $16,900 (= 33,300 − 16,400) in marketable securities. If the cash balance falls to $8,000, sell $8,400 of marketable securities for cash.

Exam focus point

Variance = standard deviation[2] so if you are given the standard deviation, you will need to square it to calculate the **variance**. If you are given the annual interest rate, you will need to divide it by 365 to obtain the **daily** interest rate.

The **usefulness of the Miller-Orr model** is limited by the assumptions on which it is based. In practice, cash inflows and outflows are unlikely to be entirely **unpredictable** as the model assumes: for example, for a retailer, seasonal factors are likely to affect cash inflows.

However, the Miller-Orr model may save management time which might otherwise be spent in responding to those cash inflows and outflows which cannot be predicted.

5 Investing surplus cash

FAST FORWARD

Temporary surpluses of cash can be invested in a variety of financial instruments. Longer-term surpluses should be returned to shareholders if there is a lack of investment opportunities.

Companies and other organisations sometimes have a **surplus of cash** and become 'cash rich'. A cash surplus is likely to be **temporary**, but while it exists the company should invest or deposit the cash bearing the following considerations in mind:

(a) **Liquidity** – money should be available to take advantage of favourable short-term interest rates on bank deposits, or to grasp a strategic opportunity, for example paying cash to take over another company

(b) **Profitability** – the company should seek to obtain a **good return** for the **risk** incurred

(c) **Safety** – the company should **avoid** the risk of a **capital loss**

Other factors that organisations need to consider include:

(a) Whether to invest at **fixed or floating rates.** Floating rate investments are likely to be chosen if interest rates are expected to rise.

(b) **Term to maturity.** The terms chosen will be affected by the business's desire for **liquidity** and **expectations** about future rates of interest – if there are major uncertainties about future interest rate levels it will be better to choose short-term investments. There may also be **penalties** for **early liquidation**.

(c) How easy it will be to **realise** the investment.

(d) Whether a **minimum amount** has to be invested in certain investments.

(e) Whether to invest on **international markets**.

If a company has no plans to grow or to invest, then surplus cash not required for transactions or precautionary purposes should normally be **returned to shareholders**.

Surplus cash may be returned to shareholders by:

(a) Increasing the usual level of the annual **dividends** which are paid

(b) Making a one-off **special dividend payment** (for example, National Power plc and BT plc have made such payments in recent years)

(c) Using the money to **buy back its own shares** from some of its shareholders. This will reduce the total number of shares in issue, and should therefore raise the level of **earnings per share**.

If surplus cash is to be invested on a regular basis, organisations should have investment guidelines in place covering the following issues.

(a) Surplus funds can only be invested in **specified types of investment** (eg no equity shares).

(b) All investments must be **convertible into cash** within a set number of days.

(c) Investments should be **ranked**: surplus funds are to be invested in higher risk instruments only when a sufficiency has been invested in lower risk items (so that there is always a cushion of safety).

(d) If a firm invests in certain financial instruments, a **credit rating** should be obtained. Credit rating agencies, discussed earlier, issue gradings according to risk.

5.1 Short-term investments

Temporary cash surpluses are likely to be:

(a) **Deposited** with a **bank** or similar financial institution

(b) Invested in **short-term debt instruments**, such as Treasury bills or CDs (Debt instruments are debt securities which can be traded.)

(c) Invested in **longer-term debt instruments** such as government bonds, which can be sold when the company eventually needs the cash

(d) Invested in **shares of listed companies**, which can be sold on the stock market when the company eventually needs the cash; investing in equities is fairly high risk, since share prices can fall substantially, resulting in large losses on investment

5.2 Short-term deposits

Cash can of course be put into a **bank deposit** to **earn interest**. The rate of interest obtainable depends on the size of the deposit, and varies from bank to bank.

There are other types of deposit.

(a) **Money market lending**

There is a very large money market in the UK for interbank lending. The interest rates in the market are related to the London Interbank Offer Rate (LIBOR) and the London Interbank Bid Rate (LIBID).

(b) **Local authority deposits**

Local authorities often need **short-term cash**, and investors can deposit funds with them for periods ranging from overnight up to one year or more.

(c) **Finance house deposits**

These are **time deposits** with finance houses (usually subsidiaries of banks).

5.3 Short-term debt instruments

There are a number of **short-term debt instruments** which an investor can resell before the debt matures and is repaid. These debt instruments include **certificates of deposit** (CDs) and **Treasury bills**.

These have already been described in the context of money market instruments.

5.3.1 Certificates of deposit (CDs)

A **CD** is a security that is issued by a bank, acknowledging that a certain amount of money has been deposited with it for a certain period of time (usually a short term). The CD is issued to the **depositor**, and attracts a **stated amount of interest**.

CDs are negotiable and traded on the CD market (a money market), so if a CD holder wishes to obtain immediate cash they can sell the CD on the market at any time. This secondhand market in CDs makes them attractive, flexible investments for organisations with excess cash. A company with a temporary cash surplus may therefore buy a CD as an investment.

5.3.2 Treasury bills

Treasury bills are issued weekly by the Government to finance short-term cash deficiencies in the Government's expenditure programme. They are **IOUs** issued by the Government, giving a promise to pay a certain amount to their holder on maturity. Treasury bills have a term of **91 days to maturity**, after which the holder is paid the full value of the bill.

The market for Treasury bills is very liquid, and bills can be bought or sold at any time.

6 Working capital funding strategies   12/09, 6/12

> Working capital can be funded by a mixture of short- and long-term funding. Businesses should be aware of the distinction between **fluctuating** and **permanent** assets.

6.1 The working capital requirement

Computing the working capital requirement is a matter of calculating the value of current assets less current liabilities, perhaps by taking averages over a one-year period.

6.2 Example: Working capital requirements

The following data relate to Corn Co, a manufacturing company.

Revenue for the year	$1,500,000

Costs as percentages of sales	%
Direct materials	30
Direct labour	25
Variable overheads	10
Fixed overheads	15
Selling and distribution	5

On average:

(a) Accounts receivable take 2.5 months before payment.

(b) Raw materials are in inventory for three months.

(c) Work in progress represents two months' worth of half produced goods.

(d) Finished goods represents one month's production.

(e) Credit is taken as follows:

(i)	Direct materials	2 months
(ii)	Direct labour	1 week
(iii)	Variable overheads	1 month
(iv)	Fixed overheads	1 month
(v)	Selling and distribution	0.5 months

Work in progress and finished goods are valued at material, labour and variable expense cost.

Compute the working capital requirement of Corn Co assuming the labour force is paid for 50 working weeks a year.

Solution

(a) The annual costs incurred will be as follows.

		$
Direct materials	30% of $1,500,000	450,000
Direct labour	25% of $1,500,000	375,000
Variable overheads	10% of $1,500,000	150,000
Fixed overheads	15% of $1,500,000	225,000
Selling and distribution	5% of $1,500,000	75,000

(b) The average value of current assets will be as follows.

		$	$
Raw materials	3/12 × $450,000		112,500
Work in progress			
Materials (50% complete)	1/12 × $450,000	37,500	
Labour (50% complete)	1/12 × $375,000	31,250	
Variable overheads (50% complete)	1/12 × $150,000	12,500	
			81,250
Finished goods			
Materials	1/12 × $450,000	37,500	
Labour	1/12 × $375,000	31,250	
Variable overheads	1/12 × $150,000	12,500	
			81,250
Accounts receivable	2.5/12 × $1,500,000		312,500
			587,500

(c)   Average value of current liabilities will be as follows.

Materials	2/12 × $450,000	75,000
Labour	1/50 × $375,000	7,500
Variable overheads	1/12 × $150,000	12,500
Fixed overheads	1/12 × $225,000	18,750
Selling and distribution	0.5/12 × $75,000	3,125
		116,875

(d)   Working capital required is ($(587,500 – 116,875))   470,625

It has been assumed that all the direct materials are allocated to work in progress when production starts.

6.3 Working capital investment policy   6/08, 12/13

Organisations have to decide what the most important **risks** relating to working capital are, and therefore whether to adopt a **conservative**, **aggressive** or **moderate** approach to investment in working capital.

6.3.1 A conservative approach

A conservative working capital investment policy aims to **reduce the risk** of system breakdown by holding **high** levels of working capital.

Customers are allowed generous payment terms to stimulate demand, finished goods inventories are high to ensure availability for customers, and raw materials and work in progress are high to minimise the risk of running out of inventory and consequent downtime in the manufacturing process. Suppliers are paid promptly to ensure their goodwill, again to minimise the chance of stock-outs.

However, the cumulative effect on these policies can be that the firm carries a high burden of unproductive assets, resulting in a **financing cost** that can **destroy profitability**. A period of rapid expansion may also cause severe cash flow problems, as working capital requirements outstrip available finance. Further problems may arise from inventory obsolescence and lack of flexibility to customer demands.

6.3.2 An aggressive approach

An aggressive working capital investment policy aims to **reduce this financing cost** and **increase profitability** by cutting inventories, speeding up collections from customers and delaying payments to suppliers.

The potential disadvantage of this policy is an **increase** in the chances of **system breakdown** through running out of inventory or **loss of goodwill** with customers and suppliers.

However, modern manufacturing techniques encourage inventory and work in progress reductions through just-in-time policies, flexible production facilities and improved quality management. Improved customer satisfaction through a quality and effective response to customer demand can also mean that credit periods are shortened.

6.3.3 A moderate approach

A moderate working capital investment policy is a **middle way** between the aggressive and conservative approaches.

These characteristics are useful for comparing and analysing the different ways that individual organisations deal with working capital and the **trade-off** between **risk and return**.

6.4 Permanent and fluctuating current assets

In order to understand working capital financing decisions, assets can be divided into three different types.

(a)   **Non-current (fixed) assets** are long-term assets from which an organisation expects to derive benefit over a number of periods; for example, buildings or machinery.

(b)   **Permanent current assets** are the amount required to meet long-term minimum needs and sustain normal trading activity; for example, inventory and the average level of accounts receivable.

(c)   **Fluctuating current assets** are the current assets which vary according to normal business activity; for example, due to seasonal variations.

Fluctuating current assets together with **permanent** current assets form part of the working capital of the business, which may be financed by either long-term funding (including equity capital) or by current liabilities (short-term funding).

6.5 Working capital financing policy   12/09

There are different ways in which the funding of the current and non-current assets of a business can be achieved by employing long- and short-term sources of funding.

Short-term sources of funding are usually **cheaper** and **more flexible** than long-term ones. However, short-term sources are **riskier** for the borrower, as interest rates are more volatile in the short term and they may not be renewed.

The diagram below illustrates three alternative types of policy: A, B and C. The dotted lines A, B and C are the cut-off levels between short-term and long-term funding for each of the policies A, B and C respectively: assets above the relevant dotted line are financed by short-term funding while assets below the dotted line are financed by long-term funding.

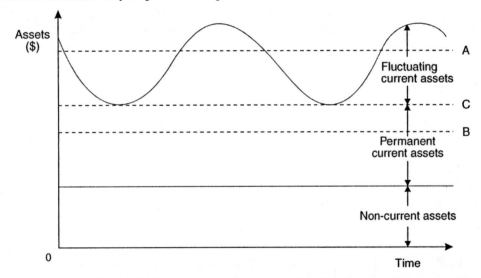

(a)   Policy A can be characterised as a **conservative approach** to financing working capital. All non-current assets and permanent current assets, as well as part of the fluctuating current assets, are financed by long-term funding. There is only a need to call on short-term financing at times when fluctuations in current assets push total assets above the level of dotted line A. At times when fluctuating current assets are low and total assets fall below line A, there will be **surplus cash** which the company will be able to invest in marketable securities.

(b)   Policy B is a more **aggressive approach** to financing working capital. Not only are fluctuating current assets all financed out of short-term sources, but so are some of the permanent current assets. This policy represents an **increased risk** of liquidity and cash flow problems, although potential returns will be increased if short-term financing can be obtained more cheaply than long-term finance.

(c)   A **balance** between risk and return might be best achieved by the **moderate approach** of policy C, a policy of **maturity matching** in which long-term funds finance permanent assets while short-term funds finance non-permanent assets. This means that the maturity of the funds **matches** the maturity of the assets.

6.6 Other factors

The trend of overall working capital management will be complicated by the following factors.

(a) **Industry norms**
These are of particular importance for the **management of receivables**. It will be difficult to offer a much shorter credit period than competitors.

(b) **Products**
The **production process**, and therefore the amount of work in progress, is obviously much greater for some products and in some industries.

(c) **Management issues**
How **working capital** is **managed** may have a significant impact on the actual length of the working capital cycle whatever the overall strategy might be. Factors to consider include:

(i) The size of the organisation

(ii) The degree of centralisation (which may allow a more aggressive approach to be adopted, though this depends on how efficient the centralised departments actually are)

(iii) Management attitudes to risk

(iv) Previous funding decisions

Chapter Roundup

- **Cash flow forecasts** show the expected receipts and payments during a forecast period and are a vital management control tool, especially during times of recession.

- **Cash shortages** can be eased by postponing capital expenditure, selling assets, taking longer to pay accounts payable and pressing accounts receivable for earlier payment.

- A large organisation will have a **treasury department** to manage liquidity, short-term investment, borrowings, foreign exchange risk and other, specialised areas such as forward contracts and futures.

- Optimal **cash** holding levels can be calculated from formal models, such as the **Baumol model** and the **Miller-Orr model.**

- **Temporary surpluses** of cash can be invested in a variety of financial instruments. Longer-term surpluses should be returned to shareholders if there is a lack of investment opportunities.

- Working capital can be funded by a mixture of short- and long-term funding. Businesses should be aware of the distinction between **fluctuating** and **permanent** assets.

Quick Quiz

1   Which of the following should be included in a cash flow forecast?

	Include	Do not include
Funds from the issue of share capital		
Revaluation of a non-current asset		
Receipts of dividends from outside the business		
Depreciation of production machinery		
Bad debts written off		
Repayment of a bank loan		

2   Match the appropriate management action to the cash position shown by a cash budget.

Position

(a)   Short-term surplus
(b)   Short-term deficit
(c)   Long-term surplus
(d)   Long-term deficit

Action

1   Diversify
2   Issue share capital
3   Reduce accounts receivable
4   Increase accounts receivable
5   Increase accounts payable
6   Expand

3   In the Miller-Orr cash management model:

Return point = Lower limit + ... × Spread

4   Which of the following is most likely to reduce a firm's working capital?

A   Adopting the Miller-Orr model of cash management
B   Lengthening the period of credit given to accounts receivable
C   Buying new machinery
D   Adopting just-in-time procurement and lean manufacturing

5   Which type of policy is characterised by all non-current assets and permanent current assets being financed by long-term funding?

1

	Include	Do not include
Funds from the issue of share capital	✓	
Revaluation of a non-current asset		✓
Receipts of dividends from outside the business	✓	
Depreciation of production machinery		✓
Bad debts written off		✓
Repayment of a bank loan	✓	

2   (a)   4
       (b)   3, 5
       (c)   1, 6
       (d)   2

3   One-third

4   D   The aim of using these methods is to minimise inventory holdings. The impact of using the Miller-Orr model will depend on how the firm was managing cash before (A). Giving more credit to accounts receivable will increase working capital (B). New machinery is not part of working capital (C); the impact, if any, on working capital will depend on how the purchase is financed.

5   Conservative

Now try the questions below from the Practice Question Bank

Number	Level	Marks	Approximate time
Section A Q14	Examination	2	4 mins
Section C Q4	Examination	20	39 mins
Section C Q5	Examination	20	39 mins

Investment appraisal

7

Investment decisions

Topic list	Syllabus reference
1 Investment and the capital budgeting process	Revision
2 Relevant cash flows	D1 (a)
3 Payback period	D1 (b)
4 Return on capital employed	D1 (d)

Introduction

This chapter introduces **investment appraisal** and covers the manner in which
investment opportunities are identified. It also introduces two relatively
straightforward, but widely used, investment appraisal methods: **payback
period** and **return on capital employed**. Chapter 8 will look at investment
appraisal using the more sophisticated **discounted cash flow (DCF)** methods,
which address some of the weaknesses of the traditional approaches covered
in this chapter (make sure you know what these are!).

Study guide

		Intellectual level
D1	Investment appraisal techniques	
(a)	Identify and calculate relevant cash flows for investment projects.	2
(b)	Calculate payback period and discuss the usefulness of payback as an investment appraisal method.	2
(d)	Calculate return on capital employed (accounting rate of return) and discuss its usefulness as an investment appraisal method.	2

Exam guide

As well as using the techniques covered in this chapter, you may be asked to discuss their drawbacks. You must be able to apply your knowledge.

1 Investment and the capital budgeting process (Brought forward knowledge)

1.1 Investment

> Knowledge brought forward from earlier studies

> You should be able to distinguish between capital and revenue expenditure, and between non-current assets and working capital investment. The following section is for revision only.

Investment can be divided into two categories: **capital expenditure** and **revenue expenditure**.

Suppose that a business purchases a building for $30,000. It then adds an extension to the building at a cost of $10,000. The building needs to have a few broken windows mended, its floors polished and some missing roof tiles replaced. These cleaning and maintenance jobs cost $900.

The original purchase ($30,000) and the cost of the extension ($10,000) are **capital expenditure** because they are incurred to **acquire** and then **improve** a non-current asset. The other costs of $900 are **revenue expenditure** because they merely maintain the building and thus the earning capacity of the building.

Capital expenditure is expenditure which results in the **acquisition** of non-current assets or an **improvement** in their earning capacity. It is not charged as an expense in the statement of profit or loss; the expenditure appears as a non-current asset in the statement of financial position.

Revenue expenditure is charged to the statement of profit or loss and is expenditure which is incurred:

(a)   For the purpose of the trade of the business – this includes expenditure classified as selling and distribution expenses, administration expenses and finance charges

(b)   To maintain the existing earning capacity of non-current assets

1.1.1 Non-current asset investment and working capital investment

Investment can be made in **non-current assets** or **working capital**.

(a)   **Investment in non-current assets** involves a significant amount of time between the commitment of funds and recovering the investment. Money is paid out to acquire resources which are going to be used on a continuing basis within the organisation.

(b)   **Investment in working capital** arises from the need to pay out money for resources (such as raw materials) before it can be recovered from sales of the finished product or service. The funds are therefore only committed for a short period of time.

1.1.2 Investment by the commercial sector

Investment by commercial organisations might include investment in:

- Plant and machinery
- Research and development
- Advertising
- Warehouse facilities

The overriding feature of a commercial sector investment is that it is generally **based on financial considerations alone**. The various capital expenditure appraisal techniques that we will be looking at assess the financial aspects of capital investment.

1.1.3 Investment by not for profit organisations

Investment by not for profit organisations differs from investment by commercial organisations for several reasons.

(a)   Relatively few not for profit organisations' capital investments are made with the **intention** of earning a **financial return**.

(b)   When there are two or more ways of achieving the same objective (mutually exclusive investment opportunities), a commercial organisation might prefer the option with the **lowest present value of cost**.

Not for profit organisations, however, rather than just considering financial cost and financial benefits, will often have regard to the **social costs** and **social benefits** of investments.

(c)   The **cost of capital** that is applied to project cash flows by the public sector will not be a 'commercial' rate of return, but one that is **determined** by the **Government**. Any targets that a public sector investment has to meet before being accepted will therefore not be based on the same criteria as those in the commercial sector.

1.2 The capital budgeting process

Knowledge brought forward from earlier studies

You should be familiar with the capital budgeting process and the investment decision-making process. This section is included for revision only.

1.2.1 Creation of capital budgets

The capital budget will normally be prepared to cover a **longer period** than sales, production and resource budgets, say from three to five years, although it should be **broken down** into periods matching those of other budgets.

It should indicate the expenditure required to cover **capital projects already underway** and those it is **anticipated will start** in the three- to five-year period (say) of the capital budget.

The budget should therefore be based on the current production budget, future expected levels of production and the long-term development of the organisation, and industry, as a whole.

Budget limits or constraints might be imposed internally or externally.

(a)   The imposition of **internal constraints**, which are often imposed when managerial resources are limited, is known as **soft capital rationing**.

(b) **Hard capital rationing** occurs when **external limits** are set, perhaps because of scarcity of financing, high financing costs or restrictions on the amount of external financing an organisation can seek.

Projects can arise from **top management policy decisions** or from sources such as mandatory government regulations (health, safety and welfare capital expenditure), or be **appraised** using the techniques covered in this chapter and the next.

Overall responsibility for **authorisation and monitoring** of capital expenditure is, in most large organisations, the **responsibility of a committee**. For example:

- Expenditure up to $75,000 may be approved by individual divisional managers.
- Expenditure between $75,000 and $150,000 may be approved by divisional management.
- Expenditure over $150,000 may be approved by the board of directors.

1.2.2 The investment decision-making process

A typical **model for investment decision-making** has a number of distinct stages.

- Origination of proposals
- Project screening
- Analysis and acceptance
- Monitoring and review

1.2.3 Origination of proposals

Ideas for investment might come from those working in technical positions. A factory manager, for example, could be well placed to identify ways in which expanded capacity or new machinery could increase output or the efficiency of the manufacturing process.

Innovative ideas, such as new product lines, are more likely to come from those in higher levels of management, given their **strategic** view of the organisation's direction and their knowledge of the competitive environment.

The overriding feature of any proposal is that it should be consistent with the organisation's overall strategy to achieve its objectives.

1.2.4 Project screening

Each proposal must be subject to detailed screening. So that a **qualitative evaluation** of a proposal can be made, a number of key questions such as those below might be asked before any financial analysis is undertaken. Only if the project passes this initial screening will more detailed financial analysis begin.

- What is the purpose of the project?
- Does it 'fit' with the organisation's long-term objectives?
- Is it a mandatory investment, for example to conform with safety legislation?
- What resources are required and are they available, eg money, capacity, labour?
- Do we have the necessary management expertise to guide the project to completion?
- Does the project expose the organisation to unnecessary risk?
- How long will the project last and what factors are key to its success?
- Have all possible alternatives been considered?

1.2.5 Analysis and acceptance

The analysis stage can be broken down into a number of steps.

Step 1 Complete and submit standard format financial information as a formal investment proposal.

Step 2 Classify the project by type (to separate projects into those that require more or less rigorous financial appraisal, and those that must achieve a greater or lesser rate of return in order to be deemed acceptable).

Step 3	Carry out financial analysis of the project.
Step 4	Compare the outcome of the financial analysis to predetermined acceptance criteria.
Step 5	Consider the project in the light of the capital budget for the current and future operating periods.
Step 6	Make the **decision (go/no go)**.
Step 7	Monitor the progress of the project.

Financial analysis

The financial analysis will involve the **application of the organisation's preferred investment appraisal techniques**.

Here are examples of the type of question that will be addressed at this stage.

- What cash flows/profits will arise from the project and when?
- Has inflation been considered in the determination of the cash flows?
- What are the results of the financial appraisal?
- Has any allowance been made for risk and, if so, what was the outcome?

Some types of project, for example a marketing investment decision, may give rise to cash inflows and **returns which are so intangible and difficult to quantify that a full financial appraisal may not be possible**. In this case, more weight may be given to a consideration of the qualitative issues.

Qualitative issues

Besides reviewing the project's 'fit' with the organisation's overall objectives and whether it is a mandatory investment, there is a very wide range of other qualitative issues that may be relevant to a particular project.

(a) What are the implications of not undertaking the investment, eg adverse effect on staff morale, loss of market share?

(b) Will acceptance of this project lead to the need for further investment activity in the future?

(c) What will be the effect on the company's image?

(d) Will the organisation be more flexible as a result of the investment, and better able to respond to market and technology changes?

Go/no go decision

Go/no go decisions on projects may be **made at different levels within the organisational hierarchy**, depending on three factors.

- The type of investment
- Its perceived riskiness
- The amount of expenditure required

For example, a divisional manager may be authorised to make decisions up to $25,000, an area manager up to $150,000 and a group manager up to $300,000, with board approval for greater amounts.

Once the go/no go (or **accept/reject**) decision has been made, the organisation is committed to the project, and the decision-maker must accept that the project's success or failure reflects on their ability to make sound decisions.

1.2.6 Monitoring the progress of the project

During the project's progress, **project controls** should be applied to ensure the following.

- Capital spending does not exceed the amount authorised.
- The implementation of the project is not delayed.
- The anticipated benefits are eventually obtained.

2 Relevant cash flows

Relevant costs of investment appraisal include opportunity costs, working capital costs and wider costs such as infrastructure and human development costs. **Non-relevant costs** include past costs and committed costs.

2.1 Relevant cash flows in investment appraisals

The cash flows that should be considered in investment appraisals are those which arise as a **consequence** of the investment decision under evaluation. This means that cash flows are only relevant if they are **future incremental cash** flows.

Any costs incurred in the **past**, or any **committed costs** which will be **incurred regardless** of whether or not an investment is undertaken, are **not relevant cash flows**. They have occurred, or will occur, whatever investment decision is taken. For example, if a company has spent money on market research into the potential returns from an investment, the cost is a **sunk cost** and should not be taken into consideration when deciding about the future and whether or not the investment should go ahead.

Any costs which do not represent an actual cash flow should also be ignored.

Here are some examples of non-relevant costs.

- **Centrally allocated overheads** that are not a consequence of undertaking the project
- **Management costs** and **marketing research expenditure** already incurred
- **Depreciation**

Exam focus point

The ACCA examination team comments that students often include non-relevant costs in investment appraisals. Make sure you identify any non-relevant costs when answering questions in the exam.

The **annual cash profits** from a project can be calculated as the **incremental contribution** earned **minus any incremental fixed costs** which are additional cash items of expenditure (that is, ignoring depreciation and so on).

There are, however, other cash flows to consider. These might include the following.

2.1.1 Opportunity costs

These are the costs incurred or revenues lost from diverting existing resources from their best use.

2.1.2 Example: Opportunity costs

If a salesman, who is paid an annual salary of $30,000, is diverted to work on a new project and as a result existing sales of $50,000 are lost, the opportunity cost to the new project will be the $50,000 of lost sales. The salesman's salary of $30,000 is **not** an opportunity cost since it will be incurred however their time is spent.

2.1.3 Tax

This refers to the extra **tax** that will be payable on extra profits, or the reductions in tax arising from tax allowable depreciation or operating losses in any year. We shall consider the effect of taxation in Chapter 9.

2.1.4 Residual value

This refers to the **residual value** or **disposal** value of equipment at the end of its life, or its disposal cost.

2.1.5 Working capital

If a company invests $20,000 in working capital and earns cash profits of $50,000, the net cash receipts will be $30,000. This is because an increase in working capital reduces the net cash inflows below the amount that could be expected from the 'cash profits' for the period.

Working capital will be released again at the end of a project's life, and so there will be a cash inflow arising out of the eventual realisation into cash of the project's inventory and receivables in the final year of the project. In other words, a reduction in working capital is included in a cash flow forecast as an increase in cash.

	$
Cash flow from profits in the period	X
Minus working capital increase	(X)
or Plus working capital reduction	X
Equals adjusted cash flow for the period	X

In investment appraisal, an investment in working capital at the beginning of the investment period is treated as an outflow of cash, and a reduction in working capital to $0 at the end of the investment period is treated as an inflow of cash.

2.2 Other relevant costs

Costs that will often need to be considered include:

- **Infrastructure costs** such as additional information technology or communication systems

- **Marketing costs** may be substantial, particularly of course if the investment is in a new product or service. They will include the costs of market research, promotion and branding and the organisation of new distribution channels.

- **Human resource costs** including training costs and the costs of reorganisation arising from investments

- **Additional specific fixed costs** may need to be considered, while apportioned existing general overheads are ignored. Specific fixed costs include additional electricity costs incurred by the use of new machines.

2.3 Timing of cash flows

It is normally assumed that cash flows that arise evenly over a period of time arise at the end of that period. For example, revenues earned in Year 1 are assumed to occur at the end of Year 1.

An exception to this general rule is that cash flows occurring at the beginning of a year (or time period) are assumed to occur at the end of the previous time period. So cash flows at the beginning of Year 1, for example, are assumed to occur at the end of Year 0 (which is 'now').

2.4 Relevant benefits of investments

2.4.1 Types of benefit

The benefits from a proposed investment must also be evaluated. These might consist of benefits of several types.

(a) **Savings** because assets used currently will no longer be used. The savings should include:
   (i) Savings in **staff costs**
   (ii) Savings in **other operating costs**, such as consumable materials

(b) Extra **savings** or revenue benefits because of the improvements or enhancements that the investment **might** bring:

    (i)   **More sales revenue** and so additional contribution

    (ii)   **More efficient system operation**

    (iii)   Further savings in **staff time**, resulting perhaps in reduced future staff growth

(c) Possibly, some one-off revenue benefits from the **sale of assets** that are currently in use, but which will no longer be required

Some benefits might be **intangible**, or impossible to give a monetary value to.

(a) Greater **customer satisfaction**, arising from a more prompt service (eg because of a computerised sales and delivery service)

(b) Improved **staff morale** from working with higher-quality assets

(c) **Better decision-making** may result from better information systems

Qualitative factors may influence a decision, but cannot easily be brought into the financial analysis of a proposed investment.

2.5 Example: Relevant cash flows

Elsie is considering the manufacture of a new product which would involve the use of both a new machine (costing $150,000) and an existing machine, which cost $80,000 two years ago and has a current net book value of $60,000. There is sufficient capacity on this machine, which has so far been underutilised. Annual sales of the product would be 5,000 units, selling at $32 per unit. Unit costs would be as follows.

	$
Direct labour (4 hours at $2 per hour)	8
Direct materials	7
Fixed costs including depreciation	9
	24

The project would have a five-year life, after which the new machine would have a net residual value of $10,000. Because direct labour is continually in short supply, labour resources would have to be diverted from other work which currently earns a contribution of $1.50 per direct labour hour. The fixed overhead absorption rate would be $2.25 per hour ($9 per unit) but actual expenditure on fixed overhead would not alter.

Working capital requirements would be $10,000 in the first year, rising to $15,000 in the second year and remaining at this level until the end of the project, when it will all be recovered. The company's cost of capital is 20%. Ignore taxation.

You are required to **identify the relevant cash flows** for the decision as to whether or not the project is worthwhile.

Solution

The timing of the investment in working capital should usually be attributed to the time period when the increase occurs. With an investment, the build-up of working capital is more likely to occur at the beginning of the period rather than gradually throughout the period. It is usually therefore normal convention to allocate changes in working capital to the beginning of the year rather than the end of the year. This means that the investment in working capital in the first year happens near the beginning of the first year (= Year 0) and the further increase in the second year happens at the beginning of Year 2 (= Year 1).

The relevant cash flows are as follows.

(a)	Year 0	Purchase of new machine: cash outflow	$150,000
(b)	Year 0	Initial investment in working capital: cash outflow	$10,000
(c)	Year 1	Additional investment in working capital in Year 2	$5,000

(d) Years 1-5

	$
Contribution from new product (5,000 units × $(32 − 15))	85,000
Less contribution foregone	
(5,000 × (4 × $1.50))	30,000
Residual value of new machine	10,000
Net cash inflow	65,000

(e) Year 5 Recovery of working capital investment: net cash inflow$15,000

When the working capital tied up in the project is 'recovered' at the end of the project, it will provide an extra cash inflow (for example debtors will eventually pay up).

(f) All other costs, which are past costs, notional accounting costs or costs which would be incurred anyway without the project, are not relevant to the investment decision.

3 Payback period

FAST FORWARD

The **payback method** of investment appraisal and the **ROCE/ARR/ROI** methods of investment appraisal are popular appraisal techniques despite their limitations (of which you should be aware).

Payback is the amount of time it takes for cash inflows = cash outflows.

There are a number of ways of evaluating capital projects, two of which we will be examining in this chapter. We will look first at the payback method.

Exam focus point

Exam questions often ask about the pros and cons of the payback method. The ACCA examination team has commented that discussion questions covering payback and ROCE are often poorly attempted by students.

Key term

Payback is the time it takes the cash inflows from a capital investment project to equal the cash outflows, usually expressed in years. It is the length of time before the cash inflows from an investment pay back the investment outlay.

Payback is often used as a 'first screening method' in investment appraisal. By this, we mean that when a capital investment project is being considered, the first question to ask is: 'How long will it take to pay back its cost?' The organisation might have a **target payback**, and so it would reject a capital project unless its payback period were less than a certain number of years.

However, a project should not be evaluated on the basis of payback alone. If a project gets through the payback test, it ought then to be evaluated with a more sophisticated investment appraisal technique that takes into consideration the total return over the full investment period.

3.1 Why is payback alone an inadequate investment appraisal technique?

The reason why payback should not be used on its own to evaluate capital investments should seem fairly obvious if you look at the figures below for two mutually exclusive projects (this means that only one of them can be undertaken).

	Project P	Project Q
	$	$
Capital investment	60,000	60,000
Profits before depreciation (a rough approximation of cash flows)		
Year 1	20,000	50,000
Year 2	30,000	20,000
Year 3	40,000	5,000
Year 4	50,000	5,000
Year 5	60,000	5,000

Project P pays back in year 3 (about one quarter of the way through year 3). Project Q pays back halfway through year 2. Using payback alone to judge capital investments, project Q would be preferred.

However, the returns from project P over its life are much higher than the returns from project Q. **Project P** will earn total profits before depreciation of $140,000 on an investment of $60,000. **Project Q** will earn total profits before depreciation of only $25,000 on an investment of $60,000.

3.2 Disadvantages of the payback method

There are a number of serious drawbacks to the payback method.

(a)   It **ignores** the **timing** of cash flows within the payback period.

(b)   It ignores the cash flows after the end of the payback period and therefore the total project return.

(c)   It **ignores the time value of money** (a concept incorporated into more sophisticated appraisal methods). This means that it does not take account of the fact that $1 today is worth more than $1 in one year's time. An investor who has $1 today can either consume it immediately or alternatively can invest it at the prevailing interest rate, say 10%, to get a return of $1.10 in a year's time.

(d)   Payback is **unable to distinguish between projects** with the same payback period.

(e)   The choice of any **cut-off** payback period by an organisation is **arbitrary**.

(f)   It may lead to **excessive investment** in **short-term projects**.

(g)   It takes account of the risk of the timing of cash flows but not the **variability** of those cash flows.

3.3 Advantages of the payback method

In spite of its limitations, the payback method continues to be popular, and the following points can be made in its favour.

(a)   It is simple to calculate and simple to understand. This may be important when management resources are limited. It is similarly helpful in communicating information about minimum requirements to managers responsible for submitting projects.

(b)   It uses cash flows rather than accounting profits.

(c)   It can be used as a screening device as a first stage in eliminating obviously inappropriate projects prior to more detailed evaluation.

(d)   The fact that it tends to bias in favour of short-term projects means that it tends to minimise both financial and business risk.

(e)   It can be used when there is a capital rationing situation to identify those projects which generate additional cash for investment quickly.

4 Return on capital employed   6/09, 12/12

$$ROCE = \frac{\text{Estimated average / total profits}}{\text{Estimated average / initial investment}} \times 100\%$$

The **return on capital employed** method (ROCE) (also called the **accounting rate of return** method or the **return on investment** (ROI) method) of appraising a capital project is to estimate the accounting rate of return that the project should yield. If it exceeds a target rate of return, the project will be undertaken. In Chapter 1 we discussed how return on capital employed is measured for financial accounting purposes. Here the measure is calculated in relation to investments.

Unfortunately, there are several different definitions of 'return on capital employed'. One of the most popular is as follows.

$$ROCE = \frac{\text{Estimated average annual accounting profits}}{\text{Estimated average investment}} \times 100\%$$

$$\text{Average investment} = \frac{\text{Capital cos t} + \text{disposal value}}{2}$$

The others include:

$$ROCE = \frac{\text{Estimated total profits}}{\text{Estimated initial investment}} \times 100\%$$

$$ROCE = \frac{\text{Estimated average profits}}{\text{Estimated initial investment}} \times 100\%$$

There are arguments in favour of each of these definitions. The most important point is, however, that the method selected should be used consistently. For examination purposes we recommend the first definition unless the question clearly indicates that some other one is to be used.

Exam focus point

Previous exams have stated that the ROCE calculation should be based on the **average** investment and used the first definition.

4.1 Example: Return on capital employed

A company has a target return on capital employed of 20% for its capital investments (using the first definition from the paragraph above), and is now considering the following project.

Capital cost of asset	$80,000
Estimated life	4 years

Estimated profit before depreciation

Year 1	$20,000
Year 2	$25,000
Year 3	$35,000
Year 4	$25,000

The capital asset would be depreciated by 25% of its cost each year, and will have no residual value. You are required to assess whether the project should be undertaken.

Solution

The annual profits after depreciation, and the mid-year net book value of the asset, would be as follows.

Year	Profit after depreciation $	Mid-year net book value $	ROCE in the year %
1	0	70,000	0
2	5,000	50,000	10
3	15,000	30,000	50
4	5,000	10,000	50

As the table shows, the ROCE is low in the early stages of the project, partly because of low profits in Year 1 but mainly because the net book value of the asset is much higher early on in its life.

The project does not achieve the target ROCE of 20% in its first two years, but exceeds it in years 3 and 4. So should it be undertaken?

When the ROCE from a project varies from year to year, it makes sense to take an overall or 'average' view of the project's return. In this case, we should look at the return as a whole over the four-year period.

	$
Total profit before depreciation over four years	105,000
Total profit after depreciation over four years	25,000
Average annual profit after depreciation	6,250
Original cost of investment	80,000
Average net book value over the four-year period $\dfrac{(80,000+0)}{2}$	40,000

$$\text{ROCE} = \frac{6,250}{40,000} = 15.6\%$$

The project would not be undertaken because it would fail to yield the target return of 20%.

4.2 ROCE and the comparison of mutually exclusive projects

The ROCE method of capital investment appraisal can also be used to compare two or more projects which are mutually exclusive. The project with the highest ROCE would be selected (provided that the expected ROCE is higher than the company's target ROCE).

4.3 Example: ROCE and mutually exclusive projects

Arrow wants to buy a new item of equipment which will be used to provide a service to customers of the company. Two models of equipment are available, one with a slightly higher capacity and greater reliability than the other. The expected costs and profits of each item are as follows.

	Equipment item X	Equipment item Y
Capital cost	$80,000	$150,000
Life	5 years	5 years
Profits before depreciation	$	$
Year 1	50,000	50,000
Year 2	50,000	50,000
Year 3	30,000	60,000
Year 4	20,000	60,000
Year 5	10,000	60,000
Disposal value	0	0

ROCE is measured as the average annual profit after depreciation, divided by the average net book value of the asset. You are required to decide which item of equipment should be selected, if any, if the company's target ROCE is 30%.

Solution

	Item X $	Item Y $
Total profit over life of equipment		
Before depreciation	160,000	280,000
After depreciation	80,000	130,000
Average annual profit after depreciation	16,000	26,000
Average investment = (Capital cost + disposal value)/2	40,000	75,000
ROCE	40%	34.7%

Both projects would earn a return in excess of 30%, but since item X would earn a bigger ROCE, it would be preferred to item Y, even though the profits from Y would be higher by an average of $10,000 a year.

4.4 The drawbacks to the ROCE method of capital investment appraisal

The ROCE method of capital investment appraisal has the serious drawback that it does not take account of the **timing** of the **profits from an investment**. Whenever capital is invested in a project, money is tied up until the project begins to earn profits which pay back the investment. Money tied up in one project cannot be invested anywhere else until the profits come in. Management should be aware of the benefits of early repayments from an investment, which will provide the money for other investments.

There are a number of other disadvantages.

(a) It is based on **accounting profits** and not cash flows. Accounting profits are subject to a number of different accounting treatments.

(b) It is a **relative measure** rather than an absolute measure and therefore takes no account of the size of the investment.

(c) It takes no account of the length of the project.

(d) Like the payback method, it ignores the time value of money.

There are, however, advantages to the ROCE method.

(a) It is a quick and simple calculation.

(b) It involves the familiar concept of a percentage return. The fact that it gives a relative measure means that ROCE makes it easy to compare two investment options.

(c) It looks at the entire project life.

Chapter Roundup

- **Relevant costs** of investment appraisal include opportunity costs, working capital costs and wider costs such as infrastructure and human development costs. **Non-relevant costs** include past costs and committed costs.

- **Relevant benefits** from investments include not only **increased cash flows** but also **savings** and **better relationships** with **customers and employees**.

- The **payback method** of investment appraisal and the **ROCE/ARR/ROI** methods of investment appraisal are popular appraisal techniques despite their limitations (of which you should be aware).

  Payback is the amount of time it takes for cash inflows = cash outflows.

- $$ROCE = \frac{\text{Estimated average / total profits}}{\text{Estimated average / initial investment}} \times 100\%$$

1   One reason that capital expenditure may be incurred is to maintain the earning capacity of existing non-current assets.

   True ☐

   False ☐

2   If a machine with annual running costs of $100,000 was diverted from producing output selling for $50,000 to producing a special order worth $70,000, what would be the relevant costs of what has happened?

   A $170,000
   B $100,000
   C $50,000
   D $20,000

3   The financial benefits of a new investment consist of the increased sales revenues it generates.

   True ☐

   False ☐

4   Fill in the blank.

   ………………………… is the time it takes the cumulative cash inflows from a capital investment project to equal the cumulative cash outflows.

5   Which of the following can be used to calculate the return on capital employed?

   (a) $\dfrac{\text{Estimated average annual profits}}{\text{Estimated average investment}} \times 100\%$

   (b) $\dfrac{\text{Estimated total profits}}{\text{Estimated initial investment}} \times 100\%$

   (c) $\dfrac{\text{Estimated average annual profits}}{\text{Estimated initial investment}} \times 100\%$

6   Fill in the blanks in these statements about the advantages of the payback method.

   (a)   Focus on early payback can enhance …………………………(liquidity/profitability)

   (b)   Investment risk is ……………………………………(increased/reduced) if payback is longer.

   (c)   ……………………….. term forecasts are likely to be more reliable.

7   The return on capital employed method of investment appraisal uses accounting profits before depreciation charges.

   True ☐

   False ☐

1   False. This is a reason for incurring **revenue** expenditure.

2   C $50,000, the opportunity cost of the lost sales revenue. A and B are wrong because they include the $100,000 running costs which would be incurred anyway so are not relevant. In the absence of any further information, $20,000 (D) would be the net benefit ($70,000 – $50,000).

3   False. Financial benefits could also include the savings from not operating existing assets any more, and also proceeds from the disposal of old assets.

4   Payback

5   All three could be used, although (a) $\dfrac{\text{Estimated average annual profits}}{\text{Estimated average investment}} \times 100\%$ is generally best.

6   (a)   Liquidity
      (b)   Increased
      (c)   Shorter

7   False

Now try the questions below from the Practice Question Bank

Number	Level	Marks	Approximate time
Section A Q15	Examination	2	4 mins
Section A Q16	Examination	2	4 mins
Section A Q17	Examination	2	4 mins
Section B Q1-5	Introductory	10	20 mins

Investment appraisal using DCF methods

Topic list	Syllabus reference
1 Discounted cash flow	Revision
2 The net present value method	D1 (e)
3 The internal rate of return method	D1 (f)
4 NPV and IRR compared	D1 (h)
5 Assessment of DCF methods of project appraisal	D1 (g)

Introduction

The **payback** and **ROCE** methods of investment appraisal were considered in the previous chapter. This chapter will look at **discounted cash flow (DCF) methods** of investment appraisal which take into account changes in the value of money over time. These two methods, **Net Present Value (NPV)** and **Internal Rate of Return (IRR)**, use the technique of **discounting** to bring all cash flows resulting from the investment to a present day value by eliminating the **interest** that would have been earned on that cash flow had it happened now rather than later.

The interest rate (referred to as **discount rate** in this context) used in this calculation is specific to each organisation, and depends on the relative levels of debt and equity funding of the organisation. This links to later studies in this text concerning cost of capital and capital structure.

Chapter 9 will look at how **inflation** and **taxation** can be incorporated into appraisal techniques.

Study guide

		Intellectual level
D1	**Investment appraisal techniques**	
(e)	Calculate net present value and discuss its usefulness as an investment appraisal method.	2
(f)	Calculate internal rate of return and discuss its usefulness as an investment appraisal method.	2
(g)	Discuss the superiority of DCF methods over non-DCF methods.	2
(h)	Discuss the relative merits of NPV and IRR.	2

Exam guide

You may be asked to discuss the relative merits of the various investment appraisal techniques as well as to demonstrate your ability to apply the techniques themselves.

Performance objective 9 requires you to 'value projects, financial securities and instruments and advise on their costs and benefits to the organisation'. This chapter concentrates on valuing projects using discounted cash flow techniques.

1 Discounted cash flow (Brought forward knowledge)

Knowledge brought forward from earlier studies

You should be familiar with the concepts of interest and discounting from your earlier studies. This section is included for revision purposes only.

There are two methods of using DCF to evaluate capital investments, the NPV method and the IRR method.

Discounted cash flow, or **DCF** for short, is an investment appraisal technique which takes into account both the timings of cash flows and also total profitability over a project's life.

Three important points about DCF are as follows.

(a) DCF looks at the **cash flows** of a project, not the accounting profits. Cash flows are considered because they show the costs and benefits of a project when they actually occur and ignore notional costs such as depreciation.

(b) Only **future incremental cash** inflows and outflows are considered. This means that costs incurred in the past (sunk costs) should be ignored. Costs which would need to be incurred regardless of whether or not the project is undertaken should also be ignored.

(c) The **timing** of cash flows is taken into account by **discounting them**. $1 earned today will be worth more than $1 earned after two years. This is partly due to the effect of inflation, and partly due to the greater certainty in having $1 in hand today compared with the promise of $1 in a year's time. In addition, cash we have in hand today can be spent or invested elsewhere: for example, put into a savings account to earn annual interest.

1.1 Compounding

Suppose that a company has $10,000 to invest, and wants to earn a return of 10% (compound interest) on its investments. This means that if the $10,000 could be invested at 10%, the value of the investment with interest would build up as follows.

(a) After 1 year $10,000 × (1.10) = $11,000
(b) After 2 years $10,000 × (1.10)^2 = $12,100
(c) After 3 years $10,000 × (1.10)^3 = $13,310 and so on.

This is **compounding**. Compounding tells us how much an investment will be worth at the end, and can be used to compare two projects with the same duration. The formula for the future value of an investment plus accumulated interest after n time periods is:

$$FV = PV (1 + r)^n$$

Where   FV   is the future value of the investment with interest
PV   is the initial or 'present' value of the investment
r   is the compound rate of return per time period, expressed as a proportion
(so 10% = 0.10, 5% = 0.05, and so on)
n   is the number of time periods

1.2 Discounting

Present value is the cash equivalent now of a sum of money receivable or payable at a stated future date, discounted at a specified rate of return.

Discounting starts with the future value, and converts a future value to a present value. Discounting tells us how much an investment will be worth in today's terms. This method can be used to compare two investments with different durations.

For example, if a company expects to earn a (compound) rate of return of 10% on its investments, how much would it need to invest now to have the following investments?

(a) $11,000 after 1 year
(b) $12,100 after 2 years
(c) $13,310 after 3 years

The answer is $10,000 in each case, and we can calculate it by discounting. The discounting formula to calculate the present value of a future sum of money at the end of n time periods is:

$$PV \;=\; FV \; \frac{1}{(1+r)^n}$$

Present value of 1 = $(1+r)^{-n}$ or $\dfrac{1}{(1+r)^n}$

(a) After 1 year, $11,000 × $\dfrac{1}{1.10}$ = $10,000

(b) After 2 years, $12,100 × $\dfrac{1}{1.10^2}$ = $10,000

(c) After 3 years, $13,310 × $\dfrac{1}{1.10^3}$ = $10,000

Discounting can be applied to both money receivable and also to money payable at a future date. By discounting all payments and receipts from a capital investment to a present value, they can be compared on a common basis at a value which takes account of when the various cash flows will take place.

Spender expects the cash inflow from an investment to be $40,000 after two years and another $30,000 after three years. Its target rate of return is 12%. Calculate the present value of these future returns, and explain what this present value signifies.

Answer

(a)

Year	Cash flow $	Discount factor 12%	Present value $
2	40,000	$\dfrac{1}{(1.12)^2} = 0.797$	31,880
3	30,000	$\dfrac{1}{(1.12)^3} = 0.712$	21,360 Total PV 53,240

(b)   The present value of the future returns, discounted at 12%, is $53,240. This means that if Spender can invest now to earn a return of 12% on its investments, it would have to invest $53,240 now to earn $40,000 after two years plus $30,000 after three years.

1.3 The discount factor

In the compounding and discounting examples above, we used the company's required rate of return as the discount factor. How do companies decide the rate of return that they require?

Imagine Company A has a bank account, earning 5% interest. When considering whether or not to invest in a project, the company's directors may use the bank interest rate as a benchmark. If the investment's rate of return is 3%, would Company A invest? Probably not, because a higher level of return can be earned by simply depositing the same amount of money in the bank account. However, if the investment's rate of return is 8%, then the company will probably choose to invest.

On the other hand, consider Company B, which has no cash in hand. It will be required to borrow from a bank should it decide to invest in a project. Company B's directors may use the loan interest as a benchmark when evaluating investments to ensure that they only accept projects which sufficiently reward the company for the additional costs the company has to bear in making the investment. If the company borrows at 6%, it will most likely reject a project which yields a rate of return of 3%. However, it may consider a project that is expected to yield a rate of return of 8%.

These examples are two simplistic ways of thinking about the **cost of capital**, often used to derive a **discount rate** for DCF analysis and investment appraisal.

The cost of capital has two aspects to it.

(a)   It is the **cost of funds** that a company raises and uses.

(b)   The return that investors expect to be paid for putting funds into the company. It is therefore the **minimum return** that a company should make from its own investments, to earn the cash flows out of which investors can be paid their return.

The cost of capital is not the cost of borrowing, although the cost of borrowing may be an element in the cost of capital. We will study the cost of capital in detail in Part E of this Study Text. For the purpose of this chapter, we shall assume that the cost of capital is a known required percentage annual rate of return on investments.

2 The net present value method

FAST FORWARD ▶▶

The **NPV method** of investment appraisal is to invest in projects with a positive NPV.

An **annuity** is a constant cash flow for a number of years. A **perpetuity** is a constant annual cash flow (an annuity) that will last forever.

Key terms

Net present value or **NPV** is the value obtained by discounting all cash outflows and inflows of a capital investment project by a chosen target rate of return or **cost of capital.**

The NPV method compares the **present value (PV)** of all the **cash inflows** from an investment with the **present value** of all the **cash outflows** from an investment. The NPV is thus calculated as the PV of **cash inflows** minus the PV of **cash outflows**.

NPV	
NPV positive	Return from investment's cash inflows in excess of cost of capital ⟹ undertake project
NPV negative	Return from investment's cash inflows below cost of capital ⟹ don't undertake project
NPV 0	Return from investment's cash inflows same as cost of capital

Note. We assume that the cost of capital is the organisation's target rate of return for proposed investment projects.

2.1 Example: NPV

A company is considering a capital investment, where the estimated cash flows are as follows.

Year		Cash flow
		$
0	(ie now)	(100,000)
1		60,000
2		80,000
3		40,000
4		30,000

The company's cost of capital is 15%. You are required to calculate the NPV of the project and to assess whether it should be undertaken.

Solution

Year	Cash flow	Discount factor 15%	Present value
	$		$
0	(100,000)	1.000	(100,000)
1	60,000	$\frac{1}{(1.15)} = 0.870$	52,200
2	80,000	$\frac{1}{(1.15)^2} = 0.756$	60,480
3	40,000	$\frac{1}{(1.15)^3} = 0.658$	26,320
4	30,000	$\frac{1}{(1.15)^4} = 0.572$	17,160
		NPV =	56,160

Note. The discount factor for any cash flow 'now' (year 0) is always = 1, regardless of what the cost of capital is.

In this example, the PV of cash inflows exceeds the PV of cash outflows by $56,160, which means that the project will earn a DCF yield in excess of 15%. It should therefore be undertaken.

(It may also be predicted that the investment should add $56,160 to the value of the company.)

2.2 Timing of cash flows: conventions used in DCF

Discounted cash flow applies discounting arithmetic to the relevant costs and benefits of an investment project. Discounting, which reduces the value of future cash flows to a present value equivalent, is clearly concerned with the timing of the cash flows. As a general rule, the following guidelines may be applied.

(a) A cash outlay to be incurred at the beginning of an investment project (**'now'**) occurs in **year 0**. The present value of $1 now, in year 0, is $1 regardless of the value of r.

(b) As explained earlier, a cash outlay, saving or inflow which occurs **during the course of a time period** (say, during a year) is assumed to occur all at once **at the end of the time period** (at the end of the year). Receipts of $10,000 during year 1 are therefore taken to occur at the end of year 1.

(c) A cash outlay or receipt which occurs **at the beginning of a time period** (say, at the beginning of one year) is taken to occur **at the end of the previous year**. Therefore a cash outlay of $5,000 at the beginning of year 2 is taken to occur at the end of year 1.

Exam focus point

> The ACCA examination team's reports suggest that candidates often get the timing of cash flows wrong, particularly initial investment, working capital and tax.

2.3 Discount tables for the PV of $1

The discount factor that we use in discounting is $\dfrac{1}{(1+r)^n} = (1+r)^{-n}$

Instead of having to calculate this factor every time, we can use tables. Discount tables for the present value of $1, for different values of r and n, are shown in the Appendix to this Study Text. Use these tables to work out your own solution to the following question.

Exam focus point

> Remember that interest should **not** be included as a cash flow. Interest is allowed for in the discount rate.

 Question   Net present value

LCH manufactures product X which it sells for $5 per unit. Variable costs of production are currently $3 per unit, and fixed costs 50c per unit. A new machine is available which would cost $90,000 but which could be used to make product X for a variable cost of only $2.50 per unit. Fixed costs, however, would increase by $7,500 per annum as a direct result of purchasing the machine. The machine would have an expected life of four years and a resale value after that time of $10,000. Sales of product X are estimated to be 75,000 units per annum. LCH expects to earn at least 12% per annum from its investments. Ignore taxation.

You are required to decide whether LCH should purchase the machine.

Answer

Savings are 75,000 × ($3 − $2.50) = $37,500 per annum.

Additional costs are $7,500 per annum.

Net cash savings are therefore $30,000 per annum. (Remember, depreciation is not a cash flow and must be ignored as a 'cost'.)

The first step in calculating an NPV is to establish the relevant costs year by year. All future cash flows arising as a direct consequence of the decision should be taken into account. It is assumed that the machine will be sold for $10,000 at the end of year 4.

Year	Cash flow $	PV factor 12%	PV of cash flow $
0	(90,000)	1.000	(90,000)
1	30,000	0.893	26,790
2	30,000	0.797	23,910
3	30,000	0.712	21,360
4	40,000	0.636	25,440
			NPV = +7,500

The NPV is positive and so the project is expected to earn more than 12% per annum and is therefore acceptable.

2.4 Annuity tables

In the previous exercise, the calculations could have been simplified for years 1-3 as follows.

$$
\begin{array}{ll}
 & 30,000 \times 0.893 \\
+ & 30,000 \times 0.797 \\
+ & 30,000 \times 0.712 \\
= & 30,000 \times 2.402
\end{array}
$$

Where there is a **constant cash flow** from year to year, we can calculate the present value by adding together the discount factors for the individual years.

These total factors could be described as 'same cash flow per annum' factors, 'cumulative present value' factors or **'annuity' factors**.

The present value of an annuity can be calculated by multiplying the annual cash flow in the annuity by the sum of all the discount factors for the years in the annuity.

Annuity factors for annuities beginning in one year's time (and for different costs of capital) are shown in the table for cumulative PV factors, which is shown in the Appendix to this Study Text. (2.402, for example, is in the column for 12% per annum and the row for three years.)

Question   **Annuities**

If you have not used them before, check that you can understand annuity tables by trying the following exercise.

(a)   What is the present value of $1,000 in contribution earned each year from years 1-10, when the required return on investment is 11%?

(b)   What is the present value of $2,000 costs incurred each year from years 3-6 when the cost of capital is 5%?

Answer

(a)   The PV of $1,000 earned each year from year 1-10 when the required earning rate of money is 11% is calculated as follows.

$1,000 × 5.889 = $5,889

(b) The PV of $2,000 in costs each year from years 3-6 when the cost of capital is 5% per annum is calculated as follows.

PV of $1 per annum for years 1-6 at 5% =	5.076
Less PV of $1 per annum for years 1-2 at 5% =	1.859
PV of $1 per annum for years 3-6 =	3.217

PV = $2,000 × 3.217 = $6,434

2.5 Annual cash flows in perpetuity

You also need to know how to calculate the cumulative present value of $1 per annum for every year in perpetuity (that is, forever).

Formula to learn

When the cost of capital is r, the cumulative PV of $1 per annum in perpetuity is **$1/r**.

For example, the PV of $1 per annum in perpetuity at a discount rate of 10% would be $1/0.10 = $10.

Similarly, the PV of $1 per annum in perpetuity at a discount rate of 15% would be $1/0.15 = $6.67 and at a discount rate of 20% it would be $1/0.20 = $5.

Question   Perpetuities

An organisation with a cost of capital of 14% is considering investing in a project costing $500,000. The project would yield nothing in Year 1, but from Year 2 would yield cash inflows of $100,000 per annum in perpetuity.

Required

Assess whether the project should be undertaken.

Answer

Year	Cash flow $	Discount factor 14%	Present value $
0	(500,000)	1.000	(500,000)
1	0	0.877	0
2–∞	100,000	1/0.14 × 0.877 = 6.264	626,429
			NPV = 126,429

The perpetuity of $100,000 per annum is calculated by multiplying $100,000 by 1/0.14. This gives a cumulative present value of cash inflows at Year 2 of $714,300.

However, because the cash inflows start only at Year 2, we need to discount the cash inflows back to today's value. This is done by using the present value factor of 0.877 (or $\frac{1}{(1+0.14)}$).

The NPV is positive and so the project should be undertaken.

Exam focus point

The ACCA examination team has often commented that candidates are often unable to evaluate cash flows in perpetuity. The formula for cash flows in perpetuity will not be provided in the exam, so make sure you learn it!

2.6 NPV and shareholder wealth maximisation

If a project has a positive NPV it offers a **higher return** than the return required by the company to provide satisfactory returns to its sources of finance. This means that the **company's value** is increased and the project contributes to shareholder wealth maximisation.

3 The internal rate of return method   12/07, 6/08, 6/09, 12/11

The **internal rate of return (IRR)** of an investment is the cost of capital at which its NPV would be exactly $0.

The **IRR method** of investment appraisal is an alternative to the NPV method for investment appraisal. This method is to accept investment projects whose IRR exceeds a target rate of return. The IRR is calculated approximately using a technique called interpolation.

Using the **NPV method of discounted cash flow**, present values are calculated by discounting at a target rate of return, or cost of capital, and the difference between the PV of costs and the PV of benefits is the NPV. In contrast, the **internal rate of return (IRR)** method is to calculate the **exact DCF rate of return** which the project is expected to achieve; in other words, the rate at which the **NPV is zero**. If the expected rate of return (the IRR or DCF yield) **exceeds** a **target rate** of return, the project would be worth undertaking (ignoring risk and uncertainty factors).

Without a computer or calculator program, the calculation of the internal rate of return is made using an approximating 'hit and miss' technique known as the interpolation method.

Step 1   Calculate the net present value using the company's cost of capital.

Step 2   Having calculated the NPV using the company's cost of capital, calculate the NPV using a second discount rate.

     (a)   If the NPV is **positive**, use a second rate that is **greater** than the first rate.

     (b)   If the NPV is **negative**, use a second rate that is **less** than the first rate.

Step 3   Use the two NPV values to **estimate the IRR**. The formula to apply is as follows.

Formula to learn

$$IRR \approx a + \left(\left(\frac{NPV_a}{NPV_a - NPV_b} \right)(b-a) \right)\%$$

Where   a   =   the lower of the two rates of return used
         b   =   the higher of the two rates of return used
       NPV_a =   the NPV obtained using rate a
       NPV_b =   the NPV obtained using rate b

Note. Ideally NPV_a will be a positive value and NPV_b will be negative. (If NPV_b is negative, then in the equation above you will be subtracting a negative, ie treating it as an added positive.)

Exam focus point

Do not worry if you have two positive or two negative values, since the above formula will extrapolate as well as interpolate. In the exam you will not have time to calculate NPVs using more than two rates.

3.1 Example: The IRR method

A company is trying to decide whether to buy a machine for $80,000 which will save costs of $20,000 per annum for five years and which will have a resale value of $10,000 at the end of year 5. If it is the company's policy to undertake projects only if they are expected to yield a DCF return of 10% or more, ascertain whether this project should be undertaken.

Solution

Step 1 Calculate the first NPV, using the company's cost of capital of 10%.

Year	Cash flow $	PV factor 10%	PV of cash flow $
0	(80,000)	1.000	(80,000)
1–5	20,000	3.791	75,820
5	10,000	0.621	6,210
			NPV = 2,030

This is positive, which means that the IRR is more than 10%.

Step 2 Calculate the second NPV, using a rate that is **greater** than the first rate, as the first rate gave a positive answer.

Suppose we try 12%.

Year	Cash flow $	PV factor 12%	PV of cash flow $
0	(80,000)	1.000	(80,000)
1–5	20,000	3.605	72,100
5	10,000	0.567	5,670
			NPV = (2,230)

This is fairly close to zero and **negative**. The IRR is therefore greater than 10% (positive NPV of $2,030) but less than 12% (negative NPV of $2,230).

Step 3 Use the two NPV values to estimate the IRR.

The interpolation method assumes that the NPV rises in linear fashion between the two NPVs close to 0. The IRR is therefore assumed to be on a straight line between NPV = $2,030 at 10% and NPV = –$2,230 at 12%.

Using the formula:

$$IRR \approx a + \left(\left(\frac{NPV_a}{NPV_a - NPV_b} \right)(b-a) \right) \%$$

$$IRR \approx 10 + \left[\frac{2,030}{2,030 + 2,230} \times (12-10) \right] \% = 10.95\%, \text{ say } 11\%$$

If it is company policy to undertake investments which are expected to yield 10% or more, this project would be undertaken.

If we were to draw a graph of a 'typical' capital project, with a negative cash flow at the start of the project, and positive net cash flows afterwards up to the end of the project, we could draw a graph of the project's NPV at different costs of capital. It would look like Figure 1 below.

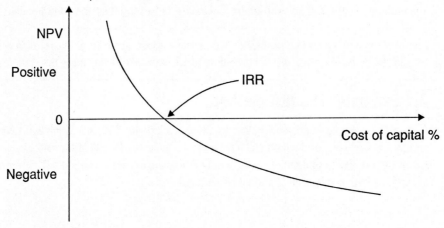

Figure 1

If we use a cost of capital where the NPV is slightly positive, and use another cost of capital where it is slightly negative, we can estimate the IRR – where the NPV is zero – by drawing a straight line between the two points on the graph that we have calculated. Figure 2 below illustrates this.

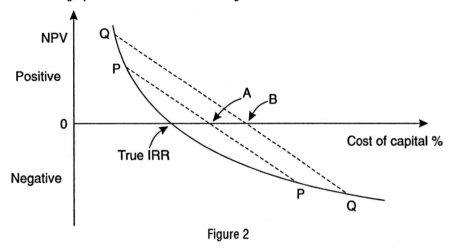

Figure 2

Consider Figure 2.

(a)   If we establish the NPVs at the two points P, we would estimate the IRR to be at point A.
(b)   If we establish the NPVs at the two points Q, we would estimate the IRR to be at point B.

The closer our NPVs are to zero, the closer our estimate will be to the true IRR.

Question
IRR

Find the IRR of the project given below and state whether the project should be accepted if the company requires a minimum return of 17%.

Time		$
0	Investment	(4,000)
1	Receipts	1,200
2	"	1,410
3	"	1,875
4	"	1,150

Answer

Time	Cash flow	Try 17% discount factor	Present value	Try 14% discount factor	Present value
	$		$		$
0	(4,000)	1.000	(4,000)	1.000	(4,000)
1	1,200	0.855	1,026	0.877	1,052
2	1,410	0.731	1,031	0.769	1,084
3	1,875	0.624	1,170	0.675	1,266
4	1,150	0.534	614	0.592	681
			NPV = (159)		NPV = 83

The IRR must be less than 17%, but higher than 14%. The NPVs at these two costs of capital will be used to estimate the IRR.

Using the interpolation formula:

$$IRR = 14\% + \left[\frac{83}{83+159} \times (17\% - 14\%) \right] = 15.03\%$$

The project should be rejected, as the IRR is less than the minimum return demanded.

4 NPV and IRR compared

6/08

 FAST FORWARD

There are **advantages and disadvantages** to each appraisal method. Make sure that you can discuss them.

Given that there are two methods of using DCF, the NPV method and the IRR method, the relative merits of each method have to be considered.

4.1 Advantages and disadvantages of IRR method

The main advantage of the IRR method is that the information it provides is **more easily understood** by managers, especially non-financial managers. For example, it is fairly easy to understand the meaning of the following statement.

'The project will be expected to have an initial capital outlay of $100,000, and to earn a yield of 25%. This is in excess of the target yield of 15% for investments.'

It is not so easy to understand the meaning of this statement.

'The project will cost $100,000 and have an NPV of $30,000 when discounted at the minimum required rate of 15%.'

However, managers may **confuse IRR** and accounting return on capital employed, **ROCE.**

The IRR method **ignores** the **relative size** of investments. Both the following projects have an IRR of 18%.

	Project A	Project B
	$	$
Cost, year 0	350,000	35,000
Annual savings, years 1-6	100,000	10,000

Clearly, project A is bigger (ten times as big) and so more 'profitable' but if the only information on which the projects were judged were to be their IRR of 18%, project B would be made to seem just as beneficial as project A, which is not the case.

4.2 Non-conventional cash flows

6/10

The projects we have considered so far have had conventional cash flows (an initial cash outflow followed by a series of inflows). When flows vary from this they are termed non-conventional. The following project has **non-conventional cash flows**.

Year	Project X
	$'000
0	(1,900)
1	4,590
2	(2,735)

Project X would have two IRRs as shown by this diagram.

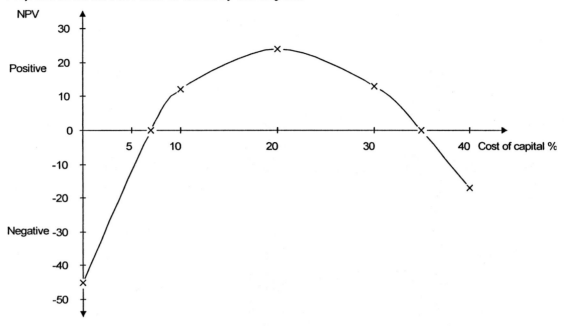

The NPV rule suggests that the project is acceptable between costs of capital of 7% and 35%.

Suppose that the required rate on project X is 10% and that the IRR of 7% is used in deciding whether to accept or reject the project. The project would be rejected since it appears that it can only yield 7%.

The diagram shows, however, that between rates of 7% and 35% the project should be accepted. Using the IRR of 35% would produce the correct decision to accept the project. **Lack of knowledge** of **multiple IRRs** could therefore lead to serious errors in the decision of whether to accept or reject a project.

In general, if the sign of the net cash flow changes in successive periods, the calculations may produce as many IRRs as there are sign changes. IRR should not normally be used when there are non-conventional cash flows.

Exam focus point	You need to be aware of the possibility of multiple IRRs, but the area is not examinable at a computational level.

4.3 Mutually exclusive projects

Mutually exclusive projects are two or more projects from which only one can be chosen. Examples include the choice of a factory location or the choice of just one of a number of machines. The IRR and NPV methods can, however, give conflicting rankings as to which project should be given priority.

Let us suppose that a company is considering two mutually exclusive options, option A and option B. The cash flows for each would be as follows.

Year		Option A $	Option B $
0	Capital outlay	(10,200)	(35,250)
1	Net cash inflow	6,000	18,000
2	Net cash inflow	5,000	15,000
3	Net cash inflow	3,000	15,000

The company's cost of capital is 16%.

The NPV of each project is calculated below.

		Option A		Option B	
Year	Discount factor	Cash flow	Present value	Cash flow	Present value
		$	$	$	$
0	1.000	(10,200)	(10,200)	(35,250)	(35,250)
1	0.862	6,000	5,172	18,000	15,516
2	0.743	5,000	3,715	15,000	11,145
3	0.641	3,000	1,923	15,000	9,615
			NPV = +610		NPV = +1,026

The IRR of option A is 20% and the IRR of option B is only 18% (workings not shown). On a comparison of NPVs, option B would be preferred, but on a comparison of IRRs, option A would be preferred.

If the projects were independent this would be irrelevant since under the NPV rule both would be accepted. With mutually exclusive projects, however, only one project can be accepted. Therefore the ranking is crucial and we cannot be indifferent to the outcomes of the NPV and IRR appraisal methods. The NPV method is preferable.

4.4 Reinvestment assumptions

An assumption underlying the NPV method is that any net cash inflows generated during the life of the project will be reinvested at the cost of capital (that is, the **discount rate**). The IRR method, on the other hand, assumes these cash flows can be reinvested to earn a return equal to the IRR of the original project.

In the example above, the NPV method assumes that the cash inflows of $6,000, $5,000 and $3,000 for option A will be reinvested at the cost of capital of 16% whereas the IRR method assumes they will be reinvested at 20%. In theory, a firm will have accepted all projects which provide a return in excess of the cost of capital. Any other funds which become available can only be reinvested at the cost of capital. This is the assumption implied in the NPV rule, but is unlikely to be the case in practice.

4.5 Summary of NPV and IRR comparison

(a) When cash flow patterns are conventional both methods give the **same** accept or reject **decision**.

(b) The IRR method is **more easily understood**.

(c) NPV is **technically superior** to IRR and simpler to calculate.

(d) **IRR** and **accounting ROCE** can be **confused**.

(e) **IRR ignores** the **relative sizes** of investments.

(f) Where cash flow patterns are non-conventional, there may be **several IRRs** which decision-makers must be aware of to avoid making the wrong decision.

(g) The **NPV method** is superior for **ranking mutually exclusive projects** in order of attractiveness.

(h) The **reinvestment assumption** underlying the **IRR** method cannot be **substantiated**.

(i) When **discount rates** are **expected to differ** over the life of the project, such **variations** can be incorporated easily into **NPV** calculations, but not into IRR calculations.

(j) Despite the advantages of the NPV method over the IRR method, the **IRR method** is **widely used** in practice.

5 Assessment of DCF methods of project appraisal   12/10

DCF methods of appraisal have a number of advantages over other appraisal methods.

- The time value of money is taken into account.
- The method takes account of all a project's cash flows.
- It allows for the timing of cash flows.
- There are universally accepted methods of calculating the NPV and IRR.

5.1 Advantages of DCF methods

DCF is a capital appraisal technique that is based on a concept known as the time value of money: the concept that $1 received today is not equal to $1 received in the future. Given the choice between receiving $100 today and $100 in one year's time, most people would opt to receive $100 today because they could spend it or invest it to earn interest. If the interest rate was 10%, you could invest $100 today and it would be worth ($100 × 1.10) = $110 in one year's time.

There are, however, other reasons why a present $1 is worth more than a future $1.

(a) **Uncertainty.** Although there might be a promise of money to come in the future, it can never be certain that the money will be received until it has actually been paid.

(b) **Inflation.** Inflation also means $1 now is worth more than $1 in the future because of inflation. The time value of money concept applies even if there is zero inflation but inflation obviously increases the discrepancy in value between monies received at different times.

Taking account of the time value of money (by discounting) is one of the principal advantages of the DCF appraisal method. Other advantages are as follows.

- The method uses **all relevant cash flows** relating to the project.
- It allows for the **timing** of the cash flows.
- There are **universally accepted methods** of calculating the NPV and the IRR.

5.2 Problems with DCF methods

Although DCF methods are theoretically the best methods of investment appraisal, you should be aware of their limitations.

(a) DCF methods use **future cash flows** that may be difficult to forecast. Although other methods use these as well, arguably the problem is greater with DCF methods that take cash flows into the longer term.

(b) The basic decision rule, accept all projects with a positive NPV, will not apply when the capital available for investment is **rationed**.

(c) The **cost of capital** used in DCF calculations may be **difficult to estimate**.

(d) The **cost of capital** may **change** over the life of the investment.

5.3 The use of appraisal methods in practice   6/11

One reason for the failure of many businesses to use NPV is that its (sometimes long-term) nature may conflict with judgements on a business that are concerned with its (short-term) profits. **Managers' remuneration** may depend on the level of annual profits, and they may thus be unwilling to risk large initial expenditure on a project that only offers good returns in the significantly uncertain long term.

In addition, the NPV method is based on the assumption that businesses seek to **maximise** the **wealth of their shareholders**. As discussed previously, this may conflict with the interests of other stakeholders. Public sector organisations will be concerned with the **social opportunity costs**.

Even when **wealth maximisation** is the key objective, there may be factors that help maximise wealth but cannot be quantified for NPV purposes, for example investment in a loss-making project for strategic reasons such as obtaining an initial share in an important market.

<table>
<tr><td>Exam focus
point</td><td>The ACCA examination team has emphasised that investment appraisal is about modelling the real world situation. Any discussion of investment appraisal techniques must be applied to the scenario in the question and should not be just a list of generally applicable points.</td></tr>
</table>

Chapter Roundup

- The **NPV method** of investment appraisal is to invest in projects with a positive NPV.

  An **annuity** is a constant cash flow for a number of years. A **perpetuity** is a constant annual cash flow (an annuity) that will last forever.

- The **internal rate of return (IRR)** of an investment is the cost of capital at which its NPV would be exactly $0.

  The **IRR method** of investment appraisal is an alternative to the NPV method for investment appraisal. This method is to accept investment projects whose IRR exceeds a target rate of return. The IRR is calculated approximately using a technique called interpolation.

- There are **advantages and disadvantages** to each appraisal method. Make sure that you can discuss them.

- **DCF methods of appraisal** have a number of **advantages** over other appraisal methods.
  - The time value of money is taken into account.
  - The method takes account of all a project's cash flows.
  - It allows for the timing of cash flows.
  - There are universally accepted methods of calculating the NPV and IRR.

Quick Quiz

1   What is the formula for calculating the future value of an investment plus accumulated interest after n time periods?

2   What is the formula for calculating the present value of a future sum of money at the end of n time periods?

3   List three cash flow timing conventions used in DCF.

4   What is the perpetuity formula?

5   List three advantages of the DCF method of project appraisal over other appraisal methods.

6   For a certain project, the net present value at a discount rate of 15% is $3,670, and at a rate of 18% the net present value is negative at ($1,390). What is the internal rate of return of the project?

   A   15.7%
   B   16.5%
   C   16.6%
   D   17.2%

7   Tick the correct box to indicate whether or not the following items are included in the cash flows when determining the net present value of a project.

	Included	Not included
(a) The disposal value of equipment at the end of its life	☐	☐
(b) Depreciation charges for the equipment	☐	☐
(c) Research costs incurred prior to the appraisal	☐	☐
(d) Interest payments on the loan to finance the investment	☐	☐

1      $FV = PV (1 + r)^n$

2      $PV = FV \dfrac{1}{(1+r)^n}$

3   (a)   A cash outlay to be incurred at the beginning of an investment project occurs in year 0.

        (b)   A cash outlay, saving or inflow which occurs during the course of a time period is assumed to occur all at once at the end of the time period.

        (c)   A cash outlay or receipt that occurs at the beginning of a time period is taken to occur at the end of the time period.

4   Annual cash flow/discount rate

5   (a)   It takes account of the time value of money.
        (b)   It uses all cash flows relating to a project.
        (c)   It allows for the timing of cash flows.

6   D $15\% + \{(3{,}670/[3{,}670 + 1{,}390]) \times 3\%\} = 17.2\%$

7   (a)   Included
        (b)   Not included (non-cash)
        (c)   Not included (past cost)
        (d)   Not included (included in the discount rate)

Now try the questions below from the Practice Question Bank

Number	Level	Marks	Approximate time
Section A Q18	Examination	2	4 mins
Section C Q6	Introductory	N/A	39 mins
Section C Q7	Examination	20	39 mins
Section C Q8	Introductory	N/A	39 mins

Allowing for inflation and taxation

Topic list	Syllabus reference
1 Allowing for inflation	D2 (a)
2 Allowing for taxation	D2 (b), (c)
3 NPV layout	D2 (b), (c)

Introduction

Having covered the more sophisticated of the investment appraisal techniques which are available in Chapter 8, we will be looking in this chapter at how to incorporate **inflation** and **taxation** into investment decisions. A key concept in this chapter which you must grasp is the difference between **nominal rates of return** and **real rates of return**, and when each is to be used as the discount rate.

The next chapter will consider how the **risk** associated with a project can be assessed and taken into account.

Study guide

		Intellectual level
D2	**Allowing for inflation and taxation in investment appraisal**	
(a)	Apply and discuss the real terms and nominal terms approaches to investment appraisal.	2
(b)	Calculate the taxation effects of relevant cash flows, including the tax benefits of capital allowances and the tax liabilities of taxable profit.	2
(c)	Calculate and apply before- and after-tax discount rates.	2

Exam guide

As well as bringing inflation into your DCF calculations, you may be asked to explain the differences between real and nominal rates. In a 20-mark question, you can expect to have to deal with inflation, tax and working capital in an NPV question.

1 Allowing for inflation 6/08, 12/08, 6/13, 12/13, 6/14, 12/14, 6/15

FAST FORWARD

Inflation is a feature of all economies, and it must be accommodated in financial planning.

Real cash flows (cash flows in current prices) should be discounted at a **real discount rate**, which is a return ignoring inflation.

Nominal cash flows (the actual expected cash flows at future prices, ie including inflationary increases) should be discounted at a **nominal discount rate**, which is a rate relating to current market rates of return.

So far we have not considered the effect of **inflation** on the appraisal of capital investment proposals. As the inflation rate increases, so will the minimum return required by an investor. For example, you might be happy with a return of 5% in an inflation-free world, but if inflation were running at 15% you would expect a considerably greater yield.

The **nominal interest rate** incorporates inflation. When the nominal rate of interest is higher than the rate of inflation, there is a **positive** real rate. When the rate of inflation is higher than the nominal rate of interest, the real rate of interest will be **negative**.

The relationship between real and nominal rates of interest is given by the Fisher formula.

Formula to learn

$$(1 + i) = (1 + r)(1 + h)$$

Where h = rate of inflation
         r = real rate of interest
         i = nominal (money) rate of interest

1.1 Example: Inflation (1)

A company is considering investing in a project with the following cash flows.

Time	Actual cash flows
	$
0	(15,000)
1	9,000
2	8,000
3	7,000

The company requires a minimum return of 20% under the present and anticipated conditions. Inflation is currently running at 10% a year, and this rate of inflation is expected to continue indefinitely. Should the company go ahead with the project?

Let us first look at the company's required rate of return. Suppose that it invested $1,000 for one year on 1 January, then on 31 December it would require a minimum return of $200. With the initial investment of $1,000, the total value of the investment by 31 December must therefore increase to $1,200. During the course of the year the purchasing value of the dollar would fall due to inflation. We can restate the amount received on 31 December in terms of the purchasing power of the dollar at 1 January as follows.

Amount received on 31 December in terms of the value of the pound at 1 January = $\dfrac{\$1,200}{(1.10)^1}$ = $1,091

In terms of the value of the dollar at 1 January, the company would make a profit of $91 which represents a rate of return of 9.1% in 'today's money' terms. This is **the real rate of return**. The required rate of 20% is a **nominal rate of return** (sometimes called a **money rate of return**). The **nominal rate** measures the return in terms of the **dollar** which is, of course, falling in value. The **real rate** measures the return in **constant price level** terms.

The two rates of return and the inflation rate are linked by the equation $(1 + i) = (1 + r)(1 + h)$ where all rates are expressed as proportions.

In our example, $(1 + 0.2)$ = $(1 + r)(1 + 0.1)$

$$1 + r \ = \ \frac{1.2}{1.1} = 1.091$$

$$r \ = \ 9.1\%$$

Exam focus point

You may be asked in the exam to explain the difference between a real and nominal terms analysis.

1.2 Do we use the real rate or the nominal rate?

The rule is as follows.

(a)   If the cash flows are expressed in terms of the **actual number of dollars** that will be **received** or **paid** on the **various future dates**, we use the **nominal rate** for discounting.

(b)   If the cash flows are expressed in terms of the **value of the dollar at time 0** (that is, in constant price level terms), we use the **real rate**.

The cash flows given above are expressed in terms of the **actual number** of **dollars** that will be received or paid at the relevant dates (nominal cash flows). We should, therefore, discount them using the **nominal rate of return**.

Time	Cash flow	Discount factor 20%	PV
	$		$
0	(15,000)	1.000	(15,000)
1	9,000	0.833	7,497
2	8,000	0.694	5,552
3	7,000	0.579	4,053
			2,102

The project has a positive net present value of $2,102.

The future cash flows can be re-expressed in terms of the value of the dollar at time 0 by deflating them as follows, given that inflation is at 10% a year.

Time	Actual cash flow $	Cash flow at time 0 price level		Cash flow at time 0 price level $
0	(15,000)			(15,000)
1	9,000	$9,000 \times \dfrac{1}{1.10}$	=	8,182
2	8,000	$8,000 \times \dfrac{1}{(1.10)^2}$	=	6,612
3	7,000	$7,000 \times \dfrac{1}{(1.10)^3}$	=	5,259

The cash flows expressed in terms of the value of the dollar at time 0 (real cash flows) can now be discounted using the real rate of 9.1%.

Time	Cash flow $	Discount factor 9.1%	PV $
0	(15,000)	1.00	(15,000)
1	8,182	$\dfrac{1}{1.091}$	7,500
2	6,612	$\dfrac{1}{(1.091)^2}$	5,555
3	5,259	$\dfrac{1}{(1.091)^3}$	4,050
			NPV = 2,105

The NPV is the same as before (and the present value of the cash flow in each year is the same as before) apart from rounding errors.

1.3 The advantages and misuses of real values and a real rate of return

Although generally companies should discount monetary values at the nominal cost of capital, there are some advantages of using real values discounted at a real cost of capital.

(a) When all costs and benefits rise at the same rate of price inflation, **real values** are the **same as current day values**, so that no **further adjustments** need to be made to cash flows before discounting. In contrast, when nominal values are discounted at the nominal cost of capital, the **prices** in **future years** must be **calculated** before discounting can begin.

(b) The Government might prefer to set a **real return** as a target for investments, being more suitable than a commercial money rate of return.

1.3.1 Costs and benefits which inflate at different rates

Not all costs and benefits will rise in line with the general level of inflation. In such cases, we can apply the **nominal rate** to **inflated values** to determine a project's NPV.

1.4 Example: Inflation (2)

Rice is considering a project which would cost $5,000 now. The annual benefits, for four years, would be a fixed income of $2,500 a year, plus other savings of $500 a year in year 1, rising by 5% each year because of inflation. Running costs will be $1,000 in the first year, but would increase at 10% each year because of inflating labour costs. The general rate of inflation is expected to be 7½% and the company's required nominal rate of return is 16%. Is the project worthwhile? Ignore taxation.

Solution

The cash flows at inflated values are as follows.

Year	Fixed income $	Other savings $	Running costs $	Net cash flow $
1	2,500	500	1,000	2,000
2	2,500	525	1,100	1,925
3	2,500	551	1,210	1,841
4	2,500	579	1,331	1,748

The NPV of the project is as follows.

Year	Cash flow $	Discount factor 16%	PV $
0	(5,000)	1.000	(5,000)
1	2,000	0.862	1,724
2	1,925	0.743	1,430
3	1,841	0.641	1,180
4	1,748	0.552	965
			+ 299

The NPV is positive and the project would therefore seem to be worthwhile.

1.4.1 Variations in the expected rate of inflation

If the rate of inflation is expected to change, the calculation of the nominal cost of capital is slightly more complicated.

1.5 Example: Inflation (3)

Mr Gable has just received a dividend of $1,000 on his shareholding in Gonwithy Windmills. The market value of the shares is $8,000 ex div. What is the (nominal) cost of the equity capital, if dividends are expected to rise because of inflation by 10% in years 1, 2 and 3, before levelling off at this year 3 amount?

Solution

The nominal cost of equity capital is the internal rate of return of the following cash flows.

Year	Cash flow $	PV factor 15%	PV at 15% $	PV factor 20%	PV at 20% $
0	(8,000)	1.000	(8,000)	1.000	(8,000)
1	1,100	0.870	957	0.833	916
2	1,210	0.756	915	0.694	840
3–∞*	1,331 pa	5.041	6,709	3.472	4,621
			581		(1,623)

The IRR is approximately $15\% + \left[\dfrac{581}{581 - - 1{,}623} \times (20 - 15) \right] \% = 16.3\%$, say 16%

* The present value factor = (Factor 1 – ∞) – (Factor yrs 1-2).

For 15%

PV factor $= \dfrac{1}{0.15} - 1.626 = 5.041$

For 20%

PV factor $= \dfrac{1}{0.2} - 1.528 = 3.472$

1.6 Expectations of inflation and the effects of inflation

When managers evaluate a particular project, or when shareholders evaluate their investments, they can only guess at what the rate of inflation is going to be. Their expectations will probably be inaccurate, because it is extremely difficult to forecast the rate of inflation correctly. The only way in which uncertainty about inflation can be allowed for in project evaluation is by **risk** and **uncertainty analysis**. Plans should be made to obtain **'contingency funds'**, for example a higher bank overdraft facility if the rate of inflation exceeds expectations.

Inflation may be **general**, affecting prices of all kinds, or **specific** to particular prices. Generalised inflation has the following effects.

(a) Since non-current assets and inventories will increase in monetary value, the same quantities of assets must be financed by **increasing amounts** of capital.

(b) Inflation means higher costs and **higher selling prices**. The effect of higher prices on demand may **not** be **easy to predict**. A company that raises its prices by 10% because the general rate of inflation is running at 10% might suffer a serious fall in demand.

(c) Inflation, because it affects financing needs, is also likely to affect **gearing**, and so the **cost of capital**.

1.7 Mid-year and end of year monetary values

You might wonder why, in all the examples so far, the cash flows have been inflated to the end of year money prices. Inflation does not usually run at a steady rate.

In DCF calculations it is more appropriate to use **end of year monetary values**. This is because, by convention, all **cash flows** are assumed to **occur** at the **end of the year**, and a discount factor appropriate to the end of the year is applied.

2 Allowing for taxation   12/07, 6/08, 12/08, 12/13, 6/14, 12/14, 6/15

FAST FORWARD

Taxation is a major practical consideration for businesses. It is vital to take it into account in making decisions.

In investment appraisal, tax is often assumed to be payable **one year in arrears**. Tax-allowable depreciation details should be checked in any question you attempt.

So far, in looking at project appraisal, we have ignored **taxation**. However, payments of tax, or reductions of tax payments, are cash flows and ought to be considered in DCF analysis. Assumptions which may be stated in questions are as follows.

(a) Tax is payable **in the year following** the one in which the taxable profits are made. Thus, if a project increases taxable profits by $10,000 in year 2, there will be a tax payment, assuming tax at 30%, of $3,000 in year 3. (However, a question may state that tax is payable in the same year as the year in which the cash flows giving rise to the tax occur. Read the question carefully.)

(b) Net operating cash flows from a project should be considered as the **taxable profits** (not just the taxable revenues) arising from the project (unless an indication is given to the contrary). This assumption means that you can ignore adjustments that may otherwise have to be made for depreciation (not an allowable charge for tax purposes) and the tax relief rules on investment.

Exam focus point

Check any question involving tax carefully to see what assumptions about tax rates are made. Also look out for questions which state that tax is payable in the same year as that in which the profits arise. The June 2014 exam contained an NPV question with a tax rate of 28%. The ACCA examination team commented that some students used a rate of 30%. Make sure that you read the question carefully to avoid this type of simple error.

2.1 Tax-allowable depreciation

Tax-allowable depreciation (capital allowances) is used to reduce taxable profits, and the consequent reduction in a tax payment should be treated as a **cash saving** arising from the acceptance of a project. Tax-allowable depreciation is not the same as the depreciation charge for the purpose of reporting profit in the financial statements.

For example, suppose tax-allowable depreciation is allowed on the cost of **plant and machinery** at the rate of 25% on a **reducing balance** basis. Thus if a company purchases plant costing $80,000, the subsequent writing down allowances would be as follows.

Year		Tax-allowable depreciation $	Reducing balance $
1	(25% of cost)	20,000	60,000
2	(25% of RB)	15,000	45,000
3	(25% of RB)	11,250	33,750
4	(25% of RB)	8,438	25,312

When the plant is eventually sold, the difference between the sale price and the reducing balance amount at the time of sale will be treated as:

(a) A taxable profit if the sale price exceeds the reducing balance
(b) A tax-allowable loss if the reducing balance exceeds the sale price

Exam focus point

Examination questions often assume that this loss will be available immediately, though in practice the balance less the sale price continues to be written off at 25% a year as part of a pool balance.

The **cash saving on tax-allowable depreciation** (or the cash payment for the charge) is calculated by multiplying the amount of the tax-allowable depreciation by the tax rate. If tax cash flows occur in the year following the year in which the item giving rise to the tax occurs, the cash flow for the tax saving from tax-allowable depreciation will occur in the year following the year in which the allowance is claimed.

In the example above, for instance, if the rate of tax on profits is 30%, the tax-allowable depreciation for Year 1 will be $6,000 (= $20,000 × 30%) and this cash flow saving will occur in Year 2.

Assumptions about tax-allowable depreciation could be **simplified** in an **exam question**. For example, you might be told that tax-allowable depreciation can be claimed at the rate of 25% of cost on a straight line basis (that is, over four years).

There are two possible assumptions about the time when tax-allowable depreciation starts to be claimed.

(a) It can be assumed that the first claim occurs at the **start** of the **project** (at year 0).
(b) Alternatively it can be assumed that the **first claim** occurs **later** in the **first year**.

Examination questions will generally indicate which of the two assumptions is required but you should state your assumptions clearly if you have to make assumptions. Assumption (b) is easier to use since there is one claim for tax-allowable depreciation for each year of the project.

Exam focus point

A common mistake in exams is to include the tax-allowable depreciation itself in the NPV calculation; it is the **tax effect** of the allowance that should be included.

2.2 Example: Taxation

A company is considering whether or not to purchase an item of machinery costing $40,000 payable immediately. It would have a life of four years, after which it would be sold for $5,000. The machinery would create annual cost savings of $14,000.

The company pays tax one year in arrears at an annual rate of 30% and can claim tax-allowable depreciation on a 25% reducing balance basis. A balancing allowance is claimed in the final year of operation. The company's cost of capital is 8%.

Should the machinery be purchased?

Solution

Year	Tax-allowable depreciation	$	Year	Tax benefits $
1	40,000 × 0.25	10,000	2	10,000 × 0.3 = 3,000
2	10,000 × 0.75	7,500	3	7,500 × 0.3 = 2,250
3	7,500 × 0.75	5,625	4	5,625 × 0.3 = 1,688
		23,125		
4	By difference	11,875	5	11,875 × 0.3 = 3,563
	40,000 – 5,000	35,000		

The extra tax payments on annual cost savings of $14,000 = 0.3 × 14,000 = $4,200

Calculation of NPV

	0 $	1 $	2 $	3 $	4 $	5 $
Machine costs	(40,000)				5,000	
Cost savings		14,000	14,000	14,000	14,000	
Tax on cost saving			(4,200)	(4,200)	(4,200)	(4,200)
Tax benefits from tax-allowable depreciation			3,000	2,250	1,688	3,563
After-tax cash flow	(40,000)	14,000	12,800	12,050	16,488	(637)
Discount factor @ 8%	1.000	0.926	0.857	0.794	0.735	0.681
Present values	(40,000)	12,964	10,970	9,568	12,119	(434)

The net present value is $5,187 and so the purchase appears to be worthwhile.

2.3 Taxation and DCF

The effect of taxation on capital budgeting is theoretically quite simple. Organisations must pay tax, and the effect of undertaking a project will be to increase or decrease tax payments each year. These incremental tax cash flows should be included in the cash flows of the project for discounting to arrive at the project's NPV.

When **taxation is ignored** in the DCF calculations, the discount rate will reflect the **pre-tax rate of return** required on capital investments. When **taxation is included** in the cash flows, a **post-tax required rate of return** should be used.

Question	DCF and taxation

A company is considering the purchase of an item of equipment, which would earn profits before tax of $25,000 a year. Depreciation charges would be $20,000 a year for six years. Tax-allowable depreciation would be $30,000 a year for the first four years. Tax is at 30%.

What would the annual net cash inflows of the project be:

(a)   For the first four years?
(b)   For the fifth and sixth years?

Assume that tax payments occur in the same year as the profits giving rise to them, and there is no balancing charge or allowance when the machine is scrapped at the end of the sixth year.

(a)

	Years 1-4	Years 5-6
	$	$
Profit before tax	25,000	25,000
Add back depreciation	20,000	20,000
Net cash inflow before tax	45,000	45,000
Less tax-allowable depreciation	30,000	0
	15,000	45,000
Tax at 30%	4,500	13,500

Years 1-4 Net cash inflow after tax $45,000 – $4,500 = $40,500

(b) Years 5-6 Net cash inflow after tax = $45,000 – $13,500 = $31,500

Question   **Tax implications**

A company is considering the purchase of a machine for $150,000. It would be sold after four years for an estimated realisable value of $50,000. By this time tax-allowable depreciation of $120,000 would have been claimed. The rate of tax is 30%.

What are the tax implications of the sale of the machine at the end of four years?

Answer

There will be a balancing charge on the sale of the machine of $(50,000 – (150,000 – 120,000)) = $20,000. This will give rise to a tax payment of 30% × $20,000 = $6,000.

Exam focus point

In reality, tax on profits may be paid quarterly but the timing is simplified in a DCF calculation and an exam question will tell you what assumptions to use.

3 NPV layout

When answering an NPV question, you may find it helpful to use the following layout. The most important thing to notice is that tax on cash profits and cash flows arising from tax-allowable depreciation can be calculated and presented separately. There is no need to combine them into a single cash flow figure for tax.

	Year 0	Year 1	Year 2	Year 3	Year 4
Sales receipts		X	X	X	
Costs	—	(X)	(X)	(X)	—
Sales less costs		X	X	X	
Taxation on profits		(X)	(X)	(X)	(X)
Capital expenditure	(X)				
Scrap value				X	
Working capital	(X)			X	
Tax benefit of tax dep'n	—	X	X	X	X
	(X)	X	X	X	(X)
Discount factors @					
post-tax cost of capital	X	X	X	X	X
Present value	(X)	X	X	X	(X)

3.1 Working capital and inflation 6/08, 12/08, 12/13

We saw how to calculate working capital cash flows in Chapter 4. This calculation is complicated when inflation is also to be considered.

When working capital is recovered at the end of the project it has a different nominal value to the working capital that was invested at the beginning. The nominal value of the investment should be inflated each period to maintain its real value. If the inflation rate is known then the incremental working capital can be included in the NPV appraisal as a relevant cost. The full nominal value of the working capital investment is recovered at the end of the project.

If for example a three-year project required $500,000 of working capital initially, the inflation rate was 5% and the working capital is recovered at the end of the project, then the relevant cash flows would be:

Year	0	1	2	3
Working capital	(500,000)	(25,000)	(26,250)	551,250

Exam focus point

> The ACCA examination team has commented that the treatment of working capital investment has been a source of regular errors.

Chapter Roundup

- **Inflation** is a feature of all economies, and it must be accommodated in financial planning.

  Real cash flows (cash flows in current prices) should be discounted at a **real discount rate**, which is a return ignoring inflation.

  Nominal cash flows (the actual expected cash flows at future prices, ie including inflationary increases) should be discounted at a nominal discount rate, which is a rate relating to current market rates of return.

- **Taxation** is a major practical consideration for businesses. It is vital to take it into account in making decisions.

  In investment appraisal, tax is often assumed to be payable **one year in arrears**. Tax-allowable depreciation details should be checked in any question you attempt.

Quick Quiz

1 What is the relationship between the nominal rate of return, the real rate of return and the rate of inflation?

2 The nominal cost of capital is 11%. The expected annual rate of inflation is 5%. What is the real cost of capital?

3 A company wants a minimum real return of 3% a year on its investments. Inflation is expected to be 8% a year. What is the company's minimum nominal cost of capital?

4 Summarise briefly how taxation is taken into consideration in capital budgeting.

5 A company is appraising an investment that will save electricity costs. Electricity prices are expected to rise at a rate of 15% per annum in future, although the general inflation rate will be 10% per annum. The nominal cost of capital for the company is 20%. What is the appropriate discount rate to apply to the forecast actual nominal cash flows for electricity?

   A   20.0%
   B   22.0%
   C   26.5%
   D   32.0%

6 Choose the correct words from those highlighted.

   Tax-allowable depreciation is used to (1) **increase/reduce** taxable profits, and the consequent reduction in a tax payment should be treated as a (2) **cash saving/cash payment** arising from the acceptance of a project.

   When the plant is eventually sold, the difference between the sales price and the reducing balance amount will be treated as a (3) **taxable profit/tax-allowable loss** if the sales price exceeds the reducing balance, and as a (4) **taxable profit/tax-allowable loss** if the reducing balance exceeds the sales price.

7 If cash flows are expressed in terms of the actual number of pounds that will be received or paid on various future dates, should the nominal rate or real rate be used for discounting?

8 Red Co is considering the purchase of a machine for $2,190,000. It would be sold after four years for an estimated realisable value of $790,000. By this time tax-allowable depreciation of $1,450,000 would have been claimed. The rate of tax is 30%.

   What is the cash flow arising as a result of tax implications on the sale of the machine at the end of four years?

   A   Inflow of $15,000
   B   Outflow of $50,000
   C   Outflow of $459,000
   D   Outflow of $15,000

1   (1 + nominal rate) = (1 + real rate) × (1 + inflation rate)

2    $\dfrac{1.11}{1.05}$ = 1.057. The real cost of capital is 5.7%.

3   1.03 × 1.08 = 1.1124. The nominal cost of capital is 11.24%.

4   If tax is included in the cash flows, the post-tax rate of required return on capital investments should be used. If tax is ignored, the discount rate should reflect the pre-tax rate of return.

5   A   The nominal rate of 20% is applied to the nominal cash flows.

6   (1)   Reduce
    (2)   Cash saving
    (3)   Taxable profit
    (4)   Tax-allowable loss

7   The nominal rate

8   D   There will be a balancing charge on the sale of the machine of $(790,000 − (2,190,000 − 1,450,000)) = $50,000. This will give rise to a tax payment of 30% × $50,000 = $15,000.

Now try the questions below from the Practice Question Bank

Number	Level	Marks	Approximate time
Section A Q19	Examination	2	4 mins
Section C Q9	Introductory	N/A	39 mins
Section C Q10	Introductory	N/A	39 mins

10

Project appraisal and risk

Topic list	Syllabus reference
1 Risk and uncertainty	D3 (a)
2 Sensitivity analysis	D3 (b)
3 Probability analysis	D3 (c)
4 Other risk adjustment techniques	D3 (d), D1 (c)

Introduction

This chapter will show some of the different methods of assessing and taking account of the **risk** and **uncertainty** associated with a project. The next chapter of this Study Text will consider two further project appraisal topics – **capital rationing** and **leasing**.

Study guide

		Intellectual level
D1	**Investment appraisal process techniques**	
(c)	Calculate discounted payback and discuss its usefulness as an investment appraisal method.	2
D3	**Adjusting for risk and uncertainty in investment appraisal**	
(a)	Describe and discuss the difference between risk and uncertainty in relation to probabilities and increasing project life.	2
(b)	Apply sensitivity analysis to investment projects and discuss the usefulness of sensitivity analysis in assisting investment decisions.	2
(c)	Apply probability analysis to investment projects and discuss the usefulness of probability analysis in assisting investment decisions.	2
(d)	Apply and discuss other techniques of adjusting for risk and uncertainty in investment appraisal, including:	
(i)	Simulation	1
(ii)	Adjusted payback	1
(iii)	Risk-adjusted discount rates	2

Exam guide

Risk and uncertainty are increasingly examinable in financial management exams and sensitivity calculations are particularly important. You will need to be able to explain these techniques as well as be confident and competent with the calculations.

1 Risk and uncertainty   12/07, 6/11

FAST FORWARD

Risk analysis can be applied to a proposed capital investment where there are several possible outcomes and, on the basis of past relevant experience, probabilities can be assigned to the various outcomes and estimated cash flows that could prevail.

Uncertainty analysis can be applied to a proposed capital investment where there are several possible outcomes but there is little past relevant experience to enable the probability of the alternative outcomes to be predicted.

There are a wide range of techniques for incorporating risk into project appraisal.

A distinction should be made between the terms risk and uncertainty.

Risk	• Several possible outcomes
	• On basis of past relevant experience, assign **probabilities** to outcomes
	• Increases as the variability of returns increases
Uncertainty	• Several possible outcomes
	• Little past experience, thus difficult to assign probabilities to outcomes
	• Increases as project life increases

A risky situation is one where we can say that there is a 70% probability that returns from a project will be $150,000 and a 30% probability that returns will be less than $50,000. This is more risky than an investment where there is a 70% probability that returns will be $110,000 and a 30% probability that returns will be $90,000. The variability of returns, which could be measured statistically, is lower with this second investment, which is why it is less risky.

If, however, no information can be provided about the probabilities of different returns from the project, we are faced with an uncertain situation. For example, we might estimate that returns from an investment could be anything between $150,000 and $50,000, but we can't estimate probabilities. This would be uncertainty about the investment returns.

In general, risky projects are those whose predicted possible future cash flows, and therefore the project returns, are more variable. The greater the variability, the greater the risk. The problem of risk is more acute with capital investment decisions than other decisions for the following reasons.

(a)   **Estimates** of capital expenditure might be for **several years ahead**, such as for major construction projects. Actual costs may escalate well above budget as the work progresses.

(b)   Estimates of **benefits** will be for **several years ahead**, sometimes 10, 15 or 20 years ahead or even longer, and such long-term estimates can at best be approximations.

2 Sensitivity analysis   12/07, 12/11, 6/12, 6/15

FAST FORWARD

Sensitivity analysis assesses how responsive the project's NPV is to changes in the variables used to calculate that NPV. Sensitivity analysis is one particular approach to uncertainty analysis. The certainty-equivalent approach is another; this involves the conversion of the expected cash flows of the project to riskless equivalent amounts.

Key term

Sensitivity analysis is one method of **analysing the uncertainty** surrounding a capital expenditure project and enables an assessment to be made of how responsive the project's NPV is to changes in the variables that are used to calculate that NPV.

The NPV could depend on a number of uncertain independent variables.

- Selling price
- Sales volume
- Cost of capital
- Initial cost
- Operating costs
- Benefits

The basic approach of sensitivity analysis is to **calculate the project's NPV** under **alternative assumptions** to determine how sensitive it is to changing conditions. An indication is thus provided of those variables to which the NPV is most sensitive (**critical variables**) and the **extent** to which those variables **may change** before the investment results in a negative NPV.

Sensitivity analysis therefore provides an indication of why a project might fail. Management should review critical variables to assess whether or not there is a strong possibility of events occurring which will lead to a negative NPV. Management should also pay particular attention to controlling those variables to which the NPV is particularly sensitive, once the decision has been taken to accept the investment.

A simple approach to deciding which variables the NPV is particularly sensitive to is to calculate the sensitivity of each variable.

$$\text{Sensitivity} = \frac{\text{NPV}}{\text{Present value of project variable}} \ \%$$

The lower the percentage, the more sensitive the NPV is to that project variable, as the variable would need to change by a smaller amount to make the project non-viable.

2.1 Example: Sensitivity analysis

Kenney Co is considering a project with the following cash flows.

Year	Initial investment $'000	Variable costs $'000	Cash inflows $'000	Net cash flows $'000
0	7,000			
1		(2,000)	6,500	4,500
2		(2,000)	6,500	4,500

Cash flows arise from selling 650,000 units at $10 per unit. Kenney Co has a cost of capital of 8%.

Required

Measure the sensitivity of the project to changes in variables.

Solution

The PVs of the cash flow are as follows.

Year	Discount factor 8%	PV of initial investment $'000	PV of variable costs $'000	PV of cash inflows $'000	PV of net cash flow $'000
0	1.000	(7,000)			(7,000)
1	0.926		(1,852)	6,019	4,167
2	0.857		(1,714)	5,571	3,857
		(7,000)	(3,566)	11,590	1,024

The project has a positive NPV and would appear to be worthwhile. The sensitivity of each project variable is as follows.

(a) **Initial investment**

$$\text{Sensitivity} = \frac{1,024}{7,000} \times 100 = 14.6\%$$

In other words, the project will only just provide the required investment return if the cost of the investment is 14.6% higher than estimated, assuming that the value of all the other cash flows for the investment are as estimated.

(b) **Sales volume**

$$\text{Sensitivity} = \frac{1,024}{11,590 - 3,566} \times 100 = 12.8\%$$

In other words, the project will only just provide the required investment return if sales volume is 12.8% lower than estimated, assuming that the value of all the other cash flows for the investment is as estimated.

(c) **Selling price**

$$\text{Sensitivity} = \frac{1,024}{11,590} \times 100 = 8.8\%$$

(d) **Variable costs**

$$\text{Sensitivity} = \frac{1,024}{3,566} \times 100 = 28.7\%$$

(e) **Cost of capital**. We need to calculate the IRR of the project. Let us try discount rates of 15% and 20%.

Year	Net cash flow $'000	Discount factor 15%	PV $'000	Discount factor 20%	PV $'000
0	(7,000)	1	(7,000)	1	(7,000)
1	4,500	0.870	3,915	0.833	3,749
2	4,500	0.756	3,402	0.694	3,123
			NPV = 317		NPV = (128)

$$IRR = 0.15 + \left[\frac{317}{317 + 128} \times (0.20 - 0.15) \right] = 18.56\%$$

The cost of capital can therefore increase by 132% before the NPV becomes negative.

The elements to which the NPV appears to be most sensitive are the selling price followed by the sales volume. Management should thus pay particular attention to these factors so that they can be carefully monitored.

2.2 Weaknesses of this approach to sensitivity analysis

These are as follows.

(a) The method requires that **changes** in each key variable are **isolated**, assuming that all other values in the estimated cash flows are unchanged. However, management may be more interested in the combination of the effects of changes in two or more key variables.

(b) Looking at factors in isolation is unrealistic since they are often **interdependent**.

(c) Sensitivity analysis is analysis when there is uncertainty. It does not examine the **probability** that any particular variation in costs or revenues might occur.

(d) **Critical factors** may be those over which managers have no control.

(e) In itself it does not provide a decision rule. Parameters defining **acceptability** of an investment project, given the uncertainty, must be laid down by managers.

Question   Sensitivity analysis

Nevers Ure Co has a cost of capital of 8% and is considering a project with the following 'most likely' cash flows.

Year	Purchase of plant $	Running costs $	Savings $
0	(7,000)		
1		2,000	6,000
2		2,500	7,000

Required

Measure the sensitivity (in percentages) of the project to changes in the levels of expected costs and savings.

Answer

The PVs of the cash flows are as follows.

Year	Discount factor 8%	PV of plant cost $	PV of running costs $	PV of savings $	PV of net cash flow $
0	1.000	(7,000)			(7,000)
1	0.926		(1,852)	5,556	3,704
2	0.857		(2,143)	5,999	3,856
		(7,000)	(3,995)	11,555	560

The project has a positive NPV and would appear to be worthwhile. Sensitivity of the project to changes in the levels of expected costs and savings is as follows.

(a) Plant costs sensitivity = $\dfrac{560}{7,000} \times 100 = 8\%$

(b) Running costs sensitivity = $\dfrac{560}{3,995} \times 100 = 14\%$

(c) Savings sensitivity = $\dfrac{560}{11,555} \times 100 = 4.8\%$

Exam focus point

The ACCA examination team has commented that sensitivity analysis is often confused with the internal rate of return.

2.3 The certainty-equivalent approach

Another method is the **certainty-equivalent approach**. By this method, the expected cash flows of the project are **converted to riskless equivalent amounts**. The greater the risk of an expected cash flow, the smaller the certainty-equivalent value (for receipts) or the larger the certainty-equivalent value (for payments).

As the cash flows are reduced to supposedly certain amounts, they should be discounted at a **risk-free rate**. This concept will be covered in detail later in this text, but the risk-free rate is effectively the level of return that can be obtained from undertaking no risk.

2.4 Example: Certainty-equivalent approach

Dark Ages Co, whose cost of capital is 10%, is considering a project with the following expected cash flows.

Year	Cash flow $	Discount factor 10%	Present value $
0	(10,000)	1.000	(10,000)
1	7,000	0.909	6,363
2	5,000	0.826	4,130
3	5,000	0.751	3,755
			NPV = +4,248

The project seems to be worthwhile. However, because of the uncertainty about the future cash receipts, the management decides to reduce them to 'certainty-equivalents' by taking only 70%, 60% and 50% of the years 1, 2 and 3 cash flows respectively. The risk-free rate is 5%.

On the basis of the information set out above, assess whether the project is worthwhile.

Solution

The risk-adjusted NPV of the project is as follows.

Year	Cash flow: certainty equivalents $	Discount factor at risk-free rate of return 5%	Present value $
0	(10,000)	1.000	(10,000)
1	4,900	0.952	4,665
2	3,000	0.907	2,721
3	2,500	0.864	2,160
			NPV = (454)

The project's certainty-equivalent NPV is negative. This means that the project is too risky and should be rejected.

The disadvantage of the 'certainty-equivalent' approach is that the amount of the adjustment to each cash flow is decided **subjectively**.

3 Probability analysis

> **FAST FORWARD**
>
> A **probability analysis** of expected cash flows can often be estimated and used both to calculate an expected NPV and to measure risk.

A **probability distribution** of '**expected cash flows**' can often be estimated, recognising that there are several possible outcomes, not just one. This may be used to do the following.

Step 1   Calculate an expected value of the NPV.

Step 2   Measure risk, for example in the following ways.

     (a)   By calculating the worst possible outcome and its probability

     (b)   By calculating the probability that the project will fail to achieve a positive NPV

     (c)   By calculating the standard deviation of the NPV

3.1 Example: Probability estimates of cash flows

A company is considering a project involving the outlay of $300,000 which it estimates will generate cash flows over its two-year life at the probabilities shown in the following table.

Cash flows for project

Year 1	Cash flow $	Probability
	100,000	0.25
	200,000	0.50
	300,000	0.25
		1.00

Year 2

If cash flow in Year 1 is: $	there is a probability of:	that the cash flow in Year 2 will be: $
100,000	0.25	Nil
	0.50	100,000
	0.25	200,000
	1.00	
200,000	0.25	100,000
	0.50	200,000
	0.25	300,000
	1.00	
300,000	0.25	200,000
	0.50	300,000
	0.25	350,000
	1.00	

The company's cost of capital for this type of project is 10% DCF.

You are required to calculate the expected value (EV) of the project's NPV and the probability that the NPV will be negative.

Solution

Step 1   Calculate expected value of the NPV.

First we need to draw up a probability distribution of the expected cash flows. We begin by calculating the present values of the cash flows.

Year	Cash flow $'000	Discount factor 10%	Present value $'000
1	100	0.909	90.9
1	200	0.909	181.8
1	300	0.909	272.7
2	100	0.826	82.6
2	200	0.826	165.2
2	300	0.826	247.8
2	350	0.826	289.1

Year 1 PV of cash flow $'000 (a)	Probability (b)	Year 2 PV of cash flow $'000 (c)	Probability (d)	Joint probability (b) × (d)	Total PV of cash inflows $'000 (a) + (c)	EV of PV of cash inflows $'000
90.9	0.25	0.0	0.25	0.0625	90.9	5.681
90.9	0.25	82.6	0.50	0.1250	173.5	21.688
90.9	0.25	165.2	0.25	0.0625	256.1	16.006
181.8	0.50	82.6	0.25	0.1250	264.4	33.050
181.8	0.50	165.2	0.50	0.2500	347.0	86.750
181.8	0.50	247.8	0.25	0.1250	429.6	53.700
272.7	0.25	165.2	0.25	0.0625	437.9	27.369
272.7	0.25	247.8	0.50	0.1250	520.5	65.063
272.7	0.25	289.1	0.25	0.0625	561.8	35.113
						344.420

	$
EV of PV of cash inflows	344,420
Less project cost	300,000
EV of NPV	44,420

Step 2   Measure risk.

Since the EV of the NPV is positive, the project should go ahead unless the risk is unacceptably high. The probability that the project will have a negative NPV is the probability that the total PV of cash inflows is less than $300,000. From the column headed 'Total PV of cash inflows', we can establish that this probability is 0.0625 + 0.125 + 0.0625 + 0.125 = 0.375 or 37.5%. This might be considered an unacceptably high risk.

3.2 Example: Probability estimates of cash flows excluding discounting

Using probabilities to assess risk need not involve discounting. Here is an example.

A company has an overdraft limit of $500,000. There are concerns that this limit may be exceeded within the next two years. As a result cash flow forecasts with their associated probabilities have been prepared for the next two periods, as follows.

The cash balance at the beginning of year 1 is $500,000.

What are the expected cash balances at the end of each year and what are the probabilities of exceeding the overdraft limit at the end of each year?

Year 1 cash flow	Probability	Year 2 cash flow	Probability
$'000		$'000	
4,000	0.20	2,500	0.10
3,000	0.50	1,000	0.65
(1,500)	0.30	(3,500)	0.25

Solution

Opening balance	Year 1 cash flow	Closing balance for year 1	Probability	Expected value
$'000	$'000	$'000		$'000
500	4,000	4,500	0.20	900
500	3,000	3,500	0.50	1,750
500	(1,500)	(1,000)	0.30	(300)
				2,350

The expected value of the cash balance at the end of year 1 is $2,350,000.

There is a 0.3 or 30% chance that the overdraft limit will be exceeded.

Year 1 closing balance	Probability	Year 2 cash flow	Probability	Year 2 closing balance	Joint probability	Expected value
$'000		$'000		$'000		$'000
(a)	(b)	(c)	(d)	(a) + (c)	(b) × (d)	
4,500	0.20	2,500	0.10	7,000	0.020	140.0
4,500	0.20	1,000	0.65	5,500	0.130	715.0
4,500	0.20	(3,500)	0.25	1,000	0.050	50.0
3,500	0.50	2,500	0.10	6,000	0.050	300.0
3,500	0.50	1,000	0.65	4,500	0.325	462.5
3,500	0.50	(3,500)	0.25	0	0.125	0.0
(1,000)	0.30	2,500	0.10	1,500	0.030	45.0
(1,000)	0.30	1,000	0.65	0	0.195	0.0
(1,000)	0.30	(3,500)	0.25	(4,500)	0.075	(337.5)
						2,375.0

The expected value of the cash balance at the end of year 2 is $2,375,000.

There is a 0.075 or 7.5% chance that the overdraft limit will be exceeded.

3.3 Problems with expected values

There are the following problems with using expected values in making investment decisions.

- An investment may be **one-off**, and 'expected' NPV may never actually occur. For example, if there is a 50% probability that the NPV will be + $10,000 and a 50% probability that it will be $(2,000), the EV of the NPV is + $4,000. On this basis the project will go ahead. However, an NPV of $4,000 is not expected to happen. The NPV will be either plus $10,000 or minus $2,000.

- **Assigning probabilities** to future events and outcomes is usually highly **subjective**.

- Expected values **do not evaluate the range** of possible NPV outcomes.

4 Other risk adjustment techniques

4.1 Simulation

FAST FORWARD

Other risk adjustment techniques include the use of simulation models, discounted payback and risk-adjusted discount rates.

Simulation will overcome problems of having a very large number of possible outcomes, as well as the correlation of cash flows (a project which is successful in its early years is more likely to be successful in its later years).

4.2 Example: Simulation model

The following probability estimates have been prepared for a proposed project.

	Year	Probability	$
Cost of equipment	0	1.00	(40,000)
Revenue each year	1-5	0.15	40,000
		0.40	50,000
		0.30	55,000
		0.15	60,000
Running costs each year	1-5	0.10	25,000
		0.25	30,000
		0.35	35,000
		0.30	40,000

The cost of capital is 12%. Assess how a simulation model might be used to assess the project's NPV.

Solution

A simulation model could be constructed by assigning a range of random number digits to each possible value for each of the uncertain variables. The random numbers must exactly match their respective probabilities. This is achieved by working upwards cumulatively from the lowest to the highest cash flow values and assigning numbers that will correspond to probability groupings, as follows.

Revenue				Running costs		
$	Prob	Random numbers		$	Prob	Random numbers
40,000	0.15	00 – 14	*	25,000	0.10	00 – 09
50,000	0.40	15 – 54	**	30,000	0.25	10 – 34
55,000	0.30	55 – 84	***	40,000	0.35	35 – 69
60,000	0.15	85 – 99		40,000	0.30	70 – 99

*   Probability is 0.15 (15%). Random numbers are 15% of range 00 – 99.
**   Probability is 0.40 (40%). Random numbers are 40% of range 00 – 99 but starting at 15.
***   Probability is 0.30 (30%). Random numbers are 30% of range 00 – 99 but starting at 55.

For revenue, the selection of a random number in the range 00 and 14 has a probability of 0.15. This probability represents revenue of $40,000. Numbers have been assigned to cash flows so that when numbers are selected at random, the cash flows have exactly the same probability of being selected as is indicated in their respective probability distribution above.

Random numbers would be generated, for example by a computer program, and these would be used to assign values to each of the uncertain variables.

For example, if random numbers 37, 84, 20, 01, 56 and 89 were generated, the values assigned to the variables would be as follows.

	Revenue		Costs	
Calculation	Random number	Value $	Random number	Value $
1	37	50,000	84	40,000
2	20	50,000	01	25,000
3	56	55,000	89	40,000

A computer would calculate the NPV many times over using the values established in this way with more random numbers, and the results would be analysed to provide the following.

(a) An **expected NPV** for the project
(b) A **statistical distribution** pattern for the possible variation in the NPV above or below this average

The decision whether to go ahead with the project would then be made on the basis of **expected return** and **risk**.

4.3 Discounted payback (adjusted payback)

> The **discounted payback period (DPP)** is the time it will take before a project's cumulative NPV turns from being negative to being positive.

The payback method of investment appraisal, discussed in Chapter 7, recognises uncertainty in investment decisions by focusing on the near future. Short-term projects are preferred to long-term projects and liquidity is emphasised.

The discounted payback period is the length of time before the cumulative PV of cash inflows from the projects begins to exceed the initial outflow. It is similar to the payback method, but uses discounted cash flows rather than non-discounted cash flows to measure the payback period.

Discounted payback uses **discounted cash flows**. This is also known as adjusted payback.

For example, if we have a cost of capital of 10% and a project with the cash flows shown below, we can calculate a discounted payback period.

Year	Cash flow $	Discount factor 10%	Present value $	Cumulative NPV $
0	(100,000)	1.000	(100,000)	(100,000)
1	30,000	0.909	27,270	(72,730)
2	50,000	0.826	41,300	(31,430)
3	40,000	0.751	30,040	(1,390)
4	30,000	0.683	20,490	19,100
5	20,000	0.621	12,420	31,520
		NPV =	31,520	

The DPP is early in year 4.

It may be approximated as 3 years + [1,390/(1,390 + 19,100)] × 12 months

= 3 years 0.8 months, say 3 years 1 month.

A company can set a target DPP, and choose not to undertake any projects with a DPP in excess of a certain number of years, say, five years.

4.4 Advantages and disadvantages of discounted payback period

The approach has **all the perceived advantages of the payback period** method of investment appraisal: it is easy to understand and calculate, and it provides a focus on liquidity where this is relevant. In addition, however, it **also takes into account the time value of money**. It therefore bridges the gap between the theoretically superior NPV method and the regular payback period method.

However, it does differ from NPV in that the discount rate used is the **unadjusted cost of capital** whereas NPV often uses an **adjusted rate to reflect project risk and uncertainty**.

Because the DPP approach takes the time value of money into consideration, it **produces a longer payback period** than the non-discounted payback approach, and **takes into account more of the project's cash flows**.

Another advantage it has over traditional payback is that it has a **clear accept or reject criterion**. Using payback, acceptance of a project depends on an arbitrarily determined cut-off time. Using DPP, a project is acceptable if it pays back within its lifetime.

DPP still shares one disadvantage with the payback period method: **cash flows which occur after the payback period are ignored** (although, as the DPP is longer than the payback period, fewer of these are ignored).

One way of dealing with risk is to **shorten** the payback period required. A **maximum payback period** can be set to reflect the fact that risk increases the longer the time period under consideration. However, the disadvantages of payback as an investment appraisal method (discussed in Section 3.2 of Chapter 7) mean that discounted payback cannot be recommended as a method of adjusting for risk.

4.5 Risk-adjusted discount rates

Investors want higher returns for higher risk investments. The greater the risk attached to future returns, the greater the risk premium required. Investors also prefer cash now to later and require a higher return for longer time periods.

In investment appraisal, a **risk-adjusted discount rate** can be used for particular types or **risk classes** of investment projects to reflect their relative risks. For example, a **high discount rate** can be used so that a cash flow which occurs quite some time in the future will have less effect on the decision. Alternatively, with the launch of a new product, a higher **initial** risk premium may be used with a decrease in the discount rate as the product becomes established.

Chapter Roundup

- **Risk analysis** can be applied to a proposed capital investment where there are several possible outcomes and, on the basis of past relevant experience, probabilities can be assigned to the various outcomes and estimated cash flows that could prevail.

  Uncertainty analysis can be applied to a proposed capital investment where there are several possible outcomes but there is little past relevant experience to enable the probability of the alternative outcomes to be predicted.

  There are a wide range of techniques for incorporating risk into project appraisal.

- **Sensitivity analysis** assesses how responsive the project's NPV is to changes in the variables used to calculate that NPV. Sensitivity analysis is one particular approach to uncertainty analysis. The certainty-equivalent approach is another; this involves the conversion of the expected cash flows of the project to riskless equivalent amounts.

- A **probability analysis** of expected cash flows can often be estimated and used both to calculate an expected NPV and to measure risk.

- Other risk adjustment techniques include the use of simulation models, discounted payback and risk-adjusted discount rates.

- The **discounted payback period (DPP)** is the time it will take before a project's cumulative NPV turns from being negative to being positive.

1   Give three examples of uncertain independent variables on which the NPV of a project may depend.

2   How are simulation models constructed?

3   Briefly list four ways in which managers can reduce risk.

4   Sensitivity analysis allows for uncertainty in project appraisal by assessing the probability of changes in the decision variables.

True ☐

False ☐

5   Fill in the blanks.

The .... is where expected cash flows are converted to riskless equivalent amounts.

6   Give two examples of ways that risk can be measured in probability analysis.

7   Expected values can help an accountant evaluate the range of possible net present value outcomes.

True ☐

False ☐

8   An investment project has the following discounted cash flows ($'000).

Year	Discount rate		
	0%	10%	20%
0	(90)	(90)	(90)
1	30	27.3	25.0
2	30	24.8	29.8
3	30	22.5	17.4
4	30	20.5	14.5
	30	5.1	(12.3)

The required rate of return on investment is 10% per annum.

What is the discounted payback period of the investment project?

A   Less than 3 years
B   3 years
C   Between 3 years and 4 years
D   More than 4 years

Answers to Quick Quiz

1   Any three of:
    (a)   Selling price
    (b)   Sales volume
    (c)   Cost of capital
    (d)   Initial cost
    (e)   Operating costs
    (f)   Benefits

2   By assigning a range of random number digits to each possible value of each of the uncertain variables.

3   (a)   Set maximum payback period
    (b)   Use high discounting rate
    (c)   Use sensitivity analysis to determine the critical factors within the decision-making process
    (d)   Use pessimistic estimates

4   False. Sensitivity analysis does not assess probability.

5   Certainty-equivalent approach

6   Calculating the worst possible outcome and its probability
Calculating the probability that the project will fail to achieve a positive NPV

7   False

8   C   At the end of year 3, $74,600 has been 'paid back'. The remaining $15,400 for payback will be received during year 4.

Now try the questions below from the Practice Question Bank

Number	Level	Marks	Time
Section A Q20	Examination	2	4 mins
Section A Q21	Examination	2	4 mins
Section C Q11	Introductory	N/A	29 mins

10: Project appraisal and risk | Part D Investment appraisal

11

Specific investment decisions

Topic list	Syllabus reference
1 Lease or buy decisions	D4 (a)
2 Asset replacement decisions	D4 (b)
3 Capital rationing	D4 (c)

Introduction

In this chapter, we consider specific investment decisions, such as whether to lease or buy an asset, when to replace an asset and how to assess projects when capital is a scarce resource.

Study guide

		Intellectual level
D4	**Specific investment decisions (lease or buy; asset replacement; capital rationing)**	
(a)	Evaluate leasing and borrowing to buy using the before- and after-tax costs of debt.	2
(b)	Evaluate asset replacement decisions using equivalent annual cost and equivalent annual benefit.	2
(c)	Evaluate investment decisions under single period capital rationing, including:	2
(i)	The calculation of profitability indexes for divisible investment projects	
(ii)	The calculation of the NPV of combinations of non-divisible investment projects	
(iii)	A discussion of the reasons for capital rationing	

Exam guide

You may be asked to calculate the results of different options and careful, methodical workings will be essential. These calculations can be quite difficult and will need lots of practice.

1 Lease or buy decisions   12/07, 12/09, 12/13

FAST FORWARD

Leasing is a commonly used source of finance.

We distinguish three types of leasing:

- **Operating leases** (**lessor** responsible for maintaining asset)
- **Finance leases** (**lessee** responsible for maintenance)
- **Sale and leaseback** arrangements

1.1 The nature of leasing

Rather than buying an asset outright, using either available cash resources or borrowed funds, a business may lease an asset.

Key terms

Leasing is a contract between a lessor and a lessee for hire of a specific asset by the lessee from a manufacturer or vendor of such assets.

The **lessor** has ownership of the asset and so provides the initial finance for the asset.

The **lessee** has possession and use of the asset on payment of specified rentals over a period.

1.1.1 Examples of lessors

- Banks
- Insurance companies

1.1.2 Types of asset leased

- Office equipment
- Computers
- Cars
- Commercial vehicles

- Aircraft
- Ships
- Buildings

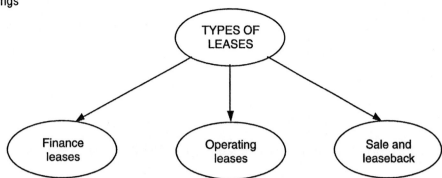

1.2 Operating leases

> **Operating lease** is a lease where the lessor retains most of the risks and rewards of ownership.

Operating leases are rental agreements between a lessor and a lessee, for a relatively short period of time. It is useful to think of operating leases as short-term rental agreements.

(a)   The lessor **supplies** the equipment to the **lessee**.

(b)   The **lessor** is **responsible** for **servicing and maintaining** the leased equipment.

(c)   The **period** of the lease is fairly **short, less** than the expected **economic life** of the asset. At the end of one lease agreement, the lessor can either lease the same equipment to someone else and obtain a good rent for it, or sell the equipment secondhand.

1.3 Finance leases

> A **finance lease** is a lease that substantially transfers all the risks and rewards of ownership of an asset to the lessee. It is an agreement between the lessee and the lessor for most or all of the asset's expected useful life.

There are other important characteristics of a finance lease.

(a)   The lessee is responsible for the **upkeep, servicing** and **maintenance** of the asset.

(b)   The lease has a **primary period** covering all or most of the useful economic life of the asset. At the end of this period, the lessor would not be able to lease the asset to someone else, because the asset would be worn out or near the end of its useful life. The lessor must therefore ensure that the lease payments during the primary period pay for the **full cost** of the asset as well as providing the lessor with a **suitable return** on their investment.

(c)   At the end of the primary period the lessee can normally continue to lease the asset for an indefinite secondary period, in return for a very low nominal rent, sometimes called a 'peppercorn rent'. Alternatively, the lessee might be allowed to sell the asset on a lessor's behalf (since the lessor is the owner) and perhaps to keep most of the sale proceeds.

1.4 Example: A motor lease

The primary period of a lease to acquire a motor car might be three years, with an agreement by the lessee to make three annual payments of $6,000 each. The lessee will be responsible for repairs and servicing, road tax, insurance and garaging. At the end of the primary period of the lease, the lessee may have the option either to continue leasing the car at a nominal rent (perhaps $250 a year) or to sell the car and pay the lessor 10% of the proceeds.

1.5 Sale and leaseback

> **Sale and leaseback** is when a business that owns an asset agrees to sell the asset to a financial institution and lease it back on terms specified in the sale and leaseback agreement.

The business retains **use** of the asset but has the **funds** from the sale, while having to pay rent.

A common form of sale and leaseback arrangement has involved commercial property. A company might sell its premises to a bank or finance company (to raise cash) and then lease back the premises under a long-term leasing arrangement.

1.6 Attractions of leasing

Attractions include the following.

(a)   The supplier of the equipment is **paid** in **full** at the beginning. The equipment is sold to the lessor and, other than guarantees, the supplier has no further financial concern about the asset.

(b)   The lessor **invests finance** by purchasing assets from suppliers and makes a **return** out of the lease payments from the lessee. The lessor will also get capital allowances (tax-allowable depreciation) on the purchase of the equipment.

(c)   Leasing may have advantages for the lessee.

   (i)   The lessee may not have enough cash to pay for the asset, and would have difficulty obtaining a bank loan to buy it. If so, the lessee has to rent the asset to obtain use of it at all.

   (ii)   Finance leasing may be cheaper than a bank loan.

   (iii)   The lessee may find the tax relief available advantageous.

Operating leases have further advantages.

(a)   The leased equipment does not have to be shown in the **lessee's** published **statement of financial position**, and so the lessee's statement shows no increase in its gearing ratio.

(b)   The equipment is leased for a **shorter period** than its expected useful life. In the case of high-technology equipment, if the equipment becomes out of date before the end of its expected life, the lessee does not have to keep on using it. The lessor will bear the risk of having to sell obsolete equipment secondhand.

A major growth area in operating leasing in the UK has been in computers and office equipment (such as photocopiers and fax machines) where technology is continually improving.

1.7 Lease or buy decisions

FAST FORWARD

> The decision whether to **lease or buy** an asset is a **financing decision** which interacts with the investment decision to buy the asset. The assumption is that the preferred financing method should be the one with the lower PV of cost. We identify the **least-cost financing option** by comparing the cash flows of purchasing and leasing. We assume that if the asset is purchased, it will be financed with a bank loan; therefore the cash flows are discounted at an **after-tax cost of borrowing**.

The decision of whether to buy or lease an asset is made once the **decision to invest** in the asset has been made.

Discounted cash flow techniques are used to evaluate the lease or buy decision so that the **least-cost financing option** can be chosen.

The cost of capital that should be applied to the cash flows for the financing decision is the **cost of borrowing**. We assume that if the organisation decided to purchase the equipment, it would finance the purchase by borrowing funds (rather than out of retained funds). We therefore compare the **cost of purchasing** with the **cash flows of leasing** by applying this cost of borrowing to the financing cash flows.

The cash flows of purchasing **do not include the interest repayments on the loan**, as these are dealt with via the cost of capital.

An important cash flow difference between leasing and buying is that:

- With buying the asset, the company receives the tax allowances (tax-allowable depreciation).
- With leasing, the lessor and not the lessee receives these allowances.

With leasing, the lease rental is allowable for tax purposes, and there are consequently savings in tax cash flows.

1.8 A simple example

Brown Co has decided to invest in a new machine which has a ten-year life and no residual value. The machine can either be purchased now for $50,000, or it can be leased for ten years with lease rental payments of $8,000 per annum payable at the end of each year.

The cost of capital to be applied is 9% and taxation should be ignored.

Solution

Present value of leasing costs

PV = Annuity factor at 9% for 10 years × $8,000
   = 6.418 × $8,000 = $51,344

If the machine was purchased now, it would cost $50,000. The purchase is therefore the least-cost financing option.

1.9 An example with taxation

Mallen and Mullins has decided to install a new milling machine. The machine costs $20,000 and it would have a useful life of five years with a trade-in value of $4,000 at the end of the fifth year. A decision now has to be taken on the method of financing the project.

(a) The company could purchase the machine for cash, using bank loan facilities on which the current rate of interest is 13% before tax.

(b) The company could lease the machine under an agreement which would entail payment of $4,800 at the end of each year for the next five years.

The rate of tax is 30%. If the machine is purchased, the company will be able to claim a tax depreciation allowance of 100% in Year 1. Tax is payable with a year's delay.

Solution

Cash flows are discounted at the after-tax cost of borrowing, which is at 13% × 70% = 9.1%, say 9%.

The present value (PV) of purchase costs

Year	Item	Cash flow $	Discount factor 9%	PV $
0	Equipment cost	(20,000)	1.000	(20,000)
5	Trade-in value	4,000	0.650	2,600
2	Tax savings, from allowances 30% × $20,000	6,000	0.842	5,052
6	Balancing charge 30% × $4,000	(1,200)	0.596	(715)
			NPV of purchase	(13,063)

The PV of leasing costs

It is assumed that the lease payments are fully tax allowable.

Year	Lease payment $	Savings in tax (30%) $	Discount factor 9%	PV $
1-5	(4,800) pa		3.890	(18,672)
2-6		1,440 pa	3.569 (W)	5,139
			NPV of leasing	(13,533)

Working

6 year cumulative present value factor 9%	4.486
1 year present value factor 9%	(0.917)
	3.569

The cheapest option would be to purchase the machine.

An alternative method of making lease or buy decisions is to carry out a single financing calculation with the payments for one method being negative and the receipts being positive, and vice versa for the other method.

Year	0 $	1 $	2 $	3 $	4 $	5 $	6 $
Saved equipment cost	20,000						
Lost trade-in value						(4,000)	
Balancing charge							1,200
Lost tax savings from allowances			(6,000)				
Lease payments		(4,800)	(4,800)	(4,800)	(4,800)	(4,800)	
Tax allowances			1,440	1,440	1,440	1,440	1,440
Net cash flow	20,000	(4,800)	(9,360)	(3,360)	(3,360)	(7,360)	2,640
Discount factor 9%	1.000	0.917	0.842	0.772	0.708	0.650	0.596
PV	20,000	(4,402)	(7,881)	(2,594)	(2,379)	(4,784)	1,573
NPV	(467)						

The negative NPV indicates that the lease is unattractive and the purchasing decision is better, as the net savings from not leasing outweigh the net costs of purchasing.

1.10 The position of the lessor

The lessor will receive tax-allowable depreciation on the expenditure, and the lease payments will be taxable income.

1.11 Example: Lessor's position

Continuing the same case of Mallen and Mullins, suppose that the lessor's required rate of return is 12% after tax. The lessor can claim 25% reducing balance tax depreciation. The lessor's cash flows will be as follows.

	Cash flow $	Discount factor 12%	PV $
Purchase costs			
Year 0	(20,000)	1.000	(20,000)
Year 5 trade-in	4,000	0.567	2,268
Tax savings			
Year 2	1,500	0.797	1,196
Year 3	1,125	0.712	801
Year 4	844	0.636	537
Year 5	633	0.567	359
Year 6	698	0.507	354
Lease payments: years 1-5	4,800	3.605	17,304
Tax on lease payments: years 2-6	(1,440)	3.218	(4,634)
NPV			(1,815)

Conclusion

The proposed level of leasing payments are not justifiable for the lessor if it seeks a required rate of return of 12%, since the resulting NPV is negative.

Question

Lease or buy

The management of a company has decided to acquire Machine X which costs $63,000 and has an operational life of four years. The expected scrap value would be zero. Tax is payable at 30% on operating cash flows one year in arrears. Tax-allowable depreciation is available at 25% a year on a reducing balance basis.

Suppose that the company has the opportunity either to purchase the machine or to lease it under a finance lease arrangement, at an annual rent of $20,000 for four years, payable at the end of each year. The company can borrow to finance the acquisition at 10%. Should the company lease or buy the machine?

Answer

Working

Tax-allowable depreciation

Year		$
1	(25% of $63,000)	15,750
2	(75% of $15,750)	11,813
3	(75% of $11,813)	8,859
		36,422
4	($63,000 − $36,422)	26,578

Note. 75% of $15,750 is also 25% × (63,000 − 15,750).

The financing decision will be appraised by discounting the relevant cash flows at the after-tax cost of borrowing, which is 10% × 70% = 7%.

(a) *Purchase option*

Year	Item	Cash flow $	Discount factor 7%	Present value $
0	Cost of machine	(63,000)	1.000	(63,000)
	Tax saved from tax-allowable depreciation			
2	30% × $15,750	4,725	0.873	4,125
3	30% × $11,813	3,544	0.816	2,892
4	30% × $8,859	2,658	0.763	2,028
5	30% × $26,578	7,973	0.713	5,685
				(48,270)

(b) *Leasing option*

It is assumed that the lease payments are tax allowable in full.

Year	Item	Cash flow $	Discount factor 7%	Present value $
1-4	Lease costs	(20,000)	3.387	(67,740)
2-5	Tax savings on lease costs (× 30%)	6,000	3.165	18,990
				(48,750)

The purchase option is cheaper, using a cost of capital based on the after-tax cost of borrowing. On the assumption that investors would regard borrowing and leasing as equally risky finance options, the purchase option is recommended.

2 Asset replacement decisions

12/09, 6/10, 6/12

FAST FORWARD

DCF techniques can assist **asset replacement decisions**, to decide how frequently an asset should be replaced. When an asset is being replaced with an identical asset, the **equivalent annual cost method** can be used to calculate an **optimum replacement cycle**.

As well as assisting with decisions between particular assets, DCF techniques can be used in **asset replacement decisions** to assess **when** and **how frequently** an asset should be replaced. When an asset is to be replaced by an 'identical' asset, the problem is to decide the optimum interval between replacements. As the asset gets older, it may cost more to maintain and operate, its residual value will decrease and it may lose some productivity/operating capability.

2.1 Equivalent annual cost method

The equivalent annual cost method is the most convenient method of analysis to use in a period of no inflation. With this method, the NPV of the cost of buying and using the asset over its life cycle is converted into an equivalent annual cost or annuity. This is a constant annual cost that is equal to the NPV of the costs over the asset life cycle. An equivalent annual cost can be calculated for each possible length of asset replacement cycle. The least-cost replacement cycle is the one with the lowest equivalent annual cost.

Step 1   Calculate the **present value of costs** for each **replacement cycle** over **one cycle only**.

These costs are not comparable because they refer to different time periods, whereas replacement is continuous.

Step 2   **Turn the present value** of costs for each replacement cycle into an **equivalent annual cost** (an annuity).

The equivalent annual cost is calculated as follows.

$$\frac{\text{The PV of cost over one replacement cycle}}{\text{The cumulative present value factor for the number of years in the cycle}}$$

For example if there are three years in the cycle, the denominator will be the present value of an annuity for three years at 10% (2.487).

2.2 Example: Replacement of an identical asset

A company operates a machine which has the following costs and resale values over its four-year life.

Purchase cost: $25,000

	Year 1	Year 2	Year 3	Year 4
	$	$	$	$
Running costs (cash expenses)	7,500	11,000	12,500	15,000
Resale value (end of year)	15,000	10,000	7,500	2,500

The organisation's cost of capital is 10%. You are required to assess how frequently the asset should be replaced.

Solution

In our example:

Step 1   Calculate the present value of costs for each replacement cycle over one cycle.

Year	Discount factors	Replace every year Cash flow $	Replace every year PV at 10% $	Replace every 2 years Cash flow $	Replace every 2 years PV at 10% $	Replace every 3 years Cash flow $	Replace every 3 years PV at 10% $	Replace every 4 years Cash flow $	Replace every 4 years PV at 10% $
0	–	(25,000)	(25,000)	(25,000)	(25,000)	(25,000)	(25,000)	(25,000)	(25,000)
1	0.909	(7,500)	(6,818)	(7,500)	(6,818)	(7,500)	(6,818)	(7,500)	(6,818)
		15,000	13,635						
2	0.826			(11,000)	(9,086)	(11,000)	(9,086)	(11,000)	(9,086)
				10,000	8,260				
3	0.751					(12,500)	(9,388)	(12,500)	(9,388)
						7,500	5,633		
4	0.683							(15,000)	(10,245)
								2,500	1,708
PV of cost over one replacement cycle			(18,183)		(32,644)		(44,659)		(58,829)

Step 2   Calculate the equivalent annual cost.

We use a discount rate of 10%.

(a)   Replacement every year:

$$\text{Equivalent annual cost} = \frac{\$(18,183)}{0.909} = \$(20,003)$$

(b)   Replacement every two years:

Equivalent annual cost = $\dfrac{\$(32,644)}{1.736}$ = $(18,804)

(c)   Replacement every three years:

Equivalent annual cost = $\dfrac{\$(44,659)}{2.487}$ = $(17,957)

(d)   Replacement every four years:

Equivalent annual cost = $\dfrac{\$(58,829)}{3.170}$ = $(18,558)

The optimum replacement policy is the one with the lowest equivalent annual cost. This is every three years.

2.3 Equivalent annual benefit

The **equivalent annual benefit** is the annual annuity with the same value as the net present value of an investment project.

The equivalent annual annuity = $\dfrac{\text{NPV of project}}{\text{Annuity factor}}$

For example, a project A with an NPV of $3.75m and a duration of 6 years, given a discount rate of 12%, will have an equivalent annual annuity of $\dfrac{3.75}{4.11} = 0.91$

An alternative project B with an NPV of $4.45m and a duration of 7 years will have an equivalent annual annuity of $\dfrac{4.45}{4.564} = 0.98$

Project B will therefore be **ranked higher** than project A. This method is a useful way of comparing projects with **unequal lives**.

You may find it useful to read the article called Equivalent Annual Costs and Benefits on the ACCA website.

3 Capital rationing   12/09, 12/11, 6/14

Capital rationing may occur due to internal factors (soft capital rationing) or external factors (hard capital rationing).

Capital rationing is a situation in which a company has a limited amount of capital to invest in potential projects, such that the different possible investments need to be compared with one another in order to allocate the capital available most effectively.

Soft capital rationing is brought about by internal factors and decisions by management.

Hard capital rationing is brought about by external factors, such as limited availability of new external finance.

If an organisation is in a **capital rationing** situation it will not be able to enter into all projects with positive NPVs because there is not enough capital for all the investments.

3.1 Soft and hard capital rationing

Soft capital rationing may arise for one of the following reasons.

(a) Management may be **reluctant** to **issue additional share capital** because of concern that this may lead to **outsiders** gaining control of the business.

(b) **Management** may be **unwilling** to **issue additional share capital** if it will lead to a **dilution of earnings** per share.

(c) Management may **not want to raise additional debt capital** because they do not wish to be committed to **large fixed interest payments**.

(d) Management may wish to **limit investment** to a level that can be financed solely from **retained earnings**.

Hard capital rationing may arise for one of the following reasons.

(a) Raising new finance through the stock market may not be possible if **share prices** are **depressed**.

(b) There may be **restrictions** on **bank lending** due to government control.

(c) Lending institutions may consider an organisation to be **too risky** to be granted further loan facilities.

(d) The **costs** associated with making small **issues** of capital may be too great.

3.2 Relaxation of capital constraints

If an organisation adopts a policy that restricts funds available for investment (soft capital rationing), the policy may be less than optimal. The organisation may reject projects with a positive net present value and forgo opportunities that would have enhanced the market value of the organisation.

A company may be able to limit the effects of hard capital rationing and exploit new opportunities.

(a) It might **seek joint venture partners** with which to share projects.

(b) As an alternative to direct investment in a project, the company may be able to consider a **licensing** or **franchising agreement** with another enterprise, under which the licensor/franchisor company would receive royalties.

(c) It may be possible to **contract out** parts of a project to reduce the initial capital outlay required.

(d) The company may seek **new** alternative **sources of capital** (subject to any restrictions which apply to it), for example:
   (i) Venture capital
   (ii) Debt finance secured on the assets of the project
   (iii) Sale and leaseback of property or equipment (see the next chapter)
   (iv) Grant aid
   (v) More effective capital management

3.3 Single period capital rationing   6/14

FAST FORWARD

When capital rationing occurs in a **single period**, projects are ranked in terms of **profitability index**. This is the ratio of the NPV of a project to its investment cost. The projects with the highest ratios should be selected for investment.

We shall begin our analysis by assuming that capital rationing occurs in a single period, and that capital is freely available at all other times.

The following further assumptions will be made.

(a) If a company does not accept and undertake a project during the period of capital rationing, the **opportunity** to undertake it is **lost**. The project cannot be postponed until a subsequent period when no capital rationing exists.

(b) There is **complete certainty** about the outcome of each project, so that the choice between projects is not affected by considerations of risk.

(c) **Projects** are **divisible**, so that it is possible to undertake, say, half of Project X in order to earn half of the net present value (NPV) of the whole project.

The basic approach is to rank all investment opportunities so that the NPVs can be maximised from the use of the available funds.

Ranking in terms of absolute NPVs will normally give incorrect results. This method leads to the **selection of large projects**, each of which has a high individual NPV but which have, in total, a lower NPV than a large number of smaller projects with lower individual NPVs. Ranking is therefore in terms of what is called the **profitability index**.

This profitability index is a ratio that measures the PV of future cash flows per $1 of investment, and so indicates which investments make the best use of the limited resources available.

> **Profitability index** is the ratio of the present value of the project's future cash flows (not including the capital investment) divided by the present value of the total capital investment.

3.4 Example: Single period capital rationing

Suppose that Hard Times Co is considering four projects, W, X, Y and Z. Relevant details are as follows.

Project	Investment required $	Present value of cash inflows $	NPV $	Profitability index (PI)	Ranking as per NPV	Ranking as per PI
W	(10,000)	11,240	1,240	1.12	3	1
X	(20,000)	20,991	991	1.05	4	4
Y	(30,000)	32,230	2,230	1.07	2	3
Z	(40,000)	43,801	3,801	1.10	1	2

Without capital rationing all four projects would be viable investments. Suppose, however, that only $60,000 was available for capital investment. Let us look at the resulting NPV if we select projects in the order of ranking per NPV.

Project	Priority	Outlay $	NPV $	
Z	1st	40,000	3,801	
Y (balance)*	2nd	20,000	1,487	(2/3 of $2,230)
		60,000	5,288	

* Projects are divisible. By spending the balancing $20,000 on project Y, two-thirds of the full investment would be made to earn two-thirds of the NPV.

Suppose, on the other hand, that we adopt the profitability index approach. The selection of projects will be as follows.

Project	Priority	Outlay $	NPV $	
W	1st	10,000	1,240	
Z	2nd	40,000	3,801	
Y (balance)	3rd	10,000	743	(1/3 of $2,230)
		60,000	5,784	

By choosing projects according to the PI, the resulting NPV (if only $60,000 is available) is increased by $496.

3.4.1 Problems with the Profitability Index method

(a) The approach can only be used if **projects** are **divisible**. If the projects are not divisible, a decision has to be made by examining the **absolute NPVs** of all possible combinations of complete projects that can be undertaken within the constraints of the capital available. The combination of projects which remains at or under the limit of available capital without any of them being divided, and which maximises the total NPV, should be chosen.

(b) The **selection criterion** is fairly **simplistic**, taking no account of the possible strategic value of individual investments in the context of the overall objectives of the organisation.

(c) The method is of limited use when projects have **differing cash flow patterns**. These patterns may be important to the company since they will affect the timing and availability of funds. With multi-period capital rationing, it is possible that the project with the highest Profitability Index is the slowest in generating returns.

(d) The Profitability Index **ignores** the **absolute size** of individual projects. A project with a high index might be very small and therefore only generate a small NPV.

Question 　　　　　　　　　　　　　　　　　　　　　　　　　　　　　　　Capital rationing

A company is experiencing capital rationing in year 0, when only $60,000 of investment finance will be available. No capital rationing is expected in future periods, but none of the three projects under consideration by the company can be postponed. The expected cash flows of the three projects are as follows.

Project	Year 0 $	Year 1 $	Year 2 $	Year 3 $	Year 4 $
A	(50,000)	(20,000)	20,000	40,000	40,000
B	(28,000)	(50,000)	40,000	40,000	20,000
C	(30,000)	(30,000)	30,000	40,000	10,000

The cost of capital is 10%. You are required to decide which projects should be undertaken in year 0, in view of the capital rationing, given that projects are divisible.

Answer

The ratio of NPV at 10% to outlay in year 0 (the year of capital rationing) is as follows.

Project	Outlay in Year 0 $	PV $	NPV $	Ratio	Ranking
A	50,000	55,700	5,700	1.114	3rd
B	28,000	31,290	3,290	1.118	2nd
C	30,000	34,380	4,380	1.146	1st

Working

Present value A

Year		$	Discount factor 10%	Present value $
1	Cash flow	(20,000)	0.909	(18,180)
2	Cash flow	20,000	0.826	16,520
3	Cash flow	40,000	0.751	30,040
4	Cash flow	40,000	0.683	27,320
				55,700

Present value B

Year		$	Discount factor 10%	Present value $
1	Cash flow	(50,000)	0.909	(45,450)
2	Cash flow	40,000	0.826	33,040
3	Cash flow	40,000	0.751	30,040
4	Cash flow	20,000	0.683	13,660
				31,290

Present value C

Year		$	Discount factor 10%	Present value $
1	Cash flow	(30,000)	0.909	(27,270)
2	Cash flow	30,000	0.826	24,780
3	Cash flow	40,000	0.751	30,040
4	Cash flow	10,000	0.683	6,830
				34,380

The optimal investment policy is as follows.

Ranking	Project	Year 0 outlay $	NPV $
1st	C	30,000	4,380
2nd	B	28,000	3,290
3rd	A (balance)	2,000 (*4% of 5,700)	228
		NPV from total investment =	7,898

*4% = (2,000/50,000)

Exam focus point

> The June 2014 exam contained a calculation question on the profitability index. The question stated that two of the projects were mutually exclusive. The ACCA examination team commented that some students did not know what mutually exclusive meant, as they included both of the projects. If two projects are mutually exclusive then only one of them can be undertaken.

3.5 Postponing projects

We have so far assumed that projects cannot be postponed until year 1. If this assumption is removed, the choice of projects in year 0 would be made by reference to the loss of NPV from **postponement**.

3.6 Example: Postponing projects

The figures in the previous exercise will be used to illustrate the method. If any project, A, B or C, were delayed by one year, the 'NPV' would now relate to year 1 values, so that in year 0 terms the NPVs would be as follows.

		NPV in Year 1 $			NPV in Year 0 Value $	Loss in NPV $
(a)	Project A	5,700 ×	$\frac{1}{1.10}$	=	5,182	518
(b)	Project B	3,290 ×	$\frac{1}{1.10}$	=	2,991	299
(c)	Project C	4,380 ×	$\frac{1}{1.10}$	=	3,982	398

An index of postponability would be calculated as follows.

Project	Loss in NPV from one-year postponement $	Outlay deferred from year 0 $	Postponability index (loss/outlay)
A	518	50,000	0.0104
B	299	28,000	0.0107
C	398	30,000	0.0133

The loss in NPV by deferring investment would be greatest for Project C, and least for Project A. It is therefore more profitable to postpone A, rather than B or C, as follows.

Investment in year 0:

Project	Outlay $	NPV $
C	30,000	4,380
B	28,000	3,290
A (balance)	2,000	228 (4% of 5,700)
	60,000	7,898

Investment in year 1 (balance):

Project A	$48,000	4,975 (96% of 5,182)
Total NPV (as at year 0) of investments in years 0 and 1		12,873

3.7 Single period rationing with non-divisible projects

If the projects are **not divisible** then the method shown above may not result in the optimal solution. Another complication which arises is that there is likely to be a small amount of **unused capital** with each combination of projects. The best way to deal with this situation is to use **trial and error** and test the NPV available from different combinations of projects. This can be a laborious process if there are a large number of projects available.

3.8 Example: Single period rationing with non-divisible projects

Short O'Funds has capital of $95,000 available for investment in the forthcoming period. The directors decide to consider projects P, Q and R only. They wish to invest only in whole projects, but surplus funds can be invested. Which combination of projects will produce the highest NPV at a cost of capital of 20%?

Project	Investment required $'000	Present value of inflows at 20% $'000
P	40	56.5
Q	50	67.0
R	30	48.8

Solution

The investment combinations we need to consider are the various possible pairs of projects P, Q and R.

Projects	Required investment $'000	PV of inflows	NPV from projects $'000
P and Q	90	123.5	33.5
P and R	70	105.3	35.3
Q and R	80	115.8	35.8

The highest NPV will be achieved by undertaking projects Q and R and investing the unused funds of $15,000 externally.

- **Leasing** is a commonly used source of finance.

  We distinguish three types of leasing:

  - **Operating leases** (**lessor** responsible for maintaining asset)
  - **Finance leases** (**lessee** responsible for maintenance)
  - **Sale and leaseback** arrangements

- The decision whether to **lease or buy** an asset is a **financing decision** which interacts with the investment decision to buy the asset. The assumption is that the preferred financing method should be the one with the lower PV of cost. We identify the **least-cost financing option** by comparing the cash flows of purchasing and leasing. We assume that if the asset is purchased, it will be financed with a bank loan; therefore the cash flows are discounted at an **after-tax cost of borrowing**.

- DCF techniques can assist **asset replacement decisions**, to decide how frequently an asset should be replaced. When an asset is being replaced with an identical asset, the **equivalent annual cost method** can be used to calculate an **optimum replacement cycle**.

- **Capital rationing** may occur due to internal factors (soft capital rationing) or external factors (hard capital rationing).

- When capital rationing occurs in a **single period**, projects are ranked in terms of **profitability index**. This is the ratio of the NPV of a project to its investment cost. The projects with the highest ratios should be selected for investment.

Quick Quiz

1   Who is responsible for the servicing of a leased asset in the case of:

(a)   An operating lease?

(b)   A finance lease?

The lessee	or	The lessor

2   The net present value of the costs of operating a machine for the next three years is $10,724 at a cost of capital of 15%. What is the equivalent annual cost of operating the machine?

A $4,697
B $3,575
C $4,111
D $3,109

3   **Hard capital rationing** occurs when a restriction on an organisation's ability to invest capital funds is caused by an internal budget ceiling imposed by management.

True ☐

False ☐

4   Profitability Index (PI) = $\dfrac{(1)}{(2)}$

What are (1) and (2)?

5   Equivalent annual cost = $\dfrac{\text{PV of costs over n years}}{\text{n year annuity factor}}$

Explain briefly what is meant by:

(a)   PV of costs
(b)   n year annuity factor

6   What is an indivisible project?

7   Give three reasons why hard capital rationing may occur.

8   What is the best way to find the optimal solution in a situation of single period rationing with indivisible projects?

9   What is the best way to find the optimal solution in a situation of single period rationing with divisible projects?

1   (a)   The lessor
    (b)   The lessee

2   A $10,724/2.283 = $4,697

3   False. This describes **soft** capital rationing.

4   (1)   Present value of cash inflows
    (2)   Initial investment

5   (a)   The purchase cost, minus the present value of any subsequent disposal proceeds at the end of the item's life

    (b)   The annuity factor at the company's cost of capital, for the number of years of the item's life

6   A project that must be undertaken completely or not at all

7   Any **three** of:

    (a)   Raising money through the stock market may not be possible if share prices are depressed.
    (b)   There are restrictions on lending due to government control.
    (c)   Lending institutions may consider the organisation to be too risky.
    (d)   The costs associated with making small issues of capital may be too great.

8   Use trial and error and test the NPV available from different project combinations.

9   Rank the projects according to their profitability index.

Now try the questions below from the Practice Question Bank

Number	Level	Marks	Approximate time
Section A Q22	Examination	2	4 mins
Section C Q12	Examination	20	39 mins
Section C Q13	Examination	20	39 mins

PART

E

Business finance

BPP
LEARNING MEDIA

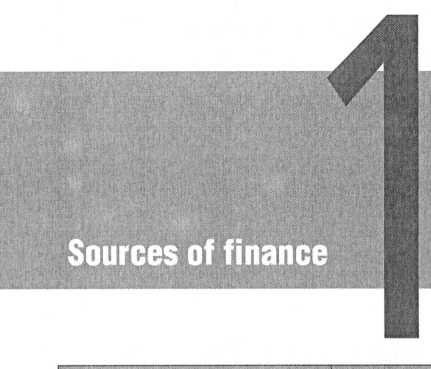

Sources of finance

Topic list	Syllabus reference
1 Short-term sources of finance	E1 (a)
2 Debt finance	E1 (b)
3 Venture capital	E1 (b)
4 Equity finance and preference shares	E1 (b), (c)
5 Islamic finance	E1 (d)

Introduction

In Part E of this study text we consider sources of finance. In this chapter we will look at the distinction between short- and long-term sources of finance.

When sources of **long-term finance** are used, large sums are usually involved, and so the financial manager needs to consider all the options available with care, looking at the possible effects on the company in the long term.

If a company decides to raise new equity finance, it needs to consider which method would be best for its circumstances.

Also considered here is the growth area of **Islamic finance** and how it differs from the other forms of financing covered.

Study guide

		Intellectual level
E1	**Sources of and raising business finance**	
(a)	Identify and discuss the range of short-term sources of finance available to businesses, including:	2
(i)	Overdraft	
(ii)	Short-term loan	
(iii)	Trade credit	
(iv)	Lease finance	
(b)	Identify and discuss the range of long-term sources of finance available to businesses, including:	2
(i)	Equity finance	
(ii)	Debt finance	
(iii)	Lease finance	
(iv)	Venture capital	
(c)	Identify and discuss methods of raising equity finance, including:	2
(i)	Rights issue	
(ii)	Placing	
(iii)	Public offer	
(iv)	Stock exchange listing	
(d)	Identify and discuss methods of raising short- and long-term Islamic finance, including:	1
(i)	Major difference between Islamic finance and the other forms of business finance	
(ii)	The concept of riba (interest) and how returns are made by Islamic financial securities	
(iii)	Islamic financial instruments available to businesses, including:	
(i)	Murabaha (trade credit)	
(ii)	Ijara (lease finance)	
(iii)	Mudaraba (equity finance)	
(iv)	Sukuk (debt finance)	
(v)	Musharaka (venture capital)	

Exam guide

Sources of finance are a major topic. You may be asked to describe appropriate sources of finance for a particular company, and also discuss in general terms when different sources of finance should be utilised and when they are likely to be available.

Performance objective 10 requires you to 'source short-term finance to improve an organisation's liquidity'. You can apply the knowledge you obtain from this chapter of the text to help to demonstrate this competence.

1 Short-term sources of finance 12/09

FAST FORWARD

A range of short-term sources of finance are available to businesses including **overdrafts**, **short-term loans**, **trade credit** and **operating lease finance**.

Short-term finance is usually needed for businesses to run their **day to day operations** including payment of wages to employees, inventory ordering and supplies. Businesses with seasonal peaks and troughs and those engaged in international trade are likely to be heavy users of short-term finance.

1.1 Overdrafts

Where payments from a current account exceed income to the account for a temporary period, the bank may agree to finance a deficit balance on the account by means of an **overdraft**. Overdrafts are the most important source of short-term finance available to businesses. They can be arranged relatively **quickly** and offer a level of **flexibility** with regard to the amount borrowed at any time, while interest is only paid when the account is overdrawn.

OVERDRAFTS	
Amount	The bank specifies an overdraft limit. The overdrawn (negative) balance on the account cannot exceed this limit. The bank usually decides the limit with reference to the borrower's known income. Overdraft borrowing is through the borrower's normal business bank account.
Margin	Interest charged at the bank's administrative base rate plus a margin. This rate is usually higher than the rate for a short-term bank loan.
	Interest is calculated daily on the amount overdrawn and is charged to the borrower's account quarterly (or monthly). An additional fee may be charged for arranging a large-size overdraft facility.
Purpose	Generally to cover short-term deficits in cash flows from normal business operations. The borrower may not want to retain large amounts of cash in a bank account, earning no interest; therefore some negative cash balances may occur.
Repayment	Technically repayable on demand. If a bank ends an overdraft facility without warning, the borrower could face a risk of insolvency.
Security	Depends on size of facility. The bank may ask for security (collateral) but often does not.
Benefits	The customer has flexible means of short-term borrowing; the bank has to accept fluctuations in amount of lending.

By providing an overdraft facility to a customer, the bank is committing itself to providing an overdraft to the customer whenever the customer wants it, up to the agreed limit. The bank will earn interest on the lending, but only to the extent that the customer **uses the facility** and goes into their overdraft. If the customer does not go into their overdraft, the bank cannot charge interest.

The bank will generally charge a **commitment fee** when a customer is granted an overdraft facility or an increase in their overdraft facility. This is a fee for granting an overdraft facility and agreeing to provide the customer with funds if and whenever they need them.

1.1.1 Overdrafts and the operating cycle

Many businesses require their bank to provide financial assistance for normal trading over the **operating cycle.**

For example, suppose that a business has the following working capital position.

	$	$
Inventories and trade receivables		10,000
Bank overdraft	1,000	
Trade payables	3,000	
		4,000
Working capital		6,000

It now buys inventory costing $2,500 for cash, using its overdraft. Working capital remains the same, $6,000, although the bank's financial stake has risen from $1,000 to $3,500.

	$	$
Inventories and trade receivables		12,500
Bank overdraft	3,500	
Trade payables	3,000	
		6,500
Working capital		6,000

A bank overdraft provides support for normal trading finance. In this example, finance for normal trading rises from $(10,000 – 3,000) = $7,000 to $(12,500 – 3,000) = $9,500 and the bank's contribution rises from $1,000 out of $7,000 to $3,500 out of $9,500.

A feature of bank lending to support normal trading finance is that the amount of the overdraft required at any time will depend on the **cash flows of the business** – the timing of receipts and payments, seasonal variations in trade patterns, and so on. The purpose of the overdraft is to bridge the gap between cash payments and cash receipts.

1.1.2 Solid core overdrafts

When a business customer has an overdraft facility, and the account is always in overdraft, then it has a **solid core** (or **hard core**) overdraft. For example, suppose that the account of a company has the following record for the previous year.

	Average balance	Range			Debit revenue
Quarter to	$	$		$	$
31 March 20X5	40,000 debit	70,000 debit	–	20,000 debit	600,000
30 June 20X5	50,000 debit	80,000 debit	–	25,000 debit	500,000
30 September 20X5	75,000 debit	105,000 debit	–	50,000 debit	700,000
31 December 20X5	80,000 debit	110,000 debit	–	60,000 debit	550,000

These figures show that the account has been permanently in overdraft, and the hard core of the overdraft has been rising steeply over the course of the year.

If the hard core element of the overdraft appears to be becoming a **long-term feature** of the business, the bank might wish, after discussions with the customer, to convert the hard core of the overdraft into a **loan**, thus giving formal recognition to its more permanent nature. Otherwise annual reductions in the hard core of an overdraft would typically be a requirement of the bank.

1.2 Short-term loans

A **term loan** is a loan for a fixed amount for a specified period, usually from a bank. The loan may have a specific purpose, such as the purchase of an asset. It is drawn in full at the beginning of the loan period and repaid at a specified time or in defined instalments. Term loans are offered with a variety of **repayment schedules**. Often, the interest and capital repayments are predetermined.

The bank establishes a separate loan account for the loan, charging interest to the account and setting off loan payments against the balance on the account.

The main advantage of lending on a loan account for the bank is that it makes **monitoring** and **control** of the advance much easier, because the loan cash flows are recorded in a separate account. The bank can see immediately when the customer is falling behind with their repayments, or struggling to make the payments. With overdraft lending, a customer's difficulties might be obscured for some time by the variety of transactions on their current account.

(a) The customer knows what they will be **expected** to **pay back** at regular intervals and the bank can also predict its future income with more certainty (depending on whether the interest rate is fixed or floating).

(b) Once the loan is agreed, the **term of** the loan must be **adhered** to, provided that the customer does not fall behind with their repayments. It is not repayable on demand by the bank.

(c) Because the bank will be committing its funds to a customer for a number of years, it may wish to insist on **building certain written safeguards** into the loan agreement, to prevent the customer from becoming overextended with their borrowing during the course of the loan. A loan **covenant** is a condition that the borrower must comply with. If the borrower does not act in accordance with the covenants, the loan can be considered in **default** and the bank can demand payment.

1.3 Overdrafts and short-term loans compared

A customer might ask the bank for an overdraft facility when the bank would wish to suggest a loan instead; alternatively, a customer might ask for a loan when an overdraft would be more appropriate.

(a) In most cases, when a customer wants finance to help with **'day to day' trading** and cash flow needs, an **overdraft** would be the appropriate method of financing. The customer should not be short of cash all the time, and should expect to be in credit in some days, but in need of an overdraft on others.

(b) When a customer wants to **borrow** from a bank **for only a short period of time**, even for the purchase of a major fixed asset, such as an item of plant or machinery, an overdraft facility might be more suitable than a loan, because the customer will stop paying interest as soon as their account goes into credit.

1.3.1 Advantages of an overdraft over a loan

(a) The customer **only pays interest** when they are **overdrawn**.

(b) The bank has the **flexibility** to review the customer's overdraft facility periodically, and perhaps agree to additional facilities, or insist on a reduction in the facility.

(c) An overdraft can do the **same job** as a loan: a facility can simply be renewed every time it comes up for review.

Bear in mind, however, that overdrafts are normally repayable on demand.

1.3.2 Advantages of a loan for longer-term lending

(a) Both the customer and the bank **know** exactly what the **repayments** of the loan will be and how much **interest** is payable, and when. This makes planning (budgeting) simpler.

(b) The interest rate on the loan balance is likely to be lower than the interest charged on overdrawn balances. The comparative cost therefore depends on the size and duration of borrowing requirements.

(c) The customer does **not** have to **worry** about the bank deciding to reduce or withdraw an overdraft facility before they are in a position to repay what is owed. There is an element of 'security' or 'peace of mind' in being able to arrange a loan for an agreed term.

(d) Loans normally carry a **facility letter** setting out the precise terms of the agreement.

However, a **mix** of overdrafts and loans might be suggested in some cases. Consider a case where a business asks for a loan, perhaps to purchase a shop with inventory. The banker might wish to suggest a loan to help with the purchase of the shop, but that inventory ought to be financed by an overdraft facility. The offer of part-loan part-overdraft is an option that might be well worth considering.

1.3.3 Calculation of repayments on a loan

We can use an annuity table to calculate the repayments on a loan.

For example, a $30,000 loan is taken out by a business at a rate of 12% over 5 years. What will be the annual payment, assuming that payments are made every 12 months and the loan provides for gradual repayment over the term of the loan?

The annuity factor for 12% over 5 years is 3.605. Therefore $30,000 = 3.605 × annual payment.

$$\text{Annual payment} = \frac{30,000}{3.605}$$

$$= \$8,321.78$$

1.3.4 The split between interest and capital repayment

A loan of $100,000 is to be repaid to the bank, over five years, in equal annual year-end instalments made up of capital repayments and interest at 9% pa.

$$\text{The annual payment} = \frac{\$100,000}{3.890} = \$25,707$$

Each payment can then be split between the repayment of capital and interest.

Year	Balance b/f	Interest @ 9%	Annual payment	Balance c/f
	$	$	$	$
1	100,000	9,000	(25,707)	83,293
2	83,293	7,496	(25,707)	65,082
3	65,082	5,857	(25,707)	45,232
4	45,232	4,071	(25,707)	23,596
5	23,596	2,111*	(25,707)	

* Rounding difference

1.4 Trade credit

Trade credit is a major source of short-term finance for a business. Current assets such as raw materials may be purchased on credit, with payment terms normally varying from between 30 and 90 days. Trade credit therefore represents an interest-free short-term loan. In a period of high inflation, purchasing via trade credit will be very helpful in keeping costs down. However, it is important to take into account the **loss of discounts** suppliers offer for early payment.

Unacceptable delays in payment will worsen a company's **credit rating** and additional credit may become difficult to obtain.

1.5 Leasing   6/11

Rather than buying an asset outright, using either available cash resources or borrowed funds, a business may **lease** an asset. Leasing is a popular source of finance.

Leasing can be defined as a contract between **lessor** and **lessee** for hire of a specific asset selected from a manufacturer or vendor of such assets by the lessee. The lessor retains ownership of the asset. The lessee has possession and use of the asset on payment of specified rentals over a period. Operating leases are in effect a short-term source of finance for non-current assets, and finance leases are a long-term source of finance. This is because the lessor purchases the asset and the lessee can use it without having to incur the initial cost immediately.

Many lessors are financial intermediaries, such as banks and insurance companies. The range of assets leased is wide, including office equipment and computers, cars and commercial vehicles, aircraft, ships and buildings.

Leasing was covered in detail in Chapter 11 of this Study Text.

1.5.1 Sale and leaseback

Sale and leaseback arrangements were also explained in Chapter 11.

A company which owns its own premises can obtain finance by selling the property to an insurance company or pension fund for immediate cash and renting it back, usually for at least 50 years with rent reviews every few years.

A company would raise more cash from sale and leaseback arrangements than from a mortgage, but there are significant **disadvantages**.

(a)   The company **loses ownership** of a valuable asset which is almost certain to appreciate over time.

(b)   The **future borrowing capacity** of the firm will be reduced, as there will be fewer assets to provide security for a loan.

(c)   The company is **contractually committed** to occupying the property for many years ahead which can be restricting.

(d)   The **real cost** is likely to be high, particularly as there will be frequent rent reviews.

2 Debt finance   12/08, 6/10, 12/10, 6/14

A range of long-term sources of finance are available to businesses including **debt finance**, **leasing**, **venture capital** and **equity finance**.

Long-term finance is used for major investments and is usually more expensive and less flexible than short-term finance.

2.1 Reasons for seeking debt finance

Sometimes businesses may need long-term funds, but may not wish to issue equity capital. Perhaps the current shareholders will be unwilling to **contribute additional capital**; possibly the company does not wish to involve outside shareholders who will have more onerous requirements than current members.

Other reasons for choosing debt finance may include **lesser cost** and **easier availability**, particularly if the company has little or no existing debt finance. Debt finance provides **tax relief** on interest payments.

2.2 Sources of debt finance

If a company does wish to raise debt finance, it will need to consider what **type** of finance will be available. If it is seeking medium-term bank finance, it ought to be in the form of a **loan**. Bank finance is an important source of both short-term and longer-term debt for small companies, and we shall consider this in greater detail in Chapter 14.

If a company is seeking to issue bonds, it must decide whether to make an issue of 'conventional' bonds, or whether investors may be attracted by a different type of bond issue, such as convertible bonds.

2.3 Factors influencing choice of debt finance

> **FAST FORWARD**
>
> The choice of **debt finance** that a company can make depends on:
>
> - The size of the company; a public issue of bonds is only available to a large company
> - The duration of the required financing
> - Whether a fixed or floating interest rate is preferred (fixed rates are more expensive, but floating rates are riskier)
> - The security (collateral) that can be offered and the security that may be demanded by a lender

In Chapter 14, we shall look in detail at the factors that determine the mix of debt and equity finance that a company chooses. For now, you need to bear in mind when reading this chapter the following considerations influencing what type of debt finance is sought.

(a) **Availability**

Only listed companies are able to make a public issue of bonds. With a 'public issue' the bonds are listed on a stock market. Most investors will not invest in bonds issued by small companies. Smaller companies are only able to obtain significant amounts of debt finance from a bank.

(b) **Credit rating**

Large companies may prefer to issue bonds if they have a strong credit rating. Credit ratings are given to bond issues by credit rating agencies. The credit rating given to a bond issue affects the interest yield that investors will require. If a company's bonds would only be given a sub-investment grade rating ('junk bond' rating), the company may prefer to seek debt finance from a bank loan.

(c) **Amount**

Bond issues are usually for large amounts. If a company wants to borrow only a small amount of money, a bank loan would be appropriate.

(d) **Duration**

If loan finance is sought to buy a particular asset to generate revenues for the business, the length of the loan should **match** the length of time that the asset will be generating revenues.

(e) **Fixed or floating rate**

Expectations of interest rate movements will determine whether a company wants to borrow at a fixed or floating rate. Fixed-rate finance may be more expensive, but the business runs the risk of adverse upward rate movements if it chooses floating rate finance. Banks may refuse to lend at a fixed rate for more than a given period of time.

(f) **Security and covenants**

The choice of finance may be determined by the assets that the business is willing or able to offer as **security**, and by the restrictions in **covenants** that the lenders wish to impose.

2.4 Bonds

> **FAST FORWARD**
>
> The term **bonds** describes various forms of long-term debt a company may issue, such as **loan notes**, which may be:
>
> - Redeemable
> - Irredeemable
>
> Bonds or loans come in various forms, including:
>
> - Floating rate loan notes
> - Zero coupon bonds
> - Convertible bonds

> **Bonds** are long-term debt capital raised by a company for which interest is paid, usually half yearly and at a fixed rate. Holders of bonds are therefore long-term payables for the company.

2.4.1 Conventional bonds

Conventional bonds are fixed-rate redeemable bonds.

Bonds have a nominal value, which is the debt owed by the company, and interest is paid at a stated 'coupon' on this amount. For example, if a company issues 10% bonds, the coupon will be 10% of the nominal value of the bonds, so that $100 of bonds will receive $10 interest each year. The rate quoted is the gross rate, before tax.

Unlike shares, debt is often issued **at nominal value**, ie with $100 payable per $100 nominal value, or close to nominal value. Bond prices are quoted per $100 nominal value of bonds, so a price of $98.65 means a market price of $98.65 per $100 nominal value.

Where the coupon rate is fixed at the time of issue, it will be set according to **prevailing market conditions** given the **credit rating** of the company issuing the debt. Subsequent changes in market (and company) conditions will cause the **market value** of the bond to fluctuate, although the coupon will stay at the fixed percentage of the nominal value.

Bonds issued by large companies are marketable, but bond markets are small. When a company issues new equity shares, the new shares rank equally with all existing equity shares, and can be bought and sold in the same market. In contrast, each bond issue is different, with its own interest rate and redemption date; the market for different bond issues by the same company cannot be combined. This is why equities may be extensively traded on a stock market, but bonds are not.

> A **loan note** is the written acknowledgement of a debt incurred by a company, normally containing provisions about the payment of interest and the eventual repayment of capital. (**Note.** For the purposes of the F9 exam, debentures is simply another word for bonds or loan notes.)

2.5 Deep discount bonds

> **Deep discount bonds** are bonds or loan notes issued at a price which is at a large discount to the nominal value of the notes, and which will be redeemable at nominal value (or above nominal value) when they eventually mature.

For example a company might issue $1,000,000 of bonds in 20X1, at a price of $50 per $100 of bond, and redeemable at nominal value in the year 20X9. The coupon rate of interest will be very low compared with yields on conventional bonds with the same maturity. For a company with specific cash flow requirements, the low servicing costs during the currency of the bond may be an attraction, coupled with a high cost of redemption at maturity.

Investors might be attracted by the **large capital gain** offered by the bonds, which is the difference between the **issue price** and the **redemption value**. However, deep discount bonds will carry a much **lower rate of interest** than other types of bond. The only tax advantage is that the gain gets taxed (as **income**) in one lump on maturity or sale, not as amounts of interest each year. The borrower can, however, **deduct notional interest** each year in computing profits.

The main benefit of deep discount bonds for a company is that the interest yield on the bonds is lower than on conventional bonds. However, it will have to pay a much larger amount at maturity than it borrowed when the bonds were issued. Deep discount bonds defer much of the cost of the debt.

2.6 Zero coupon bonds

Zero coupon bonds are bonds that are issued at a discount to their redemption value, but no interest is paid on them.

Zero coupon bonds are an extreme form of deep discount bond. For example, a company may issue zero coupon discount bonds at 75.00, pay no interest at all, but at maturity (say, five years later) redeem the bonds at 100.00. The investor gains from the difference between the issue price and the redemption value ($25 per $75 invested). There is an implied interest rate in the amount of discount at which the bonds are issued (or subsequently resold on the market).

(a) The advantage for borrowers is that zero coupon bonds can be used to **raise cash immediately**, and there is **no cash repayment** until redemption date. The cost of redemption is known at the time of issue. The borrower can plan to have funds available to redeem the bonds at maturity.

(b) The **advantage for lenders** is **restricted**, unless the rate of discount on the bonds offers a high yield. The only way of obtaining cash from the bonds before maturity is to sell them. Their **market value** will depend on the **remaining term** to maturity and **current market interest rates**.

The tax advantage of zero coupon bonds is the same as that of deep discount bonds (see 2.2.5 above).

Deep discount bonds and zero coupon bonds are not common. Companies must want to pay little or no interest and incur the main cost at redemption. Investors must have reasons for wanting to invest in these bonds, rather than in conventional bonds.

2.7 Convertible bonds   12/07, 12/12, 12/14

FAST FORWARD

Convertible bonds are bonds that give the holder the right to convert to other securities, normally ordinary shares, at a predetermined price/rate and time.

Convertible bonds are fixed-rate bonds. The coupon rate of interest is lower than on similar conventional bonds. They give the bond holders the right (but not an obligation) to convert their bonds at a specified future date into new equity shares of the company, at a conversion rate that is also specified when the bonds are issued.

For example, the conversion terms for a convertible bond may be that on 1 April 20X0, $100 of bonds can be converted into 40 ordinary shares, whereas on 1 April 20X1, the conversion rate is 45 ordinary shares per $100 of bonds. Once converted, convertible securities cannot be converted back into the original fixed return security.

If bond holders choose not to convert their bonds into shares, the bonds will be redeemed at maturity, usually at nominal rate.

2.7.1 The conversion value and the conversion premium

The current market value of ordinary shares into which a bond may be converted is known as the conversion value. The **conversion value** will be below the value of the bond at the date of issue, but will be expected to increase as the date for conversion approaches on the assumption that a company's shares ought to increase in market value over time.

Conversion value = Conversion ratio × market price per share
Conversion premium = Current market value − current conversion value

Question   Convertible debt

The 10% convertible bonds of Starchwhite are quoted at $142 per $100 nominal. The earliest date for conversion is in 4 years' time, at the rate of 30 ordinary shares per $100 nominal bond. The share price is currently $4.15. Annual interest on the bonds has just been paid.

Required

(a) Calculate the current conversion value.

(b) Calculate the conversion premium and comment on its meaning.

Answer

(a) Conversion ratio is $100 bond = 30 ordinary shares
Conversion value = 30 × $4.15 = $124.50

(b) Conversion premium = $(142 − 124.50) = $17.50 or $\dfrac{17.50}{124.50} \times 100\% = 14\%$

The share price will have to rise by 14% before the conversion rights become attractive.

2.7.2 The issue price and the market price of convertible bonds

A company will aim to issue bonds with the **greatest possible conversion premium**, as this will mean that for the amount of capital raised it will, on conversion, have to issue the lowest number of new ordinary shares. The premium that will be accepted by potential investors will depend on the company's growth potential and so on prospects for a sizeable increase in the share price.

Convertible bonds issued at nominal have a **lower coupon rate of interest** than similar conventional bonds. This lower interest rate is the price the investor has to pay for the conversion rights. It is, of course, also one of the reasons why the issue of convertible bonds is attractive to a company.

A (large) company may issue convertible bonds rather than conventional bonds in order to benefit from lower interest costs, even if this means having to issue new shares in the future, when profits and cash flows are stronger.

When convertible bonds are traded on a stock market, their **minimum market price** or **floor value** will be the price of conventional bonds with the same coupon rate of interest. If the market value falls to this minimum, it follows that the market attaches no value to the conversion rights.

The actual market price of convertible bonds will depend on:

- The **price of straight debt**
- The **current conversion value**
- The **length of time** before conversion may take place
- The **market's expectation** as to future equity returns and the risk associated with these returns

Most companies issuing convertible bonds expect them to be **converted**. They view the bonds as **delayed equity**. They are often used either because the company's ordinary share price is considered to be particularly depressed at the time of issue or because the issue of equity shares would result in an immediate and significant drop in earnings per share. There is no certainty, however, that the security holders will exercise their option to convert; therefore the bonds may run their full term and need to be redeemed.

2.7.3 Example: Convertible bonds

CD has issued 50,000 units of convertible bonds, each with a nominal value of $100 and a coupon rate of interest of 10% payable yearly. Each $100 of convertible bonds may be converted into 40 ordinary shares of CD in three years' time. Any bonds not converted will be redeemed at 110 (that is, at $110 per $100 nominal value of bond).

Estimate the likely current market price for $100 of the bonds, if investors in the bonds now require a pre-tax return of only 8%, and the expected value of CD ordinary shares on the conversion day is:

(a) $2.50 per share

(b) $3.00 per share

Solution

(a) Shares are valued at $2.50 each.

If shares are only expected to be worth $2.50 each on conversion day, the value of 40 shares will be $100, and investors in the debt will presumably therefore redeem their debt at 110 instead of converting them into shares.

The market value of $100 of the convertible debt will be the discounted present value of the expected future income stream.

Year		Cash flow $	Discount factor 8%	Present value $
1	Interest	10	0.926	9.26
2	Interest	10	0.857	8.57
3	Interest	10	0.794	7.94
3	Redemption value	110	0.794	87.34
				113.11

The estimated market value is $113.11 per $100 of debt. This is also the floor value.

(b) Shares are valued at $3 each.

If shares are expected to be worth $3 each, the debt holders will convert their debt into shares (value per $100 of bonds = 40 shares × $3 = $120) rather than redeem their debt at 110.

Year		Cash flow/value $	Discount factor 8%	Present value $
1	Interest	10	0.926	9.26
2	Interest	10	0.857	8.57
3	Interest	10	0.794	7.94
3	Value of 40 shares	120	0.794	95.28
				121.05

The estimated market value is $121.05 per $100 of debt.

2.8 Security

Bonds may be secured. Bank loans are often secured. **Security** may take the form of either a **fixed charge** or a **floating charge**.

Fixed charge	Floating charge
Security relates to specific asset/group of assets (land and buildings)	Security in event of default is whatever assets of the class secured (inventory/trade receivables) company then owns
Company can't dispose of assets without providing substitute/consent of lender	Company can dispose of assets until default takes place
	In event of default lenders appoint receiver rather than lay claim to asset

Investors are likely to expect a higher yield with **unsecured bonds** to compensate them for the extra risk. Similarly, a bank may charge higher interest for an unsecured loan compared with a similar secured loan.

2.9 The redemption of bonds

Key term

> **Redemption** is a term for the repayment of preference shares and bonds at maturity.

Bonds are usually redeemable. They are issued for a term of ten years or more, and perhaps 25 to 30 years. At the end of this period, they will 'mature' and become redeemable (at nominal value or possibly at a value above nominal value).

Most redeemable bonds have an earliest and a latest redemption date. For example, 12% Loan note 20X7/X9 is redeemable at any time between the earliest specified date (in 20X7) and the latest date (in 20X9). The **issuing company** can choose the date.

Some bonds do not have a redemption date, and are **'irredeemable'** or 'undated'. These are rare in reality and are typically only issued by governments, not companies.

2.9.1 How will a company finance the redemption of long-term debt?

There is no guarantee that a company will be able to raise a new loan to pay off a maturing debt. One item you should look for in a company's statement of financial position is the **redemption date** of current loans, to establish how much new finance is likely to be needed by the company, and when.

Occasionally, perhaps because the secured assets have fallen in value and would not realise much in a forced sale, or perhaps out of a belief that the company can improve its position soon, unpaid loan note holders may be persuaded to surrender their loan notes. In exchange they may receive an **equity interest** in the company or **convertible loan notes**, paying a lower rate of interest, but carrying the option to convert the loan notes into shares at a specified time in the future.

2.10 Tax relief on loan interest

As far as companies are concerned, debt capital is a potentially attractive source of finance because interest charges are an allowable expense for tax purposes. Interest charges **reduce the profits** chargeable to corporation tax. Dividend payments to shareholders do not attract tax relief. The after-tax cost of debt can therefore be much lower than the cost of equity.

(a) A new issue of bonds is likely to be preferable to a new issue of preference shares (preference shares are shares carrying a fixed rate of dividends).

(b) Companies might wish to **avoid dilution of shareholdings** and **increase gearing** (the ratio of fixed interest capital to equity capital) in order to improve their earnings per share by benefiting from tax relief on interest payments.

3 Venture capital   6/13

> **Venture capital** is risk capital, normally provided by a venture capital firm or individual venture capitalist, in return for an equity stake.

Venture capital is capital that is invested (or is available for investing) in private companies. The venture capital may be provided by a wealthy individual, or it may be provided by a venture capital firm that manages a venture capital fund. (A venture capital fund consists of money from investors for investing in private company equity.)

Venture capitalists seek to invest cash in return for shares in private companies with high growth potential. They seek a high return, which is often realised through a stock market listing.

Venture capital may be invested in young start-up companies, but is more commonly invested in small companies that already have a track record of business development and which need additional finance to grow. These companies may have borrowed as much money as their banks are prepared to lend, and do not have enough equity capital (from the existing owners or retained profits) to expand at the rate or scale required.

Venture capital organisations have been operating for many years. There is now quite a large number of such organisations. For example:

(a) The British Venture Capital Association is a regulatory body for all the institutions that have joined it as members.

(b) **Investors in Industry plc**, or the **3i group** as it is more commonly known, is the biggest and oldest of the venture capital organisations. It is involved in many venture capital schemes in Europe, Singapore, Japan and the US.

Venture capitalists want to invest in companies that will be successful. The 3i group's publicity material states that successful investments have certain common characteristics.

- Highly motivated individuals with a strong management team in place
- A well-defined strategy
- A clearly defined target market
- Current revenue between $1m and $100m
- A proven ability to outperform your competitors
- Innovation

The types of venture that the 3i group might invest in include the following.

(a) **Business start-ups**. When a business has been set up by someone who has already put time and money into getting it started, the group may be willing to **provide finance** to enable it to get off the ground.

(b) **Business development**. The group may be willing to **provide development capital** for a company which wants to invest in new products or new markets or to make a business acquisition, and so which needs a major capital injection.

(c) **Management buyouts**. A management buyout is the **purchase** of all or parts of a **business** from its owners by its managers.

(d) Helping a company where one of its owners wants to **realise all or part of their investment**. The 3i group may be prepared to buy some of the company's equity.

3.1 Venture capital funds

Some other organisations are engaged in the creation of **venture capital funds**. In these the organisation raises venture capital funds from investors and invests in management buyouts or expanding companies. The venture capital fund managers usually reward themselves by taking a percentage of the portfolio of the fund's investments.

3.2 Finding venture capital

When a company's directors look for help from a venture capital institution, they must recognise that:

(a) The institution will want an **equity stake** in the company.

(b) It will need convincing that the company can be successful (management buyouts of companies which already have a record of **successful trading** have been increasingly favoured by venture capitalists in recent years).

(c) It may want to have a **representative** appointed to the company's board, to look after its interests, or an **independent director** (the 3i group runs an Independent Director Scheme).

The directors of the company must then contact venture capital organisations, to try to find one or more which would be willing to offer finance. Typically, a venture capitalist will consider offering finance of $500,000 upwards. A venture capital organisation will only give funds to a company that it believes can succeed.

A venture capitalist may also agree to invest in some redeemable preference shares as well as equity, but will want a suitable proportion of the company's equity as part of the financing arrangement.

When a venture capitalist invests in new equity for a company, the company's bank may also be prepared to lend more, because the company is now seen as a lower credit risk.

A survey has indicated that around 75% of requests for venture capital are rejected on an initial screening, and only about 3% of all requests survive both this screening and further investigation and result in actual investments.

The venture capital organisation (VC) will take account of various factors in deciding whether or not to invest.

Factors in investment decisions	
The nature of the company's **product**	Viability of production and selling potential
Expertise in **production**	Technical ability to produce efficiently
Expertise in **management**	Commitment, skills and experience
The **market and competition**	Threat from rival producers or future new entrants
Future profits	Detailed business plan showing profit prospects that compensate for risks
Board membership	To take account of VC's interests and ensure that VC has say in future strategy
Risk borne by existing owners	Owners bear significant risk and invest significant part of their overall wealth

4 Equity finance and preference shares   6/11, 6/13

FAST FORWARD »

Equity finance is raised through the sale of **ordinary shares** to investors via a **new issue** or a **rights issue**.

4.1 Ordinary shares

Ordinary shares are issued to the owners of a company. Ordinary shares in many countries have a **nominal** or 'face' value, typically $1 or 50c. In some countries, equity shares no longer have a nominal value.

You should understand that the **market value** of a quoted company's shares bears **no relationship** to their nominal value except that, when ordinary shares are issued for cash, the issue price must be equal to or (more usually) more than the nominal value of the shares.

Ordinary shareholders have **rights** as a result of their ownership of the shares.

(a)   Shareholders can attend company general meetings.

(b)   They can vote on important company matters such as the appointment and re-election of directors; approving a takeover bid for another company, where the financing arrangements will involve a large new issue of shares; the appointment of auditors; or (possibly, as in the UK) approving the company's remuneration policy for senior executives.

(c)   They are entitled to receive a share of any agreed dividend.

(d)   They will receive the annual report and accounts.

(e)   They will receive a share of any assets remaining after liquidation.

(f)   They can participate in any new issue of shares, unless they agree to waive this right.

Ordinary shareholders are the ultimate bearers of **risk**, as they are at the bottom of the **creditor hierarchy** in a liquidation. This means there is a significant risk they will receive nothing after settlement of all the company's liabilities.

This high equity risk means that shareholders expect the **highest return** of long-term providers of finance, in the form of dividend yields, dividend growth and share price growth. The cost of equity finance is therefore always **higher** than the cost of debt.

4.2 Advantages of a stock market listing

A company can obtain a **stock market listing** for its shares through a **public offer** or a **placing**.

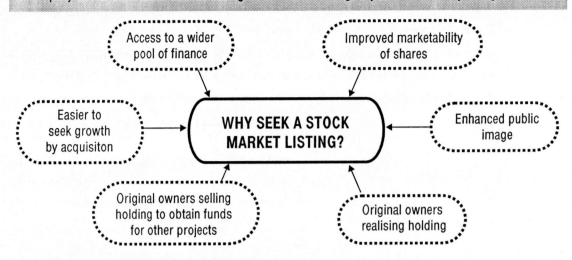

4.3 Disadvantages of a stock market listing

The owners of a company seeking a stock market listing must take the following disadvantages into account.

(a)   There will be significantly greater **public regulation, accountability** and **scrutiny**. The legal requirements the company faces will be greater, and the company will also be subject to the rules of the stock exchange on which its shares are listed.

(b)   A **wider circle of investors** with more exacting requirements will hold shares.

(c)   There will be additional costs involved in making share issues, including **brokerage commissions** and **underwriting fees**.

4.4 Methods of obtaining a listing

An unquoted company that is becoming listed for the first time can issue shares on the stock market by means of:

- **An initial public offer (IPO)**
- **A placing**
- **An introduction**

4.4.1 Initial public offer

Key term

> An **initial public offer (IPO)** is an invitation to apply for shares in a company based on information contained in a prospectus.

An **initial public offer (IPO)** is a means of selling the shares of a company to the public at large for the first time. When companies 'go public' for the first time, a **large** issue will probably take the form of an IPO. This is known as **flotation**. Subsequent issues are likely to be **placings** or **rights issues**, described later.

An IPO entails the **acquisition by an issuing house** (an investment bank acting for the company) of a large block of shares of a company, with a view to offering them for sale to the public and investing institutions.

An issuing house is usually an investment bank. It may acquire the shares either as a direct allotment from the company or by purchase from existing shareholders. In either case, the issuing house publishes an invitation to the public to apply for shares, either at a fixed price or on a tender basis. The issuing house **accepts responsibility** to the public, and gives to the issue the support of its own standing.

In an IPO, the company's shareholders may take the opportunity to sell some of their shares. They receive the money from these share sales. In addition, the company will issue new shares in the IPO to raise equity finance for investment.

4.4.2 A placing

A **placing** is an arrangement whereby, instead of offering the shares to the general public, the sponsoring investment bank arranges for most of the issue to be bought by a **small number of investors**, usually institutional investors such as pension funds and insurance companies.

4.4.3 The choice between an IPO and a placing

Is a company likely to prefer an IPO of its shares, or a placing?

(a)   **Placings** are much **cheaper**. Approaching institutional investors privately is a much cheaper way of obtaining finance, and thus placings are often used for smaller issues.

(b)   Placings are likely to be **quicker**.

(c)   Placings are likely to involve **less disclosure** of **information**.

(d)   However, most of the shares will be placed with a **relatively small number of (institutional) shareholders**, which means that most of the shares are **unlikely to be available for trading** after the flotation, and that **institutional shareholders** will have control of the **company**.

(e)   When a company first comes to the market, there may be a restriction on the proportion of shares that can be placed, or a minimum proportion that must be offered to the general public.

4.4.4 A stock exchange introduction

By this method of obtaining a quotation, no shares are made available to the market, neither existing nor newly created shares; nevertheless, the stock market grants a quotation. This will only happen where shares in a large private company are already widely held, so that a market can be seen to exist. A company might want an **introduction** to obtain **greater marketability** for the shares, a known share valuation for inheritance tax purposes and easier access in the future to additional capital.

4.5 Costs of share issues on the stock market

Companies may incur the following costs when issuing shares.

*   Underwriting costs (see below)

*   Stock market listing fee (the initial charge) for the new securities

*   Fees of the issuing house (investment bank), solicitors, auditors and public relations consultant

*   Charges for printing and distributing the prospectus: (the prospectus is the document in which the company offers its shares for sale)

*   Advertising in national newspapers

4.5.1 Underwriting

A company about to issue new securities in order to raise finance may decide to have the issue underwritten. **Underwriters** are financial institutions which agree (in exchange for a fixed fee, perhaps 2.25% of the finance to be raised) to buy at the issue price any securities which are **not subscribed** for by the investing public.

Underwriters **remove** the **risk** of a share issue's being undersubscribed, but at a cost to the company issuing the shares. It is not compulsory to have an issue underwritten. Ordinary offers for sale (IPOs) are likely to be underwritten, although rights issues may be as well.

4.6 Pricing shares for a stock market launch

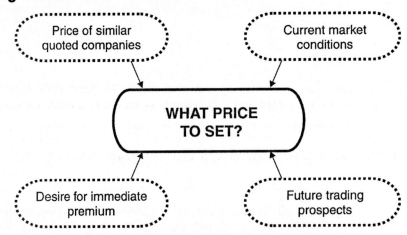

Companies will be keen to avoid **overpricing an issue**, which could result in the **issue** being **undersubscribed**, leaving underwriters with the unwelcome task of having to buy up the unsold shares. On the other hand, if the **issue price** is **too low** then the issue will be **oversubscribed** and the company would have been able to raise the required capital by issuing fewer shares.

The share price of an issue is usually advertised as being based on a certain P/E ratio, the ratio of the price to the company's most recent earnings per share figure in its audited accounts. The issuer's P/E ratio can then be compared by investors with the P/E ratios of similar quoted companies. (We covered P/E ratios in Chapter 1.)

4.7 Rights issues   12/07, 6/08, 12/08, 6/09, 12/09, 12/10, 6/14, 12/14, 6/15

> **FAST FORWARD**
>
> A **rights issue** is an offer to existing shareholders enabling them to buy more shares, usually at a price lower than the current market price, and in proportion to their existing shareholding.

A **rights issue** provides a way of raising new share capital by means of an offer to existing shareholders, inviting them to subscribe cash for new shares in proportion to their existing holdings.

For example, a rights issue on a one for four basis at 280c per share would mean that a company is inviting its existing shareholders to subscribe for one new share for every four shares they hold, at a price of 280c per new share. A rights issue may be made by any type of company. The analysis below, however, applies primarily to listed companies.

The major advantages of a rights issue are as follows.

(a) Rights issues are **cheaper** than **IPOs** to the general public. This is partly because **no prospectus** is normally required, partly because the administration is simpler and partly because the cost of underwriting will be less.

(b) Rights issues are **more beneficial** to **existing shareholders** than issues to the general public. New shares are issued at a discount to the current market price to make them attractive to investors. A rights issue **secures** the **discount** on the market price for existing shareholders, who may either keep the shares or sell them if they wish.

(c) **Relative voting** rights are **unaffected** if shareholders all take up their rights.

(d) The finance raised may be used to **reduce gearing** in book value terms by increasing share capital and/or to pay off long-term debt which will reduce gearing in market value terms. We will look at gearing in more detail in Chapter 14.

4.8 Deciding the issue price for a rights issue

The **offer price** in a rights issue will be lower than the current market price of existing shares. The size of the discount will vary, and will be larger for difficult issues. In the UK, however, the offer price must be at or above the **nominal value** of the shares, so as not to contravene company law.

A company making a rights issue must set a price which is **low enough** to **secure** the **acceptance** of shareholders, who are being asked to provide extra funds, but not too low, so as to avoid excessive dilution of the earnings per share.

4.9 Example: Rights issue (1)

Seagull can achieve a profit after tax of 20% on the capital employed. At present its capital structure is as follows.

	$
200,000 ordinary shares of $1 each	200,000
Retained earnings	100,000
	300,000

The directors propose to raise an additional $126,000 from a rights issue. The current market price is $1.80.

Required

(a) Calculate the number of shares that must be issued if the rights price is: $1.60; $1.50; $1.40; $1.20.

(b) Calculate the dilution in earnings per share in each case.

Solution

The earnings at present are 20% of $300,000 = $60,000. This gives earnings per share of 30c. The earnings after the rights issue will be 20% of $426,000 = $85,200.

Rights price $	No of new share ($126,000 ÷ rights price)	EPS ($85,200 ÷ total no of shares) Cents	Dilution Cents
1.60	78,750	30.6	+ 0.6
1.50	84,000	30.0	–
1.40	90,000	29.4	– 0.6
1.20	105,000	27.9	– 2.1

Note that at a high rights price the earnings per share are increased, not diluted. The breakeven point (zero dilution) occurs when the rights price is equal to the capital employed per share: $300,000 ÷ 200,000 = $1.50.

4.9.1 The market price of shares after a rights issue: the theoretical ex-rights price

When a rights issue is announced, all existing shareholders have the right to subscribe for new shares, and so there are rights attached to the existing shares. The shares are therefore described as being **'cum rights'** (with rights attached) and are traded cum rights. On the first day of dealings in the newly issued shares, the rights no longer exist and the old shares are now **'ex-rights'** (without rights attached).

After the announcement of a rights issue, share prices normally **fall**. The extent and duration of the fall may depend on the number of shareholders and the size of their holdings. This temporary fall is due to **uncertainty** in the market about the consequences of the issue, with respect to future profits, earnings and dividends.

After the issue has actually been made, the market price per share will normally fall, because there are more shares in issue and the new shares were issued at a discount price.

In theory, the new market price will be the consequence of an adjustment to allow for the discount price of the new issue, and a theoretical ex-rights price can be calculated.

4.9.2 Example: Rights issue (2)

Fundraiser has 1,000,000 ordinary shares of $1 in issue, which have a market price on 1 September of $2.10 per share. The company decides to make a rights issue, and offers its shareholders the right to subscribe for one new share at $1.50 each for every four shares already held. After the announcement of the issue, the share price fell to $1.95, but by the time just prior to the issue being made, it had recovered to $2 per share. This market value just before the issue is known as the cum rights price. What is the theoretical ex-rights price?

Solution

Value of the portfolio for a shareholder with 4 shares before the rights issue:

	$
4 shares @ $2.00	8.00
1 share @ $1.50	1.50
5	9.50

So the value per share after the rights issue (or TERP) is 9.50/5 = $1.90.

4.9.3 The value of rights

The value of rights is the theoretical gain a shareholder would make by exercising their rights.

(a) Using the above example, if the price offered in the rights issue is $1.50 per share, and the market price after the issue is expected to be $1.90, the value attaching to a right is $1.90 – $1.50 = $0.40. A shareholder would therefore be expected to gain 40 cents for each new share they buy.

If they do not have enough money to buy the share themselves, they could sell the right to subscribe for a new share to another investor, and receive 40 cents from the sale. This other investor would then buy the new share for $1.50, so that their total outlay to acquire the share would be $0.40 + $1.50 = $1.90, the theoretical ex-rights price.

(b) The value of rights attaching to existing shares is calculated in the same way. If the value of rights on a new share is 40 cents, and there is a one for four rights issue, the value of the rights attaching to each existing share is 40 ÷ 4 = 10 cents.

4.9.4 The theoretical gain or loss to shareholders

The possible courses of action open to shareholders are:

(a) To **'take up' or 'exercise' the rights**; that is, to buy the new shares at the rights price. Shareholders who do this will maintain their percentage holdings in the company by subscribing for the new shares.

(b) To **'renounce' the rights** and sell them on the market. Shareholders who do this will have lower percentage holdings of the company's equity after the issue than before the issue, and the total value of their shares will be less.

(c) To **renounce part of the rights and take up the remainder**. For example, a shareholder may sell enough of their rights to enable them to buy the remaining rights shares they are entitled to with the sale proceeds, and so keep the total market value of their shareholding in the company unchanged.

(d) To **do nothing**. Shareholders may be protected from the consequences of their inaction because rights not taken up are sold on a shareholder's behalf by the company. If new securities are not taken up, they may be sold by the company to new subscribers for the benefit of the shareholders who were entitled to the rights.

Gopher has issued 3,000,000 ordinary shares of $1 each, which are at present selling for $4 per share. The company plans to issue rights to purchase 1 new equity share at a price of $3.20 per share for every 3 shares held. A shareholder who owns 900 shares thinks that they will suffer a loss in their personal wealth because the new shares are being offered at a price lower than market value. On the assumption that the actual market value of shares will be equal to the theoretical ex-rights price, what would the effect on the shareholder's wealth be if:

(a)   They sell all the rights
(b)   They exercise half the rights and sell the other half
(c)   They do nothing at all

Answer

Value of the portfolio for a shareholder with 3 shares before the rights issue

	$
3 shares @ $4.00	12.00
1 share @ $3.20	3.20
4	15.20

So the value per share after the rights issue (or TERP) is 15.20/4 = 3.80.

	$
Theoretical ex-rights price	3.80
Price per new share	3.20
Value of rights per new share	0.60

The value of the rights attached to each existing share is $\dfrac{\$0.60}{3}$ = $0.20.

We will assume that a shareholder is able to sell their rights for $0.20 per existing share held.

(a)   If the shareholder sells all their rights:

	$
Sale value of rights (900 × $0.20)	180
Market value of their 900 shares ex rights (900 × $3.80)	3,420
Total wealth	3,600
Total value of 900 shares cum rights (× $4)	$3,600

The shareholder would neither gain nor lose wealth. They would not be required to provide any additional funds to the company, but their shareholding as a proportion of the total equity of the company will be lower.

(b)   If the shareholder exercises half the rights (buys 450/3 = 150 shares at $3.20) and sells the other half:

	$
Sale value of rights (450 × $0.20)	90
Market value of their 1,050 shares, ex rights (× $3.80)	3,990
	4,080
Total value of 900 shares cum rights (× $4)	3,600
Additional investment (150 × $3.20)	480
	4,080

The shareholder would neither gain nor lose wealth, although they will have increased their investment in the company by $480.

(c)   If the shareholder does nothing, but all other shareholders either exercise their rights or sell them, they would lose wealth as follows.

	$
Market value of 900 shares cum rights (× $4)	3,600
Market value of 900 shares ex rights (× $3.80)	3,420
Loss in wealth	180

It follows that the shareholder, to protect their existing investment, should either exercise their rights or sell them to another investor. If they do not exercise their rights, the new securities they were entitled to subscribe for may be sold for their benefit by the company, and this would protect them from losing wealth.

4.10 The actual market price after a rights issue   12/08

The actual market price of a share after a rights issue may differ from the theoretical ex-rights price. This will occur when:

4.10.1 Expected yield from new funds raised ≠ Earnings yield from existing funds

The market will take a view of how profitably the new funds will be invested, and will value the shares accordingly. An example will illustrate this point.

4.10.2 Example: Rights issue (3)

Musk currently has 4,000,000 ordinary shares in issue, valued at $2 each, and the company has annual earnings equal to 20% of the market value of the shares. A one for four rights issue is proposed, at an issue price of $1.50. If the market continues to value the shares on a price/earnings ratio of 5, what would the value per share be if the new funds are expected to earn, as a percentage of the money raised:

(a)   15%
(b)   20%
(c)   25%

How do these values in (a), (b) and (c) compare with the theoretical ex-rights price? Ignore issue costs.

Solution

The theoretical ex-rights price will be calculated first.

	$
Four shares have a current value (× $2) of	8.00
One new share will be issued for	1.50
Five shares would have a theoretical value of	9.50

$$\text{Theoretical ex-rights price} = \frac{1}{4+1}((4 \times 2) + 1.50)$$

$$= \$1.90$$

The new funds will raise $1,000,000 \times \$1.50 = \$1,500,000$.

Earnings as a % of money raised	Additional earnings	Current earnings	Total earnings after the issue
	$	$	$
15%	225,000	1,600,000	1,825,000
20%	300,000	1,600,000	1,900,000
25%	375,000	1,600,000	1,975,000

If the market values shares on a P/E ratio of 5, the total market value of equity and the market price per share would be as follows.

Total earnings $	Market value $	Price per share (5,000,000 shares) $
1,825,000	9,125,000	1.825
1,900,000	9,500,000	1.900
1,975,000	9,875,000	1.975

(a) If the additional funds raised are expected to generate earnings at the **same rate** as existing funds, the **actual market value** will probably be the **same** as the theoretical ex-rights price.

(b) If the new funds are expected to generate earnings at a **lower rate**, the **market value** will **fall** below the theoretical ex-rights price. If this happens, **shareholders** will **lose**.

(c) If the new funds are expected to earn at a **higher rate** than current funds, the **market value** should **rise** above the theoretical ex-rights price. If this happens, shareholders will profit by taking up their rights.

The decision by individual shareholders as to whether they take up the offer will therefore depend on:

- The **expected rate of return** on the investment (and the risk associated with it)
- The **return obtainable from other investments** (allowing for the associated risk)

4.11 New issues of shares for listed companies

A listed company can also raise new equity finance through a **public offer** or a **placing**. Usually these methods will be used as a method of refinancing or to finance growth. These methods of issuing shares will dilute the ownership of the existing shareholders. They are also more **expensive** as a method of raising equity finance than a rights issue, as the new issues can incur costs such as those covered in Section 4.5.

4.12 Stock split

A stock split occurs where, for example, each ordinary share of $1 each is split into two shares of 50c each, thus creating cheaper shares with **greater marketability**. There is possibly an added psychological advantage in that investors may expect a company which splits its shares in this way to be planning for substantial earnings growth and dividend growth in the future.

As a consequence, the market price of shares may benefit. For example, if one existing share of $1 has a market value of $6, and is then split into two shares of 50c each, the market value of the new shares might settle at, say, $3.10 instead of the expected $3, in anticipation of strong future growth in earnings and dividends.

A stock split changes the share capital but does not raise any new equity finance for the company. It also leaves the company's reserves (as shown in its statement of financial position) unaffected.

4.13 Scrip issue

A scrip issue occurs when a company issues new shares to existing shareholders in proportion to their existing holdings at no charge. The issue is made out of distributable reserves (retained profits).

A scrip issue, like a stock split, raises no extra finance for the company.

The difference between a stock split and a scrip issue is that a scrip issue converts equity reserves into share capital, whereas a stock split leaves reserves unaffected.

A company may make a scrip issue when it wants to pay a dividend to shareholders, but would prefer not to pay the dividend in cash. Scrip dividends are explained in the next chapter.

Students may find it useful to read the articles called 'Business finance' and 'Analysing the suitability of financing alternatives' on the ACCA website.

4.14 Preference shares

Preference shares are shares which give the right to receive dividends (typically a fixed percentage of the nominal value of the shares) before any dividends can be paid to ordinary shareholders.

As a source of finance, preference shares have several advantages over debt capital.

(a)   Dividends do not have to be paid if company performance is poor, whereas interest must be paid on debt capital regardless of profit.

(b)   Preference shares are not secured on company assets.

(c)   Preference shareholders usually have no voting rights so there is no dilution of control.

There is, however, a fairly significant disadvantage.

(a)   Preference share capital is not as tax efficient as debt capital, as dividends paid are not tax deductible, whereas interest on debt is.

5 Islamic finance

Islamic finance is finance that is compliant with Sharia'a law. Islamic finance has gone through an exceptional growth period in recent years. The number of fully Sharia'a compliant banks continues to increase worldwide and Sharia'a compliant financial products are not only offered by Islamic banks but also by conventional banks using specific distribution channels. The term 'conventional' is used to identify the financial institutions that have formed part of the financial infrastructure for a long time and are not specifically based on Islamic principles.

5.1 Wealth creation through trade and investment

FAST FORWARD

Islamic finance transactions are based on the concept of sharing risk and reward between the investor and the user of funds.

The object of an Islamic finance undertaking is not simply the pursuit of profit, but that the economic benefits of the enterprise should extend to goals such as social welfare and full employment. Making profits by lending alone and **the charging of interest is forbidden under Sharia'a law**. The business of trading goods and investment in Sharia'a acceptable enterprises form the core of Islamic finance.

Following the ethics of Sharia'a is important for businesses. The ethical framework recognises that capital has a cost associated with it and is in favour of wealth generation. However, **making money with money is deemed immoral**, and wealth should be generated via trade or trade-based investments.

Financial transactions are strongly based on the **sharing of risk and reward** between the provider of funds (the investor) and the user of funds (the entrepreneur).

Conventional banks aim to profit by accepting money deposits in return for the payment of interest and then lending money out in return for the payment of a higher level of interest. Islamic finance does not permit the use of interest and invests under arrangements which share the profits and losses of the enterprises. The Islamic bank arranges their business in such a way that the **bank's profitability is closely tied to that of the client**. The bank stands to take profit or make loss in line with the projects they are financing and as such must be more involved in the investment decision-making.

5.2 Riba   12/13

FAST FORWARD

Riba (interest) is forbidden in Islamic finance.

Riba is generally interpreted as the predetermined interest collected by a lender, which the lender receives over and above the principal amount it has lent out. The **Quranic ban on riba** is absolute. Riba can be viewed as unacceptable from three different perspectives, as outlined below.

- **For the borrower**

  Riba creates unfairness for the borrower when the enterprise makes a profit which is less than the interest payment, turning their profit into a loss.

- **For the lender**

  Riba creates unfairness for the lender in high inflation environments when the returns are likely to be below the rate of inflation.

- **For the economy**

  Riba can result in inefficient allocation of available resources in the economy and may contribute to instability of the system. In an interest-based economy, capital is directed to the borrower with the highest creditworthiness rather than the borrower who would make the most efficient use of the capital.

5.3 Islamic finance contracts

This section develops the discussion of Islamic finance to include the most commonly used financial arrangements which offer suitable Sharia'a compliant financial services. Forms of contract include:

- **Mudaraba** – a partnership contract
- **Musharaka** – a form of equity where a partnership exists and profits and losses are shared
- **Murabaha** – a form of credit sale
- **Ijara** – a form of lease
- **Sukuk** – similar to a bond

Unlike conventional banking where a division may exist between the lender of funds and the risks and actions of the party using the funds, Islamic finance will require that **an active role is played in the use of the asset by the fund provider** and that risks and rewards be shared. Instruments such as those listed above have varied forms and may be applied carefully to offer services comparable to those offered by conventional banks.

5.4 Mudaraba contract   6/12

A **mudaraba** transaction is a partnership transaction in which only one of the partners (the **rab al mal**) contributes capital, and the other (the **mudarib**) contributes skill and expertise. The contributor of capital has no right to interfere in the day to day operations of the business. Due to the fact that one of the partners is running the business and the other is solely providing capital, the investor has **to rely heavily on the mudarib**, their ability to manage the business and their honesty when it comes to profit share payments.

Mudaraba transactions are particularly suited to private equity investments or for clients depositing money with a bank.

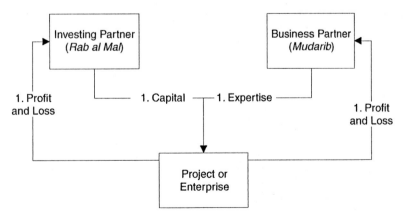

5.4.1 The roles of and the returns received by the rab al mal and mudarib under a mudaraba contract

- **Capital injection**

  The investor provides capital for the project or company. Generally, an investor will not provide any capital unless a clearly defined business plan is presented to them. In this structure, the investor provides 100% of the capital.

- **Skill and expertise**

  The business manager's contribution to the partnership is their skill and expertise in the chosen industry or area.

- **Profit and loss**

  Any profits will be **shared between the partners** according to the ratios agreed in the original contract. Any **losses are solely attributable to the investor** due to the fact that they are the sole provider of all capital to the project. In the event of a loss, the business manager does not receive any compensation (mudarib share) for their efforts. The only exception to this is when the business manager has been negligent, in which case they become liable for the total loss.

The investor in a mudaraba transaction is only liable to the **extent of the capital they have provided**. As a result, the business manager cannot commit the business for any sum which is over and above the capital provided.

The mudaraba contract can usually be **terminated at any time by either of the parties** giving a reasonable notice. Typically, conditions governing termination are included in the contract so that any damage to the business or project is eliminated in the event that the investor would like to take their equity out of the venture.

The rab al mal has no right to interfere with the operations of the business, meaning this situation is similar to an equity investment on a stock exchange.

5.5 Musharaka partnership contract

Musharaka transactions are typically suitable for investments in business ventures or specific business projects, and need to consist of at least two parties, each of which is known as **musharik**. It is widely used in equity financing.

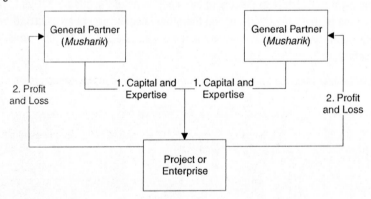

Once the contract has been agreed between the partners, the process can be broken down into the following two main components.

(a)   All partners bring a share of the capital as well as expertise to the business or project. The partners **do not have to provide equal amounts of capital or equal amounts of expertise.**

(b)   Any profits will be shared between the partners according to the ratios agreed in the original contract. To the contrary, any **losses that the project might incur are distributed to the partners strictly in proportion to capital contributions.** Although profits can be distributed in any proportion by mutual consent, it is not permissible to fix a lump sum profit for any single partner.

This transaction is similar to venture capital, for example a management buyout, where both parties contribute both capital and expertise. The venture capitalist will want board representation and therefore provides expertise and they will also want management to provide capital to demonstrate their commitment.

5.6 Murabaha contract

Instruments with predictable returns are typically favoured by banks and their regulators since the reliance on third-party profit calculations is eliminated.

A **murabaha** transaction is a **deferred payment sale or an instalment credit sale** and is mostly used for the purchase of goods for immediate delivery on deferred payment terms. In its most basic form, this transaction involves the seller and buyer of a good, as can be seen below.

Simple murabaha structure

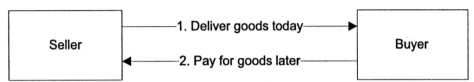

As part of the contract between the buyer and the seller, the price of the goods, the mark-up, the delivery date and payment date are agreed. The sale of the goods is immediate, against future payment. The buyer has full knowledge of the price and quality of goods they buy. In addition, **the buyer is also aware of the exact amount of mark-up they pay** for the convenience of paying later. In the context of trading, the advantage to the buyer is that they can use the goods to generate a profit in their business and subsequently use the profit to repay the original seller.

The underlying asset can vary, and can include raw materials and goods for resale.

Sharia'a prescribes that certain conditions are required for a sales contract (which include murabaha contracts) to exist.

- The object in the contract must actually exist and be owned by the seller.

- The object is offered for a price and both object and price are accepted (the price should be within fair market range).

- The object must have a value.

- The object in question and its exchange may not be prohibited by Sharia'a.

- The buyer in the contract has the right to demand that the object is of suitable quality and is not defective.

A bank can provide finance to a business in a murabaha transaction as follows.

- The manager of the business identifies an asset that the business wants to buy.

- The bank agrees to buy the asset, and to resell it to the business at an agreed (fixed) price, higher than the original purchase price of the asset.

- The bank will pay for the asset immediately but agrees to payment from the business under a deferred payment arrangement (murabaha).

- The business therefore obtains the asset 'now' and pays for it later. This is similar in effect to arranging a bank loan to purchase the asset, but it is compliant with Sharia'a law.

5.6.1 The differences between a murabaha sale and a loan of money

Murabaha is in many ways similar in its nature to a loan; however, there are key characteristics which must be present in a murabaha contract which distinguish it.

- The goods for which the financing is being arranged must effectively be owned by the financing company.

- **Penalties should not be charged** for late payment which would profit the lender. (Extensions are permissible but not for additional fees or charges.)

5.7 Ijara contract

An **ijara** transaction is the **Islamic equivalent of a lease** where one party (lessor) allows another party (lessee) to use their asset against the payment of a rental fee. Two types of leasing transactions exist: operating and finance leases. The only distinction between the two is the presence or absence of a purchase undertaking from the lessee to buy the asset at the end of the lease term. In a finance lease, this purchase undertaking is provided at the start of the contract. The lessor cannot stipulate that they will only lease the asset if the lessee signs a purchase undertaking.

Not every asset is suitable for leasing. The asset needs to be tangible, non-perishable, valuable, identifiable and quantifiable.

In an operating lease, depicted in Figure 1, the lessor leases the asset to the lessee for a pre-agreed period and the lessee pays pre-agreed periodic rentals. The rental or lease payments can either be fixed for the period or floating with periodical refixing.

Figure 1: Operating lease

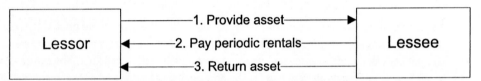

At the end of the period, the lessee can either request to extend the lease or hand the asset back to the lessor. When the asset is returned to the lessor at the end of the period, they can either lease it to another counterparty or sell the asset in the open market. If the lessor decides to sell the asset, they may offer it to the lessee.

In a finance lease, as depicted in Figure 2, the process is the same as for an operating lease, with the exception that the lessor amortises the asset over the term of the lease and at the end of the period the asset will be sold to the lessee.

Figure 2: Finance lease

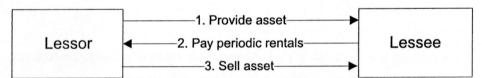

As with an operating lease, rentals can be fixed for the period or floating. As part of the lease agreement, the amount at which the lessee will purchase the asset upon expiry of the lease is specified.

In both forms of ijara the lessor is the owner of the asset and incurs all risk associated with ownership. While the lessee bears the responsibility for wear and tear, day to day maintenance and damage, the lessor is responsible for major maintenance and insurance. Due to the fact that the lessee is using the asset on a daily basis, they are often in a better position to determine maintenance requirements, and are generally appointed by the lessor as an agent to ensure all maintenance is carried out. In addition, the lessee is, in some cases, similarly appointed as agent for the lessor to insure the asset.

In the event of a total loss of the asset, the lessee is no longer obliged to pay the future periodic rentals. However, the lessor has full recourse to any insurance payments.

5.8 Islamic bond market – sukuk

From the viewpoint of Islam, conventional bonds have two major drawbacks and as a result are prohibited. Firstly, they pay interest, and secondly there is generally no underlying asset.

Unlike conventional bonds, **sukuk are normally linked to an underlying tangible asset**. The ownership of the underlying asset is transferred to the holder of the sukuk certificates together with all ownership

benefits and risks. This gives sukuk characteristics of both equity and bonds. Sukuk currently issued have a shorter term than conventional bonds and are typically three to five years.

The sukuk holder owns a proportional share of the underlying asset and the income that it generates, and has a financial right to the revenues generated by the asset. However, as mentioned before, the holder **is also subject to ownership risk**, which means that they are exposed to any risk and potential losses associated with the share of the underlying asset. Conventional bonds, on the other hand, remain part of the issuer's financial liability.

The position of a manager in a sukuk is fundamentally different to that of a manager in a company issuing bonds. When a sukuk manager sells the assets to investors to raise capital, the management of the assets remains the manager's responsibility. The sukuk manager is responsible for managing the assets on behalf of the sukuk holders. The result of this relationship is that holders will have the right to dismiss the manager if they feel that this is appropriate.

This is different to the relationship between the holders of conventional bonds and bond issuers. In this situation the issuing company is responsible for fulfilling the terms of the bond, such as paying coupons and principle, but holders of the bonds have little power to influence the actions of the issuing companies.

5.9 Summary of Islamic finance transactions

The table that follows summarises the Islamic finance transactions already covered and how they differ from other forms of business financing.

Islamic finance transaction	Similar to	Differences
Murabaha	Trade credit / loan	There is a pre-agreed mark-up to be paid in recognition of the convenience of paying later for an asset that is transferred immediately. There is no interest charged.
Musharaka	Venture capital	Profits are shared according to a pre-agreed contract. There are no dividends paid. Losses are shared according to capital contribution.
Mudaraba	Equity	Profits are shared according to a pre-agreed contract. There are no dividends paid. Losses are solely attributable to the provider of capital.
Ijara	Leasing	Whether an operating or finance transaction, in ijara the lessor is still the owner of the asset and incurs the risk of ownership. This means that the lessor will be responsible for major maintenance and insurance which is different from a conventional finance lease.
Sukuk	Bonds	There is an underlying tangible asset that the sukuk holder shares in the risk and rewards of ownership. This gives the sukuk properties of equity finance as well as debt finance.

You may find it useful to read the article called 'Introduction to Islamic finance' on the ACCA website.

 Case Study

Islamic finance 8 September 2014

Neither a borrower nor a lender be. Polonius would have approved of sukuk, instruments which provide a return but do not technically pay interest. As Goldman Sachs prepares to borrow via sukuk for the first time, Islamic financing could soon hit the mainstream. Britain has already issued sukuk and other non-Muslim countries look set to follow. One problem: the Islamic academics who interpret Sharia'a law have their focus far above the bottom line.

Goldman understands how this can happen. In 2011 it had to scrap a $2bn sukuk issue after some Islamic scholars said that its sukuk was not compliant with Sharia'a, which forbids charging interest because it is considered to be usury. Furthermore, the workarounds to meet the rules can be complicated. To comply with Sharia'a a sukuk issuer would instead pay a fixed rent on its own real estate assets to the sukuk holders, rather than typical interest, and at maturity buy back the property – a sale and leaseback structure.

For agnostic capitalists the customer is always right, even if religion must sometimes provide the guidelines. Global sukuk issuance in the first half of 2014 rose 6% to $66bn, according to the International Islamic Finance Centre, on track to beat its 2012 record of $140bn (up 50% from a decade ago). Global companies are keen to tap the new sources of wealth in the Middle East, Asia and Africa. Ernst & Young predicts that Islamic banking will grow to $3.4tn by 2018, an eightfold increase since 2010.

This time it might all go well for Goldman, though Sharia'a compliance risks remain. Demand for sukuk is on the rise. Note that Britain attracted orders of £2bn for a £200m issue in June. Global banks, such as Goldman, will want to persuade more clients to borrow via the fast-growing market. But these banks might first wish to issue some of their own sukuk, while also heeding old Polonius' advice.

Source: *Financial Times,* 8 September 2014

Chapter Roundup

- A range of short-term sources of finance are available to businesses including **overdrafts, short-term loans**, **trade credit** and **operating lease finance**.

- A range of long-term sources of finance are available to businesses including **debt finance, leasing, venture capital** and **equity finance**.

- The choice of **debt finance** that a company can make depends on:

    - The size of the company; a public issue of bonds is only available to a large company

    - The duration of the required financing

    - Whether a fixed or floating interest rate is preferred (fixed rates are more expensive, but floating rates are riskier)

    - The security (collateral) that can be offered and the security that may be demanded by a lender

- The term **bonds** describes various forms of long-term debt a company may issue, such as **loan notes**, which may be:

    - **Redeemable**
    - **Irredeemable**

    Bonds or loans come in various forms, including:

    - **Floating rate loan notes**
    - **Zero coupon bonds**
    - **Convertible bonds**

- **Convertible bonds** are bonds that give the holder the right to convert to other securities, normally ordinary shares, at a predetermined price/rate and time.

- Equity finance is raised through the sale of **ordinary shares** to investors via a **new issue** or a **rights issue**.

- A company can obtain a **stock market listing** for its shares through a **public offer** or a **placing**.

- A **rights issue** is an offer to existing shareholders enabling them to buy more shares, usually at a price lower than the current market price and in proportion to their existing shareholding.

- **Islamic finance transactions** are based on the concept of sharing risk and reward between the investor and the user of funds.

- **Riba** (interest) is forbidden in Islamic finance.

1   Identify four reasons why a company may seek a stock market listing.

2   A company's shares have a nominal value of $1 and a market value of $3. In a rights issue, one new share would be issued for every three shares at a price of $2.60. What is the theoretical ex-rights price?

3   Which of the following is least likely to be a reason for seeking a stock market flotation?

   A   Improving the existing owners' control over the business
   B   Access to a wider pool of finance
   C   Enhancement of the company's image
   D   Transfer of capital to other uses

4   Which of the following is not true of a rights issue by a listed company?

   A   Rights issues do not require a prospectus.
   B   The rights issues price can be at a discount to market price.
   C   If shareholders do not take up the rights, the rights lapse.
   D   Relative voting rights are unaffected if shareholders exercise their rights.

5   A company has 12% loan notes in issue, which have a market value of $135 per $100 nominal value. What is:

   (a)   The coupon rate?
   (b)   The amount of interest payable per annum per $100 (nominal) of loan note?

6   Convertible securities are fixed-return securities that may be converted into zero coupon bonds/ordinary shares/warrants. (Delete as appropriate.)

7   What is the value of $100 12% debt redeemable in three years' time at a premium of 20c per $ if the loan holder's required return is 10%?

1   **Four** of the following **five**: access to a wider pool of finance; improved marketability of shares; transfer of capital to other uses (eg founder members liquidating holdings); enhancement of company image; making growth by acquisition possible.

2    $\dfrac{1}{3+1} (($3 \times 3) + $2.60) = 2.90

3   A   Flotation is likely to involve a significant loss of control to a wider circle of investors.

4   C   Shareholders have the option of renouncing the rights and selling them on the market.

5   (a)   12%
      (b) $12

6   Ordinary shares

7

Years		$	Discount factor 10%	Present value $
1-3	Interest	12	2.487	29.84
3	Redemption premium	120	0.751	90.12
Value of debt				119.96

Now try the questions below from the Practice Question Bank

Number	Level	Marks	Approximate time
Section A Q23	Examination	2	4 mins
Section A Q24	Examination	2	4 mins
Section C Q14	Introductory	N/A	39 mins
Section C Q15	Examination	20	39 mins

Topic list	Syllabus reference
1 Internal sources of finance	E1 (e)(i)(ii)
2 Dividend policy	E1 (e)(iii)(iv)

Introduction

In the previous chapter we looked at **external** sources of finance. In this chapter we will consider **internal** finance in the form of surplus cash.

There is a clear link between financing decisions and the wealth of a company's shareholders. **Dividend policy** plays a big part in a company's relations with its equity shareholders, and a company must consider how the stock market will view its results.

Study guide

Exam guide

This chapter is likely to be examined as a discussion question, perhaps combined with ratio analysis.

1 Internal sources of finance

FAST FORWARD

Internal sources of finance include **retained earnings** and **increasing working capital efficiency**.

1.1 Retained earnings

Retained earnings is surplus cash that has not been needed for operating costs, interest payments, tax liabilities, asset replacement or cash dividends. For many businesses, the cash needed to finance investments will be available because the earnings the business has made have been retained within the business rather than paid out as dividends. We emphasised in Chapter 1 that this **interaction** of investment, financing and dividend policy is the most important issue facing many businesses.

Retained earnings **belong to shareholders** and are classed as **equity** financing.

A company may have substantial retained profits in its statement of financial position but no cash in the bank and therefore will not be able to finance investment from retained earnings.

1.1.1 Advantages of using retained earnings

(a) Retained earnings are a **flexible source** of finance; companies are not tied to specific amounts or specific repayment patterns.

(b) Using retained earnings does not involve a change in the pattern of shareholdings and no dilution of control.

(c) Retained earnings have no issue costs.

1.1.2 Disadvantages of using retained earnings

(a) Shareholders may be **sensitive** to the **loss of dividends** that will result from retention for reinvestment, rather than paying dividends.

(b) Not so much a disadvantage as a misconception, that retaining profits is a cost-free method of obtaining funds. There is an **opportunity cost** in that if dividends were paid, the cash received could be invested by shareholders to earn a return.

1.2 Increasing working capital management efficiency

It is important not to forget that an internal source of finance is the **savings** that can be generated from more efficient management of trade receivables, inventory, cash and trade payables. As we saw in Part C of this Study Text, efficient working capital management can reduce bank overdraft and interest charges as well as increasing cash reserves.

2 Dividend policy   12/07, 12/09, 6/10, 12/10

FAST FORWARD

Retained earnings are the most important single source of finance for companies, and financial managers should take account of the proportion of earnings that are retained as opposed to being paid as dividends. Companies generally **smooth out dividend payments** by adjusting only gradually to changes in earnings: large fluctuations might **undermine investors' confidence.**

The dividends a company pays may be treated as a **signal** to investors. A company needs to take account of different clienteles of shareholders in deciding what dividends to pay.

For any company, the amount of earnings retained within the business has a direct impact on the amount of dividends. Profit reinvested as retained earnings is profit that could have been paid as a **dividend**.

A company must restrict its self-financing through retained earnings because shareholders should be paid a **reasonable dividend**, in line with realistic expectations, even if the directors would rather keep the funds for reinvesting. At the same time, a company that is looking for extra funds will not be expected by investors (such as banks) to pay generous dividends, nor over-generous salaries to owner-directors.

The dividend policy of a business affects the **total shareholder return** and therefore **shareholder wealth** (see Chapter 1).

2.1 Dividend payments

Shareholders normally have the power to vote to **reduce** the size of the dividend at the Annual General Meeting, but **not** the power to increase the dividend. The directors of the company are therefore in a strong position with regard to shareholders when it comes to determining dividend policy. For practical purposes, shareholders will usually be obliged to accept the dividend policy that has been decided on by the directors, or otherwise to sell their shares.

2.2 Factors influencing dividend policy

When deciding on the dividends to pay out to shareholders, one of the main considerations of the directors will be the amount of earnings they wish to retain to meet **financing needs**.

As well as future financing requirements, the decision on how much of a company's profits should be retained, and how much paid out to shareholders, will be influenced by:

(a)   The **need to remain profitable**. Dividends are paid out of profits, and an unprofitable company cannot go on indefinitely paying dividends out of retained profits made in the past.

(b)   The **law on distributable profits**. Companies legislation may make companies bound to pay dividends solely out of **accumulated net realised profits**, as in the UK.

(c)   The Government may impose **direct restrictions** on the amount of dividends that companies can pay. (For example, this happened in the UK in the 1960s as part of a prices and income policy.)

(d)   Any **dividend restraints** that might be imposed by loan agreements and covenants. A loan covenant may restrict the amount of dividends that the company can pay, because this will provide protection for the lender.

(e)   The **effect of inflation**. There is also the need to retain some profit within the business just to maintain its operating capability unchanged.

(f)   The company's **gearing level**. If the company wants extra finance, the sources of funds used should strike a balance between equity and debt finance.

(g)   The company's **liquidity position**. Dividends are a cash payment, and a company must have enough cash to pay the dividends it declares.

(h)   The need to **repay debt** in the near future. The company must have enough cash to pay debts as they fall due.

(i)   The ease with which the company could raise **extra finance** from sources other than retained earnings. Small companies which find it hard to raise finance might have to rely more heavily on retained earnings than large companies.

(j)   The **signalling effect** of dividends to shareholders and the financial markets in general. See below for more details.

2.3 Dividends as a signal to investors

The ultimate objective in any financial management decisions is to **maximise shareholders' wealth**. This wealth is basically represented by the **current market value** of the company, which should largely be determined by the **cash flows arising from the investment decisions** taken by management.

Although the market would **like** to value shares on the basis of underlying cash flows on the company's projects, such information is **not readily available to investors**. But the directors do have this information. The dividend declared can be interpreted as a **signal** from directors to shareholders about the strength of underlying project cash flows.

Investors usually expect a **consistent dividend policy** from the company, with stable dividends each year or, even better, **steady dividend growth**. A large rise or fall in dividends in any year can have a marked effect on the company's share price. Stable dividends or steady dividend growth are usually needed for share price stability. A cut in dividends may be treated by investors as signalling that the future prospects of the company are weak. Thus the dividend which is paid acts, possibly without justification, **as a signal of the future prospects** of the company.

The signalling effect of a company's dividend policy may also be used by management of a company which faces a possible **takeover**. The dividend level might be increased as a defence against the takeover: investors may take the increased dividend as a signal of improved future prospects, thus driving the share price higher and making the company more expensive for a potential bidder to take over.

2.4 Theories of dividend policy

2.4.1 Residual theory

A **'residual' theory** of **dividend policy** can be summarised as follows.

*   If a company can identify projects with positive NPVs, it should invest in them.
*   Only when these investment opportunities are exhausted should dividends be paid.

Dividends should therefore be the amount of after-tax profits left over (the 'residual' amount) after setting aside money to invest in all viable business opportunities.

2.4.2 Traditional view

The **'traditional' view** of dividend policy, implicit in our earlier discussion, is to focus on the effects of dividends and dividend expectations on share price. The price of a share depends on both current dividends and expectations of future dividend growth, given shareholders' required rate of return.

2.4.3 Irrelevancy theory

In contrast to the traditional view, **Modigliani and Miller** (MM) proposed that in a perfect capital market, shareholders are indifferent between dividends and capital gains, and the value of a company is determined solely by the 'earning power' of its assets and investments.

MM argued that if a company with investment opportunities decides to pay a dividend so that **retained earnings** are **insufficient** to finance all its investments, the shortfall in funds will be made up by **obtaining additional funds** from outside sources. As a result of obtaining outside finance instead of using retained earnings:

Loss of value in existing shares = Amount of dividend paid

In answer to criticisms that certain shareholders will show a preference either for high dividends or for capital gains, MM argued that if a company pursues a consistent dividend policy, 'each corporation would tend to attract to itself a clientele consisting of those preferring its particular payout ratio, but one clientele would be entirely as good as another in terms of the valuation it would imply for the firm'. (Note that M&M's view assumes that there are no transaction costs incurred when selling shares.)

2.4.4 The case in favour of the relevance of dividend policy (and against MM's views)

There are strong arguments against MM's view that dividend policy is irrelevant as a means of affecting shareholders' wealth.

(a)   M&M's view assumes that there is no personal or corporation tax. However, differing rates of taxation on dividends and capital gains can create a preference among investors for either a high dividend or high earnings retention (for capital growth).

(b)   Dividend retention should be preferred by companies in a period of capital rationing.

(c)   Due to imperfect markets and the possible difficulties of selling shares easily at a fair price, shareholders might need high dividends in order to have funds to invest in opportunities outside the company.

(d)   Markets are not perfect. Because of transaction costs on the sale of shares, investors who want some cash from their investments will prefer to receive dividends rather than to sell some of their shares to get the cash they want.

(e)   Information available to shareholders is imperfect, and they are not aware of the future investment plans and expected profits of their company. Even if management were to provide them with profit forecasts, these forecasts would not necessarily be accurate or believable.

(f)   Perhaps the strongest argument against the MM view is that shareholders will tend to prefer a current dividend to future capital gains (or deferred dividends) because the future is more uncertain.

Exam focus point

Even if you accept that dividend policy may have some influence on share values, there may be other, more important influences.

Question   Dividend policy

Ochre is a company that is still managed by the two individuals who set it up 12 years ago. In the current year the company was launched on the stock market. Previously, all the shares had been owned by its two founders and certain employees. Now, 40% of the shares are in the hands of the investing public. The company's profit growth and dividend policy are set out below. Will a continuation of the same dividend policy as in the past be suitable now that the company is quoted on the stock market?

Year	Profits $'000	Dividend $'000	Shares in issue
4 years ago	176	88	800,000
3 years ago	200	104	800,000
2 years ago	240	120	1,000,000
1 year ago	290	150	1,000,000
Current year	444	222 (proposed)	1,500,000

Year	Dividend per share cents	Dividend as % of profit
4 years ago	11.0	50%
3 years ago	13.0	52%
2 years ago	12.0	50%
1 year ago	15.0	52%
Current year	14.8	50%

The company appears to have pursued a dividend policy of paying out half of after-tax profits in dividend. This policy is only suitable when a company achieves a stable EPS or steady EPS growth. Investors do not like a fall in dividend from one year to the next, and the fall in dividend per share in the current year is likely to be unpopular and to result in a fall in the share price.

The company would probably serve its shareholders better by paying a dividend of at least 15c per share, possibly more, in the current year, even though the dividend as a percentage of profit would then be higher.

2.5 Scrip dividends   6/11

> A **scrip dividend** is a dividend paid by the issue of additional company shares, rather than by cash.

When the directors of a company would prefer to retain funds within the business but consider that they must pay at least a certain amount of dividend, they might offer equity shareholders the choice of a **cash dividend** or a **scrip dividend**. Each shareholder would decide separately which to take.

With enhanced scrip dividends, the value of the shares offered is much greater than the cash alternative, giving investors an incentive to choose the shares.

2.5.1 Advantages of scrip dividends

(a) They can **preserve** a company's **cash position** if a substantial number of shareholders take up the share option.

(b) Investors may be able to obtain **tax advantages** if dividends are in the form of shares.

(c) Investors looking to **expand their holding** can do so **without incurring** the **transaction costs** of buying more shares.

(d) A small scrip dividend issue will **not dilute the share price significantly**. However, if cash is not offered as an alternative, empirical evidence suggests that the share price will tend to fall.

(e) A share issue will **decrease** the company's **gearing**, and may therefore **enhance** its **borrowing capacity.**

2.5.2 Disadvantages of scrip dividends

(a) Assuming that dividend per share is maintained or increased, the total cash paid as a dividend will increase.

(b) Scrip dividends may be seen as a negative signal by the market ie the company is experiencing cash flow issues.

2.6 Share repurchase

> **FAST FORWARD**

> Purchase by a company of its own shares can take place for various reasons and must be in accordance with any **requirements of legislation.**

In many countries companies have the right to **buy back shares from shareholders** who are willing to sell them, subject to certain conditions.

For a **smaller company** with few shareholders, the reason for buying back the company's own shares may be that there is no immediate willing purchaser at a time when a shareholder wishes to sell shares.

For a public company, share repurchase could provide a way of withdrawing from the share market and 'going private'.

Public companies with a large amount of surplus cash may offer to repurchase (and then cancel) some shares from its shareholders. A reason for this is to find a way of offering cash returns to investors without increasing dividend payments. Higher dividend payments would affect investor expectations about future dividends and dividend growth, whereas share buybacks would not affect dividend expectations at all. In addition, by reducing the number of shares in issue, the company should be able to increase the earnings per share (EPS) for the remaining shares.

2.6.1 Benefits of a share repurchase scheme

(a) Finding a **use for surplus cash**, which may be a 'dead asset'.

(b) **Increase in earnings per share** through a reduction in the number of shares in issue. This should lead to a higher share price than would otherwise be the case, and the company should be able to increase dividend payments on the remaining shares in issue.

(c) **Increase in gearing**. Repurchase of a company's own shares allows debt to be substituted for equity, so raising gearing. This will be of interest to a company wanting to increase its gearing without increasing its total long-term funding.

(d) **Readjustment of the company's equity base** to more appropriate levels, for a company whose business is in decline.

(e) Possibly **preventing a takeover** or enabling a quoted company to withdraw from the stock market.

2.6.2 Drawbacks of a share repurchase scheme

(a) It can be **hard to arrive at a price** that will be fair both to the vendors and to any shareholders who are not selling shares to the company.

(b) A repurchase of shares could be seen as an **admission** that the company **cannot make better use of the funds** than the shareholders.

(c) Some shareholders may suffer from being **taxed on a capital gain** following the purchase of their shares rather than receiving dividend income.

 Case Study

BASF's Chief Executive Kurt Bock told Reuters Insider TV that, unlike its largest US rivals, the German diversified chemicals group does not plan to revive its share buyback programme and would rather invest in new plant and equipment.

'We pay a handsome dividend and then the money is being spent, frankly,' Bock said. 'We are rightly leveraged, there is little money left for buybacks.'

Between 1999 and 2008, BASF purchased about 10 billion euros' ($13.7 billion) worth of its own stock.

BASF's largest US rivals Dow Chemical Co and DuPont last month sought to boost shareholder value with share buyback programmes after posting forecast-beating quarterly earnings.

Source: http://uk.reuters.com, 25 February 2014

- Internal sources of finance include **retained earnings** and **increasing working capital efficiency**.

- **Retained earnings** are the most important single source of finance for companies, and financial managers should take account of the proportion of earnings that are retained as opposed to being paid as dividends.

  Companies generally **smooth out dividend payments** by only gradually adjusting to changes in earnings: large fluctuations might **undermine investors' confidence**.

  The dividends a company pays may be treated as a **signal** to investors. A company needs to take account of different clienteles of shareholders in deciding what dividends to pay.

- Purchase by a company of its own shares can take place for various reasons and must be in accordance with any **requirements of legislation**.

Quick Quiz

1   A company offers to pay a dividend in the form of new shares which are worth more than the cash alternative which is also offered. What is this dividend in the form of shares called?

2   Which of the following sources of finance to companies is the most widely used in practice?

    A   Bank borrowings   C   New share issues

    B   Rights issues   D   Retained earnings

3   A scrip dividend is:

    A   A dividend paid at a fixed percentage rate on the nominal value of the shares

    B   A dividend paid at a fixed percentage rate on the market value of the shares on the date that the dividend is declared

    C   A dividend payment that takes the form of new shares instead of cash

    D   A cash dividend that is not fixed but is decided on by the directors and approved by the shareholders

4   Give a definition of 'signalling' in the context of dividends policy.

5   Why might shareholders prefer a current dividend to a future capital gain?

1   An enhanced scrip dividend

2   D   Retained earnings

3   C   A would most commonly be a preference dividend. D is a definition of a normal dividend.

4   The use of dividend policy to indicate the future prospects of an enterprise

5   Tax advantages or because the future capital gain will be uncertain

Now try the questions below from the Practice Question Bank

Number	Level	Marks	Approximate time
Section A Q25	Examination	2	4 mins
Section C Q16	Introductory	N/A	39 mins

14

Gearing and capital structure

Topic list	Syllabus reference
1 Gearing	E3 (c)
2 Effect on shareholder wealth	E3 (d)
3 Finance for small and medium-sized entities	E5 (a), (b), (c), (d)

Introduction

In Chapter 12, we described different methods by which a company can obtain long-term finance, in the form of both **equity** and **debt**.

This chapter looks now at the effect of sources of finance on the financial position and financial risk of a company. A central question here is: What are the implications of using different proportions of equity and debt finance?

The answer to this has to take account of the attitudes of investors to the **financial risk** associated with increasing levels of debt finance, and the **trade-off** between risk and return.

We also look at various **gearing ratios** which give us a measure of the extent to which a company is financed by debt.

In this chapter we shall also be looking at how small and medium-sized enterprises **(SMEs)** obtain finance. The sources of finance are important but this chapter also discusses why SMEs have difficulty raising finance and how they can tackle the obstacles that exist in obtaining finance.

Study guide

		Intellectual level
E3	**Sources of finance and their relative costs**	
(c)	Identify and discuss the problem of high levels of gearing.	2
(d)	Assess the impact of sources of finance on financial position, financial risk and shareholder wealth using appropriate measures, including:	
(i)	Ratio analysis using statement of financial position gearing, operational and financial gearing, interest coverage ratio and other relevant ratios	2
(ii)	Cash flow forecasting	2
(iii)	Leasing or borrowing to buy	2
E5	**Finance for small and medium-sized entities (SMEs)**	
(a)	Describe the financing needs of small businesses.	2
(b)	Describe the nature of the financing problem for small businesses in terms of the funding gap, the maturity gap and inadequate security.	2
(c)	Explain measures that may be taken to ease the financing problems of SMEs, including the responses of government departments and financial institutions.	1
(d)	Identify and evaluate the financial impact of different sources of finance for SMEs, including sources already referred to in syllabus section E1, and also:	2
(i)	Business angel financing	
(ii)	Government assistance	
(iii)	Supply chain financing	
(iv)	Crowdfunding/peer to peer funding	

Exam guide

You may be asked to explain the implications of different financing decisions on investment opportunities and the company's continued health. Capital structure is a significant topic in this exam and can be examined in conjunction with a number of other areas.

> Performance objective 11 requires you to 'identify key sources of financial risk to the organisation and how they might arise' and to 'monitor financial risks, reviewing their status and how they should be managed'. You can apply the knowledge you obtain from this chapter of the text to help to demonstrate this competence.

1 Gearing   12/07, 6/09

Key term

> **Gearing** is the amount of debt finance a company uses relative to its equity finance.

1.1 Financial risk

> Debt finance tends to be relatively low risk for the debt holder, as it is interest bearing and can be secured. The cost of debt to the company is therefore relatively low.

The greater the level of debt, the more **financial risk** (of reduced dividends after the payment of debt interest) to the shareholder of the company, so the higher their required return. The cost of equity therefore increases with higher gearing.

The assets of a business must be financed somehow and, when a business is growing, the additional assets must be financed by additional capital.

However, a high level of debt creates financial risk. **Financial risk** can be seen from different points of view.

(a) **Ordinary shareholders**

Higher levels of financial gearing increase the variability of after-tax profits and earnings per share. With a high-geared company, a small percentage change in operating profits can result in a much greater change in after-tax profits and EPS. Greater variability in returns to equity shareholders means greater financial risk.

(b) **The company as a whole**

If a company builds up debts that it cannot pay when they fall due, it will be forced into liquidation.

(c) **Suppliers / lenders**

If a company cannot pay its debts, the company will go into liquidation owing suppliers money that they are unlikely to recover in full. Lenders will therefore want a **higher interest yield** to compensate them for higher financial risk and gearing.

1.2 Gearing ratios   12/09, 6/10, 12/12

FAST FORWARD

The **financial risk** of a company's capital structure can be measured by a **gearing ratio**, a **debt ratio** or **debt/equity ratio**, or by the **interest cover**.

Financial gearing measures the relationship between **shareholders' funds (equity)** and **prior charge capital**. It indicates the degree to which the organisation's activities are funded by borrowed funds, as opposed to shareholder funds.

Operational gearing measures the relationship between **contribution** and **profit before interest and tax**. It indicates the degree to which an organisation's profits are made up of variable (as opposed to fixed) costs.

Exam focus point

You need to be able to explain **and calculate** the level of financial gearing using alternative measures.

Financial gearing measures the degree to which an organisation's activities are funded by borrowed funds, as opposed to shareholder's funds.

Commonly used measures of financial gearing are based on the **statement of financial position values** of the fixed interest and equity capital. They include:

Formula to learn

$$\text{Financial gearing} = \frac{\text{Prior charge capital}}{\text{Equity capital (including reserves)}}$$

$$\text{and} = \frac{\text{Prior charge capital}}{\text{Total capital employed}^*}$$

* Either including or excluding non-controlling (minority) interests, deferred tax and deferred income

Prior charge capital is capital which has a right to the receipt of interest or of preferred dividends in precedence to any claim on distributable earnings on the part of the ordinary shareholders. On winding up, the claims of holders of prior charge also rank before those of ordinary shareholders.

With the first definition above, a company is low geared if the gearing ratio is less than 100% (meaning it is funded less by prior charge capital than by equity capital), highly geared if the ratio is over 100% and neutrally geared if it is exactly 100%. With the second definition, a company is neutrally geared if the ratio is 50%, low geared below that, and highly geared above that.

> If the question specifies a gearing formula, for example by defining an industry average for comparison, you must use that formula.

Question

Gearing

From the following statement of financial position, compute the company's financial gearing ratio.

	$'000
Non-current assets	12,400
Current assets	1,000
	13,400
Financing	
Bonds	4,700
Bank loans	500
Provisions for liabilities and charges: deferred taxation	300
Deferred income	250
Ordinary shares	1,500
Preference shares	500
Share premium account	760
Revaluation reserve	1,200
Statement of profit or loss	2,810
	12,520
Current liabilities	
Loans	120
Bank overdraft	260
Trade payables	500
	13,400

Answer

	$'000
Prior charge capital	
Preference shares	500
Bonds	4,700
Long-term bank loans	500
Prior charge capital, ignoring short-term debt	5,700
Short-term loans	120
Overdraft	260
Prior charge capital, including short-term interest bearing debt	6,080

Either figure, $6,080,000 or $5,700,000, could be used. If gearing is calculated with capital employed in the denominator, and capital employed is net non-current assets plus **net** current assets, it would seem more reasonable to exclude short-term interest-bearing debt from prior charge capital. This is because short-term debt is set off against current assets in arriving at the figure for net current assets.

Equity = 1,500 + 760 + 1,200 + 2,810 = $6,270,000

The gearing ratio can be calculated in any of the following ways.

(a) $\dfrac{\text{Prior charge capital}}{\text{Equity}} \times 100\% = \dfrac{6,080}{6,270} \times 100\% = 97\%$

(b) $\dfrac{\text{Prior charge capital}}{\text{Equity plus prior charge capital}} \times 100\% = \dfrac{6,080}{(6,080+6,270)} \times 100\% = 49.2\%$

(c) $\dfrac{\text{Prior charge capital}}{\text{Total capital employed}} \times 100\% = \dfrac{5,700}{12,520} \times 100\% = 45.5\%$

1.2.1 Gearing ratios based on market values

An alternative method of calculating a gearing ratio is one based on **market values**.

$$\text{Financial gearing} = \frac{\text{Market value of prior charge capital}}{\text{Market value of equity} + \text{Market value of prior charge capital}}$$

The advantage of this method is that potential investors in a company are able to judge the further debt capacity of the company more clearly by reference to **market values** than they could by looking at statement of financial position values.

The disadvantage of a gearing ratio based on market values is that it **disregards** the **value** of the company's **assets**, which might be used to secure further loans. A gearing ratio based on statement of financial position values arguably gives a better indication of the security for lenders of fixed interest capital.

1.2.2 Changing financial gearing

Financial gearing is an attempt to quantify the **degree of risk** involved in holding equity shares in a company, both in terms of the company's ability to remain in business and in terms of expected ordinary dividends from the company.

The more geared the company is, the **greater the risk** that little (if anything) will be available to distribute by way of dividend to the ordinary shareholders. Interest and preference dividends on debt must continue to be paid regardless of the company's profits. A high financial gearing therefore means the company is more vulnerable to poor trading conditions.

There is therefore greater **volatility** of amount of earnings available for ordinary shareholders, and greater volatility in dividends paid to those shareholders where a company is highly geared. That is the main financial risk with high gearing. You may do extremely well or extremely badly, without a particularly large movement in the profit from operations of the company.

Gearing ultimately measures the company's ability to **remain in business**. A high-geared company has a large amount of interest to pay annually. If those borrowings are 'secured' in any way (and bonds in particular are secured), then the holders of the debt are perfectly entitled to force the company to realise assets to pay their interest if funds are not available from other sources. Clearly, the more highly geared a company, the more likely this is to occur if and when profits fall.

1.2.3 Example: Gearing

Suppose that two companies are identical in every respect except for their gearing. Both have assets of $20,000 and make the same operating profits (profit before interest and tax: PBIT). The only difference between the two companies is that Nonlever is all-equity financed and Lever is partly financed by debt capital, as follows.

	Nonlever $	Lever $
Assets	20,000	20,000
10% bonds	0	(10,000)
	20,000	10,000
Ordinary shares of $1	20,000	10,000

Because Lever has $10,000 of 10% bonds it must make a profit before interest of at least $1,000 in order to pay the interest charges. Nonlever, on the other hand, does not have any minimum PBIT requirement because it has no debt capital. A company which is lower geared is considered less risky than a higher geared company because of the greater likelihood that its PBIT will be high enough to cover interest charges and make a profit for equity shareholders.

1.2.4 Operational gearing

Financial risk, as we have seen, can be measured by financial gearing. **Business risk** refers to the risk of making only low profits, or even losses, due to the nature of the business that the company is involved in. One way of measuring business risk is by calculating a company's **operational gearing**.

$$\text{Operational gearing} = \frac{\text{Contribution}}{\text{Profit before interest and tax (PBIT)}}$$

Contribution is sales minus variable cost of sales.

Operational gearing indicates the degree to which an organisation's profits are made up of variable (as opposed to fixed) costs.

The significance of operational gearing is as follows.

(a)   **If contribution is high but PBIT is low**, the company has a high proportion of fixed costs, which are only just covered by contribution. Business risk, as measured by operational gearing, will be high.

(b)   **If contribution is not much bigger than PBIT**, the company has a low proportion of fixed costs, which are fairly easily covered by contribution. Business risk, as measured by operational gearing, will be low.

Operational gearing, like financial gearing, affects the volatility of earnings. If a company has high operational gearing, a small percentage change in sales revenue will have a much greater percentage change in operating profits. The proportional size of the change is higher than for a company with low operational gearing.

A company with both high operational gearing and high financial gearing is likely to have highly volatile earnings and earnings per share.

1.3 Interest coverage ratio

The interest cover ratio is a measure of financial risk which is designed to show the risks in terms of profit rather than in terms of capital values.

$$\text{Interest coverage ratio} = \frac{\text{Profit before interest and tax}}{\text{Interest}}$$

The reciprocal of this, the interest to profit ratio, is also sometimes used. As a general guide, an interest coverage ratio of **less than three times** is considered low, indicating that profitability is too low given the gearing of the company. An interest coverage ratio of more than seven is usually seen as safe.

1.4 The debt ratio

Another measure of financial risk is the **debt ratio**.

Debt ratio   =   Total debts : Total assets

Debt does not include long-term provisions and liabilities such as deferred taxation.

There is no firm rule on the maximum safe debt ratio but, as a general guide, you might regard 50% as a safe limit to debt.

Timothy Co is planning to invest in new machinery costing $10 million. The revenues and costs arising from the investment are as follows.

	$'000
Sales	2,500
Variable cost of sales	1,100
Other variable operating expenses	200
Other fixed operating expenses including tax-allowable depreciation	120

The purchase of the machinery will be financed solely by an issue of 7% bonds, repayable in 20X9.

Timothy's budgeted statement of profit or loss for the year ended, and statement of financial position at, 31 December 20X4 before taking into account the effects of the new investment are set out below.

STATEMENT OF PROFIT OR LOSS

	20X4
	$'000
Sales	16,000
Cost of sales (100% variable)	9,600
Gross profit	6,400
Other operating expenses (50% variable)	2,800
Profit before interest and tax	3,600
Interest	800
Profit before tax	2,800
Tax (30%)	840
Profit after tax	1,960
Dividends (Dividend cover is constant 2:1)	980
Retained earnings	980

STATEMENT OF FINANCIAL POSITION

	$'000	$'000
Non-current assets		25,000
Current assets		10,000
Total assets		35,000
Equity share capital and reserves		24,000
10% bonds 20X8	8,000	
Current liabilities	3,000	
Total liabilities		11,000
Total equity and liabilities		35,000

Required

Demonstrate the effects of the new investment on:

(a) Operational gearing

(b) Interest cover

(c) Financial gearing $(= \dfrac{\text{Prior charge capital}}{\text{Total capital employed}})$

Answer

The best approach is firstly to calculate the impact on the budgeted statement of profit or loss and the finance section of the statement of financial position.

STATEMENT OF PROFIT OR LOSS

	20X4 $'000
Sales (16,000 + 2,500)	18,500
Cost of sales (9,600 + 1,100)	10,700
Gross profit	7,800
Other variable operating expenses (50% × 2,800) + 200	1,600
Other fixed operating expenses (50% × 2,800) + 120	1,520
Profit before interest and tax	4,680
Interest (800 + (7% × 10,000))	1,500
Profit before tax	3,180
Tax (840 + (30% × (2,500 – 1,100 – 200 – 120 – 700)))	954
Profit after tax	2,226
Dividends (50% × 2,226)	1,113
Retained earnings	1,113

STATEMENT OF FINANCIAL POSITION

	$'000
7% bonds 20X9	10,000
10% bonds 20X8	8,000
	18,000
Equity share capital and reserves (24,000 + (1,113 – 980))	24,133

(a) Operational gearing $= \dfrac{\text{Contribution}}{\text{Profit before interest and tax (PBIT)}}$

Before the investment

Operational gearing $= \dfrac{16,000 - 9,600 - (50\% \times 2,800)}{3,600} = 1.39$

After the investment

Operational gearing $= \dfrac{18,500 - 10,700 - 1,600}{4,680} = 1.32$

(b) Interest cover $= \dfrac{\text{Profit before interest and tax}}{\text{Interest}}$

Before the investment

Interest cover $= \dfrac{3,600}{800} = 4.5$

After the investment

Interest cover $= \dfrac{4,680}{1,500} = 3.12$

(c) Financial gearing $= \dfrac{\text{Prior charge capital}}{\text{Total capital employed}}$

Before investment

Financial gearing $= \dfrac{8,000}{8,000 + 24,000} = 25\%$

After investment

Financial gearing $= \dfrac{8,000 + 10,000}{8,000 + 10,000 + 24,133} = 42.7\%$

A change in sources of finance could be examined by the preparation of a **cash flow forecast** which we covered in Chapter 6.

1.5 Company circumstances   6/08, 12/08

One determinant of the suitability of the gearing mix is the **stability** of the company. It may seem obvious, but it is worth stressing that debt financing will be more appropriate when:

- The company is in a **healthy competitive position**.

- **Cash flows** and **earnings** are stable.

- **Profit margins** are **reasonable**.

- **Operational gearing** is **low** (ie the fixed costs that have to be covered by profits from trading activities are low).

- The **bulk of the company's assets** are **tangible**.

- The **liquidity** and **cash flow position** is **strong**.

- The **debt-equity ratio** is **low**.

- **Share prices** are **low**.

1.6 Cost and flexibility

The **cost of debt** is likely to be lower than the cost of equity, because debt is **less risky** from the debtholders' viewpoint. As we have seen, interest has to be paid no matter what the level of profits, and debt capital can be secured by **fixed** and **floating charges**.

Interest rates on longer-term debt may be higher than interest rates on shorter-term debt, because many lenders believe longer-term lending to be riskier. However, **issue costs** or **arrangement fees** will be **higher** for shorter-term debt, as it has to be renewed more frequently.

A business may also find itself locked into **longer-term debt**, with adverse interest rates and large penalties if it repays the debt early. Both **inflation** and **uncertainty** about future interest rate changes are reasons why companies are unwilling to borrow long term at high rates of interest and investors are unwilling to lend long term when they think that interest yields might go even higher.

1.7 Optimal capital structure

When we consider the capital structure decision, the question arises of whether there is an optimal mix of capital and debt which a company should try to achieve. We will consider this issue in detail in Chapter 16 of this Study Text.

2 Effect on shareholder wealth   6/08

FAST FORWARD

If a company can generate returns on capital in excess of the interest payable on debt, financial gearing will raise the EPS. Gearing will, however, also increase **the variability of returns** for shareholders and increase the chance of corporate **failure**.

A company will only be able to raise finance if investors think the returns they can expect are satisfactory in view of the risks they are taking.

2.1 Earnings per share

Remember the definition of earnings per share.

Key term

> **Basic earnings per share** should be calculated by dividing the net profit or loss for the period attributable to ordinary shareholders by the weighted average number of ordinary shares outstanding during the period.

One measure of gearing uses earnings per share.

$$\text{Financial gearing at a given level of sales} = \frac{\text{\% change in earnings per share}}{\text{\% change in profits before interest and tax}}$$

The relationship between these two figures can be used to evaluate alternative financing plans by examining their effect on earnings per share over a range of PBIT levels. Its objective is to determine the PBIT indifference points among the various alternative financing plans. The indifference points between any two methods of financing can be determined by solving for PBIT the following equation.

$$\frac{(PBIT - I)(1 - t)}{S1} = \frac{(PBIT - I)(1 - t)}{S2}$$

Where t = tax rate, I = interest payable, S1 and S2 = number of shares after financing for plans 1 and 2

2.2 Example: PBIT and EPS

Edted Company has 10,000m €1 shares in issue and wants to raise €5,000m to fund an investment by either:

(a)   Selling 2,500m shares at €2 each, or
(b)   Issuing €5,000m 10% loan stock at par.

The income tax rate is 40%.

In order to calculate the indifference point between issuing equity shares and issuing debt, we use the above equation.

$$\frac{(PBIT - 0)(1 - 0.4)}{12,500} = \frac{(PBIT - 500)(1 - 0.4)}{10,000}$$

$10,000 \times 0.6 \times PBIT = 12,500 \times 0.6 \times (PBIT - 500)$

$6,000\ PBIT = 7,500\ PBIT - 3,750,000$

$1,500\ PBIT = 3,750,000$

$PBIT = 2,500$

We can prove this calculation as follows.

	Issues equity €m	Issues debt €m
PBIT	2,500	2,500
Interest		(500)
PBT	2,500	2,000
Tax	(1,000)	(800)
Earnings after tax	1,500	1,200
Number of shares	12,500	10,000
Earnings per share	€0.12	€0.12

At a level of PBIT above €2,500 million, it will be better to issue debt, as every € extra of earnings will be distributed between fewer shareholders. At a level of PBIT below €2,500 million, it will be better to issue equity, as the loss of each € will be shared by more shareholders.

The company's attitude will depend on what levels of earnings it expects and also the **variability** of **possible earnings** limits. Variations from what is expected will have a greater impact on earnings per share if the company chooses debt finance.

2.3 Price-earnings ratio

You will remember that the price-earnings ratio is calculated in the following way.

Key term

$$\text{Price-earnings (P/E) ratio} = \frac{\text{Market price per share}}{\text{Earnings per share}}$$

You will also recall that the **value of the P/E ratio** reflects the market's appraisal of the share's future prospects. If earnings per share falls because of an increased burden arising from increased gearing, an increased P/E ratio will mean that the share price has not fallen as much as earnings, indicating the market views positively the projects that the increased gearing will fund.

2.4 Dividend cover

You will recall that the **dividend cover** is the number of times the actual dividend could be paid out of current profits.

Key term

$$\text{Dividend cover} = \frac{\text{Earnings per share}}{\text{Dividend per share}}$$

To judge the effect of increased gearing on dividend cover, you should consider changes in the dividend levels and changes in dividend cover. If earnings decrease because of an increased burden of interest payments, then:

(a) The directors may decide to make **corresponding reductions in dividend** to maintain levels of dividend cover.

(b) Alternatively the directions may choose to maintain dividend levels, in which case **dividend cover will fall**. This will indicate to shareholders an **increased risk** that the company will not be able to maintain the same dividend payments in future years, should earnings fall.

2.5 Dividend yield

Remember that the dividend yield is calculated as follows.

Key term

$$\text{Dividend yield} = \frac{\text{Dividend per share}}{\text{Market price per share}} \times 100\%$$

We have discussed how increased gearing might affect dividends and dividend cover. However, with dividend yield, we are also looking at the effect on the **market price of shares**. If the additional debt finance is expected to be used to generate good returns in the long term, it is possible that the dividend yield might fall significantly in the short term because of a fall in short-term dividends, but also an increase in the market price reflecting market expectations of enhanced long-term returns. How shareholders view this movement will depend on their preference between short-term and long-term returns.

Question   Gearing

A summarised statement of financial position of Rufus is as follows.

	$m
Assets less current liabilities	150
Debt capital	(70)
	80
Share capital (20 million shares of $1)	20
Reserves	60
	80

The company's profits in the year just ended are as follows.

	$m
Profit from operations	21.0
Interest	6.0
Profit before tax	15.0
Taxation at 30%	4.5
Profit after tax (earnings)	10.5
Dividends	6.5
Retained profits	4.0

The company is now considering an investment of $25 million. This will add $5 million each year to profits before interest and tax.

(a) There are two ways of financing this investment. One would be to borrow $25 million at a cost of 8% per annum in interest. The other would be to raise the money by means of a one for four rights issue.

(b) Whichever financing method is used, the company will increase dividends per share next year from 32.5c to 35c.

(c) The company does not intend to allow its gearing level, measured as debt finance as a proportion of equity capital plus debt finance, to exceed 55% as at the end of any financial year. In addition, the company will not accept any dilution in earnings per share.

Assume that the rate of taxation will remain at 30% and that debt interest costs will be $6 million plus the interest cost of any new debt capital.

Required

(a) Produce a profit forecast for next year, assuming that the new project is undertaken and is financed (i) by debt capital or (ii) by a rights issue.

(b) Calculate the earnings per share next year, with each financing method.

(c) Calculate the effect on gearing as at the end of next year, with each financing method.

(d) Explain whether either or both methods of funding would be acceptable.

Answer

Current earnings per share are $10.5 million/20 million shares = 52.5c

If the project is financed by $25 million of debt at 8%, interest charges will rise by $2 million. If the project is financed by a one for four rights issue, there will be 25 million shares in issue.

	Finance with debt $m	Finance with rights issue $m
Profit before interest and tax (+ 5.0)	26.00	26.00
Interest	8.00	6.00
	18.00	20.00
Taxation (30%)	5.40	6.00
Profit after tax	12.60	14.00
Dividends (35c per share)	7.00	8.75
Retained profits	5.60	5.25
Earnings (profits after tax)	$12.6m	$14.0m
Number of shares	20 million	25 million
Earnings per share	63c	56c

The projected statement of financial position as at the end of the year will be:

	Finance with debt $m	Finance with rights issue $m
Assets less current liabilities	180.6	180.25
(150 + new capital 25 + retained profits)		
Debt capital	(95.0)	(70.00)
	85.6	110.25
Share capital	20.0	25.00
Reserves	65.6	85.25*
	85.6	110.25

* The rights issue raises $25 million, of which $5 million is represented in the statement of financial position by share capital and the remaining $20 million by share premium. The reserves are therefore the current amount ($60 million) plus the share premium of $20 million plus accumulated profits of $5.25 million.

	Finance with debt	Finance with rights issue
Debt capital	95.0	70.0
Debt capital plus equity finance	(95.0 + 85.6)	(70.0 + 110.25)
Gearing	53%	39%

Either financing method would be acceptable, since the company's requirements for no dilution in EPS would be met with a rights issue as well as by borrowing, and the company's requirement for the gearing level to remain below 55% is (just) met even if the company were to borrow the money.

3 Finance for small and medium-sized entities

SMEs are generally:

- Unquoted private companies
- Owned by a small number of individuals
- Not micro businesses

Key term

Small and medium-sized entities (SMEs) have the following characteristics.

(a) Firms are likely to be unquoted private companies.

(b) The business is owned by a few individuals, typically a family group.

(c) They are not micro businesses – very small businesses that act as the owners' medium for self-employment.

The SME sector accounts for between a third and a half of sales and employment in the UK. The sector is particularly associated with the service sector and niche markets. If market conditions change, small businesses may be **more adaptable**.

There is, however, a significant failure rate among small firms. According to a study by the US Small Business Association, only two-thirds of small business start-ups survive for two years and less than half make it to four years after commencing trading.

3.1 The problems of financing SMEs

> **FAST FORWARD**
>
> SMEs may **not know about** the sources of finance available.
>
> Finance may be difficult to obtain because of the **risks** faced by SMEs.

SMEs are restricted in their sources of new equity finance. They are private companies, with a limited number of shareholders. Unless the shareholders are wealthy, there is a limit to the amount of extra capital they may be able to invest in the company.

SMEs therefore rely heavily on retained profits for new equity finance, but there is a limit to the amount of equity that can be obtained from this source, especially when profits are low.

It is not easy for SMEs to attract venture capital. They must be able to demonstrate strong opportunities for profit growth.

So if SMEs are restricted in the amount of new equity they can obtain, they may rely on borrowing to supplement their finances.

Government policy can have a major influence on the level of funds available for borrowing.

(a)   **Tax policy** including concessions given to businesses to invest (tax-allowable depreciation) and taxes on distributions (higher taxes on dividends mean less income for investors) can have an impact.

(b)   **Interest rate policy** can affect lending to SMEs. High interest rates work in different ways – borrowing for SMEs becomes more expensive, but the supply of funds is also greater, as higher rates give greater incentives to investors to save.

SMEs, however, also face **competition** for funds. Investors have opportunities to invest in all sizes of organisation, as well as overseas and in government debt.

The main handicap that SMEs face in accessing funds is the problem of **uncertainty** and **risk** for lenders.

(a)   Whatever the details provided to potential investors, SMEs have **neither the business history nor the longer track record** that larger organisations possess.

(b)   Larger enterprises are subject by law to **more public scrutiny**: their financial statements have to contain more detail and be audited, they receive more press coverage, and so on.

(c)   Because of the uncertainties involved, banks use **credit scoring systems** and **control their exposure** to the SME business sector.

SMEs will have to provide extensive information about their business to a bank when they seek loan finance. They will need to give a business plan, a list of the firm's assets, details of the experience of directors and managers and show how they intend to provide security for sums advanced.

Prospective lenders, usually banks, will then make a decision based on the information provided. The terms of the loan (interest rate, term, security, repayment details) will depend on the **risk** involved, and the lender will also want to monitor their investment.

A common problem is often that the banks will be **unwilling** to increase loan funding without an increase in **security** given in the form of assets (which the owners may be unwilling or unable to give), or an increase in equity funding (which may be difficult to obtain).

A further problem for SMEs is the **maturity gap**. It is particularly difficult for SMEs to obtain medium-term loans due to a mismatching of the maturity of assets and liabilities. Longer-term loans are easier to obtain than medium-term loans, as longer loans can be secured with mortgages against property.

3.2 Sources of finance for SMEs

Potential sources of financing for small and medium-sized companies include the following.

(a) Owner financing
(b) Overdraft financing (covered in Chapter 12)
(c) Bank loans (covered in Chapter 12)
(d) Trade credit (covered in Chapter 5)
(e) Equity finance
(f) Business angel financing
(g) Venture capital (covered in Chapter 12)
(h) Leasing (covered in Chapter 12)
(i) Factoring (covered in Chapter 5)
(j) Government assistance (covered in Chapter 2)
(k) Supply chain finance
(l) Crowdfunding/peer to peer funding

Surveys have suggested that small firms have problems accessing different sources of finance because managers are **insufficiently informed** about what is available. However, the increased amount of literature and government agencies designed to help small businesses have resulted in a reduction in this difficulty.

3.2.1 Owner financing

Finance from the owner(s)' personal resources or those of family connections is generally the initial source of finance. At this stage, because many assets are intangible, external funding may be difficult to obtain.

3.2.2 Equity finance

Other than investment by owners or business angels, businesses with few tangible assets will probably have difficulty obtaining equity finance when they are formed (a problem known as the **equity gap**).

However, once small firms have become established, they do not necessarily need to seek a market listing to obtain equity financing; shares can be **placed privately**. Letting external shareholders invest does not necessarily mean that the original owners have to cede control, particularly if the shares are held by a number of small investors. However, small companies may find it difficult to obtain large sums by this means.

As noted above, owners will need to invest a certain amount of capital when the business starts up. However, owners can subsequently choose whether they withdraw profits from the business or reinvest them.

Surveys have suggested that the amount of equity invested by owners in a business after start-up and retained earnings are relatively low compared with other sources of finance. However, the failure of owners to invest limits the assets that can be acquired, and therefore the amount of security that can be given for debt capital.

A major problem with obtaining equity finance can be the inability of the small firm to offer an easy **exit route** for any investors who wish to sell their stake.

(a) The **firm** can **purchase its own shares** back from the shareholders, but this involves the use of cash that could be better employed elsewhere.

(b) The **firm** can obtain a **market listing** but not all small firms do.

(c) The 'exit route' for equity investors in small businesses is often a **sale of the business to a larger company**.

3.2.3 Business angel financing

Business angel financing can be an important initial source of business finance. Business angels are wealthy individuals or groups of individuals who invest directly in small businesses. They are prepared to take **high risks** in the hope of **high returns**.

The main problem with business angel financing is that it is **informal** in terms of a market and can be difficult to set up. However, informality can be a strength. There may be less need to provide business angels with **detailed information** about the company, since business angels generally have prior knowledge of the industry.

Surveys suggest that business angels are often more patient than providers of other sources of finance. However, the money available from individual business angels may be limited, and large sums may only be available from a consortium of business angels.

There is a useful article on the ACCA website called 'Being an angel'.

3.2.4 Supply chain finance (SCF)

In June 2014, ACCA published a report aimed at CFOs and FDs called 'A study of the business case for supply chain finance'. In the glossary, ACCA defines SCF as 'The use of financial instruments, practices and technologies to optimise the management of the working capital and liquidity tied up in supply chain processes for collaborating business partners'.

The most widely used form of SCF is **reverse factoring**. Rather confusingly, reverse factoring is sometimes simply referred to as SCF.

Reverse factoring is a method of **financing** by **selling invoices** at a small **discount** (interest rate) in order to obtain the **cash in advance** of the invoice due date. This is achieved through an intermediary fund provider such as a bank, who provides early payment to the supplier in exchange for the discount, and in turn receives later payment from the buyer. This is a technology-based process which links the buyer, the seller and the fund provider. The process works as follows.

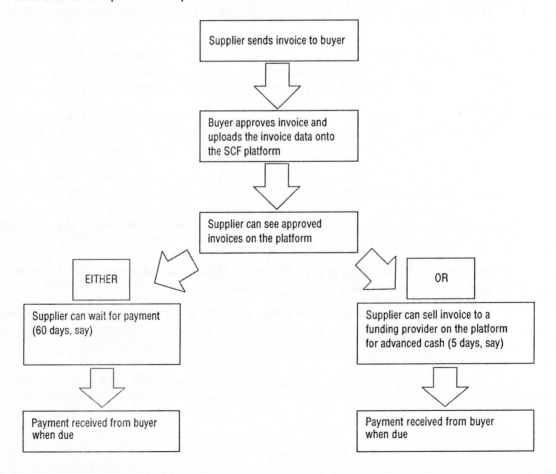

When the invoice is due, the buyer pays the fund provider. So the buyer has the advantage of taking 60 days, say, to pay and the supplier has the advantage of being paid in 5 days, say.

SCF relies on **efficient automation** and **real-time visibility** of invoice information. Note also that the funding provider relies on the **creditworthiness of the buyer** and the buyer is usually a large company with a good credit rating.

The good credit rating means that low interest rates are charged to the supplier to purchase the invoice. Therefore a small or medium-sized supplier has access to a lower interest rate than would normally be available to them.

3.2.5 Crowdfunding/peer to peer funding

SMEs are finding it increasingly difficult to obtain funding in the traditional way, ie from a bank. At the same time, investors are finding that banks are offering very low returns for their money. This situation has led to the development of crowdfunding.

Crowdfunding is the funding of a project by raising money from a **large number of people**. It is usually carried out **via the internet** and involves the initiator, the people willing to support the project and a **platform** to bring them together. Various platforms are now in existence, such as www.crowdcube.com and www.seedrs.com.

 Case Study

Can the crowd still crowdfund? By Elaine Moore, *The Financial Times*

There are lots of things that the bankrupt city of Detroit could do with. Whether those things include a 10ft tall statue of a robot/policeman hybrid is immaterial, because that's what it's going to get following a $60,000 'Detroit needs a statue of RoboCop!' campaign. That's the thing about crowdfunding websites such as Kickstarter and Indiegogo – they make it very easy for people to raise a lot of money for very esoteric projects.

As crowdfunding edges its way into the mainstream, the types of campaigns using the sites are getting broader. I've supported a few worthy, interesting projects on crowdfunding sites over the past year, but a quick inventory of the things I've put money behind also throws up a film of a TV show I haven't watched in a decade and probably won't go to see, and a graphic novel I supported, mostly because I liked the video pitch.

Crowdfunding allows interested individuals to club together to fund projects or businesses that might otherwise struggle to get off the ground and it is one of the more interesting innovations within financial services.

My foray into the sector has so far been limited to a few pounds in so-called 'reward-based' funding, where all that is promised in return is a product, such as a book or t-shirt.

Equity crowdfunding, in which investors provide money in exchange for a share of the venture, sets the stakes far higher. Appetite from investors for this form of fundraising is high. In recent months, fund manager Nicola Horlick has raised £150,000 to fund a business backing films through Seedrs and Kevin McCloud, presenter of Channel 4's Grand Designs, raised £1.5m through Crowdcube to build customised homes.

Italy recently became the first country in Europe to implement equity-crowdfunding laws and in the US the JOBS Act, designed to help new companies raise capital, legalised equity-based crowdfunding, boosting investor interest as a result.

In the UK, equity crowdfunding is not yet regulated and there are some heated discussions going on about how oversight of the sector should work.

As the recent collapse of crowdfunded beauty business Bubble & Balm showed, investors in a crowdfunded project that fails have little or no protection, and some people are worried that not all investors realise this is the case.

There are reports that the UK financial regulator is thinking about preventing investors from putting in anything less than £1,000 through equity crowdfunding, to dissuade inexperienced investors from investing money they cannot afford to lose. But at this week's UK Crowdfunding Association's autumn conference, companies complained that this would turn direct, online investment into a sort of club for the wealthy. That would be a shame. Direct, consumer investment – whether crowdfunding or via peer to peer websites – is an area in which the UK is a global leader.

The Financial Conduct Authority will take responsibility for crowdfunding in April 2014, and in the next month will release a paper looking at ways to regulate the sector. Let's hope it doesn't lock out the crowd.

Source: *www.ft.com* <accessed 10/09/14>

3.3 Capital structure

Significant influences on the capital structure of small firms are:

- The **lack of separation** between **ownership** and **management**
- The **lack of equity finance**

Studies have suggested that the owners' preference and market considerations are also significant. Small firms tend not to have target debt ratios.

Other studies suggest that the **life cycle** of the firm is important. Debt finance is an important early source, its availability depending on the security available.

As firms mature, however, the reliance on debt declines. There seems to be little evidence of a relationship between gearing, and profitability and risk levels.

3.4 Government aid for SMEs

FAST FORWARD

Government aid schemes are country-specific.

Exam focus point

Availability of government assistance is country-specific. For the exam, at a minimum, you should be aware of the possibilities of such assistance and the major schemes operating in at least one country.

Some governments provide assistance schemes to help businesses. Some schemes may be designed to encourage lenders and investors to make finance available to small and unquoted businesses.

3.4.1 Loan schemes

Some governments may provide loan schemes to facilitate lending to viable businesses that have been turned down for a normal commercial loan due to a lack of security or a proven track record.

3.4.2 Grants

A grant is a sum of money given to an individual or business for a specific project or purpose. A grant usually covers only part of the total costs involved.

Grants to help with **business development** are available from a variety of sources, such as the Government, European Union, Regional Growth Fund, local authorities and some charitable organisations.

These grants may be linked to business activity or a specific industry sector. Some grants are linked to specific geographical areas, eg those in need of economic regeneration.

Ella, a small company, is currently considering a major capital investment project for which additional finance will be required. It is not currently feasible to raise additional equity finance; consequently, debt finance is being considered. The decision has not yet been finalised as to whether this debt finance will be short or long term and if it is to be at fixed or variable rates. The financial controller has asked you for your assistance in the preparation of a report for a forthcoming meeting of the board of directors.

Required

Prepare a draft report to the board of directors which identifies and briefly explains:

(a)   The main factors to be considered when deciding on the appropriate mix of short-, medium- or long-term debt finance for Ella.

(b)   The practical considerations which could be factors in restricting the amount of debt which Ella could raise.

Answer

(a)   To: Board
      From: Accountant
      Date: 8 January 20X2
      Re: Debt finance

The term of the finance

The term should be appropriate to the **asset** being acquired. As a general rule, long-term **assets** should be **financed** from **long-term finance** sources. Cheaper short-term funds should be used to finance short-term requirements, such as fluctuations in the level of working capital.

Flexibility

Short-term debt is a **more flexible** source of finance; there may be penalties for repaying long-term debt early. If the company takes out long-term debt and interest rates fall, it will find itself locked into unfavourable terms.

Repayment terms

The company must have **sufficient funds** to be able to **meet repayment schedules** laid down in loan agreements, and to cover interest costs. Although there may be no specific terms of repayment laid down for short-term debt, it may possibly be **repayable on demand**, so it may be risky to finance long-term capital investments in this way.

Costs

Interest on short-term debt is usually **less** than on long-term debt. However, if short-term debt has to be renewed frequently, issue expenses may raise its cost significantly.

Availability

It may be **difficult to renew short-term finance** in the future if the company's position or economic conditions change adversely.

Effect on gearing

Certain types of short-term debt (bank overdrafts, increased credit from suppliers) will not be included in gearing calculations. If a company is seen as **too highly geared**, lenders may be **unwilling to lend money**, or judge that the high risk of default must be compensated by higher interest rates or restrictive covenants.

(b) **Previous record of company**

If the company (or possibly its directors or even shareholders) has a **low credit rating** with credit reference agencies, investors may be unwilling to subscribe for loan notes. Banks may be influenced by this, and also by their own experiences of the company as customer (has the company exceeded overdraft limits in the past on a regular basis).

Restrictions in memorandum and articles

The company should examine the legal documents carefully to see if they place any restrictions on what the company can borrow, and for what purposes.

Restrictions of current borrowing

The **terms** of any **loans** to the company that are **currently outstanding** may contain restrictions about further borrowing that can be taken out.

Uncertainty over project

The project is a significant one, and presumably the **interest and ultimately repayment** that lenders obtain may be very dependent on the success of the project. If the results are uncertain, lenders may not be willing to take the risk.

Security

The company may be **unwilling to provide the security** that lenders require, particularly if it is faced **with restrictions** on what it can do with the **assets secured**.

Alternatively, it may have **insufficient assets** to provide the necessary security.

Exam focus point

You may find it useful to read the article called Business Finance for SMEs on the ACCA website.

Chapter Roundup

- Debt finance tends to be relatively low risk for the debt holder, as it is interest bearing and can be secured. The cost of debt to the company is therefore relatively low.

  The greater the level of debt, the more **financial risk** (of reduced dividends after the payment of debt interest) to the shareholder of the company, so the higher is their required return. The cost of equity therefore increases with higher gearing.

- The **financial risk** of a company's capital structure can be measured by a **gearing ratio**, a **debt ratio** or **debt/equity ratio**, or by the **interest cover**.

  Financial gearing measures the relationship between **shareholders' funds (equity)** and **prior charge capital**. It indicates the degree to which the organisation's activities are funded by borrowed funds, as opposed to shareholder funds.

  Operational gearing measures the relationship between **contribution** and **profit before interest and tax**. It indicates the degree to which an organisation's profits are made up of variable (as opposed to fixed) costs.

- If a company can generate returns on capital in excess of the interest payable on debt, financial gearing will raise the EPS. Gearing will, however, also increase **the variability of returns** for shareholders and increase the chance of corporate **failure**.

- **SMEs** are generally:

  – Unquoted private companies
  – Owned by a small number of individuals
  – Not micro businesses

- SMEs may **not know about** the sources of finance available.

  Finance may be difficult to obtain because of the **risks** faced by SMEs.

- **Government aid** schemes are country-specific.

Quick Quiz

1 Fill in the blank.

$$\text{.................................. gearing} = \frac{\text{Prior charge capital}}{\text{Total capital employed}}$$

2 Fill in the blank.

$$\text{.................................. gearing} = \frac{\text{Contribution}}{\text{Profit before interest and tax}}$$

3 Fill in the blank.

Interest coverage ratio = ...

4 What condition has to be fulfilled for increased financial gearing to result in increased earnings per share?

5 What is the debt ratio?

6 What are the main characteristics of small and medium-sized enterprises?

7 What is business angel financing?

1. **Financial** gearing = $\dfrac{\text{Prior charge capital}}{\text{Total capital employed}}$

2. **Operational** gearing = $\dfrac{\text{Contribution}}{\text{Profit before interest and tax}}$

3. Interest coverage ratio = $\dfrac{\text{Profit before interest and tax}}{\text{Interest}}$

4. The returns on capital investment must exceed the interest payable on the extra debt used to finance the investment.

5. Total debt: Total assets

6. (a) Firms are likely to be unquoted.
    (b) Ownership of the business is restricted to a few individuals, typically a family group.
    (c) They are not micro businesses that offer a medium for self-employment of their owners.

7. Direct investment in SMEs by individuals or small groups of investors

Now try the questions below from the Practice Question Bank

Number	Level	Marks	Approximate time
Section A Q26	Examination	2	4 mins
Section C Q17	Examination	20	39 mins

The cost of capital

15

Topic list	Syllabus reference
1 Cost of capital	E3 (a), (b)
2 Dividend growth model	E2 (a)(i)
3 Capital asset pricing model (CAPM)	E2 (a)(ii)(iii)(iv)
4 Cost of debt	E2 (b)
5 Weighted average cost of capital (WACC)	E2 (c)

Introduction

In this chapter we examine the concept of the **cost of capital**, which can be used as a **discount rate** in evaluating the investments of an organisation.

We firstly base **cost of equity** calculations on the **dividend valuation model**. We then look at a way of establishing the cost of equity that takes risk into account: the **capital asset pricing model**.

We then calculate the cost of capital for a range of debt instruments and then estimate the **cost of capital**.

Study guide

		Intellectual level
E2	**Estimating the cost of capital**	
(a)	Estimate the cost of equity including:	2
(i)	Application of the dividend growth model and discussion of its weaknesses	
(ii)	Explanation and discussion of systematic and unsystematic risk	
(iii)	Relationship between portfolio theory and the capital asset pricing model (CAPM)	
(iv)	Application of the CAPM, its assumptions, advantages and disadvantages	
(b)	Estimating the cost of debt:	2
(i)	Irredeemable debt	
(ii)	Redeemable debt	
(iii)	Convertible debt	
(iv)	Preference shares	
(v)	Bank debt	
(c)	Estimating the overall cost of capital including:	2
(i)	Distinguishing between average and marginal cost of capital	
(ii)	Calculating the weighted average cost of capital (WACC) using book value and market value weightings	
E3	**Sources of finance and their relative costs**	
(a)	Describe the relative risk-return relationship and describe the relative costs of equity and debt.	2
(b)	Describe the creditor hierarchy and its connection with the relative costs of sources of finance.	2

Exam guide

In the exam you may be asked to calculate the **weighted average cost of capital** and its component costs, either as a separate sub-question, or as part of a larger question, most likely an investment appraisal. Remember that questions won't just involve calculations; you may be asked to discuss the problems with the methods of calculation you've used or the relevance of the costs of capital to investment decisions.

1 Cost of capital   6/08

FAST FORWARD

> The **cost of capital** is the rate of return that the enterprise must pay to satisfy the providers of funds, and it reflects the riskiness of providing funds.

1.1 Aspects of the cost of capital

The cost of capital has two aspects to it.

(a) The **cost of funds** that a company raises and uses
(b) The return that investors expect to be paid for putting funds into the company

It is therefore the **minimum return** that a company should make on its own investments, to earn the cash flows out of which investors can be paid their return.

The cost of capital can therefore be measured by studying the returns required by investors. The cost of capital can then be used to derive a discount rate for DCF analysis and investment appraisal.

Each form of capital has its own cost. For example, equity has a cost and each bank loan or bond issue has a different cost. A company must make sufficient returns from its investments to satisfy the requirements for return of all the different finance providers.

1.2 The cost of capital as an opportunity cost of finance

The cost of capital is an **opportunity cost of finance**, because it is the minimum return that investors require. If they do not get this return, they will transfer some or all of their investment somewhere else. Here are two examples.

(a) If a bank offers to lend money to a company, the interest rate it charges is the **yield** that the bank wants to receive from investing in the company, because it can get just as good a return from lending the money to someone else. In other words, the interest rate is the opportunity cost of lending for the bank.

(b) When shareholders invest in a company, the returns that they can expect must be sufficient to persuade them not to sell some or all of their shares and invest the money somewhere else. The yield on the shares is therefore the **opportunity cost** to the **shareholders of not investing somewhere else**.

1.3 The cost of capital and risk

The cost of capital can be analysed into three elements.

Risk-free rate of return +
Premium for business risk +
Premium for financial risk
COST OF CAPITAL

(a) **Risk-free rate of return**

This is the return which would be required from an investment if it were completely free from risk. Typically, a risk-free yield is the **yield on government securities**.

(b) **Premium for business risk**

This is an increase in the required rate of return due to the existence of **uncertainty about** the future and about a **firm's business prospects**. The actual returns from an investment may not be as high as they are expected to be. Business risk will be higher for some firms than for others, and some types of project undertaken by a firm may be more risky than other types of project that it undertakes.

(c) **Premium for financial risk**

This relates to the danger of high debt levels (high gearing). The higher the gearing of a company's capital structure, the greater will be the financial risk to ordinary shareholders, and this should be reflected in a higher risk premium and therefore a higher cost of capital.

Because different companies are in different types of business (varying business risk) and have different capital structures (varying financial risk) the cost of capital applied to one company may differ radically from the cost of capital of another.

1.4 The relative costs of sources of finance

The cost of debt (the rate a firm pays on its current loans, bonds and other debts) is likely to be **lower** than the cost of equity (the return paid to its shareholders). This is because debt is **less risky** from the debtholders' viewpoint. In the event of liquidation, the **creditor hierarchy** dictates the priority of claims and debt finance is paid off before equity. This makes debt a safer investment than equity and hence debt investors demand a lower rate of return than equity investors.

Debt interest is also corporation **tax deductible** (unlike equity dividends), making it even cheaper to a taxpaying company. Arrangement costs are usually lower on debt finance than on equity finance and once again, unlike equity arrangement costs, they are also tax deductible.

1.5 The creditor (payables) hierarchy

Increasing risk →

1   Creditors with a fixed charge
2   Creditors with a floating charge
3   Unsecured creditors
4   Preference shareholders
5   Ordinary shareholders

This means that the **cheapest type of finance is debt** (especially if secured) and the **most expensive type of finance is equity** (ordinary shares).

2 Dividend growth model   6/08, 12/13, 6/14

The **dividend growth model** can be used to estimate a cost of equity, on the assumption that the market value of share is directly related to the expected future dividends from the shares.

2.1 The cost of ordinary share capital

New funds from equity shareholders are obtained either from **new issues of shares** or from **retained earnings**. Both of these sources of funds have a cost.

(a)   Shareholders will **not** be prepared to **provide funds** for a **new issue** of **shares** unless the return on their investment is sufficiently attractive.

(b)   Retained earnings also have a cost. This is an **opportunity cost**, the dividend forgone by shareholders.

The cost of equity can be estimated using several different methods or models. These include the dividend valuation model, the dividend growth model and the capital asset pricing model. Each method is a way of estimating the cost of equity, so in theory they should produce identical answers. However, as each involves different sources of data and estimates, in practice they would probably result in differing estimates for the cost of equity.

2.2 The dividend valuation model   6/12, 6/13

If we begin by ignoring share issue costs, the cost of equity, both for new issues and retained earnings, could be estimated by means of a **dividend valuation model**, on the assumption that the market value of shares is directly related to expected future dividends on the shares.

Remember the formula for a perpetuity:

$$PV = \frac{c}{r}, \text{ or } r = \frac{c}{PV}$$

Where c is the constant cash flow every period, and r is the cost of capital.

If the future dividend per share is expected to be **constant** in amount, the present value of future dividends is a perpetuity. It is no surprise, then, that the **ex dividend** share price is calculated by the formula:

$$P_0 = \frac{d}{(1+k_e)} + \frac{d}{(1+k_e)^2} + \frac{d}{(1+k_e)^3} + \ldots = \frac{d}{k_e}, \text{ so } k_e = \frac{d}{P_0}$$

Where k_e is the cost of equity capital

      d   is the annual dividend per share, starting at year 1 and then continuing annually in perpetuity

P_0 is the ex-dividend share price (the price of a share where the share's new owner is **not** entitled to the dividend that is soon to be paid)

We shall look at the dividend valuation model again in Chapter 18, in the context of valuation of shares.

2.3 Example: Dividend valuation model

Cygnus has a dividend cover ratio of 4.0 times and expects zero growth in dividends. The company has one million $1 ordinary shares in issue and the market capitalisation (value) of the company is $50 million. After-tax profits for next year are expected to be $20 million.

What is the cost of equity capital?

Solution

Total dividends = 20 million/4 = $5 million.

k_e = 5/50 = 10%

2.4 The dividend growth model

Shareholders will normally expect dividends to increase year by year and not to remain constant in perpetuity. The **fundamental theory of share values** states that the market price of a share is the present value of the discounted future cash flows of revenues from the share, so the market value given an expected constant annual growth in dividends would be:

$$P_0 = \frac{d_0(1+g)}{(1+k_e)} + \frac{d_0(1+g)^2}{(1+k_e)^2} + ...$$

where P_0 is the current market price (ex div)
d_0 is the current net dividend
k_e is the cost of equity capital
g is the expected annual growth in dividend payments

and both k_e and g are expressed as proportions.

It is often convenient to assume a constant expected dividend growth rate in perpetuity. The formula above then simplifies to:

$$P_0 = \frac{d_0(1+g)}{(k_e - g)} = \frac{d_1}{(k_e - g)}$$

Rearranging this, we get a formula for the ordinary shareholders' cost of capital.

Formula to learn

Cost of ordinary (equity) share capital, having a current ex div price, P_0, having just paid a dividend, d_0, with the dividend growing in perpetuity by a constant g% per annum:

$$k_e = \frac{d_0(1+g)}{P_0} + g \qquad \text{or } k_e = \frac{d_1}{P_0} + g$$

Look at the second formula above, and you will notice how it derives from the formula for constant dividends in Section 2.2. This will help you to remember the formula in the exam.

✏️ **Question**   Cost of equity

A share has a current market value of 96c, and the last dividend was 12c. If the expected annual growth rate of dividends is 4%, calculate the cost of equity capital.

$$\text{Cost of capital} = \frac{12(1 + 0.04)}{96} + 0.04$$

$$= 0.13 + 0.04$$

$$= 0.17$$

$$= 17\%$$

2.4.1 Estimating the growth rate

There are two methods for estimating the growth rate that you need to be familiar with.

Firstly, the future growth rate can be predicted from an **analysis of the growth in dividends** over the past few years.

Year	Dividends $	Earnings $
20X1	150,000	400,000
20X2	192,000	510,000
20X3	206,000	550,000
20X4	245,000	650,000
20X5	262,350	700,000

Dividends have risen from $150,000 in 20X1 to $262,350 in 20X5. The increase represents four years' growth. (Check that you can see that there are four years' growth, and not five years' growth, in the table.) The average growth rate, g, may be calculated as follows.

$$\text{Dividend in 20X1} \times (1 + g)^4 = \text{Dividend in 20X5}$$

$$(1+g)^4 = \frac{\text{Dividend in 20X5}}{\text{Dividend in 20X1}}$$

$$= \frac{\$262,350}{\$150,000}$$

$$= 1.749$$

$$1 + g = \sqrt[4]{1.749} = 1.15$$

$$g = 0.15, \text{ ie } 15\%$$

The growth rate over the last four years is assumed to be expected by shareholders into the indefinite future. If the company is financed entirely by equity and there are 1,000,000 shares in issue, each with a market value of $3.35 ex div, the cost of equity, K_e, is:

$$\frac{d_0(1+g)}{P_0} + g = \frac{0.26235(1.15)}{3.35} + 0.15 = 0.24, \text{ ie } 24\%$$

2.4.2 Gordon's growth approximation

Alternatively, the growth rate can be estimated using **Gordon's growth approximation**. The **rate of growth in dividends** is sometimes expressed theoretically as:

Formula to learn

> $g = br$
>
> Where g is the annual growth rate in dividends
>
> b is the proportion of profits that are retained
>
> r is the rate of return on new investments

So, if a company retains 65% of its earnings for capital investment projects it has identified and these projects are expected to have an average return of 8%:

$g = br = 65\% \times 8 = 5.2\%$

2.5 Weaknesses of the dividend growth model   6/08

(a)   The model does not explicitly incorporate risk.

(b)   Dividends do not grow smoothly in reality, so g is only an approximation.

(c)   The model fails to take capital gains into account; however, it is argued that a change of share ownership does not affect the present value of the dividend stream.

(d)   No allowance is made for the effects of taxation although the model can be modified to incorporate tax.

(e)   It assumes there are no issue costs for new shares.

(f)   It does not produce meaningful results where no dividend is paid (if d is zero, K_e is 0).

3 Capital asset pricing model (CAPM)   6/08

FAST FORWARD

> The **capital asset pricing model** can be used to calculate a cost of equity and incorporates **risk**.
>
> The CAPM is based on a comparison of the **systematic risk** of **individual investments** with the **risks of all shares** in the **market**.

3.1 Portfolio theory   6/14

Different investments react differently to events in the market. **Portfolio theory** suggests that investors can reduce the total risk on their investments by diversifying their portfolio of investments. Because each investment is exposed to different risks, investors should consider how the value of each of their investments changes in relation to every other investment when making new investments.

Provided that the investor **diversifies** their investments in a suitably wide portfolio, the investments which perform well and those which perform badly should tend to cancel each other out, and much risk can be diversified away. In the same way, a company which invests in a number of projects will find that some do well and some do badly, but taking the whole portfolio of investments, average returns should turn out much as expected.

A concept in portfolio theory that is used in the capital asset pricing model is the **market portfolio**. The market portfolio is a portfolio of investments, excluding risk-free investments, that represents a basket of risky investments each weighted in proportion to their overall size. Usually 'risky investments' is taken to mean stock market investments. An investor in a portfolio of investments that reflects the market as a whole should therefore expect returns that are equal to the average returns for the market as a whole (excluding returns on risk-free investments). The return available on a market 'index' measure like the FTSE 100 in the UK or the Dow Jones in the US is often used to measure this.

3.2 Systematic risk and unsystematic risk

FAST FORWARD

> The total **risk** involved in holding securities (shares) divides into **risk specific** to the company (unsystematic) and risk due to **variations** in **market activity** (systematic).
>
> **Unsystematic risk** can be diversified away, while **systematic or market risk** cannot. Investors may mix a diversified market portfolio with risk-free assets to achieve a preferred mix of risk and return.

Whenever an investor invests in some shares, or a company invests in a new project, there will be some risk involved. The actual return on the investment might be better or worse than that hoped for. To some extent, risk is unavoidable (unless the investor settles for risk-free securities, such as gilts).

We have looked at how diversification reduces the risks of investment according to the portfolio theory. However, not all risks can be diversified away.

Risks that can be diversified away are referred to as **unsystematic risk**. But there is another sort of risk too. Some markets are by their very nature more risky than others. This has nothing to do with chance variations up or down in actual returns compared with what an investor should expect. This **inherent risk** – the **systematic risk** or **market risk** – cannot be diversified away. Systematic risk includes, for example, the risk that the market crashes as a result of a global recession, war or natural catastrophe.

Key terms

Risk is the risk of variability in investment returns.

Market risk or **systematic risk** cannot be diversified away. **Non-systematic** or **unsystematic risk** applies to a single investment or class of investments, and can be reduced or eliminated by diversification.

In return for accepting systematic risk, a **risk-averse investor** will expect to **earn a return** which is **higher** than the return on a risk-free investment.

Exam focus
point

Common errors on this topic in exams include:

- Assuming risk-averse investors wish to eliminate risk; risk-averse investors are prepared to accept risk, in exchange for higher returns
- Failing to link the risks of an investment with its returns
- Mixing up systematic and unsystematic risk

3.3 Systematic risk and unsystematic risk: implications for investments

The implications of systematic risk and unsystematic risk are therefore as follows.

(a) If an investor wants to **avoid risk** altogether, they must **invest entirely** in **risk-free securities**.

(b) If an investor **holds shares in just a few companies**, there will be **some unsystematic risk** as well as systematic risk in their portfolio, because they will not have spread their risk enough to diversify away the unsystematic risk. To eliminate unsystematic risk, they must build up a well-diversified portfolio of investments.

(c) If an investor holds a **balanced portfolio** of all the stocks and shares on the stock market, they will incur systematic risk which is exactly equal to the average systematic risk in the stock market as a whole.

(d) **Shares in individual companies** will have **different systematic risk characteristics** to this market average. Some shares will be less risky and some will be more risky than the stock market average. Similarly, some investments will be more risky and some will be less risky than a company's 'average' investments.

3.4 Systematic risk and the CAPM

FAST FORWARD

The systematic risk in individual company shares can be measured statistically, by analysing historical returns.

The CAPM model uses a **beta factor** to measure a share's volatility in terms of systematic risk.

In accordance with portfolio theory, unsystematic risk is ignored in the CAPM, as it is assumed unsystematic risk can be diversified away.

The Capital Asset Pricing Model (CAPM) is mainly concerned with how systematic risk is measured, and how systematic risk affects required returns and share prices. **Systematic risk** is measured using **beta factors**.

Beta factor is the measure of the systematic risk of a security relative to the average market portfolio. The higher the beta factor, the more sensitive the security is to systematic risk (the more volatile its returns in response to factors that affect market returns generally).

Beta factors	
1	This is the measurement of systematic risk for the stock market as a whole.
0	This is the systematic risk for risk-free investments. Returns on risk-free investments are unaffected by market risk and variations in market returns.
Less than 1	Systematic risk is lower than for the market on average.
More than 1	Systematic risk is higher than for the market on average.

The beta factor reflects the fact that different market sectors, and individual companies within each market sector, are exposed to different degrees of systematic risk. Supermarkets are relatively unaffected by systematic risk, for example, so are likely to have a low beta factor. On the other hand, the banking and tourism industries are impacted to a much greater degree by systematic risk. They will have a high beta factor.

CAPM theory includes the following propositions.

(a) Investors in shares require a **return** in **excess of the risk-free rate**, to compensate them for systematic risk.

(b) Investors should **not require** a **premium** for **unsystematic risk**, because this can be diversified away by holding a wide portfolio of investments. In this, CAPM builds on **portfolio theory**.

(c) Because systematic risk varies between companies, investors will require a **higher return** from shares in those companies where the systematic risk is bigger.

The same propositions can be applied to capital investments by companies.

(a) Companies will want a **return on a project** to **exceed** the **risk-free rate**, to compensate them for systematic risk.

(b) **Unsystematic risk** can be **diversified away**, and so a premium for unsystematic risk should not be required.

(c) Companies should want a **bigger return** on projects where **systematic risk is greater**.

3.5 Market risk and returns

Market risk (systematic risk) is the average risk of the market as a whole. Taking all the shares on a stock market together, the total expected returns from the market will vary because of systematic risk. The market as a whole might do well or it might do badly.

3.6 Risk and returns from an individual security

In the same way, an individual security may offer prospects of a return of x%, but with some risk (business risk and financial risk) attached. The return (the x%) that investors will require from the individual security will be higher or lower than the market return, depending on whether the security's systematic risk is greater or less than the market average. A major **assumption in CAPM** is that there is a linear relationship between the return obtained from an individual security and the average return from all securities in the market.

3.7 Example: CAPM (1)

The following information is available about the performance of an individual company's shares and the stock market as a whole.

	Individual company	Stock market as a whole
Price at start of period	105.0	480.0
Price at end of period	110.0	490.0
Dividend during period	7.6	39.2

The return on the company's shares R_i (total shareholder return) and the expected return on the 'market portfolio' of shares $E(r_m)$ may be calculated as:

$$\frac{\text{Capital gain (or loss)} + \text{dividend}}{\text{Price at start of period}} = \frac{P_1 - P_0 + D_1}{P_0}$$

$$R_i = \frac{(110 - 105) + 7.6}{105} = 12\% \qquad E(r_m) = \frac{(490 - 480) + 39.2}{480} = 10.25\%$$

A statistical analysis of 'historical' returns from a security and from the 'average' market may suggest that a linear relationship can be assumed to exist between them. A series of comparative figures could be prepared of the return from a company's shares and the average return of the market as a whole. The results could be drawn on a scattergraph and a 'line of best fit' drawn (using linear regression techniques) as shown below.

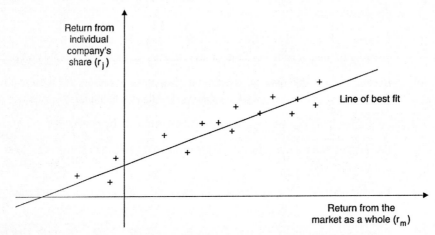

This analysis would show three things.

(a)   The **return from** the **security** and the **return from** the **market** as a whole **will tend to rise or fall together**.

(b)   The **return from the security** may be **higher or lower** than the **market return**. This is because the systematic risk of the individual security differs from that of the market as a whole.

(c)   The scattergraph may **not give a good line of best fit**, unless a large number of data items are plotted, because actual returns are affected by unsystematic risk as well as by systematic risk.

Note that returns can be negative. A share price fall represents a capital loss, which is a negative return.

The conclusion from this analysis is that individual securities will be either more or less risky than the market average in a fairly **predictable** way. The measure of this relationship between market returns and an individual security's returns, reflecting differences in systematic risk characteristics, can be developed into a beta factor for the individual security.

3.8 The equity risk premium

Key term

> **Market risk premium** or **equity risk premium** is the difference between the expected rate of return on a market portfolio and the risk-free rate of return over the same period.

The equity risk premium $E(r_m - R_f)$ represents the excess of market returns over those associated with investing in risk-free assets.

The CAPM makes use of the principle that **returns on shares** in the **market** as a whole are expected to be higher than the returns on risk-free investments. The difference between market returns and risk-free returns is called an **excess return**. For example, if the return on British Government stocks is 9% and market returns are 13%, the **excess** return on the market's shares as a whole is 4%.

The difference between the risk-free return and the expected return on an individual security can be measured as the **excess return for the market as a whole multiplied** by **the security's beta factor**.

3.9 The CAPM formula   6/08, 12/08, 12/09, 6/14

The capital asset pricing model is a statement of the principles explained above. It can be stated as follows.

Formula to learn

$E(r_i) = R_f + \beta_i(E(r_m) - R_f)$

Where $E(r_i)$ is the cost of equity capital   Note: $E(r_m) - R_f$ = equity risk premium
       R_f is the risk-free rate of return
       $E(r_m)$ is the return from the market as a whole
       β_i is the beta factor of the individual security

3.10 Example: CAPM (2)

Shares in Louie and Dewie have a beta of 0.9. The expected returns to the market are 10% and the risk-free rate of return is 4%. What is the cost of equity capital for Louie and Dewie?

Solution

$E(r_i) = R_f + \beta_i(E(r_m) - R_f)$

   $= 4 + 0.9\,(10 - 4)$

   $= 9.4\%$

3.11 Example: CAPM (3)

Investors have an expected rate of return of 8% from ordinary shares in Algol, which have a beta of 1.2. The expected returns to the market are 7%.

What will be the expected rate of return from ordinary shares in Rigel, which have a beta of 1.8?

Solution

Algol: $E(r_i)$ $= R_f + \beta_i(E(r_m) - R_f)$

          8 $= R_f + 1.2(7 - R_f)$

          8 $= R_f + 8.4 - 1.2\,R_f$

   $0.2\,R_f$ $= 0.4$

      R_f $= 2\%$

Rigel: $E(r_i)$ $= 2 + (7 - 2)\,1.8$

          $= 11\%$

Question   Returns

The risk-free rate of return is 7%. The average market return is 11%.

(a)   What will be the return expected from a share whose β factor is 0.9?

(b)   What would be the share's expected value if it is expected to earn an annual dividend of 5.3c, with no capital growth?

Answer

(a)   7% + 0.9 (11% – 7%) = 10.6%

(b) $\dfrac{5.3c}{10.6\%}$ = 50c

3.12 Problems with applying the CAPM in practice   6/08

FAST FORWARD

Problems of CAPM include **unrealistic assumptions** and the **required estimates being difficult to make**.

(a)   The need to **determine** the **excess return** $(E(r_m) - R_f)$. Expected, rather than historical, returns should be used, although historical returns are used in practice, since beta factors are derived from statistical analysis of historical returns.

(b)   The need to **determine** the **risk-free rate**. A risk-free investment might be a government security. However, interest rates vary with the term of the lending.

(c)   **Errors** in the **statistical analysis used** to calculate β values are an issue.

(d)   Betas may also **change over** time and changes may not be identified quickly through historical statistical analysis.

(e)   The CAPM is also **unable to forecast returns accurately** for companies with **low price/earnings** ratios and to take account of seasonal 'month of the year' effects and 'day of the week' effects that appear to influence returns on shares.

Question   Beta factor

(a)   What does beta measure, and what do betas of 0.5, 1 and 1.5 mean?
(b)   What factors determine the level of beta which a company may have?

Answer

(a)   **Beta measures** the systematic risk of a risky investment, such as a share in a company. The total risk of the share can be subdivided into two parts, known as **systematic (or market) risk** and **unsystematic (or unique) risk**. The systematic risk depends on the sensitivity of the return of the share to general economic and market factors, such as periods of boom and recession. The capital asset pricing model shows how the return which investors expect from shares should depend only on systematic risk, not on unsystematic risk, which can be eliminated by holding a well-diversified portfolio.

Beta is calibrated such that the average risk of stock market investments has a **beta of 1**. Thus shares with betas of 0.5 or 1.5 would have half or 1½ times the average sensitivity to market variations respectively.

This is reflected by higher volatility of share prices for shares with a beta of 1.5 than for those with a beta of 0.5. For example, a 10% increase in general stock market prices would be expected to be reflected as a 5% increase for a share with a beta of 0.5 and a 15% increase for a share with a beta of 1.5, with a similar effect for price reductions.

(b)   The beta of a company will be the **weighted average** of the beta of its shares and the beta of its debt. The beta of debt is very low, but not zero, because corporate debt bears default risk, which in turn is dependent on the volatility of the company's cash flows.

Factors determining the beta of a company's equity shares include:

(i)   **Sensitivity** of the company's **cash flows** to economic factors, as stated above. For example sales of new cars are more sensitive than sales of basic foods and necessities.

(ii) The company's **operating gearing**. A high level of fixed costs in the company's cost structure will cause high variations in operating profit compared with variations in sales.

(iii) The company's **financial gearing**. High borrowing and interest costs will cause high variations in equity earnings compared with variations in operating profit, increasing the equity beta as equity returns become more variable in relation to the market as a whole. This effect will be countered by the low beta of debt when computing the weighted average beta of the whole company.

3.13 Dividend growth model and CAPM

The dividend growth model and CAPM will not necessarily give the same cost of equity, and in your exam you may have to calculate the cost of equity using either, or both, models.

3.13.1 Example: Dividend growth model and CAPM

The following data relates to the ordinary shares of Stilton.

Current market price, 31 December 20X1	250c
Dividend per share, 20X1	3c
Expected growth rate in dividends and earnings	10% pa
Average market return	8%
Risk-free rate of return	5%
Beta factor of Stilton equity shares	1.40

(a)   What is the estimated cost of equity using the dividend growth model?
(b)   What is the estimated cost of equity using the capital asset pricing model?

Solution

(a) $k_e = \dfrac{d_0(1+g)}{P_0} + g$

$= \dfrac{3(1.10)}{250} + 0.10$

$= 0.1132 \text{ or } 11.32\%$

(b) $k_e = 5 + 1.40\,(8 - 5) = 9.2\%$

4 Cost of debt   6/08, 12/09, 6/10, 12/10

FAST FORWARD

The **cost of debt** is the return an enterprise must pay to its lenders.

- For **irredeemable debt**, this is the (post-tax) interest as a percentage of the ex interest market value of the bonds (or preferred shares).

- For **redeemable debt**, the cost is given by the internal rate of return of the cash flows involved (interest and capital gain or loss at redemption).

Interest is tax deductible and this is taken into account in the calculations.

4.1 The cost of debt capital

Lenders are only willing to lend if their initial outlay of money is fully compensated by future cash inflows. Therefore, the cost of capital is the rate at which lenders recover their initial outlay of money, and the price of debt equals the present value of cash inflows. For the borrowing company this represents:

(a)   The cost of **continuing to use the finance** rather than redeem the securities at their current market price; and

(b)   The cost of raising **additional fixed interest capital** if we assume that the cost of the additional capital would be equal to the cost of that already issued. If a company has not already issued any fixed interest capital, it may estimate the cost of doing so by making a similar calculation for another company which is judged to be similar as regards risk.

4.2 Irredeemable debt capital

Again, remember the formula for a perpetuity: $PV = \dfrac{c}{r}$

Irredeemable debt capital is a perpetuity. Rearrange the perpetuity formula and the cost of irredeemable debt capital, paying interest i in perpetuity, and having a current ex-interest price is as follows.

$$P_0 = \frac{i}{K_d} \text{ and } k_d = \frac{i}{P_0}$$

4.3 Example: Cost of debt capital (1)

Lepus has issued bonds of $100 nominal value with annual interest of 9% per year, based on the nominal value. The current market price of the bonds is $90. What is the cost of the bonds?

Solution

$k_d = 9/90 = 10\%$

4.4 Example: Cost of debt capital (2)

Henryted has 12% irredeemable bonds in issue with a nominal value of $100. The market price is $95 ex interest. Calculate the cost of capital if interest is paid half-yearly.

Solution

If interest is 12% annually, therefore 6% is payable half-yearly.

$$\text{Cost of loan capital} = \left(1 + \frac{6}{95}\right)^2 - 1 = 13.0\%$$

4.5 Redeemable debt capital   6/11

If the debt is **redeemable** then in the year of redemption the interest payment will be received by the holder as well as the amount payable on redemption, so:

$$P_0 = \frac{i}{(1+k_{d\,net})} + \frac{i}{(1+k_{d\,net})^2} + \ldots + \frac{i + p_n}{(1+k_{d\,net})^n}$$

Where p_n = the amount payable on redemption in year n

The above equation cannot be simplified, so 'r' will have to be calculated by trial and error, as an **internal rate of return (IRR)**.

The best trial and error figure to start with in calculating the cost of redeemable debt is to take the cost of debt capital as if it were irredeemable and then add the annualised capital profit that will be made from the present time to the time of redemption.

4.6 Example: Cost of debt capital (3)

Owen Allot has in issue 10% bonds of a nominal value of $100. The market price is $90 ex interest. Calculate the cost of this capital if the bond is:

(a)   Irredeemable
(b)   Redeemable at par after ten years

Ignore taxation.

Solution

(a)   **The cost of irredeemable debt capital** is $\dfrac{i}{P_0} = \dfrac{\$10}{\$90} \times 100\% = 11.1\%$

(b)   **The cost of redeemable debt capital**. The capital profit that will be made from now to the date of redemption is $10 ($100 – $90). This profit will be made over a period of ten years which gives an annualised profit of $1 which is about 1% of current market value. The best trial and error figure to try first is therefore 12%.

Year		Cash flow $	Discount factor 12%	PV $	Discount factor 11%	PV $
0	Market value	(90)	1.000	(90.00)	1.000	(90.00)
1-10	Interest	10	5.650	56.50	5.889	58.89
10	Capital repayment	100	0.322	32.20	0.352	35.20
				(1.30)		+4.09

The approximate cost of redeemable debt capital is therefore:

$(11 + \dfrac{4.09}{(4.09 - -1.30)} \times 1) = 11.76\%$

4.7 Debt capital and taxation

The interest on debt capital is likely to be an allowable deduction for the purposes of taxation and so the cost of debt capital and the cost of share capital are not properly comparable costs. This tax relief on interest ought to be recognised in computations. The **after-tax cost of irredeemable debt** capital is:

$k_{d\,net} = \dfrac{i(1-T)}{P_0}$

Where $k_{d\,net}$ is the after-tax cost of debt capital

i   is the annual interest payment

P_0 is the current market price of the debt capital ex interest (that is, after payment of the current interest)

T   is the rate of corporation tax

Note. This is only a variant of the cost of irredeemable debt capital formula in Section 4.2.

Cost of irredeemable debt capital, paying annual net interest $i(1 - T)$, and having a current ex-interest price P_0:

$$k_{d\,net} = \frac{i(1-T)}{P_0}$$

Therefore if a company pays $10,000 a year interest on irredeemable bonds with a nominal value of $100,000 and a market price of $80,000, and the rate of tax is 30%, the cost of the debt would be:

$$\frac{10,000}{80,000}(1 - 0.30) = 0.0875 = 8.75\%$$

The higher the rate of tax, the greater the tax benefits in having debt finance will be compared with equity finance. In the example above, if the rate of tax had been 50%, the cost of debt after tax would have been:

$$\frac{10,000}{80,000}(1 - 0.50) = 0.0625 = 6.25\%$$

Students often don't remember that debt attracts tax relief in most jurisdictions.

In the case of **redeemable debt**, the capital repayment is not allowable for tax. To calculate the cost of the debt capital to include in the weighted average cost of capital, it is necessary to calculate an internal rate of return which takes account of tax relief on the interest.

4.8 Example: Cost of debt capital (4)

(a) A company has outstanding $660,000 of 8% bonds on which the interest is payable annually on 31 December. The debt is due for redemption at par on 1 January 20X6. The market price of the bonds at 28 December 20X2 was $95. Ignoring any question of personal taxation, what do you estimate to be the current cost of debt?

(b) If the pre-tax cost of debt rises to 12%, what effect will this have on the market price?

(c) If the effective rate of tax on company profits is 30%, what would be the after-tax cost of debt of the bonds in (a) above? Tax is paid each 31 December on profits earned in that year.

Solution

(a) The current cost of debt is found by calculating the pre-tax internal rate of return of the cash flows shown in the table below. A discount rate of 10% is chosen for a trial and error start to the calculation.

Item and date		Year	Cash flow $	Discount factor 10%	Present value $
Market value	28.12.X2	0	(95)	1.000	(95.0)
Interest	31.12.X3	1	8	0.909	7.3
Interest	31.12.X4	2	8	0.826	6.6
Interest	31.12.X5	3	8	0.751	6.0
Redemption	1.1.X6	3	100	0.751	75.1
NPV					0.0

By coincidence, the cost of debt is 10% since the NPV of the cash flows above is zero. This is the pre-tax cost of the debt.

(b) If the cost of debt rises to 12%, the market price will fall to reflect the new rate of return required by the bond holder. The new market price will be the discounted value of all future cash flows up to the redemption date in 20X6, using a discount rate of 12%.

Item and date		Year	Cash flow	Discount factor 12%	Present value
			$		$
Interest	31.12.X2	0	8	1.000	8.0
Interest	31.12.X3	1	8	0.893	7.1
Interest	31.12.X4	2	8	0.797	6.4
Interest	31.12.X5	3	8	0.712	5.7
Redemption	1.1.X6	3	100	0.712	71.2
NPV					98.4

The estimated market price would be $98.40.

(c)

Item and date		Year	Cash flow after tax	Try 5% PV	Try 10% PV
			$	$	$
Market value		0	(95.0)	(95.0)	(95.0)
Interest (8 × (1 − 0.3))	31.12.X3	1	5.6	5.3	5.1
Interest	31.12.X4	2	5.6	5.1	4.6
Interest	31.12.X5	3	5.6	4.8	4.3
Redemption	1.1.X6	3	100.0	86.4	75.1
NPV				6.6	(5.9)

The estimated after-tax cost of debt is: $5\% + (\dfrac{6.6}{(6.6+5.9)} \times 5\%) = 7.6\%$

4.9 Cost of floating rate debt

If a firm has variable or **'floating rate' debt**, then the cost of an equivalent fixed interest debt should be substituted. 'Equivalent' usually means fixed interest debt with a similar term to maturity in a firm of similar standing, although if the cost of capital is to be used for project appraisal purposes, there is an argument for using debt of the same duration as the project under consideration.

The short-term funds such as bank loans and overdrafts is the current interest being charged on such funds. Alternatively, the cost of debt of ordinary or straight bonds could be used.

4.10 Cost of convertible debt

The cost of capital of convertible to debt is harder to determine. The calculation will depend on whether or not conversion is likely to happen. Debt holders will only convert if the value of the shares is greater than the redemption value of the debt.

(a) If conversion is **not** expected, the conversion value is ignored and the bond is treated as **redeemable debt**, using the IRR method described in Section 4.6.

(b) If conversion **is** expected, the IRR method for calculating the cost of redeemable debt is used, but the number of years to redemption is replaced by the **number of years to conversion** and the redemption value is replaced by the **conversion value** ie the market value of the shares into which the debt is to be converted.

Conversion value = $P_0 (1 + g)^n R$

Where
- P_0 is the current ex-dividend ordinary share price
- g is the expected annual growth of the ordinary share price
- n is the number of years to conversion
- R is the number of shares received on conversion

4.11 Example: Cost of convertible debt

A company has issued 8% convertible bonds which are due to be redeemed in five years' time. They are currently quoted at $82 per $100 nominal. The bonds can be converted into 25 shares in five years' time. The share price is currently $3.50 and is expected to grow at a rate of 3% pa. Assume a 30% rate of tax.

Calculate the cost of the convertible debt.

Solution

$$\text{Conversion value} = P_0(1+g)^n R$$
$$= 3.50 \times (1+0.03)^5 \times 25$$
$$= \$101.44$$

As the redemption value is $100, investors would **choose to convert** the bonds so the **conversion value** is used in the IRR calculation.

Year	Cash flow $		Discount factor 8%	PV $	Discount factor 12%	PV $
0	Market value	(82.00)	1.000	(82.00)	1.000	(82.00)
1-5	Interest (8 ×(1 − 0.3))	5.60	3.993	22.36	3.605	20.19
5	Conversion value	101.44	0.681	69.08	0.567	57.52
				9.44		(4.29)

$$\text{Cost of debt} = 8\% + \frac{9.44}{9.44 + 4.29} (12\% - 8\%) = 10.75\%$$

4.12 Cost of preference shares

For preference shares the future cash flows are the dividend payments in perpetuity.

The relationship between the market price of the preference shares and the annual dividend is expressed by the formula:

$$P_0 = \frac{d}{(1+k_{pref})} + \frac{d}{(1+k_{pref})^2} + \frac{d}{(1+k_{pref})^3} + \text{(in perpetuity)}$$

Where

- P_0 is the current market price of preference share capital after payment of the current dividend
- d is the dividend received
- k_{pref} is the cost of preference share capital

$$\frac{d}{(1+k_{pref})} + \frac{d}{(1+k_{pref})^2} + \frac{d}{(1+k_{pref})^3} \ldots\ldots$$

This simplifies to $P_0 = \dfrac{d}{k_{pref}}$

Rearranging: $k_{pref} = d/P_0$

The cost of preference shares can be calculated as $k_{pref} = \dfrac{d}{P_0}$.

Again, this is the 'in perpetuity' formula.

Don't forget that tax relief is not given for preference share dividends.

When calculating the weighted average cost of capital (see Section 5), the cost of preference shares is a separate component and should **not** be combined with the cost of debt or the cost of equity.

5 Weighted average cost of capital (WACC)
12/07, 6/08, 12/08, 6/09, 12/09, 6/10, 12/10, 6/11, 6/12, 12/12, 6/13, 6/14, 12/14

FAST FORWARD

The **weighted average cost of capital** (WACC) is the average cost of capital for all the company's long-term sources of finance, weighted to allow for the relative proportions of each type of capital in the overall capital structure.

The WACC is calculated by weighting the costs of the individual sources of finance according to their **relative** importance as sources of finance.

The WACC represents the return that the company should make on its investments to be able to provide the returns required by its finance providers.

5.1 Computing a discount rate

We have looked at the costs of individual sources of capital for a company. But how does this help us to work out the cost of capital as a whole, or the discount rate to apply in DCF investment appraisals?

In many cases it will be difficult to associate a particular project with a particular form of finance. A company's funds may be viewed as a **pool of resources**. Money is withdrawn from this pool of funds to invest in new projects and added to the pool as new finance is raised or profits are retained. Under these circumstances it might seem appropriate to use an average cost of capital as the discount rate.

The correct cost of capital to use in investment appraisal is the **marginal cost of the funds** raised (or earnings retained) to finance the investment. The weighted average cost of capital (WACC) might be considered the most **reliable guide** to the **marginal cost of capital**, but only on the assumption that the company continues to invest in the future, in projects of a standard level of business risk, by raising funds in the same proportions as its existing capital structure.

Weighted average cost of capital is the average cost of the company's finance (equity, bonds, bank loans) weighted according to the proportion each element bears to the total pool of capital.

5.2 General formula for the WACC

A general formula for the weighted average cost of capital (WACC) k_0 is as follows. This formula assumes that the capital structure has just two elements, equity and debt.

$$\text{WACC} = \left[\frac{V_e}{V_e + V_d}\right] k_e + \left[\frac{V_d}{V_e + V_d}\right] k_d (1 - T)$$

where k_e is the cost of equity
k_d is the cost of debt
V_e is the market value of equity in the firm
V_d is the market value of debt in the firm
T   is the rate of company tax

5.3 Example: Weighted average cost of capital

An entity has the following information in its statement of financial position.

	$'000
Ordinary shares of 50c	2,500
12% unsecured bonds	1,000

The ordinary shares are currently quoted at 130c each and the bonds are trading at $72 per $100 nominal. The ordinary dividend of 15c has just been paid with an expected growth rate of 10%. Corporation tax is currently 30%.

Calculate the weighted average cost of capital for this entity.

Solution

Market values:

		$'000
Equity (V_e):	$\dfrac{2,500}{0.5} \times 1.30$	6,500
Bonds (V_d):	$1,000 \times 0.72$	720
		7,220

Cost of equity:

$$k_e = \frac{d_0(1+g)}{P_0} + g = \frac{0.15(1+0.1)}{1.3} + 0.1 = 0.2269 = 22.69\%$$

Cost of debt:

$$k_d = \frac{i}{P_0} = \frac{0.12}{0.72} = 0.1667 = 16.67\%$$

Weighted average cost of capital:

$$\text{WACC} = \left[\frac{V_e}{V_e + V_d}\right] k_e + \left[\frac{V_d}{V_e + V_d}\right] k_d (1 - T)$$

$V_e + V_d = 7,220$

$$\text{WACC} = \left[\left(\frac{6,500}{7,220}\right) \times 22.69\%\right] + \left[\left(\frac{720}{7,220}\right) \times 16.67\% \times 0.7\right] = 20.43\% + 1.16\% = 21.59\%$$

5.4 Weighting

Two methods of weighting could be used.

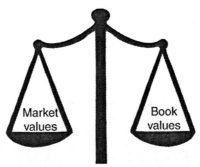

Market values should always be used if data is available. Although book values are often easier to obtain, they are based on historical costs and their use will seriously **understate** the impact of the cost of equity finance on the average cost of capital. If the WACC is underestimated, unprofitable projects will be accepted.

5.5 Marginal cost of capital approach

The **marginal cost of capital** approach involves calculating a marginal cut-off rate for acceptable investment projects by:

(a)   **Establishing rates of return** for each component of capital structure, except retained earnings, based on its value if it were to be raised under current market conditions.

(b)   **Relating dividends or interest** to these values to obtain a marginal cost for each component.

(c)   **Applying the marginal cost** to each component depending on its proportionate weight within the capital structure and adding the resultant costs to give a weighted average.

It can be argued that the current weighted average cost of capital should be used to evaluate projects. Where a company's capital structure changes only very **slowly** over time, the marginal cost of new capital should be roughly **equal** to the weighted average cost of current capital.

Where gearing levels fluctuate significantly, or the finance for a new project carries a significantly different level of risks to that of the existing company, there is good reason to seek an alternative marginal cost of capital.

5.6 Example: Marginal cost of capital

Georgebear has the following capital structure.

Source	After-tax cost %	Market value $m	After-tax cost × Market value
Equity	12	10	1.2
Preference	10	2	0.2
Bonds	7.5	8	0.6
		20	2.0

Weighted average cost of capital $= \dfrac{2 \times 100\%}{20}$

$= 10\%$

Note that this is a simplified calculation of WACC. The full calculation will give the same answer of 10%.

Georgebear's directors have decided to embark on major capital expenditure, which will be financed by a major issue of funds. The estimated project cost is $3,000,000, 1/3 of which will be financed by equity, 2/3 of which will be financed by bonds. As a result of undertaking the project, the cost of equity (existing and new shares) will rise from 12% to 14%. The cost of preference shares and the cost of existing bonds will remain the same, while the after-tax cost of the new bonds will be 9%.

Required

Calculate the company's new weighted average cost of capital, and its marginal cost of capital.

Solution

New weighted average cost of capital

Source	After-tax cost %	Market value $m	After-tax cost × Market value
Equity	14	11	1.54
Preference	10	2	0.20
Existing bonds	7.5	8	0.60
New bonds	9	2	0.18
		23	2.52

$$\text{WACC} = \frac{2.52 \times 100\%}{23}$$

$$= 11.0\%$$

$$\text{Marginal cost of capital} = \frac{(2.52 - 2.0) \times 100\%}{23 - 20}$$

$$= 17.3\%$$

Chapter Roundup

- The **cost of capital** is the rate of return that the enterprise must pay to satisfy the providers of funds, and it reflects the riskiness of providing funds.

- The **dividend growth model** can be used to estimate a cost of equity, on the assumption that the market value of share is directly related to the expected future dividends from the shares.

- The **capital asset pricing model** can be used to calculate a cost of equity and incorporates **risk**.

  The CAPM is based on a comparison of the **systematic risk** of **individual investments** with the **risks of all shares** in the **market**.

- The total **risk** involved in holding securities (shares) divides into **risk specific** to the company (unsystematic) and risk due to **variations** in **market activity** (systematic).

  Unsystematic risk can be diversified away, while **systematic or market risk** cannot. Investors may mix a diversified market portfolio with risk-free assets to achieve a preferred mix of risk and return.

- The systematic risk in individual company shares can be measured statistically, by analysing historical returns.

  The CAPM model uses a **beta factor** to measure a share's volatility in terms of systematic risk.

  In accordance with portfolio theory, unsystematic risk is ignored in the CAPM, as it is assumed that unsystematic risk can be diversified away.

- Problems of CAPM include **unrealistic assumptions** and the **required estimates being difficult to make**.

- The **cost of debt** is the return an enterprise must pay to its lenders.

  - For **irredeemable debt**, this is the (post-tax) interest as a percentage of the ex interest market value of the bonds (or preferred shares).

  - For **redeemable debt**, the cost is given by the internal rate of return of the cash flows involved (interest and capital gain or loss at redemption).

  Interest is tax deductible and this is taken into account in the calculations.

- The **weighted average cost of capital** (WACC) is the average cost of capital for all the company's long-term sources of finance, weighted to allow for the relative proportions of each type of capital in the overall capital structure.

  The WACC is calculated by weighting the costs of the individual sources of finance according to their **relative** importance as sources of finance.

  The WACC represents the return that the company should make on its investments to be able to provide the returns required by its finance providers.

1 Fill in the blanks.

Cost of capital = (1) .... + (2) premium for .... risk +
(3) premium for .... risk.

2 A share has a current market value of 120c and the last dividend was 10c. If the expected annual growth rate of dividends is 5%, calculate the cost of equity capital.

3 What type of risk arises from the existing operations of a business and cannot be diversified away?

4 Which of the following risks can be eliminated by diversification?

A   Inherent risk
B   Systematic risk
C   Market risk
D   Unsystematic risk

5 Unsystematic risk is measured by beta factors.

True   ☐

False   ☐

6 A portfolio consisting entirely of risk-free securities will have a beta factor of (tick one box):

−1   ☐

0   ☐

1   ☐

7 The risk-free rate of return is 8%. Average market return is 14%. A share's beta factor is 0.5. What will its expected return be?

8 Identify the variables k_e, k_d, V_e and V_d in the following weighted average cost of capital formula.

$$WACC = \left[\frac{V_e}{V_e + V_d}\right] k_e + \left[\frac{V_d}{V_e + V_d}\right] k_d (1 - T)$$

9 When calculating the weighted average cost of capital, which of the following is the preferred method of weighting?

A   Book values of debt and equity
B   Average levels of the market values of debt and equity (ignoring reserves) over five years
C   Current market values of debt and equity (ignoring reserves)
D   Current market values of debt and equity (plus reserves)

10 What is the cost of $1 irredeemable debt capital paying an annual rate of interest of 7%, and having a current market price of $1.50?

1   (1)   Risk-free rate of return
    (2)   Business
    (3)   Financial

2   $\dfrac{10(1+0.05)}{120} + 0.05 = 13.75\%$

3   Systematic or market risk

4   D   Unsystematic risk is risk that is specific to sectors, companies or projects. Systematic risk (also known as inherent risk or market risk) affects the whole market and therefore cannot be reduced by diversification.

5   False. Beta factors measure systematic risk.

6   Zero

7   Expected return = 8 + 0.5 (14 − 8) = 11%

8   k_e is the cost of equity
    k_d is the cost of debt
    V_e is the market value of equity in the firm
    V_d is the market value of debt in the firm

9   C   Current market values of debt and equity (ignoring reserves)

10 Cost of debt = $\dfrac{0.07}{1.50} = 4.67\%$

Now try the questions below from the Practice Question Bank

Number	Level	Marks	Approximate time
Section A Q27	Examination	2	4 mins
Section B Q6 – Q10	Examination	10	20 mins
Section C Q18	Introductory	N/A	39 mins

Capital structure

Topic list	Syllabus reference
1 Capital structure theories	E4 (a), (b), (c), (d)
2 Impact of cost of capital on investments	E3 (e)(i)(ii)(iii)(iv)

Introduction

This chapter considers the impact of **capital structure** on the cost of capital.
The **practical application** of this comes in Section 2 where we consider various
ways of incorporating the effects of changing capital structure into cost of
capital and net present value calculations.

Study guide

		Intellectual level
E3	**Sources of finance and their relative costs**	
(e)	Impact of cost of capital on investments including:	2
(i)	The relationship between company value and cost of capital	
(ii)	The circumstances under which WACC can be used in investment appraisal	
(iii)	The advantages of the CAPM over WACC in determining a project-specific cost of capital	
(iv)	Application of CAPM in calculating a project-specific discount rate	
E4	**Capital structure theories and practical considerations**	
(a)	Describe the traditional view of capital structure and its assumptions.	2
(b)	Describe the views of Miller and Modigliani on capital structure, both without and with corporate taxation, and their assumptions.	2
(c)	Identify a range of capital market imperfections and describe their impact on the views of Miller and Modigliani on capital structure.	2
(d)	Explain the relevance of pecking order theory to the selection of sources of finance.	1

Exam guide

The theories covered in this chapter could be needed in a discussion part of a question. Gearing and ungearing a beta is an essential technique to master using the formula which will be given to you in the exam.

1 Capital structure theories   6/09, 6/11, 12/13

FAST FORWARD

> Some commentators believe that an **optimal mix of finance** exists at which the company's **cost of capital** will be minimised.

A company should seek to minimise its weighted average cost of capital. By doing so, it minimises its cost of funds. The weighted average cost of capital is an average cost of all the different sources of finance that a company uses. By changing the proportions of each type of finance, it will alter its WACC.

So how can a company adjust its financing structure in such a way that its WACC is minimised?

There are different views on the answer to this question. One is the so-called 'traditional' view. Another is a view proposed by Modigliani and Miller.

The **traditional view** concludes that there is an optimal capital mix of equity and debt at which the **weighted average cost of capital is minimised.**

However, the alternative view of **Modigliani and Miller** (assuming no tax) is that the firm's overall **weighted average cost of capital** is **not influenced** by changes in its **capital structure**.

Both views agree that:

- The cost of equity is higher than the cost of debt.

- As the level of gearing increases, the larger proportion of debt in the capital structure means that there is a larger proportion of lower-cost finance.

- However, as the level of gearing rises, the cost of equity also rises to compensate shareholders for the higher risk.

- As gearing increases, the higher proportion of low-cost debt but the rising cost of equity pull the WACC in opposite directions.

1.1 The traditional view

Under the **traditional theory of cost of capital**, the weighted average cost of capital declines initially as gearing increases, but then rises as gearing increases further. The **optimal capital structure** is at the gearing level where WACC is lowest.

The **traditional view** is as follows.

(a)   As the **level of gearing increases**, the **cost of debt** remains **unchanged** up to a certain level of gearing. Beyond this level, the cost of debt will increase.

(b)   The **cost of equity** rises as the level of **gearing increases** and financial risk increases. There is a non-linear relationship between the cost of equity and gearing.

(c)   The **weighted average cost of capital** does **not remain constant**, but rather falls initially as the proportion of debt capital increases, and then begins to increase as the rising cost of equity (and possibly of debt) becomes more significant.

(d)   The optimum level of gearing is where the company's weighted average cost of capital is minimised.

The traditional view about the cost of capital is illustrated in the following figure.

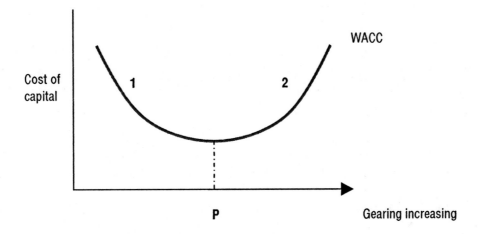

At point 1, the cost of capital falls as the level of debt finance increases. This is because debt is cheaper than equity.

Point P shows the optimum level of debt: cheap debt finance minimises the cost of capital.

At point 2, the cost of capital increases as the level of debt finance continues to increase. This is because above the optimum level of debt finance, the company is perceived to be high risk by shareholders and lenders, who start to demand a higher level of return.

The figure below shows the same cycle, illustrating the changes in cost of capital, cost of debt and cost of equity.

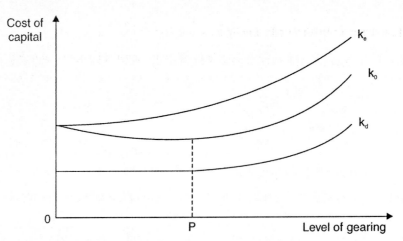

Where k_e is the cost of equity in the geared company
$\quad k_d$ is the cost of debt
$\quad k_0$ is the weighted average cost of capital

1.2 Net operating income view of WACC: Modigliani-Miller (MM)

FAST FORWARD

Modigliani and Miller stated that, in the absence of tax relief on debt interest, a company's **capital structure** would have **no impact** on its WACC. WACC would be the same regardless of the company's capital structure.

The net operating income approach takes a different view of the effect of gearing on WACC. In their 1958 theory, Modigliani and Miller (MM) proposed that the total market value of a company, in the absence of tax relief on debt interest, will be determined only by two factors.

*   The **total earnings** of the company
*   The **level of operating (business) risk** attached to those earnings

The total market value would be computed by discounting the total earnings at a rate that is appropriate to the level of operating risk. This rate would represent the WACC of the company.

Thus Modigliani and Miller concluded that **the capital structure of a company would have no effect on its overall value or WACC.**

1.2.1 Assumptions of net operating income approach

Modigliani and Miller made various assumptions in arriving at this conclusion, including:

(a)   A **perfect capital market** exists, in which investors have the same information, on which they act rationally, to arrive at the same expectations about future earnings and risks.

(b)   There are no **tax or transaction costs**.

(c)   **Debt is risk free** and freely available at the same cost to investors and companies alike.

Modigliani and Miller justified their approach by the use of **arbitrage**.

Key term

Arbitrage is when a purchase and sale of a security takes place simultaneously in different markets, with the aim of making a risk-free profit through the exploitation of any price difference between the markets.

Arbitrage can be used to show that once all opportunities for profit have been exploited, the market values of two companies with the same earnings in equivalent business risk classes will have moved to an equal value.

Exam focus point

The proof of Modigliani and Miller's theory by arbitrage is not examinable.

If Modigliani and Miller's theory holds, it implies:

(a) The **cost of debt remains unchanged** as the level of gearing increases.
(b) The **cost of equity rises** in such a way as to keep the **weighted average cost of capital constant**.

This would be represented on a graph as shown below.

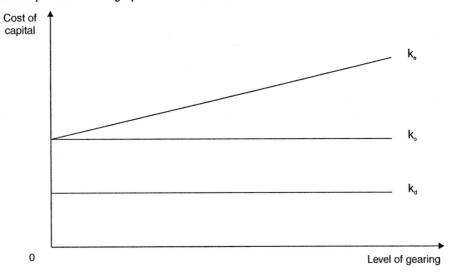

1.3 Example: Net operating income approach

A company has $5,000 of debt at 10% interest, and earns $5,000 a year before interest is paid. There are 2,250 issued shares, and the weighted average cost of capital of the company is 20%.

The market value of the company should be as follows.

Earnings	$5,000
Weighted average cost of capital	0.2
	$
Market value of the company ($5,000 ÷ 0.2)	25,000
Less market value of debt	5,000
Market value of equity	20,000

The cost of equity is therefore $\dfrac{5,000-500}{20,000} = \dfrac{4,500}{20,000} = 22.5\%$

and the market value per share is $\dfrac{4,500}{2,250} \times \dfrac{1}{0.225} = \$8.89$

Suppose that the level of gearing is increased by issuing $5,000 more of debt at 10% interest to repurchase 562 shares (at a market value of $8.89 per share) leaving 1,688 shares in issue.

The weighted average cost of capital will, according to the net operating income approach, remain unchanged at 20%. The market value of the company should still therefore be $25,000.

Earnings	$5,000
Weighted average cost of capital	0.2
	$
Market value of the company	25,000
Less market value of debt	10,000
Market value of equity	15,000

Annual dividends will now be $5,000 – $1,000 interest = $4,000.

The cost of equity has risen to $\dfrac{4,000}{15,000}$ = 26.667% and the market value per share is still:

$$\frac{4,000}{1,688} \times \frac{1}{0.2667} = \$8.89$$

The conclusion of the net operating income approach is that the level of gearing is a matter of indifference to an investor, because it does not affect the market value of the company, nor of an individual share. This is because as the level of gearing rises, so does the cost of equity in such a way as to keep both the weighted average cost of capital and the market value of the shares constant. Although, in our example, the dividend per share rises from $2 to $2.37, the increase in the cost of equity is such that the market value per share remains at $8.89.

1.4 Market imperfections

In 1963 Modigliani and Miller modified their theory to admit that **tax relief** on interest payments does lower the weighted average cost of capital. The savings arising from tax relief on debt interest are the **tax shield**.

However, whereas the traditional approach to gearing and WACC is that there is an optimal level of gearing where WACC is minimised, MM took a different view. They argued that the weighted average cost of capital continues to fall, up to gearing of 100%.

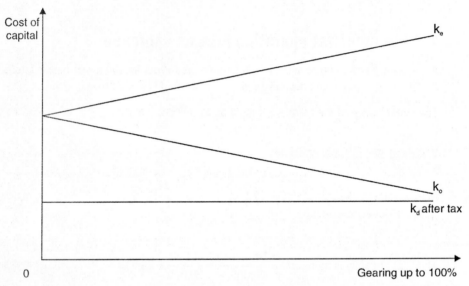

This suggests that companies should have a capital structure made up entirely of debt. This does not happen in practice due to the existence of other **market imperfections** which undermine the tax advantages of debt finance.

1.4.1 Bankruptcy costs

MM's theory assumes perfect capital markets so a company would always be able to raise finance and avoid bankruptcy. In reality, however, at higher levels of gearing there is an increasing risk of the company being unable to meet its interest payments and being declared bankrupt. At these higher levels of gearing, the bankruptcy risk means that shareholders will require a higher rate of return as compensation.

1.4.2 Agency costs

At higher levels of gearing there are also agency costs as a result of action taken by concerned debt holders. Providers of debt finance are likely to impose **restrictive covenants**, such as restriction of future dividends or the imposition of minimum levels of liquidity in order to protect their investment. They may also increase their level of monitoring and require more financial information.

1.4.3 Tax exhaustion

As companies increase their gearing they may reach a point where there are not enough profits from which to obtain all available tax benefits. They will still be subject to increased bankruptcy and agency costs but will not be able to benefit from the increased tax shield.

1.5 Pecking order theory

Pecking order theory has been developed as an alternative to traditional theory. This theory is based on the view that companies will not seek to minimise their WACC. Instead they will seek additional finance in an order of preference, or 'pecking order'.

Pecking order theory states that firms will prefer retained earnings to any other source of finance, and then will choose debt, and last of all equity. The order of preference will be:

- Retained earnings
- Straight debt (bank loans or bonds)
- Convertible debt
- Preference shares
- Issue new equity shares

1.5.1 Reasons for following pecking order

(a)   It is easier to **use retained earnings** than go to the trouble of obtaining external finance and have to live up to the demands of external finance providers.

(b)   There are **no issue costs** if retained earnings are used, and the issue costs of debt are lower than those of equity.

(c)   Investors prefer **safer securities**; that is, debt with its guaranteed income and priority on liquidation.

(d)   Some managers believe that debt issues have a better **signalling effect** than equity issues because the market believes that managers are better informed about shares' true worth than the market itself is. Their view is that the market will interpret debt issues as a sign of confidence, that businesses are confident of making sufficient profits to fulfil their obligations on debt and that the shares are **undervalued**.

By contrast, the market will interpret equity issues as a measure of last resort, that managers believe that equity is currently **overvalued** and hence are trying to achieve high proceeds while they can.

However, an issue of debt may **imply a similar lack of confidence** to an **issue of equity**; managers may issue debt when they believe that the **cost of debt** is **low** due to the market underestimating the risk of default and therefore undervaluing the risk premium in the cost of debt. If the market recognises this lack of confidence, it is likely to respond by raising the cost of debt.

1.5.2 Consequences of pecking order theory

(a)   Businesses will try to match **investment opportunities** with **internal finance** provided this does not mean excessive changes in dividend payout ratios.

(b)   If it is **not possible** to **match investment opportunities** with **internal finance**, surplus internal funds will be invested; if there is a deficiency of internal funds, external finance will be issued in the pecking order, starting with straight debt.

(c)   Establishing an **ideal debt-equity mix** will be problematic, since internal equity funds will be the first source of finance that businesses choose, and external equity funds the last.

1.5.3 Limitations of pecking order theory

(a) It fails to take into account **taxation, financial distress, agency costs** or how the **investment opportunities** that are available may influence the choice of finance.

(b) Pecking order theory is an explanation of what businesses **actually** do, rather than what they **should** do.

Studies suggest that the businesses that are most likely to follow pecking order theory are those that are **operating profitably** in markets where **growth prospects** are **poor**. There will thus be limited opportunities to invest funds, and these businesses will be content to rely on retained earnings for the limited resources that they need.

2 Impact of cost of capital on investments   6/08, 12/08

FAST FORWARD

The lower a company's WACC, the higher the NPV of its future cash flows and the higher its market value.

2.1 The relationship between company value and cost of capital

The market value of a company depends on its cost of capital. The lower a company's WACC, the higher the net present value of its future cash flows will be and therefore the higher its market value. We will consider business valuations in more detail in Part G of this Study Text.

2.2 Using the WACC in investment appraisal

The weighted average cost of capital can be used in investment appraisal if:

(a) The project being appraised is **small relative** to the company.
(b) The **existing capital structure** will be maintained (same financial risk).
(c) The project has the same **business risk** as the company.

2.3 Arguments against using the WACC   6/10

(a) New investments undertaken by a company might have different **business risk** characteristics from the company's existing operations. As a consequence, the return required by investors might go up (or down) if the investments are undertaken, because their business risk is perceived to be higher (or lower).

(b) The finance that is raised to fund a new investment might substantially change the capital structure and the perceived **financial risk** of investing in the company. Depending on whether the project is financed by equity or by debt capital, the perceived financial risk of the entire company might change. This must be taken into account when appraising investments.

(c) Many companies raise **floating-rate** debt capital as well as fixed interest debt capital. With floating-rate debt capital, the interest rate is variable, and is altered every three or six months or so in line with changes in current market interest rates. The cost of debt capital will therefore fluctuate as market conditions vary. Floating-rate debt is difficult to incorporate into a WACC computation, and the best that can be done is to substitute an 'equivalent' fixed interest debt capital cost in place of the floating-rate debt cost.

2.4 Using CAPM in investment appraisal   6/13

We looked at how the CAPM can be used to calculate a cost of equity incorporating risk in Chapter 15. It can also be used to calculate a **project-specific cost of capital**.

The CAPM produces a required return based on the expected return of the market $E(r_m)$, the risk-free interest rate (R_f) and the variability of project returns relative to the market returns (β). Its main advantage when used for investment appraisal is that it produces a discount rate which is based on the **systematic** risk of the individual investment.

It can be used to **compare projects of all different risk classes** and is therefore superior to an NPV approach which uses only one discount rate for all projects, regardless of their risk.

The model was developed with respect to securities; by applying it to an investment within the firm, the company is assuming that the shareholder wishes investments to be evaluated as if they were securities in the capital market and thus assumes that all shareholders will hold **diversified portfolios** and will not look to the company to achieve diversification for them.

2.5 Example: Required return

Panda is all-equity financed. It wishes to invest in a project with an estimated beta of 1.5. The project has significantly different business risk characteristics from Panda's current operations. The project requires an outlay of $10,000 and will generate expected returns of $12,000.

The market rate of return is 12% and the risk-free rate of return is 6%.

Required

Estimate the minimum return that Panda will require from the project and assess whether the project is worthwhile, based on the figures you are given.

Solution

We do not need to know Panda's current weighted average cost of capital, as the new project has different business characteristics from its current operations. Instead we use the capital asset pricing model so that:

$$\text{Required return} = R_f + \beta (E (r_m) - R_f)$$
$$= 6 + 1.5(12 - 6)$$
$$= 15\%$$

$$\text{Expected return} = \frac{12,000 - 10,000}{10,000}$$
$$= 20\%$$

Thus the project is worthwhile, as expected return exceeds required return.

2.6 Limitations of using CAPM in investment decisions   12/08

The greatest practical problems with the use of the CAPM in capital investment decisions are as follows.

(a)   It is **hard to estimate** returns on projects under different economic environments, market returns under different economic environments and the probabilities of the various environments.

(b)   The CAPM is really just a **single period model**. Few investment projects last for one year only and to extend the use of the return estimated from the model to more than one time period would require both project performance relative to the market and the economic environment to be reasonably stable.

        In theory, it should be possible to apply the CAPM for each time period, thus arriving at successive discount rates, one for each year of the project's life. In practice, this would exacerbate the estimation problems mentioned above and also make the discounting process much more cumbersome.

(c)   It may be **hard to determine the risk-free rate of return**. Government securities are usually taken to be risk free, but the return on these securities varies according to their term to maturity.

(d)   Some experts have argued that betas calculated using complicated statistical techniques often overestimate high betas and underestimate low betas, particularly for small companies.

2.7 CAPM and MM combined – geared betas

FAST FORWARD ⟩⟩

When an investment has differing business and finance risks from the existing business, **geared betas** may be used to obtain an appropriate cost of capital and required rate of return for an investment.

Geared betas are calculated by:

- Ungearing industry betas
- Converting ungeared betas back into a geared beta that reflects the company's own gearing ratio

2.7.1 Beta values and the effect of gearing

The gearing of a company will affect the risk of its equity. If a company is geared and its **financial risk is therefore higher** than the risk of an all-equity company, then the β value of the geared company's equity will be higher than the β value of a similar ungeared company's equity.

The earnings of a company with gearing are more volatile than the earnings of an all-equity company. This means that the beta factor (a measure of its systematic risk) is larger for a geared company than an ungeared company. Similarly, the beta factor of a high-geared company is greater than the beta factor of a low-geared company, because the volatility in its earnings is greater.

The CAPM is consistent with the propositions of Modigliani and Miller. MM argue that as gearing rises, the cost of equity rises to compensate shareholders for the extra financial risk of investing in a geared company. This financial risk is an aspect of systematic risk, and ought to be reflected in a company's beta factor.

2.7.2 Geared betas and ungeared betas

The connection between MM theory and the CAPM means that it is possible to establish a mathematical relationship between the β value of an ungeared company and the β value of a similar, but geared, company. The β value of a geared company will be higher than the β value of a company identical in every respect except that it is all-equity financed. This is because of the extra financial risk. The mathematical relationship between the 'ungeared' (or asset) and 'geared' betas is as follows.

Exam formula

$$\beta_a = \left[\frac{V_e}{(V_e + V_d(1-T))} \beta_e \right] + \left[\frac{V_d(1-T)}{(V_e + V_d(1-T))} \beta_d \right]$$

This is the **asset beta formula** on the exam formula sheet.

Where β_a is the asset beta or ungeared beta
β_e is the equity beta or geared beta
β_d is the beta factor of debt in the geared company
V_d is the market value of the debt capital in the geared company
V_e is the market value of the equity capital in the geared company
T is the rate of corporate tax

Debt is often assumed to be risk free and its beta (β_d) is then taken as zero, in which case the formula above reduces to the following form.

$$\beta_a = \beta_e \times \frac{V_e}{V_e + V_d(1-T)} \quad \text{or, without tax,} \quad \beta_a = \beta_e \times \frac{V_e}{V_e + V_d}$$

2.7.3 Example: CAPM and geared betas

Two companies are identical in every respect except for their capital structure. Their market values are in equilibrium, as follows.

	Geared	Ungeared
	$'000	$'000
Annual profit before interest and tax	1,000	1,000
Less interest (4,000 × 8%)	320	0
	680	1,000
Less tax at 30%	204	300
Profit after tax = dividends	476	700
Market value of equity	3,900	6,600
Market value of debt	4,180	0
Total market value of company	8,080	6,600

The total value of Geared is higher than the total value of Ungeared, which is consistent with MM.

All profits after tax are paid out as dividends, and so there is no dividend growth. The beta value of Ungeared has been calculated as 1.0. The debt capital of Geared can be regarded as risk free.

Calculate:

(a)   The cost of equity in Geared
(b)   The market return R_m
(c)   The beta value of Geared

Solution

(a)   Since its market value (MV) is in equilibrium, the cost of equity in Geared can be calculated as:

$$\frac{d}{MV} = \frac{476}{3,900} = 12.20\%$$

(b)   The beta value of Ungeared is 1.0, which means that the expected returns from Ungeared are exactly the same as the market returns, and $R_m = 700/6,600 = 10.6\%$.

(c) $\beta_e = \beta_a \times \dfrac{V_e + V_d(1-T)}{V_e}$

$= 1.0 \times \dfrac{3,900 + (4,180 \times 0.70)}{3,900} = 1.75$

The beta of Geared, as we should expect, is higher than the beta of Ungeared.

2.7.4 Using the geared and ungeared beta formula to estimate a beta factor

So what is the relevance of geared and ungeared betas?

A private company may want to evaluate a proposed new investment using DCF and so wants to identify a suitable cost of capital to use as the discount rate. Because it is a private company, it does not have a beta factor. However, it may identify a listed company that is similar to itself in many ways, and whose beta factor it can use to establish its own cost of equity. If the listed company and the private company are similar in every respect except for their gearing, it would be appropriate to adjust the estimated beta factor for the private company by making an adjustment for the difference in gearing levels between the two companies.

If a company plans to invest in a project which involves diversification into a new business, the investment will involve a different level of systematic risk from that applying to the company's existing business. A discount rate should be calculated which is specific to the project, and which takes account of both the project's systematic risk and the company's gearing level. The discount rate can be found using the CAPM.

Step 1 Get an estimate of the systematic risk characteristics of the project's operating cash flows by obtaining published beta values for companies in the industry into which the company is planning to diversify.

Step 2 Adjust these beta values to allow for the company's capital gearing level. This adjustment is done in two stages.

(a) Convert the beta values of other companies in the industry to ungeared betas, using the formula:

$$\beta_a = \beta_e \left(\frac{V_e}{V_e + V_d(1-T)} \right)$$

(b) Having obtained an ungeared beta value β_a, convert it back to a geared beta β_e, which reflects the company's own gearing ratio, using the formula:

$$\beta_e = \beta_a \frac{V_e + V_d(1-T)}{V_e}$$

Step 3 Having estimated a project-specific geared beta, use the CAPM to estimate a project-specific cost of equity. Having calculated a cost of equity, it may be necessary to calculate a weighted average cost of capital if there is also debt capital in the financing.

This may seem complicated. An example will be used to illustrate the method.

2.7.5 Gearing and ungearing betas

A company's debt:equity ratio, by market values, is 2:5. The corporate debt, which is assumed to be risk free, yields 11% before tax. The beta value of the company's equity is currently 1.1. The average returns on stock market equity are 16%.

The company is now proposing to invest in a project which would involve diversification into a new industry, and the following information is available about this industry.

(a) Average beta coefficient of equity capital = 1.59
(b) Average debt:equity ratio in the industry = 1:2 (by market value)

The rate of corporation tax is 30%. What would be a suitable cost of capital to apply to the project?

Solution

The company should not use its existing WACC as the discount rate for the planned project, because the investment will be in a different industry or market sector where the systematic risk is different.

Instead it can use the average systematic risk in the 'new' industry to determine a cost of capital. A problem is that the beta factor for listed companies that are already in the industry is different to some extent because of the different gearing level.

To get round this problem, we calculate a geared beta for the company based on the average geared betas of companies already in the industry, adjusted to allow for the difference in gearing.

This is essentially a three-step process.

(1) Convert the geared beta for the new industry into an ungeared beta.

(2) Use the ungeared beta to calculate a geared beta that reflects the company's own capital structure.

(3) Use this geared beta to calculate an appropriate cost of equity for the investment. This cost of equity should be used to determine an appropriate weighted cost of capital to use as the discount rate.

The beta value for the industry is 1.59.

Step 1   Convert the geared beta value for the industry to an ungeared beta (asset beta) for the industry.

$$\beta_a = 1.59 \left(\frac{2}{2+(1(1-0.30))} \right) = 1.18$$

Step 2   Convert this ungeared industry beta back into a geared beta, which reflects the company's own gearing level of 2:5.

$$\beta_e = 1.18 \left(\frac{5+(2(1-0.30))}{5} \right) = 1.51$$

Step 3   (a) This is a project-specific beta for the firm's equity capital and so, using the CAPM, we can estimate the project-specific cost of equity as:

$$k_{eg} = 11\% + (16\% - 11\%)\,1.51 = 18.55\%$$

  (b) The project will presumably be financed in a gearing ratio of 2:5 debt to equity, and so the project-specific cost of capital ought to be:

$$[5/7 \times 18.55\%] + [2/7 \times 70\% \times 11\%] = 15.45\%$$

Question   Ungeared and geared betas

Two companies are identical in every respect except for their capital structure. XY has a debt:equity ratio of 1:3, and its equity has a β value of 1.20. PQ has a debt:equity ratio of 2:3. Corporation tax is at 30%. Estimate a β value for PQ's equity.

Answer

Estimate an ungeared beta from XY data.

$$\beta_a = 1.20 \frac{3}{3+(1(1-0.30))} = 0.973$$

Estimate a geared beta for PQ using this ungeared beta.

$$\beta_e = 0.973 \frac{3+(2(1-0.30))}{3} = 1.427$$

2.7.6 Weaknesses in the formula

The problems with using the geared and ungeared beta formula for calculating a firm's equity beta from data about other firms are as follows.

(a) It is **difficult to identify other firms with identical operating characteristics**.

(b) **Estimates of beta values** from **share price information are not wholly accurate**. They are based on statistical analysis of historical data and, as the previous example shows, estimates using one firm's data will differ from estimates using another firm's data.

(c) There may be **differences in beta values** between firms caused by:

  (i)   Different cost structures (eg the ratio of fixed costs to variable costs)
  (ii)   Size differences between firms
  (iii) Debt capital not being risk free

(d) If the firm for which an equity beta is being estimated has **opportunities for growth** that are recognised by investors, and which will affect its equity beta, estimates of the equity beta based on other firms' data will be inaccurate, because the opportunities for growth will not be allowed for.

Perhaps the most significant simplifying assumption is that, to link MM theory to the CAPM, it must be assumed that the **cost of debt** is a **risk-free rate of return**. This could obviously be unrealistic. Companies may default on interest payments or capital repayments on their loans. It has been estimated that corporate debt has a beta value of 0.2 or 0.3.

The consequence of making the assumption that debt is risk free is that the formulae tend to **overstate** the financial risk in a geared company and to **understate** the business risk in geared and ungeared companies by a compensating amount.

Question   Gearing and ungearing betas

Backwoods is a major international company with its head office in the UK, wanting to raise £150 million to establish a new production plant in the eastern region of Germany. Backwoods evaluates its investments using NPV, but is not sure what cost of capital to use in the discounting process for this project evaluation.

The company is also proposing to increase its equity finance in the near future for UK expansion, resulting overall in little change in the company's market-weighted capital gearing.

The summarised financial data for the company before the expansion are shown below.

STATEMENT OF PROFIT OR LOSS (EXTRACTS) FOR THE YEAR ENDED 31 DECEMBER 20X1

	£m
Revenue	1,984
Gross profit	432
Profit after tax	81
Dividends	37
Retained earnings	44

STATEMENT OF FINANCIAL POSITION (EXTRACTS) AS AT 31 DECEMBER 20X1

	£m
Non-current assets	846
Current assets	350
Total assets	1,196
Issued ordinary shares of £0.50 each nominal value	225
Reserves	761
	986
Medium-term and long-term loans (see note below)	210
Total equity and liabilities	1,196

Note on borrowings

These include £75m 14% fixed rate bonds due to mature in five years' time and redeemable at par. The current market price of these bonds is £120 and they have an after-tax cost of debt of 9%. Other medium- and long-term loans are floating-rate UK bank loans at LIBOR plus 1%, with an after-tax cost of debt of 7%.

Company rate of tax may be assumed to be at the rate of 30%. The company's ordinary shares are currently trading at 376p.

The equity beta of Backwoods is estimated to be 1.18. The systematic risk of debt may be assumed to be zero. The risk-free rate is 7.75% and market return is 14.5%.

The estimated equity beta of the main German competitor in the same industry as the new proposed plant in the eastern region of Germany is 1.5, and the competitor's capital gearing is 35% equity and 65% debt by book values, and 60% equity and 40% debt by market values.

Required

Estimate the cost of capital that the company should use as the discount rate for its proposed investment in eastern Germany. State clearly any assumptions that you make.

Answer

The discount rate that should be used is the weighted average cost of capital (WACC), with weightings based on market values. The cost of capital should take into account the systematic risk of the new investment, and therefore it will not be appropriate to use the company's existing equity beta. Instead, the estimated equity beta of the main German competitor in the same industry as the new proposed plant will be ungeared, and then the capital structure of Backwoods applied to find the WACC to be used for the discount rate.

Since the systematic risk of debt can be assumed to be zero, the German equity beta can be 'ungeared' using the following expression.

$$\beta_a = \beta_e \frac{V_e}{V_e + V_d (1-T)}$$

where: β_a = asset beta
β_e = equity beta
V_e = proportion of equity in capital structure
V_d = proportion of debt in capital structure
T = tax rate

For the German company:

$$\beta_a = 1.5 \left(\frac{60}{60 + 40(1-0.30)} \right) = 1.023$$

The next step is to calculate the debt and equity of Backwoods based on market values.

		£m
Equity	450m shares at 376p	1,692.0
Debt: bank loans	(210 – 75)	135.0
Debt: bonds	(75 million × 1.20)	90.0
Total debt		225.0
Total market value		1,917.0

The beta can now be re-geared

$$\beta_e = \frac{1.023(1,692 + 225 (1 - 0.3))}{1,692} = 1.118$$

This can now be substituted into the capital asset pricing model (CAPM) to find the cost of equity.

$$E(r_i) = R_f + \beta (E (r_m) - R_f)$$

where: $E(r_i)$ = cost of equity
R_f = risk-free rate of return
$E(r_m)$ = market rate of return
$E(r_i)$ = 7.75% + (14.5% – 7.75%) × 1.118 = 15.30%

The WACC can now be calculated:

$$\left[15.3 \times \frac{1,692}{1,917} \right] + \left[7 \times \frac{135}{1,917} \right] + \left[9 \times \frac{90}{1,917} \right] = 14.4\%$$

An exam question may ask you to explain how CAPM can be used in investment appraisal rather than requiring a calculation.

There is a series of articles on CAPM available on www.accaglobal.com.

Chapter Roundup

- Some commentators believe that an **optimal mix of finance** exists at which the company's **cost of capital** will be minimised.

- Under the **traditional theory of cost of capital**, the weighted average cost of capital declines initially as gearing increases, but then rises as gearing increases further. The **optimal capital structure** is at the gearing level where WACC is lowest.

- Modigliani and Miller stated that, in the absence of tax relief on debt interest, a company's **capital structure** would have **no impact** on its WACC. WACC would be the same regardless of the company's capital structure.

- The lower a company's WACC, the higher the NPV of its future cash flows and the higher its market value.

- When an investment has differing business and finance risks from the existing business, **geared betas** may be used to obtain an appropriate cost of capital and required rate of return for an investment.

  Geared betas are calculated by:

  - Ungearing industry betas
  - Converting ungeared betas back into a geared beta that reflects the company's own gearing ratio

Quick Quiz

1   What are the main problems in using geared and ungeared betas to calculate a firm's equity beta?

2   Explain the significance of lines 1 to 3 and point 4 in the diagram below illustrating the traditional view of the WACC.

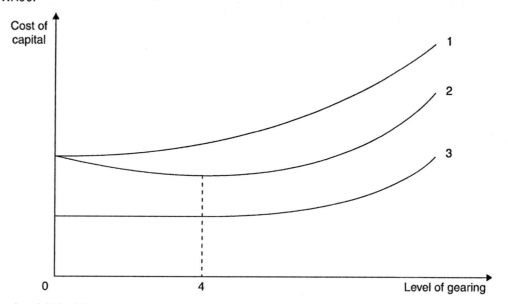

3   Assuming debt is risk free β_a = ?

4   To use WACC as the discount rate in an investment appraisal, the project must have the same business risk as the overall company. Why is this?

5   Why, in the real world, do businesses not adopt the Modigliani and Miller (with taxation) theory that a business should be solely funded by debt?

1   (a)   It is difficult to identify other firms with identical operating characteristics.
     (b)   Estimates of beta values from share price information are not wholly accurate.
     (c)   There may be firm-specific causes of differences in beta values.
     (d)   The market may recognise opportunities for future growth for some firms but not others.

2   Line 1 is the cost of equity in the geared company.
     Line 2 is the weighted average cost of capital.
     Line 3 is the cost of debt.
     Point 4 is the optimal level of gearing.

3    $\beta_a = \beta_e \times \dfrac{V_e}{V_e + V_d(1-T)}$

4   If a new investment has different business risks from the company as a whole then investors may seek a higher return if they deem the project to be riskier. Conversely, a lower return may be required if the project is deemed to be less risky.

5   The Modigliani and Miller theory is based on perfect capital markets which do not exist in the real world.

Now try the questions below from the Practice Question Bank

Number	Level	Marks	Approximate time
Section A Q28	Examination	2	4 mins
Section C Q19	Examination	20	39 mins

Business valuations

17

Business valuations

Topic list	Syllabus reference
1 The nature and purpose of business valuations	F1 (a), (b)
2 Asset valuation bases	F2 (a)
3 Income-based valuation bases	F2 (b)
4 Cash flow based valuation models	F2 (c)
5 Valuation of debt	F3 (a)

Introduction

In Part F we shall be concentrating on the valuation of businesses. In this chapter, we will cover the **reasons** why businesses are valued and the main **methods of valuation**.

Study guide

		Intellectual level
F1	**Nature and purpose of the valuation of business and financial assets**	
(a)	Identify and discuss reasons for valuing businesses and financial assets.	2
(b)	Identify information requirements for valuation and discuss the limitations of different types of information.	2
F2	**Models for the valuation of shares**	
(a)	Asset-based valuation models, including:	2
(i)	Net book value (statement of financial position basis)	
(ii)	Net realisable value basis	
(iii)	Net replacement cost basis	
(b)	Income-based valuation models, including:	2
(i)	Price/earnings ratio method	
(ii)	Earnings yield method	
(c)	Cash flow based valuation models, including:	2
(i)	Dividend valuation model and the dividend growth model	
(ii)	Discounted cash flow basis	
F3	**The valuation of debt and other financial assets**	
(a)	Apply appropriate valuation methods to:	2
(i)	Irredeemable debt	
(ii)	Redeemable debt	
(iii)	Convertible debt	
(iv)	Preference shares	

Exam guide

Business valuations are highly examinable. You might be asked to apply different valuation methods and discuss their advantages and disadvantages.

1 The nature and purpose of business valuations

There are a number of different ways of **putting a value on a business**, or on shares in an unquoted company. It makes sense to use **several methods** of valuation, and to compare the values they produce.

1.1 When valuations are required

Given quoted share prices on a stock exchange, why devise techniques for estimating the value of a share? A share valuation will be necessary:

(a) For **quoted companies**, when there is a takeover bid and the offer price is an estimated 'fair value' in excess of the current market price of the shares

Key term

A **takeover** is the acquisition by a company of a controlling interest in the voting share capital of another company, usually achieved by the purchase of a majority of the voting shares.

(b) For **unquoted companies**, when:

  (i) The company wishes to 'go public' and must fix an issue price for its shares.

  (ii) There is a scheme of merger with another company.

  (iii) Shares are sold.

  (iv) Shares need to be valued for the purposes of taxation.

  (v) Shares are pledged as collateral for a loan and the bank wants to put a value to the collateral.

  (vi) Another company is proposing to take over the unquoted company by making an offer to buy all its shares.

(c) For **subsidiary companies**, when the group's holding company is negotiating the sale of the subsidiary to a management buyout team or to an external buyer

(d) For **any company**, where a shareholder wishes to dispose of their holding – some of the valuation methods we describe will be most appropriate if a large or controlling interest is being sold; however, even a small shareholding may be a significant disposal, if the purchasers can increase their holding to a controlling interest as a result of the acquisition

If you are asked to value a business, check the wording of the question carefully to establish whether you are being asked to estimate a value for the business as a whole, or just its equity shares.

1.2 Business valuation methods

There are a number of different methods of valuing a business. Each of the methods give different values, and are suitable in different situations.

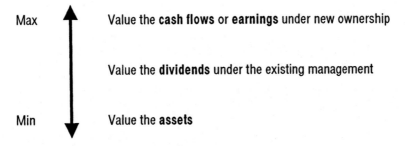

Max — Value the **cash flows** or **earnings** under new ownership

Value the **dividends** under the existing management

Min — Value the **assets**

We will look at each of the valuation methods in this chapter.

1.3 Information requirements for valuation

There is a wide range of information that can be used to value a business.

- Financial statements: statements of financial position and comprehensive income, statements of changes in financial position and statements of shareholders' equity for the past five years

- Summary of non-current assets and depreciation schedule

- Aged accounts-receivable summary

- Aged accounts-payable summary

- List of marketable securities

- Inventory summary

- Details of any existing contracts: eg leases, supplier agreements

- List of shareholders with number of shares owned by each

- Budgets or projections, for a minimum of five years

- Information about the company's industry and economic environment

- List of major customers by sales
- Organisation chart and management roles and responsibilities
- Profit forecasts or budgets

This list is not exhaustive and there are **limitations** to some of the information. For example, statement of financial position values of assets may be out of date and unrealistic, projections may be unduly optimistic or pessimistic and much of the information used in business valuation is **subjective**. We will look at this in more detail under each valuation method.

In an exam question as well as in practice, it is unlikely that one method would be used in isolation. Several valuations might be made, each using a different technique or different assumptions. The valuations could then be compared, and a final price reached as a compromise between the different values. Remember that some methods may be more appropriate for valuing a small parcel of shares, others for valuing a whole company.

1.4 Market capitalisation   6/08, 12/12

Market capitalisation is the market value of a company's shares. This is the share price multiplied by the number of issued shares.

For quoted companies, calculating the market capitalisation of its shares is therefore a straightforward process.

However, if the shares of the company do not have a liquid secondary market, its quoted market price may not be a fair reflection of value. In these cases, where a valuation of the business is required, other methods of valuation in addition to market capitalisation may be worth making to assess whether the market capitalisation seems reasonable.

In June 2008, the ACCA examination team used the term 'market capitalisation' to ask for a calculation of the value of a company. Some students were confused by this terminology.

2 Asset valuation bases

FAST FORWARD

The **net assets valuation** method can be used as one of many valuation methods, or to provide a lower limit for the value of a company. By itself it is unlikely to produce the most realistic value.

2.1 Net assets method of share valuation   12/10, 12/11, 12/12

In the December 2011 exam, many candidates struggled to calculate the net asset value of a company based on a set of financial statements. There should be fairly easy marks so make sure you can do this.

Using this method of valuation, the value of an equity share is equal to the **net tangible assets** divided by the **number of shares**.

Net tangible assets are the value in the statement of financial position of the tangible non-current assets (net of depreciation) plus current assets, minus all liabilities.

Intangible assets (including goodwill) should be excluded, unless they have a market value (for example patents and copyrights, which could be sold).

(a) **Goodwill**, if shown in the financial statements, is unlikely to be shown at a true figure for purposes of valuation, and the value of goodwill should be reflected in another method of valuation (for example the earnings basis).

(b) **Development expenditure**, if shown in the financial statements, would also have a value which is related to future profits rather than to the worth of the company's physical assets.

2.2 Example: net assets method of share valuation

The summary statement of financial position of Cactus is as follows.

Assets	$
Non-current assets	
Land and buildings	160,000
Plant and machinery	80,000
Motor vehicles	20,000
Goodwill	20,000
	280,000
Current assets	
Inventory	80,000
Receivables	60,000
Short-term investments	15,000
Cash	5,000
	160,000
Total assets	440,000
Equity and liabilities	
Ordinary shares of $1	80,000
Reserves	140,000
Total equity	220,000
Non-current liabilities	
12% bonds	60,000
Deferred taxation	10,000
4.9% redeemable preference shares of $1	50,000
	120,000
Current liabilities	
Payables	60,000
Taxation	20,000
Declared ordinary dividend	20,000
	100,000
Total liabilities	220,000
Total equity and liabilities	440,000

What is the value of an ordinary share using the net assets basis of valuation?

Solution

If the figures given for asset values are not questioned, the valuation would be as follows.

	$
Total assets	440,000
Less goodwill	(20,000)
Less total liabilities	(220,000)
Net asset value of equity	200,000
Number of ordinary shares	80,000
Value per share	$2.50

2.3 Choice of valuation bases

The difficulty in an asset valuation method is establishing the **asset values** to use. Values ought to be realistic. The figure attached to an individual asset may vary considerably depending on whether it is valued on a **going concern** or a **break-up** basis.

Possibilities include:

- **Historical cost basis (net book value)** – unlikely to give a realistic value, as it is dependent on the business's depreciation and amortisation policy

- **Realisable basis** – if the assets are to be sold, or the business as a whole broken up. This won't be relevant if a minority (non-controlling) shareholder is selling their stake, as the assets will continue in the business's use

- **Replacement basis** – if the assets are to be used on an ongoing basis

The following list should give you some idea of the factors that must be considered.

(a)   Do the assets need **professional valuation**? If so, how much will this cost?

(b)   Have the **liabilities** been accurately quantified, for example deferred taxation? Are there any contingent liabilities? Will any balancing tax charges arise on disposal?

(c)   How have the **current assets** been valued? Are all receivables collectable? Is all inventory realisable? Can all the assets be physically located and brought into a saleable condition? This may be difficult in certain circumstances where the assets are situated abroad.

(d)   Can any **hidden liabilities** be accurately assessed? Would there be redundancy payments and closure costs?

(e)   Is there an **available market** in which the assets can be realised (on a break-up basis)? If so, do the statement of financial position values truly reflect these break-up values?

(f)   Are there any **prior charges** on the assets?

(g)   Does the business have a regular **revaluation and replacement** policy? What are the bases of the valuation? As a broad rule, valuations will be more useful the better they estimate the **future cash flows** that are derived from the asset.

(h)   Are there factors that might indicate that the **going concern valuation** of the business **as a whole** is **significantly higher** than the valuation of the individual assets?

(i)   **What shareholdings are being sold?** If a non-controlling interest is being disposed of, realisable value is of limited relevance, as the assets will not be sold.

2.4 Use of net asset basis

The net assets basis of valuation might be used in the following circumstances.

(a)   **As a measure of the 'security' in a share value**. A share might be valued using an earnings basis. This valuation might be **higher or lower than the net asset value per share**. If the earnings basis is higher, then if the company went into liquidation, the investor could not expect to receive the full value of their shares when the underlying assets were realised.

The **asset backing** for shares thus provides a measure of the **possible loss** if the company fails to make the expected earnings or dividend payments. Valuable tangible assets may be a good reason for acquiring a company, especially freehold property which might be expected to increase in value over time.

(b)   **As a measure of comparison in a scheme of merger**

Key term

> A **merger** is essentially a business combination of two or more companies, of which none obtains control over any other.

For example, if company A, which has a low asset backing, is planning a merger with company B, which has a high asset backing, the shareholders of B might consider that their shares' value ought to reflect this. It might therefore be agreed that something should be added to the value of the company B shares to allow for this difference in asset backing.

(c) As a **'floor value'** for a business that is up for sale. Shareholders will be reluctant to sell for less than the NAV. However, if the sale is essential for cash flow purposes or to realign with corporate strategy, even the asset value may not be realised.

For these reasons, it is always advisable to calculate the net assets per share.

3 Income-based valuation bases

FAST FORWARD **P/E ratios** may be used to value equity shares when a large block of shares, or a whole business, is being valued. This method can be problematic when P/E ratios for quoted companies are used to value unquoted companies.

3.1 P/E ratio (earnings) method of valuation
12/07, 6/08, 12/08, 6/09, 6/12, 12/12, 12/14

A P/E ratio-based valuation of equity shares may be used to value a **controlling interest** in the shares of a company, where the owner can decide on **dividend** and **retentions policy**. The P/E ratio relates earnings per share to a share's value.

Since P/E ratio = $\dfrac{\text{Market value}}{\text{EPS}}$,

then market value per share = EPS $\times$ P/E ratio

Exam focus point

Remember that earnings per share (EPS) = $\dfrac{\text{Profit / loss attributable to ordinary shareholders}}{\text{Weighted average number of ordinary shares}}$

The ACCA examination team has commented in the past that students often calculate earnings per share incorrectly.

The P/E ratio produces an **earnings-based** valuation of shares by deciding a suitable P/E ratio and multiplying this by the EPS for the shares which are being valued.

Market valuation or capitalisation =

(for individual shares) **P/E ratio $\times$ Earnings per share**, or

(for all the company's equity) **P/E ratio $\times$ Total earnings**

The EPS could be a historical EPS or a prospective future EPS. For a given EPS figure, a higher P/E ratio will result in a higher price.

3.2 Significance of high P/E ratio

A high P/E ratio may indicate:

(a) **Expectations that the EPS will grow rapidly**

A **high price is being paid for future profit prospects**. Many small but successful and fast-growing companies are valued on the stock market on a high P/E ratio. Some stocks (for example those of some software companies in the 2010s) have reached high valuations before making any profits at all, on the strength of expected future earnings.

(b) **Security of earnings**

A well-established low-risk company would be valued on a higher P/E ratio than a similar company whose earnings are subject to greater uncertainty.

(c) **Status**

If a quoted company (the bidder) made a share for share takeover bid for an unquoted company (the target), it would normally expect its own shares to be valued on a higher P/E ratio than the target company's shares. This is because a quoted company ought to be a lower-risk company; but in addition, there is an advantage in having shares which are quoted on a stock market: the shares can be readily sold. The P/E ratio of an unquoted company's shares might be around 50% to 60% of the P/E ratio of a similar public company with a full stock market listing.

3.3 Problems with using P/E ratios

However, using the P/E ratios of quoted companies to value **unquoted** companies may be problematic. This is because a P/E ratio must be guessed at, using the P/E ratios for similar quoted companies as a guide.

- Finding a quoted company with a **similar range of activities** may be difficult. Quoted companies are often **diversified**.

- A **single year's P/E ratio** may not be a good basis if earnings are volatile, or the quoted company's share price is at an abnormal level, due for example to the expectation of a takeover bid.

- If a P/E ratio trend is used, then **historical data** will be used to value how the unquoted company will do in the future.

- The quoted company may have a **different capital structure** to the unquoted company.

3.4 Guidelines for a P/E ratio-based valuation

When a company is thinking of acquiring an **unquoted** company in a takeover, the final offer price will be agreed by **negotiation**, but a list of some of the factors affecting the valuer's choice of P/E ratio is given below.

(a)   The general **economic** and **financial** conditions will have an impact.

(b)   The type of **industry** and the prospects of that industry. Use of current P/E ratios may give an unrealistically low valuation if these ratios are being affected by a lack of confidence throughout the industry.

(c)   The **size** of the undertaking and its **status** within its industry. If an unquoted company's earnings are growing annually, then it could probably seek a listing in its own right, and a higher P/E ratio should therefore be used when valuing its shares.

(d)   **Marketability**. The market in shares which do not have a stock market quotation is always a restricted one and a higher yield is therefore required.

(e)   The **diversity** of shareholdings and the **financial status** of any principal shareholders will be factors.

(f)   The **reliability** of profit estimates and the past profit record. Use of profits and P/E ratios over time may give a more reliable valuation, especially if they are being compared with industry levels over that time.

(g)   Asset **backing** and **liquidity** are both factors.

(h)   The **nature of the assets** will be considered, for example whether some of the non-current assets are of a highly specialised nature, and so have only a small break-up value.

(i)   **Gearing**. A relatively high gearing ratio will generally mean greater financial risk for ordinary shareholders and call for a higher rate of return on equity.

(j)   The extent to which the business is dependent on the **technical skills** of one or more individuals will be considered.

(k)   The bidder may need to be particularly careful when valuing an unlisted company of using a P/E ratio of a **'similar' listed company**. The bidder should obtain reasonable evidence that the listed

company does have the same risk and growth characteristics, and has similar policies on significant areas, such as directors' remuneration.

3.4.1 Use of a bidder's P/E ratio

A bidder company may sometimes use its higher P/E ratio to value a target company. This assumes that the bidder **can improve the target's business**, which may be a dangerous assumption to make. It may be better to use an adjusted industry P/E ratio, or some other method.

3.4.2 Use of forecast earnings

When one company is thinking about taking over another, it should look at the target company's **forecast earnings**, not just its historical results.

<table>
<tr><td>Exam focus point</td><td>Make sure the earnings you use are **future maintainable earnings**. One-off income or expenses must be excluded.</td></tr>
</table>

Forecasts of **earnings growth** should only be used if:

(a)   There are good reasons to believe that earnings growth will be achieved.

(b)   A reasonable estimate of growth can be made.

(c)   Forecasts supplied by the target company's directors are made in good faith and using reasonable assumptions and fair accounting policies.

Question   Valuations

Flycatcher wishes to make a takeover bid for the shares of an unquoted company, Mayfly. The earnings of Mayfly over the past five years have been as follows.

20X0	$50,000	20X3	$71,000
20X1	$72,000	20X4	$75,000
20X2	$68,000		

The average P/E ratio of quoted companies in the industry in which Mayfly operates is 10. Quoted companies which are similar in many respects to Mayfly are:

(a)   Bumblebee, which has a P/E ratio of 15, but is a company with very good growth prospects

(b)   Wasp, which has had a poor profit record for several years, and has a P/E ratio of 7

What would be a suitable range of valuations for the shares of Mayfly?

(a) **Earnings**. Average earnings over the last five years have been $67,200, and over the last four years $71,500. There might appear to be some growth prospects, but estimates of future earnings are uncertain.

A low estimate of earnings in 20X5 would be, perhaps, $71,500.

A high estimate of earnings might be $75,000 or more. This solution will use the most recent earnings figure of $75,000 as the high estimate.

(b) **P/E ratio**. A P/E ratio of 15 (Bumblebee's) would be much too high for Mayfly, because the growth of Mayfly earnings is not as certain, and Mayfly is an unquoted company.

On the other hand, Mayfly's expectations of earnings are probably better than those of Wasp. A suitable P/E ratio might be based on the industry's average, 10; but since Mayfly is an unquoted company and therefore more risky, a lower P/E ratio might be more appropriate: perhaps 60% to 70% of 10 = 6 or 7, or conceivably even as low as 50% of 10 = 5.

The valuation of Mayfly's shares might therefore range between:

high P/E ratio and high earnings: 7 × $75,000 = $525,000; and
low P/E ratio and low earnings: 5 × $71,500 = $357,500.

3.5 Earnings yield valuation method
12/11, 6/15

In the December 2011 exam, candidates were required to calculate the value of a company based on the earnings yield method. Few were able to do so and many confused this with the price/earnings ratio valuation method, which was not asked for.

Another income-based valuation model is the earnings yield method.

$$\text{Earnings yield (EY)} = \frac{\text{EPS}}{\text{Market price per share}} \times 100\%$$

This method is effectively a variation on the P/E method (the EY being the reciprocal of the P/E ratio), using an appropriate earnings yield as a discount rate to value the earnings.

$$\text{Market value} = \frac{\text{Earnings}}{\text{EY}}$$

Exactly the same guidelines apply to this method as for the P/E method. Note that where **high growth** is envisaged, **the EY will be low**, as current earnings will be low relative to a market price that has built in future earnings growth. A stable earnings yield may suggest a company with low-risk characteristics.

We can incorporate earnings growth into this method in the same way as the growth model that we will discuss in Section 4.2.

$$\text{Market value} = \frac{\text{Earnings} \times (1 + g)}{(\text{EY} - g)}$$

This is similar to the formula given on your formula sheet as $P_0 = \frac{D_0(1+g)}{K_e - g}$.

A company has the following results.

	20X1 $m	20X2 $m	20X3 $m	20X4 $m
Profit after tax	6.0	6.2	6.3	6.3

The company's earnings yield is 12%.

Required

Calculate the value of the company based on the present value of expected earnings.

Answer

Market value = $\dfrac{\text{Earnings} \times (1+g)}{(EY - g)}$

Earnings = $6.3m

EY = 12%

$g = \sqrt[3]{\dfrac{6.3}{6.0}} - 1 = 0.0164$ or 1.64%

Market value = $\dfrac{6.3 \times 1.0164}{0.12 - 0.0164}$

= $61.81m

4 Cash flow based valuation models

Cash flow based valuation models include the **dividend valuation model**, the **dividend growth model** and valuation on a **discounted cash flow basis**.

4.1 Dividend valuation model   12/07, 6/08

The dividend valuation model is based on the theory that an equilibrium price for any share (or bond) on a stock market is:

- The **future expected stream of income** from the security
- **Discounted** at a suitable **cost of capital**

Equilibrium market price is thus a **present value** of a **future expected income stream**. The annual income stream for a share is the expected dividend every year in perpetuity.

The basic dividend-based formula for the market value of shares is expressed in the **dividend valuation model** as follows.

$$MV \text{ (ex div)} = \frac{D}{1+k_e} + \frac{D}{(1+k_e)^2} + \frac{D}{(1+k_e)^3} + \dots = \frac{D}{k_e}$$

where   MV = Ex-dividend market value of the shares
          D = Constant annual dividend
          k_e = Shareholders' required rate of return

This should look familiar. We used the dividend valuation model in Chapter 15 to calculate a cost of equity, given the annual dividend and share price.

Here the same model is used to calculate a share price, given the annual dividend and the cost of equity.

For example, if a company is expected to pay an annual dividend of $0.50 per share on its equity shares into the foreseeable future, and the cost of equity is 8%, the market value of the share would be $0.50/0.08 = $6.25.

4.2 The dividend growth model   12/08, 6/09, 12/09, 6/10, 12/10, 12/12, 6/15

Remember the formula for the cost of equity in Chapter 15? This is the **dividend growth model**, which was also introduced in Chapter 15.

$$P_0 = \frac{D_0(1+g)}{(1+k_e)} + \frac{D_0(1+g)^2}{(1+k_e)^2} + ... = \frac{D_0(1+g)}{(k_e-g)}$$

$$= \frac{D_1}{k_e - g}$$

where

	D_0	=	Current year's dividend
	g	=	Growth rate in earnings and dividends
	$D_0(1+g)$	=	Expected dividend in one year's time (D_1)
	k_e	=	Shareholders' required rate of return
	P_0	=	Market value excluding any dividend currently payable

In Chapter 15, we used this model to calculate a cost of equity, given the share price, the current annual dividend and expectations of future dividend growth. Here, we calculate a market value per share, given the current annual dividend, expectations of future dividend growth and a cost of equity.

Question

DVM

Target paid a dividend of $250,000 this year. The current return to shareholders of companies in the same industry as Target is 12%, although it is expected that an additional risk premium of 2% will be applicable to Target, being a smaller and unquoted company. Compute the expected valuation of Target, if:

(a)   The current level of dividend is expected to continue into the foreseeable future.
(b)   The dividend is expected to grow at a rate of 4% pa into the foreseeable future.
(c)   The dividend is expected to grow at a 3% rate for 3 years and 2% afterwards.

Answer

k_e = 12% + 2% = 14% (0.14) D_0 = $250,000   g (in (b)) = 4% or 0.04

(a) $P_0 = \dfrac{d_0}{k_e} = \dfrac{\$250,000}{0.14} = \$1,785,714$

(b) $P_0 = \dfrac{d_0(1+g)}{k_e-g} = \dfrac{\$250,000(1.04)}{0.14-0.04} = \$2,600,000$

(c)

Time	1	2	3	4 onwards
Dividend ($'000)	258	266	274	279
Annuity to infinity $1/(k_e-g)$				8.333
Present value at Year 3				2,325
Discount factor @ 14%	0.877	0.769	0.675	0.675
	226	205	185	1,569

Total $2,185,000

4.3 Assumptions in the dividend valuation model

The dividend valuation model is underpinned by a number of assumptions that you should bear in mind.

(a) Investors act **rationally** and **homogenously**. The model fails to take into account the **different expectations** of shareholders, or how much they are motivated by a preference for dividends over future capital appreciation on their shares.

(b) The current year's dividend (D_0 figure) does **not vary significantly** from the **trend of dividends**. If D_0 does appear to be a rogue figure, it may be better to use an adjusted trend figure, calculated on the basis of the past few years' dividends.

(c) The **estimates** of future dividends and prices used and also the cost of capital are **reasonable**. As with other methods, it may be difficult to make a confident estimate of the cost of capital. Dividend estimates may be made from historical trends that may not be a good guide for a future, or derived from uncertain forecasts about future earnings.

(d) Investors' attitudes to receiving different cash flows at different times can be modelled using **discounted cash flow arithmetic**.

(e) Directors use dividends to **signal** the strength of the company's position. (However, companies that pay zero dividends do not have zero share values.)

(f) Dividends either show **no growth** or **constant growth**. If the growth rate is estimated using Gordon's growth approximation ($g = br$), then the model assumes that the percentage of profits retained in the business and the return on those retained profits, b and r, are constant values.

(g) **Other influences** on share prices are **ignored**.

(h) The company's **earnings** will **increase** sufficiently to maintain dividend growth levels.

(i) The **discount rate** used exceeds the **dividend growth rate**.

4.4 Discounted cash flow basis of valuation

A DCF method of share valuation may be appropriate when one company intends to buy the assets of another company and to make further investments in order to improve cash flows in the future.

The steps in this method of valuation are:

Step 1 Estimate the cash flows that will be obtained each year from the acquired business. The cash flows may be estimated for a maximum number of years (say, for ten years). Alternatively, there may be an assumption about annual cash flows from the business into perpetuity.

If the proposal is to buy the equity shares only, the cash flows should be cash flows after interest payments on debt of the target company and tax on the profits.

If the proposal is to buy the entire business, including liability for its debts, the cash flows should be cash flows before interest payments on debt of the target company.

Step 2 Discount these cash flows at an appropriate cost of capital. This produces a value either for the equity shares or for the business as a whole.

4.4.1 Example: Discounted future cash flows method of share valuation

Diversification wishes to make a bid for Tadpole. Tadpole makes after-tax profits of $40,000 a year. Diversification believes that if further money is spent on additional investments, the after-tax cash flows (ignoring the purchase consideration) could be as follows.

Year	Cash flow (net of tax)
	$
0	(100,000)
1	(80,000)
2	60,000
3	100,000
4	150,000
5	150,000

The after-tax cost of capital of Diversification is 15% and the company expects all its investments to pay back, in discounted terms, within five years.

(a)　What is the maximum price that the company should be willing to pay for the shares of Tadpole?

(b)　What is the maximum price that the company should be willing to pay for the shares of Tadpole if it decides to value the business on the basis of its cash flows in perpetuity, and annual cash flows from Year 6 onwards are expected to be $120,000?

Solution

(a)　The maximum price is one which would make the return from the total investment exactly 15% over five years, so that the NPV at 15% would be 0.

Year	Cash flows ignoring purchase consideration $	Discount factor (from tables) 15%	Present value $
0	(100,000)	1.000	(100,000)
1	(80,000)	0.870	(69,600)
2	60,000	0.756	45,360
3	100,000	0.658	65,800
4	150,000	0.572	85,800
5	150,000	0.497	74,550
Maximum purchase price			101,910

(b)　If the shares are valued on the basis of cash flows in perpetuity, we need to add the PV of annual cash flows from Year 6 onwards.

The value of the cash flows from Year 6 onwards, in perpetuity, at a Year 5 present value = $120,000/0.15 = $800,000.

Discounting this to a Year 0 PV: $800,000 × 0.497 = $397,600.

This increases the valuation from $101,910 to $499,510.

The difference between this valuation and the valuation in (a) is huge. It may illustrate that business valuations depend crucially on the assumptions that are used to reach the valuation.

4.4.2 Selection of an appropriate cost of capital

In the above example, Diversification used its own cost of capital to discount the cash flows of Tadpole. There are a number of reasons why this may not be appropriate.

(a)　The **business risk** of the new investment may not match that of the investing company. If Tadpole is in a completely different line of business from Diversification, its cash flows are likely to be subject to differing degrees of risk, and this should be taken into account when valuing them.

(b)　The **method of finance** of the new investment may not match the current debt/equity mix of the investing company, which may have an effect on the cost of capital to be used.

Profed provides a tuition service for professional students. This includes courses of lectures provided on their own premises and provision of study material for home study. Most of the lecturers are qualified professionals with many years' experience in both their profession and tuition. Study materials are written and word processed in-house, but sent out to an external printers.

The business was started 15 years ago, and now employs around 40 full-time lecturers, 10 authors and 20 support staff. Freelance lecturers and authors are employed from time to time in times of peak demand.

The shareholders of Profed mainly comprise the original founders of the business who would now like to realise their investment. In order to arrive at an estimate of what they believe the business to be worth, they have identified a long-established quoted company, City Tutors, who have a similar business, although they also publish texts for external sale to universities, colleges, etc.

Summary financial statistics for the two companies for the most recent financial year are as follows.

	Profed	City Tutors
Issued shares (million)	4	10
Net asset values ($m)	7.2	15
Earnings per share (cents)	35	20
Dividend per share (cents)	20	18
Debt: equity ratio	1:7	1:65
Share price (cents)		362
Expected rate of growth in earnings/dividends	9% pa	7.5% pa

Notes

1   The net assets of Profed are the net book values of tangible non-current assets plus net working capital. However:

   •   A recent valuation of the buildings was $1.5m above book value.

   •   Inventory includes past editions of textbooks which have a realisable value of $100,000 below their cost.

   •   Due to a dispute with one of their clients, an additional allowance for bad debts of $750,000 could prudently be made.

2   Growth rates should be assumed to be constant per annum; Profed's earnings growth rate estimate was provided by the marketing manager, based on expected growth in sales adjusted by normal profit margins. City Tutors' growth rates were gleaned from press reports.

3   Profed uses a discount rate of 15% to appraise its investments, and has done for many years.

Required

(a)   Compute a range of valuations for the business of Profed, using the information available and stating any assumptions made.

(b)   Comment on the strengths and weaknesses of the methods you used in (a) and their suitability for valuing Profed.

Answer

(a)   The information provided allows us to value Profed on three bases: net assets, P/E ratio and dividend valuation.

   All three will be computed, even though their validity may be questioned in part (b) of the answer.

Assets based

	$'000
Net assets at book value	7,200
Add increased valuation of buildings	1,500
Less decreased value of inventory and receivables	(850)
Net asset value of equity	7,850

Value per share = $1.96

P/E ratio

	Profed	City Tutors
Issued shares (million)	4	10
Share price (cents)		362
Market value ($m)		36.2
Earnings per share (cents)	35	20
P/E ratio (share price ÷ EPS)		18.1

The P/E for a similar quoted company is 18.1. This will take account of such factors as marketability of shares, status of company and growth potential that will differ from those for Profed. Profed's growth rate has been estimated as higher than that of City Tutors, possibly because it is a younger, developing company, although the basis for the estimate may be questionable.

All other things being equal, the P/E ratio for an unquoted company should be taken as between one-half to two-thirds of that of an equivalent quoted company. Being generous, in view of the possible higher growth prospects of Profed, we might estimate an appropriate P/E ratio of around 12, assuming that Profed is to remain a private company.

This will value Profed at 12 × $0.35 = $4.20 per share, a total valuation of $16.8m.

Dividend valuation model

The dividend valuation method gives the share price as:

$$\frac{\text{Next year's dividend}}{\text{Cost of equity} - \text{Growth rate}}$$

which assumes dividends being paid into perpetuity, and growth at a constant rate.

For Profed, next year's dividend = $0.20 × 1.09 = $0.218 per share

While we are given a discount rate of 15% as being traditionally used by the directors of Profed for investment appraisal, there appears to be no rational basis for this. We can instead use the information for City Tutors to estimate a cost of equity for Profed. This is assuming the business risks to be similar, and ignoring the small difference in their gearing ratio.

Again, from the DVM, cost of equity = $\dfrac{\text{next year's dividend}}{\text{market price}}$ + growth rate

For City Tutors, cost of equity = $\dfrac{\$0.18 \times 1.075}{\$3.62} + 0.075 = 12.84\%$

Using, say, 13% as a cost of equity for Profed (it could be argued that this should be higher since Profed is unquoted so riskier than the quoted City Tutors):

Share price = $\dfrac{\$0.218}{0.13 - 0.09} = \$5.45$

This values the whole of the share capital at $21.8 million.

Range for valuation

The three methods used have thus come up with a range of value of Profed, as follows.

	Value per share $	Total valuation $m
Net assets	1.96	7.9
P/E ratio	4.20	16.8
Dividend valuation	5.45	21.8

(b) **Comment on relative merits of the methods used, and their suitability**

Asset-based valuation

Valuing a company on the **basis of its asset values** alone is rarely appropriate if it is to be sold on a going concern basis. Exceptions would include property investment companies and investment trusts, the market values of the assets of which will bear a close relationship to their earning capacities.

Profed is typical of a lot of service companies, a large part of whose value lies in the **skill, knowledge and reputation of its personnel**. This is not reflected in the net asset values, and renders this method quite inappropriate. A potential purchaser of Profed will generally value its intangible assets, such as knowledge, expertise, customer/supplier relationships and brands, more highly than those that can be measured in accounting terms.

Knowledge of the net asset value (NAV) of a company will, however, be important as a **floor value** for a company which is in financial difficulties or subject to a takeover bid. Shareholders will be reluctant to sell for less than the NAV even if future prospects are poor.

P/E ratio valuation

The P/E ratio measures the **multiple of the current year's earnings** that is reflected in the **market price** of a share. It is thus a method that reflects the earnings potential of a company from a market point of view. Provided the marketing is efficient, it is likely to give the most meaningful basis for valuation.

One of the first things to say is that the market price of a share at any point in time is determined by supply and demand forces prevalent during small transactions, and will be dependent on a lot of factors in addition to a realistic appraisal of future prospects. A downturn in the market economies and political changes can all affect the day to day price of a share and thus its prevailing P/E ratio. It is not known whether the share price given for City Tutors was taken on one particular day, or was some sort of average over a period. The latter would perhaps give a sounder basis from which to compute an applicable P/E ratio.

Even if the P/E ratio of City Tutors can be taken to be **indicative of its true worth**, using it as a basis to value a smaller, unquoted company in the same industry can be problematic.

The status and marketability of shares in a quoted company have tangible effects on value but these are difficult to measure.

The P/E ratio will also be affected by **growth prospects** – the higher the growth expected, the higher the ratio. The growth rate incorporated by the shareholders of City Tutors is probably based on a more rational approach than that used by Profed.

If the growth prospects of Profed, as would be perceived by the market, did not coincide with those of **Profed management** it is difficult to see how the P/E ratio should be adjusted for relative levels of growth. The earnings yield method of valuation could, however, be useful here.

In the valuation in (a) a crude adjustment has been made to City Tutors' P/E ratio to arrive at a ratio to use to value Profed's earnings. This can result in a very inaccurate result if account has not been taken of all the differences involved.

Dividend-based valuation

The dividend valuation model (DVM) is a **cash flow based approach**, which values the dividends that the shareholders expect to receive from the company by discounting them at their required rate of return. It is perhaps more appropriate for valuing a non-controlling shareholding where the holder has no influence over the level of dividends to be paid than for valuing a whole company, where the total cash flows will be of greater relevance.

The practical problems with the dividend valuation model lie mainly in its **assumptions**. Even accepting that the required 'perfect capital market' assumptions may be satisfied to some extent, in reality the formula used in (a) assumes constant growth rates and constant required rates of return in perpetuity.

Determination of an **appropriate cost of equity** is particularly difficult for a unquoted company, and the use of an 'equivalent' quoted company's data carries the same drawbacks as discussed above. Similar problems arise in estimating future growth rates, and the results from the model are highly sensitive to changes in both these inputs.

It is also highly dependent on the **current year's dividend** being a representative base from which to start.

The dividend valuation model valuation provided in (a) results in a higher valuation than that under the P/E ratio approach. Reasons for this may be:

- The **share price** for City Tutors may be currently **depressed below its normal level**, resulting in an inappropriately low P/E ratio.

- The **adjustment** to get to an **appropriate P/E ratio** for Profed may have been too harsh, particularly in light of its apparently better growth prospects.

- The **cost of equity** used in the dividend valuation model was that of City Tutors. The validity of this will largely depend on the relative levels of risk of the two companies. Although they both operate the same type of business, the fact that City Tutors sells its material externally means it is perhaps less reliant on a fixed customer base.

- Even if business risks and gearing risk may be thought to be comparable, a prospective buyer of Profed may consider investment in a **younger, unquoted company** to carry **greater personal risk**. Their required return may thus be higher than that envisaged in the dividend valuation model, reducing the valuation.

5 Valuation of debt

12/08

In Chapter 15, we looked at how to calculate the cost of debt and other financial assets. The same formulae can be rearranged so that we can calculate their value.

For **irredeemable debt**:

Market price, ex interest (P_0) $= \dfrac{I}{K_d}$

$= \dfrac{i(1-T) \text{ with tax}}{K_{dnet}}$

For **redeemable debt**, the market value is **the discounted present value of future interest receivable**, up to the year of redemption, plus the **discounted present value of the redemption payment**.

5.1 Debt calculations – a few notes

(a) Debt is always quoted in **$100 nominal units**, or blocks; always use $100 nominal values as the basis to your calculations.

(b) Debt can be quoted in **%** or as a **value**, eg 97% or $97. Both mean that $100 nominal value of debt is worth $97 market value.

(c) Interest on debt is stated as a **percentage** of **nominal value**. This is known as the coupon rate. It is **not** the same as the redemption yield on debt or the cost of debt.

(d) The ACCA examination team sometimes quotes an **interest yield, defined as coupon/market price**.

(e) Always use **ex-interest prices** in any calculations.

5.2 Irredeemable debt

For **irredeemable bonds** where the company will go on paying interest every year in perpetuity, without ever having to redeem the loan (ignoring taxation):

Formula to learn

$$P_0 = \frac{i}{K_d}$$

where P_0 is the market price of the bond ex interest; that is, excluding any interest payment that might soon be due

i is the annual interest payment on the bond

K_d is the return required by the bond investors

With taxation, we have the following:

Formula to learn

Irredeemable (undated) debt, paying annual after-tax interest $i(1 - T)$ in perpetuity, where P_0 is the ex-interest value:

$$P_0 = \frac{i(1 - T)}{K_{dnet}}$$

For example, if the cost of debt is 7% before tax and 5.6% after tax, and the rate of tax is 20%, the market value of irredeemable debt with a coupon rate of 6% will be:

$P_0 = 6/0.07 = 85.71$, or
$P_0 = 6(1 - 0.20)/0.056 = 85.71$

Both formulae produce the same valuation.

5.3 Redeemable debt

The valuation of redeemable debt spends on future expected receipts. The market value is the discounted present value of future interest receivable, up to the year of redemption, **plus** the discounted present value of the redemption payment.

Formula to learn

Value of debt = (Interest earnings × annuity factor) + (Redemption value × Discounted cash flow factor)

5.4 Example: Valuation of debt   12/08

Furry has in issue 12% bonds with par value $100,000 and redemption value $110,000, with interest payable quarterly. The cost of debt on the bonds is 8% annually and 2% quarterly. The bonds are redeemable on 30 June 20X4 and it is now 31 December 20X0.

Required

Calculate the market value of the bonds.

Solution

You need to use the cost of debt as the discount rate, and remember to use an annuity factor for the interest. We are discounting over 14 periods (quarters) using the quarterly discount rate (8%/4).

Period		Cash flow $	Discount factor 2%	Present value $
1-14	Interest	3,000	12.11	36,330
14	Redemption	110,000	0.758	83,380
				119,710

The market value is $119,710.

Question   Value of redeemable debt

A company has issued some 9% bonds, which are now redeemable at par in three years' time. Investors now require a redemption yield of 10%. What will the current market value of each $100 of bond be?

Answer

Year		Cash flow $	Discount factor 10%	Present value $
1	Interest	9	0.909	8.18
2	Interest	9	0.826	7.43
3	Interest	9	0.751	6.76
3	Redemption value	100	0.751	75.10
				97.47

Each $100 of bond will have a market value of $97.47.

5.5 Convertible debt   6/08

Convertible bonds were discussed in Section 2 of Chapter 12. As a reminder, when convertible bonds are traded on a stock market, its **minimum market price** will be the price of straight bonds with the same coupon rate of interest. If the market value falls to this minimum, it follows that the market attaches no value to the conversion rights.

The actual market price of convertible bonds will depend on:

- The price of straight debt
- The current conversion value
- The length of time before conversion may take place
- The market's expectation as to future equity returns and the associated risk

If the conversion value rises above the straight debt value then the price of convertible bonds will normally reflect this increase.

Formula to learn

> **Conversion value** = $P_0 (1 + g)^n R$
>
> where P_0 is the current ex-dividend ordinary share price
> g is the expected annual growth of the ordinary share price
> n is the number of years to conversion
> R is the number of shares received on conversion

The current **market value** of a convertible bond where conversion is expected is the sum of the present values of the future interest payments and the present value of the bond's conversion value.

5.6 Example: Valuation of convertible debt

What is the value of a 9% convertible bond if it can be converted in 5 years' time into 35 ordinary shares or redeemed at par on the same date? An investor's required return is 10% and the current market price of the underlying share is $2.50 which is expected to grow by 4% per annum.

Solution

Conversion value = $P_0 (1 + g)^n R = 2.50 \times 1.04^5 \times 35 = \$106.46$

Present value of $9 interest per annum for 5 years at 10% = $9 \times 3.791 = \$34.12$

Present value of the conversion value = $106.46 \times 0.621 = \$66.11$

Current market value of convertible bond = $34.12 + 66.11 = \$100.23$

5.7 Preference shares

Preference shares pay a fixed-rate dividend which is not tax deductible for the company.

Formula to learn

The current ex-dividend value P_0 paying a constant annual dividend d and having a cost of capital k_{pref}:

$$P_0 = \frac{d}{k_{pref}}$$

Chapter Roundup

- There are a number of different ways of **putting a value on a business**, or on shares in an unquoted company. It makes sense to use **several methods** of valuation, and to compare the values they produce.

- The **net assets valuation** method can be used as one of many valuation methods, or to provide a lower limit for the value of a company. By itself it is unlikely to produce the most realistic value.

- **P/E ratios** may be used to value equity shares when a large block of shares, or a whole business, is being valued. This method can be problematic when P/E ratios for quoted companies are used to value unquoted companies.

- Cash flow based valuation models include the **dividend valuation model**, the **dividend growth model** and valuation on a **discounted cash flow basis**.

- For **irredeemable debt**:

  Market price, ex interest (P_0) $= \dfrac{I}{K_d}$

  $= \dfrac{i(1-T) \text{ with tax}}{K_{dnet}}$

  For **redeemable debt**, the market value is **the discounted present value of future interest receivable**, up to the year of redemption, plus the **discounted present value of the redemption payment**.

Quick Quiz

1. Give four circumstances in which the shares of an unquoted company might need to be valued.

2. How is the P/E ratio related to EPS?

3. What is meant by 'multiples' in the context of share valuation?

4. Suggest two circumstances in which net assets might be used as a basis for valuation of a company.

5. Cum interest prices should always be used in calculations involving debt. True/False?

6. Fill in the blanks. For redeemable bonds:

   Market value = ... + ...

Answers to Quick Quiz

1. (a) Setting an issue price if the company is floating its shares
   (b) When shares are sold
   (c) For tax purposes
   (d) When shares are pledged as collateral for a loan

2. P/E ratio = Share price/EPS

3. The P/E ratio: the multiple of earnings at which a company's shares are traded

4. (a) As a measure of asset backing
   (b) For comparison, in a scheme of merger

5. False. Ex-interest prices should be used.

6. Market value

   = Discounted present value of future interest receivable up to year of redemption
   + Discounted present value of redemption payment

Now try the questions below from the Practice Question Bank

Number	Level	Marks	Approximate time
Section A Q29	Examination	2	4 mins
Section B Q11-15	Examination	10	20 mins
Section B Q16-20	Examination	10	20 mins
Section C Q20	Introductory	N/A	39 mins
Section C Q21	Introductory	N/A	39 mins

Market efficiency

18

Topic list	Syllabus reference
1 The efficient market hypothesis	F4 (a)
2 The valuation of shares	F4 (b), (c)

Introduction

This chapter deals with the determination of share prices. As we shall see, there are various theories which seek to provide a rationale for share price movement. The most important of these is the **efficient market hypothesis**, which provides theoretical underpinning for how markets take into account new information.

The chapter also looks at practical issues that may affect the market valuation of shares.

Study guide

Exam guide

Market efficiency may need to be discussed as part of a business valuation question.

1 The efficient market hypothesis   12/07, 6/08, 12/10, 6/14

FAST FORWARD

The theory behind share price movements can be explained by the three forms of the **efficient market hypothesis.**

- **Weak form efficiency** implies that prices reflect all relevant information about past price movements and their implications.
- **Semi-strong form efficiency** implies that prices reflect past price movements and publicly available knowledge.
- **Strong form efficiency** implies that prices reflect past price movements, publicly available knowledge and inside knowledge.

Key term

The **efficient market hypothesis** provides a rationale for explaining how share prices react to new information about a company, and when any such change in share price occurs. Stock market reaction to new information depends on the strength of the stock market efficiency.

1.1 Definition of market efficiency

Different types of efficiency can be distinguished in the context of the operation of financial markets.

(a) **Allocative efficiency**

If financial markets allow funds to be directed towards firms which make the most productive use of them, then there is **allocative efficiency** in these markets.

(b) **Operational efficiency**

Transaction costs are incurred by **participants** in financial markets, for example commissions on share transactions, margins between interest rates for lending and for borrowing, and loan arrangement fees. Financial markets have **operational efficiency** if transaction costs are kept as low as possible. Transaction costs are kept low where there is open competition between brokers and other market participants.

(c) **Information processing efficiency**

The **information processing efficiency** of a stock market means the ability of a stock market to price stocks and shares fairly and quickly. An efficient market in this sense is one in which the market prices of all securities reflect all the available information.

The efficient markets hypothesis is concerned with the information processing efficiency of stock markets.

1.2 Varying degrees of efficiency

There are three degrees or 'forms' of stock market **efficiency**: **weak form**, **semi-strong form** and **strong form**.

1.2.1 Weak form efficiency

If a stock market has weak form efficiency, it is not efficient at responding to events that affect companies and should affect share prices. It does not react to much of the information that is available about a company. Instead, when stock market efficiency is weak, share prices respond to all available historical published information and information about **past** changes in the share price.

1.2.2 Semi-strong form efficiency

If a stock market displays semi-strong efficiency, current share prices reflect:

- **All relevant information** about **past price movements** and their implications
- All publicly available **knowledge** about companies and market returns

Share prices respond quickly to new information as it becomes available.

This means that individuals cannot 'beat the market' by reading the newspapers or annual reports, since the information contained in these will already be reflected in share prices.

Tests to prove semi-strong efficiency have concentrated on the speed and accuracy of stock market response to information and on the ability of the market to **anticipate share price changes** before new information is formally announced. For example, if two companies plan a merger, share prices of the two companies will inevitably change once the merger plans are formally announced. The market would show semi-strong efficiency, however, if it were able to anticipate such an announcement, so that share prices of the companies concerned would change in advance of the merger plans being confirmed.

Research in both the UK and the US has suggested that market prices anticipate mergers several months before they are formally announced, and the conclusion drawn is that the stock markets in these countries **do** exhibit semi-strong efficiency.

1.2.3 Strong form efficiency

If a stock market displays a strong form of efficiency, share prices reflect **all** information, whether it is publicly available or not:

- From past price changes
- From public knowledge or anticipation
- From specialists' or experts' insider knowledge (eg the inside knowledge of investment managers about unpublished facts)

If a stock market has strong form efficiency, share prices will respond to new developments and events before they even become public knowledge.

1.3 Features of efficient markets

Stock markets that are efficient (or semi-efficient) are therefore markets in which:

(a) The prices of securities bought and sold **reflect all the relevant information** available to the buyers and sellers, and share prices change quickly to reflect all new information about future prospects.

(b)   No individual dominates the market.

(c)   **Transaction costs** of buying and selling are not so high as to discourage trading significantly.

(d)   Investors are **rational** and so make rational buying and selling decisions, and value shares in a rational way.

(e)   There are low, or no, costs of **acquiring information**.

1.4 Impact of efficiency on share prices

If the stock market is efficient, share prices should vary in a rational way.

(a)   If a company makes an investment with a **positive net present value** (NPV), shareholders will get to know about it and the market price of its shares will rise in anticipation of future dividend increases.

(b)   If a company makes a **bad investment**, shareholders will find out and so the **price** of its **shares will fall**.

(c)   If interest rates rise, **shareholders will want a higher return** from their investments, so market prices will fall.

1.5 Implications of efficient market hypothesis for the financial manager

If the markets are quite strongly efficient, the main consequence for financial managers will be that they simply need to **concentrate on maximising the net present value** of the **company's investments** in order to maximise the wealth of shareholders. Managers need not worry, for example, about the effect on share prices of financial results in the published accounts because investors will make **allowances** for **low profits** or **dividends** in the current year if higher profits or dividends are expected in the future.

If the market is strongly efficient, there is little point in financial managers attempting strategies that will attempt to mislead the markets.

(a)   There is no point for example in trying to identify a correct date when **shares** should be **issued**, since share prices will always reflect the true worth of the company.

(b)   The market will identify any attempts to **window dress the accounts** and put an optimistic spin on the figures.

(c)   The market will decide what **level of return** it requires for the risk involved in making an investment in the company. It is pointless for the company to try to change the market's view by issuing different types of capital instruments.

Similarly, if the company is looking to expand, the directors will be wasting their time if they seek as **takeover targets** companies whose shares are undervalued, since the market will fairly value all companies' shares.

Only if the market is semi-strongly efficient, and the financial managers possess **inside information** that would significantly alter the price of the company's shares if released to the market, could they perhaps gain an advantage. However, attempts to take account of this inside information may breach insider dealing laws.

The different characteristics of a semi-strong form and a strong form efficient market thus affect the **timing** of share price movements, in cases where the relevant information becomes available to the market eventually. The difference between the two forms of market efficiency concerns **when** the share prices change, not by how much prices eventually change.

2 The valuation of shares

Fundamental analysis is based on the theory that share prices can be derived from a rational analysis of future dividends.

Technical analysts or **chartists** work on the basis that past price patterns will be repeated, therefore future price movements can be predicted from historical patterns of share price movements in the past, and there are some patterns that continually reappear.

Random walk theory is based on the idea that share prices will alter when new information becomes available.

Share prices are also affected by **marketability** and **liquidity** of shares, availability and sources of information, **market imperfections** and **pricing anomalies**, **market capitalisation** and **investor speculation**.

2.1 The fundamental theory of share values

We discussed the fundamental theory of share values in the last chapter. Remember that it is based on the theory that the realistic market price of a share can be derived from a valuation of estimated future dividends. The value of a share will be the discounted present value of all future expected dividends on the shares, discounted at the shareholders' cost of capital. The theory therefore supports the view that 'realistic' share prices can be determined by valuation models, such as the dividend growth model.

If the fundamental analysis theory of share values is correct, the price of any share will be **predictable**, provided that all investors have the same information about a company's expected future profits and dividends, and a known cost of capital.

Question
Share valuation

The management of Crocus is trying to decide on the dividend policy of the company.

There are two options that are being considered.

(a)   The company could pay a constant annual dividend of 8c per share.

(b)   The company could pay a dividend of 6c per share this year, and use the retained earnings to achieve an annual growth of 3% in dividends for each year after that.

The shareholders' cost of capital is thought to be 10%. Which dividend policy would maximise the wealth of shareholders, by maximising the share price?

Answer

(a)   With a constant annual dividend

Share price = $\dfrac{8}{0.1}$ = 80c

(b)   With dividend growth

Share price $= \dfrac{6(1.03)}{(0.1-0.03)} = \dfrac{6.18}{0.07} = 88c$

The dividend of 6c per share with 3% annual growth would be preferred.

2.2 Charting or technical analysis

Chartists or **'technical analysts'** attempt to predict share price movements by assuming that past price patterns will be repeated. There is no real theoretical justification for this approach, but it can at times be spectacularly successful. Studies have suggested that the degree of success is greater than could be expected merely from chance.

Chartists do not attempt to predict every price change. They are primarily interested in trend reversals, for example when the price of a share has been rising for several months but suddenly starts to fall.

Moving averages help the chartist to examine overall trends. For example, they may calculate and plot moving averages of share prices for 20 days, 60 days and 240 days. The 20 day figures will give a reasonable representation of the actual movement in share prices after eliminating day to day fluctuations. The other two moving averages give a good idea of longer-term trends.

One of the main problems with chartism is that it is **often difficult to see a new trend until after it has happened**. By the time the chartist has detected a signal, other chartists will have as well, and the resulting mass movement to buy or sell will push the price so as to eliminate any advantage.

With the use of sophisticated computer programs to simulate the work of a chartist, academic studies have found that the **results obtained were no better or worse** than those obtained from a simple 'buy and hold' strategy of a **well-diversified portfolio of shares**.

This may be explained by research that has found that there are no regular patterns or cycles in share price movements over time – they follow a **random walk**.

2.3 Random walk theory

Random walk theory is consistent with the fundamental theory of share values. It accepts that a share should have an intrinsic price dependent on the fortunes of the company and the expectations of investors. One of its underlying assumptions is that **all relevant information about a company is available to all potential investors** who will act on the information in a **rational** manner.

The key feature of random walk theory is that, although share prices will have an **intrinsic or fundamental value**, this value will be altered as new information becomes available, and that the behaviour of investors is such that the actual share price will fluctuate from day to day around the intrinsic value.

2.4 Marketability and liquidity of shares

In financial markets, **liquidity** is the **ease of dealing** in the shares; how easily the shares can be bought and sold without significantly moving the price.

In general, large companies, with hundreds of millions of shares in issue, and high numbers of shares changing hands every day, have good liquidity. In contrast, small companies with few shares in issue and thin trading volumes can have very poor liquidity.

The **marketability** of shares in a private company, particularly a minority shareholding, is generally very limited, a consequence being that the price can be difficult to determine.

Shares with restricted marketability may be subject to sudden and large falls in value and companies may act to improve the marketability of their shares with a **stock split**. A stock split occurs where, for example, each ordinary share of $1 each is split into two shares of 50c each, thus creating cheaper shares with **greater marketability**. There is possibly an added psychological advantage in that investors may expect a company which splits its shares in this way to be planning for substantial earnings growth and dividend growth in the future.

As a consequence, the market price of shares may benefit. For example, if one existing share of $1 has a market value of $6, and is then split into two shares of 50c each, the market value of the new shares might settle at, say, $3.10 instead of the expected $3, in anticipation of strong future growth in earnings and dividends.

2.5 Availability and sources of information

In Section 1 of this chapter it was stated that an efficient market is one where the prices of securities bought and sold reflect all the **relevant information** available. Efficiency relates to how quickly and how accurately prices adjust to new information.

Information comes from financial statements, financial databases, the financial press and the internet.

2.5.1 Dividend information

It has been argued that shareholders see dividend decisions as passing on **new information** about the company and its prospects. A dividend increase is usually seen by markets to be good news and a dividend decrease to be bad news, but it may be that the market will react to the difference between the actual dividend payments and the market's **expectations** of the level of dividend. For example, the market may be expecting a cut in dividend but if the actual decrease is less than expected, the share price may rise.

2.6 Market imperfections and pricing anomalies

Various types of anomaly appear to support the views that irrationality often drives the stock market, including the following.

(a) **Seasonal month of the year effects**, day of the week effects and also hour of the day effects seem to occur, so that share prices might tend to rise or fall at a particular time of the year, week or day.

(b) There may be a **short-run overreaction** to recent events. For example, during the stock market crash in 1987, the market went into free fall, losing 20% in a few hours.

(c) Individual shares or shares in small companies may be neglected.

The paradox of efficient markets is that an efficient market requires people to believe that the market is inefficient so that they trade securities in an attempt to outperform the market.

A **noise trader** is a trader who buys and sells irrationally and erratically; for example, overreacting to good or bad news. Noise traders can cause prices and risk levels to change from expected levels.

2.7 Market capitalisation

The **market capitalisation** is the market value of a company's shares multiplied by the number of issued shares.

The market capitalisation or **size** of a company has also produced some pricing anomalies.

The return from investing in **smaller** companies has been shown to be **greater** than the average return from all companies in the long run. This increased return may compensate for the greater risk associated with smaller companies, or it may be due to a start from a lower base.

2.8 Behavioural finance

Speculation by investors and market sentiment is a major factor in the behaviour of share prices. **Behavioural finance** is an alternative view to the efficient market hypothesis. It attempts to explain the market implications of the **psychological** factors behind investor decisions and suggests that **irrational investor behaviour** may significantly affect share price movements. These factors may explain why share prices appear sometimes to overreact to past price changes.

Behavioural finance considers the emotional and 'illogical' factors that affect the decision-making of investors. These behavioural factors may explain why investors often do not act rationally. For example, behavioural theory may explain stock market bubbles, such as inexplicable bubbles in the share prices of technology stocks (in the early 2000s and the 2010s in the US) and a stock market crash, like the crashes of 1929 and 1987.

- The theory behind share price movements can be explained by the three forms of the **efficient market hypothesis**.

  - **Weak form efficiency** implies that prices reflect all relevant information about past price movements and their implications.

  - **Semi-strong form efficiency** implies that prices reflect past price movements and publicly available knowledge.

  - **Strong form efficiency** implies that prices reflect past price movements, publicly available knowledge and inside knowledge.

- **Fundamental analysis** is based on the theory that share prices can be derived from a rational analysis of **future dividends**.

  Technical analysts or **chartists** work on the basis that past price patterns will be repeated, therefore future price movements can be predicted from historical patterns of share price movements in the past, and there are some patterns that continually reappear.

  Random walk theory is based on the idea that share prices will alter when new information becomes available.

  Share prices are also affected by **marketability** and **liquidity** of shares, availability and sources of **information**, **market imperfections** and **pricing anomalies**, **market capitalisation** and **investor speculation**.

1   Which theory of share price behaviour does the following statement describe?

'The analysis of external and internal influences on the operations of a company with a view to assisting in investment decisions.'

A   Technical analysis
B   Random walk theory
C   Fundamental analysis theory
D   Chartism

2   What is meant by 'efficiency' in the context of the efficient market hypothesis?

3   The different 'forms' of the efficient market hypothesis state that share prices reflect **which** types of information? Tick all that apply.

	Form of EMH		
	Weak	*Semi-strong*	*Strong*
No information	☐	☐	☐
All information in past share price record	☐	☐	☐
All other publicly available information	☐	☐	☐
Specialists' and experts' 'insider' knowledge	☐	☐	☐

4   Which theory makes which assertions?

(a)   Chartism

(i)   A share price can be expected to fluctuate around its 'intrinsic' value.

(b)   Random walk theory

(ii)   Past share price patterns tend to be repeated.

(c)   Fundamental analysis theory

(iii) The value of a share is the discounted present value of all future expected dividends on the share, discounted at the shareholders' cost of capital.

5   List three factors affecting share price behaviour.

1   C   Fundamental analysis theory

2   Efficiency in processing information in the pricing of stocks and shares

3

	Form of EMH		
	Weak	*Semi-strong*	*Strong*
No information	☐	☐	☐
All information in past share price record	☑	☑	☑
All other publicly available information	☐	☑	☑
Specialists' and experts' 'insider' knowledge	☐	☐	☑

4   (a)   (ii)
    (b)   (i)
    (c)   (iii)

5   Any three of:

   (a) Investor speculation
   (b) Marketability and liquidity of shares
   (c) Information
   (d) Market imperfections
   (e) Pricing anomalies
   (f) Market capitalisation

Now try the questions below from the Practice Question Bank

Number	Level	Marks	Approximate time
Section A Q30	Examination	2	4 mins
Section C Q22	Introductory	N/A	39 mins

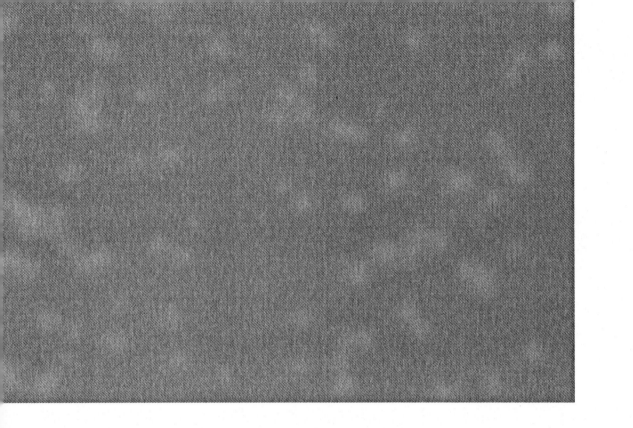

Risk management

Foreign currency risk

Topic list	Syllabus reference
1 Exchange rates	G1 (a)
2 Foreign currency risk	G1 (a)
3 The causes of exchange rate fluctuations	G2 (a), (b)
4 Foreign currency risk management	B3 (a)(iii), G3 (a), (b)
5 Foreign currency derivatives	G3 (c)

Introduction

In Part G, we look at various techniques for the management of **risk**, in particular **foreign currency risk** and **interest rate risk**. In this chapter, we are particularly concerned with risks related to **exchange rate fluctuations**.

The first section contains some very important basic concepts so make sure you're happy with how foreign exchange rates are quoted and the **causes** of exchange rate fluctuations.

The techniques to **hedge** foreign currency risk are covered in Section 4. Forward exchange rate calculations are straightforward, but you need to use a step by step approach to tackle money market hedges. Don't feel overwhelmed by the terminology in the derivatives section; you need to identify the main types of derivative and will not need to perform any calculations.

Study guide

		Intellectual level
B3	**The nature and role of money market**	
(a)	Describe the role of money markets in:	1
(iii)	Allowing an organisation to manage its exposure to foreign currency risk and interest rate risk	
G1	**The nature and types of risk and approaches to risk management**	
(a)	Describe and discuss different types of foreign currency risk:	2
(i)	Translation risk	
(ii)	Transaction risk	
(iii)	Economic risk	
G2	**Causes of exchange rate differences and interest rate fluctuations**	
(a)	Describe the causes of exchange rate fluctuations, including:	
(i)	Balance of payments	1
(ii)	Purchasing power parity theory	2
(iii)	Interest rate parity theory	2
(iv)	Four-way equivalence	2
(b)	Forecast exchange rates using:	2
(i)	Purchasing power parity	
(ii)	Interest rate parity	
G3	**Hedging techniques for foreign currency risk**	
(a)	Discuss and apply traditional and basic methods of foreign currency risk management, including:	
(i)	Currency of invoice	1
(ii)	Netting and matching	2
(iii)	Leading and lagging	2
(iv)	Forward exchange contracts	2
(v)	Money market hedging	2
(vi)	Asset and liability management	1
(b)	Compare and evaluate traditional methods of foreign currency risk management.	2
(c)	Identify the main types of foreign currency derivatives used to hedge foreign currency risk and explain how they are used in hedging.	1

Exam guide

This is an important chapter. You need to have a good understanding of various hedging methods, and be able to determine in a given situation what exposure needs hedging and how best to do it.

1 Exchange rates

1.1 Exchange rates

Key terms

> An **exchange rate** is the rate at which one country's currency can be traded in exchange for another country's currency.
>
> The **spot rate** is the exchange rate currently offered on a particular currency for **immediate delivery**.
>
> A **forward rate** is an exchange rate set now for currencies to be exchanged at a future date.

Every traded currency in fact has many exchange rates. There is an exchange rate with every other traded currency on the foreign exchange markets. Foreign exchange dealers make their profit by buying currency for less than they sell it, and so there are really two exchange rates, a selling rate and a buying rate. Rates change continually, because there is a huge volume of transactions daily in the foreign exchange (FX) markets globally.

1.2 Foreign exchange demand

If an importer has to pay a foreign supplier in a foreign currency, they might ask their bank to sell them the required amount of the currency, so that they can make the payment. For example, suppose that a UK bank's customer, a trading company, has imported goods for which it must now pay US$10,000.

(a)   The company will ask the bank to sell it US$10,000. If the company is buying currency, the bank is selling it.

(b)   When the bank agrees to sell US$10,000 to the company, it will tell the company what the spot rate of exchange will be for the transaction. If the bank's selling rate (known as the **'offer'**, or **'ask'** price) is, say, $1.5135 per £1 for the currency, the bank will charge the company:

$10,000/$1.5135 per £1 = £6,607.20

Similarly, if an exporter is paid, say, $10,000 by a foreign customer in the US, they may wish to exchange the dollars to obtain sterling. They will therefore ask the bank to buy the dollars from them. Since the exporter is selling currency to the bank, the bank is buying the currency.

If the bank quotes a buying rate (known as the **bid** price) of, say, $1.5195 per £1, for the currency the bank will pay the exporter:

$10,000/$1.5195 per £1 = £6,581.11

A bank expects to make a profit from selling and buying currency, and it does so by offering a rate for selling a currency which is different from the rate for buying the currency.

Question   Sterling receipts

Calculate how much sterling exporters would receive or how much sterling importers would pay, ignoring the bank's commission, in each of the following situations, if they were to exchange currency and sterling at the spot rate.

(a)   A UK exporter receives a payment from a Danish customer of 150,000 kroner.
(b)   A UK importer buys goods from a Japanese supplier and pays 1 million yen.

Spot rates are as follows.

	Bank sells (offer)		Bank buys (bid)
Danish Kr/£	9.4340	–	9.5380
Japan Y/£	168.650	–	170.781

(a)   The bank is being asked to buy the Danish kroner and will give the exporter:

$\dfrac{150{,}000}{9.5380}$ = £15,726.57 in exchange

(b)   The bank is being asked to sell the yen to the importer and will charge for the currency:

1,000,000/168.650 = £5,929.44

1.3 The foreign exchange (FX) markets

Banks buy currency from customers and sell currency to customers – typically, **exporting and importing firms**. Banks may buy currency from a **government** or sell currency to a government. Banks also buy and sell currency **between themselves**.

International trade involves foreign currency, for either the buyer, the seller, or both (for example, a Saudi Arabian firm might sell goods to a Malaysian buyer and invoice for the goods in US dollars). As a consequence, it is quite likely that exporters might want to sell foreign currency earnings to a bank in exchange for domestic currency, and that importers might want to buy foreign currency from a bank in order to pay a foreign supplier.

Since most foreign exchange rates are not fixed but are allowed to vary, rates are continually changing and each bank will offer new rates for new customer enquiries according to how its dealers judge the market situation.

Exam focus point

> You may find it useful to read 'Foreign currency risk and its management', on the ACCA website.

2 Foreign currency risk   12/09, 6/13

FAST FORWARD

> **Currency risk** is the risk of changes in an exchange rate or in the foreign exchange value of a currency. It is a two-way risk.
>
> Currency risk occurs in three forms: **transaction exposure** (short-term), **economic exposure** (effect on present value of longer-term cash flows) and **translation exposure** (book gains or losses).

2.1 The nature of foreign exchange risk

Foreign exchange risk, also called currency risk or FX risk, is the risk arising from unforeseen changes in an exchange rate or the value of a currency.

Business decisions may be made now, but the profits or returns from those decisions may depend on exchange rates in the future.

Foreign currency risk is a two-way risk. This means that exchange rate movements may be favourable as well as adverse, so the term 'risk' can be misleading.

For example, say a UK company buys goods from a US supplier costing $336,000, for settlement in three months' time. If the current spot rate of exchange is $1.50 = $1, the expected cost of the goods for the UK buyer will be £224,000 (= $336,000/$1.50).

If the UK company does nothing to protect itself against the risk of exchange rate movement, it may do nothing for three months, and then buy the $336,000 at whatever the spot rate is at that time. If the spot rate after three months is $1.40 = £1, the cost of the goods will be £240,000, which is £16,000 more than expected. However, if the spot exchange rate is $1.60, the cost of the goods will be £210,000, which is £14,000 less than expected.

The UK company should consider the seriousness of the risk, and the potential consequences of an adverse movement in the exchange rate. The seriousness of the risk will depend to some extent on expectations of future movements in the dollar-sterling spot exchange rate.

2.2 Translation risk

Translation risk is the risk that the organisation will make exchange losses when the **accounting** results of its foreign branches or subsidiaries are translated into the home currency. Translation losses can result, for example, from re-stating the book value of a foreign subsidiary's assets at the exchange rate on the statement of financial position date.

The effect of translation risk is to create gains or losses in the reported financial results of the parent group, but they do not create cash flow gains or losses.

2.3 Transaction risk

Transaction risk is the risk of adverse exchange rate movements occurring in the course of **normal international trading transactions**. This arises when the prices of imports or exports are fixed in foreign currency terms and there is movement in the exchange rate between the date when the price is agreed and the date when the cash is paid or received in settlement.

For example, if an Australian company buys goods from a US supplier for an agreed price of US$1,000,000, with payment in two months' time, it is exposed to a transaction risk, that the US dollar may strengthen in value against the Australian dollar during the two-month credit period.

Much international trade involves credit. An importer will take credit often for several months and sometimes longer, and an exporter will grant credit. One consequence of taking and granting credit is that international traders will know in advance about the receipts and payments arising from their trade. They will know:

- What foreign currency they will receive or pay
- When the receipt or payment will occur
- How much of the currency will be received or paid

The great danger to profit margins is in the **movement in exchange rates**. The risk is faced by (i) exporters who invoice in a foreign currency and (ii) importers who pay in a foreign currency.

Question   Changes in exchange rates

Bulldog Ltd, a UK company, buys goods from Redland which cost 100,000 Reds (the local currency). The goods are resold in the UK for £32,000. At the time of the import purchase the exchange rate for Reds against sterling is Red3.5650 – Red3.5800 per £1.

Required

(a)   What is the expected profit on the resale?

(b)   What would the actual profit be if the spot rate at the time when the currency is received has moved to:

     (i)   Red3.0800 – Red3.0950 per £1?
     (ii)   Red4.0650 – Red4.0800 per £1?

Ignore bank commission charges.

(a) Bulldog must buy Reds to pay the supplier, and so the bank is selling Reds. The expected profit is as follows.

	£
Revenue from resale of goods	32,000.00
Less cost of 100,000 Reds in sterling (÷ 3.5650)	28,050.49
Expected profit	3,949.51

(b) (i) If the actual spot rate for Bulldog to buy and the bank to sell the Reds is 3.0800, the result is as follows.

	£
Revenue from resale	32,000.00
Less cost (100,000 ÷ 3.0800)	32,467.53
Loss	(467.53)

(ii) If the actual spot rate for Bulldog to buy and the bank to sell the Reds is 4.0650, the result is as follows.

	£
Revenue from resale	32,000.00
Less cost (100,000 ÷ 4.0650)	24,600.25
Profit	7,399.75

This variation in the final sterling cost of the goods (and thus the profit) illustrates the concept of transaction risk.

2.4 Economic risk

This refers to the effect of exchange rate movements on the **international competitiveness** of a company and refers to the effect on the present value of longer-term cash flows.

It is the risk that over time a currency will depreciate or appreciate in value against other currencies, so that a country's economy becomes more or less competitive.

For example, a UK company might use raw materials which are priced in US dollars, but export its products mainly within the EU, pricing its exports in sterling. A depreciation of sterling against the dollar or an appreciation of sterling against other EU currencies will erode the competitiveness of the company.

Economic exposure can be difficult to avoid, although **diversification of the supplier and customer base** across different countries will reduce this kind of exposure to risk.

3 The causes of exchange rate fluctuations

3.1 Currency supply and demand

FAST FORWARD

Factors influencing the exchange rate include the comparative rates of inflation in different countries (**purchasing power parity**), comparative interest rates in different countries (**interest rate parity**), the underlying balance of payments, speculation and government policy on managing or fixing exchange rates.

The exchange rate between two currencies – ie the buying and selling rates, both spot and forward – is determined primarily by **supply and demand** in the foreign exchange markets. Demand comes from individuals, firms and governments who want to buy a currency. Supply comes from those who want to sell it.

Supply and demand for currencies are in turn influenced by:

- The rate of inflation, compared with the rate of inflation in other countries
- Interest rates, compared with interest rates in other countries
- The balance of payments in goods and services
- Transactions of a capital nature, such as inward or outward foreign investment
- Sentiment of foreign exchange market participants regarding economic prospects
- Speculation
- Government policy on intervention to influence the exchange rate

3.2 Interest rate parity   6/11, 12/14

Key term

> **Interest rate parity** is a method of predicting foreign exchange rates based on the hypothesis that the difference between the interest rates in the two countries should offset the difference between the spot rates and the forward foreign exchange rates over the same period.

The difference between spot and forward rates reflects differences in interest rates. In other words, the expected dollar return on dollar deposits is equal to the expected dollar return on foreign deposits. If this were not so, then investors holding the currency with the lower interest rates would switch to the other currency for (say) three months, ensuring that they would not lose on returning to the original currency by fixing the exchange rate in advance at the forward rate.

If enough investors acted in this way (known as **arbitrage**), forces of supply and demand would lead to a change in the forward rate to prevent such risk-free profit making.

The principle of **interest rate parity** links the foreign exchange markets and the international money markets and capital markets. The theory states that over time movements in the spot exchange rate between two currencies are determined by differences in the interest rates between the two countries.

The principle can be stated as follows.

Formula to learn

$$F_0 = S_0 \times \frac{(1+i_c)}{(1+i_b)}$$

Where F_0 = forward rate

S_0 = current spot rate

i_c = interest rate in country c (the overseas country) up to the future date

i_b = interest rate in country b (the base country) up to the future date

Exam focus point

> Try to remember that **interest rate parity** predicts the **forward rate**.

To help apply the formula the following may be useful. If there are two countries, C and B, then country C's interest rate will be the numerator when the exchange rates are expressed as the quantity of the currency of C required to purchase one unit of the currency of B. The formula is given in the exam on the formula sheet.

3.2.1 Example: Interest rate parity

Exchange rates between two currencies, the Northland florin (NF) and the Southland dollar (S$), are listed in the financial press as follows.

Spot rates	$S1 = NF4.7250
	NF1 = $S0.21164
90-day forward rates	NF4.7506 per $S1
	$S0.21050 per NF1

The money market interest rate for 90-day deposits in Northland florins is 7.5% annualised. What is implied about interest rates in Southland?

Assume a 365-day year. (**Note**. In practice, foreign currency interest rates are often calculated on an alternative **360-day** basis, one month being treated as 30 days.)

Solution

Today, \$S1.000 buys NF4.7250.

NF4.7250 could be placed on deposit for 90 days to earn interest of $NF(4.7250 \times 0.075 \times 90/365) = NF0.0874$, thus growing to $NF(4.7250 + 0.0874) = NF4.8124$.

This is then worth \$S1.0130 at the 90-day forward exchange rate (4.8124/4.7506).

This tells us that the annualised expected interest rate on 90-day deposits in Southland is $0.013 \times 365/90 = 5.3\%$.

Alternatively, applying the formula given earlier, we have the following.

Northland interest rate on 90-day deposit = i_n = 7.5% × 90/365 = 1.85%

Southland interest rate on 90-day deposit = i_s

90-day forward exchange rate = F_0 = 0.21050

Spot exchange rate = S_0 = 0.21164

$$\therefore 0.2150 = 0.21164 \times \frac{(1+i_s)}{1+0.0185}$$

$$\therefore \frac{1+i_s}{1+0.0185} = \frac{0.21050}{0.21164}$$

$1 + i_s = 1.0185 \times 0.21050 \div 0.21164 = 1.013$

$i_s = 0.013$, or 1.3%

Annualised, this is $0.013 \times 365/90 = 5.3\%$

3.2.2 Example: Interest rate parity

A Canadian company is expecting to receive Kuwaiti dinars in one year's time. The spot rate is Canadian dollar 5.4670 per 1 dinar. The company could borrow in dinars at 9% or in Canadian dollars at 14%. There is no forward rate for one year's time. Predict what the exchange rate is likely to be in one year.

Solution

Using interest rate parity, the Canadian dollar is the numerator and the Kuwaiti dinar is the denominator. So the expected future exchange rate dollar/dinar is given by:

$$5.4670 \times \frac{1.14}{1.09} = 5.7178$$

This prediction is subject to great inaccuracy, but note that the company could 'lock into' this exchange rate, working a money market hedge by borrowing today in dinars at 9%, converting the cash to dollars at spot and repaying any 14% dollar debt. When the dinar cash is received from the customer, the dinar loan is repaid.

3.3 Purchasing power parity   6/11, 6/12

Key term

> **Purchasing power parity** theory states that the exchange rate between two currencies is the same in equilibrium when the purchasing power of currency is the same in each country.

Interest rate parity should not be confused with **purchasing power parity** (PPP).

Purchasing power parity theory is an alternative theory for predicting movements in a spot exchange rate over time.

Purchasing power parity theory predicts that the exchange value of foreign currency depends on the relative purchasing power of each currency in its own country and that **spot exchange rates will vary over time according to relative price changes**.

Formally, purchasing power parity can be expressed in the following formula.

$$S_1 = S_0 \times \frac{(1+h_c)}{(1+h_b)}$$

Where S_1 = expected spot rate
S_0 = current spot rate
h_c = expected inflation rate in country c (a foreign country)
h_b = expected inflation rate in country b (the investor's country)

Note this formula is given in the exam.

Exam focus point

Try to remember that **purchasing power parity** predicts the **future spot rate** and **interest rate parity** predicts the **forward rate**.

Note. The expected future spot rate will not necessarily coincide with the 'forward exchange rate' currently quoted.

3.4 Example: Purchasing power parity

The spot exchange rate between UK sterling and the Danish krone is £1 = 8.00 kroner. Assuming that there is now purchasing parity, an amount of a commodity costing £110 in the UK will cost 880 kroner in Denmark. Over the next year, price inflation in Denmark is expected to be 5% while inflation in the UK is expected to be 8%. What is the 'expected spot exchange rate' at the end of the year?

Using the formula above:

Future (forward) rate, S_1 $= 8 \times \dfrac{1.05}{1.08}$

$= 7.78$

This is the same figure as we get if we compare the inflated prices for the commodity. At the end of the year:

UK price	=	£110 × 1.08 = £118.80
Denmark price	=	Kr880 × 1.05 = Kr924
S_t	=	924 ÷ 118.80 = 7.78

In the real world, exchange rates move towards purchasing power parity only over the **long term**. However, the theory is sometimes used to predict future exchange rates in **investment appraisal problems** where forecasts of relative inflation rates are available.

 Case Study

An amusing example of purchasing power parity is *The Economist*'s Big Mac index. Under PPP, movements in countries' exchange rates should in the long-term mean that the prices of an identical basket of goods or services are equalised. The McDonalds Big Mac represents this basket.

The index compares local Big Mac prices with the price of Big Macs in America. This comparison is used to forecast what exchange rates should be, and this is then compared with the actual exchange rates to decide which currencies are over- and under-valued.

For example, in July 2015, the price of a Big Mac in America was $4.79. At market exchange rates, the price of a Big Mac in China was $2.74. So the Big Mac index suggests that the yuan was undervalued by 43% at the time.

3.5 The Fisher effect

The term **Fisher effect** is sometimes used in looking at the relationship between **interest** rates and expected rates of **inflation** (see Chapter 9, Section 1).

The rate of interest is seen as being made up of two parts: the real required rate of return (real interest rate) plus a premium for inflation. Then:

Exam formula

[1 + nominal (money) rate] = [1 + real interest rate] [1 + inflation rate]

$(1 + i) = (1 + r)(1 + h)$

Countries with relatively **high** rates of inflation will generally have high nominal rates of interest, partly because high interest rates are a mechanism for reducing inflation, and partly because of the Fisher effect: higher nominal interest rates serve to allow investors to obtain a high enough real rate of return where inflation is relatively high.

According to the **international Fisher effect**, nominal interest rate differentials between countries provide an unbiased predictor of future changes in spot exchange rates. The currency of countries with relatively high interest rates is expected to depreciate against currencies with lower interest rates, because the higher interest rates are considered necessary to compensate for the anticipated currency depreciation. Given free movement of capital internationally, this idea suggests that the real rate of return in different countries will equalise as a result of adjustments to spot exchange rates.

The international Fisher effect can be expressed as:

$$\frac{1 + i_a}{1 + i_b} = \frac{1 + h_a}{1 + h_b}$$

Where i_a is the nominal interest rate in country a
i_b is the nominal interest rate in country b
h_a is the inflation rate in country a
h_b is the inflation rate in country b

3.6 Four-way equivalence

The **four-way equivalence model** states that in equilibrium, differences between forward and spot rates, differences in interest rates, expected differences in inflation rates and expected changes in spot rates are **equal** to one another.

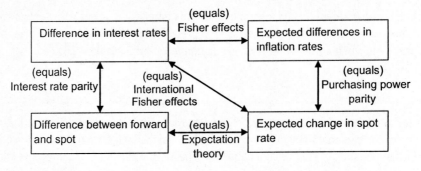

4 Foreign currency risk management

> **FAST FORWARD**
>
> Foreign currency risk can be managed, in order to reduce or eliminate the risk. Measures to reduce currency risk are known as 'hedging'.
>
> Basic methods of hedging risk include **matching receipts and payments, invoicing in own currency**, and **leading and lagging** the times that cash is received and paid. Other common hedging methods are the use of forward exchange contracts and money market hedging.

4.1 Risk and risk management

Risk management describes the policies which a firm may adopt and the techniques it may use to manage the risks it faces. **Exposure** means being open to or vulnerable to risk. If entrepreneurship is about risk, why should businesses want to 'manage' risk? Broadly, there are two reasons why risk management makes good business sense.

(a) Firstly, a business may wish to reduce **risks** to which it is exposed to acceptable levels. What is an acceptable level of risk may depend on various factors, including the scale of operations of the business and the degree to which its proprietors or shareholders are risk averse.

(b) Secondly, a business may wish to avoid **particular kinds of risks**. For example, a business may be averse to taking risks with exchange rates. The reasons may include the fact that the risks are simply **too great** for the business to bear, for example if adverse exchange rate movements could easily wipe out the expected profit on business transactions.

4.2 Currency of invoice

One way of avoiding exchange risk is for exporters to **invoice their foreign customer in their domestic currency**, or for importers to arrange with their **foreign supplier to be invoiced in their domestic currency**. However, although either the exporter or the importer can avoid the transaction risk through invoicing in domestic currency, only one of them can do it. The other must deal in a foreign currency and must accept the exchange risk. This is the risk of adverse movement in the exchange rate up to the date of settlement of the invoice.

For example, if a UK exporter is able to quote and invoice an overseas buyer in sterling, then the foreign exchange risk is in effect **transferred** to the overseas buyer.

An alternative method of achieving the same result is to negotiate contracts expressed in the foreign currency but specifying a fixed rate of exchange as a condition of the contract.

There are certain advantages in invoicing in a foreign currency which might persuade an exporter to take on the exchange risk.

(a) There is the possible **marketing advantage** by proposing to invoice in the buyer's own currency, when there is competition for the sales contract.

(b) The exporter may also be able to **offset** payments to their own suppliers in a particular foreign currency against receipts in that currency.

(c) By arranging to sell goods to customers in a foreign currency, an exporter might be able to **obtain a loan** in that currency, and at the same time obtain cover against exchange risks by arranging to repay the loan out of the proceeds from the sales in that currency.

4.3 Matching receipts and payments

A company may be able to reduce or eliminate its foreign exchange transaction exposure by **matching** receipts and payments in a foreign currency. Wherever possible, a company that expects to make

payments and have receipts in the same foreign currency should plan to **offset its payments against its receipts in the currency**.

Since the company will be setting off foreign currency receipts against foreign currency payments, it does not matter whether the currency strengthens or weakens against the company's 'domestic' currency because there will be no purchase or sale of the currency.

The process of matching receipts and payments is made possible by having one or more **foreign currency accounts** with a bank. Receipts of the foreign currency can be paid into the account, and payments made from the account.

4.4 Matching assets and liabilities

A company which expects to receive a substantial amount of income in a foreign currency will be concerned that this currency may weaken. It can hedge against this possibility by borrowing in the foreign currency and using the foreign receipts to repay the loan. For example, US dollar receivables can be hedged by taking out a US dollar overdraft. In the same way, US dollar trade payables can be matched against a US dollar bank account which is used to pay the suppliers.

A company which has a long-term foreign investment, for example an overseas subsidiary, may also try to **match its foreign assets** (property, plant, etc) by a **long-term loan in the foreign currency**. This would reduce its risk from translation exposure.

4.5 Leading and lagging

In order to take advantage of foreign exchange rate movements, companies might try to use:

- **Lead payments** (payments in advance for goods purchased in a foreign currency)

- **Lagged payments** (delaying payments beyond their due date for goods purchased in a foreign currency)

Payments in a foreign currency may be made in advance when the company expects the foreign currency to increase in value up to the settlement date for the transaction.

With a lead payment, paying in advance of the due date, there is a **finance cost** to consider. This is the interest cost on the money used to make the payment, but early settlement discounts may be available.

Payments in a foreign currency may be delayed until after the due settlement date when it is expected that the currency will soon fall in value. However, delaying payments and taking more than the agreed amount of credit is questionable business practice.

4.6 Netting

Unlike matching, netting is not technically a method of managing exchange risk. However, it is conveniently dealt with at this stage. The objective is simply to save transactions costs by netting off inter-company balances before arranging payment. Many **multinational groups** of companies engage in **intra-group trading**. Where related companies located in different countries trade with one another, there is likely to be inter-company indebtedness denominated in different currencies.

Key term

> **Netting** is a process in which credit balances are netted off against debit balances so that only the reduced net amounts remain due to be paid by actual currency flows.

Netting has the following advantages.

(a) **Foreign exchange purchase** costs, including commission and the spread between selling and buying rates, and money transmission costs are **reduced**.

(b) There is **less loss in interest** from having money in transit.

Local laws and regulations need to be considered before netting is used, as netting is restricted by some countries.

4.6.1 Example: Netting

A and B are respectively UK- and US-based subsidiaries of a Swiss-based holding company. At 31 March 20X5, A owed B SFr300,000 and B owed A SFr220,000. Netting can reduce the value of the inter-company debts: the two inter-company balances are set against each other, leaving a net debt owed by A to B of SFr 80,000 (SFr300,000 – 220,000).

4.7 Forward exchange contracts   12/08, 6/12, 6/13, 12/14

FAST FORWARD

> A forward exchange contract is a contract made now for the purchase or sale of a quantity of currency in exchange for another currency, for settlement at a future date, and at a rate of exchange that is fixed in the contract.
>
> A **forward contract** therefore fixes in advance the rate at which a specified quantity of currency will be bought and sold.

4.7.1 The purpose of forward contracts

The purpose of a forward contract is to fix an exchange rate now for the settlement of a transaction at a future date. This removes uncertainty about what the exchange rate will be at the future date.

Currency risk is a two-way risk. By arranging a forward contract, a company can hedge against the risk of an adverse movement in the spot exchange rate up to the date of settlement, but at the same time it loses the opportunity to gain from a favourable movement in the spot rate.

Forward contracts can be arranged for settlement up to several months ahead, or possibly as much as one year ahead, depending on the nature of the money markets in the two currencies. They may therefore be used to manage exposures to transaction risk, but cannot be used as a hedge against currency risk in the long term.

4.7.2 Forward exchange rates

Forward exchange rates are determined by the current spot rate and differences in interest rates between the two currencies.

A forward exchange rate may be higher or lower than the spot rate. When a currency is more expensive forward than spot, it is quoted forward 'at a premium' to the spot rate. When a currency is cheaper forward than spot, it is quoted forward 'at a discount' to the spot rate.

For example, suppose that:

- The spot rate for Swiss francs against sterling is SFr1.4460 – SFr1.4560 per £1, and
- The three-month forward rate is SFr1.4680 – SFr1.4800 per £1.

(a) A bank would sell 20,000 Swiss francs:

    (i) At the spot rate, now, for (20,000/1.4460) £13,831.26

    (ii) Under a forward contract for settlement in three months' time, for (20,000/1.4680) £13,623.98

(b) A bank would buy 20,000 Swiss francs:

    (i) At the spot rate, for (20,000/1.4560) £13,736.26

    (ii) Under a forward contract for settlement in three months' time, for (20,000/1.4800) £13,513.51

In both cases, the quoted currency (Swiss franc) would be quoted forward at a discount to the spot rate.

The forward rate can be calculated today without making any estimates of future exchange rates. **Future exchange rates** depend largely on future events and will often turn out to be very different from the forward rate. However, the forward rate is probably an **unbiased predictor of the expected value of the**

future exchange rate, based on the information available today. It is also likely that the spot rate will move in the direction indicated by the forward rate.

4.7.3 Forward exchange contracts

Forward exchange contracts are legally binding contracts. They hedge against transaction exposure by allowing the importer or exporter to arrange for a bank to sell or buy a quantity of foreign currency at a future date, at a **rate of exchange determined** when the **forward contract is made**. The trader will know in advance either how much local currency they will receive (if they are selling foreign currency to the bank) or how much local currency they must pay (if they are buying foreign currency from the bank).

Forward contracts are very popular with small companies as a method of hedging currency risk and taking away uncertainty about the exchange rate. The current spot price is irrelevant to the outcome of a forward contract.

A **forward exchange contract** is defined as:

(a)   An immediately firm and binding contract, eg between a bank and its customer

(b)   For the purchase or sale of a specified quantity of a stated foreign currency

(c)   At a rate of exchange fixed at the time the contract is made

(d)   For performance (delivery of the currency and payment for it) at a future time which is agreed when making the contract (This future time will be either a specified date, or any time between two specified dates.)

4.7.4 Example: Forward exchange contracts (1)

A UK importer knows on 1 April that they must pay a foreign seller 26,500 Swiss francs in one month's time, on 1 May. They can arrange a one-month forward exchange contract with the bank on 1 April, whereby the bank undertakes to sell the importer 26,500 Swiss francs. The bank's forward rates for one month are:

SFr/ £1   1.4396 – 1.4504

Because the importer is buying Swiss francs and the bank is selling the francs, the appropriate rate is 1.4396.

The UK importer can be certain that whatever the spot rate is on 1 May, they will have to pay at this forward rate. The cost in sterling will be:

(26,500/1.4396) £18,407.89.

(a)   If the spot rate is **lower than 1.4396** on 1 May, the importer would have successfully protected themselves against a fall in the value of sterling, and would have avoided paying more sterling at the spot rate to obtain the Swiss francs.

(b)   If the spot rate is **higher than 1.4396** on 1 May, the importer would pay more at the forward rate than if they had obtained the francs at the spot rate on 1 May. They cannot avoid this extra cost because a forward contract is binding.

4.7.5 What happens if a customer cannot satisfy a forward contract?

A company may arrange a forward contract and then subsequently discover that it does not need to buy or sell the currency.

(a)   An **importer** might find that:

(i)   Their supplier **fails to deliver the goods** as specified, so the importer will not accept the goods delivered and will not agree to pay for them.

(ii)   The **supplier sends fewer goods** than expected, perhaps because of supply shortages, and so the importer has less to pay for.

(iii) The supplier is **late with the delivery**, and so the importer does not have to pay for the goods until later than expected.

(b) An **exporter** might experience the same types of situation, but in reverse, so that they do not receive any payment at all, or they receive more or less than originally expected, or they receive the expected amount, but only after some delay.

4.7.6 Close-out of forward contracts

If a customer cannot satisfy a forward exchange contract, the bank will make the customer fulfil the contract.

(a) If the customer has arranged for the bank to buy currency but then cannot deliver the currency for the bank to buy, the bank will:

(i) **Sell currency** to the **customer** at the **spot rate** (when the contract falls due for performance)

(ii) Buy the currency back, under the terms of the forward exchange contract

(b) If the customer has contracted for the bank to sell them currency, the bank will:

(i) **Sell** the customer the **specified amount of currency** at the **forward exchange rate**
(ii) **Buy back** the **unwanted currency** at the **spot rate**

Thus, the bank arranges for the customer to perform their part of the forward exchange contract by either selling or buying the 'missing' currency at the spot rate. These arrangements are known as **closing out** a forward exchange contract.

4.8 Money market hedging   12/08, 6/12, 6/13, 6/15

FAST FORWARD

Money market hedging involves borrowing in one currency, converting the money borrowed into another currency and putting the money on deposit until the time the transaction is completed, hoping to take advantage of favourable exchange rate movements.

Because of the close relationship between forward exchange rates and the interest rates in two currencies, it is possible to 'manufacture' a forward rate by using the spot exchange rate and money market lending or borrowing. This technique is known as a **money market hedge** or **synthetic forward**.

4.8.1 Setting up a money market hedge for a foreign currency payment

Suppose a British company needs to **pay** a supplier in Swiss francs in three months' time. It does not have enough cash to pay now, but will do in three months' time. Instead of negotiating a forward contract, the company could:

Step 1   Borrow the appropriate amount in sterling now.

Step 2   Convert the sterling to francs immediately at the spot rate.

Step 3   Put the francs on deposit in a Swiss franc bank account.

Step 4 When the time comes to pay the company:

(a) Pay the supplier out of the franc bank account.

(b) Repay the sterling loan.

The effect is exactly the same as using a forward contract, and will usually cost almost exactly the same amount. If the results from a money market hedge were very different from a forward hedge, speculators could make money without taking a risk. Market forces therefore ensure that the two hedges produce very similar results.

This transaction is called a money market hedge because the company is borrowing and investing in the money markets to create the currency hedge.

4.8.2 Example: Money market hedge (1)

A UK company owes a Danish supplier Kr3,500,000 which is payable in three months' time. The spot exchange rate is Kr7.5509 – Kr7.5548 per £1. The company can borrow in sterling for three months at 8.60% per annum and can deposit kroner for three months at 10% per annum. What is the cost in pounds with a money market hedge and what effective forward rate would this represent?

Solution

The interest rates for three months are 2.15% (= 8.60%/4) to borrow in pounds and 2.5% (= 10%/4) to deposit in kroner. The company needs to deposit enough kroner now so that the total including interest will be Kr3,500,000 in three months' time. This means depositing:

Kr3,500,000/(1 + 0.025) = Kr3,414,634.

These kroner will cost £452,215 (spot rate Kr7.5509 = £1). The company must borrow this amount and, with three months' interest at 2.15%, will have to repay:

£452,215 × (1 + 0.0215) = £461,938.

Thus, in three months, the Danish supplier will be paid out of the Danish bank account and the company will effectively be paying £461,938 to satisfy this debt. The effective forward rate which the company has 'manufactured' is 3,500,000/461,938 = Kr7.5768 = £1. This effective forward rate shows the krone at a discount to sterling because the krone interest rate is higher than the sterling rate.

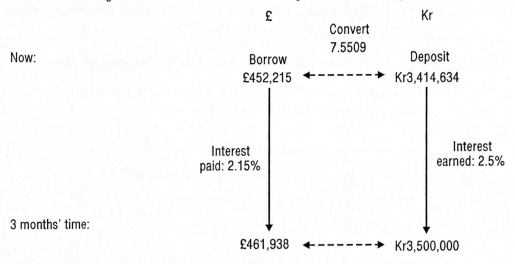

The foreign currency **asset hedges** the foreign currency **liability**.

4.8.3 Setting up a money market hedge for a foreign currency receipt

A similar technique can be used to cover a foreign currency **receipt** from a trade receivable. To manufacture a forward exchange rate, follow the steps below.

Step 1   Borrow an appropriate amount in the foreign currency today.

Step 2   Convert it immediately to home currency at the spot rate.

Step 3   Place this on deposit in the home currency.

Step 4   When the receivable's cash is received:
  (a)   Repay the foreign currency loan.
  (b)   Take the cash from the home currency deposit account.

4.8.4 Example: Money market hedge (2)

A UK company is owed SFr 2,500,000, receivable in 3 months' time from a Swiss company. The spot exchange rate is SFr1.4498 – SFr1.4510 per £1. The company can deposit in sterling for 3 months at 8.00% per annum and can borrow Swiss francs for 3 months at 7.00% per annum. What is the receipt in sterling with a money market hedge and what effective forward rate would this represent?

Solution

The interest rates for 3 months are 2.00% to deposit in sterling and 1.75% to borrow in Swiss francs. The company should borrow SFr2,500,000/1.0175 = SFr 2,457,002 today. After 3 months, SFr 2,500,000 will be repayable, including interest.

These Swiss francs will be converted to £ at 2,457,002/1.4510 = £1,693,316. The company must deposit this amount for 3 months, when it will have increased in value with interest (2% for the three months) to:

£1,693,316 × 1.02 = £1,727,182

Thus, in 3 months, the loan will be repaid out of the proceeds from the trade receivable and the company will receive £1,727,182. The effective forward rate which the company has 'manufactured' is 2,500,000/1,727,182 = SFr1.4474 = £1. This effective forward rate shows the Swiss franc at a premium to the pound because the Swiss franc interest rate is lower than the sterling rate.

```
                           SFr                              £

                                      Convert
Now:                    Borrow         2.2510      Deposit
                        SFr 2,457,002 <-------->   £1,091,516


                        Interest                   Interest
                        paid: 1.75%                earned: 2.0%



                           SFr        <-------->   £1,113,346
3 months' time:         2,500,000
```

4.9 Choosing between a forward contract and a money market hedge

The choice between a forward contract and a money market hedge is generally made on the basis of which method is **cheaper**, with other factors being of limited significance.

4.9.1 Choosing the hedging method

When a company expects to receive or pay a sum of foreign currency in the next few months, it can choose between using the **forward exchange market** and the **money market** to hedge against the foreign exchange risk. Other methods may also be possible, such as **making lead payments**. The cheapest method available is the one that ought to be chosen.

Often, the costs of using a forward contract and money market hedge are very similar. In such cases, transaction costs must be considered.

4.9.2 Example: Choosing the cheapest method

Trumpton plc has bought goods from a US supplier, and must pay $4,000,000 for them in three months' time. The company's finance director wishes to hedge against the foreign exchange risk, and the three methods which the company usually considers are:

- Using **forward exchange contracts**
- Using **money market borrowing or lending**
- Making **lead payments**

The following annual interest rates and exchange rates are currently available.

	US dollar		Sterling	
	Deposit rate	Borrowing rate	Deposit rate	Borrowing rate
	%	%	%	%
1 month	7	10.25	10.75	14.00
3 months	7	10.75	11.00	14.25

	Exchange rate per £1
Spot	$1.8625 – $1.8635
1 month forward	$1.8565 – $1.8577
3 months forward	$1.8445 – $1.8460

Which is the cheapest method for Trumpton plc? Ignore commission costs (the bank charges for arranging a forward contract or a loan).

Solution

The three choices must be compared on a similar basis, which means working out the cost of each to Trumpton either now or in three months' time. In the following paragraphs, the cost to Trumpton now will be determined.

Choice 1: The forward exchange market

Trumpton must buy dollars in order to pay the US supplier. The exchange rate in a forward exchange contract to buy $4,000,000 in 3 months' time (bank sells) is $1.8445 = £1.

The cost of the $4,000,000 to Trumpton in 3 months' time will be:

$$\frac{\$4,000,000}{1.8445} = £2,168,609.38$$

This is the cost in **three months**. To work out the cost now, we could say that by deferring payment for three months, the company is:

- Saving having to borrow money now at 14.25% a year to make the payment now; or
- Avoiding the loss of interest on cash on deposit, earning 11% a year.

The choice depends on whether Trumpton plc (a) needs to borrow to make any current payment or (b) is cash rich. Here, assumption (a) is selected, but (b) might in fact apply.

At an annual interest rate of 14.25% the rate for 3 months is 14.25/4 = 3.5625%. The 'present cost' of £2,168,609.38 in 3 months' time is:

$$\frac{£2,168,609.38}{1.035625} = £2,094,010.26$$

Choice 2: The money markets

Using the money markets involves:

(a) **Borrowing in the foreign currency**, if the company will eventually receive the currency

(b) **Lending in the foreign currency**, if the company will eventually pay the currency. Here, Trumpton will pay $4,000,000 and so it would lend US dollars.

It would lend enough US dollars for 3 months, so that the principal repaid in 3 months' time plus interest will amount to the payment due of $4,000,000.

(a) Since the US dollar deposit rate is 7%, the rate for 3 months is approximately 7/4 = 1.75%.

(b) To earn $4,000,000 in 3 months' time at 1.75% interest, Trumpton would have to lend now:

$$\frac{\$4,000,000}{1.0175} = \$3,931,203.93$$

These dollars would have to be purchased now at the spot rate of (bank sells) $1.8625 = £1. The cost would be:

$$\frac{\$3,931,203.93}{1.8625} = £2,110,713.52$$

By lending US dollars for three months, Trumpton is matching eventual receipts and payments in US dollars, and so has hedged against foreign exchange risk.

Choice 3: Lead payments

Lead payments should be considered when the currency of payment is expected to strengthen over time, and is quoted forward at a premium on the foreign exchange market. Here, the cost of a lead payment (paying $4,000,000 now) would be $4,000,000 ÷ 1.8625 = £2,147,651.01.

Summary

	£
Forward exchange contract	2,094,010.26 (cheapest)
Currency lending	2,110,713.52
Lead payment	2,147,651.01

Exam focus point

> If the exam question includes payments and receipts in the same foreign currency at the same time, the payments and receipts can be netted off against each other.

5 Foreign currency derivatives

FAST FORWARD

> **Foreign currency derivatives** can be used to hedge foreign currency risk. **Futures contracts, options** and **swaps** are types of derivative.

5.1 Currency futures

FAST FORWARD

> **Currency futures** are standardised contracts for the sale or purchase at a set future date of a set quantity of currency.

Currency futures can be used to hedge currency risk in the same way as forward contracts. Futures are exchange-traded instruments whereas forward contracts are over the counter transactions. Forward contracts are used much more extensively than currency futures.

Key term

> A **currency future** is a standardised, market-traded contract to buy or sell a specified quantity of foreign currency.

The following table summarises the differences between currency futures and forward contracts.

Currency futures	Forward contracts
Standard contracts	Bespoke contracts
Traded on the open market (futures exchange)	Traded over the counter
Contract price in US dollars	Contract price in any currency offered by the bank
Flexible close out dates	Fixed date of settlement
Underlying transactions take place at the spot rate; the difference between the spot rate and futures rate is settled between two parties	Underlying transactions take place at the forward rate
Cheaper than forwards	Relatively high premium required

A **futures market** is an exchange-traded market for the purchase or sale of a standard quantity of an underlying item, such as currencies, commodities or shares, for settlement at a future date and at an agreed price.

The **contract size** is the fixed minimum quantity of commodity which can be bought or sold using a futures contract. In general, dealing on futures markets must be in a **whole number** of contracts.

The **contract price** is the price at which the futures contract can be bought or sold. For all currency futures the contract price is in US dollars. The contract price is the figure which is traded on the futures exchange. It changes continuously and is the basis for computing gains or losses.

The **settlement date** (or delivery date, or expiry date) is the date when trading on a particular futures contract stops and all accounts are settled. On the International Monetary Market (IMM), the settlement dates for all currency futures are at the end of March, June, September and December.

A future's price may be different from the spot price, and this difference is the **basis**.

Basis = Spot price – Futures price

One **tick** is the smallest measured movement in the contract price. For currency futures this is a movement in the fourth decimal place.

Market traders will compute gains or losses on their futures positions by reference to the number of ticks by which the contract price has moved.

5.1.1 Example: Futures contract

Exam focus point

> You will **not** be expected to do futures calculations in the exam but the following example will help you to understand how they work.

A US company buys goods worth €720,000 from a German company payable in 30 days. The US company wants to hedge against the € strengthening against the dollar.

Current spot is $0.9215 – $0.9221 per €1 and the € futures rate is $0.9245 per €1.

The standard size of a three-month € futures contract is €125,000.

In 30 days' time the spot is $0.9345 – $0.9351 per €1.

Closing futures price will be $0.9367 per €1.

Evaluate the hedge.

Solution

Step 1 **Setup**

   (a) **Which contract?**

       We assume that the three month contract is the best available.

   (b) **Type of contract**

       We need to buy € or sell $.

       As the futures contract is in €, we need to buy futures.

   (c) **Number of contracts**

$$\frac{720,000}{125,000} = 5.76, \text{ say 6 contracts}$$

   (d) **Tick size**

       Minimum price movement × contract size = 0.0001 × 125,000 = \$12.50

Step 2 **Closing futures price**

We're told it will be 0.9367.

Step 3 **Hedge outcome**

   (a) **Outcome in futures market**

Opening futures price	0.9245	Buy at low price
Closing futures price	0.9367	Sell at high price
Movement in ticks	122 ticks	Profit
Futures profit/loss	122 × \$12.50 × 6 contracts = \$9,150	

   (b) **Net outcome**

	$
Spot market payment (720,000 × 0.9351 $/£)	673,272
Futures market profit	(9,150)
	664,122

5.1.2 Advantages of futures

(a) **Transaction** costs should be **lower** than other hedging methods.

(b) Futures are **tradeable** and can be bought and sold on a secondary market so there is **pricing transparency**, unlike forward contracts where prices are set by financial institutions.

(c) The **exact date** of **receipt** or **payment** of the currency does **not have to be known**, because the futures contract does not have to be closed out until the actual cash receipt or payment is made.

5.1.3 Disadvantages of futures

(a) The **contracts cannot be tailored** to the user's exact requirements.

(b) **Hedge inefficiencies** are caused by having to deal in a **whole number of contracts** and by **basis risk** (the risk that the futures contract price may move by a different amount from the price of the underlying currency or commodity).

(c) Only a **limited number of currencies** are the subject of futures contracts (although the number of currencies is growing, especially with the rapid development of Asian economies).

(d) Unlike options (see below), they do not allow a company to take advantage of favourable currency movements.

5.2 Currency options

FAST FORWARD

Currency options protect against **adverse exchange rate movements** while allowing the investor to take advantage of favourable exchange rate movements. They are particularly useful in situations where the cash flow is not certain to occur (eg when tendering for overseas contracts).

Key term

A currency **option** is a right of an option holder to buy (call) or sell (put) a quantity of one currency in exchange for another, at a specific exchange rate (the exercise rate, exercise price or strike price) on or before a future expiry date. If a buyer exercises the option, the option seller must sell or buy at this rate. If an option is not exercised, it lapses at the expiry date.

The exercise price for the option may be the same as the current spot rate, or it may be more favourable or less favourable to the option holder than the current spot rate.

Companies can choose whether to buy:

(a) A tailor-made currency option from a bank, suited to the company's specific needs. These are **over the counter** (OTC) or **negotiated** options; or

(b) A standard option, in certain currencies only, from an options exchange. Such options are **traded** or **exchange-traded** options.

Because of the flexibility offered by currency options – the holder can exercise the option at any point, or choose to sell the option – it allows the holder to enjoy the upside without a risk of suffering the downside.

However, buying a currency option involves **paying a premium to the option seller**. The option premium is a cost of using an option. It is the most the buyer of the option can lose by hedging an exposure to currency risk with an option: this maximum loss occurs if the option is not exercised, but is allowed to lapse.

5.2.1 Example: Currency options

Currency options will be exercised by the option holder only if the exercise rate in the option is more favourable than the spot rate at the exercise date for the option.

For example, a company may buy a currency call option, giving it the right to buy US$6,000,000 in 2 months' time in exchange for sterling at an exercise rate of $1.5000. Buying the dollars at this rate would cost £4,000,000.

(a) If the spot exchange rate at the exercise date is $1.60, the option holder will let the option lapse and will buy the dollars at the spot rate for £3,750,000.

(b) If the spot exchange rate at the exercise date is $1.40, the option holder will exercise the option and will buy the dollars at the exercise rate of $1.50. (Buying at the spot rate would cost £4,285,714.)

Similarly, a company may buy a currency put option, giving it the right to sell US$2,800,000 in 2 months' time in exchange for sterling at an exercise rate of $1.4000. The dollars could be sold at this rate for £2,000,000.

(a) If the spot exchange rate at the exercise date is $1.35, the option holder will let the option lapse and will sell the dollars at the spot rate for £2,074,074.

(b) If the spot exchange rate at the exercise date is $1.45, the option holder will exercise the option and will sell the dollars at the exercise rate of $1.40. (Selling at the spot rate would earn £1,931,034.)

5.2.2 The purposes of currency options

The purpose of currency options is to reduce or eliminate exposure to currency risks, and they are particularly useful for companies in the following situations.

(a) Where there is **uncertainty** about **foreign currency receipts or payments**, either in timing or amount. Should the foreign exchange transaction not materialise, the option can be sold on the market (if it has any value) or exercised if this would make a profit.

(b) To **support the tender** for an **overseas contract** by a company, priced in a foreign currency. The option would be to sell the currency earned from the contract. If the company does not win the contract, it can let the option lapse (or make a profit on a favourable movement in the spot rate). In this situation, an option would be preferable to a binding forward contract, because it does not know whether or not it will need to sell any currency.

(c) To allow **the publication of price lists** for its goods **in a foreign currency**. A company can arrange a number of currency options to sell a quantity of the foreign currency in exchange for its domestic currency, covering the time period for which the price list remains valid.

In both situations (b) and (c), the company would not know whether it had won any export sales or would have any foreign currency income at the time that it announces its selling prices. It cannot make a forward exchange contract to sell foreign currency without becoming exposed in the currency.

5.2.3 Drawbacks of currency options

- They have a cost (the 'option premium'). The **cost** depends on the **expected volatility** of the **exchange rate**, the choice of **exercise rate** and **the length of time to the expiry date for the option**.
- Options must be paid for **as soon** as they are **bought**.
- **Tailor-made** options (arranged over the counter with a bank) **lack negotiability**.
- Traded options are **not available** in **every currency**.

5.3 Currency swaps

FAST FORWARD

Currency swaps effectively involve the exchange of debt from one currency to another.

Currency swaps can provide a **hedge** against exchange rate movements for longer periods than the forward market, and can be a means of obtaining finance from new countries.

Key term

A **swap** is a formal agreement whereby two organisations contractually agree to exchange payments on different terms, eg in different currencies, or one at a fixed rate and the other at a floating rate.

In a **currency swap**, the parties agree to swap equivalent amounts of currency for a period. This effectively involves the exchange of debt from one currency to another. Liability on the main debt (the principal) is not transferred and the parties are liable to **counterparty risk**: if the other party defaults on the agreement to pay interest, the original borrower remains liable to the lender.

Consider a UK company X with a subsidiary Y in France which owns vineyards. Assume a spot rate of £1 = 1.6 euros. Suppose the parent company X wishes to raise a loan of 1.6 million euros for the purpose of buying another French wine company. At the same time, the French subsidiary Y wishes to raise £1 million to pay for new up to date capital equipment imported from the UK. The UK parent company X could borrow the £1 million sterling and the French subsidiary Y could borrow the 1.6 million euros, each effectively borrowing on the other's behalf. They would then swap currencies.

5.3.1 Benefits of currency swaps

(a) Swaps are **easy to arrange** and are **flexible** since they can be arranged in any size.

(b) **Transaction costs are low**, only amounting to legal fees, since there is no commission or premium to be paid.

(c) The parties can **obtain the currency they require** without subjecting themselves to the **uncertainties** of the spot foreign exchange markets.

(d) The company can gain **access to debt finance in another country** and currency where it is little known, and consequently has a poorer credit rating, than in its home country. It can therefore take advantage of lower interest rates than it could obtain if it arranged the currency loan itself.

(e) Currency swaps may be used to **restructure the currency base** of the company's liabilities. This may be important where the company is trading overseas and receiving revenues in foreign currencies, but its borrowings are denominated in the currency of its home country. Currency swaps therefore provide a means of reducing exchange rate exposure.

(f) A currency swap could be used to **absorb excess liquidity** in one currency which is not needed immediately in order to create funds in another where there is a need.

In practice, most currency swaps are conducted between banks and their customers. An agreement should only be necessary if the swap were for longer than, say, one year. For shorter periods, a forward exchange contract should be arranged if a currency hedge is required.

5.3.2 Example: Currency swap

Step 1 Edted, a UK company, wishes to invest in Germany. It borrows £20 million from its bank and pays interest at 5%. To invest in Germany, the £20 million will be converted into euros at a spot rate of £1 = €1.50. The earnings from the German investment will be in euros, but Edted will have to pay interest on the swap. The company arranges to swap the £20 million for €30 million with Gordonbear, a company in the euro currency zone. Gordonbear is thus the counterparty in this transaction. Interest of 6% is payable on the €30 million. Edted can use the €30 million it receives to invest in Germany.

Step 2 Each year when interest is due:

(a) Edted receives from its German investment cash remittances of €1.8 million (€30 million × 6%).

(b) Edted passes this €1.8 million to Gordonbear so that Gordonbear can settle its interest liability.

(c) Gordonbear passes to Edted £1 million (£20 million × 5%).

(d) Edted settles its interest liability of £1 million with its lender.

Step 3 At the end of the useful life of the investment the original payments are reversed with Edted paying back the €30 million it originally received and receiving back from Gordonbear the £20 million. Edted uses this £20 million to repay the loan it originally received from its UK lender.

Chapter Roundup

- **Currency risk** is the risk of changes in an exchange rate or in the foreign exchange value of a currency. It is a two-way risk.

  Currency risk occurs in three forms: **transaction exposure** (short-term), **economic exposure** (effect on present value of longer-term cash flows) and **translation exposure** (book gains or losses).

- Factors influencing the exchange rate include the comparative rates of inflation in different countries (**purchasing power parity**), comparative interest rates in different countries (**interest rate parity**), the underlying balance of payments, speculation and government policy on managing or fixing exchange rates.

- Foreign currency risk can be managed, in order to reduce or eliminate the risk. Measures to reduce currency risk are known as 'hedging'.

  Basic methods of hedging risk include **matching receipts and payments**, **invoicing in own currency**, and **leading and lagging** the times that cash is received and paid. Other common hedging methods are the use of forward exchange contracts and money market hedging.

- A forward exchange contract is a contract made now for the purchase or sale of a quantity of currency in exchange for another currency, for settlement at a future date, and at a rate of exchange that is fixed in the contract.

  A **forward contract** therefore fixes in advance the rate at which a specified quantity of currency will be bought and sold.

- **Money market hedging** involves borrowing in one currency, converting the money borrowed into another currency and putting the money on deposit until the time the transaction is completed, hoping to take advantage of favourable exchange rate movements.

- The choice between a forward contract and a money market hedge is generally made on the basis of which method is **cheaper**, with other factors being of limited significance.

- **Foreign currency derivatives** can be used to hedge foreign currency risk. **Futures contracts, options** and **swaps** are types of derivative.

- **Currency futures** are standardised contracts for the sale or purchase at a set future date of a set quantity of currency.

- **Currency options** protect against **adverse exchange rate movements** while allowing the investor to take advantage of favourable exchange rate movements. They are particularly useful in situations where the cash flow is not certain to occur (eg when tendering for overseas contracts).

- **Currency swaps** effectively involve the exchange of debt from one currency to another.

  Currency swaps can provide a **hedge** against exchange rate movements for longer periods than the forward market, and can be a means of obtaining finance from new countries.

1 Identify the three types of currency risk.

2 Define a 'forward exchange rate'.

3 The principle of purchasing power parity must always hold.

True ☐

False ☐

4 Fill in the blanks.

(a) Forward rate higher than spot rate is quoted at a _____

(b) Forward rate lower than spot rate is quoted at a _____

5 Name three methods of foreign currency risk management.

6 Name three types of foreign currency derivative used to hedge foreign currency risk.

1 (a) Transaction risk
   (b) Translation risk
   (c) Economic risk

2 An exchange rate set for the exchange of currencies at some future date

3 False. In reality commodity prices do differ significantly in different countries.

4 (a) Discount
   (b) Premium

5 Any three of:

   (a) Currency of invoice
   (b) Netting and matching
   (c) Leading and lagging
   (d) Forward exchange contracts
   (e) Money market hedging
   (f) Asset and liability management

6 (a) Currency futures
   (b) Currency options
   (c) Currency swaps

Now try the questions below from the Practice Question Bank

Number	Level	Marks	Approximate time
Section A Q31	Examination	2	4 mins
Section C Q23	Examination	20	39 mins

Interest rate risk

Topic list	Syllabus reference
1 Interest rates	G1 (b)
2 Interest rate risk	G1 (b)
3 The causes of interest rate fluctuations	G2 (c)
4 Interest rate risk management	G4 (a)
5 Interest rate derivatives	G4 (b)

Introduction

Here we consider **interest rate risk** and some of the financial instruments which are now available for managing financial risks, including **derivatives** such as **options**. However, the risk of interest rate changes is less significant in most cases than the risk of currency fluctuations. If the risk of currency fluctuations is not hedged, it can in some cases fairly easily wipe out profits.

Study guide

		Intellectual level
G1	**The nature and types of risk and approaches to risk management**	
(b)	Describe and discuss different types of interest rate risk:	1
(i)	Gap exposure	
(ii)	Basis risk	
G2	**Causes of exchange rate differences and interest rate fluctuations**	
(c)	Describe the causes of interest rate fluctuations, including:	2
(i)	Structure of interest rates and yield curves	
(ii)	Expectations theory	
(iii)	Liquidity preference theory	
(iv)	Market segmentation	
G4	**Hedging techniques for interest rate risk**	
(a)	Discuss and apply traditional and basic methods of interest rate risk management, including:	
(i)	Matching and smoothing	1
(ii)	Asset and liability management	1
(iii)	Forward rate agreements	2
(b)	Identify the main types of interest rate derivatives used to hedge interest rate risk and explain how they are used in hedging.	1

Exam guide

The material in this chapter, if it appears in a Section B question, will be examined almost entirely as a discussion question. It is important that you understand and can explain the terminology.

1 Interest rates

FAST FORWARD

The **interest rates** on financial assets are influenced by the **risk** of the assets, the **duration** of the lending, and the **size** of the loan.

There is a **trade-off** between **risk and return**. Investors in riskier assets expect to be compensated for the risk.

Interest rates are effectively prices for lending and costs for borrowing. We discussed interest rates in Section 4 of Chapter 3.

2 Interest rate risk

FAST FORWARD

Interest rate risk relates to the sensitivity of profit and cash flows to changes in interest rates.

Interest rate risk is faced by companies with floating (variable) and fixed rate debt. It can arise from **gap exposure** and **basis risk**.

Interest rate risk is the risk of a change in interest rates, and the effect that this will have on profits and cash flows. This type of risk is greatest for organisations with large amounts of assets that yield interest or liabilities on which interest is payable. Banks and investment institutions are therefore heavily exposed to interest rate risk, but so too are companies with large borrowings.

An organisation will need to analyse how its profits and cash flows might be affected by changes in interest rates and decide whether to take action to hedge the exposure to the risk.

2.1 Floating interest rate debt

The most common form of interest rate risk faced by a non-bank company is the **volatility of cash flows** associated with a high proportion of **floating** interest rate debt (also known as variable interest rate debt). Interest rates on this debt will rise or fall in line with changes in a benchmark interest rate, such as the bank's base rate or the London Interbank Offered Rate (LIBOR).

Some interest rate risks to which a firm is exposed may **cancel each other out**, where it has both assets and liabilities that are sensitive to changes in interest rates. If interest rates rise, more interest will be payable on loans and other liabilities, but this will be **compensated for** by higher interest received on assets, such as money market deposits.

2.2 Fixed interest rate debt

A company with a high proportion of fixed interest rate debt has a commitment to fixed interest payments. If interest rates fall sharply, the company will suffer from a loss of **competitive advantage** compared with companies using floating rate borrowing whose interest costs and cost of capital will fall.

This means that a company with fixed rate debt has exposure to interest rate risk, just as a company with floating rate debt is exposed to interest rate risk.

2.3 Gap exposure

The degree to which a firm is exposed to interest rate risk can be identified by using the method of **gap analysis**. Gap analysis is based on the principle of **grouping together** assets and liabilities which are sensitive to interest rate changes according to their maturity dates. Two different types of 'gap' may occur.

(a) **A negative gap**

   A negative gap occurs when a firm has a larger amount of interest-sensitive liabilities maturing at a certain time or in a certain period than it has interest-sensitive assets maturing at the same time. The difference between the two amounts indicates the net exposure.

(b) **A positive gap**

   There is a positive gap if the amount of interest-sensitive assets maturing at a particular time exceeds the amount of interest-sensitive liabilities maturing at the same time.

With a **negative** gap, the company faces exposure if interest rates **rise** by the time of maturity. With a **positive** gap, the company will lose out if interest rates **fall** by maturity.

2.4 Basis risk

It may appear that a company which has size-matched assets and liabilities, and is both receiving and paying interest, may not have any interest rate exposure. However, the two floating rates may not be determined using the same **basis** or **benchmark**. For example, one loan may be linked to one-month LIBOR and the other to six-month LIBOR.

Key term

> **LIBOR** or the London Interbank Offered Rate is the rate of interest applying to wholesale money market lending between London banks. There are different LIBOR rates for loans and deposits with different maturities.

Basis risk makes it unlikely that the two floating rates will move perfectly **in line** with each other. As one rate increases, the other rate may change by a different amount or may change later.

3 The causes of interest rate fluctuations

> The **causes** of interest rate fluctuations include the **structure of interest rates and yield curves** and changing economic factors.

3.1 The structure of interest rates   12/13

There are several reasons why interest rates differ in different markets and market segments.

(a) **Risk**

Higher risk borrowers must pay higher rates on their borrowing, to compensate lenders for the greater risk involved. For example, governments can borrow at lower rates than companies, because lending to government is generally considered a much lower risk. Similarly, lending to a large listed company is less risky than lending to a small start-up business, and large companies can therefore borrow at a much lower cost.

(b) **The need to make a profit on re-lending**

Financial intermediaries make their profits from re-lending at a higher rate of interest than the cost of their borrowing.

(c) **The size of the loan**

Deposits above a certain amount with a bank or building society may attract higher rates of interest than smaller deposits.

(d) **Different types of financial asset**

Different types of financial asset attract different rates of interest. This is largely because of the competition for deposits between different types of financial institution.

(e) **The duration of the lending**. This is discussed below.

3.1.1 The term structure of interest rates

The **term structure of interest rates** refers to the way in which the yield on a security varies according to the term of the borrowing. The interest rate for different maturities of a debt security can be shown graphically in a **yield curve**.

(a) Normally, the longer the term to maturity, the higher the rate of interest. This is shown by the **normal yield curve** in the diagram below.

(b) Occasionally, interest rates may be higher for short-term maturities than longer-term maturities. When this happens, there is a **negative yield curve**, which is also illustrated in the diagram below.

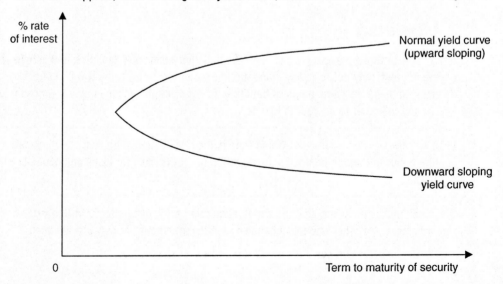

There are several different reasons why interest rates on a debt security or loan may differ for different maturities.

(a) **Liquidity preference theory** provides a reason why, in theory, the yield curve is normally upward sloping, so that long-term financial assets offer a higher yield than short-term assets.

Liquidity preference means that investors prefer having cash now to deferring the use of the cash by lending or investing it. Investors also prefer having cash sooner to having cash later. They therefore want **compensation** in the form of a **higher return** for being unable to use their cash now. The required return increases with the length of time for which the cash is unavailable. Because of this, long-term interest rates, such as bond yields, tend to be higher than short-term yields, and the yield curve slopes upward.

(b) **Expectations theory** states that interest rates reflect expectations of future changes in interest rates. If interest rates are expected to rise in the future, the yield curve will slope upwards. When interest rates are expected to fall, short-term rates may be higher than long-term rates, and the yield curve downward sloping. Thus, the shape of the yield curve gives an indication about how interest rates are expected to move in the future.

(c) The **market segmentation theory** of interest rates suggests that the slope of the yield curve will reflect conditions in different segments of the market. This theory holds that the major investors are confined to a particular segment of the market and will not switch segment even if the forecast of likely future interest rates changes.

(d) **Government policy** on interest rates may be significant too. A government policy of keeping interest rates relatively high may have the effect of forcing short-term interest rates higher than long-term rates. Similarly, a government may have a policy of very low short-term interest rates. In the US, the eurozone and the UK, the central banks are responsible for managing short-term interest rates, through the rates at which the central bank lends to banks.

3.2 The general level of interest rates

Interest rates on any one type of financial asset will vary over time. In other words, the general level of interest rates might go up or down. The general level of interest rates is affected by several factors.

(a) **Need for a real return**

Investors normally want to **earn a 'real' rate of return** on their investment. The appropriate 'real' rate of return will depend on such factors as investment risk.

(b) **Inflation**

Nominal rates of interest should be sufficient to **cover expected rates of inflation** over the term of the investment and to provide a real return.

(c) **Uncertainty about future rates of inflation**

When investors are uncertain about inflation and therefore about what future nominal and real interest rates will be, they are likely to require **higher interest yields** to persuade them to take the risk of investing, especially in the longer term.

(d) **Liquidity preference of investors and the demand for borrowing**

Higher interest rates have to be offered to persuade savers to invest their surplus money. When the demand to borrow increases, interest rates will rise.

(e) **Balance of payments**

When a country has a continuing deficit on the current account of its balance of payments, and the authorities are unwilling to allow the exchange rate to depreciate by more than a certain amount, interest rates may have to be raised to **attract capital** into the country. The country can then finance the deficit by borrowing from abroad.

(f)   **Monetary policy**

As explained above, the monetary policy of a government may be to try to control the rate of inflation through management of short-term interest rates. This is done by the central bank, which can control very short-term interest rates through the rates at which it lends to banks. However, although the central bank can act to change just short-term interest rates, it may expect that increases or reductions in short-term rates will eventually work through to increases or reductions in longer-term interest rates.

3.3 Interest rate risk management   12/08, 12/12

Exam focus point

You may find it useful to read the article called Hedging Techniques for Interest Rate Risk on the ACCA website.

FAST FORWARD

Interest rate risk can be managed using **internal hedging** in the form of asset and liability management, matching and smoothing or using **external hedging** instruments, such as forward rate agreements and interest rate derivatives.

3.4 Asset and liability management

Fixed interest rates for payments or earnings may have different maturity time scales. Asset and liability management aims to achieve similar durations for payments and earnings. For example, say a business has a 10 year mortgage on a building at a fixed rate of interest of 5% per year. It rents out the building for 6 years at a rate of 7% per year. This is fine for 6 years but then if rental yields fall to 4% per year, the business will start to lose money. A safer option would have been to match the loan period to the rental period.

3.5 Matching and smoothing

Matching and smoothing are two methods of **internal hedging** used to manage interest rate risk.

Key term

Matching is where liabilities and assets with a common interest rate are matched.

For example, subsidiary A of a company might be investing in the money markets at LIBOR and subsidiary B is borrowing through the same market at LIBOR. If LIBOR increases, subsidiary A's borrowing cost increases and subsidiary B's returns increase. The **interest rates** on the assets and liabilities are therefore **matched**.

This method is most widely used by financial institutions, such as banks, who find it easier to match the magnitudes and characteristics of their assets and liabilities than commercial or industrial companies.

Key term

Smoothing is where a company keeps a **balance** between its fixed rate and floating rate borrowing. Some loans or deposits have fixed rates of interest and some have variable rates.

A rise in interest rates will make the variable rate loan more expensive but this will be **compensated** for by the less expensive fixed rate loan. However, the company may incur increased transaction and arrangement costs.

Major companies with large amounts of borrowing may try to maintain a balance between fixed rate and floating rate debt.

3.6 Forward rate agreements (FRAs)   6/15

FAST FORWARD

Forward rate agreements hedge risk by **fixing the interest rate** on future short-term borrowing.

A forward rate agreement (FRA) for interest rates is similar in many respects to a forward exchange contract for currencies.

- FRAs are arranged with a bank as an over the counter transaction.

- An FRA is a binding contract that fixes an interest rate for short-term lending/investing or short-term borrowing, for an interest rate period that begins at a future date.

In other words, an FRA fixes an interest rate now for a future short-term lending/investing/borrowing transaction.

However, an FRA is not an agreement to lend or borrow. It is an agreement that fixes an interest rate on a notional amount of principal.

A company can enter into a FRA with a bank that **fixes the rate of interest** for short-term borrowing from a certain time in the future. If the actual interest rate at that date proves to be higher than the rate in the FRA, the bank pays the company the difference. If the actual interest rate is lower than the FRA rate, the company pays the bank the difference. The FRA does not need to be with the same bank as the loan, as the FRA is a hedging method independent of any loan agreement.

One **limitation** of FRAs is that they are usually only available on large loans. They are also likely to be **difficult to obtain for periods of over one year**.

An **advantage** of FRAs is that, for the period of the FRA at least, they **protect the borrower** from adverse market interest rate movements to levels above the rate negotiated for the FRA. With a normal variable rate loan (for example linked to a bank's base rate or to LIBOR) the borrower is exposed to the risk of such adverse market movements. On the other hand, the borrower will similarly not benefit from the effects of favourable market interest rate movements.

The **interest rates** for which banks arrange FRAs will reflect their current expectations of interest rate movements. If it is expected that interest rates are going to rise during the term for which the FRA is being negotiated, the bank is likely to seek a higher FRA rate than the spot rate of interest which is current at the time of negotiating the FRA.

3.6.1 FRA terminology

The terminology is as follows.

(a) 5.75-5.70 means that you can fix a borrowing rate at 5.75% (and a deposit rate at 5.70%). The interest rate in the FRA will be compared with a reference rate or benchmark rate of interest, which is specified by the FRA agreement. The reference rate may be, for example, the 3-month LIBOR rate or the 6-month LIBOR rate.

(b) A '3-6' forward rate agreement is an agreement that fixes an interest rate for a period starting in 3 months' time and lasting for 3 months to the end of month 6. Similarly, a '3-12' FRA fixes the interest rate for a 9-month period starting in 3 months' time.

(c) A basis point is 0.01%.

3.6.2 Example: Forward rate agreement

Lynn plc is a UK listed company. It is 30 June. Lynn will need a £10 million 6-month fixed rate loan from 1 October. Lynn wants to hedge its exposure to the risk of a rise in the 6-month interest rate between the end of June and 1 October, using an FRA. The relevant FRA rate is 6% on 30 June and the reference rate for the FRA is the 6-month LIBOR rate. The current 6-month FRA rate is 6.25%.

(a) State what FRA is required.

(b) What is the result of the FRA and the effective loan rate if the spot 6-month LIBOR rate (the benchmark or reference rate for the FRA) is:

(i) 5%
(ii) 9%

Solution

(a) The FRA required is '3-9'. It is for a period beginning after 3 months and lasting for 6 months. The FRA is for Lynn to borrow a notional sum of £10 million for 6 months at a fixed rate of 6%, starting on 1 October.

Lynn has fixed the effective borrowing rate with the FRA, even though it may not be borrowing the £10 million from the bank that has arranged the FRA.

(b) (i) If the 6-month LIBOR rate on 1 October is 5%, the LIBOR rate will have fallen since 30 June. The FRA is a binding contract, so Lynn must borrow the notional sum of £10 million for 6 months at 6%. In practice, there is no actual lending. Instead, Lynn makes a payment for the difference between interest for 6 months at the FRA rate of 6% and the spot rate of 5%.

The payment is £10 million $\times$ (6% − 5%) $\times\,^{6}/_{12}$ = £50,000.

Let's suppose that Lynn is able to borrow for 6 months at the LIBOR rate. It will borrow £10 million on 1 October for 6 months at an interest rate of 5%. Taking the cost of the actual loan interest with the cost of the FRA payment, the effective cost of borrowing for the 6 months is an annual rate of 6%. This is the rate in the FRA.

	£
FRA payment £10 million $\times$ (6% − 5%) $\times\,^{6}/_{12}$	(50,000)
Interest payment on actual loan 5% $\times$ £10 million $\times\,^{6}/_{12}$	(250,000)
Total cost	(300,000)
Effective annual interest rate on loan	6%

(ii) If the 6-month LIBOR rate on 1 October is 9%, the LIBOR rate will have fallen since 30 June. To settle the FRA contract, the bank must pay Lynn: £10 million $\times$ (9% − 6%) $\times\,^{6}/_{12}$ = £150,000.

Let's suppose again that Lynn is able to borrow for 6 months at the LIBOR rate. It will borrow £10 million on 1 October for 6 months at an interest rate of 9%. Taking the cost of the actual loan interest with the revenue from the FRA contract, the effective cost of borrowing for the 6 months is an annual rate of 6%. This is the rate in the FRA.

	£
FRA receipt £10 million $\times$ (9% − 6%) $\times\,^{6}/_{12}$	150,000
Payment on actual loan at market rate 9% $\times$ £10 million $\times\,^{6}/_{12}$	(450,000)
Net payment	(300,000)
Effective interest rate on loan	6%

Note that the FRA and loan need not be with the same bank.

> **Exam focus point**
>
> The examiner's report for the June 2015 exam noted that many students gained very low marks in Q1(b). This 5-mark question asked for an explanation of the nature of a forward rate agreement (FRA) and how it can be used to manage interest rate risk. Many students thought that a FRA was a forward exchange contract and discussed exchange rate risk instead of interest rate risk. Make sure you read questions carefully and try not to confuse interest rate and exchange rate risk.

4 Interest rate derivatives

FAST FORWARD

Interest rate derivatives can be used to hedge against the risk of interest rate changes. They include interest rate futures, interest rate options and interest rate swaps.

4.1 Interest rate futures

Interest rate futures offer a means of hedging against the risk of interest rate movements. Such contracts are effectively a gamble on whether interest rates will rise or fall. Like other futures contracts, interest rate futures offer a way in which **speculators can 'bet'** on market movements just as they offer others who are more risk averse a way of **hedging risks**.

Interest rate futures are similar in effect to FRAs, except that the terms, amounts and periods are **standardised**. For example, a company can contract to buy (or sell) £100,000 of a notional 30-year Treasury bond bearing an 8% coupon in, say, 6 months' time, at an agreed price. The basic principles behind such a decision are:

(a)   The futures price is likely to vary with changes in interest rates, and this acts as a **hedge** against adverse interest rate movements.

(b)   The outlay to buy futures is much less than for buying the financial instrument itself, and so a company can hedge large exposures of cash with a relatively **small initial employment of cash**.

4.1.1 Nature of interest rate futures contracts

The **standardised nature** of interest rate futures is a limitation on their use by the corporate treasurer as a means of hedging, because they **cannot always be matched** with specific interest rate exposures. Futures contracts are frequently used by banks and other financial institutions as a means of hedging their portfolios: such institutions are often not concerned with achieving an exact match with their underlying exposure.

4.1.2 Entitlement with contracts

With interest rate futures what we **buy** is the entitlement to **interest receipts** and what we **sell** is the promise to make **interest** payments. So when a lender buys one three-month sterling contract they have the right to receive interest for three months in pounds. When a borrower sells a three-month sterling contract they incur an obligation to make interest payments for three months.

(a)   **Selling** a future creates the obligation to **borrow** money and the obligation to **pay interest**. **Borrowers** will wish to hedge against an interest rate rise by **selling futures now** and **buying futures** on the day that the interest rate is fixed.

(b)   **Buying** a future creates the obligation to **deposit** money and the right to **receive interest**. **Lenders** will wish to hedge against the possibility of falling interest rates by **buying futures now** and **selling futures** on the date that the actual lending starts.

Exam focus point

> The examiner's report for the June 2015 exam noted that many students were unable to identify the incorrect statement in the MCQ on interest rate futures. The incorrect statement said 'Borrowers hedging against an interest rate risk increase will buy interest rate futures now and sell them at a future date'. This is incorrect because borrowers *sell* futures now and buy them at a later date. You need to know details like this to be able to answer the MCQs in Section A of the exam. You also need to read the questions carefully so as not to miss details like this.

4.1.3 Other factors to consider

(a)   **Short-term interest rate futures** contracts normally represent interest receivable or payable on notional lending or borrowing **for a three-month period** beginning on a standard future date. The contract size depends on the currency in which the lending or borrowing takes place. For example, the three-month sterling interest rate futures March contract represents the interest on notional lending or borrowing of £500,000 for three months, starting at the end of March. £500,000 is the contract size.

(b)   As with all futures, a **whole number of contracts** must be dealt with. Note that the notional **period of lending or borrowing starts** when the **contract expires**, at the **end of March**.

(c)   On LIFFE (London International Financial Futures and Options Exchange), futures contracts are available with **maturity dates** at the end of March, June, September and December. The three-month eurodollar interest rate futures contract is for notional lending or borrowing in US dollars. The contract size is $1 million.

4.2 Interest rate options

FAST FORWARD

Interest rate options allow an organisation to limit its exposure to adverse interest rate movements, while allowing it to take advantage of favourable interest rate movements.

Key term

> An **interest rate option** grants the buyer of it the right, but **not the obligation,** to deal at an agreed interest rate (strike rate) at a future maturity date (the expiry date for the option).
>
> On the date of expiry of the option, the buyer must decide whether or not to exercise the right.

Options are like insurance policies. A premium is paid and then the option can be exercised or ignored. Clearly, a buyer of an **option to borrow** will **not wish to exercise** it if the **market interest rate** is now **below** that specified in the option agreement. Conversely, an **option to lend** will not be worth exercising if **market rates** have **risen above** the rate specified in the option by the time the option has expired.

Tailor-made **'over the counter' interest rate options** can be purchased from major banks, with specific values, periods of maturity, denominated currencies and rates of agreed interest. The cost of the option is the 'premium'. Interest rate options offer more **flexibility** and are more **expensive** than FRAs.

Note that an option to sell is known as a **put** option and an option to buy is known as a **call** option.

4.3 Interest rate caps, collars and floors

FAST FORWARD

Caps set a ceiling to the interest rate; a **floor** sets a lower limit. A **collar** is the simultaneous purchase of a cap and sale of floor.

Various **cap** and **collar** agreements are possible.

Key terms

> (a)   An interest rate **cap** is an option which sets an interest rate ceiling.
>
> (b)   A **floor** is an option which sets a lower limit to interest rates.
>
> (c)   Using a **'collar'** arrangement, the borrower can buy an interest rate cap and at the same time sell an interest rate floor. This limits the cost for the company, as it receives a premium for the option it's sold.

The cost of a collar is lower than for buying an option alone. However, the borrowing company forgoes the benefit of movements in interest rates **below the floor limit** in exchange for this cost reduction and an investing company forgoes the benefit of **movements in interest rates above the cap level.** A **zero cost collar** can even be negotiated sometimes, if the **premium paid** for buying the cap **equals** the **premium received** for selling the floor.

4.4 Interest rate swaps

FAST FORWARD

Interest rate swaps are where two parties agree to exchange interest rate payments.

Interest rate swaps can act as a means of **switching** from paying one type of interest to another, raising **less expensive loans** and **securing better** deposit **rates.**

A **fixed to floating rate currency swap** is a combination of a currency and interest rate swap.

Key term

> **Interest rate swap** is an agreement whereby the parties to the agreement exchange interest rate commitments.

4.4.1 Swap procedures

Interest rate swaps involve two parties agreeing to exchange interest payments with each other over an agreed period. In practice, however, the major players in the swaps market are banks and many other types of institution can become involved, for example national and local governments and international institutions.

In the simplest form of interest rate swap, party A agrees to pay the interest on party B's loan, while party B reciprocates by paying the interest on A's loan. If the swap is to make sense, **the two parties must swap interest which has different characteristics**. Assuming that the interest swapped is in the same currency, the most common motivation for the swap is to switch from paying floating rate interest to fixed interest or *vice versa*. This type of swap is known as a **'plain vanilla'** or **generic** swap.

4.4.2 Why bother to swap?

Obvious questions to ask are:

- Why do the companies bother swapping interest payments with each other?
- Why don't they just terminate their original loan and take out a new one?

The answer is that **transaction costs** may be too high. Terminating an original loan early may involve a significant termination fee and taking out a new loan will involve issue costs. Arranging a swap can be significantly cheaper, even if a banker is used as an intermediary. Because the banker is simply acting as an agent on the swap arrangement and has to bear no default risk, the arrangement fee can be kept low.

Exam focus point

If you have to discuss which instrument should be used to hedge interest rate risk, consider **cost**, **flexibility**, **expectations** and **ability to benefit** from favourable interest rate movements.

- The **interest rates** on financial assets are influenced by the **risk** of the assets, the **duration** of the lending, and the **size** of the loan.

  There is a **trade-off** between **risk and return**. Investors in riskier assets expect to be compensated for the risk.

- Interest rate risk relates to the sensitivity of profit and cash flows to changes in interest rates.

  Interest rate risk is faced by companies with floating and fixed rate debt. It can arise from **gap exposure** and **basis risk**.

- The **causes** of interest rate fluctuations include the **structure of interest rates and yield curves** and **changing economic factors**.

- Interest rate risk can be managed using **internal hedging** in the form of asset and liability management, matching and smoothing or using **external hedging** instruments, such as forward rate agreements and interest rate derivatives.

- **Forward rate agreements** hedge risk by **fixing the interest rate** on future short-term borrowing.

- **Interest rate derivatives** can be used to hedge against the risk of interest rate changes. They include **interest rate futures, interest rate options and interest rate swaps**.

- **Interest rate options** allow an organisation to limit its exposure to adverse interest rate movements, while allowing it to take advantage of favourable interest rate movements.

- **Caps** set a ceiling to the interest rate; a **floor** sets a lower limit. A **collar** is the simultaneous purchase of a cap and sale of floor.

- **Interest rate swaps** are where two parties agree to exchange interest rate payments.

  Interest rate swaps can act as a means of **switching** from paying one type of interest to another, raising **less expensive loans** and **securing better** deposit **rates**.

  A **fixed to floating rate currency swap** is a combination of a currency and interest rate swap.

Quick Quiz

1   What is LIBOR?

2   Which of the following is **not** an explanation for a downward slope in the yield curve?

    A   Liquidity preference
    B   Expectations theory
    C   Government policy
    D   Market segmentation

3   What is basis risk?

4   How do forward rate agreements hedge risk?

5   Fill in the blanks.

    With a **collar**, the borrower buys (1) ...…..................... and at the same time sells (2) ....

6   What is gap exposure?

7   Name three types of interest rate derivative used to hedge interest rate risk.

Answers to Quick Quiz

1. The rate of interest that applies to wholesale money market lending between London banks

2. A   Liquidity preference (and thus compensating investors for a longer period of time) is an explanation of why the liquidity curve slopes upwards.

3. Basis risk is where a company has assets and liabilities of similar sizes, both with floating rates but the rates are not determined using the same basis.

4. Forward rate agreements hedge risk by fixing the interest rate on future borrowing.

5. (1)   An interest rate cap
    (2)   An interest rate floor

6. Gap exposure is where a firm is exposed to interest rate risk form differing maturities of interest-sensitive assets and liabilities.

7. Any three of:

    (a)   Futures contracts
    (b)   Interest rate options
    (c)   Caps, collars and floors
    (d)   Interest rate swaps

Now try the questions below from the Practice Question Bank

Number	Level	Marks	Approximate time
Section A Q32	Examination	2	4 mins
Section B Q21-25	Examination	10	20 mins
Section C Q24	Introductory	N/A	39 mins

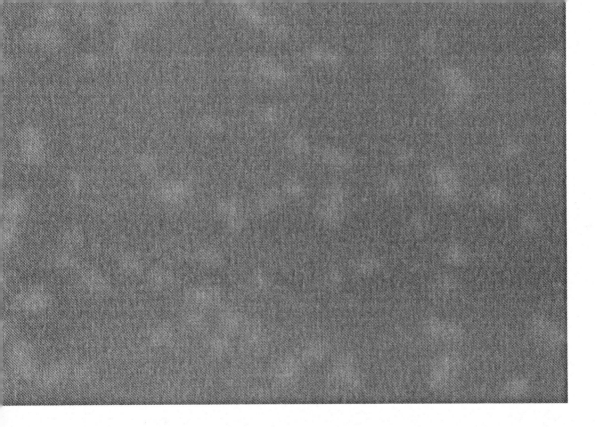

Mathematical tables

Present Value Table

Present value of 1 ie $(1+r)^{-n}$

Where r = discount rate
             n = number of periods until payment

Discount rate (r)

Periods (n)	1%	2%	3%	4%	5%	6%	7%	8%	9%	10%	
1	0·990	0·980	0·971	0·962	0·952	0·943	0·935	0·926	0·917	0·909	1
2	0·980	0·961	0·943	0·925	0·907	0·890	0·873	0·857	0·842	0·826	2
3	0·971	0·942	0·915	0·889	0·864	0·840	0·816	0·794	0·772	0·751	3
4	0·961	0·924	0·888	0·855	0·823	0·792	0·763	0·735	0·708	0·683	4
5	0·951	0·906	0·863	0·822	0·784	0·747	0·713	0·681	0·650	0·621	5
6	0·942	0·888	0·837	0·790	0·746	0·705	0·666	0·630	0·596	0·564	6
7	0·933	0·871	0·813	0·760	0·711	0·665	0·623	0·583	0·547	0·513	7
8	0·923	0·853	0·789	0·731	0·677	0·627	0·582	0·540	0·502	0·467	8
9	0·914	0·837	0·766	0·703	0·645	0·592	0·544	0·500	0·460	0·424	9
10	0·905	0·820	0·744	0·676	0·614	0·558	0·508	0·463	0·422	0·386	10
11	0·896	0·804	0·722	0·650	0·585	0·527	0·475	0·429	0·388	0·350	11
12	0·887	0·788	0·701	0·625	0·557	0·497	0·444	0·397	0·356	0·319	12
13	0·879	0·773	0·681	0·601	0·530	0·469	0·415	0·368	0·326	0·290	13
14	0·870	0·758	0·661	0·577	0·505	0·442	0·388	0·340	0·299	0·263	14
15	0·861	0·743	0·642	0·555	0·481	0·417	0·362	0·315	0·275	0·239	15

(n)	11%	12%	13%	14%	15%	16%	17%	18%	19%	20%	
1	0·901	0·893	0·885	0·877	0·870	0·862	0·855	0·847	0·840	0·833	1
2	0·812	0·797	0·783	0·769	0·756	0·743	0·731	0·718	0·706	0·694	2
3	0·731	0·712	0·693	0·675	0·658	0·641	0·624	0·609	0·593	0·579	3
4	0·659	0·636	0·613	0·592	0·572	0·552	0·534	0·516	0·499	0·482	4
5	0·593	0·567	0·543	0·519	0·497	0·476	0·456	0·437	0·419	0·402	5
6	0·535	0·507	0·480	0·456	0·432	0·410	0·390	0·370	0·352	0·335	6
7	0·482	0·452	0·425	0·400	0·376	0·354	0·333	0·314	0·296	0·279	7
8	0·434	0·404	0·376	0·351	0·327	0·305	0·285	0·266	0·249	0·233	8
9	0·391	0·361	0·333	0·308	0·284	0·263	0·243	0·225	0·209	0·194	9
10	0·352	0·322	0·295	0·270	0·247	0·227	0·208	0·191	0·176	0·162	10
11	0·317	0·287	0·261	0·237	0·215	0·195	0·178	0·162	0·148	0·135	11
12	0·286	0·257	0·231	0·208	0·187	0·168	0·152	0·137	0·124	0·112	12
13	0·258	0·229	0·204	0·182	0·163	0·145	0·130	0·116	0·104	0·093	13
14	0·232	0·205	0·181	0·160	0·141	0·125	0·111	0·099	0·088	0·078	14
15	0·209	0·183	0·160	0·140	0·123	0·108	0·095	0·084	0·074	0·065	15

Annuity Table

Present value of an annuity of ie $\quad \dfrac{1-(1+r)^{-n}}{r}$

Where r = discount rate

             n = number of periods

Discount rate (r)

Periods (n)	1%	2%	3%	4%	5%	6%	7%	8%	9%	10%	
1	0·990	0·980	0·971	0·962	0·952	0·943	0·935	0·926	0·917	0·909	1
2	1·970	1·942	1·913	1·886	1·859	1·833	1·808	1·783	1·759	1·736	2
3	2·941	2·884	2·829	2·775	2·723	2·673	2·624	2·577	2·531	2·487	3
4	3·902	3·808	3·717	3·630	3·546	3·465	3·387	3·312	3·240	3·170	4
5	4·853	4·713	4·580	4·452	4·329	4·212	4·100	3·993	3·890	3·791	5
6	5·795	5·601	5·417	5·242	5·076	4·917	4·767	4·623	4·486	4·355	6
7	6·728	6·472	6·230	6·002	5·786	5·582	5·389	5·206	5·033	4·868	7
8	7·652	7·325	7·020	6·733	6·463	6·210	5·971	5·747	5·535	5·335	8
9	8·566	8·162	7·786	7·435	7·108	6·802	6·515	6·247	5·995	5·759	9
10	9·471	8·983	8·530	8·111	7·722	7·360	7·024	6·710	6·418	6·145	10
11	10·37	9·787	9·253	8·760	8·306	7·887	7·499	7·139	6·805	6·495	11
12	11·26	10·58	9·954	9·385	8·863	8·384	7·943	7·536	7·161	6·814	12
13	12·13	11·35	10·63	9·986	9·394	8·853	8·358	7·904	7·487	7·103	13
14	13·00	12·11	11·30	10·56	9·899	9·295	8·745	8·244	7·786	7·367	14
15	13·87	12·85	11·94	11·12	10·38	9·712	9·108	8·559	8·061	7·606	15

(n)	11%	12%	13%	14%	15%	16%	17%	18%	19%	20%	
1	0·901	0·893	0·885	0·877	0·870	0·862	0·855	0·847	0·840	0·833	1
2	1·713	1·690	1·668	1·647	1·626	1·605	1·585	1·566	1·547	1·528	2
3	2·444	2·402	2·361	2·322	2·283	2·246	2·210	2·174	2·140	2·106	3
4	3·102	3·037	2·974	2·914	2·855	2·798	2·743	2·690	2·639	2·589	4
5	3·696	3·605	3·517	3·433	3·352	3·274	3·199	3·127	3·058	2·991	5
6	4·231	4·111	3·998	3·889	3·784	3·685	3·589	3·498	3·410	3·326	6
7	4·712	4·564	4·423	4·288	4·160	4·039	3·922	3·812	3·706	3·605	7
8	5·146	4·968	4·799	4·639	4·487	4·344	4·207	4·078	3·954	3·837	8
9	5·537	5·328	5·132	4·946	4·772	4·607	4·451	4·303	4·163	4·031	9
10	5·889	5·650	5·426	5·216	5·019	4·833	4·659	4·494	4·339	4·192	10
11	6·207	5·938	5·687	5·453	5·234	5·029	4·836	4·656	4·486	4·327	11
12	6·492	6·194	5·918	5·660	5·421	5·197	4·988	4·793	4·611	4·439	12
13	6·750	6·424	6·122	5·842	5·583	5·342	5·118	4·910	4·715	4·533	13
14	6·982	6·628	6·302	6·002	5·724	5·468	5·229	5·008	4·802	4·611	14
15	7·191	6·811	6·462	6·142	5·847	5·575	5·324	5·092	4·876	4·675	15

Practice question and answer bank

Section A questions

1   The following statements relate to various functions within a business.

    1   The financial management function makes decisions relating to finance.
    2   Financial accounts are used as a future planning tool.

    Are the statements true or false?

    A   Both statements are true
    B   Both statements are false
    C   Statement 1 is true and statement 2 is false
    D   Statement 2 is true and statement 1 is false   **(2 marks)**

2   Which of the following is true?

    A   Most management accounting information is of a monetary nature
    B   Financial accounts act as a future planning tool
    C   Financial management decisions include dividend decisions
    D   Management accounting is the management of finance   **(2 marks)**

3   Which of the following is NOT a connected stakeholder?

    A   Shareholders
    B   Customers
    C   Competitors
    D   Local community   **(2 marks)**

4   The following statements relate to fiscal policy and demand management.

    1   If a government spends more by borrowing more, it will raise demand in the economy.
    2   A government can reduce demand in an economy by raising taxes.

    Are the statements true or false?

    A   Both statements are true
    B   Both statements are false
    C   Statement 1 is true and statement 2 is false
    D   Statement 2 is true and statement 1 is false   **(2 marks)**

5   The following statements relate to business and the economic environment.

    1   To create jobs and growth, there must be an increase in aggregate demand.
    2   High interest rates encourage companies to make investments.

    Are the statements true or false?

    A   Both statements are true
    B   Both statements are false
    C   Statement 1 is true and statement 2 is false
    D   Statement 2 is true and statement 1 is false   **(2 marks)**

6   The following statements relate to business and the economic environment.

    1   Raising taxes or reducing government spending is a contractionary policy.

    2   Fiscal policy seeks to influence the economy by managing government spending and taxation.

    Are the statements true or false?

    A   Both statements are true
    B   Both statements are false
    C   Statement 1 is true and statement 2 is false
    D   Statement 2 is true and statement 1 is false   **(2 marks)**

7   Which of the following statements is NOT correct?

   A   Money markets are markets for short-term capital

   B   Money markets are operated by banks and other financial institutions

   C   Money market instruments include interest-bearing instruments, discount instruments and
        derivatives

   D   Money market derivatives include certificates of deposits and money market deposits

                                                                                    (2 marks)

8   Which of the following is/are financial intermediaries?

   1   Commercial banks
   2   Pension funds
   3   Finance houses

   A   1 only
   B   1 and 3 only
   C   2 and 3 only
   D   1, 2 and 3   **(2 marks)**

9   Which of the following is/are derivatives?

   1   Treasury bills
   2   Swaps
   3   Certificates of deposit

   A   2 only
   B   3 only
   C   1 and 2 only
   D   1 and 3 only   **(2 marks)**

10   Which of the following would lengthen the working capital cycle?

   A   Delaying payments made to suppliers
   B   Reducing raw material inventory
   C   Increasing the turnover of finished goods inventory
   D   Increasing credit given to customers   **(2 marks)**

11   Which of the following is/are symptoms of overtrading?

   1   A rapid increase in sales revenue
   2   A decrease in the volume of current assets

   A   1 only
   B   2 only
   C   Both 1 and 2
   D   Neither 1 nor 2   **(2 marks)**

12   The following statements relate to working capital.

   1   Working capital is excessive in a company that is over-capitalised
   2   A conservative approach to working capital results in large levels of inventory

   Are the statements true or false?

   A   Both statements are true
   B   Both statements are false
   C   Statement 1 is true and statement 2 is false
   D   Statement 2 is true and statement 1 is false   **(2 marks)**

13   A company is offering its customers a choice of a cash discount of 2% for payment within 10 days of the invoice date or paying in full within 40 days.

What is the effective annual interest rate of cash discount?

A   20.2%
B   27.9%
C   44.9%
D   78.2%   (2 marks)

14   Sub Co is a subsidiary of Dub Co. Sub Co requires $5 million in finance to be easily spread over the coming year which Dub Co will supply. Research shows:

There is a standing bank fee of $250 for each drawdown.

The interest cost of holding cash (ie finance cost less deposit interest) is 6% pa.

How much should Sub Co draw down at a time (to the nearest $'000)?

A $14,000
B $204,000
C $417,000
D $32,000   (2 marks)

15   In decision-making, costs which need to be considered are said to be relevant costs.

Which of the following are characteristics associated with relevant costs?

1   Future costs
2   Unavoidable costs
3   Incremental costs
4   Cash costs

A   1 and 3 only
B   1 and 2 only
C   1, 3 and 4 only
D   All of them   (2 marks)

16   Which of the following is/are relevant costs for investment appraisal of a new machine?

1   Depreciation of the machine
2   Research into different types of machine
3   Annual maintenance costs for the machine

A   1 and 2 only
B   2 only
C   3 only
D   1 and 3 only   (2 marks)

17   Which of the following is/are true of the payback method of investment appraisal?

1   It tends to maximise financial and business risk
2   It's a fairly complex technique and not easy to understand
3   It cannot be used when there is a capital rationing situation

A   None of these
B   All of these
C   1 only
D   2 and 3 only   (2 marks)

18   Using a discount rate of 10% per year the net present value (NPV) of a project has been correctly
        calculated as $50. If the discount rate is increased by 1% the NPV of the project falls by $20.

        What is the internal rate of return (IRR) of the project?

        A   7.5%
        B   11.7%
        C   12.5%
        D   20.0%   (2 marks)

19   The details of an investment project are as follows.

        Life of the project   10 years
        Cost of asset bought at the start of the project $100,000
        Annual cash inflow $20,000
        Cost of capital, after tax   8% each year

        Corporation tax is 30% and is paid half in the year and half in the following year, in equal quarterly
        instalments. The instalments are in the seventh and tenth months of the year in which the profit
        was earned and in the first and fourth months of the following year.

        Tax-allowable depreciation of 25% reducing balance will be claimed each year.

        (Assume the asset is bought on the first day of the tax year and that the company's other projects
        generate healthy profits.)

        (Round all cash flows to the nearest $ and discount end of year cash flows.)

        What is the present value of the cash flows that occur in the second year of the project?

        A $17,622
        B $18,426
        C $20,193
        D $22,764   (2 marks)

20   A company has a cost of capital of 10%. Project A has the following present values.

                                                                        $
        Initial investment   300,000
        Cash inflows   600,000
        Cash outflows   100,000

        What is the sensitivity of Project A to changes in the cash inflows?

        A   33%
        B   40%
        C   67%
        D   300%   (2 marks)

21   R Co is deciding whether to launch a new product. The initial outlay for the product is $20,000. The
        forecast possible annual cash inflows and their associated probabilities are shown below.

| | Probability | Year 1 | Year 2 | Year 3 |
		$	$	$
Optimistic	0.20	10,000	12,000	9,000
Most likely	0.50	7,000	8,000	7,600
Pessimistic	0.30	6,400	7,200	6,200

        The company's cost of capital is 10% per annum.

        Assume the cash inflows are received at the end of the year and that the cash inflows for each year are
        independent.

What is the expected net present value for the product?

A $(582)
B $582
C $ (19,418)
D $19,418   **(2 marks)**

22   TS operates a fleet of vehicles and is considering whether to replace the vehicles on a 1, 2 or 3 year cycle. Each vehicle costs $25,000. The operating costs per vehicle for each year and the resale value at the end of each year are as follows.

	Year 1	Year 2	Year 3
	$	$	$
Operating costs	5,000	8,000	11,000
Resale value	18,000	15,000	5,000

The cost of capital is 6% per annum.
You should assume that the initial investment is incurred at the beginning of year 1 and that all other cash flows arise at the end of the year.

What is the equivalent annual cost of replacing the vehicles every two years?

A $11,743
B $12,812
C $13,511
D $15,666   **(2 marks)**

23   AD Co announced its intention to make a rights issue of one share at $1.45 for every four existing shares. After the announcement of the issue the share price fell by 40c to $2.20. The price per share just prior to the rights issue is $2.45 ex dividend.

What is the theoretical ex-rights price per share?

A $2.05
B $2.25
C $2.37
D $2.45   **(2 marks)**

24   The following statements refer to Islamic financial instruments.

(1)   Sukuk (debt finance) holders have little influence over the actions of the Sukuk manager

(2)   Under a Musharaka contract (venture capital) profits are shared between partners according to ratios in the contract

(3)   An Ijara transaction is the Islamic equivalent of a lease

Which of these statements is/are correct?

A   1 only
B   2 only
C   2 and 3 only
D   1, 2 and 3   **(2 marks)**

25   The following statements relate to dividend policy.

1   According to Modigliani and Miller, in a perfect capital market, shareholders are indifferent between dividends and capital gains.

2   Residual theory states that dividends should be paid ahead of investing in positive NPV projects.

Are the statements true or false?

A   Both statements are true
B   Both statements are false
C   Statement 1 is true and statement 2 is false
D   Statement 2 is true and statement 1 is false   (2 marks)

26   CTF Co has the following information relating to its ordinary shares.

Dividend cover   5
Earnings per share   150
Published dividend yield 3.75%

What is the price of CTF Co's ordinary shares?

A   30c
B   113c
C   563c
D   800c   (2 marks)

27   The equity shares of HF Co have a beta value of 0.90. This risk-free rate of return is 6% and the market risk premium is 4%. Tax is 30%.

What is the return on shares of HF Co?

A   6.6%
B   6.7%
C   9.4%
D   9.6%   (2 marks)

28   The following statements relate to capital structure theory.

1   The traditional view is that, in the absence of tax, a company's capital structure would have no impact on its weighted cost of capital (WACC).

2   The net operating income approach (MM) assumes that debt is risk free.

Are the statements true or false?

A   Both statements are true
B   Both statements are false
C   Statement 1 is true and statement 2 is false
D   Statement 2 is true and statement 1 is false   (2 marks)

29   Sparrow Co has just paid an ordinary dividend of 30c per share. The shares are now trading at 480c.

If dividend growth is expected to be 3% per annum, what is the company's cost of equity to the nearest whole number?

A   6%
B   7%
C   8%
D   9%   (2 marks)

30   The following statements relate to the valuation of shares and market efficiency.

1   Technical analysis is based on the theory that share prices can be derived from an analysis of future dividends.

2   Under the strong form hypothesis of market efficiency, share prices reflect all available information about past changes in the share price.

Are the statements true or false?

A   Both statements are true
B   Both statements are false
C   Statement 1 is true and statement 2 is false
D   Statement 2 is true and statement 1 is false   **(2 marks)**

31   A company from Northland is expecting to receive Southland Krone in one year's time. The spot rate is Northland dollar 3.4670 per 1 Krone. The company could borrow in Krone at 8% or in Northland dollars at 13%. There is no forward rate for one year's time.

What would interest rate parity predict the exchange rate to be in one year?

A   0.1734
B   3.3136
C   3.6275
D   5.2251   **(2 marks)**

32   The following statements relate to currency risk.

1   Transaction risk is the risk that the organisation will make exchange losses when the accounting results of its foreign branches are shown in the home currency.

2   Economic risk is the effect on the present value of longer-term cash flows.

Are the statements true or false?

A   Both statements are true
B   Both statements are false
C   Statement 1 is true and statement 2 is false
D   Statement 2 is true and statement 1 is false   **(2 marks)**

Section B questions

The following scenario relates to questions 1 – 5.

A company is considering two capital expenditure proposals. Both proposals are for similar products and both are expected to operate for four years. Only one proposal can be accepted.

The following information is available.

	Profit/(loss)	
	Proposal A	Proposal B
	$	$
Initial investment	46,000	46,000
Year 1	6,500	4,500
Year 2	3,500	2,500
Year 3	13,500	4,500
Year 4	(1,500)	14,500
Estimated scrap value at the end of year 4	4,000	4,000

Depreciation is charged on the straight line basis.

1   What is the annual cash flow for year 4 for Proposal A?

    A $2,500
    B $9,000
    C $13,000
    D $15,000   **(2 marks)**

2   What is the payback period for Proposal B?

    A   2.6 years
    B   3.1 years
    C   4.0 years
    D   It doesn't pay back   **(2 marks)**

3   What is the return on capital employed on average investment for Proposal A?

    A   4.5%
    B   22.0%
    C   26.0%
    D   26.2%   **(2 marks)**

4   Which of the following are true of the payback period?

    1   It is a measure used by external analysts
    2   It reduces risk
    3   It looks at the entire project life
    4   It may lead to excessive investment in short-term projects

    A   2 and 4 only
    B   1, 2 and 3 only
    C   1 and 4 only
    D   1, 2, 3 and 4   **(2 marks)**

5   Which of the following are true of ROCE?

    1   It can be used to compare two investment options
    2   It takes account of the length of a project
    3   It ignores the time value of money
    4   It is subject to the company's accounting treatment

    A   1 and 2 only
    B   1, 3 and 4 only
    C   2 and 3 only
    D   4 only   **(2 marks)**

The following scenario relates to questions 6 – 10.

Florrie Co currently has the following long-term capital structure.

	$m	$m
Equity finance	75	
Ordinary shares	96	
Reserves		171
Non-current liabilities		
Bank loans	37.5	
7% convertible loan notes	40.0	
5% redeemable preference shares	37.5	
		115
Total equity and liabilities		286

The 7% loan notes are convertible into ten ordinary shares per loan note in six years' time. If not converted, the loan notes can be redeemed on the same future date at their nominal value of $100. Florrie Co has a cost of debt of 8% per year.

The ordinary shares of Florrie Co have a nominal value of $1 per share. The current ex dividend share price of the company is $11.20 per share and share prices are expected to grow by 5% per year for the foreseeable future. The equity beta of Florrie Co is 0.98.

6   What are the cheapest and most expensive sources of finance?

	Cheapest	Most expensive
A	Debt with a fixed charge	Ordinary shares
B	Debt with a floating charge	Ordinary shares
C	Debt with a fixed charge	Preference shares
D	Debt with a floating charge	Preference shares

(2 marks)

7   What is the conversion value of the 7% loan notes of Florrie Co after six years?

A $15.01
B $150.10
C $177.73
D $600.40

(2 marks)

8   Assuming that the conversion value after six years is $192.36, what is the current market value of the 7% loan notes of Florrie Co?

A $88.83
B $153.55
C $166.25
D $893.69

(2 marks)

9   Which of the following statements relating to the capital asset pricing model is correct?

A   The equity beta of Florrie Co reflects systematic and financial risk
B   The debt beta of Florrie Co is zero
C   It is assumed that systematic risk can be diversified away
D   Systematic risk for Florrie Co is higher than for the market on average

(2 marks)

10 Which of the following statements relating to the weighted average cost of capital (WACC) are true?

A   If WACC is overestimated, unprofitable projects will be accepted
B   Book values should always be used if the data is available
C   WACC assumes the long term gearing of the company will change
D   WACC assumes new investments have the same risk as current ones

(2 marks)

The following scenario relates to questions 11 – 15.

Mathilda Co is a listed company which is seen as a potential target for acquisition by financial analysts. The value of the company has therefore been a matter of public debate in recent weeks and the following financial information is available:

Year	20X4	20X3	20X2	20X1
Profit after tax ($m)	25.3	24.3	22.3	21.3
Total dividends ($m)	15.0	14.0	13.0	12.5

Statement of financial position information for 20X4

	$m	$m
Non-current assets		227.5
Current assets		
Inventory	9.5	
Trade receivables	11.3	20.8
Total assets		248.3
Equity finance		
Ordinary shares	50.0	
Reserves	118.0	168.0
Non-current liabilities		
8% bonds		62.5
Current liabilities		17.8
Total liabilities		248.3

The shares of Mathilda Co have a nominal value of 50c per share and a market value of $10.00 per share. The business sector of Mathilda Co has an average price/earnings ratio of 16 times.

The expected net realisable values of the non-current assets and the inventory are $215.0m and $10.5m, respectively. In the event of liquidation, only 90% of the trade receivables are expected to be collectible.

11   What is the value of Mathilda Co using market capitalisation (equity market value)?

    A $50m
    B $250m
    C $500m
    D $1,000m   **(2 marks)**

12   What is the value of Mathilda Co using the net asset value (liquidation basis)?

    A $147.20m
    B $155.37m
    C $217.87m
    D $248.30m   **(2 marks)**

13   What is the value of Mathilda Co using the price/earnings ratio method (business sector average price/earnings ratio)?

    A $269.87m
    B $404.8m
    C $155.37m
    D $240m   **(2 marks)**

14   What is the average historic dividend growth rate for Mathilda Co?

    A   4.66%
    B   5.90%
    C   6.27%
    D   35.72%   **(2 marks)**

15 Which of the following statements are problems in using the price/earnings ratio to value a company?

1   It can be difficult to find a quoted company with a similar range of activities.
2   A single year's P/E ratio may not be representative
3   It is the reciprocal of the earnings yield
4   It combines stock market information with corporate information

A   1 and 2 only
B   3 and 4 only
C   1, 3 and 4 only
D   1, 2, 3 and 4   (2 marks)

The following scenario relates to questions 16 –20

Daisy Co is listed on the stock market and has increased earnings over the last year. As a result, the board of directors has increased the dividend payout ratio from 36% for the year to June 20X4 to 37.1% for the year to June 20X5. Daisy Co has a cost of equity of 13%. The following information is also available:

Year to June	20X4	20X5
	$'000	$'000
Earnings	12,100	12,700
Ordinary shares	7,000	7,000

The nominal value of the ordinary shares of Daisy Co is $0.50 per share. Listed companies similar to Daisy Co have an earnings yield of 9.2%

16 What is the equity market value of Daisy Co using the dividend growth model?

A $39m
B $92m
C $97m
D $105.5m   (2 marks)

17 What is the equity market value of Daisy Co using the earnings yield method?

A $12m
B $105.5m
C $132m
D $138m   (2 marks)

18 The following statements relate to the dividend growth model (DGM) and the earnings yield method (EYM).

1   The EYM uses profit (rather than cash) so is the preferable method for Daisy Co.

2   In an acquisition context, the EYM is used to value a minority shareholding in a target company.

Are the statements true or false?

A   Both statements are true
B   Both statements are false
C   Statement 1 is true and statement 2 is false
D   Statement 2 is true and statement 1 is false   (2 marks)

19 How is the net assets method of share valuation calculated?

A   Net current assets ÷ number of shares
B   Net tangible assets ÷ number of shares
C   Total net assets ÷ number of shares
D   Tangible assets less current liabilities ÷ number of shares   (2 marks)

20   In which of the following circumstances might net assets be used as a basis for valuing a company?

1   As a floor value
2   As a measure of asset backing for shares
3   In a merger

A   1 and 2 only
B   2 only
C   3 only
D   1, 2 and 3   (2 marks)

The following scenario relates to questions 21 – 25.

Robin Co expects to receive €800,000 from a credit customer in the European Union in six months' time. The spot exchange rate is €2.413 per $1 and the six month forward rate is €2.476 per $1. The following commercial interest rates are available to Robin Co:

	Deposit rate	Borrow rate
Euros	3.0% per year	7.0% per year
Dollars	1.0% per year	2.5% per year

Robin Co does not have any surplus cash to use in hedging the future euro receipt.

21   What could Robin Co do to reduce the risk of the euro value dropping relative to the dollar before the €800,000 is received?

1   Deposit €800,000 immediately
2   Enter into a forward contract to sell €800,000 in six months
3   Enter into an interest rate swap for six months

A   1 or 2 only
B   2 only
C   3 only
D   1, 2 or 3   (2 marks)

22   What is the dollar value of a forward market hedge?

A $323,102
B $331,538
C $1,930,400
D $1,980,800   (2 marks)

23   If Robin Co used a money market hedge, what would be the percentage borrowing rate for the period?

A   1.25%
B   2.5%
C   3.5%
D   7%   (2 marks)

24   Which of the following statements about forward rate agreements (FRAs) are true?

1   They fix the borrowing rate on a sum of money for an agreed period
2   They are arranged with a bank as an over-the-counter transaction
3   The allow companies to benefit from favourable interest rate movements
4   They can be used to hedge against foreign exchange risk

A   1, 2, 3 and 4
B   1 and 2 only
C   3 and 4 only
D   2, 3 and 4 only   (2 marks)

25   Which of the following statements about interest rate theories are true?

1   Expectations theory provides a reason why the interest yield curve is normally upward sloping

2   Market segmentation theory states that interest rates reflect expectations of future changes in interest rates

A   Statement 1 is true and statement 2 is false
B   Statement 2 is true and statement 1 is false
C   Both statements are true
D   Both statements are false   (2 marks)

Section C style questions

1 Gustaffson
39 mins

(a) Briefly explain what is meant by the term 'overtrading'. **(3 marks)**

(b) Gustaffson is a toy manufacturing company. It manufactures Polly Playtime, the latest doll craze amongst young girls. The company is now at full production of the doll. The final accounts for 20X9 have just been published and are as follows. 20X8's accounts are also shown for comparison purposes.

STATEMENT OF PROFIT OR LOSS Y/E 31 DECEMBER

	20X9	20X8
	$'000	$'000
Sales	30,000	20,000
Cost of sales	20,000	11,000
Operating profit	10,000	9,000
Interest	450	400
Profit before tax	9,550	8,600
Tax	2,000	1,200
Profit after tax	7,550	7,400

Dividends paid were $2.5m in both years.

STATEMENT OF FINANCIAL POSITION AS AT 31 DECEMBER

	20X9		20X8	
	$'000	$'000	$'000	$'000
Non-current assets		1,500		1,400
Current assets				
Inventory	7,350		3,000	
Accounts receivable	10,000		6,000	
Cash	2,500		4,500	
		19,850		13,500
		21,350		14,900
Ordinary shares (25c)		5,000		5,000
Profit		6,450		1,400
8% bonds		1,200		3,500
Current liabilities				
Overdraft	2,000		–	
Dividends owing	2,500		2,500	
Trade accounts payable	4,200		2,500	
		8,700		5,000
		21,350		14,900

(i) By studying the above accounts and using ratio analysis, identify the main problems facing Gustaffson. **(13 marks)**

(ii) Provide possible solutions to the problems identified in (i). **(4 marks)**

(Total = 20 marks)

2 H Finance

39 mins

H Finance Co is prepared to advance 80% of D Co's sales invoicing, provided its specialist collection services are used by D Co. H Finance Co would charge an additional 0.5% of D Co's revenue for this service. D Co would avoid administration costs it currently incurs amounting to $80,000 per annum.

The history of D Co's accounts receivable ledgers may be summarised as follows:

	20X8	20X9	20Y0
Revenue ($'000)	78,147	81,941	98,714
% accounts receivable at year end	17	20	22
% accounts receivable of 90+ days (of revenue)	1.5	2	2.5
Bad debts ($'000)	340	497	615

D Co estimates that the aggressive collection procedures adopted by the finance company are likely to result in lost revenue of some 10% of otherwise expected levels.

Currently, each $1 of revenue generates 18 cents additional profit before taxation. D Co turns its capital over, on average, three times each year. On receipt by H Finance Co of amounts due from D Co's customers, a further 15% of the amounts are to be remitted to D Co. The cheapest alternative form of finance would cost 20% per annum.

Required

(a) Calculate whether the factoring of D Co's accounts receivable ledger would be worthwhile.
(b) Explain how the factoring of sales invoicing may assist a firm's financial performance.

(Introductory question)

3 Victory

39 mins

Victory is a retailer, specialising in vitamin supplements and health foods claimed to enhance performance. One of the products purchased by Victory for resale is a performance enhancing vitamin drink called 'Buzz'.

Victory sells a fixed quantity of 200 bottles of Buzz per week. The estimated storage costs for a bottle of Buzz are $2.00 per annum per bottle.

Delivery from Victory's existing supplier takes two weeks and the purchase price per bottle delivered is $20. The current supplier charges a fixed $75 order processing charge for each order, regardless of the order size.

Victory has recently been approached by another supplier of Buzz with the following offer:

1 The cost to Victory per bottle will be $19 each.
2 There will be a fixed order processing charge of $250 regardless of order size.
3 Delivery time will be one week.
4 Victory estimates that due to packaging differences, the storage cost per bottle will be $1.80 per annum per bottle.

Note

The economic order quantity Q, which will minimise costs, is:

$$Q = \sqrt{\frac{2C_0 D}{Ch}}$$

Where C_0 = The cost of making one order
   D = Annual demand
   Ch = The holding cost per unit per annum

Required

(a) Assuming Victory continues to purchase from the existing supplier, calculate:

    (i)   Economic order quantity

    (ii)   Reorder level

    (iii) Total cost of stocking Buzz for one year to the nearest $

(b) (i)   Calculate the economic order quantity if Victory changes to the new supplier and determine if it would be financially viable to change to this new supplier.

    (ii)   Discuss TWO limitations of the above calculations and briefly describe THREE other non-financial factors to be taken into account before a final decision is made.

(c) Explain what is meant by a Just-in-Time (JIT) system and briefly describe FOUR of its main features.

(Introductory question)

4 ZX

39 mins

ZX is a relatively small company in the agricultural industry. It is highly mechanised and uses modern techniques and equipment. In the past, it has operated a very conservative policy in respect of the management of its working capital. Assume that you are a newly recruited management accountant. The finance director, who is responsible for both financial control and treasury functions, has asked you to review this policy.

You assemble the following information about the company's forecast end-of-year financial outcomes. The company's year end is in six months' time.

	$'000
Receivables	2,500
Inventory	2,000
Cash at bank	500
Current assets	5,000
Non-current assets	1,250
Current liabilities	1,850
Forecast sales for the full year	8,000
Forecast operating profit (18% of sales)	1,440

You wish to evaluate the likely effect on the company if it introduced one or two alternative approaches to working capital management. The finance director suggests you adjust the figures in accordance with the following parameters.

	'Moderate' policy	*'Aggressive' policy*
Receivables and inventory	−20%	−30%
Cash	Reduce to $250,000	Reduce to $100,000
Non-current assets	No change	No change
Current liabilities	+10%	+20%
Forecast sales	+2%	+4%
Forecast profit	No change in percentage profit/sales	

Required

Write a report to the finance director that includes the following.

(a) An explanation of a conservative and aggressive working capital policy. **(5 marks)**

(b) Calculations of the return on net assets and the current ratio under each of three scenarios shown below.

    • The company continues with its present policy.
    • The company adopts the 'moderate' policy.
    • The company adopts the 'aggressive' policy. **(8 marks)**

(c)   A recommendation for the company of a proposed course of action. Your recommendation should be based on your evaluation as discussed above and on your opinion of what further action is necessary before a final decision can be taken.   **(7 marks)**

(Total = 20 marks)

5 Velm Co   39 mins

Velm Co sells stationery and office supplies on a wholesale basis and has an annual revenue of $4,000,000. The company employs four people in its sales ledger and credit control department at an annual salary of $12,000 each. All sales are on 40 days' credit with no discount for early payment. Bad debts represent 3% of revenue and Velm Co pays annual interest of 9% on its overdraft. The most recent accounts of the company offer the following financial information:

Velm Co: Statement of financial position as at 31 December 20X2

	$'000	$'000
Non-current assets		
Tangible non-current assets		17,500
Current assets		
Inventory of goods for resale	900	
Receivables	550	
Cash	120	
		1,570
Total assets		19,070
Equity and liabilities		
Ordinary shares	3,500	
Reserves	11,640	
		15,140
Non-current liabilities		
12% Bonds due 20Y0		2,400
Current liabilities		
Trade payables	330	
Overdraft	1,200	
		1,530
Total equity and liabilities		19,070

Velm Co is considering offering a discount of 1% to customers paying within 14 days, which it believes will reduce bad debts to 2.4% of revenue. The company also expects that offering a discount for early payment will reduce the average credit period taken by its customers to 26 days. The consequent reduction in the time spent chasing customers where payments are overdue will allow one member of the credit control team to take early retirement. Two-thirds of customers are expected to take advantage of the discount.

Required

(a)   Using the information provided, determine whether a discount for early payment of 1 per cent will lead to an increase in profitability for Velm Co.   **(5 marks)**

(b)   Discuss the relative merits of short-term and long-term debt sources for the financing of working capital.   **(8 marks)**

(c)   Discuss the different policies that may be adopted by a company towards the financing of working capital needs and indicate which policy has been adopted by Velm Co.   **(7 marks)**

(Total = 20 marks)

6 Knuckle Down

The management of Knuckle Down are reviewing the company's capital investment options for the coming year, and are considering six projects.

Project A would cost $29,000 now, and would earn the following cash profits.

1st year	$8,000	3rd year	$10,000
2nd year	$12,000	4th year	$ 6,000

The capital equipment purchased at the start of the project could be resold for $5,000 at the start of the fifth year.

Project B would involve a current outlay of $44,000 on capital equipment and $20,000 on working capital. The profits from the project would be as follows.

Year	Sales	Variable costs	Contribution	Fixed costs	Profit
	$	$	$	$	$
1	75,000	50,000	25,000	10,000	15,000
2	90,000	60,000	30,000	10,000	20,000
3	42,000	28,000	14,000	8,000	6,000

Fixed costs include an annual charge of $4,000 for depreciation. At the end of the third year the working capital investment would be recovered and the equipment would be sold for $5,000.

Project C would involve a current outlay of $50,000 on equipment and $15,000 on working capital. The investment in working capital would be increased to $21,000 at the end of the first year. Annual cash profits would be $18,000 for five years, at the end of which the investment in working capital would be recovered.

Project D would involve an outlay of $20,000 now and a further outlay of $20,000 after one year. Cash profits thereafter would be as follows.

2nd year	$15,000
3rd year	$12,000
4th to 8th years	$8,000 pa

Project E is a long-term project, involving an immediate outlay of $32,000 and annual cash profits of $4,500 in perpetuity.

Project F is another long-term project, involving an immediate outlay of $20,000 and annual cash profits as follows.

1st to 5th years	$5,000
6th to 10th years	$4,000
11th year onwards for ever	$3,000

The company discounts all projects of ten years duration or less at a cost of capital of 12%, and all other projects at a cost of 15%.

Ignore taxation.

Required

(a)   Calculate the NPV of each project, and determine which should be undertaken by the company on financial grounds.

(b)   Calculate the IRR of projects A, C and E.

(Introductory question)

7 Mezen

39 mins

Mezen is currently considering the launch of a new product. A market survey was recently commissioned to assess the likely demand for the product and this showed that the product has an expected life of four years. The survey cost $30,000 and this is due for payment in four months' time. On the basis of the survey information as well as internal management accounting information relating to costs, the assistant accountant prepared the following profit forecasts for the product.

Year	1	2	3	4
	$'000	$'000	$'000	$'000
Sales	180	200	160	120
Cost of sales	(115)	(140)	(110)	(85)
Gross profit	65	60	50	35
Variable overheads	(27)	(30)	(24)	(18)
Fixed overheads	(25)	(25)	(25)	(25)
Market survey written off	(30)	–	–	–
Net profit/(loss)	(17)	5	1	(8)

These profit forecasts were viewed with disappointment by the directors and there was a general feeling that the new product should not be launched. The Chief Executive pointed out that the product achieved profits in only two years of its four-year life and that over the four-year period as a whole, a net loss was expected. However, before a meeting that had been arranged to decide formally the future of the product, the following additional information became available:

(i)   The new product will require the use of an existing machine. This has a written down value of $80,000 but could be sold for $70,000 immediately if the new product is not launched. If the product is launched, it will be sold at the end of the four-year period for $10,000.

(ii)   Additional working capital of $20,000 will be required immediately and will be needed over the four-year period. It will be released at the end of the period.

(iii)   The fixed overheads include a figure of $15,000 per year for depreciation of the machine and $5,000 per year for the re-allocation of existing overheads of the business.

The company has a cost of capital of 10%.

Ignore taxation.

Required

(a)   Calculate the net present value of the new product.   **(10 marks)**
(b)   Calculate the approximate internal rate of return of the product.   **(5 marks)**
(c)   Explain, with reasons, whether or not the product should be launched.   **(5 marks)**

(Total = 20 marks)

8 Auriga

39 mins

Auriga (Healthcare) has invested $220,000 over the past two years in the development of a personal stress-monitoring device (PSMD). The device is designed for busy individuals wishing to check their stress levels. Market research that was commissioned earlier in the year at a cost of $45,000 suggests that the price for the PSMD should be $22 per unit and that the expected product life cycle of the device is four years.

In order to produce the device, the business must purchase immediately specialist machinery and equipment at a cost of $300,000. This machinery and equipment has an expected life of four years and will have no residual value at the end of this period. The machinery and equipment can produce a maximum of 15,000 PSMDs per year over four years. To ensure that the maximum output is achieved, the business will spend $50,000 a year in advertising the device over the next four years.

Based on the maximum output of 15,000 units per year, the PSMD has the following expected costs per unit (excluding the advertising costs above):

	Notes	$
Materials	(1)	6.50
Labour	(2)	5.50
Overheads	(3)	8.50
		20.50

Notes

(1)   The materials figure above includes a charge of $2 for a polymer that is currently in stock and can be used for this project. Each PSMD requires 200 grams of the polymer and the charge is based on the original cost of $1 per 100 grams for the polymer. It is a material that is currently used in other areas of the business and the cost of replacing the polymer is $1.50 per 100 grams. The polymer could easily be sold at a price of $1.25 per 100 grams.

(2)   The labour costs relate to payments made to employees that will be directly involved in producing the PSMD. These employees have no work at present and, if the PSMD is not produced, they will be made redundant immediately at a cost of $230,000. If, however, the PSMD is produced, the employees are likely to be found other work at the end of the four-year period and so no redundancy costs will be incurred.

(3)   The figure includes a depreciation charge for the new machinery and equipment. The policy of the business is to depreciate non-current assets in equal instalments over their expected life. All other overheads included in the above figure are incurred in production of the new device.

(4)   Auriga uses a cost of capital of 10% to assess projects.

Ignore taxation.

Required

(a)   Calculate the net present value of the project.

(b)   Calculate the required reduction in annual net cash flows from operations before the project becomes unprofitable.

(Introductory question)

9 Bridgeford

39 mins

Bridgeford is considering whether or not to invest in the development of a new product, which would have an expected market life of 5 years.

The managing director is in favour of the project, because its estimated accounting rate of return (ARR) would be over 15%.

His estimates for the project are as follows:

Year	0	1	2	3	4	5
	$'000	$'000	$'000	$'000	$'000	$'000
Cost of equipment	2,000					
Total investment in working capital	200	250	300	350	350	
Sales		2,500	3,000	3,500	3,500	3,000
Materials costs		500	600	700	700	600
Labour costs		750	900	1,100	1,100	1,000
Overhead costs		300	350	350	350	350
Interest		240	240	240	240	240
Depreciation		400	400	400	400	400
Total costs		2,190	2,490	2,790	2,790	2,590
Profit		310	510	710	710	410

The average annual profit before tax is $530,000 and with corporation tax at 35%, the average annual profit after tax is $344,500. This gives an ARR of 15.7% on the initial investment of $2,200,000.

As finance director, you have some criticisms of the managing director's estimates. His figures ignore both inflation and capital allowances on the equipment, and you decide to prepare an amended assessment of the project with the following data.

(1) Selling prices and overhead expenses will increase with inflation by 5% pa.

(2) Materials costs, labour costs and the working capital requirements, will increase by 10% pa.

(3) For taxation purposes, capital allowances will be available against the taxable profits of the project, at 25% pa on a reducing balance basis.

(4) The rate of corporation tax on taxable profits is 35% and tax is paid one year in arrears.

(5) The equipment will have a zero salvage value at the end of the project's life.

(6) The company's real after-tax weighted average cost of capital is estimated to be 7% pa, and its nominal after-tax weighted average cost of capital is 12%.

Required

(a) Estimate the net present value of the project, and recommend, on the basis of the NPV, whether or not the project should be undertaken.

(b) Outline the strengths and weaknesses of the internal rate of return method as a basis for investment appraisal.

(Introductory question)

10 Dinard   39 mins

(a) Explain the difference between real rates of return and nominal rates of return.

(b) Dinard Co has just developed a new product to be called Rance and is now considering whether to put it into production. The following information is available.

   (i) Costs incurred in the development of Rance amount to $480,000.

   (ii) Production of Rance will require the purchase of new machinery at a cost of $2,400,000 payable immediately. This machinery is specific to the production of Rance and will be obsolete and valueless when that production ceases. The machinery has a production life of four years and a production capacity of 30,000 units per annum.

   (iii) Production costs of Rance (at year 1 prices) are estimated as follows.

	$
Variable materials	8.00
Variable labour	12.00
Variable overheads	12.00

   In addition, fixed production costs (at year 1 prices), including straight line depreciation on plant and machinery, will amount to $800,000 per annum.

   (iv) The selling price of Rance will be $80.00 per unit (at year 1 prices). Demand is expected to be 25,000 units per annum for the next four years.

   (v) The retail price index is expected to increase at 5% per annum for the next four years and the selling price of Rance is expected to increase at the same rate. Annual inflation rates for production costs are expected to be as follows.

	%
Variable materials	4
Variable labour	10
Variable overheads	4
Fixed costs	5

   (vi) The company's weighted average cost of capital in nominal terms is expected to be 15%.

Required

Advise the directors of Dinard Co whether it should produce Rance on the basis of the information above.

(Introductory question)

Note. Unless otherwise specified all costs and revenues should be assumed to rise at the end of each year. Ignore taxation.

11 Muggins

39 mins

Muggins is evaluating a project to produce a new product. The product has an expected life of four years. Costs associated with the product are expected to be as follows.

Variable costs per unit

Labour: $30

Materials:

6 kg of material X at $1.64 per kg
3 units of component Y at $4.20 per unit

Other variable costs: $4.40

Indirect cost each year

Apportionment of head office salaries $118,000

Apportionment of general building occupancy $168,000

Other overheads $80,000, of which $60,000 represent additional cash expenditures (including rent of machinery)

To manufacture the product, a product manager will have to be recruited at an annual gross cost of $34,000, and one assistant manager, whose current annual salary is $30,000, will be transferred from another department, where he will be replaced by a new appointee at a cost of $27,000 a year.

The necessary machinery will be rented. It will be installed in the company's factory. This will take up space that would otherwise be rented to another local company for $135,000 a year. This rent (for the factory space) is not subject to any uncertainty, as a binding four-year lease would be created.

60,000 kg of material X are already in inventory, at a purchase value of $98,400. They have no use other than the manufacture of the new product. Their disposal value is $50,000.

Expected sales volumes of the product, at the proposed selling price of $125 a unit, are as follows.

Year	Expected sales
	Units
1	10,000
2	18,000
3	18,000
4	19,000

All sales and costs will be on a cash basis and should be assumed to occur at the end of the year. Ignore taxation.

The company requires that certainty-equivalent cash flows have a positive NPV at a discount rate of 5%. Adjustment factors to arrive at certainty-equivalent amounts are as follows.

Year	Costs	Benefits
1	1.1	0.9
2	1.3	0.8
3	1.4	0.7
4	1.5	0.6

Required

Assess on financial grounds whether the project is acceptable.

(Introductory question)

12 Banden

39 mins

Banden is a highly geared company that wishes to expand its operations. Six possible capital investments have been identified, but the company only has access to a total of $620,000. The projects are not divisible and may not be postponed until a future period. After the project's end it is unlikely that similar investment opportunities will occur.

Expected net cash inflows (including salvage value)

Project	Year 1	Year 2	Year 3	Year 4	Year 5	Initial outlay
	$	$	$	$	$	$
A	70,000	70,000	70,000	70,000	70,000	246,000
B	75,000	87,000	64,000			180,000
C	48,000	48,000	63,000	73,000		175,000
D	62,000	62,000	62,000	62,000		180,000
E	40,000	50,000	60,000	70,000	40,000	180,000
F	35,000	82,000	82,000			150,000

Projects A and E are mutually exclusive. All projects are believed to be of similar risk to the company's existing capital investments.

Any surplus funds may be invested in the money market to earn a return of 9% per year. The money market may be assumed to be an efficient market.

Banden's cost of capital is 12% a year.

Required

(a) (i) Calculate the expected net present value for each of the six projects.

(ii) Calculate the expected profitability index associated with each of the six projects.

(iii) Rank the projects according to both of these investment appraisal methods. Explain briefly why these rankings differ.   **(12 marks)**

(b) Give reasoned advice to Banden recommending which projects should be selected.   **(8 marks)**

(Total = 20 marks)

13 ANT

39 mins

ANT, a multi-product company, is considering four investment projects, details of which are given below.

Development costs already incurred on the projects are as follows.

A	B	C	D
$	$	$	$
100,000	75,000	80,000	60,000

Each project will require an immediate outlay on plant and machinery, the cost of which is estimated as follows.

A	B	C	D
$	$	$	$
2,100,000	1,400,000	2,400,000	600,000

In all four cases the plant and machinery has a useful life of five years at the end of which it will be valueless.

Unit sales per annum, for each project, are expected to be as follows.

A	B	C	D
150,000	75,000	80,000	120,000

Selling price and variable costs per unit for each project are estimated below.

	A	B	C	D
	$	$	$	$
Selling price	30.00	40.00	25.00	50.00
Materials	7.60	12.00	4.50	25.00
Labour	9.80	12.00	5.00	10.00
Variable overheads	6.00	7.00	2.50	10.50

The company charges depreciation on plant and machinery on a straight line basis over the useful life of the plant and machinery. Development costs of projects are written off in the year that they are incurred. The company apportions general administration costs to projects at a rate of 5% of selling price. None of the above projects will lead to any actual increase in the company's administration costs.

Working capital requirements for each project will amount to 20% of the expected annual sales value. In each case this investment will be made immediately and will be recovered in full when the projects end in five years time.

Funds available for investment are limited to $5,200,000. The company's cost of capital is estimated to be 18%.

Required

(a) Calculate the NPV of each project. **(12 marks)**

(b) Calculate the profitability index for each project and advise the company which of the new projects, if any, to undertake. You may assume that each of the projects can be undertaken on a reduced scale for a proportionate reduction in cash flows. Your advice should state clearly your order of preference for the four projects, what proportion you would take of any project that is scaled down, and the total NPV generated by your choice. **(4 marks)**

(c) Briefly discuss the limitations of the profitability index as a means of dealing with capital rationing problems. **(4 marks)**

Ignore taxation. **(Total = 20 marks)**

14 Sagitta   39 mins

Sagitta is a large fashion retailer that opened stores in India and China three years ago. This has proved to be less successful than expected and so the directors of the company have decided to withdraw from the overseas market and to concentrate on the home market. To raise the finance necessary to close the overseas stores, the directors have also decided to make a one-for-five rights issue at a discount of 30% on the current market value. The most recent statement of profit or loss of the business is as follows.

STATEMENT OF PROFIT OR LOSS FOR THE YEAR ENDED 31 MAY 20X4

	$m
Sales	1,400.00
Net profit before interest and taxation	52.0
Interest payable	24.0
Net profit before taxation	28.0
Company tax	7.0
Net profit after taxation	21.0

Dividends paid are $14 million.

The capital and reserves of the business as at 31 May 20X4 are as follows.

	$m
$0.25 ordinary shares	60.0
Accumulated profits	320.0
	380.0

The shares of the business are currently traded on the Stock Exchange at a P/E ratio of 16 times. An investor owning 10,000 ordinary shares in the business has received information of the forthcoming rights issue but cannot decide whether to take up the rights issue, sell the rights or allow the rights offer to lapse.

Required

(a)   Calculate the theoretical ex-rights price of an ordinary share in Sagitta.
(b)   Calculate the price at which the rights in Sagitta are likely to be traded.
(c)   Evaluate each of the options available to the investor with 10,000 ordinary shares.
(d)   Discuss, from the viewpoint of the business, how critical the pricing of a rights issue is likely to be.

Sagitta's finance director has looked into alternative sources of finance, particularly Islamic finance. She knows that there is a transaction type called Murabaha, but she is unsure how it differs from a conventional loan.

Required

(e)   Explain how a simple Murabaha transaction works and discuss the differences from a conventional loan.

(Introductory question)

15 Headwater   39 mins

It is now August 20X6. In 20X0, the current management team of Headwater, a manufacturer of car and motorcycle parts, bought the company from its conglomerate parent company in a management buyout deal. Six years on, the managers are considering the possibility of obtaining a listing for the company's shares on the stock market. The following information is available.

HEADWATER
STATEMENT OF PROFIT OR LOSS FOR THE YEAR ENDED 30 JUNE 20X6

	$ million
Revenue	36.5
Cost of sales	(31.6)
Profit before interest and taxation	4.9
Interest	(1.3)
Profit before taxation	3.6
Taxation	(0.5)
Profit attributable to ordinary shareholders	3.1

Dividends paid were $300,000.

STATEMENT OF FINANCIAL POSITION AS AT 30 JUNE 20X6

	$ million	$ million
Non-current assets (at cost less accumulated depreciation)		
Land and buildings		3.6
Plant and machinery		9.9
		13.5
Current assets		
Inventories	4.4	
Accounts receivable	4.7	
Cash at bank	1.0	
		10.1
		23.6
Ordinary $1 shares		
Voting		1.8
'A' shares (non-voting)		0.9
Reserves		9.7
Accounts payable due after more than one year: 12% Debenture 20X8		2.2
Current liabilities		
Trade accounts payable	7.0	
Bank overdraft	2.0	
		9.0
		23.6

Average performance ratios for the industry sector in which Headwater operates are given below.

Industry sector ratios

Return before interest and tax on long-term capital employed	24%
Return after tax on equity	16%
Operating profit as percentage of sales	11%
Current ratio	1.6:1
Quick (acid test) ratio	1.0:1
Total debt: equity (gearing)	24%
Dividend cover	4.0
Interest cover	4.5
Price/earnings ratio	10.0

Required

(a) Evaluate the financial state and performance of Headwater by comparing it with that of its industry sector. **(10 marks)**

(b) Discuss the probable reasons why the management of Headwater is considering a Stock Exchange listing. **(5 marks)**

(c) Explain how you think Headwater should restructure its statement of financial position before becoming a listed company. **(5 marks)**

(Total = 20 marks)

16 ABC

39 mins

The managing directors of three profitable listed companies discussed their company's dividend policies at a business lunch.

Company A has deliberately paid no dividends for the last five years.

Company B always pays a dividend of 50% of earnings after taxation.

Company C maintains a low but constant dividend per share (after adjusting for the general price index), and offers regular scrip issues and shareholder concessions.

Each managing director is convinced that his company's policy is maximising shareholder wealth.

Required

Discuss the advantages and disadvantages of the alternative dividend policies of the three, and the circumstances under which each managing director might be correct in his belief that his company's dividend policy is maximising shareholder wealth. State clearly any assumptions that you make.

(Introductory question)

17 DF

39 mins

DF is a manufacturer of sports equipment. All of the shares of DF are held by the Wong family.

The company has recently won a major 3-year contract to supply FF with a range of sports equipment. FF is a large company with over 100 sports shops. The contract may be renewed after 3 years.

The new contract is expected to double DF's existing total annual sales, but demand from FF will vary considerably from month to month.

The contract will, however, mean a significant additional investment in both non-current and current assets. A loan from the bank is to be used to finance the additional non-current assets, as the Wong family is currently unable to supply any further share capital. Also, the Wong family does not wish to raise new capital by issuing shares to non-family members.

The financing of the additional current assets is yet to be decided. In particular, the contract with FF will require orders to be delivered within two days. This delivery period gives DF insufficient time to manufacture items, thus significant inventories need to be held at all times. Also, FF requires 90 days' credit from its suppliers. This will result in a significant additional investment in accounts receivable by DF.

If the company borrows from the bank to finance current assets, either using a loan or an overdraft, it expects to be charged annual interest at 12%. Consequently, DF is considering alternative methods of financing current assets. These include debt factoring, invoice discounting and offering a 3% cash discount to FF for settlement within 10 days rather than the normal 90 days.

Required

(a) Calculate the annual equivalent rate of interest implicit in offering a 3% discount to FF for settlement of debts within 10 days rather than 90 days.

Briefly explain the factors, other than the rate of interest, that DF would need to consider before deciding on whether to offer a cash discount. **(6 marks)**

(b) Write a report to the Wong family shareholders explaining the various methods of financing available to DF to finance the additional current assets arising from the new FF contract. The report should include the following headings:

- Bank loan
- Overdraft
- Debt factoring
- Invoice discounting **(14 marks)**

(Total = 20 marks)

18 CRY

39 mins

The following figures have been extracted from the most recent accounts of CRY

STATEMENT OF FINANCIAL POSITION AS ON 30 JUNE 20X9

	$'000	$'000
Non-current assets	10,936	
Current assets	3,658	
		14,594
3,000,000 ordinary shares of $1	3,000	
Reserves	7,125	
Total equity		10,125
7% Bonds	1,300	
Current liabilities	1,735	
Corporation tax payable	1,434	
		4,469
		14,594

Summary of profits and dividends

Year ended 30 June:	20X5	20X6	20X7	20X8	20X9
	$'000	$'000	$'000	$'000	$'000
Profit before tax	1,737	2,090	1,940	1,866	2,179
Less tax	573	690	640	616	719
Profit after tax	1,164	1,400	1,300	1,250	1,460
Less dividends	620	680	740	740	810
Retained earnings	544	720	560	510	650

The current (1 July 20X9) market value of CRY's ordinary shares is $3.00 per share ex div. The bonds are redeemable at par in ten years time. Their current market value is $77.10. Annual interest has just been paid on the bonds. There have been no issues or redemptions of ordinary shares or bonds during the past five years.

The current rate of corporation tax is 30%. Assume that there have been no changes in the system or rates of taxation during the last five years.

Required

(a) Calculate the cost of capital which CRY should use as a discount rate when appraising new investment opportunities.

(b) Discuss any difficulties and uncertainties in your estimates.

(Introductory question)

19 Katash

39 mins

Katash is a major international company with its head office in the UK. Its shares and bonds are quoted on a major international stock exchange.

Katash is evaluating the potential for investment in an area in which it has not previously been involved. This investment will require $900 million to purchase premises, equipment and provide working capital.

Extracts from the most recent (20X1) statement of financial position of Katash are shown below:

	$m
Non-current assets	2,880
Current assets	3,760
	6,640

Equity	
Share capital (Shares of $1)	450
Retained earnings	2,290
	2,740

Non-current liabilities	
10% Secured bonds repayable at par 20X6	1,800
Current liabilities	2,100
	6,640

Current share price (pence)	500
Bond price ($100)	105
Equity beta	1.2

Katash proposes to finance the $900 million investment with a combination of debt and equity as follows:

- $390 million in debt paying interest at 9.5% per annum, secured on the new premises and repayable in 20X8.

- $510 million in equity via a rights issue. A discount of 15% on the current share price is likely.

A marginally positive NPV of the proposed investment has been calculated using a discount rate of 15%. This is the entity's cost of equity plus a small premium, a rate judged to reflect the risk of this venture. The Chief Executive of Katash thinks this is too marginal and is doubtful whether the investment should go ahead. However, there is some disagreement among the Directors about how this project was evaluated, in particular about the discount rate that has been used.

Director A: Suggests the entity's current WACC is more appropriate.

Director B: Suggests calculating a discount rate using data from Chlopop, a quoted entity, the main competitor in the new business area. Relevant data for this entity is as follows:

- Shares in issue: 600 million currently quoted at 560 cents each
- Debt outstanding: $525 million variable rate bank loan
- Equity beta: 1.6

Other relevant information

- The risk-free rate is estimated at 5% per annum and the return on the market 12% per annum. These rates are not expected to change in the foreseeable future.

- Katash pays corporate tax at 30% and this rate is not expected to change in the foreseeable future.

- Issue costs should be ignored.

Required

(a) Calculate the current WACC for Katash.   **(7 marks)**

(b) Calculate a project specific cost of equity for the new investment.   **(5 marks)**

(c) Discuss whether financial management theory suggests that Katash can reduce its WACC to a minimum level.   **(8 marks)**

(Total = 20 marks)

20 Black Raven

Black Raven is a prosperous private company, whose owners are also the directors. The directors have decided to sell their business, and have begun a search for organisations interested in its purchase. They have asked for your assessment of the price per ordinary share a purchaser might be expected to offer. Relevant information is as follows.

MOST RECENT STATEMENT OF FINANCIAL POSITION

	$'000	$'000
Non-current assets (net book value)		
Land and buildings		800
Plant and equipment		450
Motor vehicles		55
Patents		2
		1,307
Current assets		
Inventory	250	
Receivables	125	
Cash	8	
		383
		1,690
Share capital (300,000 ordinary shares of $1)		300
Reserves		760
Long-term liability		
Loan secured on property		400
Current liabilities		
Payables	180	
Taxation	50	
		230
		1,690

The profits after tax and interest but before dividends over the last five years have been as follows.

Year	$
1	90,000
2	80,000
3	105,000
4	90,000
5 (most recent)	100,000

The company's five year plan forecasts an after-tax profit of $100,000 for the next 12 months, with an increase of 4% a year over each of the next four years. The annual dividend has been $45,000 (gross) for the last six years.

As part of their preparations to sell the company, the directors of Black Raven have had the non-current assets revalued by an independent expert, with the following results.

	$
Land and buildings	1,075,000
Plant and equipment	480,000
Motor vehicles	45,000

The gross dividend yields and P/E ratios of three quoted companies in the same industry as Black Raven Ltd over the last three years have been as follows.

	Albatross		Bullfinch		Crow	
	Div. yield	P/E ratio	Div. yield	P/E ratio	Div. yield	P/E ratio
	%		%		%	
Recent year	12	8.5	11.0	9.0	13.0	10.0
Previous year	12	8.0	10.6	8.5	12.6	9.5
Three years ago	12	8.5	9.3	8.0	12.4	9.0
Average	12	8.33	10.3	8.5	12.7	9.5

Large companies in the industry apply an after-tax cost of capital of about 18% to acquisition proposals when the investment is not backed by tangible assets, as opposed to a rate of only 14% on the net tangible assets.

Your assessment of the net cash flows which would accrue to a purchasing company, allowing for taxation and the capital expenditure required after the acquisition to achieve the company's target five year plan, is as follows.

	$
Year 1	120,000
Year 2	120,000
Year 3	140,000
Year 4	70,000
Year 5	120,000

Required

Use the information provided to suggest a range of valuations which prospective purchasers might make.

(Hint: Asset based valuation, earnings based valuation, dividend yield basis without growth, dividend yield basis with growth, discounted value of future cash flows.)

(Introductory question)

21 Bases of valuation   39 mins

The directors of Carmen, a large conglomerate, are considering the acquisition of the entire share capital of Manon, which manufactures a range of engineering machinery. Neither company has any long-term debt capital. The directors of Carmen believe that if Manon is taken over, the business risk of Carmen will not be affected.

The accounting reference date of Manon is 31 July. Its statement of financial position as on 31 July 20X4 is expected to be as follows.

	$	$
Non-current assets (net of depreciation)		651,600
Current assets: inventory and work in progress	515,900	
receivables	745,000	
bank balances	158,100	
	1,419,000	
		2,070,600
Capital and reserves: issued ordinary shares of $1 each		50,000
distributable reserves		404,100
Current liabilities: payables	753,600	
bank overdraft	862,900	
		1,616,500
		2,070,600

Manon's summarised financial record for the five years to 31 July 20X4 is as follows.

Year ended 31 July	20X0	20X1	20X2	20X3	20X4 (estimated)
	$	$	$	$	$
Profit after tax	33,300	66,800	43,300	38,400	52,200
Less dividends	20,500	22,600	25,000	25,000	25,000
Added to reserves	12,800	44,200	18,300	13,400	27,200

The following additional information is available.

(1)   There have been no changes in the issued share capital of Manon during the past five years.

(2)   The estimated values of Manon's non-current assets and inventory and work in progress as on 31 July 20X4 are as follows.

	Replacement cost	Realisable value
	$	$
Non-current assets	725,000	450,000
Inventory and work in progress	550,000	570,000

(3)   It is expected that 2% of Manon's receivables at 31 July 20X4 will be uncollectable if the company is liquidated.

(4)   The cost of capital of Carmen plc is 9%. The directors of Manon estimate that the shareholders of Manon require a minimum return of 12% per annum from their investment in the company.

(5)   The current P/E ratio of Carmen is 12. Quoted companies with business activities and profitability similar to those of Manon have P/E ratios of approximately 10, although these companies tend to be much larger than Manon.

Required

(a)   Estimate the value of the total equity of Manon as on 31 July 20X4 using each of the following bases:

   (i)   Statement of financial position value;
   (ii)   Replacement cost of the assets;
   (iii)   Realisable value of the assets;
   (iv)   The dividend valuation model;
   (v)   The P/E ratio model.

(b)   Explain the role and limitations of each of the above five valuation bases in the process by which a price might be agreed for the purchase by Carmen of the total equity capital of Manon.

Ignore taxation.   **(Introductory question)**

22 Market efficiency   39 mins

Describe the various forms of market efficiency and explain whether it is possible for institutions to out-perform the market.

(Introductory question)

23 Expo Co   39 mins

Expo Co is an importer/exporter of textiles and textile machinery. It is based in the US but trades extensively with countries throughout Europe. The company is about to invoice a European customer for €750,000, payable in three months' time. Expo's treasurer is considering two methods of hedging the exchange risk. These are:

Method 1: Borrow Euros now, converting the loan into dollars and repaying the Euro loan from the expected receipt in three months' time.

Method 2: Enter into a 3-month forward exchange contract with the company's bank to sell €750,000.

The spot rate of exchange is €0.7834 = $1. The 3-month forward rate of exchange is €0.7688 = $1. Annual interest rates for 3 months' borrowing in: Euros is 3% for investing in dollars, 5%.

Required

(a) Advise the treasurer on:
   (i)   Which of the two methods is the most financially advantageous for Expo, and
   (ii)   The factors to consider before deciding whether to hedge the risk using the foreign currency markets

   Include relevant calculations in your advice.   **(10 marks)**

(b) Advise the treasurer on other methods to hedge exchange rate risk.   **(10 marks)**

                                                                          (Total = 20 marks)

24 Yields   **39 mins**

(a) Describe what a yield curve is.

(b) Explain the extent to which the shape of the yield curve depends on expectations about the future.

                                                                    (Introductory question)

Section A answers

1   C   Statement 1 is true and statement 2 is false. Management accounts are used as a future planning tool (not financial accounts).

2   C   Option A is incorrect. Most financial accounting information is of a monetary nature. Option B is incorrect. Management accounts act as a future planning tool. Option D is false. Financial management is the management of finance.

3   D   Options A, B and C are all connected stakeholders but the local community is an external stakeholder.

4   A   Both statements are true. If a government spends more, for example, on public services such as hospitals without raising more money in taxation, it will increase expenditure in the economy and raise demand. A government can reduce demand in the economy by raising taxes or reducing its expenditure.

5   C   Statement 1 is true and statement 2 is false. Aggregate demand is the total amount of goods and services demanded in the economy at a given overall price level and in a given time period. As it increases, more jobs are created and growth occurs. Statement 2 is false. High interest rates appear to deter companies from investing.

6   A   Both statements are true. Raising taxes or reducing government spending are methods that the government uses to reduce demand in the economy. 'Fiscal policy' is a term for the ways in which a government will attempt to manage the economy through taxation, spending, and borrowing.

7   D   Certificates of deposits and money market deposits are interest-bearing instruments (not derivatives).

8   D   Commercial banks, pension funds and finance houses are all financial intermediaries.

9   A   Derivatives include forwards, swaps, futures and options. Treasury bills are discount instruments. Certificates of deposit are interest-bearing instruments.

10   D   Increasing credit given to customers. Increasing credit given to customers will increase the level of receivables and this will lengthen the working capital cycle.

11   A   Symptoms of overtrading include a rapid increase in sales revenue and volume of current assets. So statement 1 is a symptom and statement 2 is not.

12   A   Statement 1 is true. If there are excessive inventories, receivables and cash and few payables, there will be an over investment by the company in current assets. Statement 2 is true. A conservative approach results in high levels of cash tied up in excessive inventories and receivables and harms profits.

13   B   Payment will be made 30 days early.

Number of compounding periods $= \dfrac{365}{30} = 12.167$

$$1 + r = \left(\dfrac{1.00}{0.98}\right)^{12.167}$$

$$= 1.279$$

$$\therefore r = 27.9\%$$

14 B   The Baumol model applies here. This is effectively economic order quantity applied to cash draw-downs, as follows.

$$\sqrt{\frac{2 \times \text{cost of ordering} \times \text{annual cash required}}{\text{Net interest of holding \$1 for 1 year}}}$$

$$= \sqrt{\frac{2 \times 250 \times \$5\text{m}}{0.06}}$$

= \$204,124 = \$204,000 to the nearest \$'000

15 C   A decision is about the future, therefore relevant costs are future costs (1). If a cost is unavoidable then any decision taken about the future will not affect the cost, therefore unavoidable costs are not relevant costs (2). Incremental costs are extra costs which will be incurred in the future therefore relevant costs are incremental costs (3). Cash costs are associated with relevant costs, as relevant costs are cash flows (4).

16 C   Depreciation is not a cash flow and so is not relevant. Research into different types of machine is a sunk cost and therefore not relevant. Annual maintenance costs will be a future incremental cash flow and so are relevant.

17 A   Statement 1 is not true. Payback tends to favour short-term projects and therefore minimises financial and business risk. Statement 2 is untrue. It is simple to understand. Statement 3 is not true because payback helps to identify those projects which generate additional cash for investment quickly.

18 C $$\text{IRR} = A + \left[\frac{a}{a-b} \times (B-A) \right]$$

$$= 0.10 + \left[\frac{50}{50-30} \times (0.01) \right]$$

$$= 0.125$$

$$= 12.5\%$$

19 A   Tax-allowable depreciation in year 1 = \$100,000 × 25% = \$25,000

Tax saved in year 2 = \$25,000 × 50% × 30% = \$3,750 (other half saved in year 1)

Reducing balance of asset at beginning of year 2 = \$100,000 − \$25,000 = \$75,000

∴ tax-allowable depreciation in year 2 = \$75,000 × 25% = \$18,750

Tax saved in year 2 = \$18,750 × 50% × 30% = \$2,813 (other half saved in year 3)

	Cash flows
	$
Annual cash inflow	20,000
Tax on inflow at 30% *	(6,000)
Tax saved (year 1)	3,750
(year 2)	2,813
	20,563
× 8% discount factor for year 2	× 0.857
PV	17,622

* \$3,000 of this relates to year 1 annual cash inflow, \$3,000 to year 2 annual cash inflow.

20 A   NPV = −300,000 + 600,000 − 100,000 = 200,000

$$\text{Sensitivity} = \frac{\text{NPV}}{\text{PV of project variable}}\%$$

$$= 200/600 \times 100\%$$

$$= 33\%$$

21	A	EV of year 1 cash flow = $0.2 \times \$10{,}000 + 0.5 \times \$7{,}000 + 0.3 \times \$6{,}400 = \$7{,}420$			

21   A   EV of year 1 cash flow = $0.2 \times \$10{,}000 + 0.5 \times \$7{,}000 + 0.3 \times \$6{,}400 = \$7{,}420$

EV of year 2 cash flow = $0.2 \times \$12{,}000 + 0.5 \times \$8{,}000 + 0.3 \times \$7{,}200 = \$8{,}560$

EV of year 3 cash flow = $0.2 \times \$9{,}000 + 0.5 \times \$7{,}600 + 0.3 \times \$6{,}200 \quad = \$7{,}460$

Year	Cash flow $	Discount factor 10%	PV $
0	(20,000)	1.000	(20,000.00)
1	7,420	0.909	6,744.78
2	8,560	0.826	7,070.56
3	7,460	0.751	5,602.46
			(582.20)

22   B $12,812

Replace every 2 years

Year	Cash flow $	PV at 6% $
0	(25,000)	(25,000)
1	(5,000)	(4,715)
2	7,000 *	6,230
PV of cost		(23,485)
÷ CDF		1.833
Annualised equivalent cost		(12,812)

* Resale value – running costs

23   B $2.25

	$
Four current shares have an ex-div value of (× $2.45)	9.80
One new share – subscription price $1.45	1.45
Theoretical ex-rights value of five shares	11.25
Theoretical ex-rights price per share (÷ 5)	2.25

24   C   Statement (1) is incorrect. The Sukuk manager is responsible for managing the assets on behalf of the Sukuk holders and the holders have the right to dismiss the manager if they feel it is appropriate. This is different from the relationship between the holder of conventional bonds and bond issuers.

Statements (2) and (3) are correct.

25   C   Statement 1 is true and statement 2 is false. M&M proposed that the value of the company is determined solely by the earning power of its assets and investments and that shareholders are indifferent between dividends and capital gains. Residual theory states that a company should invest in projects with a positive NPV. Only when these investment opportunities are exhausted should dividends be paid.

26   D   Step 1: Calculate the dividend amount using dividend cover.

Dividend cover	= EPS / Dividend per share
∴ Dividend per share	= EPS / Dividend cover
	= 150 / 5
	= 30c per share

Step 2: Calculate the market price per share using dividend yield.

Dividend yield	= Dividend per share / Ex-div market price per share
∴ Market price per share	= Dividend per share / Dividend yield
	= 30c / 0.0375
	= 800c per share

27   D   CAPM $E(r_i) = R_f + \beta_i(E(r_m) - R_f)$

               $E(r_m) - R_f$ = market risk premium = 4%

            $\therefore \; E(r_i)$ $= 0.06 + (0.9 \times 0.04)$

                          $= 0.096$

                          $= 9.6\%$

28   D   Statement 1 is false. The traditional view is that there is an optimal mix at which the average cost of capital, weighted according to the different forms of capital employed, is minimised. Statement 2 is true. One of the assumptions of the net operating income approach is that debt is risk free and freely available at the same cost to investors and companies alike.

29   D   The cost of equity is $\dfrac{d(1+g)}{P_0} + g$

     $\therefore$ cost of equity $= \dfrac{30 \times 1.03}{480} + 0.03 = 0.094 = 9\%$

30   B   Both statements are false. Technical analysis assumes that past price patterns will be repeated. Under the weak form (rather than strong form) hypothesis of market efficiency, share prices reflect all available information about past changes in the share price.

31   C   Using interest rate parity the expected future exchange rate dollar/krone is given by:

     $3.4670 \times \dfrac{1.13}{1.08} = 3.6275$

32   D   Statement 2 is true and statement 1 is false. The risk that the organisation will make exchange losses when the accounting results of its foreign branches are shown in the home currency is known as translation risk (not transaction risk).

Section B answers

1   C   Depreciation must first be added back to the annual profit figures to arrive at the annual cash flows.

$$\text{Depreciation} = \frac{\text{Initial investment \$46,000} - \text{scrap value \$4,000}}{4 \text{ years}} = \$10,500$$

Cash flow in year 4 = $4,000 -$1,500 + $10,500 = $13,000

2   B   Depreciation must first be added back to the annual profit figures to arrive at the annual cash flows.

$$\text{Depreciation} = \frac{\text{Initial investment \$46,000} - \text{scrap value \$4,000}}{4 \text{ years}} = \$10,500$$

Adding $10,500 per annum to the profit figures produces the cash flows for the proposal.

Proposal B

Year	Annual cash flow $	Cumulative cash flow $
0	(46,000)	(46,000)
1	15,000	31,000
2	13,000	(18,000)
3	15,000	(3,000)
4	25,000	22,000
4	4,000	26,000

Proposal B

$$\text{Payback period} = 3 + \left(\frac{3,000}{25,000} \times 1 \text{ year} \right) = 3.1 \text{ years}$$

3   B   The return on capital employed (ROCE) is calculated using the accounting profits given in the question.

$$\text{Average investment} = \frac{46,000 + 4,000}{2} = 25,000$$

Proposal A

$$\text{Average profit} = \frac{\$(6,500 + 3,500 + 13,500 - 1,500)}{4} = \frac{\$22,000}{4} = \$5,500$$

$$\text{ROCE on average investment} = \frac{\$5,500}{\$25,000} \times 100\% = 22\%$$

4   A   Statement 1 is false. ROCE (not payback) is used by analysts. Statement 2 is true. Because payback favours short-term projects, it tends to minimise both financial and business risk. Statement 3 is false. Payback only looks at the period up to the payback and ignores the cash flows after payback. Statement 4 is true. If payback is used, it may lead to excessive investment in short-term projects.

5   B   Statement 1 is true. ROCE can be used to compare two or more investment options. Statement 2 is false. Unlike payback, ROCE takes no account of the length of the project. Statement 3 is true. Both payback and ROCE ignore the time value of money. Statement 4 is true. ROCE is based on accounting profits and not cash flows. Accounting profits are subject to a number of different accounting treatments.

6	A	In the creditor hierarchy, debt with a fixed charge is the cheapest and ordinary shares are the most expensive.

7 B Future share price after six years = $11.20 × 1.05^6 = $15.01 per share.

Conversion value of each loan note = $15.01 × 10 = $150.10 per loan note.

8 B Market value of each loan note

= ($7 × 8% annuity factor for six years) + ($192.36 × 8% discount factor for year 6)

= ($7 × 4.623) + ($192.36 ×0.630)

= $32.36 + $121.19

= $153.55

9 A The equity beta of Florrie Co reflects both systematic and financial risk. The equity beta of 0.98 means that systematic risk is lower (not higher) than for the market on average. It is assumed that unsystematic risk (not systematic risk) can be diversified away.

10 D If WACC is underestimated then unprofitable projects will be accepted. Market values (rather than book values) should be used. WACC assumes the long term gearing of the company will not change.

11 D Market capitalisation = number of shares × market value.

$$= (\$50m / \$0.5) \times \$10.00 = \$1,000m$$

12 B The net realisable value of assets at liquidation = non-current assets + inventory + trade receivables – current liabilities – bonds

= $215m + $10m + ($11.3m × 90%) - $17.8m - $62.5m

= $155.37m

13 B Historic earnings based on 20X4 profit are after tax = $25.3m

Average P/E ratio in industry = 16 times

Assuming no adjustment required to P/E ratio (Mathilda is a listed company so no need to adjust for transferability) and using historic earnings:

P/E ratio value = 16 × $25.3m = $404.8m

14 C Historic growth dividend rate = $\left(\dfrac{15m}{12.5m} \right)^{\frac{1}{3}} - 1 = 0.0627 = 6.27\%$

15 A It can be difficult to find a quoted company with a similar range of activities. Quoted companies are often diversified. A single year's P/E ratio may not be a good basis if earnings are volatile or the quoted company's share price is at an abnormal level.

16 D Total dividend has increased from $12,100,000 × 0.36 = $4,356,000 to $12,700,000 × 0.371 = $4,711,700.

This represents a growth of $4,711,700 / $4,356,000 × 100% = 8.17%

Equity market value using the dividend growth model is therefore:

($4,711,700 × 1.0817) / (0.13 – 0.0817) = $105,520,619 or $105.5m

17 D Market value = Earnings / earnings yield = $12,700,000 / 0.092 = $138m

18	B	Both statements are false. Cash-flow valuation models tend to be preferred to profit-based valuation methods and so the DGM would be preferred as it uses cash. In an acquisition context, the DGM values a minority shareholding in a target company, while the earnings yield valuation gives a value from the perspective of the acquirer, provided the earnings yield used is appropriate.
19	B	Net tangible assets ÷ number of shares. Intangible assets should be excluded unless they have a market value (for example, copyrights, which could be sold).
20	D	Circumstances 1, 2 and 3. The net asset basis can be used as a floor value for a business that is up for sale. Shareholders will be reluctant to sell for less than the net asset value.
		A share might be valued using an earnings basis. This valuation might be higher or lower than the net asset value per share. If the earnings basis is higher and the company went into liquidation, the investor could not expect to receive the full value of their shares when the underlying assets were realised. The asset backing thus provides a measure of the possible loss if the company fails to make the expected earnings or dividend payments.
		The net asset basis can also be used as a measure of comparison in a scheme of merger. For example if two companies have different asset backings then one might consider that their shares' value should reflect this.
21	B	Robin Co should enter into a forward contract to sell €800,000 in six months. Statement 1 is incorrect. Robin Co could use a money market hedge but €800,000 would have to be borrowed, then converted into dollars and then placed on deposit. Statement 3 is incorrect. An interest rate swap, swaps one type of interest payment (such as fixed interest) for another (such as floating rate interest). Therefore it would not be suitable.
22	A	Future value = €800,000 / 2.476 = $323,102.
23	C	Robin Co is expecting a euro receipt in six months' time and it can hedge this receipt in the money markets by borrowing euros to create a euro liability. Euro borrowing rate for six months = 7.0% / 2 = 3.5%.
24	B	Statement 3 is false. A company is locked into the FRA borrowing rate and so it cannot benefit from favourable rate movements. Statement 4 is false. FRAs hedge against interest rate risk (although they are similar to a forward exchange contract for currencies).
25	D	Statement 1 is false. It is liquidity theory which provides a reason why the interest yield curve is normally upward sloping . Expectations theory states that interest rates reflect expectations of future changes in interest rates. Therefore statement 2 is also false.

Section C style answers

1 Gustaffson

> **Top tips.** Part (a) should be fairly straightforward. Part (b) should be approached by using your calculations to determine whether overtrading exists rather than just calculating random ratios. This means examining the short-term ratios in company finance, as well as sales growth, profit margins, liquidity ratios and working capital ratios. Do not be surprised however if not all the ratios show the same results; here the company is keeping up its payment schedule to accounts payable despite its other problems.
>
> (b) concludes by highlighting the most important indicators of overtrading. It is important to do this in an answer where you have given a lot of detail, as you need to pick out where the greatest threats to the business lie. In this question the threats highlighted at the end of part (b) will be those for which remedies are identified in (c).

(a)   **Overtrading**

'**Overtrading**' commonly occurs when a company is expanding rapidly, and the term refers to the situation where the company becomes **over-reliant** on **short-term finance** to support its growing operations. This is risky because short-term finance may be withdrawn relatively quickly if accounts payable **lose confidence** in the business, or if there is a general tightening of credit in the economy, and this may result in a liquidity crisis and even bankruptcy, even though the firm is profitable. The fundamental solution to overtrading is to replace short term finance with longer term finance such as term loans or equity funds.

(b)   (i)   The company has become significantly more reliant on short term liabilities to finance its operations as shown by the following analysis:

	20X9		20X8	
	$'000		$'000	
Total assets	21,350		14,900	
Short-term liabilities	8,700	40.7%	5,000	33.6%
Long-term funds (equity and debt)	12,650	59.3%	9,900	66.4%
	21,350		14,900	

Overtrading

A major reason for this is classic overtrading: sales increased by 50% in one year, but the operating profit margin fell from 9,000/20,000 = 45% in 20X8 to 10,000/30,000 = 33% in 20X9.

Refinancing

However, the effect is **compounded** by the **repayment** of $2.3 million (66%) of the 8% bonds and replacement with a $2 million bank overdraft and increased trade creditor finance. Although this may be because the interest rate on the overdraft is cheaper than on the bonds, it is generally not advisable in the context of the risk of short term debt.

However, if it is felt that the current sales volume is abnormal and that, when the Polly Playtime doll reaches the end of its product life cycle, sales will stabilise at a lower level, the use of shorter term debt is justified.

Liquidity ratios

As a result of overtrading, the company's **current ratio** has deteriorated from 13,500/5000 = 2.7 in 20X8 to 19,850/8700 = 2.28 in 20X9. The **quick assets ratio** (or 'acid test') has deteriorated from 10,500/5,000 = 2.1 to 12,500/8,700 = 1.44. However these figures are acceptable and only if they continue to deteriorate is there likely to be a liquidity problem. In the 20X9 accounts the company continues to have a healthy bank balance, although this has been achieved partly by halting dividend growth.

Investment in non-current assets

The company has **not maintained an investment in non-current assets** to match its sales growth. Sales/non-current assets has increased from 20,000/1,400 = 14.3 times to 30,000/1,500 = 20 times. This may be putting the quality of production at risk, but may be justified, however, if sales are expected to decline when the doll loses popularity.

Working capital ratios

An investigation of working capital ratios shows that:

(1)   **Inventory turnover** has **decreased** from 11,000/3,000 = 3.67 times to 20,000/7,350 = 2.72 times. This indicates that there has been a large investment in inventory. The question of whether this is justified again depends on expected future sales, but the strategy appears to be the opposite of that adopted for non-current assets.

(2)   The **average accounts receivable payment period has increased** from 6,000/20,000 × 365 = 110 days to 10,000/30,000 × 365 = 122 days, indicating a lack of credit control. This has contributed to a weakening of the cash position. There appears to be no evidence of prompt payment discounts to accounts receivable.

(3)   The **payment period to accounts payable** (roughly estimated) has **decreased** from 2,500/11,000 × 365 = 83 days to 4,200/20,000 × 365 = 77 days. This result is unexpected, indicating that there has been no increase in delaying payment to accounts payable over the year. Suppliers are being paid in a significantly shorter period than the period of credit taken by customers.

(4)   The sales/net working capital ratio has **increased** from 20,000/8,500 = 2.35 times to 30,000/11,150 = 2.69 times. This indicates that working capital has not increased in line with sales and this may indicate future liquidity problems.

Conclusion

In summary, the main problem facing Gustaffson is its increasing overdependence on short term finance, caused in the main by:

(1)   A major investment in inventory to satisfy a rapid increase in sales volumes
(2)   Deteriorating profit margins
(3)   Poor credit control of accounts receivable
(4)   Repayment of bond capital

(ii)   Future sales

Possible solutions to the above problems depend on **future sales** and **product projections**. If the rapid increase in sales has been a one-product phenomenon, there is little point in over-capitalising by borrowing long term and investing in a major expansion of non-current assets. If, however, sales of this and future products are expected to continue increasing, and further investment is needed, the company's growth should be underpinned by an injection of equity capital and an issue of longer term debt.

Better working capital management

Regardless of the above, various working capital strategies could be improved. **Credit customers** should be encouraged to **pay more promptly**. This is best done by instituting **proper credit control procedures. Longer credit periods** could probably be negotiated with accounts payable and quantity discounts should be investigated.

2 H Finance

> **Top tips.** In the exam you probably would not get a complete question on factoring. The arrangement would most likely be examined in combination with other methods such as invoice discounting or credit insurance.
>
> However the question is typical of the sort of things that might be asked about factoring, combining calculation with discussion of the general issues involved. When comparing the costs of two possibilities, sometimes as here you would calculate the total costs of each arrangement. On other occasions you would use the differences between each method in your calculation. (a) shows where the differences are likely to lie.
>
> To answer (b) well you needed to bring out benefits in different areas (factoring as a source of finance, use of factors as means of improving working capital management and decreasing administration time and costs.) As far as the effect on the accounts is concerned, the gearing point is significant but note the uncertain effect on return on capital employed.

(a) Assuming that the historical data presented is a reasonable guide to what will happen in the future, we can use some approximate calculations to assess whether the factoring of the debts would be worthwhile as follows. The 20Y0 figures are assumed below to be typical.

Cost	$000s	Benefit	$000s
(1) Cost of funds advanced	4,442	(2) Saved administration costs	80
(2) Administration costs	444	(3) Possible savings in bad debts	615
(3) Lost profits	1,777	(1) Saved finance costs	3,909
Total	6,663	Total	4,604

Cost exceeds benefit so using the factor would not be worthwhile.

(1) **Cost of finance**

The cost of the finance provided by the factor is 5% of sales, since 80% and then a further 15% is remitted by the factor. If sales are 10% lower due to the aggressive collection procedures, then this is $0.05 \times 98,714 \times 0.9 = 4,442$.

Assuming that 80% of receivables will be factored, and that these will be lower in the future because of the lost sales of $0.22 \times 98,714 \times 0.9 = 19,545$, this will save the finance cost associated with these receivables of $19,545 \times 0.2 = 3,909$.

Note: If D Co was using an overdraft there would also be an interest saving on the reduction in the overdraft from using the reduced receivables to reduce the overdraft.

(2) **Administration costs**

In addition, there would be administration costs of $0.5\% \times 98.7m \times 0.9 = 444$. This amounts to considerably more than the amount of $80,000 saved in D's own administration costs.

(3) **Bad debts**

There may be some saving through a reduction in bad debts, which in 20Y0 amounted to 615 which is 0.6% of revenue. However there is against this a loss of contribution amounting to $18\% \times 10\% \times 98,714 = 1,777$ as a result of the factor's aggressive collection procedures.

(b) **Aspects of factoring**

The three main aspects of factoring are as follows.

(i) **Administration** of the client's invoicing, sales accounting and debt collection service.

(ii) **Credit protection** for the client's debts, whereby the factor takes over the risk of loss from bad debts and so 'insures' the client against such losses. This service is also referred to as 'debt underwriting' or the 'purchase of a client's debts'. The factor usually purchases these debts 'without recourse' to the client, which means that in the event that the client's accounts receivable are unable to pay what they owe, the factor will not ask for his money back from the client.

(iii)   **Making payments** to the client in **advance** of collecting the debts. This might be referred to as 'factor finance' because the factor is providing cash to the client against outstanding debts.

Benefits of factoring

The benefits of factoring for a business customer include the following.

(i)   The business can **pay** its **suppliers promptly**, and so can take advantage of any early payment discounts that are available.

(ii)   **Optimum inventory** levels can be **maintained**, because the business will have enough cash to pay for the inventories it needs.

(iii)   **Growth** can be **financed** through sales rather than by injecting fresh external capital.

(iv)   The business gets **finance linked** to its **volume of sales**. In contrast, overdraft limits tend to be determined by historical statements of financial position.

(v)   The managers of the business do **not have to spend their time** on the **problems** of slow-paying accounts receivable.

(vi)   The business does **not incur the costs** of **running its own sales ledger department**.

Effect on accounts

Factoring of sales invoicing leads to a **reduction of accounts receivable** and therefore of assets employed in the business, accompanied by a reduction in profit as a result of the costs involved. Part of these 'costs' are generally reflected in the fact that less than 100% of the debt is paid to the company by the factor. The effect on the **return on capital employed** will depend upon the cost of factoring and the level of profits without factoring relative to assets employed.

Since they reduce assets, the funds advanced by the factor do not show up as **borrowings** in the statement of financial position. The apparent gearing will therefore improve. Factoring is attractive to some companies as a method of avoiding borrowing limits or covenants being breached. It provides a means of financing accounts receivable, which are otherwise unsuitable for secured lending because of their volatility.

Disadvantages of factoring

The main disadvantage of factoring is that it is a **relatively expensive form** of finance compared to loan finance. Some businesses will also find it undesirable for customer relations if the administration of debt collection is passed to a third party.

3 Victory

> **Top tips.** Always note how long it will take to deliver orders as this is an important detail, even though it isn't brought into the economic order quantity calculation.
>
> In (a)(iii) and (b)(i) you need to bring purchasing costs in as they will be affected by the discount.
>
> For questions like (b)(ii) focus on what might differ in the real world from what is assumed to happen for the purposes of the calculation, and think about non-financial factors.
>
> Remember for questions such as (c) that just-in-time is a philosophy that impacts upon the whole production process, not just delivery of inventory. That said, relationships with suppliers are critical and do need to be stressed.

(a) (i) Using the economic order quantity (EOQ) model:

$$Q = \sqrt{\frac{2C_0 D}{C_h}}$$

where: C_0 = cost of making one order = $75

D = annual demand = $200 \times 52 = 10{,}400$

C_h = holding cost per unit per annum = $2

$$Q = \sqrt{\frac{(2 \times \$75 \times 10{,}400)}{\$2}}$$

$$Q = \sqrt{780{,}000}$$

$$Q = 883.2 \text{ units}$$

The economic order quantity is therefore 883 units (to the nearest unit).

(ii) Demand is fixed at 200 bottles per week, and delivery from the supplier takes two weeks. Victory must therefore reorder when inventory falls to 400 units (2 weeks demand).

(iii) The total cost of stocking Buzz for one year will be:

		$
Purchase cost		
10,400 units $20 each		208,000
Ordering cost		
Annual demand (units)	10,400	
Order size (units)	883	
Number of orders per year	11.78	
Cost of placing one order	$75	
Annual ordering cost		883
Holding cost		
Average inventory (883/2)	441.5	
Holding cost per unit pa	$2	
Annual holding cost		883
Total annual cost		209,766

(b) (i) The factors for the new supplier are as follows:

$C_0 = \$250$

$D = 10{,}400$

$C_h = \$1.80$

$$Q = \sqrt{\frac{(2 \times \$250 \times 10{,}400)}{\$1.80}}$$

$$= 1{,}699.7$$

The economic order quantity is therefore 1,700 units (to the nearest unit).

To determine whether it is financially viable to change supplier we must calculate the total annual cost of ordering from this supplier and to compare this with the existing annual cost.

	$
Purchase cost	
10,400 units $19 each	197,600

Ordering cost		
Annual demand (units)	10,400	
Order size (units)	1,700	
Number of orders per year	6.12	
Cost of placing one order	$250	
Annual ordering cost		1,530

Holding cost		
Average inventory (1,700/2)	850	
Holding cost per unit pa	$1.80	
Annual holding cost		1,530
Total annual cost		200,660

This is $9,106 less than the existing annual purchasing cost, and therefore it would be financially beneficial to switch suppliers.

(ii) Limitations of the calculations include the following:

   (1) **Demand is assumed to be the same** throughout the year. In practice, there are likely to be variations.

   (2) **It is assumed that the lead-time is constant** and that the **suppliers** are both **completely dependable.**

   (3) **It is assumed that purchase costs are constant.** In practice it is necessary to allow for the effects of differing discount and credit policies.

   Non-financial factors to be considered include:

   (1) **Quality** must be consistent and reliable from both suppliers.

   (2) **Packaging differences** must be acceptable, and the product from both suppliers must be equally attractive to consumers.

   (3) **Flexibility**. Both suppliers must be able to respond quickly and efficiently to variations in the level of demand.

   (4) **Environmental effects**. Victory must ensure that the suppliers' production facilities meet any agreed environmental standards that the company requires.

(c) **Just-in-time (JIT) manufacturing** involves obtaining goods from suppliers at the **latest possible time** (ie when they are needed on the production line), thereby **avoiding the need to carry** any materials or components inventory. Reduced inventory levels mean that a **lower level of investment in working capital** will be required. In certain environments where the cost of a stock-out is high, JIT is inappropriate, eg in a hospital, the cost of a stock-out for certain items could be fatal.

The main features of a JIT system include the following:

   (i) **Deliveries** will be **small and frequent**, rather than in bulk. **Production runs** will also be shorter.

   (ii) **Supplier relationships** must **be close**, since high demands will be placed on suppliers to deliver on time and with 100% quality.

   (iii) **Unit purchasing prices** may need to be **higher** than in a conventional system to compensate suppliers for their need to hold higher inventories and to meet more rigorous quality and delivery requirements. However, savings in production costs and reductions in working capital should offset these costs.

   (iv) **Improved labour productivity** should result from a smoother flow of materials through the process.

   (v) **Production process improvements** may be required for a JIT system to function to full effectiveness. In particular set-up time for machinery may have to be reduced, workforce teams reorganised, and movement of materials within the production process minimised.

4 ZX

> **Top tips.** The key point to emphasise is that holding too much working capital is expensive whereas holding too little can result in system breakdown. However, modern manufacturing techniques and re-engineering of business processes can help achieve the best of both worlds: low working capital *and* efficient production and sales systems.
>
> In (b) you need to show the effects on assets and liabilities, sales and profits, and current ratios and return on assets to score maximum marks. In (c) a couple of marks are available specifically for a recommendation, with the remaining marks being available for the effect on various stakeholders (staff, customers and suppliers) and possible disadvantages.

To: Finance Director
From: Financial Manager
Date: 4 December 20X1
Subject: Working capital policy

(a) **Conservative working capital policy**

A conservative policy, such as we adopt at present, aims to **reduce the risk of system breakdown** by holding high levels of working capital. Thus customers are allowed **generous payment terms** to stimulate demand, **inventory** of finished goods is **high** to ensure availability for customers, and raw materials and work in progress are high to minimise the risk of running out of inventory and consequent downtime in the manufacturing process. Suppliers are paid promptly to ensure their goodwill, again to minimise the chance of stock-outs.

Aggressive working capital policy

An aggressive working capital investment policy aims to reduce this financing cost and increase profitability by **cutting inventory**, **speeding up collections from customers**, and **delaying payments to suppliers**. The potential disadvantage of this policy is an increase in the chances of **system breakdown** through **running out of inventory** or **loss of goodwill** with customers and suppliers. However, modern manufacturing techniques encourage inventory and work in progress reductions through just–in–time policies, flexible production facilities and improved quality management. Improved customer satisfaction through quality and effective response to customer demand can also enable the shortening of credit periods. Our **modern production facility** gives the company the potential to implement radical new management techniques, including those mentioned above, and to move along the working capital policy spectrum towards a more aggressive stance.

(b) **Ratio analysis**

Policy:	Conservative (present)	Change	Moderate	Change	Aggressive
	$'000	%	$'000	%	$'000
Receivables	2,500	−20	2,000	−30	1,750
Inventory	2,000	−20	1,600	−30	1,400
Cash at bank	500		250		100
Current assets	5,000		3,850		3,250
Current liabilities	(1,850)	10	(2,035)	20	(2,220)
Net current assets	3,150		1,815		1,030
Non-current assets	1,250		1,250		1,250
Net assets	4,400		3,065		2,280
Forecast sales	8,000	2	8,160	4	8,320
Operating profit margin	18%		18%		18%
Forecast operating profit	1,440		1,469		1,498
Return on net assets	33%		48%		66%
Current ratio	2.70		1.89		1.46

Notes

(1)   Return on net assets = $\dfrac{\text{operating profit}}{\text{net assets}}$.

(2)   There is no logical reason why sales should increase as a result of a more aggressive working capital policy. The reasoning behind this assumption is unclear.

(c)   **Recommended course of action**

The conclusion to be drawn from the figures in (b) above is that **substantial funds** can be released by moving from a conservative to an aggressive working capital position ($4.40m – $2.28m = $2.12m). These funds could be **repaid to shareholders, invested** or used to **reduce borrowings** depending on the company's situation.

Moderate working capital position

My first recommendation is that the company should attempt to move towards a moderate working capital position by **tightening up** its **debt collection procedures, buying inventory** in **smaller batches** and **negotiating longer credit periods** from suppliers. Our small size does not help us in this respect but, if achievable, this would result in a significant increase in return on net assets and an acceptable current ratio.

Use of modern techniques

However, further moves towards more aggressive working capital arrangements should be the outcome rather than the driver of policy changes. The key changes that need to be made in our firm are concerned with the adoption of **modern supply chain** and **manufacturing techniques**. These will enable us not only to reduce working capital while avoiding system breakdown but also to improve quality and flexibility and to increase customer demand. At the moment, we have modern equipment but are not taking full advantage of its potential. I therefore recommend that a **comprehensive study** of our **key business processes** is undertaken. I will be happy to evaluate the financial effects of the possible scenarios.

5 Velm Co

> **Top tips.** There isn't much to calculate here so just make sure you know your receivable days formula and think about the relationship between receivables and cash flow.
>
> Most of the marks on this question are for a discussion of working capital in one form or another. So think about sources of finance and policies for managing working capital.

(a)   Receivables are currently taking on average ($550,000/$4,000,000) × 365 = 50 days to pay. This is in excess of Velm's stated terms. The discount, to be taken up by 2/3 of customers, will cost the company $4,000,000 × 1% × 2/3 = $26,667. It is stated that this will bring the receivables' payment period down to 26 days, which is represented by a new receivables level of ($4,000,000 – $26,667) × 26/365 = $283,000. This is a reduction in receivables of $267,000. At current overdraft costs of 9%, this would be a saving of $267,000 × 0.09 = $24,030.

Bad debts would decrease from 3% to 2.4% of revenue, which saves a total of $4,000,000 × 0.006 = $24,000. There would also be a salary saving from early retirement of $12,000.

So the net effect on Velm's profitability is as follows:

	$
Saving on overdraft costs	24,030
Decreased bad debts	24,000
Salary saving	12,000
Less: cost of discount	(26,667)
Net saving	33,363

(b) Short-term sources of finance include overdrafts and short-term loans. Long-term sources of finance include loan notes and long-term loans. The choice is between cheaper but riskier short-term finance and more expensive but less risky long-term debt. A customer might ask the bank for a short term overdraft facility when the bank would wish to suggest a loan instead; alternatively, a customer might ask for a loan when an overdraft would be more appropriate.

In most cases, when a customer wants finance to help with **'day to day' trading** and cash flow needs, an overdraft would be the appropriate method of financing. The customer should not be short of cash all the time, and should expect to be in credit in some days, but in need of an overdraft on others.

When a customer wants to borrow from a bank for only a short period of time, even for the purchase of a major non-current asset such as an item of plant or machinery, an overdraft facility might be **more suitable** than a loan, because the customer will stop paying interest as soon as his account goes into credit.

However, when a customer wants to borrow from a bank, but cannot see his way to repaying the bank except over the course of a few years, the required financing is best catered for by the provision of a loan rather than an overdraft facility.

Advantages of an overdraft over a loan

(i) The customer **only pays interest when he is overdrawn**.

(ii) The bank has the flexibility to **review** the customer's overdraft facility periodically, and perhaps agree to additional facilities, or insist on a reduction in the facility.

(iii) An overdraft can do the same job as a **loan**: a facility can simply be renewed every time it comes up for review.

(iv) Being short-term debt, an overdraft will not affect the calculation of a company's **gearing**.

Bear in mind, however, that overdrafts are technically **repayable on demand**, so even though they are cheaper than longer term sources of debt finance, they are more risky.

Advantages of a long term loan

(i) Both the customer and the bank know exactly what the repayments of the loan will be and how much interest is payable, and when. This makes planning (budgeting) simpler.

(ii) The customer does not have to worry about the bank deciding to reduce or withdraw an overdraft facility before he is in a position to repay what is owed. There is an element of 'security' or 'peace of mind' in being able to arrange a loan for an agreed term. However, long term finance is generally more expensive than short term finance.

(iii) Loans normally carry a facility letter setting out the precise terms of the agreement.

Working capital policies can be characterised as **conservative**, **moderate** and **aggressive**. A conservative policy would finance working capital needs primarily from long term sources of finance, so all long term assets and some fluctuating current assets. However, Velm Co is following an aggressive financing policy as long term debt only makes up 2.75% (40/1,450) of non-cash current assets and most finance is provided by short term debt ($1,530k).

(c) As a general rule, assets which yield profits over a long period of time should be financed by long-term funds. This is an application of the **matching principle**.

In this way, the returns made by the asset will be sufficient to pay either the interest cost of the loans raised to buy it, or dividends on its equity funding.

If, however a long-term asset is financed by short-term funds, the company cannot be certain that when the loan becomes repayable, it will have enough cash (from profits) to repay it.

Under a moderate or matching approach, a company would normally finance short-term assets partly with short-term funding and partly with long-term funding. However, Velm appears to be conducting an aggressive financing policy, as short term finance is being used for most of its current assets. This is a higher risk source of finance.

6 Knuckle Down

(a)   (i)   Project A

Year	Cash flow $	Discount factor 12%	Present value $
0	(29,000)	1.000	(29,000)
1	8,000	0.893	7,144
2	12,000	0.797	9,564
3	10,000	0.712	7,120
4	11,000	0.636	6,996
		Net present value =	1,824

(ii)   Project B

Year	Equipment $	Working capital $	Cash profit $	Net cash flow $	Discount factor 12%	Present value $
0	(44,000)	(20,000)		(64,000)	1.000	(64,000)
1			19,000	19,000	0.893	16,967
2			24,000	24,000	0.797	19,128
3	5,000	20,000	10,000	35,000	0.712	24,920
					Net present value =	(2,985)

(iii)   Project C

Year	Equipment $	Working capital $	Cash profit $	Net cash flow $	Discount factor 12%	Present value $
0	(50,000)	(15,000)		(65,000)	1.000	(65,000)
1		(6,000)		(6,000)	0.893	(5,358)
1–5			18,000	18,000	3.605	64,890
5		21,000		21,000	0.567	11,907
					Net present value =	6,439

(iv)   *Project D*

Year	Cash flow $	Discount factor 12%	Present value $
0	(20,000)	1.000	(20,000)
1	(20,000)	0.893	(17,860)
2	15,000	0.797	11,955
3	12,000	0.712	8,544
4–8	8,000	2.566	20,528
		Net present value =	3,167

Discount factor at 12%, years 1 to 8	4.968
Less discount factor at 12%, years 1 to 3	2.402
Discount factor at 12%, years 4 to 8	2.566

(v)   *Project E*

The cumulative discount factor for a perpetuity at 15% is 1/0.15 = 6.667.

Year	Cash flow $	Discount factor 15%	Present value $
0	(32,000)	1.000	(32,000)
1–∞	4,500	6.667	30,000
		Net present value =	(2,000)

(vi)   *Project F*

		$
1	Present value (at 15%) of $3,000 a year from year 1 in perpetuity	20,000
	Less present value of $3,000 a year for years 1 to 10 (× 5.019)	15,057
	Present value of $3,000 a year from year 11 in perpetuity	4,943
2	Discount factor at 15%, years 1 to 10	5.019
	Less discount factor at 15%, years 1 to 5	3.352
	Discount factor at 15%, years 6 to 10	1.667

3	Year	Net cash flow $	Discount factor 15%	Present value $
	0	(20,000)	1.000	(20,000)
	1–5	5,000	3.352	16,760
	6–10	4,000	1.667	6,668
	11–∞	3,000	See above	4,943
			Net present value =	8,371

(vii)   Projects A, C, D and F have positive net present values and should be undertaken. Projects B and E should not be undertaken.

(b)   (i)   The IRR of project A is above 12% (where the NPV is $1,826). We will calculate the NPV at 15%.

Year	Cash flow $	Discount factor 15%	Present value $
0	(29,000)	1.000	(29,000)
1	8,000	0.870	6,960
2	12,000	0.756	9,072
3	10,000	0.658	6,580
4	11,000	0.572	6,292
		Net present value =	(96)

The IRR is between 12% and 15%. By interpolation, we can estimate the IRR as about

$$12\% + \left[\frac{1{,}826}{(1{,}826 - -96)} \times (15 - 12) \right]\% = 14.85\%$$

(ii) The IRR of project C is above 12%, where the NPV is $6,439. Try 20%.

Year	Net cash flow	Discount factor 20%	Present value
	$		$
0	(65,000)	1.000	(65,000)
1	(6,000)	0.833	(4,998)
1–5	18,000	2.991	53,838
5	21,000	0.402	8,442
		Net present value =	(7,718)

The IRR is approximately $12\% + \left[\dfrac{6{,}439}{(6{,}439 - -7{,}718)} \times (20 - 12) \right]\% = 15.6\%$

(iii) The IRR, r, of project E is found as follows.

PV of cost = PV of benefits

$$(32{,}000) = \frac{4{,}500}{r}$$

$$r = \frac{4{,}500}{32{,}000} = 0.141$$

IRR = 14.1%

7 Mezen

> **Top tips.** In (a), if you failed to identify which costs were relevant correctly, make sure you understand why. Part (c) makes the important point about sensitivity of cash flows. Even if a project has a positive NPV, or an acceptable IRR, a company may not go ahead if the profits are felt to be too marginal, and the risk of loss too great.

(a) **Incremental cash flows**

The survey has been undertaken already, even though it has not yet been paid for, and therefore the $30,000 is a sunk cost.

The depreciation charge of $15,000 is not a cash-flow. The re-allocated fixed overheads will be incurred whether or Mezen goes ahead with the product. Both of these amounts may be subtracted from the $25,000 of fixed overheads in the original calculations.

The company forgoes $70,000 of immediate income from the sale of the machine.

	Time 0	Time 1	Time 2	Time 3	Time 4	NPV
	$'000	$'000	$'000	$'000	$'000	$'000
Sales		180	200	160	120	
Cost of sales		(115)	(140)	(110)	(85)	
Variable overheads		(27)	(30)	(24)	(18)	
Fixed overheads		(5)	(5)	(5)	(5)	
Machine	(70)				10	
Working capital	(20)				20	
Incremental cash flows	(90)	33	25	21	42	
× 10% discount factor	1.00	0.909	0.826	0.751	0.683	
Present value	(90.00)	30.00	20.65	15.77	28.69	5.11

(b) Approximate internal rate of return

	Time 0 $'000	Time 1 $'000	Time 2 $'000	Time 3 $'000	Time 4 $'000	NPV $'000
Incremental cash flows	(90)	33	25	21	42	
× 14% discount factor	1.000	0.877	0.769	0.675	0.592	
Present value	(90.00)	28.94	19.23	14.18	24.86	(2.79)

$$IRR = a + \left[\frac{NPV_a}{NPV_a - NPV_b} \times (b - a)\right]\%$$

where a is the lower rate of return, b is the higher rate of return, NPV_a is the NPV discounted at a, and NPV_b is the NPV discounted at b.

$$IRR = 10 + \left[\frac{5.11}{5.11 - (-2.79)} \times (14 - 10)\right]\% = 12.59\%$$

(c) The product has a positive net present value and an IRR that exceeds the company's cost of capital, and this suggests that it should be launched.

The decision is very marginal, however. It would certainly not be worthwhile if the market survey had not yet been commissioned, in which case the cost of $30,000 would need to be included. A relatively small drop in sales or a small increase in costs would result in a negative NPV. The company may well be able to find better uses for the $20,000 that will be spent now, and for the immediate income of $70,000 on the sale of the machine.

8 Auriga

> **Top tips.** (a) is another question that requires careful identification of relevant costs.
> Work carefully through part (b).

(a) Net present value

	0 $'000	1 $'000	2 $'000	3 $'000	4 $'000
Machinery	(300.00)				
Advertising		(50.00)	(50.00)	(50.00)	(50.00)
Sales ($22 × 15,000)		330.00	330.00	330.00	330.00
Materials (W1)		(112.50)	(112.50)	(112.50)	(112.50)
Labour ($5.50 × 15,000)		(82.50)	(82.50)	(82.50)	(82.50)
Redundancy cost saving	230.00				
Overheads (W2)		(52.50)	(52.50)	(52.50)	(52.50)
Net cash flow	(70.00)	32.50	32.50	32.50	32.50
Discount factor @ 10%	1.00	0.91	0.83	0.75	0.68
Present value	(70.00)	29.60	27.00	24.40	22.10
Net present value	33.10				

Workings

1 *Materials*

	$
Cost per unit	
Without polymer (6.50 – 2.0)	4.50
Replacement cost (2 × $1.50)	3.00
	7.50

Total material cost 15,000 × $7.50 = $112,500

2   Overheads

	$
Total overheads ($8.50 × 15,000)	127,500
Depreciation (300,000/4)	(75,000)
Cash flow	(52,500)

(b)   X = annual net cash flow from operations

Project becomes unprofitable when NPV is zero ie where net present value of annual cash flows is equal to the initial cash outflow of $70,000.

(X × 4 year annuity factor)	= $70,000
X × (0.91 + 0.83 + 0.75 + 0.68)	= $70,000
3.17X	= $70,000
X	= $22,082

Therefore if the net cash flows reduce from $32,500 per annum to $22,082 per annum the net present value will be zero. This is a reduction of $10,418.

9 Bridgeford

(a)   **NPV calculations**

It is assumed that the after-tax nominal weighted average cost of capital is the appropriate cost of capital to use, although the method of financing implied in the managing director's estimates of interest charges for the project raises questions about what the most appropriate cost of capital should be.

Year	0	1	2	3	4	5	6
	$'000	$'000	$'000	$'000	$'000	$'000	
Sales		2,625	3,308	4,052	4,254	3,829	
Operating costs (W1)		(1,690)	(2,201)	(2,801)	(3,061)	(3,024)	
Contribution		935	1,107	1,251	1,193	805	
Tax @ 35%			(327)	(387)	(438)	(418)	(282)
Capital expenditure	(2,000)						
Working capital (W2)	(200)	(75)	(88)	(103)	(46)	512	
Tax benefit of tax depreciation (W3)			175	131	98	74	222
Net cash flow	(2,200)	860	867	892	807	973	(60)
Discount factor @ 12%	1.000	0.893	0.797	0.712	0.636	0.567	0.507
Present value	(2,200)	768	691	635	513	552	(30)
NPV	**929**						

* Assumed that working capital as at the end of year 5 will all be recovered at the beginning of year 6, giving a total net cash inflow of $512,000.

The NPV is positive, + $929,000, and so the project should be undertaken.

Workings

1   *Operating costs*

Year	1	2	3	4	5
	$'000	$'000	$'000	$'000	$'000
Materials costs	550	726	932	1,025	966
Labour costs	825	1,089	1,464	1,611	1,611
Overhead costs	315	386	405	425	447
Total operating costs	1,690	2,201	2,801	3,061	3,024

2   *Working capital*

Year	1	2	3	4	5
	$'000	$'000	$'000	$'000	$'000
Total investment in working capital*	275	363	466	512	
Cash flow effect of working capital changes	(75)	(88)	(103)	(46)	
Sales	2,625	3,308	4,052	4,254	3,829
Materials costs	550	726	932	1,025	966
Labour costs	825	1,089	1,464	1,611	1,611
Overhead costs**	315	386	405	425	447

* Working capital in Year 1 = 250×1.1, in Year 2 = 300×1.1^2 etc

** All are assumed to involve cash outflows.

3   *Tax depreciation*

It is assumed that the capital allowances will be claimed from year 1, and will have an effect on cash flows one year later.

Year of claim		Allowance	Tax benefit
		$'000	$'000
1	(25% of $2,000)	500	175
2	(75% of $500)	375	131
3	(75% of $375)	281	98
4	(75% of $281)	211	74
		1,367	
5	(2,000 – 1,367)	633	222

(b)   The **internal rate of return (IRR)** is the rate of return that results in a NPV of zero. The rule with the **internal rate of return (IRR)** method of project evaluation is that a project should be undertaken if it is expected to achieve a return in excess of the company's cost of capital. A project that has an IRR in excess of the cost of capital must have a positive NPV.

Strengths

The main **advantage** of the IRR method is that the information it provides may be more easily understood by managers, especially non-financial managers.

It is sometimes said that IRR is difficult to calculate, but **both** NPV and IRR are actually **very easy to calculate** with a **spreadsheet**.

Weaknesses

However, it might be tempting for some managers to **confuse IRR** and **accounting return** on capital employed (ROCE). The accounting ROCE and the IRR are two completely different measures. If managers were given information about both ROCE (or ROI) and IRR, it might be easy to get their relative meaning and significance mixed up.

The IRR method also ignores the **relative size of investments**: for example a project with an annual return of $50 on an initial investment of $100 would have the same IRR as a project with an annual return of $5,000 on an initial investment of $10,000, although the latter is clearly preferable.

IRR **favours projects that are less sensitive to increases in the discount rate** and therefore the IRR method may sometimes indicate that a project that yields a smaller increase in shareholder wealth should be preferred to one that yields a larger increase, whereas the opposite is the case. NPV should therefore be used to **decide** between **mutually exclusive projects**.

10 Dinard

> **Top tips.** (a) allows you to demonstrate that you understand the topic of real and nominal returns by explaining the difference between them.
>
> (b) introduces the complication of what you should do if you are told what current (or year 1) prices are but are also given information about price increases over the period of investment. Because the costs are increasing at different rates, the nominal rate (which you are given) has to be used, and the revenues and costs inflated each year. If the rate of increase for everything had been the same, you could either have used the nominal rate (and inflated costs and revenues), or calculated the real rate (and used uninflated costs and revenues). Since calculating the real rate only involves one calculation, you should really have chosen that option.
>
> Again don't forget to exclude depreciation as it is not a cash flow. Development costs of $480,000 are sunk costs and should also be excluded from the calculation. Because you are told to confine your answer to the information given, you should not discuss any wider issues that might be involved in the investment.

(a)   The **real rate of return** is the rate of return which an investment would show in the **absence of inflation**. For example, if a company invests $100, inflation is 0%, and the investment at the end of the year is worth $110, then the real rate of return is 10%.

In reality however, there is likely to be an element of inflation in the returns due to the change in the purchasing power of money over the period. In the example above, if inflation was running at 5%, then to show a real rate of return of 10%, the investment would need to be worth $115.50 at the end of the year. In this case the nominal rate of return is 15.5% which is made up of the real return of 10% and inflation at 5%.

The relationship between the nominal ('money') rate of return and the real rate of return can be expressed as follows:

(1 + nominal rate) = (1 + real rate) × (1 + inflation rate)

(b)   *Workings*

	Year 1	Year 2	Year 3	Year 4
Sales volume	25,000	25,000	25,000	25,000
Unit price ($)	80	84	88	93
Variable material cost ($)	8.00	8.32	8.65	9.00
Variable labour cost ($)	12.00	13.20	14.52	15.97
Variable overhead ($)	12.00	12.48	12.98	13.50

Notes. Evaluation of investment

(All figures $'000)

	Year 0	Year 1	Year 2	Year 3	Year 4
Capital outlay	(2,400)				
Sales		2,000	2,100	2,205	2,315
Direct costs					
Materials		(200)	(208)	(216)	(225)
Labour		(300)	(330)	(363)	(399)
Overhead		(300)	(312)	(324)	(337)
Fixed overheads		(200)	(210)	(221)	(232)
Gross cash flow	(2,400)	1,000	1,040	1,081	1,122
Discount at 15%	1.000	0.870	0.756	0.658	0.572
Present value	(2,400)	870	786	711	642
Cumulative PV	(2,400)	(1,530)	(744)	(33)	608

The investment yields a net present value at the end of four years of $608,000. In the absence of other factors such as a capital rationing situation, production of the Rance should be undertaken.

11 Muggins

> **Top tips.** A methodical set of workings is key to answering this question well (also not confusing the adjustment factors for costs and benefits).
>
> Apart from testing your ability to use the certainty-equivalent approach, the question is a good test of your understanding of relevant costs and opportunity costs.
>
> - Apportioned costs are not incurred by the project and should not be included.
> - Only the additional element of other overheads should be included.
> - The current assistant manager's salary of $30,000 will be incurred anyway and should not be included; the $27,000 salary of the new manager should however be included since it has been incurred because the current assistant manager is needed on the project.
> - The company will not be able to obtain the rental of $135,000 on the factory space if it undertakes the project; thus the rental is an opportunity cost which should be included.
> - The 60,000 kg of material X currently in inventory should not be included at purchase price since this is a sunk cost. However by undertaking the project, the company forgoes the opportunity to sell the raw materials in inventory, and they should thus be included at selling price.

Certainty-equivalent cash flows

	Year 1	Year 2	Year 3	Year 4
	$'000	$'000	$'000	$'000
Sales (W1)	1,125	1,800	1,575	1,425
Material X (W2)	50	230	248	280
Other variable costs (W3)	517	1,100	1,184	1,340
Management salaries (W4)	67	79	85	92
Rental: opportunity cost	135	135	135	135
Other overheads (× 1.1, 1.3, 1.4, 1.5)	66	78	84	90
	835	1,622	1,736	1,937
Sales less cash costs	290	178	(161)	(512)
Discount factor at 5%	0.952	0.907	0.864	0.823
Present value	276	161	(139)	(421)

The net present value is –$123,000, so the project is not acceptable.

Workings

1	*Sales*	Year 1	$10,000 \times \$125 \times 0.9$
		Year 2	$18,000 \times \$125 \times 0.8$
		Year 3	$18,000 \times \$125 \times 0.7$
		Year 4	$19,000 \times \$125 \times 0.6$

2	*Material X*	Year 1	$50,000 opportunity cost
		Year 2	$18,000 \times 6 \times \$1.64 \times 1.3$
		Year 3	$18,000 \times 6 \times \$1.64 \times 1.4$
		Year 4	$19,000 \times 6 \times \$1.64 \times 1.5$

3	*Other variable costs*	Per unit: $\$30 + (3 \times \$4.20) + \$4.40 = \$47$	
		Year 1	$10,000 \times \$47 \times 1.1$
		Year 2	$18,000 \times \$47 \times 1.3$
		Year 3	$18,000 \times \$47 \times 1.4$
		Year 4	$19,000 \times \$47 \times 1.5$

4	*Management salaries*	Year 1	$34,000 + $27,000 = $61,000 x 1.1
		Year 2	$61,000 × 1.3
		Year 3	$61,000 × 1.4
		Year 4	$61,000 × 1.5

12 Banden

Top tips. This question gives you practice in doing NPV calculations rapidly. Note how the NPV calculations are laid out in a way that enables you to show clearly how the profitability index is calculated. It would be less time consuming to use the proforma we have used than to do the NPV calculations, and then separately to do the profitability index calculations. What this emphasises is the usefulness of taking a few moments to plan the most efficient way of carrying out calculations.

In (b) because of the constraints you have to calculate the combined NPV of various possible combinations. It is obvious looking at the figures that the company will be undertaking some combination of three of the projects. However you would be penalised (and waste time) if you calculated the NPV of all combinations of three of the six. Any combinations including C should be excluded as the project makes a loss. It is also not possible for a combination to include A and E as they are mutually exclusive.

Our answer shows only those possible combinations of projects that cost less than $620,000. It would also be fine if you showed the cost of combinations that cost more than $620,000; however you should have then stated that they could not be undertaken, and should not have calculated their NPV.

(a)   The profitability index will be calculated as the ratio of the PV of net cash inflows to the year 0 capital outlay.

	Year	Cash flow $	Discount factor 12%		Present value $	Profitability index
Project A	1–5	70,000	3.605		252,350	252,350
	0	(246,000)	1.000		(246,000)	246,000
				NPV =	6,350	= 1.026
Project B	1	75,000	0.893		66,975	
	2	87,000	0.797		69,339	
	3	64,000	0.712		45,568	
					181,882	181,882
	0	(180,000)	1.000		(180,000)	180,000
				NPV =	1,882	= 1.010
Project C	1	48,000	0.893		42,864	
	2	48,000	0.797		38,256	
	3	63,000	0.712		44,856	
	4	73,000	0.636		46,428	
					172,404	172,404
	0	(175,000)	1.000		(175,000)	175,000
				NPV =	(2,596)	= 0.985
Project D	1–4	62,000	3.037		188,294	188,294
	0	(180,000)	1.000		(180,000)	180,000
				NPV =	8,294	= 1.046

	Year	Cash flow $	Discount factor 12%	Present value $	Profitability index
Project E	1	40,000	0.893	35,720	
	2	50,000	0.797	39,850	
	3	60,000	0.712	42,720	
	4	70,000	0.636	44,520	
	5	40,000	0.567	22,680	
				185,490	185,490
	0	(180,000)	1	(180,000)	180,000
				NPV = 5,490	= 1.031
Project F	1	35,000	0.893	31,255	
	2	82,000	0.797	65,354	
	3	82,000	0.712	58,384	
				154,993	154,993
	0	(150,000)	1	(150,000)	150,000
				4,993	= 1.033

Ranking	NPV	Profitability index
1st	D	D
2nd	A	F
3rd	E	E
4th	F	A
5th	B	B
6th	C	C

The rankings differ because the project's capital outlays differ. NPV shows the absolute benefit from a project, while profitability index scales that benefit according to the project's size.

(b) Project C comes sixth and last in the ranking according to both NPV and profitability index. It has a negative NPV and should not be undertaken.

Banden cannot afford to undertake more than three projects, given the maximum available capital of $620,000. It should not undertake project C, and it cannot undertake A and E simultaneously. The various feasible options are as follows.

Capital outlay

Projects	In total $	NPV in total $
D, F, E	510,000	18,777
D, F, A	576,000	19,637
D, F, B	510,000	15,169
D, E, B	540,000	15,666
D, A, B	606,000	16,526
F, A, B	576,000	13,225
F, E, B	510,000	12,365

Banden should not invest any funds in the money markets, because the return would only be 9% pa and the cost of capital for Banden is higher, at 12% pa.

It is assumed that the company does not have to use more funds than it needs to, and so there will not be any surplus funds which have to be invested somewhere.

Recommendation. The company should use $576,000 and invest in projects D, F and A.

13 ANT

(a) The first step is to calculate the **annual contribution** from each project, together with the working capital cash flows. These cash flows, together with the initial outlay, can then be **discounted** at the **cost of capital** to arrive at the NPV of each project. Development costs already incurred are irrelevant. There are no additional administration costs associated with the projects, and depreciation is also irrelevant since it has no cash effect.

First, calculate annual contribution.

	A	B	C	D
Unit sales	150,000	75,000	80,000	120,000
	$	$	$	$
Selling price per unit	30.00	40.00	25.00	50.00
Material cost per unit	7.60	12.00	4.50	25.00
Labour cost per unit	9.80	12.00	5.00	10.00
Variable overheads per unit	6.00	7.00	2.50	10.50
	$'000	$'000	$'000	$'000
Sales per annum	4,500	3,000	2,000	6,000
Materials	1,140	900	360	3,000
Labour	1,470	900	400	1,200
Variable overheads	900	525	200	1,260
Annual contribution	990	675	1,040	540

	A	B	C	D
	$'000	$'000	$'000	$'000
Working capital requirement (20% annual sales value)	900	600	400	1,200

It is assumed that working capital will be recovered at the end of year 5. The initial outlay will be made in year 0.

The NPV of each project can now be calculated.

Cash flows

Year	A Gross pa $'000	A Net $'000	B Gross pa $'000	B Net $'000	C Gross pa $'000	C Net $'000	D Gross pa $'000	D Net $'000	Discount factor 18%
0	(3,000)	(3,000)	(2,000)	(2,000)	(2,800)	(2,800)	(1,800)	(1,800)	1
1–4	990	2,663	675	1,816	1,040	2,798	540	1,453	2.690
5	1,890	826	1,275	557	1,440	629	1,740	760	0.437
		489		373		627		413	

(b) The **profitability** index provides a **means** of **optimising the NPV** when there are more projects available which yield a positive NPV than funds to invest in them. The profitability index measures the ratio of the present value of **cash inflows** to the **initial outlay** and represents the net present value per $1 invested.

Project	PV of inflows $'000	Initial outlay $'000	Ratio	Ranking
A	3,489	3,000	1.163	4
B	2,373	2,000	1.187	3
C	3,427	2,800	1.224	2
D	2,213	1,800	1.229	1

Project D has the highest PI ranking and is therefore the first choice for investment. On this basis the funds available should be invested as follows.

Project	Initial outlay $'000	Total NPV $'000	% taken	Cumulative outlay $'000	Actual NPV $'000
D	1,800	413	100	1,800	413
C	2,800	627	100	4,600	627
B	2,000	373	30	5,200	112
A	3,000	491	0	5,200	0
Total NPV generated					1,152

(c) The profitability index (PI) approach can be applied only if the projects under consideration fulfil certain criteria, such as:

(i) There is **only one constraint on investment**, in this case capital. The PI ensures that maximum return per unit of scarce resource (capital) is obtained.

(ii) **Each investment** can be **accepted** or **rejected** in its entirety or alternatively accepted on a partial basis.

(iii) The NPV generated by a given project is **directly proportional** to the percentage of the investment undertaken.

If **additional funds** are **available** but at a higher cost, then the simple PI approach cannot be used since it is not possible to calculate unambiguous individual NPVs.

If certain of the projects that may be undertaken are **mutually exclusive** then **sub-problems** must be **defined** and **calculations made** for different combinations of projects.

Possibly a more serious constraint is the assumption that the company's only concern is to **maximise NPV**. It is possible that there may be long-term strategic reasons which mean that an investment with a lower NPV should be undertaken instead of one with a higher NPV, and the ratio approach takes no account of the relative degrees of risk associated with making the different investments.

14 Sagitta

> **Top tips.** Remember in (b) that the value of rights is **not** the cost of the rights share. (c) emphasises that taking up and selling the rights should have identical effects.

(a) Current total market value
= $21m × 16
= $336m

Market value per share
= $336m/(60m × 4)
= $1.40

Rights issue price
= $1.40 × 0.70
= $0.98

Theoretical ex-rights price

	$
5 shares @ $1.40	7.00
1 share @ $0.98	0.98
6 shares	7.98

Theoretical ex-rights price = $7.98/6
= $1.33

(b) **Rights price**

	$
Theoretical ex-rights price	1.33
Cost of rights share	0.98
Value of rights	0.35

(c) **Take up rights issue**

	$
Value of shares after rights issue (10,000 × 6/5 × $1.33)	15,960
Cost of rights (2,000 × $0.98)	(1,960)
	14,000

Sell rights

	$
Value of shares (10,000 × $1.33)	13,300
Sale of rights (2,000 × $0.35)	700
	14,000

Allow rights offer to lapse

	$
Value of shares (10,000 × $1.33)	13,300

If the investor either takes up the rights issue or sells his rights then his wealth will remain the same. The difference is that if he takes up the rights issue he will maintain his relative shareholding but if he sells his rights his percentage shareholding will fall, although he will gain $700 in cash.

However if the investor allows the rights to lapse his wealth will decrease by $700.

(d) Sagitta clearly needs to raise $47.04 million which is why it was decided to make a 1 for 5 rights issue of 48 million additional shares at a price of $0.98. Provided that this amount is raised it could have been done (for example) by issuing 96 million new shares as a two for five rights issue with the issue price at $0.49 per share.

The **price of the issue** and the **number of shares should not be important** in a competitive market as the value of the business will not change and nor will the shareholders' percentage shareholding.

However the critical factor about the **price of the rights issue** is that it **must be below the market value** at the time of the rights issue. If the rights issue price is higher than the market value then there is no incentive to shareholders to purchase the additional shares and the rights issue will fail. As far as the business is concerned the details of the rights issue including the price must be determined a considerable time before the rights issue actually takes place, therefore there is always the risk that the share price might fall in the intervening period.

(e) A Murabaha transaction is a form of credit sale. There is an immediate transfer of an asset, with the buyer making payment in the future (possibly in instalments). The total payment will include a mark-up on the value of the asset in recognition of the convenience of paying later. The asset can be sold to raise funds for the future payment. There is a contract between the buyer and the seller stating the value of the asset transferred and the mark-up amount.

A conventional loan has capital borrowed and then interest is to be repaid on top and there is no transfer of an asset to the borrower. For a Murabaha transaction, there must be an underlying asset that exists and has a value within a fair market range. Although the asset can vary for transactions it **must not be prohibited by Sharia'a**. Another difference is that in Murabaha transactions penalties for late payments that would profit the seller are not allowed.

In Islamic finance riba (or interest) is forbidden, therefore under Murabaha there is an agreed upon mark-up, which should allow both parties to share in the profit from the sale of the asset.

15 Headwater

> **Top tips.** The bulk of the marks in (a) would be available for the written comparisons with the rest of the industry, particularly as you are told which ratios to calculate rather than having to select them yourself. You need to provide sensible explanations for differences with the industry and highlight areas for concern, in particular here the problems over sources of finance.
>
> In (b) you need to show that the company can gain more funds not only because more investors can put money in, but also that listed status provides more reasons for investors to buy a stake (improved marketability of shares being probably the most important).
>
> When answering (c) you should examine the statement of financial position and consider how different elements might be made more attractive to investors. This includes looking at share capital and considering whether the issue price of each share is likely to be too high.

(a)   The performance and financial health of Headwater in relation to that of the industry sector as a whole can be evaluated by comparing its financial ratios with the industry averages, as follows.

Headwater	*Industry average*
Return on (long-term) capital employed	
Operating profit (PBIT): Equity + long-term debt	
$4.9m: ($12.4m + $2.2m) = 33.6%	24%
Return on equity	
Profit attributable to equity shareholders	
$3.1m: $12.4m = 25%	16%
Operating profit margin	
Operating profit : Sales	
$4.9m: $36.5m = 13.4%	11%
Current ratio	
Current assets: Current liabilities	
$10.1m: $9.0m = 1.12:1	1.6:1
Acid test	
Current assets excluding inventory: Current liabilities	
$5.7m: $9.0m = 0.63:1	1.0:1
Gearing	
Debt: Equity	
($2m + $2.2m): $12.4m = 33.9%	24%
Dividend cover	
Profit attributable to equity shareholders	
$3.1m: $0.3m = 10.3 times	4.0
Interest cover	
Profit before interest and tax (PBIT): Interest	
$4.9m: $1.3m = 3.77 times	4.5

These ratios can be used to evaluate performance in terms of profitability, liquidity and financial security.

Profitability

Headwater's return on capital employed, return on equity and operating profit margin are all significantly above the industry averages. Although the first two measures could be inflated due to assets being shown at low book values, the profit margin indicates that Headwater is managing to make good profits, which could be due to successful marketing, a low cost base or to its occupation of a particularly profitable niche in the market.

Liquidity

Both the current and the quick (acid test) ratios are well below the industry averages. This suggests that Headwater is either short of liquid resources or is managing its working capital poorly. However, the three key working capital ratios modify this impression.

Receivables days: $365 \times 4.7/36.5 = 47$ days
Inventory turnover: $365 \times 4.4/31.6 = 51$ days
Payment period: $365 \times 7.0/31.6 = 81$ days

Although the industry averages are not known, these ratios appear to be very good by general standards. It therefore appears that Headwater has become under-capitalised, perhaps through the use of working capital to finance growth.

Financial security

Gearing is **high** in comparison with the rest of the industry, and 48% of the debt is in the form of overdraft which is generally repayable on demand. This is therefore a risky form of debt to use in large amounts. The debenture is repayable in two years and will need to be refinanced since Headwater cannot redeem it out of existing resources. Interest cover is also poor, and this together with the poor liquidity probably account for the low payout ratio (the inverse of the dividend cover).

In summary, profit performance is strong, but there are significant weaknesses in both the liquidity and the financial structure. These problems need to be addressed if Headwater is to be able to maintain its record of strong and consistent growth.

(b)   A company such as Headwater may seek a stock market listing for the following reasons.

      (i)   To **allow access** to a **wider pool of finance**: companies that are growing fast may need to raise larger sums than is possible privately. Obtaining a listing widens the potential number of equity investors, and may also result in an improved credit rating, thus reducing the cost of additional debt finance.

      (ii)   To **improve the marketability of the shares**: shares that are traded on the stock market can be bought and sold in relatively small quantities at any time. This means that it is easier for existing investors to realise a part of their holding.

      (iii)   To **allow capital to be transferred** to other ventures: founder owners may wish to liquidate the major part of their holding either for personal reasons or for investment in other new business opportunities.

      (iv)   To **improve the company image**: quoted companies are commonly believed to be more financially stable, and this may improve the image of the company with its customers and suppliers, allowing it to gain additional business and to improve its buying power.

      (v)   **Growth by acquisition** is easier: a listed company is in a better position to make a paper offer for a target company than an unlisted one.

(c)   Restructuring its statement of financial position prior to flotation will help to make Headwater appear a sounder prospect to potential investors who know little about its past performance. Methods available include the following.

Disposal of surplus assets. This will improve both gearing and liquidity.

Non-current asset revaluation. Land and buildings may well be shown in the accounts at values that are significantly below the current market valuation. Adjustment to market values will improve the gearing ratio and the value of shareholders' funds, although the effect of this will be to depress the reported return on capital employed and return on equity. However, since these are currently well above industry averages this should not present too much of a problem.

Liquidity improvement. Although there does not appear to be much scope for tightening the control of working capital, Headwater may be able to improve its cash flow by other means, for example by reducing overheads and delaying the purchase of additional fixed assets.

Sale and leaseback. If Headwater owns valuable freehold premises it may be able to release cash by selling them and exchanging the freehold for an operating lease. This would improve both the liquidity position and the reported return on capital employed although the gearing would be little affected.

Elimination of non-voting 'A' shares. These are not permitted by the Stock Exchange for companies newly entering the market.

Share split. On the basis of the industry average P/E of 10, the shares would be priced at $11.48 (= $10 \times 3.1m/(1.8m + 0.9m)$). A highly priced new issue is likely to deter potential small investors. This problem could be overcome by reducing the nominal value of the shares by means of a share split.

16 ABC

> **Top tips**. The wisdom of the dividend policy each company adopts is somewhat dependent upon its current and future plans – whether in fact it can make 'better' use of the profits by re-investing them. The answer stresses the importance of stability in dividend payments – this is a very important 'real-world' issue. The scrip issues and other concessions by C are unlikely to be harmful, although their positive effect may not be very great.
>
> The key element in the second part of the question is the **clientele effect**. You need to stress the importance of the shareholders' tax position here.

A's policy

Company A, which has deliberately avoided paying any dividends in the last five years, is pursuing a sensible policy for a rapidly growing company. All its post-tax profits are being **reinvested** in the company's business. By adopting this strategy, Company A reduces to a minimum its need to raise new capital from the market. **Issue costs** are **reduced** or **eliminated** and the company has **greater** flexibility in its investment programme since decision taking is not dependent on gaining market approval. Furthermore, since the company is probably investing heavily its taxation liability may well be small.

B's policy

At first sight the policy pursued by Company B, of distributing 50% of post-tax profits, appears to offer the shareholders **predictability**. In fact, however, with changes in the company's operating profits and in the tax regime, the post-tax earnings may fluctuate considerably. **Reducing** the **dividend** of a quoted company normally causes its **share price** to **fall sharply**, since the market takes this as casting considerable doubt on its future earnings potential. But, the more **mature** and **predictable** that Company B's business is, the **greater the merit** in its **dividend policy**. A mature business usually needs less new capital investment than a growing one and so a higher level of dividend is justified. Distributing profits allows shareholders to make some adjustment to the risk and return profile of their portfolios without incurring the transaction costs of buying and selling.

C's policy

Company C's policy falls between those of A and B in that a dividend is paid, albeit a small one. The **predictability** of the dividend will be welcomed by shareholders, since it allows them to make their financial plans with more certainty than would otherwise be possible. It also gives C part of A's advantage; **retained earnings** can be used as the principal source of investment capital. To the extent that they are relevant at all, **scrip issues** are likely to increase a company's market value, since they are often made to increase the **marketability** of the shares. Shareholder concessions are simply a means of attracting the 'small' shareholder who can benefit from them personally, and have no impact on dividend policy.

Effect on shareholders

In addition to looking at the cash flows of each company, we must also consider the impact of these dividend policies on the after tax wealth of shareholders. Shareholders can be divided into groups or **'clienteles'**. Different clienteles may be attracted to invest in each of the three firms, depending on their tax situation. It is worth noting that one clientele is as good as another in terms of the valuation it implies for the firm.

Company A would be particularly attractive to individuals who do not require an income stream from their investment and prefer to obtain a **return** through **capital growth**. Company B's clientele prefer a much higher proportion of their return to be in the form of **income**, although it would not be income on which they rely since it may be very variable from year to year. **Tax exempt funds**, such as pension funds, are indifferent between returns in the form of income or capital and might well invest in B since they need a flow of income to meet their day to day obligations. A large, diversified portfolio would reduce the effect of variability in the dividend. Company C is more likely to appeal to the **private investor** since most of the return is in the form of capital growth and there are shareholder concessions too.

So, each company may maximise the wealth of its shareholders. If the theorists are right, A, B and C all **maximise shareholder wealth** because the value of the companies is unaffected by dividend policy. Alternatively, each company's group of shareholders may favour their company's policy (and so their wealth is maximised) because the dividend policy is appropriate to their tax position and so maximises their post-tax returns.

17 DF

Top tips. The nature of the calculation in (a) should have suggested to you that the majority of marks would be available for the discussion. The answer looks well beyond the relationship with FF, considering the effect on relations with other customers, the effect on DF itself, and whether there are alternative sources of finance for DF.

(b) goes on to cover those alternative sources of finance. Various criteria can be used to consider them:

- **Costs** (including costs saved)
- **Flexibility** (a company knows when and how much interest and principal it has to pay on a loan but still has to pay it; by contrast an overdraft facility only has interest charged on it if it is used, but it is repayable on demand.)
- **Commitment** (security that has to be given, how much the company is tied into the arrangement)
- **Appearances** (effect on gearing, effect on accounts receivable if factor organisation is employed)

Although the question directs you towards discussing certain sources of finance, it does not confine you to those sources. Therefore, although the bulk of your answer to (b) should discuss the sources listed, a section briefly mentioning other sources should also be included.

Don't forget also in (b) to bear in mind the likely level of financial knowledge of the recipients of your report; don't assume a high level of understanding.

(a) **Cost of discount**

The **percentage cost** of an **early settlement discount** to the company giving it can be estimated by the formula:

$$1 - \left[\frac{100}{100 - d} \right]^{\frac{365}{t}}$$

Where d is the size of discount (%)

t is the reduction in payment period in days necessary to achieve discount

d = 3%
t = 90 − 10 = 80

$$\% \text{ cost} = 1 - \left[\frac{100}{100 - 3} \right]^{\frac{365}{80}} = 14.9\%$$

The **annual equivalent rate of interest** in offering a 3% cash discount is therefore 14.9%.

Offer of discount

Other factors that DF should take into account before deciding on whether to offer a discount include:

(i) The **attractiveness** of the **discount** to FF, and the probability that it will be taken up

(ii) Whether the **discount** will encourage FF to **purchase larger volumes** than it would if the discount was not available

(iii) The **relative effect** of the **different financing alternatives** on the administration costs of DF

(iv) The **ease** with which DF will be **able to raise alternative sources of finance,** the effect on **gearing** of these sources and the need for **security**

(v) The interest **other customers** might show in taking a discount

(vi) The possibility of **withdrawing** from the discount arrangement without loss of FF's goodwill in the future

(b) To: Shareholders in DF
From: Management Accountant
Date: 11 December 20X1
Subject: Alternative methods of financing current assets

Introduction

The contract to supply FF means that DF will need to make a **significant additional permanent investment** in **current assets** (in the form of additional inventories and higher accounts receivable). There will also be an additional temporary element which **fluctuates** with the level of sales. This will increase the amount of money needed by the company to finance these assets. There are a number of different sources of finance that could be considered.

Bank loan

A bank loan would normally be for a **fixed amount of money** for a fixed term and at a fixed rate of interest. It is not clear whether or not the company has any existing debt finance. However, it has already been decided to use a bank loan to fund the purchase of the additional non-current assets. The **size of this loan** and the **quality of security** available will be key factors in determining whether the bank is willing to make a further advance to cover the investment in current assets. Assuming that a further loan is forthcoming, the company will need to evaluate the effect of this in terms of **cost** and the **effect on the capital structure**.

Advantages of bank loan

(i) **Bank finance** is **cheaper** than the cost of allowing a 3% **settlement discount**, and is also likely to be cheaper than using debt factoring or invoice discounting.

(ii) The **loan** can be **negotiated** for a **fixed term** and a **fixed amount**, and this is less risky than for example using an overdraft, which is repayable on demand.

Disadvantages of bank loan

(i) The company will have to **pay interest** on the **full amount of the loan** for the entire period. This could make it more expensive in absolute terms than using an alternative source of finance where interest is only payable on the amount outstanding.

(ii) The loan will **increase the level** of the company's **financial gearing**. This means that there could be greater volatility in the returns attributable to the ordinary shareholders.

(iii) The bank is likely to **require security**. If there are questions as to the quality of the asset base, the bank may also require personal guarantees or additional security from the directors or shareholders.

Overdraft

An overdraft is a form of lending that is **repayable on demand**. The bank grants the customer a **facility** up to a certain limit, and the customer can take advantage of this as necessary. Overdrafts are essentially short-term finance, but are renewable and may become a near-permanent source.

Advantages of overdraft

The attraction of using an overdraft to finance current assets is that **interest** is only **payable** on the **amount of the facility actually in use** at any one time. This means that the **effective cost of the overdraft** will be **lower** than that of the **bank loan**. This is particularly attractive for a company such as DF, where demand is expected to fluctuate significantly from month to month, and consequently there are likely to be large variations in the level of working capital. It is also likely to be cheaper than the other alternatives being considered.

Disadvantages of overdraft

The main drawback to using an overdraft is that it will be **repayable on demand**, and therefore the company is in a more vulnerable position than it would be if a bank loan were used instead. A long-term overdraft may be included in the **gearing** calculations, and the bank may require **security.**

Debt factoring

Factoring is an arrangement to have **debts collected** by a **factor company**, which advances a proportion of the money it is due to collect. Services offered by the factor would normally include the following:

(i)   **Administration** of the client's invoicing, sales accounting and debt collection service.

(ii)   **Credit protection** for the client's debts, whereby the factor takes over the risk of loss from bad debts and so 'insures' the client against such losses.

(iii)   **Making advance payments** to the client before the debts are collected.

Benefits of factoring

(i)   **Growth** is **effectively financed through sales**, which provide the security to the factor. DF would not have to provide the additional security that might be required by the bank.

(ii)   The **managers** of the business will **not** have to **spend time** on the problem of **slow paying accounts receivable.**

(iii)   **Administration costs** will be **reduced** since the company will not have to run its own sales ledger department.

Disadvantages of factoring

(i)   The **level of finance** is **geared** to the **level of sales**; in other words, finance lags sales. In practice, DF will need finance ahead of sales in order to build up sufficient inventorys to meet demand.

(ii)   Factoring may be **more expensive** than bank finance. Service charges are generally around 2% of total invoice value, in addition to finance charges at levels comparable to bank overdraft rates.

(iii)   The fact that accounts receivable will be making payments direct to the factor may present a **negative picture** of the firm.

Invoice discounting

Invoice discounting is related to factoring and many factors will provide an invoice discounting service. Invoice discounting is the **purchase of a selection of invoices**, at a discount. The discounter does **not take over** the **administration** of the client's sales ledger, and the arrangement is purely for the advance of cash.

Advantages of discounting

The arrangement is thus a **purely financial transaction** that can be used to release working capital, and therefore shares some of the benefits of factoring in that **further security** is **not required**. The discounter will make an assessment of the risk involved, and only good quality invoices will be purchased, but this should not be a problem to DF since FF is a large well established company.

Disadvantages of discounting

The main disadvantage is that **invoice discounting** is likely to be **more expensive** than any of the other alternatives. It is normally only used to cover a temporary cash shortage, and not for the routine provision of working capital.

Other options

(i) Finance can be obtained by **delaying payment to accounts payable.** In theory this is potentially a **cheap source of finance.** The main disadvantage may be a **loss of supplier goodwill,** at a time when the company needs supplier co-operation to fulfil the new order.

(ii) Other methods of loan finance, notably debenture issue, are not appropriate as they are essentially **long-term,** and the **debenture holders** may require **security** that the company is unable to give.

(iii) Although we are told that **increased inventory levels** will be needed to **fulfil FF's requirements,** there may be scope for **reducing the inventory levels** necessary to fulfil other customers' requirements.

Conclusions

Of the options considered, factoring or some form of bank finance is likely to be the most appropriate. The final decision must take into account the full cost implications, and not just the relative rates of interest on the finance. DF must also consider the effect of the type of finance selected on the statement of financial position, and the type of security that will be required. This could also impact on the ability of the company to raise further finance in the future.

18 CRY

Top tips. (a) demonstrates the complications that may occur in weighted average cost of capital calculations.

With bonds, the most serious mistake you can make is to treat redeemable bonds as irredeemable. Because the bonds are redeemable, you need to carry out an IRR analysis. Remember this calculation is done from the viewpoint of the investor. The investor pays the market price for the bonds at time 0, and then receives the interest and the conversion value in subsequent years. You must bring tax into your calculation, although you could have assumed that tax was paid with a one year time delay.

Lastly don't forget that the weightings in the WACC calculation are based on **market values, not book values**.

(b) demonstrates that the calculation of the weighted average cost of capital is not a purely mechanical process. It makes assumptions about the shareholders, the proposed investment and the company's capital structure and future dividend prospects. Given all the assumptions involved, the result of the calculations may need to be taken with a large pinch of salt!

(a) The post-tax weighted average cost of capital should first be calculated.

(i) **Ordinary shares**

The formula for calculating the cost of equity when there is dividend growth is:

$$k_e = \frac{D_0(1 + g)}{P_0} + g$$

where k_e = cost of equity

D_0 = current dividend

g = rate of growth

P_0 = current ex div market value.

In this case we shall estimate the future rate of growth (g) from the average growth in dividends over the past four years.

$$810 = 620 (1 + g)^4$$

$$(1 + g)^4 = \frac{810}{620}$$

$$= 1.3065$$

$$(1 + g) = 1.069$$

$$g = 0.069 = 6.9\%$$

$$k_e = \frac{0.27 \times 1.069}{3} + 0.069 = 16.5\%$$

(ii) **7% Bonds**

In order to find the post-tax cost of the bonds, which are redeemable in ten years time, it is necessary to find the discount rate (IRR) which will give the future post-tax cash flows a present value of $77.10.

The relevant cash flows for a single bond with a nominal value of $100 are:

(1) Annual interest payments, net of tax, which are $100 \times 7\% \times 70\% = \$4.90$ (for ten years)

(2) A capital repayment of $100 (in ten years time)

It is assumed that tax relief on the bond interest arises at the same time as the interest payment. In practice the cash flow effect is unlikely to be felt for about a year, but this will have no significant effect on the calculations.

Try 10%

	Present value $'000
Current market value of bonds	(77.1)
Annual interest payments net of tax $4.90 × 6.145 (10% for 10 years)	30.1
Capital repayment $100 × 0.386 (10% in ten years time)	38.6
NPV	(8.4)

Try 5%

	$'000
Current market value of bonds	(77.1)
Annual interest payments net of tax $4.90 × 7.722	37.8
Capital repayment 100 × 0.614	61.4
NPV	22.1

$$IRR = 5\% + \left[\frac{22.1}{22.1--8.4} \times (10-5)\right]\% = 8.6\%$$

(iii) **The weighted average cost of capital**

	Market value $'000	Cost %
Equity	9,000	16.5
7% Bonds	1,002	8.6
	10,002	

$$WACC = \left(\frac{V_e}{V_e + V_d}\right) K_e + \left(\frac{V_d}{V_e + V_d}\right) K_d (1-T)$$

$$WACC = \left(\frac{9,000}{10,002}\right) \times 16.5 + \left(\frac{1,002}{10,002}\right) \times 8.6$$

(The K_d is already post-tax so it is not multiplied by $1 - T$)

$$= 14.85 + 0.86 = 15.7\%$$

The above calculations suggest that a discount rate in the region of 16% might be appropriate for the appraisal of new investment opportunities.

(b) Difficulties and uncertainties in the above estimates arise in a number of areas.

(i) **The cost of equity**. The above calculation assumes that all shareholders have the same marginal cost of capital and the same dividend expectations, which is unrealistic. In addition, it is assumed that dividend growth has been and will be at a constant rate of 6.9%. In fact, actual growth in the years 20X5/6 and 20X8/9 was in excess of 9%, while in the year 20X7/8 there was no dividend growth. 6.9% is merely the average rate of growth for the past four years. The rate of future growth will depend more on the return from future projects undertaken than on the past dividend record.

(ii) **The use of the weighted average cost of capital**. Use of the weighted average cost of capital as a discount rate is only justified where the company in question has achieved what it believes to be the **optimal capital structure** (the mix of debt and equity) and where it intends to maintain this structure in the long term.

(iii) **The projects themselves**. The weighted average cost of capital makes **no allowance** for the **business risk** of **individual projects**. In practice some companies, having calculated the WACC, then add a premium for risk. In this case, for example, if one used a risk premium of 5% the final discount rate would be 21%. Ideally the risk premium should vary from project to project, since not all projects are equally risky. In general, the riskier the project the higher the discount rate which should be used.

19 Katash

Top tips. Use clear workings and a logical approach to the calculations in parts (a) and (b). They should be straightforward if you have done enough practice but make sure you do not spend too long on them.

The discussion in part (c) covers a very important and highly examinable area. You must be familiar with both the traditional view and that of Modigliani and Miller.

Easy marks. There are plenty of marks available for some straightforward calculations.

(a) **Current WACC**

Cost of debt

Year		Cash flow	Discount factor	PV	Discount factor	PV
		$	7%	$	5%	$
0	Bond price	(105.00)	1.000	(105.00)	1.000	(105.00)
1-5	Interest (10 × (1 − 0.3))	7.00	4.100	28.70	4.329	30.30
5	Repayment	100.00	0.713	71.30	0.784	78.40
				(5.00)		3.70

Calculate the cost of debt using an IRR calculation.

$$\text{IRR} = a\% + \left[\frac{NPV_a}{NPV_a - NPV_b} \times (b-a)\right]\%$$

$$\text{Cost of debt} = 5 + \left[\frac{3.7}{3.7+5}(7-5)\right]$$

$$= 5.85\%$$

Cost of equity

$$k_e = R_f + (R_m - R_f)\beta$$

$$
\begin{aligned}
R_f &= 5\% \\
R_m &= 12\% \\
\beta &= 1.2 \\
k_e &= 5\% + (12\% - 5\%)1.2 \\
&= 13.40\%
\end{aligned}
$$

Weighted average cost of capital

$$V_E = 450 \times 5 = \$2{,}250m$$

$$V_D = 1{,}800 \times 1.05 = \$1{,}890m$$

$$\text{WACC} = k_e\left[\frac{V_E}{V_E + V_D}\right] + k_d\left[\frac{V_D}{V_E + V_D}\right]$$

$$= \left[13.40\% \times \frac{2.250}{4{,}140}\right] + \left[5.85\% \times \frac{1{,}890}{4{,}140}\right]$$

$$= 7.28\% + 2.67\%$$

$$= 9.95\%$$

(b) **Project specific cost of equity**

Ungear Chlopop beta

$$\beta_u = \beta_g \frac{V_E}{V_E + V_D(1-t)}$$

For Chlopop:
$$V_E = 600 \times 5.60 = \$3{,}360m$$
$$V_D = \$525m$$

$$\beta_u = 1.6 \times (3{,}360/(3{,}360 + (525 \times 0.7)))$$

$$= 1.44$$

Re-gearing

$V_E = \$510m$

$V_D = \$390m$

$$\beta_g = \beta_u \times \frac{V_E + V_D(1-t)}{V_E}$$

$$\beta_g = 1.44 \times \frac{510 + (390 \times 0.7)}{510} = 2.211$$

Cost of equity

$$k_e = R_f + (R_m - R_f)\,\beta$$
$$= 5\% + (12\% - 5\%)2.211$$
$$= 20.48\%$$

(c) **Sources of finance**

The sources of long-term finance for Katash are ordinary shares and bonds and the rate of return expected by investors depends on the **relative risks** of each type of finance. Equity is the most risky and therefore has the highest cost of capital. The bonds are the least risky with the lowest cost of capital.

Therefore, if we ignore taxation, the weighted average cost of capital would be expected to decrease if equity is replaced by debt.

Traditional view

In the **traditional view** of capital structure, ordinary shareholders are relatively **indifferent** to the addition of small amounts of debt so the WACC falls as a company gears up.

However, as equity is replaced by debt and gearing increases, **financial risk** will increase so the cost of equity will rise and this will offset the effect of cheaper debt.

The before-tax cost of debt will also increase at high levels of gearing due to the risk of bankruptcy. This **bankruptcy risk** will further increase the cost of equity.

A company can therefore gear up using debt and reduce its WACC to a **minimum**. When the WACC is minimised, the **market value** of the company, equal to the present value of its cash flows, will be maximised.

Beyond this minimum point, the WACC will increase due to the effect of increasing financial and bankruptcy risk.

Modigliani and Miller

In contrast to this traditional view, **Modigliani and Miller**, assuming a perfect market and ignoring tax, demonstrated that the WACC remained constant as a company increased its gearing. They argued that the increase in the cost of equity due to financial risk **exactly balanced** the decrease in WACC caused by the lower before-tax cost of debt.

In a perfect capital market, there is no bankruptcy risk so the WACC and therefore the market value of the company is constant at all gearing levels. The market value of a company depends on its **business risk** only. This means that Katash cannot change its WACC.

However, corporate tax does exist and interest payments on debt reduce tax liability. It could thus be argued that WACC falls as gearing increases, and Katash could therefore reduce its WACC to a minimum by taking on as much debt as possible.

The assumption of a perfect capital market is unrealistic. Bankruptcy risk and other costs of servicing debt will increase as gearing increases and this will offset the value of the tax shield.

Conclusion

In conclusion, Katash should be able to reduce its WACC by gearing up, but the minimum WACC achievable may be hard to determine.

20 Black Raven

Top tips. This introductory question may have taken you more than 36 minutes but it provides comprehensive practice of valuation techniques. In the exam you would most likely be expected to use these techniques to carry out calculations that would form the basis of discussions. Even in this question, you do need to make clear the basis of your calculations and the assumptions you are making.

Other important issues which this question raises include:

- Valuation (if any) of intangible assets
- Lack of likelihood that asset valuation basis would be used
- Adjustment to P/E ratios used in calculations because company is unquoted

Don't take all of the figures used in this answer as the only possibilities. You could for example have made adjustments to estimated earnings to allow for uncertainty, or used a different figure to 17% for the required yield in the calculation of a valuation based upon dividend yield. when

(a) **An assets basis valuation**

If we assume that a purchaser would accept the revaluation of assets by the independent valuer, an assets valuation of equity would be as follows.

	$	$
Non-current assets		
(ignore patents, assumed to have no market value)		
Land and buildings		1,075,000
Plant and equipment		480,000
Motor vehicles		45,000
		1,600,000
Current assets		383,000
		1,983,000
Less: current liabilities	230,000	
loan	400,000	
		630,000
Asset value of equity (300,000 shares)		1,353,000

Value per share = $4.51

Unless the purchasing company intends to sell the assets acquired, it is more likely that a valuation would be based on earnings.

(b) **Earnings basis valuations**

If the purchaser believes that earnings over the last five years are an appropriate measure for valuation, we could take average earnings in these years, which were:

$$\frac{\$465,000}{5} = \$93,000$$

An appropriate P/E ratio for an earnings basis valuation might be the average of the three publicly quoted companies for the recent year. (A trend towards an increase in the P/E ratio over three years is assumed, and even though average earnings have been taken, the most recent year's P/E ratios are considered to be the only figures which are appropriate.)

	P/E ratio
Albatross	8.5
Bullfinch	9.0
Crow	10.0
Average	9.167 (i)
Reduce by about 40% to allow for unquoted status	5.5 (ii)

Share valuations on a past earnings basis are as follows.

	P/E ratio	Earnings $'000	Valuation $'000	Number of shares	Value per share $
(i)	9.167	93	852.5	300,000	2.84
(ii)	5.5	93	511.5	300,000	1.71

Because of the unquoted status of Black Raven, purchasers would probably apply a lower P/E ratio, and an offer of about $1.71 per share would be more likely than one of $2.84.

Future earnings might be used. Forecast earnings based on the company's five year plan will be used.

		$
Expected earnings:	Year 1	100,000
	Year 2	104,000
	Year 3	108,160
	Year 4	112,486
	Year 5	116,986
	Average	108,326.4 (say $108,000)

A share valuation on an expected earnings basis would be as follows.

P/E ratio	Average future earnings	Valuation	Value per share
5.5	$108,000	$594,000	$1.98

It is not clear whether the purchasing company would accept Black Raven's own estimates of earnings.

(c) **A dividend yield basis of valuation with no growth**

There seems to have been a general pattern of increase in dividend yields to shareholders in quoted companies, and it is reasonable to suppose that investors in Black Raven would require at least the same yield.

An average yield for the recent year for the three quoted companies will be used. This is 12%. The only reliable dividend figure for Black Raven is $45,000 a year gross, in spite of the expected increase in future earnings. A yield basis valuation would therefore be:

$$\frac{\$45,000}{12\%} = \$375,000 \text{ or } \$1.25 \text{ per share}$$

A purchasing company would, however, be more concerned with earnings than with dividends if it intended to buy the entire company, and an offer price of $1.25 should be considered too low. On the other hand, since Black Raven is an unquoted company, a higher yield than 12% might be expected.

(d) **A dividend yield basis of valuation, with growth**

Since earnings are expected to increase by 4% a year, it could be argued that a similar growth rate in dividends would be expected. We shall assume that the required yield is 17%, rather more than the 12% for quoted companies because Black Raven is unquoted. However, in the absence of information about the expected growth of dividends in the quoted companies, the choice of 12%, 17% or whatever, is not much better than a guess.

$$P_0 = \frac{D_0(1+g)}{(r-g)} = \frac{45,000(1.04)}{(0.17-0.04)} = \$360,000 \text{ or } \$1.20 \text{ per share}$$

(e) **The discounted value of future cash flows**

The present value of cash inflows from an investment by a purchaser of Black Raven's shares would be discounted at either 18% or 14%, depending on the view taken of Black Raven's assets. Although the loan of $400,000 is secured on some of the company's property, there are enough assets against which there is no charge to assume that a purchaser would consider the investment to be backed by tangible assets.

The present value of the benefits from the investment would be as follows.

Year	Cash flow $'000	Discount factor 14%	PV of cash flow $'000
1	120	0.877	105.24
2	120	0.769	92.28
3	140	0.675	94.50
4	70	0.592	41.44
5	120	0.519	62.28
			395.74

A valuation per share of $1.32 might therefore be made. This basis of valuation is one which a purchasing company ought to consider. It might be argued that cash flows beyond year 5 should be considered and a higher valuation could be appropriate, but a figure of less than $2 per share would be offered on a DCF valuation basis.

Summary

Any of the preceding valuations might be made, but since share valuation is largely a subjective matter, many other prices might be offered. In view of the high asset values of the company an asset stripping purchaser might come forward.

21 Bases of valuation

(a) (i) **Statement of financial position value** = $ (2,070,600 − 1,616,500) = $454,100.

(ii) **Replacement cost value** = $454,100 + $(725,000 − 651,600) + $(550,000 − 515,900) = $561,600.

(iii) **Realisable value** = $454,100 + $(450,000 − 651,600) + (570,000 − 515,900) - $14,900 = $291,700.

Bad debts are 2% × $745,000 = $14,900. Bad debts are assumed not to be relevant to statement of financial position and replacement cost values.

(iv) The **dividend growth model value** depends on an estimate of growth, which is far from clear given the wide variations in earnings over the five years.

1 The lowest possible value, assuming zero growth, is as follows.

$$\text{Value ex div} = \frac{\$25,000}{0.12} = \$208,333$$

It is not likely that this will be the basis taken.

2 Looking at dividend growth over the past five years we have:

20X4 dividend = $25,000

20X0 dividend = $20,500.

If the annual growth rate in dividends is g

$$(1 + g)^4 = \frac{(25,000)}{20,500} = 1.2195$$

$$1 + g = 1.0508$$

$$g = 0.0508, \text{ say } 5.1\%$$

$$\text{Then, MV ex div} = \frac{\text{Dividend in 1 year}}{0.12 - g}$$

$$= \frac{25,000(1.051)}{0.069}$$

$$= \$380,797$$

3   Using the rb model, we have:

Average proportion retained =

$$\frac{12,800 + 44,200 + 18,300 + 13,400 + 27,200}{33,300 + 66,800 + 43,300 + 38,400 + 52,200} = 0.495 \text{ (say } b = 0.5)$$

$$\text{Return on investment this year } = \frac{52,200}{\text{average investment}}$$

$$= \frac{52,200}{\left[(454,100 + 454,100 - 27,200]/2\right.}$$

$$= 0.1185 \text{ (say } r = 12\%).$$

Then g = 0.5 × 12% = 6%

so MV ex div = $\dfrac{\$25,000(1.06)}{0.06} = \$441,667$

(v) P/E ratio model

Comparable quoted companies to Manon have P/E ratios of about 10. Manon is much smaller and being unquoted its P/E ratio would be less than 10, but how much less?

If we take a P/E ratio of 5, we have MV = $52,200 × 5 = $261,000.

If we take a P/E ratio of 10 × 2/3, we have MV = $52,200 × 10 × 2/3 = $348,000.

If we take a P/E ratio of 10, we have MV = $522,000.

(b) (i)   The statement of financial position value

The statement of financial position value should not play a part in the negotiation process. Historical costs are not relevant to a decision on the future value of the company.

(ii) The replacement cost

This gives the cost of setting up a similar business. Since this gives a higher figure than any other valuation in this case, it could show the maximum price for Carmen to offer. There is clearly no goodwill to value.

(iii) The realisable value

This shows the cash which the shareholders in Manon could get by liquidating the business. It is therefore the minimum price which they would accept.

All the methods (i) to (iii) suffer from the limitation that they do not look at the going concern value of the business as a whole. Methods (iv) and (v) do consider this value. However, the realisable value is of use in assessing the risk attached to the business as a going concern, as it gives the base value if things go wrong and the business has to be abandoned.

(iv) The dividend model

The figures have been calculated using Manon's K_e (12%). If (2) or (3) were followed, the value would be the minimum that Manon's shareholders would accept, as the value in use exceeds scrap value in (iii). The relevance of a dividend valuation to Carmen will depend on whether the current retention and reinvestment policies would be continued. Certainly the value to Carmen should be based on 9% rather than 12%. Both companies are ungeared and in the same risk class so the different required returns must be due to their relative sizes and the fact that Carmen's shares are more marketable.

One of the main limitations on the dividend growth model is the problem of estimating the future value of g.

(v) **The P/E ratio model**

The P/E ratio model is an attempt to get at the value which the market would put on a company like Manon. It does provide an external yardstick, but is a very crude measure. As already stated, the P/E ratio which applies to larger quoted companies must be lowered to allow for the size of Manon and the non-marketability of its shares. Another limitation of P/E ratios is that the ratio is very dependent on the expected future growth of the firm. It is therefore not easy to find a P/E ratio of a 'similar firm'. However, in practice the P/E model may well feature in the negotiations over price simply because it is an easily understood yardstick.

22 Market efficiency

Top tips. The efficient market hypothesis may be the subject of a part question in this exam. An answer focusing on a technical concept should always start with a clear definition of that concept, including as appropriate the key assumptions. Here the answer goes on to discuss the various forms of the efficient market hypothesis, concentrating on the differences between them (the amount of information available).

It is also important when discussing a theory that attempts to model actual behaviour to bring in evidence of how much it applies in practice. Here that is a key distinction between the strong form and other forms.

If a theory does not appear to work in practice, you need to indicate why this might be so, or at least that there is no obvious explanation why the theory does not work. Here the strong form hypothesis does not work, so you consider why when discussing the hypothesis. In addition there is the general point that some financial institutions do perform better than expected. Because this applies to all forms of the efficient market hypothesis, and because the subject is highlighted in the question you need a separate paragraph covering why performance of financial institutions might deviate from what is anticipated.

Generally written questions will benefit from a conclusion that sums up the answer and is supported by the preceding discussion.

The **efficient market hypothesis** contends that some capital markets (in the UK and US for instance) are 'efficient markets' in which the prices at which securities are traded reflect all the **relevant information** available. In other words, this information is freely available to all participants in the market and is fully reflected in share prices. Further, it is assumed that **transaction costs** are **insignificant** and do not discourage trading in shares, and that no single individual or group of individuals dominates the market.

The theory exists in three forms: weak form, semi-strong form and strong form.

Weak form efficiency

Weak form efficiency contends that prices only change when new factual information becomes available. Information about past prices is in the public domain and equally available to all players in the market, and thus if this form of the hypothesis is correct, no one player should be able to outperform the market consistently. Thus the fact that financial institutions rarely outperform the market on a regular basis lends weight to this form of the theory.

Semi strong efficiency

The semi-strong form of the theory holds that in addition to responding to information that is publicly available, the market also reflects all other knowledge that is publicly available and relevant to the share valuation. Thus to take the example used above, the share prices of companies involved in a takeover bid will change in **advance of the bid** being **formally announced** as the market anticipates the bid. Once again, this form of the theory is based upon the assumption that all the knowledge upon which share price movements are based is in **the public domain** and **freely available**. Thus no single player or group of players should be able consistently to outperform the market. This form of the theory is supported by empirical research which suggests that share price movements do anticipate merger announcements. The fact that the neither the financial institutions nor any other group of investors regularly beat the market also supports this version of the hypothesis.

Strong form efficiency

The strong form of the theory holds that the market price of securities reflects **all information** that is **available**. This includes knowledge of past performance and anticipated events as in the semi-strong form, and also **'insider' knowledge** not publicly available. This form can be tested by investigating the effect on the share price of the effect of releasing a piece of information previously confidential to the firm; if the strong form of the hypothesis is valid, then this should already be factored into the share value and a significant price movement should not result. The implication is that this sort of information is only available to specialists who are in regular contact with the company, such as investment trust managers, and that as a result they could use their privileged position to outperform other investors. Empirical work suggests that this form of the hypothesis is not valid, and this is what one would expect since insider dealing is illegal in the UK.

Why institutions may perform well

If an institution **does consistently perform well**, it is probably more related to the fund managers' understanding of the structure of the industries and markets in which they invest, and their ability to hold a more widely diversified portfolio than the small investor. This means that they are in a better position to avoid the risk of large losses. The fact that they are in daily contact with the markets also means that they are in practice able to react more quickly to new information that becomes available than is the small investor.

Conclusion

Thus the fact that the financial institutions in general do **not consistently outperform** the **market supports** both the weak and semi-strong forms of the efficient market hypothesis.

23 Expo plc

> **Top tips.** This question is a good example of how you might be tested on calculations involving forward and money market alternatives to hedging. You can expect to have to also answer discussion questions on this topic.

(a) To: The Treasurer
   From: Assistant
   Date: 12 November 20X7

 (i) Comparison of two methods of hedging exchange risk

  Method 1

  3 month borrowing rate = $3 \times \dfrac{3}{12}$ = 0.75%

  750,000/1.0075 = 744,417 Euros

  Dollars at spot rate = $\dfrac{744,417}{0.7834}$ = \$950,239

  3 month dollar deposit rate = $5 \times \dfrac{3}{12}$ = 1.25%

  Dollar value of deposit in 3 months = \$950,239 × 1.0125 = \$962,117

  Method 2

  The exchange rate is agreed in advance. Cash received in three months is converted to produce 750,000/0.7688 = \$975,546.

  Conclusion

  On the basis of the above calculations, Method 2 gives a slightly better receipt. Banker's commission has been omitted from the figures.

(ii)   **Factors to consider before deciding whether to hedge foreign exchange risk using the foreign currency markets**

Risk-averse strategy

The company should have a clear strategy concerning how much foreign exchange risk it is prepared to bear. A highly **risk-averse** or **'defensive'** strategy of **hedging all transactions** is expensive in terms of commission costs but recognises that floating exchange rates are very unpredictable and can cause losses high enough to bankrupt the company.

Predictive strategy

An alternative 'predictive' strategy recognises that if all transactions are hedged, then the chance of currency gains is lost. The company could therefore attempt to forecast foreign exchange movements and only **hedge those transactions** where **currency losses** are **predicted**. The fact is that some currencies are relatively predictable (for example, if inflation is high the currency will devalue and there is little to be gained by hedging payments in that currency).

This is, of course, a much more risky strategy but in the long run, if predictions are made sensibly, the strategy should lead to a higher expected value than that of hedging everything and will incur lower commission costs as well. The risk remains, though, that a single large uncovered transaction could cause severe problems if the currency moves in the opposite direction to that predicted.

Best strategy

A sensible strategy for our company could be to set a **cash size** for a foreign currency exposure above which all amounts must be hedged, but below this limit a predictive approach is taken or even, possibly, all amounts are left unhedged.

(b)   The other methods used to hedge exchange rate risk include the following.

Currency of invoice which is where an exporter invoices his foreign customer in his domestic currency, or an importer arranges with his foreign supplier to be invoiced in his domestic currency. However, although either the exporter or the importer can avoid any exchange risk in this way, only one of them can deal in his domestic currency. The other must accept the exchange risk, since there will be a period of time elapsing between agreeing a contract and paying for the goods (unless payment is made with the order).

Matching receipts and payments is where a company that expects to make payments and have receipts in the same foreign currency **offsets its payments against its receipts in the currency**. Since the company will be setting off foreign currency receipts against foreign currency payments, it does not matter whether the currency strengthens or weakens against the company's 'domestic' currency because there will be no purchase or sale of the currency.

Matching assets and liabilities is where a company which expects to receive a substantial amount of income in a foreign currency hedges against a weakening of the currency by borrowing in the foreign currency and using the foreign receipts to repay the loan. For example, US dollar receivables can be hedged by taking out a US dollar overdraft. In the same way, US dollar trade payables can be matched against a US dollar bank account which is used to pay the creditors.

Leading and lagging is where a company makes payments in advance or delays payments beyond their due date in order to take advantage of foreign exchange movements.

Netting is where inter-company balances are netted off before arranging payment. It reduces foreign exchange purchase costs and there is less loss in interest from having money in transit.

Foreign currency derivatives such as futures contracts, options and swaps can be used to hedge foreign currency risk.

24 Yields

(a)   A **yield curve** is a curve that can be drawn showing the relationship between the **yield on an asset** (usually long-term government stocks) and the **term to maturity** of that same asset. It shows how the rate of interest (yield) varies with different maturities. To construct a yield curve you need to gather information about the interest rates on short-term stocks, medium-term stocks and long-term stocks. These rates can then be **plotted on a diagram** against the maturity dates of those same stocks.

A normal yield curve looks like Figure 1.

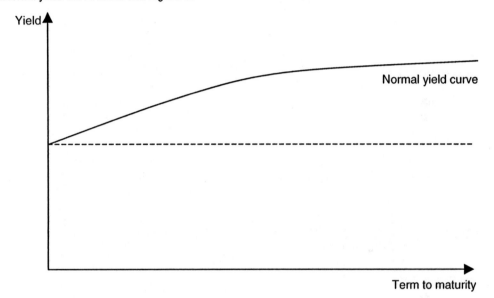

Figure 1

LEARNIN

(b) **Importance of expectations**

The **shape of the yield curve** depends very much on **expectations about the future.** Reward for loss of liquidity is likely to remain fairly constant. Reward for possible default is likely to remain constant also. Reward for the risk of having to cash in before maturity and suffering a loss are also likely to stay fairly constant. The only factor which will vary widely is expectations - in particular, expectations about future short-term interest rates.

Expectations about the future level of short-term interest rates are the most important factor in determining the shape of the yield curve. Although the normal yield curve is upward sloping, with higher yields being expected for longer maturity periods, expectations of rises in future interest rates can cause the yield curve to be steeper than the normal curve. Expectations of falls in interest rates can cause the yield to flatten, or, if substantial falls are expected, to become downward-sloping (Figure 2).

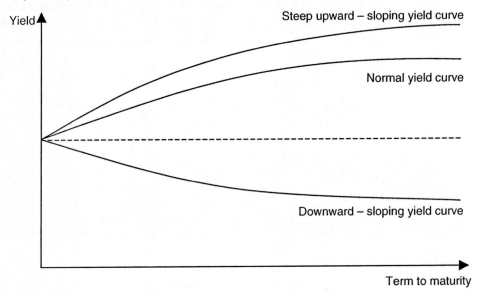

Figure 2

Rising interest rates

If interest rates are now **expected to rise**, investors will not wish to lock in to lower interest rates and will therefore sell short. Borrowers will wish to borrow at lower long-term rates to avoid exposure to the higher rates expected in the future. These demand and supply factors will result in a shortage of long-term funds, which will push up long-term money market rates, and to an excess supply of short-term funds, which will lead to a reduction in short-term rates. The resulting yield curve will be more steeply upward-sloping than the normal curve.

Falling interest rates

If there are **new expectations that interest rates will fall,** investors will prefer to lock in at higher long rates, while borrowers will not wish to be committed to higher long term rates and will prefer to borrow short. There will be an excess supply of funds at long maturities and a shortage of funds at short maturities. This will tend to lower the yield curve, possibly resulting in a flat curve or even in a downward-sloping curve.

Inflation

Short-term interest rates are in turn determined partly by **expectations of inflation** rates in the near future. If high inflation is expected, investors will seek higher nominal rates of interest in order to achieve a real return. If people believe that inflation is falling, then they will not require such a high return.

Practice answer bank

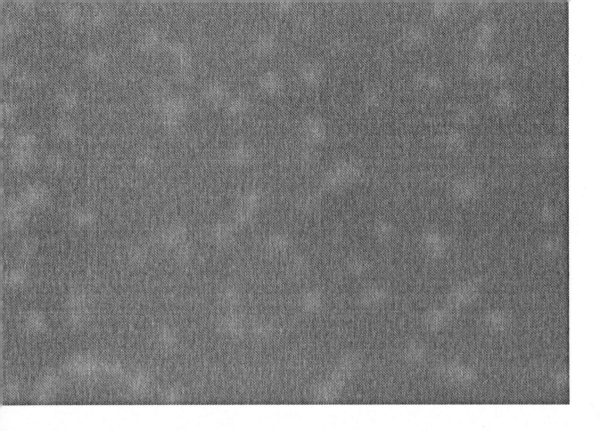

Index